Katherine

Oct. 1987.

Statics and Applied Strength of Materials

Raymond F. Neathery

Division of Engineering Technology
Oklahoma State University

JOHN WILEY & SONS

New York   Chichester   Brisbane   Toronto   Singapore

To Kay, Raymond, Paige, and Neal

Library of Congress Cataloging in Publication Data:

Neathery, Raymond F. (Raymond Franklin), 1939–
  Statics and applied strength of materials.

  Includes index.
  1. Statics.   2. Strength of materials.   I. Title.
TA351.N43 1985   620.1'12   85-6432
ISBN 0-471-88811-7

Printed in the United States of America

10 9 8 7 6 5 4 3 2 1

Preface

Mechanics is a subject that can be studied at various levels of mathematical and analytical sophistication, as even a casual examination of available texts will quickly reveal. Some books on the subject require a working knowledge of arithmetic only; algebra is eliminated entirely by the provision of all possible variations of formulas. Often such texts do not draw upon previous mathematics or science courses the student may have taken; indeed, in some textbooks the latter chapters are actually independent of the earlier ones.

While such books assume no mathematical maturity and do little to develop it, at the other end of the spectrum there are texts employing partial differential equations and tensor analysis. These books are written with the expectation that students will take giant steps in understanding mathematical analyses. They present problems requiring great resourcefulness on the part of the student.

This book has been written on the assumption that the reader has a working knowledge of algebra and trigonometry and will mature mathematically as he or she goes along. Thus, steps will get bigger and the analysis more complicated as the text advances. In most cases the student will have had, or will be currently enrolled in, a first course in technical calculus. Accordingly, calculus is used very lightly in the statics portion—but enough so that instructors may emphasize, reinforce, and apply the principles of calculus, should they wish to do so. Hence, the early usage is light enough to serve as an introduction to calculus, or even to be ignored altogether if desired.

As we proceed to strength of materials, however, the use of calculus and the level of mathematical sophistication increase. Many of the derivations and a few problems are calculus-based. Yet the material is presented and the problems structured such that those who do not wish to emphasize calculus can satisfactorily use this book. (This of course precludes those solutions which are calculus-based, such as finding beam deflections by successive integration.)

Engineering technology has been described as applied engineering. A book written for engineering technology must emphasize the potential applications and practical importance of the material, but it should also—and fundamentally—emphasize an understanding of the material. Students should know when an equation applies and when it does not, what its limitations are, and what is going on physically. Forces need to be intuitively understood as well as calculated. Stress patterns should be visualized, and their equivalence to the forces producing them should be appreciated. Throughout the book, therefore, I have emphasized application *and* understanding, and have avoided rote substitution of unfamiliar variables into even less familiar formulas.

I have tried to write a book that will be read, bearing in mind that students tend to read books that are either sexy, violent, funny, or helpful. Lacking the talent or experience for the first two, I have concentrated on the last two. If, as you read, you occasionally smile, I will be pleased. In attempting to be helpful, I've included a large number of example problems. In most cases enough detail is presented to allow the reader to understand the material without the assistance of the instructor. I have tried to be sensitive to those concepts we expect students to know but find that many have difficulty with. To convey the idea that I'm on the student's side, I have used a conversational tone. (This is not a style I recommend for technical papers, however!)

The order of the material is traditional. Topics and entire chapters may be omitted without loss of continuity for shorter courses or those with a different emphasis. In such cases the instructor must be selective in assigning problems. The amount of material exceeds that normally covered in a two-semester sequence. A solutions manual is available that includes suggested topics for courses of various lengths.

Because understanding of the material is a primary objective of this book, most equations are presented with some argument justifying their existence. Sometimes these arguments are intuitive; sometimes they are mathematical; sometimes they are both. I firmly believe that a student who understands where an equation comes from is far less likely to misuse it. I also believe that many technology students are put off by derivations regardless of their utility or mathematical elegance. These students are convinced by example—and since all students are helped by example, in this book examples abound. They are followed by a large number of student problems; answers to two-thirds of them (excluding those divisible by three) are in the appendix.

A unique feature of this book is the use of unit vector notation. This is presented in an optional fashion. Some students who use this text will study mechanics further; others will work in environments where they will encounter this notation. It is therefore presented here in friendly territory for their benefit. No use is made of vector algebra (dot or cross product) or vector calculus.

The strength of materials portion of this text is based on the author's *Applied Strength of Materials*. Reviewers for that text were: Donald E. Breyer, California State Polytechnic University, Pomona; T. M. Brittain, University of Akron; Stanley M. Brodsky, New York City Technical College; Donald S. Bunk, Dutchess Community College; Eugene F. Kruetzer, Illinois Valley Community College; Dan M. Parker, Southern Technical Institute; John O. Pautz, Middlesex County College; Richard S. Rossignol, Central Virginia Community College. The statics portion of this text was reviewed by Stanley M. Brodsky, New York City Technical College; Karl S. Webster, University of Maine at Orono; James Ehrenberg, California Polytechnic State University; Donald Buchwald, Kansas Technical Institute; John Jackson, Vermont Technical College; and Donald E. Keyt, Spring Garden College. My colleagues at Oklahoma State University, Jack Bayles, John Scheihing, and Larry Simmons, used the material at various stages of development and made many helpful suggestions.

My editor at John Wiley, Susan Weiss, has been a gentle taskmaster and friend. Fran Maurizzi typed the portion on strength of materials, and my children, Raymond and Paige, typed the statics portion. My friend Charles Kroell of General Motors picked more nits than I care to mention, but niggling was needed. To all I offer my thanks.

Raymond F. Neathery

Contents

1

Introduction

As you begin this study, you begin an adventure that can reward you throughout your technical career. For some of you this constitutes a "related" course, one that you are required to take, perhaps without really understanding why. Maybe you've heard it's difficult and are apprehensive. It is true that many find it so, for various reasons. It is also true that if this is a "related" course, your professional life will not be heavily dependent on it. You are not likely to routinely work problems of the type found in this text. Nonetheless the course can be a rewarding lifelong adventure in two aspects. First, the problem-solving approach presented, reviewed, assigned, summarized, exercised, tested, and—if possible—pounded into your head, has value on its own. Successful completion of the course should result in the ability to reliably quantify and analyze. These skills are extremely valuable to anyone working in the engineering field. Second, virtually all areas of modern technology—electronics, fluidics, microcomputers, fiber optics, aerospace, astronautics, robotics, communications, and so on—have mechanical handles. We interact with this technology mechanically. A thorough understanding of mechanics will allow us to manage the interface.

For others this study will be not only a rewarding adventure, it will be an essential journey. For those who will design, manufacture, or construct our automobiles, bridges, airplanes, homes, refrigerators (the list goes on and on), or their components, this subject is a basic science. These people *must* understand mechanics, and in their professional lives, many will routinely solve problems based on this subject.

1.1 MECHANICS (WITHOUT A TOOLBOX)

As a freshman in college I visited an elderly woman who had watched me grow from infancy. She was extremely pleased to learn I was in college and asked what I was studying. I puffed up and beamed as I told her I was going to be an engineer! I was certain that I faintly heard a minor drumroll and a trumpet fanfare as I proudly proclaimed my proposed profession. The music was halted abruptly as she responded, "Aw, Raymond, you don't want to drive no train!" She was right, of course; I never have driven one. Given her response to "engineer," I am glad I did not know at the time that I would ultimately study "mechanics"!

Just to clear the air early, our study of mechanics will have nothing to do with the repair of automobiles. With all due respect to "Mr. Goodwrench," our tools will not be screwdrivers, ball peen hammers, socket wrenches, or ignition analyzers. We will have tools of an entirely different sort, and we hope to add to our toolbox as we go. The "basic beginner's set" includes an understanding of and computational ability in algebra and trigonometry, the ability to read carefully and to translate words into physical situations, the ability to interpret drawings, the ability to follow directions, and the ability to reason logically. As the course progresses, we will improve our skills with these tools and add to them as well.

Well, if a course in mechanics is not about dropping the transmission in the old Chevy, what is it about? Mechanics is the study of forces and the effect they have on objects. It includes the transmission of forces, how they are carried internally, and the motion they produce. In this course, statics, we are concerned primarily with forces on bodies at rest. Unless you are reading on the bus, the seat you are sitting on is not moving; it is at rest. From the principles of statics we can determine the force you exert on a chair and the forces the chair exerts in turn on the floor. The floor reacts with opposite forces on the chair as shown in Fig. 1.1. We

A   *B*

FIG. 1.1 The floor exerts forces on the chair.

can further find the *internal* forces in the legs of the chair. From mechanics of materials (or strength of materials, as it is commonly called) we can determine how this load is carried and the deflection it produces. In the study of dynamics we are concerned with bodies in motion. We study the description of the motion as well as the forces causing it. We can also study the mechanics of fluids—statically and dynamically. That is done in courses in fluid mechanics or hydraulics.

1.2 GETTING THERE IS HALF THE FUN: AN APPROACH TO PROBLEMS

A major benefit of a course in mechanics is the development of good work habits in the solution of analytical problems. We emphasize that now and throughout the text. You should begin now to emphasize it and continue throughout the course because, if for no other reason, many instructors will begin to emphasize it now—in their grading. We illustrate what we mean by the following problem.

Example Problem 1.1

A ballast is to be cut from steel bar stock that is 2 in. wide and $\frac{3}{4}$ in. thick. The ballast should weigh 12 lb. How long does the ballast need to be?

The solution to this problem is given in Fig. 1.2. Follow along in the figure as we go through the solution. The first thing to notice is the paper itself. Using a grid paper keeps the work neat and orderly. It also helps in making sketches, which are very important in solving mechanics problems. Use sketches generously, copiously, even redundantly! The "engineer's pad," which lets the grid printed on its back side show through faintly, has become very common and popular. I recommend it.

The first step in solving the ballast problem is to read it carefully. Some students write the question out in longhand to force themselves to examine the problem thoroughly. You should try this on a few problems and see if it helps you, but I'll not emphasize it. Instead I'll read through the problem in detail and list the essential data. This is shown as step 1 in Fig. 1.2. (Of course, it's not necessary to write "step 1," etc., in your solution.) Step 1 is to find what is "given." As we reread the problem we note that the material is steel and record that under "Given." Next we note that the cross-sectional area is 2 in. by $\frac{3}{4}$ in. We record this, and the desired 12-lb weight. We note the length is to be found and record this dimension under "Find." We also give length the symbol L so that we may manipulate it algebraically. The "Find" statement is labeled step 2. In step 3 we make a sketch of the problem. We label and assign values to the elements of the sketch. The sketch will help us to take all the given information into account, get a physical grasp of the problem, and suggest a method of solution. We have indicated these three steps as being sequential, but more often than not they are interactive. In any case, all three should be completed before proceeding.

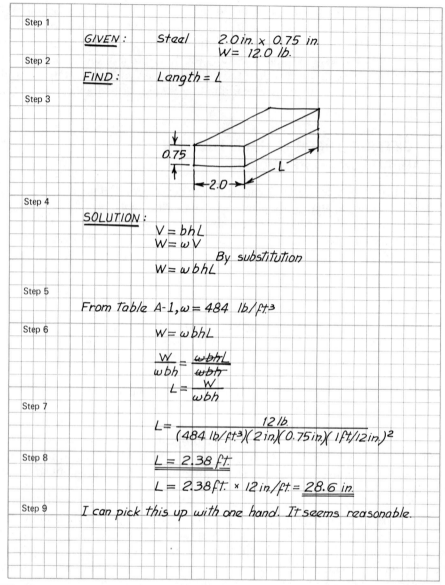

Step 1

GIVEN :   Steel   2.0 in. x 0.75 in.
                    W= 12.0 lb.
Step 2

FIND :   Length = L

Step 3

0.75

←2.0→   L

Step 4

SOLUTION :
        V = bhL
        W = ωV
                By substitution
        W = ωbhL

Step 5

From Table A-1, ω = 484 lb/ft³

Step 6

W = ωbhL

$$\frac{W}{\omega bh} = \frac{\omega bhL}{\omega bh}$$
$$L = \frac{W}{\omega bh}$$

Step 7

$$L = \frac{12\ lb.}{(484\ lb/ft^3)(2\ in.)(0.75\ in.)(1ft/12in.)^2}$$

Step 8

L = 2.38 ft.

L = 2.38 ft. × 12 in./ft. = 28.6 in.

Step 9

I can pick this up with one hand. It seems reasonable.

FIG. 1.2 Solution format.

Step 4 begins our solution. We recognize the volume to be

$$V = bhL$$

where b = width
        h = height
        L = length

and the weight is

$$W = wV$$

where w is the weight per unit volume (commonly but inaccurately called density). We record these in step 4 and recognize that neither L nor w is known. The material property w is not given in the problem, but such data are commonly available in tables such as Table A-1 in the Appendix. From this table we have $w = 484$ lb/ft^3. In step 5 we cite the source of this value.

It is important to document references. This leaves us with the single unknown, L, which we seek. Solve algebraically for L *before* substituting in any values. This approach has all sorts of advantages over plugging in numbers and starting to do arithmetic—most importantly, it is less work and less vulnerable to error. As a rule, one should not pass up propositions that are less work and produce better results! Thus, in step 6 we solve for L. This solution is general. We can readily exercise it for different values of W, b, h, or w. We can even program the solution on our computer.

Now we solve our specific problem by substituting in the values we have (step 7). It is a good practice to write the units that go with numbers as we substitute them into the equation. Performing the algebra on the units will give us the units for the answer. We note that we have length in both inches and feet and make the appropriate conversion. Finally, at step 8 we write the result to an appropriate number of significant figures and with proper units. If desired we may convert the answer to other units. We mark the answer clearly so that it may be readily identified later.

Step 9 is often overlooked, even though it may be the most important of all. For this step we move back and look at the whole solution to see if it is logical, reasonable, and valid. Then we look at the answer itself. Here we want to test the answer against our intuition. Sometimes our intuition will indicate that there is an error in the solution; in some cases the solution will correct our intuition, and in other cases it is a standoff—we don't learn anything either way. As the great Dizzy Dean used to say regarding baseball, "You win some, you lose some, and some are rained out!" But this is no rainout. We can imagine picking up this bar with one hand, and we know we can pick up 12 lb. So we conclude that based on our intuition, it's satisfactory, although frankly, it's a little longer than I expected.

Figure 1.3 shows step 6 through the end of the solution in bad form. In addition to a wrong answer (although the arithmetic is correct), what other bad practices can you identify?

Many students believe that if they turn in neat and orderly work, they will receive a good grade and impress the instructor with their neatness and orderliness. As a result, students who solve problems in the most unorganized manner, actually doing the work on discarded computer paper, newsprint, paper bags, stationary pilfered from the office, fish wrappers, and who knows what else, often recopy it in the neatest possible format. Lettering approaches Leroy quality and multicolor presentations are not unknown. This totally misses the point! The process just explained is for the student's benefit, not the instructor's. This process will help

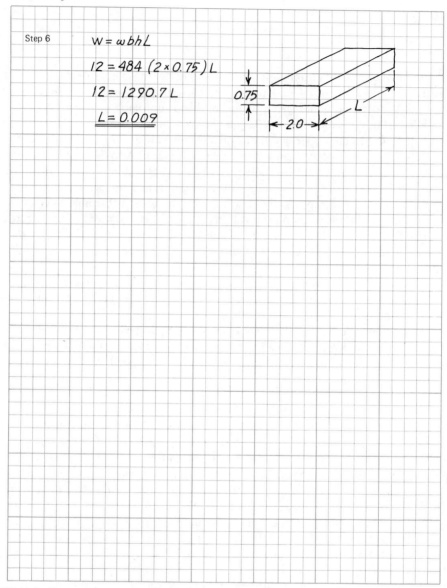

$$w = \omega b h L$$

$$12 = 484\ (2 \times 0.75)\,L$$

$$12 = 1290.7\,L$$

$$L = 0.009$$

FIG. 1.3 Poor solution process.

you grasp the problem, understand its solution, find and correct errors, and so on. Rather than a flawlessly lettered, sterile, antiseptic, and copied output, the solution should be the result of real work, with its erasures, mark-throughs, corrected errors, coffee stains, tears, and occasionally a little blood. The point is to make it easier to solve the problems, document assumptions, and find errors, not to pretend that errors don't occur. (And your instructor will smile more.)

1.3 "YOU DON'T KNOW ME THAT WELL!" (ON THE PROPER USE OF SIGNIFICANT FIGURES)

In his entertaining book on the wonders of mathematics, George Gamov offers this limerick.*

"There was a young fellow from Trinity
Who took the square-root of infinity
    But the number of digits
    Gave him the fidgets;
He dropped Math and took up Divinity."

All too often today the number of digits is giving me the fidgets. The culprit is the little hand calculator, which works every problem as precisely as it knows how. Although this handy-dandy device is extremely fast and efficient, and a wonderful work saver, and always gets the decimal point in the right place (if we do), and can solve trigonometry problems with lightning speed, it is too simple-minded to handle significant figures. It must rely on its intelligent human operator for that, and if the intelligent human operator is going to handle significant figures, he needs to know what they are.

Let's define what we mean by significant figures. The number of significant figures indicates the precision with which a quantity is known. We cannot measure any physical quantity *exactly*—all measurements are approximations. We can, of course, count exactly, but as the number grows larger we often resort to less precise estimates. For the remainder of this discussion we will exclude exact counts.

Let's say we measure a piece of steel with a ruler and find it to be 2.0 in. long. We then measure it with a vernier caliper and find it to be 2.01 in. long. Last, we measure it with a micrometer and find it to be 2.008 in. Each successive instrument allows for a more precise estimate of the length of the piece, proceeding from two to three and then to four significant figures. The difference in these three numbers is the precision with which they indicate the value. None is exact and all are attempts at the same measurement.

To determine the number of significant figures, move left to right on the number. Start counting at the first nonzero and continue to the last nonzero.

308.2
xxxx → 4 significant figures

418,000
xxx   → 3 significant figures

If the last nonzero is to the right of the decimal, keep counting until the last zero. This gives the number of significant figures. For example:

0.0012300
xxxxx → 5 significant figures

0.0012
xx → 2 significant figures

---

* From *One, Two, Three . . . Infinity* by George Gamow. Copyright 1947, 1961 by George Gamow. Copyright renewed © 1974 by Barbara Gamow. Reprinted by permission of Viking Penguin Inc.

Note that lead zeros do not count, middle zeros do. Trailing zeros do not count unless they are to the right of the decimal or are followed by some that are.

The example of 418,000 can be ambiguous. Scientific notation eliminates this ambiguity. With it we write

$$4.18 \times 10^5 \text{ or}$$
$$4.180 \times 10^5 \text{ or}$$
$$4.1800 \times 10^5$$

or

$$4.18000 \times 10^5$$

according to our intent, three, four, five, or six significant figures.

Because neither computers nor typists like to use superscripts, we have taken to writing "computerese." We will often write

$$4.18 \times 10^5 \qquad \text{as} \quad 4.18 \, E5$$

in the manner of an IBM 360 or even my hand-held calculator. I think you'll find it convenient, too.

Let us consider now the number 2. By it we mean some number between 1.5 and 2.5. With only 2 we absolutely cannot distinguish between 1.7 and 2.2. We represent this as follows:

$$2 = \begin{cases} 1.5 \\ 2.5 \end{cases}$$

In a similar manner,

$$3 = \begin{cases} 2.5 \\ 3.5 \end{cases}$$

Next consider the product 2×3. We evaluate this and its extremes:

$$1.5 \times 2.5 = 3.75$$
$$2 \times 3 = 6$$
$$2.5 \times 3.5 = 8.75$$

We see that 2×3 really includes any value from 3.75 to 8.75—a very wide range. We say that the answer is:

$$6 = \begin{cases} 5.5 \\ 6.5 \end{cases} \simeq \begin{cases} 3.75 \\ 8.75 \end{cases}$$

As can be seen from the above, when we say $2 \times 3 = 6$ we are limiting the answer to a range of possible values that is a small portion (20%) of the actual range. This cannot be avoided without writing the number with tolerances (which is sometimes necessary). We should, however, point out the absurdity of saying:

$$2 \times 3 = 6.0 = \begin{cases} 5.95 \\ 6.05 \end{cases}$$

which includes only 2% of the possible values.

It will be helpful for comparison to consider the product 2.00×3.00 and its extremes:

$$1.995 \times 2.995 = 5.975$$
$$2.00 \times 3.00 = 6.00 \ = \begin{cases} 5.995 \\ 6.005 \end{cases}$$
$$2.005 \times 3.005 = 6.025$$

Again we see that by preserving the original number of significant figures, three, we indicate a range of answers that is approximately 20% of the range of possible answers. Greater precision (6.000) is clearly ludicrous. Since 6.00 is overly precise, why not drop to 6.0? That gives

$$6.0 = \begin{cases} 5.95 \\ 6.05 \end{cases}$$

This range is twice as large as the actual range 5.975 to 6.025. We are faced with the dilemma of either overspecifying the answer as 6.00 or underspecifying the answer as 6.0. The absurd option of 6.000 and finer tuned numbers is clearly not acceptable. We opt to use 6.00, because it does not enlarge the original uncertainty of the numbers. Additional operations will continually degrade the precision of the numbers.

In most calculations it is not necessary or desirable to do this type of error analysis. We can get by just fine by applying a simple rule:

The number of significant figures in an answer can be no more than the smallest number of significant figures in any of the factors forming the answer.

This is simplified further in our application, since most of the factors we will deal with can be conveniently determined to three significant figures. Unless otherwise indicated, we will assume that all given values are accurate to three significant figures. Therefore, all derived answers will be good to three significant figures.

One additional note may be needed. We have mentioned that our calculator works with a precision of 8 to 10 figures, although we rarely give it information that precise. When we write down answers from the calculator we will round off to three significant figures. But we will *not* round off the numbers *in* the calculator. Such adjustments would be artificial and certainly are not justified, given the uncertainty of input data. Following this practice will result in differences in the third digit of an answer for some calculations depending on calculator precision and storage, the method of solution, and intermediate round-off. These differences are not important and should not cause concern. If after a lengthy computation you get 793, and I have 795; your answer is as good as mine. Differences of less than a couple of percentage points are acceptable. Answers do not have to be *identical* to three significant figures to be correct.

1.4 UNITS AND DIMENSIONAL CONSISTENCY

In the United States engineering calculations have traditionally been made using the English or U.S. customary units, especially in mechanical and civil fields. This is being replaced by the Système International d'Unités, abbreviated SI. In English

TABLE 1.1   METRIC AND ENGLISH UNITS

Dimension	International System (SI) Unit	Common English Unit
Length	meter (m)	foot (ft) or inch (in.)
Mass	kilogram (kg)	$\left(\dfrac{\text{lb-s}^2}{\text{ft}}\right)$ or slug
Time	second (s)	second (s)
Force	newton (N) or $\left(\dfrac{\text{kg}\cdot\text{m}}{\text{s}^2}\right)$	pound (lb)
Stress or pressure	pascal (Pa) or $\left(\dfrac{\text{N}}{\text{m}^2}\right)$	$\left(\dfrac{\text{lb}}{\text{in.}^2}\right)$ (psi)
Energy or work	joule (J) or N·m	ft-lb
Angle	radian (rad)	degree (°)
Power	watt (W), $\left(\dfrac{\text{N}\cdot\text{m}}{\text{s}}\right)$, or (J/s)	$\left(\dfrac{\text{ft-lb}}{\text{s}}\right)$ horsepower (hp), watt (W), etc.
Area	m^2	in.^{2}, etc.
Volume	m^3	in.^{3}, etc.
Velocity	$\left(\dfrac{\text{m}}{\text{s}}\right)$	$\left(\dfrac{\text{ft}}{\text{s}}\right)$

it is called the International System of Units, but still abbreviated SI. Table 1.1 gives the common units used in mechanics in both systems.

In statics we work mostly with forces in pounds (lb), kilopounds (kip: meaning 1000 lb), ounce (oz), and ton (2000 lb) in the U.S. system, and newtons (N) in the SI. For length we use feet (ft), inches (in.), yards (yd), and mile (mi) in the U.S. system and meter (m) in the SI. That's metre if you talk funny.

The SI is commonly referred to as the metric system. It is *a* metric system, but its adoption in countries that were already using a metric system requires changes too. Its key features, in addition to having units that are multiples of 10, are:

1. A world-wide universal system is being adopted.
2. Abbreviations are standardized.
3. Generally there is a single unit for each physical term.
4. It is coherent.

"Coherent" means in this case that all derived units come from the straightforward combination of basic units. For example, power is the rate or doing work—a force acting through a distance over a period of time. In the English system we use

$$1 \text{ horsepower} = 550\,\frac{\text{ft-lb}}{\text{s}}$$

In the SI we use

$$1 \text{ watt} = 1\,\frac{\text{N}\cdot\text{m}}{\text{s}}$$

Notice that the conversion factor is 1. In the SI the conversion factor is always 1 because the system is coherent.

In this text we will work with both systems of units. However, to keep our focus on mechanics, rather than units conversion, we will generally work problems in one system or the other, not combinations of the two. Appendix Table A-3 gives the conversion factors we will use. Occasionally you may want to convert a problem just to gain a better feel for the magnitude of units in the SI.

Of course, a key feature of any metric system is the generation of very large or very small units by using an appropriate multiplying prefix. The SI continues this and, in addition, gives a preference for prefixes representing an exponent that is a multiple of 3, such as 10^3 or 10^{-3}. Recommended prefixes of concern to us are given in Table A-4. The most common exception to this is the centimeter (cm). We will avoid all other exceptions.

In this text we handle conversions of units by physically multiplying by a fraction equal to one. All the conversion ratios given in Table A-3 are physically one. We arrive at this conclusion as follows. First we note

$$1 \text{ ft} = 0.3048 \text{ m}$$

Dividing both sides of the equation by 1 ft gives

$$\frac{1 \text{ ft}}{1 \text{ ft}} = 1 = \frac{0.3048 \text{ m}}{1 \text{ ft}}$$

Thus we conclude that this factor is physically one. We use the factor as follows.

Example Problem 1.2

Convert a torque of 135 in.-lb to newton-meters (N · m).

GIVEN $T = 135$ in.-lb

FIND T in N·m

Solution

$$T = 135 \text{ in.-lb} \frac{1 \text{ ft}}{12 \text{ in.}} \left(\frac{0.3048 \text{ m}}{\text{ft}}\right)\left(\frac{4.448 \text{ N}}{\text{lb}}\right)$$

Each of the conversion factors is a fraction equal to one. We do the arithmetic on the numbers and the algebra on the units.

$$T = \frac{135(0.3048)(4.448)}{12} \text{ in.-lb} \left(\frac{\text{ft}}{\text{in.}}\right)\left(\frac{\text{m}}{\text{ft}}\right)\left(\frac{\text{N}}{\text{lb}}\right)$$

$$T = 15.252192 \text{ N·m}$$

This is the answer my calculator gives. However, since the torque was given to three significant figures, the answer is valid only to three significant figures. The conversion factors 12 and 0.3048 are exact. That means we can add as many trailing zeros as are needed to preserve the precision. The factor 4.448 is good for four significant figures. Thus, the answer is limited to three significant figures, and rounding off we write

$$T = 15.3 \text{ N·m}$$

EVALUATION   My intuition on this answer is not much help, so I just register a ratio of approximately 10:1 between the units.

Example Problem 1.3

Express the power consumed by a 100-W light bulb in inch-pounds per second (in.-lb/s).

GIVEN $P = 100$ W

FIND P in in.-lb/s

Solution

$$P = 100 \text{ W} = 100 \text{ N·m/s}$$

$$P = 100 \frac{\text{N·m}}{\text{s}} \left(\frac{\text{lb}}{4.448 \text{ N}} \right) \left(\frac{\text{ft}}{0.3048} \right) \left(\frac{12 \text{ in.}}{\text{ft}} \right)$$

$$= \frac{100 \,(12)}{4.448(0.3048)} \frac{\cancel{\text{N·m}}}{\text{s}} \left(\frac{\text{lb}}{\cancel{\text{N}}} \right) \left(\frac{\cancel{\text{ft}}}{\cancel{\text{m}}} \right) \left(\frac{\text{in.}}{\cancel{\text{ft}}} \right)$$

$$P = 885 \, \frac{\textbf{in.-lb}}{\text{s}}$$

Notice that in this case the conversion factors are inverted, but we are still multiplying by one and carrying out the algebra with the units. We assume the 100 W to be accurate to three significant figures and round off the answer to three significant figures.

EVALUATION   We went from newton-meters per second to inch-pounds per second. Since the denominator is in seconds in both cases, the numerators form the relevant factors. This gives a transition from N·m to in.-lb. Again we observe an approximate 10:1 ratio.

It is important to note that in Example Problems 1.2 and 1.3 the conversion of units was accomplished by dealing with the units algebraically. Much information is carried by the units, and careful attention should always be given to the units or dimensions of an equation.

When we talk about the dimensions of an equation, we are using a general term for the units. If we say something is 12 ft long, the unit is foot and the dimension is length. If we say a car is moving at 60 mph, the units are miles per hour and the dimensions are length per unit time. Other units of velocity are feet per second, meters per second, and furlongs per fortnight. These different units all have the same dimensions—length per unit time.

An important principle is that if terms are physically related by an equation, they must be dimensionally equivalent as well. That is, all physical equations must be dimensionally homogeneous. For example, if a body moves at constant velocity, its displacement is its velocity multiplied by the elasped time, or

$$s = vt \qquad\qquad\qquad (1.1)$$

This equation says that if we travel at 60 mph for 2 h, we will have traveled 120 mi, found by:

$$s = \left(60 \, \frac{\text{mi}}{\text{h}}\right) 2 \, \text{h} = 60(2) \left(\frac{\text{mi}}{\text{h}}\right) (\text{h})$$

$$s = 120 \, \text{mi}$$

Note that in arriving at this answer we do the algebra on the numbers *and* the units. The algebra of the units determines the units for distance traveled. We may examine units dimensionally as follows:

$$s \overset{D}{=} \frac{\text{mi}}{\text{h}} (\text{h}) \overset{D}{=} \text{miles}$$

The equal sign with a D over it means "s is equal dimensionally to." Other illustrative equations are as follows.

$$a = \frac{v}{t} \overset{D}{=} \frac{\text{ft}}{\text{s}} \cdot \frac{1}{\text{s}} \overset{D}{=} \frac{\text{ft}}{\text{s}^2}$$

$$s = v_1 t + \tfrac{1}{2} a t^2$$

$$s \overset{D}{=} \left(\frac{\text{ft}}{\text{s}}\right) s + \frac{\text{ft}}{(\text{s})^2} (\text{s})^2$$

$$s \overset{D}{=} \text{ft} + \text{ft} \overset{D}{=} \text{ft}$$

The second equation above illustrates another use of this principle. It calls for adding $v_1 t$ to $\tfrac{1}{2} a t^2$. The units for $v_1 t$ and $\tfrac{1}{2} a t^2$ must be the same; otherwise meaningful addition cannot occur. This point also allows us to check the accuracy of equations about which we have doubt. If we were not sure whether the last term were $\tfrac{1}{2} a t^2$ or $\tfrac{1}{2} a t$, the dimensions would dictate $\tfrac{1}{2} a t^2$. On the other hand, the $\tfrac{1}{2}$ is a dimensionless constant, and this analysis is blind to it.

There is a class of equations that is confounding to this principle. These are empirical equations and design equations that contain constants that carry dimensions. Constants in basic physical equations never carry dimensions. An example of a design equation is:

$$H = \frac{s_s N D^3}{321{,}000}$$

This equation gives the power in horsepower that can be carried by a shaft turning at N revolutions per minute, of diameter D, in inches, and of an allowable shear stress s_s, in pounds per square inch. This equation is dimensionally consistent only when the 321,000 carries with it the units of pound-revolutions per horsepower-minute. If these units are not written with the constant—and they usually are not—the equation has only limited application. It is further handicapped by the fact that it is valid only when s_s, N, and D are entered with the proper units. It is, however, quite valuable if we are routinely making this calculation, because it relieves us of repeatedly doing the same units conversion.

Equations of this type can be generally recognized by their uneven constants.

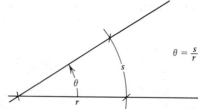

FIG. 1.4 Angle definition.

Naturally occurring constants that are usually dimensionless are integers, π, e, and the like.

One final note is in order concerning the units for angles. As shown in Fig. 1.4 the angle θ is defined as the arc length s divided by the radius r.

$$\theta = \frac{s}{r}$$

In this equation, if s is equal to r, the radius, the angle defined is one radian. By dimensional algebra we see:

$$\theta \overset{\text{D}}{=} \frac{\text{ft}}{\text{ft}} = \text{dimensionless}$$

Thus we conclude that an angle (being the ratio of two lengths) is, in fact, dimensionless when measured in radians. Any other unit of angular measure will not be dimensionless. Basic equations involving angles invariably call for their measurement in radians. It is not surprising that the SI calls for angular measurement in radians.

1.5 GEOMETRIC PRINCIPLES: IF ALL ELSE FAILS, DRAW THE DARN THING!

The title of this section is intended to provoke a little chuckle. Beyond that, it is excellent advice. Many geometric problems can be solved quite nicely by simply drawing them to scale and measuring angles and lengths. This approach, of course, will not work when an answer is needed in equation form for programming into a computer or when your instructor *insists* on an analytical solution. But when it will work and when the analytical solution is very difficult and when it's your option, draw it! As a matter of fact, it is good practice always to use a graphical solution—at least approximately—to confirm our analytical solution. To do this we just make a sketch to scale, approximate the results, and compare them with the analytical solution. The previously mentioned "engineer's pad" (or grid paper), a 10-units-to-the-inch scale, a small protractor, and a compass are the tools you need. This small investment will pay large dividends.

Let us briefly recall a few geometric principles that will be important in our analysis of statics problems. Figure 1.5 shows two parallel lines intersected by a third line. We observe the following relationships between the angles formed.

$$A = C = E = G \quad \text{and} \quad B = D = F = H$$

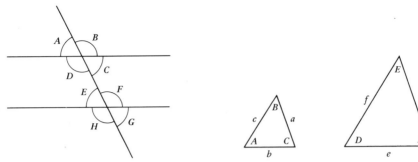

FIG. 1.5 Angle relationships between parallel and intersecting lines.

FIG. 1.6 Similar triangles.

In Fig. 1.6 two similar triangles are shown. Triangles are similar if the following relationships hold for the angles:

$$A = D$$
$$B = E$$
$$C = F$$

or if corresponding sides are proportional:

$$\frac{a}{d} = \frac{b}{e} = \frac{c}{f}$$

The first condition (angles) implies the second (sides), and vice versa.

Figure 1.7 shows an arc of a circle. We construct a line *ab* that is *tangent* to the circle at *A*; that is, it touches the circle at only one point, namely, *A*. Next we construct the line *cd* perpendicular to *ab* and through the point of tangency *A*. This line is said to be *normal* to the circle. In this context, "normal" is another way of saying perpendicular. At a distance of *r,* the radius of the circle, is the point 0, the center of the circle. This is also referred to as the center of curvature of the arc *AB*. At *B* a second tangent *ef* is drawn. A second normal *gh* is drawn through *B*. The lines *gh* and *cd* will intersect at O. The distance from O to *A* or *B* is known as the radius of curvature of the arc *AB*. In the case of a complete

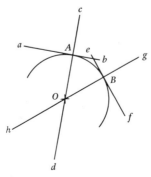

FIG. 1.7 Properties of a circular arc.

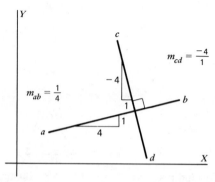

FIG. 1.8 Perpendicular lines.

circle it is just the radius. If an arc of unknown radius is given, its center may be found by constructing two normals.

Another useful relation can be seen by noting that if two lines are perpendicular, the slope of one is the negative reciprocal of the other. This is illustrated in Fig. 1.8, where line *cd*, which has a slope of -4, is perpendicular to line *ab*, which has a slope of $+\frac{1}{4}$.

1.6 A NOTE ON ALGEBRA

This chapter has emphasized the desirability of a neat, logical, and orderly approach to the solution of problems. In Example Problem 1.1 it was emphasized that once a problem is set up it is usually best to complete an algebraic solution before doing the arithmetic. That is very important. We recognize that the job in analysis is to generate as many equations as we have unknowns. Once that has been done, all that is required for solution is the careful, systematic algebraic manipulation of the equations.

Before we can manipulate an equation, we must have an equation. Be careful to write complete equations, not just expressions. For example,

$$A + 100 - 50$$

is an expression. There are several things we can do to this expression, but none of them will tell us what the value of *A* is. If, on the other hand, we have an equation such as

$$A + 100 - 50 = 0$$

we can execute certain algebraic steps and arrive at a value for *A*. Notice that an equation has something *equal* to something. As long as we do the same thing to both sides of the equation, we're OK. By subtracting 50 from each side, we arrive at

$$A = -50$$

But we can't do anything until we have an equation—so remember, WRITE COMPLETE EQUATIONS!

1.7 THE BERMUDA TRIANGLE AND OTHER TRIGONOMETRIC CONUNDRUMS

You've no doubt heard of the Bermuda Triangle, where ships and planes disappear without a trace. It is only slightly better known than the infamous Buford Triangle—a triangular region in northern Georgia that has corners formed by the towns of Dawsonville, New Holland, and, of course, Buford. In one 6-week period in the summer of 1978 thirteen pickup trucks and six semis disappeared without so much as a skid mark. It is known that eight of the pickups carried campers, all of which sported at least one large decal of a bass. It is further known that all the semi drivers were CBers ("gear jammers" in their lingo). Alas, their "handles" are gone forever. The Bermuda and the less publicized Buford triangles may represent man's encounter with the "twilight zone," unsolvable conundrums (puzzles) painted in undistinguishable grays on the canvas of the unknown.

So much for my impression of Rod Serling. Unfortunately, many seem to approach trigonometry as though it were similarly mysterious. It is not. We encounter trigonometry in two areas; trigonometric functions and the solution of triangles. Our primary application will be in solving triangles.

TRIANGLES

Triangles have six parts: three angles (hence the name) and three sides. We can determine all six parts if we know any three parts except all three angles. (In a few cases *two* solutions are possible.)

When we know only three angles, there is an infinite set of similar triangles that have that set of angles. We classify triangles as right (if they contain a 90° angle) and nonright (if they do not). In the case of a right triangle we may solve for all parts if we know two additional parts, one of which is a side. We may solve right triangles using definitions of angles based on a right triangle. These definitions are (Fig. 1.9):

$$\sin \theta = \frac{\text{side opposite}}{\text{hypotenuse}} = \frac{a}{c} \tag{1.2}$$

$$\cos \theta = \frac{\text{side adjacent}}{\text{hypotenuse}} = \frac{b}{c} \tag{1.3}$$

$$\tan \theta = \frac{\text{side opposite}}{\text{side adjacent}} = \frac{a}{b} \tag{1.4}$$

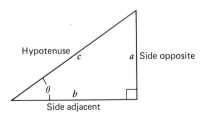

FIG. 1.9 Right triangle.

These definitions should be known for any orientation of a triangle. There are three other functions of angles, (secant, cosecant, and cotangent), which are redundant and not needed. An additional principle is the Pythagorean theorem, which is:

$$c^2 = a^2 + b^2 \qquad (1.5)$$

And the angles must sum to 180°: $A + B + C = 180°$.

Using an electronic calculator, it will be convenient to determine components of the triangle using trig functions and to reserve the Pythagorean theorem for a check.

Example Problem 1.4

Solve for parts a, b and the angle B in the triangle shown in Fig. 1.10.

GIVEN   A side and angle in a right triangle.

FIND a, b and B.

Solution

We observe:

$$\sin A = \frac{a}{c}$$

Solving for a:

$$a = c \sin A$$
$$a = 48.3 \sin 28° = \textbf{22.7 m}$$

Store 48.3 and 28 in memories as they are entered into the calculator. Store 22.7 before proceeding. Then:

$$\cos A = \frac{b}{c}$$

$$b = c \cos A$$
$$b = 48.3 \cos 28° = \textbf{42.6 m}$$

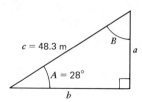

FIG. 1.10   Example Problem 1.4.

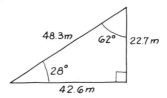

FIG. 1.11   Sketch of solution.

This can be evaluated by recalling the values from the calculator memory. We then check the answer using the Pythagorean theorem and the values stored in the calculator

$$(22.7)^2 + (42.6)^2 = (48.3)^2 \qquad \textbf{check}$$

Then find B:

$$B = 90° - 28° = \textbf{62.0°}$$

Last we sketch our solution approximately to scale (Fig 1.11) and note that the indicated angles are in proper order, their opposite sides are in proportion, and the hypotenuse is the largest side but less than the sum of the other two sides.

The second type of triangle does not have a right angle (Fig. 1.12). The equations used to solve for triangles like this are:

Law of sines:

$$\frac{a}{\sin A} = \frac{b}{\sin B} = \frac{c}{\sin C} \qquad (1.6)$$

Law of cosines:

$$c^2 = a^2 + b^2 - 2ab \cos C \qquad (1.7)$$

If in the three known parts there is a known side opposite a known angle, the law of sines is used. Otherwise we must use the law of cosines, switching to the law of sines once the above conditions have been satisfied.

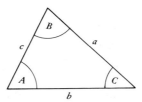

FIG. 1.12   Nonright triangle.

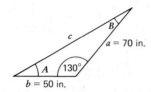

FIG. 1.13   Example Problem 1.5.

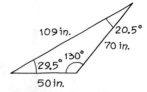

FIG. 1.14   Sketch of solution.

Example Problem 1.5

Find the side c and the angles A and B in Fig. 1.13.

GIVEN   Two sides and an included angle.

FIND A, B, and c.

Solution

Since we do not have a side opposite an angle, we use the law of cosines:

$$c^2 = a^2 + b^2 - 2ab \cos C$$
$$c^2 = (50)^2 + (70)^2 - 2(50)(70) \cos 130°$$

(Most calculators will evaluate $\cos 130°$ as -0.643. If yours will not handle the sign, s-i-g-n, then use:

$$\cos 130° = -\cos 50°$$
$$c^2 = 2500 + 4900 - 2(50)(70)(-0.643)$$
$$= 11,900$$
$$c = \mathbf{109 \text{ in.}}$$

Then by the law of sines:

$$\frac{\sin C}{c} = \frac{\sin A}{a}$$

$$\sin A = \frac{a}{c} \sin C$$

$$\sin A = \frac{70}{109} \sin 130°$$

$$\sin A = 0.492$$
$$A = \mathbf{29.5°}$$
$$B = 180 - 130 - 29.5 = \mathbf{20.5°} = B$$

Once again we sketch and label the triangle to check our solution (Fig. 1.14). We note that the indicated angles are in proper order. The larger sides are opposite the larger angles, and the longest side is less than the sum of the

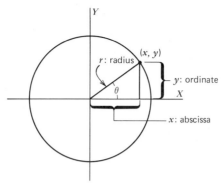

FIG. 1.15 Unit circle definition of trigonometric functions.

remaining two. We would have an even better check of the results if we drew the triangle to scale. Indeed we could have solved the problem this way!

TRIGONOMETRIC FUNCTIONS

We have defined trigonometric functions using a right triangle. A unit circle definition is more general and allows us to interpret functions of angles greater than 90° ($\pi/2$ rad). Based on the terminology from Fig. 1.15, we define:

$$\sin \theta = \frac{\text{ordinate}}{\text{radius}} = \frac{y}{r} \tag{1.8}$$

$$\cos \theta = \frac{\text{abscissa}}{\text{radius}} = \frac{x}{r} \tag{1.9}$$

$$\tan \theta = \frac{\text{ordinate}}{\text{abscissa}} = \frac{y}{x} \tag{1.10}$$

The advantage of these definitions is that they are general; that is; they apply for all values of θ. For example, Fig. 1.16 shows a second-quadrant angle. Equations

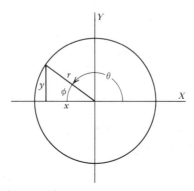

FIG. 1.16 A second-quadrant angle.

1.8 through 1.10 define the angle in the second, third, or fourth quadrants as well as the first. So:

$$\sin \theta = \frac{y}{r}$$

and

$$\sin \phi = \frac{y}{r}$$

from Fig. 1.16. Thus:

$$\sin \theta = \sin \phi$$

Since

$$\phi = 180 - \theta$$

we conclude:

$$\sin \theta = \sin(180° - \theta)$$

Thus, in addition to giving general definitions of the functions Equations 1.8 through 1.10 lead us to many trig identities. Table A.5 lists a number of useful relationships.

1.8 ARLIN'S TOOLBOX

We have an expert craftsman named Arlin Harris in our machine shop. Arlin is helpful, cheerful, and kind. If you need a widget made just so, Arlin will (1) show you how to make a widget just so or (2) make a widget just so for you. He is very generous. He'll take you to coffee, he'll take you to lunch, he'll even take you fishing where the big ones are.

In the cubby hole in the corner of our shop where Arlin dwells when he is not being helpful is a wooden case that has several little drawers, chrome hardware, and a natural wood finish. Daily Arlin dusts this box and wipes finger smudges from it. Frequently he'll open it for this or that. He never has to look for anything because each item is always in its place. He can find anything in it in the dark. He'll take some object from the box and caress it like a fine jewel before carefully returning it to its exact location. This is, of course, Arlin's toolbox!

You can ride Arlin's bike, drive his car, fish his pond, or even kick his dog, but you better not mess with Arlin's toolbox. There is a Dr. Jekyll–Mr. Hyde transformation in this man when it comes to his toolbox. You might as well insult his wife. Now why would this otherwise benevolent man become so disagreeable over a toolbox? Because it contains *his* tools. In this case "his" is not just possession; it's an extension of the person.

Any craftsman worth the term has *his* tools: tools gathered over time, tools that have served 20 and 30 years, tools with individual characteristics, just the right thing for the right job; tools that are an extension of the mechanic; tools that contribute substantially to the machinist's or mechanic's ability to do the job, and without which he is incomplete.

What are the tools of those who work in the engineering field? For an aircraft structural designer, tools might include drafting instruments. For many—a growing many—tools include a computer terminal or microcomputer. But for all, tools include their books: books that become old friends; books that say it just the way you understand it; books that have the right explanation where you can find it and in words you know; books that are dog-eared and soiled from use; books that have just the right table in the right place; books that have their margins scribbled with private jokes, the score from the game when we won, and one or two insults for your instructor. Books are your tools! Get to know them, mark them, index them, and most of all *keep them!*

PROBLEMS

1.1 Write each of the following numbers to four, three, two, and one significant figures.

(a) 866,723
(b) 942.06
(c) 0.00012345
(d) Exactly 2
(e) Exactly 0.02
(f) π (i.e., 3.14159)

1.2 Compute the range of values covered by each of the following products; compare that with the range represented when the answer is given to the same number of significant figures contained in the original factors.

(a) 4×5
(b) 4.0×5.0
(c) 4.00×5.00

1.3 Convert the following values to the units indicated:

(a) 42.3 ft-lb to in.-lb
(b) 1250 lb/ft² to lb/in.²
(c) 86.0 hp-days to ft-lb
(d) 928 lb-ft²/in.⁴ to lb/in.²
(e) 650 rpm to rads/s

1.4 Convert each of the following terms to the indicated units.

(a) 30 psi to Pa
(b) 215 ft³ to m³
(c) 22 ft/s to km/h
(d) 225 lb/ft to N/m
(e) 20,000 ft-lb/min to W

1.5 Do Problem 1.3, observing the rules for three significant figures.

1.6 Are the conversion factors in Table A-3 adequate to convert 938.73 ft-lb to newton-meters? Explain your answer.

1.7 The right triangle shown in Fig. 1.17 has the values indicated in the accompanying tabulation. Find the missing values and sketch the triangle approximately to scale.

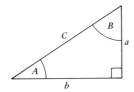

FIG. 1.17 Problem 1.7.

	a	b	c	A (deg)	B (deg)
(a)	10.0 in.	20.0 in.			
(b)	15.0 m		30.0 m		
(c)		20.0 ft	30.0 ft		
(d)	18.0 km			35.6	
(e)	20.0 mi				22.0
(f)				78.0	12.0
(g)			55.0 yd	57.3	
(h)		20.0 mm		30.0	
(i)		30.0 lb			42.0

1.8 The triangle shown in Fig. 1.18 has the values indicated below. Find the missing values and sketch the triangle approximately to scale, drawing side c horizontal.

	a	b	c	A (deg)	B (deg)	C (deg)
(a)	10.0 in.	20.0 in.	25.0 in.			
(b)	10.0 m	20.0 m		30.0		
(c)	10.0 ft	20.0 ft			30.0	
(d)	10.0 km	20.0 km				30.0
(e)	150.0 mi			70.0	80.0	
(f)	150.0 yd				60.0	50.0
(g)				80.0	40.0	60.0
(h)		1100.0 mm	200.0 mm	50.0		
(i)			200.0 lb	40.0		70.0

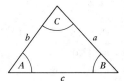

FIG. 1.18   Problem 1.8.

2

Forces in a Plane

Forces are everywhere and common to the experience of everyone. We see the effect of gravity on our bodies when we descend the stairs. We see the bruises that forces produce on the athletic field. Many of us can recall "woodshed" experiences where forces were applied to the learning center of our anatomy in an effort to modify our behavior. We experience the thrust of a great airplane as it lifts off the ground. We see a small leaf move back and forth in a gentle breeze. We see the aftermath of a vicious tornado. We hear the noise of a small child beating on her highchair tray. We see a crumpled automobile as two vehicles collide, and sadly too often, we see human bodies literally torn apart by the tremendous forces of an accident. A wise few have experienced the tug of seat and shoulder belts restraining them as they avoid disaster and death.

We see and experience the effect of forces in many settings. As a result of our substantial experience with forces, our intuition is usually quite effective in explaining what will happen or has happened. As we learn to quantify forces and their effect, we will want to rely on this intuition and build on it.

For the time being, we will limit our attention to forces in a plane—that is, two-dimensional problems. This is not a serious limitation, since a great portion of the analysis of forces and most of the phenomena can be adequately managed on a two-dimensional basis.

2.1 VECTORS AND SCALARS

Most physical phenomena may be described in terms of either scalars or vectors. *Scalars* are quantities that can be described by a single number (e.g., the number of pages in this book, the number of dollars in your wallet, the length of a string of spaghetti, the distance traveled by a television signal beamed to a satellite and bounced back to earth, the weight of a flea's knee, the size of the national debt). Some of these numbers are small, some are enormous, but in each case we have a single *number*.

But let's say I am in Houston, Texas, and take a trip of 250 miles before stopping for dinner. Given the single number, 250 miles, I might be eating barbeque ribs in Dallas, fried crawfish in Louisiana, or a taco on the border, or dodging a shark in the Gulf as we debate who is the diner and who is the "dinee." The single number, 250 miles, does not fix my destination. I also need to know in which direction: south? north? east? west? If I want those crawfish in Shreveport, I may have to set my course to 20° east of north, using a second number. To determine my destination, a *second* number is essential. If I say just "north," the second number is implied—0 degrees—but it is still essential.

We observe that to adequately describe a displacement, two numbers are required: How far, and which way? Displacement is a *vector* quantity. Vector quantities require two numbers to fully describe them (in two dimensions: you need three numbers in three dimensions). Vector quantities include velocity (how fast and which way?), acceleration, and of course force.

In Fig. 2.1, we represent a vector graphically as an arrow of appropriate length. In this case the vector represents a displacement from point A to point B. The vector is written as:

$$\textbf{AB} = 12 \text{ in. at } 35°$$

The two numbers required to describe this vector are 12 and 35. It is understood that the angle is measured positively counterclockwise from a positive X axis. In writing a vector by hand we put a bar ($\overline{AB}$) or arrow ($\overrightarrow{AB}$) over it. In print it is shown in boldface. Thus $\textbf{AB}$ means that the quantity being discussed is a vector and requires two numbers to fully describe it. If we simply write AB we mean the *magnitude* of the vector $\textbf{AB}$. In the case we are discussing,

$$\textbf{AB} = 12 \text{ in. at } 35°$$

and

$$AB = 12 \text{ in.}$$

We note the vector from B to A called $-\textbf{AB}$ is one with the same magnitude and line-of-action (or direction) as $\textbf{AB}$; but of opposite sense. This is illustrated in Fig. 2.2. We also note that a scalar times a vector gives another vector of different magnitude but the same direction. If

$$\textbf{AB} = 12 \text{ in. at } 35°$$

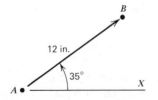

FIG. 2.1 Displacement as a vector.

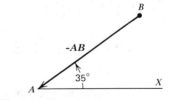

FIG. 2.2 Negative vector.

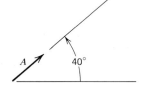 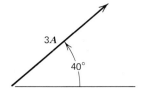

FIG. 2.3 Scalar multiplication of a vector.

Then

$$3(AB) = 36 \text{ in. at } 35°$$

Figure 2.3 further illustrates this point.

Both scalars and vectors must carry the appropriate sign and the proper units.

2.2 ADDITION OF VECTORS

In response to the question, "What is a vector?" an instructor facetiously replied "A vector is anything that behaves like a vector!" That sounds a bit like double-talk, yet it is a pretty good definition. The next question should be, "How does a vector behave?" In particular, we want to know how vectors behave in addition. We will address vectors generally, so that the conclusions we reach will be valid for any quantity that can be described as a vector (force, velocity, etc.).

Vectors are said to follow the "parallelogram law" for addition. This is illustrated in Fig. 2.4, where we get the sum of the vectors A and B. We describe this sum as R and call it the *resultant*. The resultant is the diagonal of the parallelogram formed by the vectors A and B and sides parallel to them when A, B, and R have a common origin as illustrated in Fig. 2.4. We can also write the vector equation

$$R = A + B$$

Note that each of the three quantities in this equation is a vector and each requires two numbers to fully describe it.

In Fig. 2.5, an alternate application of the parallelogram law, the vectors A and B have been drawn tip-to-tail. A resultant vector R is drawn from the origin to the terminal point. Of course the resultant is independent of the order of addition and we may write

$$R = A + B = B + A$$

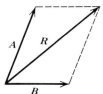 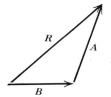

FIG. 2.4 Parallelogram law of vector addition.

FIG. 2.5 Vector addition by linking vectors tip-to-tail.

This principle gives us two methods of finding the resultant of two vectors. We can obtain a *graphical solution* by drawing the vectors to scale, tip-to-tail, drawing a resultant from the origin to the terminal point and scaling its magnitude and direction. This is the *graphical method*. Alternately we may simply sketch this triangle and solve for the unknown parts of the triangle formed *analytically*. We call this the *analytical method*. The following example problem illustrates both methods.

Example Problem 2.1

Add the vectors *A* and *B* shown in Fig. 2.6.

Solution

Graphical Solution

The parallelogram is constructed with the diagonal *R*. Careful drawing with hand-held instruments on an engineer's pad will yield results approaching three significant figures. The diagram should fill approximately half the sheet. Greater accuracy may be obtained at a drafting table. A graphical solution may also be obtained by using the tip-to-tail diagram shown in Fig. 2.7. The diagonal in Fig. 2.6 is scaled to give

$$R = 156 \text{ lb at } 56.3°$$

Analytical Solution

Sketch the force polygon as in Fig. 2.7 and note that the angle opposite *R* is 120°. Then by the law of cosines:

$$c^2 = a^2 + b^2 - 2ab \cos C$$
$$R^2 = (100)^2 + (80)^2 - 2(100)(80) \cos 120°$$
$$R^2 = 10{,}000 + 6400 - (-8000)$$
$$R^2 = 24{,}400$$
$$R = 156 \text{ lb}$$

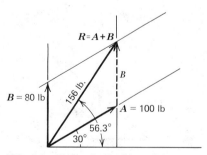

FIG. 2.6 Example Problem 2.1.

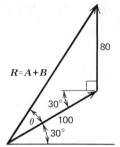

FIG. 2.7 Force triangle for Example Problem 2.1.

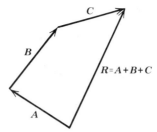

FIG. 2.8 Resultant of three vectors.

Then by the law of sines:

$$\frac{\sin\theta}{80} = \frac{\sin 120°}{156}$$

$$\sin\theta = \frac{80}{156}\sin 120° = 0.444$$

$$\theta = 26.3°$$

When added to 30° this gives:

$$R = A + B = 156 \text{ lb at } 56.3°$$

If we have more than two vectors to add, we can continue to add them tip-to-tail, producing a vector polygon as shown in Fig. 2.8. The resultant is still found by drawing a vector from the origin to the terminal point. Graphical addition for more than two vectors presents no special problems. However the analytical solution will require solving for an additional triangle for each additional vector. This quickly generates excessive calculations and will cause us to seek other methods of analytically handling such problems.

For Fig. 2.8 we write

$$R = A + B + C$$

or more generally

$$R = F_1 + F_2 + F_3 + \cdots$$

which will be valid for any number of vectors. We abbreviate this as follows:

$$R = \sum F_i$$

where $\sum$, the capital Greek letter sigma, which is equivalent to "S," stands for summation. We read this as "The resultant vector R equals the sum of the vectors."

Subtraction of vectors is a straightforward extension of vector addition. The equation

$$R = A - B$$

may be rewritten as

$$R = A + (-B)$$

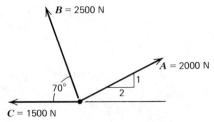

FIG. 2.9 Example Problem 2.2.

and we see that to subtract a vector is to add its negative. That is, we add a vector of the same magnitude and direction, but with a reversed sense.

Example Problem 2.2

Add the vectors *A*, *B*, and *C* shown in Fig. 2.9 *graphically*.

Solution

The force polygon is constructed by laying out the vectors to scale and in the proper direction in tip-to-tail fashion. A scale is selected that will fill half a page of an engineer's pad. Scales that are multiples of 5 to the inch and can be read conveniently off the grid are best. The force *A* is drawn first from *O* to *P* in Fig. 2.10, although the order does not matter. Then the vector *B* is drawn from *P* to *Q*, and then *C* from *Q* to *S*. Finally the resultant is drawn from the starting point *O* to the terminal point *S*. It is scaled and its direction measured, from which:

$$R = 3300 \text{ N at } 99.9°$$

To solve this problem analytically we would find the side *OQ* of the triangle *OPQ* (*OQ* is shown only for this discussion). Then we would find side *OS* of

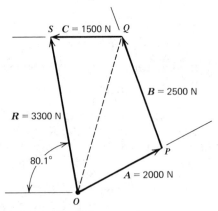

FIG. 2.10 Graphical solution to Example Problem 2.2.

triangle OQS. Because the amount of work goes up directly with the number of vectors to be added, the analytical method is generally not used for adding more than two vectors.

2.3 COMPONENTS OF VECTORS

In Fig. 2.4 we observed that the vector R was to be the *resultant* of the two vectors A and B. An alternate description of this situation is that the vectors A and B are *components* of the vector R. That is, we may resolve the vector into its components A and B. Any vector may be resolved into two or more components. The components are such that when they're added tip-to-tail, they will produce the original vector as a resultant. As before, we write:

$$R = A + B$$

A resultant vector, a force of 120 kN at 45°, is shown in Fig. 2.11. In Fig. 2.12 the force has been resolved into two components, A and B. There is an infinite number of pairs of components that will produce the given vector. In Fig. 2.13 the given force is resolved into three components. This can be continued ad infinitum. Figure 2.14 shows a particular pair of components that are perpendicular to each other. They are called rectangular components. We will have great interest in these components and will return to them shortly.

To find a particular pair of components, we work the inverse of Example Problem 2.1. Again, we may find components graphically or analytically.

Example Problem 2.3

Find components of the 1800-N force in Fig. 2.15 along the lines *ab* and *cd*.

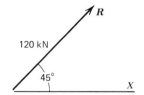

FIG. 2.11 Resultant vector.

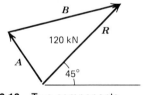

FIG. 2.12 Two components.

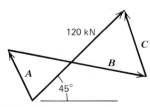

FIG. 2.13 Three components.

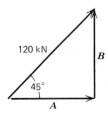

FIG. 2.14 Rectangular components.

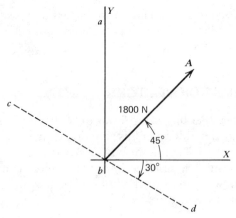

FIG. 2.15 Example Problem 2.3.

Solution

Graphical Solution

A graphical solution is obtained by drawing the 1800-N vector to scale and with the proper orientation, Fig. 2.16. One line is then constructed through the origin parallel to *ab*. A second line is constructed parallel to *cd* through the end point of *A*. The intersection of these two lines, point *P*, gives the third point on the force triangle. Arrowheads with the appropriate sense are added so that

$$A = B + C$$

We then scale *B* and *C*, yielding

$$B = 2010 \text{ N at } 90.0°$$
$$C = 1470 \text{ N at } -30.0°$$

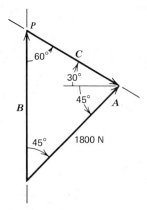

FIG. 2.16 Graphical Solution for Example Problem 2.3.

The order of **B** and **C** is not important. Reversing the order gives the other half of the parallelogram, but the same results.

Analytical Solution

The analytical solution requires at least a sketch of Fig. 2.16. Making this sketch roughly to scale gives us an approximate graphical solution as well. From Fig. 2.15 we can determine the angles included in the triangle; these are as indicated in Fig. 2.16. We must solve a nonright triangle. In this case, we have a 60° angle opposite the 1800-N side, which calls for the law of sines.

$$\frac{A}{\sin 60°} = \frac{B}{\sin 75°} = \frac{C}{\sin 45°}$$

$$B = 1800 \frac{\sin 75°}{\sin 60°} = 2010$$

$$\mathbf{B = 2010 \text{ N at } 90.0°}$$

$$C = 1800 \frac{\sin 45°}{\sin 60°} = 1470$$

$$\mathbf{C = 1470 \text{ N at } -30.0°}$$

We intuitively examine this solution, noting that the sides are proportional to the angles.

2.4 RECTANGULAR COMPONENTS

We have discussed components in general. Now we are concerned with a special pair of components, which will be *extremely* useful. The special pair is the rectangular pair, that is, a horizontal component and a vertical component. We will also be interested in other rectangular components from time to time, but mostly we will see horizontal and vertical. Figure 2.17 shows a vector A, which makes an angle θ with the X axis. We may find the components A_x and A_y by projecting

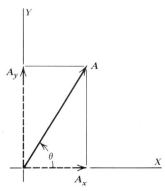

FIG. 2.17 Rectangular components.

the vector A onto the respective axes. This can be done graphically, but to no particular advantage. Since we have a right triangle, we observe:

$$\sin \theta = \frac{A_y}{A}$$

from which

$$A_y = A \sin \theta \tag{2.1}$$

Similarly

$$\cos \theta = \frac{A_x}{A}$$

and

$$A_x = A \cos \theta \tag{2.2}$$

Equations 2.1 and 2.2 are general for any value of θ as long as it is measured from the X axis and carries the proper sign.

Example Problem 2.4

Find the horizontal and vertical components of the force shown in Fig. 2.18.

Solution

We can blindly apply Eqs. 2.1 and 2.2. First we note that θ should be measured from the X axis, so we write:

$$\theta = 180° - 35° = 145°$$

Then we have:

$$C_x = C \cos \theta = 25.0 \cos 145°$$
$$\mathbf{C_x = -20.5 \ kip}$$
$$C_y = C \sin \theta = 25.0 \sin 145°$$
$$\mathbf{C_y = 14.3 \ kips}$$

In examining the solution we note that C_x is negative, which agrees with the Fig. 2.18; C_y is positive.

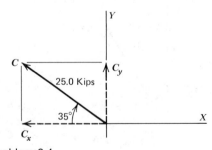

FIG. 2.18   Example Problem 2.4.

Referring once again to Fig. 2.17, we note that:

$$A = A_x + A_y \qquad (2.3)$$

This equation says that a resultant vector is the vector sum of its components. Suppose we have a second vector B, for which:

$$B = B_x + B_y$$

If we desire the vector sum of A and B, we have, in Fig. 2.19,

$$R = A + B$$

Substituting from above,

$$R = A_x + A_y + B_x + B_y$$

We recognize that R may also be expressed as the sum of its components.

$$R = R_x + R_y$$

Then

$$R_x + R_y = A_x + B_x + A_y + B_y$$

and it follows, as illustrated in Fig. 2.19, that

$$R_x = A_x + B_x$$

and

$$R_y = A_y + B_y$$

Since in each of the last two equations all the vectors are in the same direction, X or Y, we may replace the vector equation with two scalar equations.

$$R_x = A_x + B_x \qquad (2.4)$$
$$R_y = A_y + B_y \qquad (2.5)$$

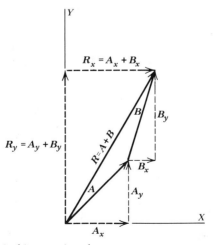

FIG. 2.19 The resultant of two vectors by components.

and

$$R = R_x + R_y \qquad (2.6)$$

These three equations will allow us to find resultant vectors using components. Of course A_x, B_x, A_y, and B_y all carry appropriate positive or negative signs. Finally, we have

$$\tan \phi = \frac{R_y}{R_x} \qquad (2.7)$$

and

$$R^2 = R_x^2 + R_y^2 \qquad (2.8)$$

which give the direction and magnitude of R.

Example Problem 2.5

Add vectors A and B shown in Fig. 2.20 using *components*.

Solution

Find the components of A.

$$A_x = A \cos \theta = 100 \cos 30°$$
$$A_x = 86.6 \text{ lb}$$
$$A_y = A \sin \theta = 100 \sin 30°$$
$$A_y = 50.0 \text{ lb}$$

Find the components of B.

$$B_x = B \cos \theta = 80 \cos 90° = 0$$
$$B_y = B \sin \theta = 80 \sin 90° = 80.0 \text{ lb}$$

Then

$$R_x = A_x + B_x$$
$$R_x = 86.6 + 0 = 86.6 \text{ lb}$$
$$R_y = A_y + B_y$$
$$R_y = 50.0 + 80.0 = 130 \text{ lb}$$

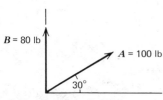

FIG. 2.20 Example Problem 2.5.

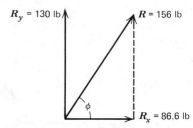

FIG. 2.21 Resultant of components.

The components are resolved into the vector R as shown in Fig. 2.21.

$$\tan \phi = \frac{130}{86.6} = 1.50$$

$$\phi = 56.3°$$

$$\sin \phi = \frac{R_y}{R}$$

$$R = \frac{R_y}{\sin \phi} = \frac{130}{\sin 56.3°}$$

$$R = 156 \text{ lb at } 56.3°$$

If this problem seems familiar, it should. This resultant agrees with Example Problem 2.1.

2.5 VECTOR NOTATION

Vector notation is a system that gives us greater efficiency in writing vector equations. With it we can replace two or three scalar equations with one vector equation. Most of the advanced work in mechanics uses vector mathematics including vector notation. In this text we simply introduce the notation without getting into the algebra or calculus of vectors. For our purposes vector notation offers a minor convenience and will prepare the student to recognize it in more advanced texts or articles. Nothing in the text that follows depends on vector notation, so this section is optional. We will, however, show a number of alternate solutions using this notation.

The first concept we need to grasp is that of the *unit vector*. A unit vector is simply a vector that has a magnitude of one. It can point in any direction. Figure 2.22 shows two unit vectors in which we are especially interested, labeled i and j and directed along the X and Y axes respectively. Recall that when we multiply a vector by a scalar, we get another vector with the same direction and a different magnitude. The sense will also be reversed if the scalar is a negative value. Based on this, we write:

$$A = 10i \qquad \text{(lb)}$$

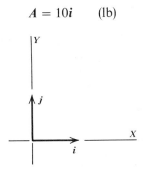

FIG. 2.22 Unit vectors.

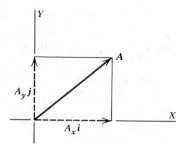

FIG. 2.23 Expressing a vector in terms of unit vectors.

meaning a force of 10 lb in the X direction. Or we write:

$$\boldsymbol{B} = -8\boldsymbol{i} \qquad \text{(lb)}$$

meaning a force of 8 lb in the negative X direction. Since any vector can be resolved into horizontal and vertical components, we can write

$$\boldsymbol{A} = A_x\boldsymbol{i} + A_y\boldsymbol{j} \qquad (2.9)$$

as illustrated in Fig. 2.23. Substituting in Eqs. 2.1 and 2.2 gives:

$$\boldsymbol{A} = A\cos\theta\boldsymbol{i} + A\sin\theta\boldsymbol{j} \qquad (2.10)$$

For instance, for Example Problem 2.5 we wrote the result as follows:

$$\boldsymbol{R} = 156 \text{ lb at } 56.3°$$

But we could just as well have written

$$\boldsymbol{R} = 86.6\boldsymbol{i} + 130\boldsymbol{j} \qquad \text{(lb)}$$

Although we will not use (this convention) in our discussion of plane problems, it is worth noting that a unit vector in the direction of the Z axis is denoted by $\boldsymbol{k}$. A positive Z axis comes out of the paper toward the reader in Fig. 2.22. This in accordance with the "right-hand rule," which is derived from observing that the thumb, forefinger, and middle finger of the right hand correspond to the X, Y, and Z, axes respectively. We will also have occasion to use an arbitrarily directed unit vector, which we will designate $\boldsymbol{u}$.

Example Problem 2.6

Find the magnitude and direction of the vector:

$$\boldsymbol{A} = 10\boldsymbol{i} + 12\boldsymbol{j}$$

Sketch the components and the resultant.

Solution

The components are sketched in Fig. 2.24, and we note that A is the hypotenuse of the triangle that has the components as sides. We note

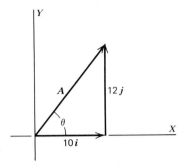

FIG. 2.24 Example Problem 2.6.

$$\tan \theta = \frac{12}{10} = 1.20$$

$$\theta = 50.2°$$

$$\sin \theta = \frac{12}{A}$$

$$A = \frac{12}{\sin \theta} = 15.6$$

$$A = \textbf{15.6 at 50.2°}$$

We note that the resultant is greater than either component and the angle is greater than 45°, which we would have expected. Also, in each case two numbers are required to totally define the vector A. In the first case, 10 and 12; in the latter, 15.6 and 50.2.

Example Problem 2.7

Add the vectors A, B, and C using vector notation, where

$$A = 10i + 12j$$
$$B = 8i - 6j$$
$$C = -4i + 4j$$

Solution

Using vector notation, we combine Eqs. 2.4, 2.5, and 2.6 into a single equation.

$$R = A + B + C$$
$$R = (10i + 12j) + (8i - 6j) + (-4i + 4j)$$
$$R = (10i + 8i - 4i) + (12j - 6j + 4j)$$
$$R = (10 + 8 - 4)i + (12 - 6 + 4)j$$
$$R = 14i + 10j$$

In the future only the fourth and final steps should be necessary. Later a vector in component form will be acceptable. For the time being, however, we will find the magnitude and direction of the resultant.

$$\tan \phi = \frac{R_y}{R_x} = \frac{10}{14} = 0.714$$

$$\phi = 35.5°$$

$$R = \frac{R_y}{\sin \phi} = \frac{10}{\sin 35.5°} = 17.2$$

R = 17.2 at 35.5°

2.6 RESULTANT FORCES

Thus far we have examined vectors somewhat generally. In statics our primary interest in vectors will be as forces. We learned that vectors in a plane require two numbers to be fully defined. These two numbers may be magnitude and direction or two components, primarily rectangular components, and in particular corresponding to X and Y axes. We have learned three methods of adding vectors, which we will apply to forces. They are:

1. Graphical addition.
2. Analytical addition.
3. Addition by components.

GRAPHICAL ADDITION

Forces are drawn to scale and in the proper direction and are placed tip-to-tail as in Fig. 2.8. The resultant is found by constructing a line from the beginning point to the terminal point, completing the force polygon. The resulting magnitude and direction are scaled. Using an engineer's pad and hand instruments, an accuracy of two to three significant figures can be achieved with careful work. This can be improved by working at a drawing board with instruments and using a larger scale. The difficulty of this method does not depend on the number of forces to be added. It is good practice to always use an approximate graphical solution for a quick and easy visual check of results. This method cannot be easily extended to three dimensions.

ANALYTICAL ADDITION

As in the graphical method, a force polygon is constructed, although it does not have to be to scale. The parts of the force polygon are found using the laws of sines and cosines. If two forces are to be added, analytical addition is quite acceptable. However for each additional force, an additional nonright triangle must be solved, making this method unattractive for more than two forces. The method can be extended to three dimensions but becomes very awkward. Although quite limited, occasionally it is the preferred method.

ADDITION BY COMPONENTS

Addition by components is based on Eqs. 2.4 through 2.8, and is superior to the analytical method for more than two forces and superior to the graphical method for three-dimensional problems. For most students this will become the preferred and regularly used method of adding forces. It can be used without even drawing a figure, but that is not recommended. For solving statics problems using the computer, this is the preferred method, and some hand-held calculators are pre-programmed to solve problems this way.

2.7 SUMMARY

A scalar quantity requires one number to describe it; a vector needs two (in two dimensions). We describe a vector by its magnitude and direction or by the magnitude of its rectangular components. A negative vector is one of the same magnitude as the corresponding positive vector, but opposite sense.

Vectors add according to the parallelogram law or by constructing a vector polygon by adding the vectors tip-to-tail. Results may be obtained graphically, or analytically, using the laws of sines and cosines. A vector may be resolved into any number of components. Of primary interest to us are rectangular components. For the vector A we write

$$A_y = A \sin \theta \qquad (2.1)$$
$$A_x = A \cos \theta \qquad (2.2)$$

and

$$A = A_x + A_y \qquad (2.3)$$

or using unit vector notation we may write

$$A = A_x i + A_y j \qquad (2.9)$$

Using components gives an additional method of addition:

$$R_x = A_x + B_x \qquad (2.4)$$
$$R_y = A_y + B_y \qquad (2.5)$$

and

$$R = R_x + R_y \qquad (2.6)$$

or using unit vector notation

$$R = R_x i + R_y j$$

Our primary interest in vector addition will be for forces. We will gravitate to the component method of force addition, but should not lose sight of the other two.

PROBLEMS

2.1 For each pair of forces in the indicated figure, find the resultant force *graphically.*

    (a) Fig. 2.25   (b) Fig. 2.26   (c) Fig. 2.27   (d) Fig. 2.28

2.2 For each pair of forces in the indicated figure, find the resultant force by sketching the force polygon and solving *analytically.*

    (a) Fig. 2.25   (b) Fig. 2.26   (c) Fig. 2.27   (d) Fig. 2.28

2.3 Find the resultant of *A* and *B graphically.*

	A	*B*
(a)	50 lb at 30°	100 lb at 75°
(b)	100 lb at 30°	50 lb at 75°
(c)	800 lb at 45°	800 lb at 135°
(d)	60 kips at 90°	80 kips at $-135°$
(e)	300 N at $-20°$	400 N at $-80°$
(f)	10 kN at $-(\pi/4)$ rad	25 kN at $+(\pi/4)$ rad
(g)	25 kN at $(3\pi/4)$ rad	10 kN at $(\pi/6)$ rad

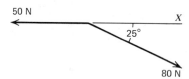

FIG. 2.25 Problems 2.1a, 2.2a, 2.5, 2.14a, 2.18, 2.19a.

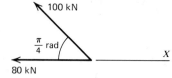

FIG. 2.26 Problems 2.1b, 2.2b, 2.6, 2.14b, 2.19b, 2.20.

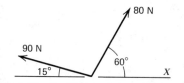

FIG. 2.27 Problems 2.1c, 2.2c, 2.5, 2.14c, 2.18, 2.19c.

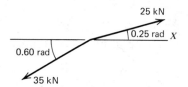

FIG. 2.28 Problems 2.1d, 2.2d, 2.6, 2.14d, 2.19d, 2.20.

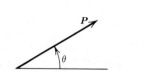

FIG. 2.29 Problems 2.8, 2.10, 2.11.

FIG. 2.30 Problem 2.9.

2.4 Find the resultant of *A* and *B* for the assigned part in Problem 2.3 by sketching the force polygon and using the laws of sines and cosines.

2.5 Add the four forces given in Figs. 2.25 and 2.27 *graphically.*

2.6 Add the four forces given in Figs. 2.26 and 2.28 *graphically.*

2.7 Add the following forces *graphically.*

	A	*B*	*C*	*D*
(a)	50 lb at 30°	100 lb at 75°	100 lb at 30°	50 lb at 75°
(b)	60 kips at 90°	80 kips at −135°	50 kips at 135°	60 kips at −45°
(c)	10 kN at −($\pi/4$) rad	25 kN at ($\pi/4$) rad	25 kN at ($3\pi/4$) rad	10 kN at ($\pi/6$) rad
(d)	300 N at 90°	400 N at 180°	500 N at 135°	600 N at 120°

2.8 Resolve the force *P* into horizontal and vertical components for the following values of *P* and θ for Fig. 2.29.

	P	θ		*P*	θ
(a)	100 lb	30°	(d)	50 kN	0.3 rad
(b)	100 lb	60°	(e)	50 kN	0.6 rad
(c)	100 lb	75°	(f)	50 kN	1.0 rad

2.9 Resolve the force *P* into horizontal and vertical components for the following values of *P* and θ for Fig. 2.30. (Note: 1 kip is 1000 lb.)

	P	θ		*P*	θ
(a)	250 kips	20°	(d)	1800 N	0.40 rad
(b)	250 kips	40°	(e)	1800 N	0.80 rad
(c)	250 kips	80°	(f)	1800 N	1.20 rad

2.10 Resolve the force *P* into horizontal and vertical components for the following values of *P* and θ for Fig. 2.29.

	P	θ		*P*	θ
(a)	18 tons	+35°	(d)	18 tons	+125°
(b)	18 tons	−35°	(e)	18 tons	+215°
(c)	18 tons	−125°	(f)	18 tons	−215°

2.11 Resolve the force *P* into horizontal and vertical components for the following values of *P* and θ for Fig. 2.29.

	P	θ		*P*	θ
(a)	25 kN	($\pi/4$) rad	(d)	25 kN	−($3\pi/4$) rad
(b)	25 kN	−($\pi/4$) rad	(e)	25 kN	($5\pi/4$) rad
(c)	25 kN	($3\pi/4$) rad	(f)	25 kN	−($5\pi/4$) rad

2.12 Find the resultant force (that means magnitude *and* direction, without our saying so) from the following components:

	R_x	R_y			R_x	R_y
(a)	30 lb	40 lb		(g)	20 kips	− 30 kips
(b)	30 lb	− 40 lb		(h)	30 kips	20 kips
(c)	− 50 lb	− 120 lb		(i)	400 kN	600 kN
(d)	− 50 lb	+ 120 lb		(j)	− 400 kN	600 kN
(e)	120 N	50 N		(k)	− 400 kN	− 600 kN
(f)	− 120 N	− 50 N		(l)	400 kN	− 600 kN

2.13 Find the resultant of *A* and *B* for the assigned part of Problem 2.3 *by summing components*.

2.14 For each pair of forces shown, find the resultant force *by components*.

   (a) Fig. 2.25   (b) Fig. 2.26   (c) Fig. 2.27   (d) Fig. 2.28

2.15 From Problem 2.12 add the three forces of parts (a), (b), and (c).

   (a) *Graphically*   (b) *By components*

2.16 From Problem 2.12 add the forces of parts (i), (j), and (k).

   (a) *Graphically*   (b) *By components*

2.17 Add the forces in the assigned part of Problem 2.7 *using components*.

2.18 Add the forces of Figs. 2.25 and 2.27 by components.

The following problems denoted by an asterisk (*) are optional.

*2.19 For each pair of forces shown, find the resultant force by *components using vector notation*.

   (a) Fig. 2.25   (b) Fig. 2.26   (c) Fig. 2.27   (d) Fig. 2.28

*2.20 Add the forces of Figs. 2.26 and 2.28 *by components using vector notation*.

*2.21 Add the forces in the assigned part of Problem 2.7 *using components and unit vector notation*.

*2.22 Find the resultant of *A* and *B* for the assigned part in Problem 2.3 *using vector notation and components*.

*2.23 Three vectors are defined as follows.

$$A = 10i + 14j \quad \text{(N)}$$
$$B = -4i + 6j \quad \text{(N)}$$
$$C = i - 9j \quad \text{(N)}$$

Find the indicated resultant.

   (a) $R = A + B + C$ (b) $R = A - B - C$ (c) $R = B + C - 2A$

3

Statics of a
Particle in a Plane

We have reviewed the concepts we will need to be successful and have examined the characteristics of vectors—in particular, forces. We now begin the study of statics proper; that is, we will determine the forces required to hold bodies at rest. This state is called *static equilibrium*. If you look around, you will observe many objects that are at rest and therefore in static equilibrium. The book you're reading is *at rest*; the table it lies on is *at rest*; the chair on which you sit is *at rest*; the floor that supports the table and chair is *at rest*. The building of which the floor is a part is *at rest*, and things that are at rest are said to be in static equilibrium. In this chapter we will learn to determine the forces required to keep a body at rest.

Having emphasized that a body at rest is in static equilibrium, I must hastily add that a body in motion at a constant velocity is also in equilibrium. That is an extremely important physics principle, but we won't be too much concerned with it in statics. A frame of reference fixed to the earth's surface is adequate for our purposes.

3.1   WHEN A 40-TON LOCOMOTIVE IS A PARTICLE

When you hear the term "particle," what do you think of? Something very small, perhaps insignificant as well? Sure. Maybe a speck of dust in the eye, a tiny grain of sand in the core of a pearl, an infinitesimal impurity observed under a microscope in the structure of a metal, or one of those tiny bits within the nucleus of an atom, which physicists seem to chase endlessly. We will use the term "particle" to refer to entities such as these and many more as well. We'll use it to refer to green peas, billiard balls, basketballs, chairs, tables, automobiles, tracks, airplanes, and 40-ton locomotives. Forty-ton locomotives and things much bigger! In fact, there is probably nothing that cannot appropriately be viewed as a particle in some analysis—that is, in some cases, but unfortunately not all. The problem is to know which.

For reasons we will explore later, a body may be treated as a particle if all the forces acting on it pass through a common point. We use the term *concurrent* to refer to things that come together in time or space; thus we call these *concurrent forces.* If all the forces acting on a body are concurrent the body may be treated as a particle. Returning to our 40-ton locomotive, suppose it is sitting on an incline when the brakes fail. Fortunately SUPERPERSON . . . Yes, SUPERPERSON, that way we don't offend nobody! Anyway, SUPERPERSON is nearby and holds the locomotive in place (as shown in Fig. 3.1) by pushing with a force of about 7000 lb. Now SUPERPERSON must be smart as well as strong, since the 7000-lb force needs to pass through the intersection of the 80,000-lb weight of the locomotive and the ground reaction force. All three forces pass through a common point; we have a system of concurrent forces; we've treated the locomotive as a particle; and SUPERPERSON have saved the day!

Knowing when to treat a body as a particle in many cases comes from experience and judgment. For the time being assume it's OK. Later we will work problems where it's not OK. By the time we are through with the course, you will have had some experience and developed some judgment in the matter.

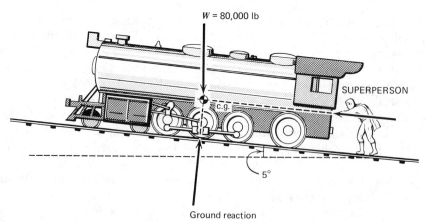

FIG. 3.1   Forty-ton locomotive being held in place by SUPERPERSON.

In Fig. 3.1 the weight (80,000 lb) was treated as a concentrated force acting through the center of gravity (cg). We will continue this practice until Chapter 6, where we will see why and when we can do this.

3.2 NEWTON'S LAWS OF MOTION

The fundamental principles of mechanics are Newton's three laws. These are:

1. *If the sum of forces acting on a body is zero, the body will remain at rest or continue in motion at a constant velocity, and vice versa.*
2. *If the sum of forces acting on a body is not zero, the body will be accelerated proportional to and in the direction of the unbalanced force.*
3. *For every action there is a reaction that is equal in magnitude and opposite in sense.*

Statics is based squarely on the first and third laws. Dynamics is based on the second.

Recall that forces are vectors. Thus we express the first law in equation form as

$$\sum F = 0 \tag{3.1}$$

We read this as "the sum of the forces is zero," recalling that $\sum$ (sigma) means summation. A vector equation in two dimensions is equivalent to two scalar equations, which we write as follows:

$$\sum F_x = 0 \tag{3.2}$$
$$\sum F_y = 0 \tag{3.3}$$

We could pick any two directions and on occasion we will pick others, but mainly we will sum forces in the X and Y or horizontal and vertical directions. In the preceding chapter we found the resultant force, R by summing forces.

$$\sum F = R$$

Newton's first law requires that this resultant force R be zero for bodies at rest. Recognizing this will allow us to extend the methods of Chapter 2 to this one.

A body that satisfies the first law is said to be in *equilibrium*. I can determine *equilibrium* from either of its provisions. If on the one hand I sum the forces acting on a body and find zero, I declare the body to be in equilibrium; and I know it must be at rest or moving at constant velocity. On the other hand, if I look at my cup and see it just sitting there at rest, I know it is in equilibrium and must satisfy Eq. 3.1. It is more difficult to determine whether the velocity of a body in motion is constant; but if that is determined, then this body must also satisfy Eq. 3.1, hence it is in equilibrium. When SUPERPERSON holds the locomotive in place in Fig. 3.1, it is at rest and in equilibrium. The forces acting on it must therefore satisfy Eq. 3.1.

3.3 EQUILIBRIUM AND THE FREE BODY DIAGRAM

If you were learning statics from a computer, at this point the program would give you a fanfare or drumroll. It's time to sit up and pay attention!

In Section 3.2 we introduced Newton's first law and the condition it describes—equilibrium. We will apply the equilibrium equations (3.2 and 3.3) over and over again during this course. To apply them systematically, and also to help us visualize what they represent, we will use one of the fundamental tools of mechanics, a *free body diagram*. That is a phrase you are sure to grow weary of. It is repeated so often by teachers of mechanics that they frequently acquire it as a nickname. So take it from ol' "Free Body" Neathery: it is a fundamental tool, and it will remove much of the mystery and difficulty from mechanics.

Well now that everyone is in favor of it, we might as well find out what it is. It's pretty much what its name says: a *diagram* of a *body* that has been cut *free* of all supports. Figure 3.2 shows the 40-ton locomotive we have been discussing being held in place by SUPERPERSON. This is a diagram of the locomotive as we might see it. To obtain a free body diagram, we observe the following steps.

1. Select a body.
2. Show all externally applied forces.
3. Remove each support and replace it with an appropriate force.
4. Label all forces and important dimensions.

Step 1 We decide to draw a free body diagram of the locomotive in Fig. 3.2, so the locomotive is our body. Figure 3.3 shows the body. We may wish to be fairly simplistic in our sketch as in this figure. Those with an artistic flair may

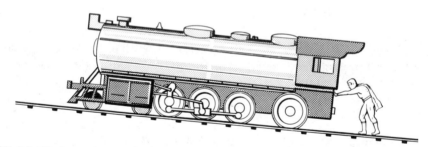

FIG. 3.2 Forty-ton locomotive.

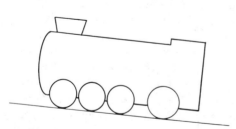

FIG. 3.3 Diagram of a body.

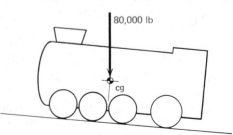

FIG. 3.4 Diagram of body with externally applied load.

want to flaunt it. That's OK, but if you need the help of a straight edge and template to write your signature, then use one for free body diagrams too. The main thing is that your diagrams should pictorially convey essential detail. The use of an engineer's pad will make sketching easier.

Step 2   The only externally applied load on the locomotive is its weight. The weight is shown to act through the body's center of gravity (cg) as seen in Fig. 3.4. Weight is always present, but it is not always necessary to show it. In some cases it acts perpendicular to the plane of interest. If for instance we wish to analyze forces between colliding billiard balls on a horizontal table, the weight of the balls is perpendicular to the plane of the table and has little importance. In other cases weight is very small compared to the other forces present and may be neglected. This is often the case when metals and engineering plastics are loaded to capacity. If we analyze the forces on a wrench in tightening a bolt, we may safely ignore the weight of the wrench. On the other hand, weight is totally responsible for the other forces in our locomotive problem. Other types of externally applied loads will be seen as we proceed in the text.

Step 3   The locomotive is supported in two areas: at its wheels and at the back, where SUPERPERSON (*SP*) is pushing. We visualize removing the roadway under each wheel. As the support for each wheel is removed, the reacting force must be supplied—in this case N_1, N_2, N_3, and N_4, as shown in Fig. 3.5. There will be a reacting force in each direction in which motion is prevented. The wheel cannot punch through the track, so a force perpendicular (or normal) to the track must be present to prevent this motion. If friction were present, there would also be a friction force at each wheel parallel to the track. In this case there is none. We will assume this to be the case for a wheel unless stated otherwise. The four forces (N_1–N_4) were represented as a single force in Fig. 3.1. We'll see later how to handle this situation.

The remaining support is where SUPERPERSON is pushing at the back of the locomotive. This is assumed to be normal to the back. In the more general case there would also be a component parallel to the back.

Now the body is free from all supports, and is therefore a *free body*. It is important to remember to cut *all* supports.

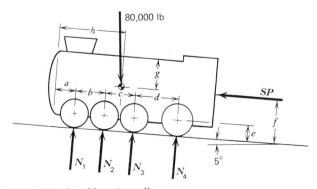

FIG. 3.5   Diagram of body with externally applied load and reactions.

Step 4   We have supplied labels to Fig. 3.5 as we proceeded. Each force and its location must be clearly and uniquely labeled. In the next chapter important dimensions will become more apparent.

Figure 3.5 is a completed free body diagram of a body in equilibrium; that is, it must satisfy Eqs. 3.2 and 3.3. If it is accurate and complete, all that is required to solve a statics problem is an accurate listing of what has been drawn and a little algebra. If the free body diagram is incorrect, no amount of mathematical manipulation can salvage the problem.

Example Problem 3.1

Make a free body diagram of the wheelbarrow in Fig. 3.6.

Solution

Step 1   The wheelbarrow is specified in the problem as the body.

Step 2   The weight (W) of the wheelbarrow and its cargo is shown acting through the combined center of gravity in Fig. 3.7.

Step 3   The ground support is removed, and the force N, normal to the ground, is drawn. The friction force F, which resists rolling, is shown parallel to the ground. The force exerted by the worker on the handle is shown by two components, P and L, parallel and perpendicular to the handles. Any other pair of components, such as horizontal and vertical, would do as well.

Step 4   The forces have been labeled. To proceed, the dimensions required to locate the forces would be added.

FIG. 3.6   Example Problem 3.1.

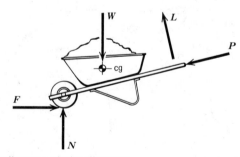

FIG. 3.7   Free body diagram of wheelbarrow.

3.4   THE PRINCIPLE OF TRANSMISSIBILITY

Figure 3.8 shows five forces that have a common magnitude, direction, sense, and line of action. Any of the forces would have exactly the same tendency to produce motion in body A. Any one of the forces will require the same set of additional forces to prevent the body A from moving. We conclude that it does not matter where along the line PP' the force is applied. The static effect will be the same. In Fig. 3.9 we see that SUPERPERSON has grown tired of pushing and has started pulling. As long as the pull is along the same line of action and of the same magnitude, the effect will be the same. This is known as the principle of transmissibility.

Based on the principle of transmissibility, we may move a force forward or backward along its line of action as we please. Moving the force along its line of action will not alter the effect of the force on the body. This principle will prove useful in the construction of free body diagrams.

3.5   CONCURRENT FORCE PROBLEMS: ANALYTICALLY

"Concurrent" refers to things that come together in *space* or *time*. We will use this term to refer to forces that come together in space, that is, forces that act through a common point. Since a particle is a point in space, the forces acting on a particle are always *concurrent*. The forces on a rigid body may also be concurrent but are not necessarily so. According to Newton's first law, a body will be at rest if the

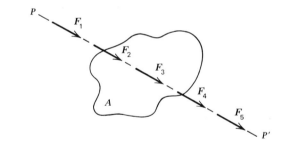

FIG. 3.8   Principle of transmissibility.

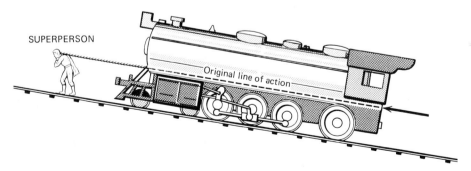

FIG. 3.9   SUPERPERSON demonstrates the principle of transmissibility.

sum of these concurrent forces is zero. Alternately, if it is at rest, the resultant will be zero. Figure 3.10 shows a particle with forces acting on it. If this particle is at rest, the sum of the forces must be zero. In this section we determine the unknown force *A analytically*. In sections that follow, we will solve the same problem *graphically* and *by components*. Each method has it advantages, and you should become familiar with all three.

Newton's first law is expressed by Eqs. 3.1 (or 3.2 and 3.3) for coplanar problems. Since we have two equations, we can solve for two unknowns. Recall that a force is a vector quantity, and in two dimensions, two numbers are required to fully define it.

Example Problem 3.2

Find the force *A* required to keep the particle in Fig. 3.10 in equilibrium.

Solution

The first step is to draw a free body diagram, that is, a sketch of the body and all the forces acting on it. Careful observation will show that Fig. 3.10 is a free body diagram, so we proceed.

For the particle to be in equilibrium, Eq. 3.1 must be satisfied.

$$\sum F = 0 \qquad (3.1)$$

We add these vectors tip-to-tail as shown in Fig. 3.11. We sketch the known vectors of 120 N and 200 N at the appropriate angles as shown. For the sum of the three forces to be zero, the remaining vector, *A*, must close the force polygon. That is, it must return to the starting point *q*. Note that it is *from p to q*, not the reverse. (The reverse is the *resultant* force.) *All* the vectors in the polygon are joined tip-to-tail.

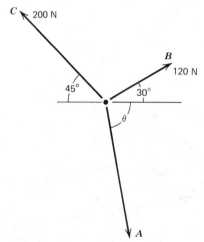

FIG. 3.10 A system of concurrent forces acting on a particle.

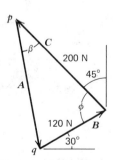

FIG. 3.11 Example Problem 3.2.

In the case of three forces, the force polygon is a force triangle. In general, we can solve for two unknowns. We solve for the angle ϕ by

$$\phi = 180° - 45° - 60° = 75°$$

We now have two sides and the included angle, so using the law of cosines:

$$c^2 = a^2 + b^2 - 2ab \cos C$$
$$A^2 = 200^2 + 120^2 - 2(200)(120) \cos 75°$$
$$A = 205 \text{ N}$$

Then by the law of sines:

$$\frac{a}{\sin A} = \frac{b}{\sin B}$$

$$\frac{120}{\sin \beta} = \frac{A}{\sin 75°}$$

$$\sin \beta = \frac{120}{205} \sin 75° = 0.566$$

$$\beta = 34.5°$$

The angle A makes with the horizontal is

$$34.5° + 45° = 79.5°$$

and

$$A = \textbf{205 N at 79.5°}$$

The answer looks reasonable, assuming that our sketch is approximately to scale. We note it is less than the sum of the other two sides.

We call this method—sketching the force polygon and solving analytically—the analytical method. It works well for three forces that give a triangle for a force polygon. If we have more than three forces, the method becomes overly tedious and one of the other methods will be preferred.

3.6 CONCURRENT FORCE PROBLEMS: GRAPHICALLY

The graphical method is very similar to the analytical method. A free body diagram is drawn. Then a force polygon is drawn to scale, joining the vectors tip-to-tail, and the unknown sides and angles are measured.

This method is not limited by the number of forces. However, it cannot be extended to three-dimensional problems easily. Using graphical methods, fairly difficult statics problems can be solved easily and quickly, although computer methods are replacing this approach. A very important use of this method is to obtain a rough solution (by an approximate sketch) to problems that are solved by other methods.

Example Problem 3.3

Solve Example Problem 3.2 graphically.

Solution

Again Fig. 3.10 is the free body diagram, so we proceed to draw the force polygon. The problem is to draw the triangle accurately and at an appropriate scale. If one works carefully, accuracy of two to three significant figures can be obtained using an $8\frac{1}{2} \times 11$ in. engineer's pad and hand instruments. Greater accuracy may be achieved using a drawing board and drafting machine. In Fig. 3.12 we draw the line a–b and lay off the vector B at 120 units. From the tip of B we draw the line c–d at the proper angle and lay off C at 200 units, terminating it at e. From e we draw a line back to the starting point a. The line e–a represents the force A. We scale this to be 205 units at 79.8° below the horizontal. Thus

$$A = 205 \text{ N at } 79.8°$$

This differs slightly from the more accurate analytical result.

Example Problem 3.4

The ring in Fig. 3.13 is held by a post. Find the force the post must exert on the ring to keep it from moving.

Solution

A free body diagram of the ring is drawn in Fig. 3.14 with the unknown force labeled D. Since there are four forces on this diagram, an analytical solution would be tedious. A graphical solution, however, requires only that the additional force be drawn on the force polygon. We proceed by laying out

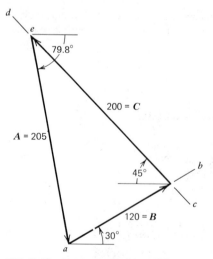

FIG. 3.12   Example Problem 3.3.

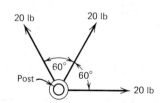

FIG. 3.13   Example Problem 3.4.

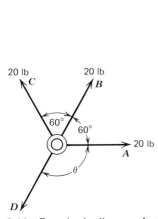

FIG. 3.14 Free body diagram for Example Problem 3.4.

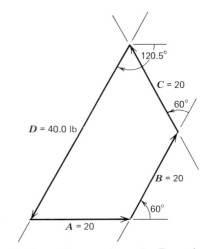

FIG. 3.15 Force polygon for Example Problem 3.4.

the forces *A*, *B*, and *C* to scale, in the proper direction and tip-to-tail in Fig. 3.15. Then we construct the vector *D* from the terminal point of *C* to the beginning point of *A*. We measure it and find it to be 40.0 lb at an angle of $-120.5°$. Thus:

$$D = \textbf{40.0 lb at } -120.5°$$

This is the force the post must exert on the ring to hold it in place.

3.7 HOW TO HANDLE PULLEYS AND TWO-FORCE MEMBERS WITHOUT KNOWING WHY

In Chapter 5 we will see why pulleys and two-force members behave as they do. For the present we simply observe how they behave and learn to handle them in statics problems. There are two reasons for taking this approach. First, by presenting these important elements twice, we stand a better chance of mastering them. Second, we can consider a more interesting variety of concurrent force problems in this chapter.

In the pulley shown in Fig. 3.16*a*, we can see the tensions T_1 and T_2 in the cable or belt. Figure 3.16*b*, a free body diagram of the pulley, illustrates that if the

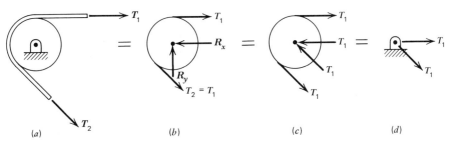

FIG. 3.16 How to handle a pulley.

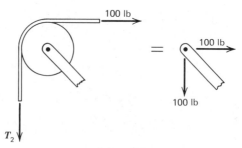

FIG. 3.17 Cable forces are transmitted to the pin.

pulley is frictionless, the tension in the cable will be the same everywhere (i.e., $T_1 = T_2$). Figure 3.16b also shows that the cable force may be represented as forces tangent to the pulley at the point of contact. Finally Fig. 3.16b shows that there will be a reaction at the pin that in general may be represented by the horizontal and vertical components R_x and R_y. Figure 3.16c shows that this pin reaction is equal and opposite the cable forces. It should be obvious that the sum of the forces on the pulley in Fig. 3.16c is zero. If the pin exerts on the pulley the forces shown in Fig. 3.16c, then according to Newton's third law the pulley does just the opposite to the pin, as shown in Fig. 3.16d. Thus we conclude that the forces in a cable on a frictionless pulley are the same everywhere, and the cable forces act on the pin supporting the pulley. This is illustrated further in Fig. 3.17.

Example Problem 3.5

Find the force P required to lift the 7-ton weight in Fig. 3.18 and find the reaction at the pin support of pulley 1.

Solution

A free body diagram for pulley 2 is drawn in Fig. 3.19a by passing a cutting plane through the supporting cables. The tension in the cable is everywhere

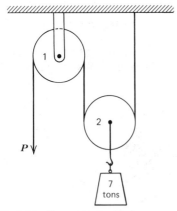

FIG. 3.18 Example Problem 3.5.

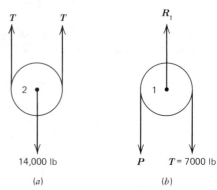

FIG. 3.19 Free body diagrams for Example Problem 3.5.

the same, so we label this T for both cases. The downward force due to the weight is 7 tons or 14,000 lb. Then:

$$\sum F_y = 0 = T + T - 14{,}000$$

$$T = \frac{14{,}000}{2} = 7000 \text{ lb}$$

Drawing next the free body diagram for pulley 1 (Fig. 3.19b), we see that the tension between the two pulleys is 7000 lb or T. The applied force $\boldsymbol{P}$ is on the other side. The upward reaction at the pin is labeled $\boldsymbol{R}_1$. Since this is a pin, there is a potential for a horizontal component also. But all the loading is vertical, so there will be no horizontal component at the pin and for this simple free body diagram, we leave the horizontal component off. This is commonly done by an experienced analysts, but if in doubt, include it. The value of P is obtained by again recognizing the tension in the cable remains the same around the pulley. Thus:

$$\boldsymbol{P} = \textbf{7000 lb}$$

We find the pin reaction R_1 by

$$\sum F_y = 0 = +R_1 - P - 7000$$
$$\boldsymbol{R_1} = \textbf{14,000 lb}$$

Next we come to *two-force members*. More correctly we will examine members that have forces applied *at only two locations*. In Fig. 3.20 member AC is a two-force member because forces are applied only at A and C. Member BC is a two-force member because forces are applied only at B and C. In general the pins at A and B will exert a reaction with two unknowns as shown in the free body diagram in

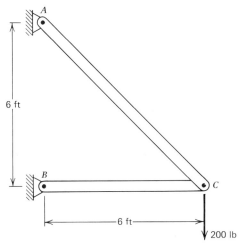

FIG. 3.20 Two-force members.

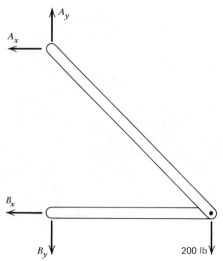

FIG. 3.21   Free body diagram showing pin reactions.

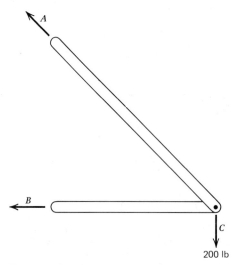

FIG. 3.21   Free body diagram showing pin reactions.

Fig. 3.21. However, by recognizing members AC and BC to be two-force members, we may redraw this free body diagram as in Fig. 3.22. For AC to be a straight two-force member, the forces on it must be along it. Thus we know the direction of the reaction at A. Similarly we know the reaction at B is along the member BC. Thus Fig. 3.22 shows only two unknowns, whereas Fig. 3.21 shows four. We might also note that the reactions A and B pass through point C, and this free body diagram represents a concurrent force problem.

To recap, a two-force member has forces applied at two locations only. These forces (as well as the internal forces in the member) must be along the member if the member is straight.

Another useful concept we will apply without development is that of center of gravity. Most students at this stage of education have some understanding of the center of gravity and know that for many problems the weight of an object may be treated as though it acts there. They also understand that the center of gravity is located at the "center" of an object if one can be identified. By "center" they mean the geometric center. We will explore certain limitations to this point of view later; for the time being, we use this understanding.

Example Problem 3.6

The frictionless pulley in Fig. 3.23 weighs 50 lb. Find the forces in members *AB* and *BC* including the weight of the pulley.

Solution

A free body diagram of the pin at the center of the pulley is drawn in Fig. 3.24. The tension in the cable is 100 lb everywhere. The 100-lb force down and the 100 lb in the length *ED* are tangent to the pulley as the cable is cut. However the pair may be transferred to the center of the pulley producing the 100-lb forces to the right and down in Fig. 3.24. The weight of the pulley, 50 lb, acts at its center and down. Members *AB* and *BC* are two-force members. Thus the direction of the forces acting on them will be along each member, and we draw *AB* and *BC* in known directions as shown. This results in the complete free body diagram of Fig. 3.24, which has only two unknowns, the magnitude of *AB* and *BC*. For concurrent force problems, two unknowns may be found.

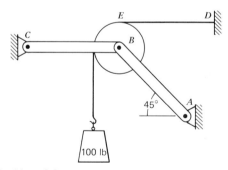

FIG. 3.23   Example Problem 3.6.

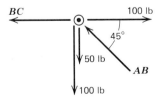

FIG. 3.24   Free body diagram for Example Problem 3.6.

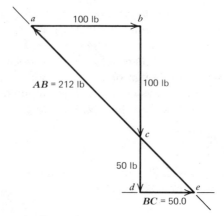

FIG. 3.25 Force polygon for Example Problem 3.6.

Since there are five forces making up this free body diagram, we choose the graphical method of solution over the analytical. In Fig. 3.25 we draw the known vectors as a–b, b–c, and c–d tip-to-tail. Through d we draw a horizontal line parallel to the force $\mathbf{BC}$ and through a we draw a line parallel to the forces $\mathbf{AB}$. These two lines intersect at e and the force polygon is completed. $\mathbf{BC}$ and $\mathbf{AB}$ are assigned senses so that the force polygon closes (i.e., returns to point a). Finally, we scale their magnitudes getting

$$\mathbf{BC} = \mathbf{50.0\ lb\ at\ 0.0°}$$

and

$$\mathbf{AB} = \mathbf{212\ lb\ at\ 135.0°}$$

Note that the sense assumed for $\mathbf{AB}$ was correct while that for $\mathbf{BC}$ was not. Furthermore, the result does not depend on the order in which the vectors are added. A different order changes the shape of the force polygon but not the result. You may want to add the vectors in a different order to verify this statement.

3.8 CONCURRENT FORCE PROBLEMS: COMPONENTS

Our third method of solving concurrent force problems, that of components, will become the method most commonly used because it is applicable to nonconcurrent problems and three-dimensional ones also.

The equilibrium principle was presented as the vector equation 3.1 or the two scalar equations 3.2 and 3.3. The latter relations are *component* equations, thus the name of the method. The equations imply summing forces in the horizontal and vertical directions. Actually any two directions will do, and we occasionally choose others. The method is illustrated in Example Problems 3.7 through 3.9.

Example Problem 3.7

Find the forces in members AC and BC in Fig. 3.20 on page 57 using components.

Solution

The first step is still to draw a free body diagram. This is done in Fig. 3.22 on page 58, recognizing AC and BC to be two-force members. It should be noted that where a single two-force member acts on a pin, the pin reaction and the force in the member are the same. Also note that all three forces act through the point C.

A second step is to replace inclined forces with horizontal and vertical components. In Fig. 3.26 this has been done. The forces also can be shown at point C by moving them along their line of action. In Fig. 3.26a the vector A is represented in component form by broken lines. In Fig. 3.26b A is marked out and replaced with its components. Either form is acceptable. Care should be taken, however, not to represent the force A and its components A_x and A_y by the same notation, as is done in Fig. 3.27. This figure is incorrect and will lead to incorrect force equations.

Once the free body diagram has been drawn and components have been found, the statics problem reduces to bookkeeping. We must accurately write Eqs. 3.2 and 3.3 for this free body, and that requires just a simple listing. Do be careful to note the sense of the forces shown in the diagram, listing up and to the

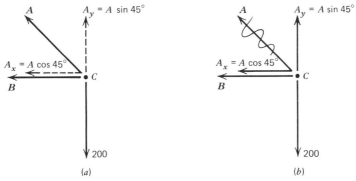

FIG. 3.26 Equivalent free body diagrams for Example Problem 3.7.

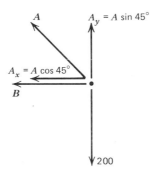

FIG. 3.27 *Incorrect* equivalent free body diagram.

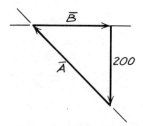

FIG. 3.28   Hand sketch of the force polygon for Example Problem 3.7.

right as positive and down and to the left as negative. Thus we write

$$\sum F_x = -B - A \cos 45° = 0$$

and

$$\sum F_y = +A \sin 45° - 200 = 0$$

Solving for A, we write

$$A = \frac{200}{\sin 45°} = +283 \text{ lb}$$

The positive sign for A means that the assumed sense for A was correct; that is, it is indeed up and to the left, or link AC is in tension. Substituting this into the first equation we have

$$B = -(283) \cos 45° = -200 \text{ lb}$$

The minus sign means the assumed sense of B was incorrect and that it is in fact to the right, or link BC is in compression. Finally we make a hand sketch of the force polygon for a visual check of the results (Fig. 3.28).

Optional Solution Using Vector Notation

Optional material and problems are denoted by an asterisk (*). An alternate solution using vector notation is as follows. Equation 3.1 is:

$$\sum F = 0 = -Bi - 200j - A_x i + A_y j$$

Gathering the j components gives:

$$-200 + A_y = 0$$
$$A_y = 200$$

then observing:

$$A_x = A_y = 200$$

and gathering the i components:

$$-B - A_x = 0$$
$$B = -A_x = -200$$

Hence

$$A = -200i + 200j \qquad \textbf{(lb)}$$

and

$$B = 200i \qquad \textbf{(lb)}$$

Example Problem 3.8

Find the reactions at A and B in Fig. 3.29 by components.

Solution

Draw a free body diagram of pin C (Fig. 3.30) as follows. The forces in the cable are 500 lb downward and 500 lb to the right. Assuming the pulley to

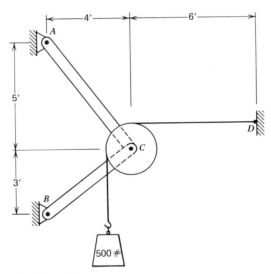

FIG. 3.29 Example Problem 3.8.

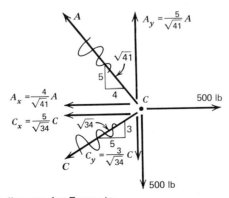

FIG. 3.30 Free body diagram for Example Problems 3.8 and 3.9.

be frictionless, these are transferred to the pin C. We recognize members AC and BC to be two-force members; therefore, their forces will be along them. We assume both to be in tension and show them as A and C to Fig. 3.30. We replace A with its components. We can find the angle A makes with the horizontal and work with trigonometric functions or with proportions. We deal similarly with C. Be sure to mark out the vectors A and C as they are replaced with their components or use some alternate designation for the components. If the free body diagram is *complete* and *accurate*, we are again ready for the bookkeeping. If not, even H & R Block won't help!

We proceed by writing Eqs. 3.2 and 3.3 for our problem. Again be careful to note the sense of the component when entering it into the equation.

$$\sum F_x = -\frac{4}{\sqrt{41}} A - \frac{5}{\sqrt{34}} C + 500 = 0$$

$$\sum F_y = +\frac{5}{\sqrt{41}} A - \frac{3}{\sqrt{34}} C - 500 = 0$$

Sometimes one of these equations can be solved explicitly for a single variable. Here neither can, and we have the general case of two equations and two unknowns. Reducing the coefficients to decimals and putting the equations in standard form, we have:

$$0.625A + 0.857C = 500$$

and

$$0.781A - 0.514C = 500$$

Solving the first equation for A, we write:

$$A = 800 - 1.371C$$

Substituting this into the second equation gives:

$$0.781(800 - 1.371C) - 0.514C = 500$$
$$-1.585C = -124.8$$
$$\mathbf{C = 78.7\ lb}$$

and

$$A = 800 - 1.371(78.7) = \mathbf{692\ lb}$$

Both have positive signs, indicating the assumed senses to be correct, and both are in tension. Fig. 3.31 is a sketch of the force polygon that confirms these values.

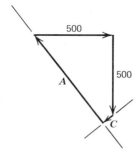

500

500

A

C

FIG. 3.31 Sketch of force polygon for
Example Problem 3.8.

*Example Problem 3.9

Solve Example Problem 3.8 using vector notation.

Solution

Figure 3.29 shows the problem, and Fig. 3.30 is a free body diagram with
the components indicated. Using vector notation we note the forces to be:

$$500i \quad \text{and} \quad -500j$$

$$A = -\frac{4}{\sqrt{41}} Ai + \frac{5}{\sqrt{41}} Aj$$

$$C = -\frac{5}{\sqrt{34}} Ci - \frac{3}{\sqrt{34}} Cj$$

In vector form, Newton's first law is:

$$\sum F = 0$$

from which we get:

$$\sum F = 500i - 500j - \frac{4}{\sqrt{41}} Ai + \frac{5}{\sqrt{41}} Aj - \frac{5}{\sqrt{34}} Ci$$

$$-\frac{3}{\sqrt{34}} Cj = 0$$

This equation can be satisfied only when both the i and j components are
zero. Thus:

$$i: \quad 500 - \frac{4}{\sqrt{41}} A - \frac{5}{\sqrt{34}} C = 0$$

$$j: \quad -500 + \frac{5}{41} A - \frac{3}{34} C = 0$$

These are identical to the component equations in Example Problem 3.8, where the algebra yielded:

$$A = 692 \text{ lb}$$
$$C = 78.7 \text{ lb}$$

Thus:

$$A = -\frac{4}{\sqrt{41}}(692)i + \frac{5}{\sqrt{41}}(692)j$$

$$A = -432i + 540j \qquad \textbf{(lb)}$$

and

$$C = -\frac{5}{\sqrt{34}}(78.7)i - \frac{3}{\sqrt{34}}(78.7)j$$

$$C = -67.5i - 40.5j \qquad \textbf{(lb)}$$

3.9 SUMMARY

We have seen that many large bodies may be treated as *particles*. When analyzing a body as a particle, all the forces act through a common point. Such systems of forces are called *concurrent*. The following points are important.

1. *Newton's first law* says that a body at rest or moving at constant velocity has a zero resultant force. The converse is also true. In equation form, we have:

$$\sum F_x = 0 \quad \text{and} \quad \sum F_y = 0$$

2. The *free body diagram* depicts a body that has been cut free of all external supports. Each support is replaced by the appropriate reaction. The diagram also shows all externally applied loads. Drawing the free body diagram is the first step in the solution of statics problems.
3. The *principle of transmissibility* says that a force may be treated as acting anywhere along its line of action.
4. *Pulleys* may be handled in free body diagrams by showing the cable forces as acting at the center of the pulley.
5. A *two-force member* has forces applied at two locations only. The resultant forces at each location act along a line between the two points and are equal in magnitude but opposite in sense.

Three methods were examined for solving concurrent force problems. All three require the initial step of drawing a free body diagram. Additional steps specific to the method are as follows.

1. *Analytically*   Sketch the polygon and solve for its parts using trigonometry. This method is limited to two dimensional problems and becomes undesirable if the number of forces exceeds three.

2. *Graphically* Draw the force polygon to scale and measure the desired unknowns. This method is limited to two-dimensional problems, but does not become excessively difficult as the number of forces increases.

3. *Components* Resolve the forces into components and write the equations:

$$\sum F_x = 0 \quad \text{and} \quad \sum F_y = 0$$

Solve algebraically for the unknowns. This method is easily extended to three-dimensional problems and easily accommodates a large number of forces. Vector notation is a convenient method of handling a large number of forces or three-dimensional problems.

PROBLEMS

3.1 Draw a free body diagram of the wheel on the wheelbarrow in Fig. 3.32.

3.2 Draw a free body diagram of the wheelbarrow in Fig. 3.32 excluding its wheel.

3.3 Draw a free body diagram of the disk in Fig. 3.33.

3.4 Draw a free body diagram of the disk in Fig. 3.34.

FIG. 3.32   Problems 3.1, 3.2.

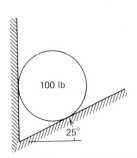

FIG. 3.33   Problems 3.3, 3.11a, 3.20a, 3.40a, 3.54a.

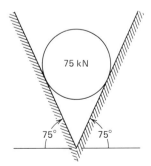

FIG. 3.34   Problems 3.4, 3.11b, 3.20b, 3.40b, 3.54b.

3.5 Draw a free body diagram of the rod in Fig. 3.35.

3.6 Draw a free body diagram of the rod in Fig. 3.36.

3.7 A particle is acted on by a 1500-lb horizontal force, to the right, and a 3000-lb vertical force, upward. *Analytically* find the force required to keep this particle in equilibrium.

3.8 A particle is acted on by a 1200-N upward vertical force and a 900-N horizontal force to the left. *Analytically* find the force required to keep this particle in equilibrium.

3.9 *Analytically* find the force **C** required for equilibrium of the particle in Fig. 3.37.

3.10 *Analytically* find the force **C** required for equilibrium of the particle in Fig. 3.38.

3.11 Assuming that the walls are smooth, *analytically* find the forces acting on the disk in:

(a)   Fig. 3.33   (b)   Fig. 3.34

Hint: The reaction force on the disk by the wall will be perpendicular to the wall.

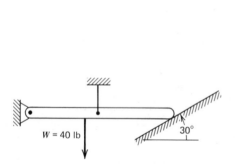

FIG. 3.35 Problem 3.5.

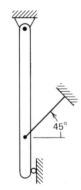

FIG. 3.36 Problem 3.6.

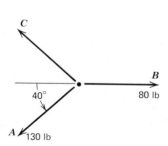

FIG. 3.37 Problems 3.9, 3.18, 3.38, 3.57.

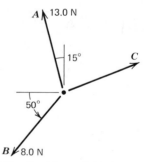

FIG. 3.38 Problems 3.10, 3.19, 3.39, 3.58.

3.12 The ball in Fig. 3.39 weighs 5 lb and is hanging on a string. It is acted on by a 2-lb force **P**. What angle will the string make with the vertical, and what will be the magnitude of the force in it? Solve *analytically*.

3.13 The ball in Fig. 3.39 weighs 40 N and is hanging on a string. It is acted on by a 20-N force **P**. What angle will the string make with the vertical and what will be the magnitude of the force in it? Solve *analytically*.

3.14 Fig. 3.40 shows a block that has a weight *W* of 35 lb on a frictionless inclined plane. The plane makes an angle θ equal to 20° with the horizontal. The force *N* is the reaction of the plane on the block and is normal to the plane. If the force **P** is parallel to the plane (i.e., $\phi = 0$), find the magnitude of **P** and *N*. Solve this problem *analytically*.

3.15 Fig. 3.40 shows a block that has a weight *W* of 80 N on a frictionless inclined plane. The plane makes an angle θ equal to 35° with the horizontal. The force *N* is the reaction of the plane on the block and is normal to the plane. The force **P** makes an angle of 15° with the horizontal (i.e., $\phi = 15°$). Find the magnitude of **P** and *N* *analytically*.

3.16 Solve Problem 3.7 *graphically*.

3.17 Solve Problem 3.8 *graphically*.

3.18 Solve Problem 3.9 *graphically*.

3.19 Solve Problem 3.10 *graphically*.

3.20 Solve *graphically*:

(a) Problem 3.11a   (b) Problem 3.11b.

3.21 Solve Problem 3.12 *graphically*.

3.22 Solve Problem 3.13 *graphically*.

3.23 Solve Problem 3.14 *graphically*.

3.24 Solve Problem 3.15 *graphically*.

3.25 Find the force **D** required to hold the particle in Fig. 3.41 in place. Solve *graphically*.

3.26 Find the force **D** required to hold the particle in Fig. 3.42 in place. Solve *graphically*.

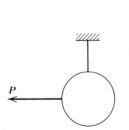

FIG. 3.39 Problems 3.12, 3.13, 3.21, 3.22, 3.41, 3.42.

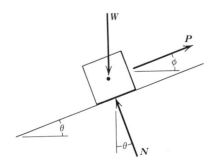

FIG. 3.40 Problems 3.14, 3.15, 3.23, 3.24, 3.43, 3.44, 3.59, 3.60.

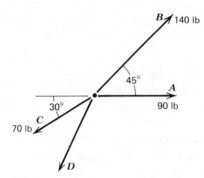

FIG. 3.41 Problems 3.25, 3.45, 3.61.

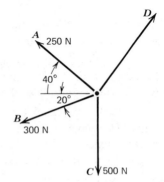

FIG. 3.42 Problems 3.26, 3.46, 3.62.

3.27 The disk in Fig. 3.43 weighs 200 lb. The force *P* is 80 lb and *θ* is 50°. Graphically find the reactions at the walls if the walls are smooth.

3.28 The disk in Fig. 3.43 weighs 10 kN. The force *P* is 8 kN and *θ* is 35°. Graphically find the reactions at the walls if the walls are smooth.

3.29 Find the force *P* required to lift the 8-kN weight in Fig. 3.44 and the pin reaction on pulley 1 when *θ* is 60°. Also find *P* and the pin reactions when *θ* is 45°. Discuss the differences found.

3.30 The force *P* in Fig. 3.45 is 900 lb. What weight *W* can be lifted by this pulley system? What is the reaction at *A*? For small-diameter pulleys *BC* may be assumed to be vertical.

3.31 The force *P* in Fig. 3.45 is 16 N. What weight *W* can be lifted by the pulley system? What is the reaction at *A*? For small-diameter pulleys *BC* may be assumed to be vertical.

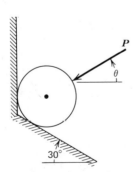

FIG. 3.43 Problems 3.27, 3.28, 3.47, 3.48.

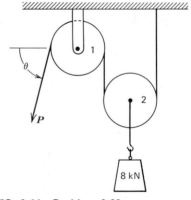

FIG. 3.44 Problem 3.29.

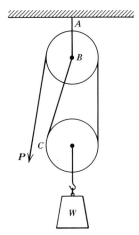

FIG. 3.45 Problems 3.30, 3.31.

3.32 The block *W* in Fig. 3.46 weighs 2000 lb.

    (a) Find the force *P* required to hold it in place.

    (b) Find the tension in each length of cable.

    (c) Find the reaction at the pin at *l* if θ equals 50°.

3.33 The force *P* (Fig. 3.46) is 16 kN and θ is 70°.

    (a) Find the weight *W* that can be held.

    (b) Find the tension in each length of cable.

    (c) Find the reaction at the pin *l*.

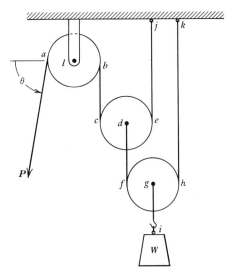

FIG. 3.46 Problems 3.32, 3.33.

3.34 For *P* equal to 40 lb, find the load *W* that can be held by the pulley system in Fig. 3.47. Assume the weight *W* is positioned so that it remains level. Also find the tension in each cable length.

3.35 The weight *W* in Fig. 3.47 is 2.7 MN. Find the force *P* required to hold it in place, assuming it is positioned so that it will remain level. Also find the tension in each cable length.

3.36 Solve Problem 3.7 by *components*.

3.37 Solve Problem 3.8 by *components*.

3.38 Solve Problem 3.9 by *components*.

3.39 Solve Problem 3.10 by *components*.

3.40 Solve by *components*:

    (a) Problem 3.11a   (b) Problem 3.11b

3.41 Solve Problem 3.12 by *components*.

3.42 Solve Problem 3.13 by *components*.

3.43 Solve Problem 3.14 by *components*.

3.44 Solve Problem 3.15 by *components*.

3.45 Solve Problem 3.25 by *components*.

3.46 Solve Problem 3.26 by *components*.

3.47 Solve Problem 3.27 by *components*.

3.48 Solve Problem 3.28 by *components*.

3.49 For Fig. 3.48 find the forces in members *AC* and *BC* for the values given.

	h	l	W
(a)	6 m	3 m	400 N
(b)	10 m	4 m	800 N
(c)	8 m	12 m	1200 N

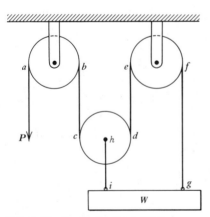

FIG. 3.47 Problems 3.34, 3.35.

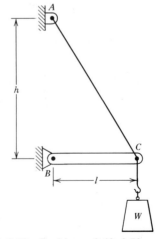

FIG. 3.48 Problems 3.49, 3.50.

3.50 For Fig. 3.48 find the forces in the members *AC* and *BC* for the values given.

	h	*l*	*W*
(a)	5 ft	10 ft	15 tons
(b)	10 ft	5 ft	15 tons
(c)	16 in.	30 in.	250 lb

3.51 For Fig. 3.49 find the loads in members *AC* and *BC*.

3.52 For Fig. 3.50 find the loads in members *AC* and *BC*.

3.53 For Fig. 3.51 find the loads in members *AC* and *BC*.

The following problems, denoted by an asterisk (*), are optional.

*3.54 Solve by *components using vector notation*:

    (a)   Problem 3.11a   (b)   Problem 3.11b

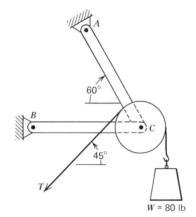

FIG. 3.49   Problem 3.51.

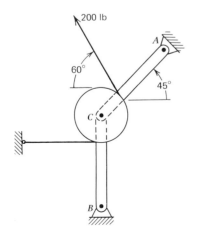

FIG. 3.50   Problem 3.52.

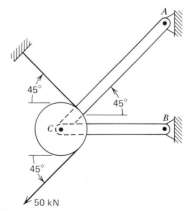

FIG. 3.51   Problem 3.53.

*3.55 Solve Problem 3.7 by *components using vector notation.*

*3.56 Solve Problem 3.8 by *components using vector notation.*

*3.57 Solve Problem 3.9 by *components using vector notation.*

*3.58 Solve Problem 3.10 by *components using vector notation.*

*3.59 Solve Problem 3.14 by *components using vector notation.*

*3.60 Solve Problem 3.15 by *components using vector notation.*

*3.61 Solve Problem 3.25 by *components using vector notation.*

*3.62 Solve Problem 3.26 by *components using vector notation.*

4

Moments of Plane Forces and Couples

We have noted that the magnitude of a force is a measure of the force's tendency to cause motion (specifically translation) in the direction of the force. If I take a wrench to tighten a bolt as shown in Fig. 4.1, the force applied does not produce translation. Instead, the wrench rotates about the center of the bolt, and we see that a force can also produce rotation. We know that if the force is increased, the tendency to rotate is increased. We also know that we can affect the tendency to rotate by changing the location of the force. If we move in on the handle, for example, the tendency to rotate is decreased. The tendency of the force to cause rotation

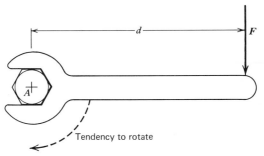

FIG. 4.1   A force can cause rotation.

75

is measured by the *moment* of the force, which is defined in Section 4.1. In general an applied force will tend to translate *and* to rotate a body. Later we will see a special case of a moment of force known as a *couple*. A couple has a tendency to rotate a body but not to translate it.

A moment of force that tends to bend a body such as a beam is called a *bending moment*. A moment of force that tends to twist an object is called a *torque*. Both, however, are just moments of force and are equivalent terms in statics.

4.1   MOMENT OF A FORCE ABOUT A POINT

The wrench shown in Fig. 4.1 allows the force F to rotate the bolt. The tendency of this force to rotate the bolt is known as the moment of the force F about the center of the bolt A. It can be calculated by:

$$M = F \times d \qquad (4.1)$$

where d is the *perpendicular distance* between A and the force F (also the shortest distance), and M is the moment of the force F about the point A.

The direction of the tendency to rotate will be in agreement with the sense of the force. In Fig. 4.1, it is clockwise. Dimensionally a moment of force will be a force times a distance. In the U.S. customary system this will be foot-pounds or inch-pounds (or some write pound-foot—the order doesn't matter to most). In the SI we have the newton-meter (N·m). This is one of the few frequent combinations of SI units that does not get a new name. If we are talking about work, the newton-meter is a joule (J), but for a moment of force it remains N·m (a minor advantage of the SI).

Example Problem 4.1

Find the moment of the force shown in Fig. 4.2 about the point A.

Solution

The distance from point A to point B is 5 ft. However, this is *not* the perpendicular distance, and the moment of force is *not* 5 ft times 200 lb or 1000 ft-lb. To find the perpendicular distance, we extend the line of action of the 200-lb force. (Remember the principle of transmissibility?) Construct the line AC perpendicular to CB. We observe the angle ABC to be 30° in the right triangle

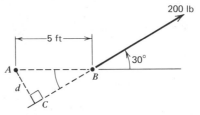

FIG. 4.2 Example Problem 4.1.

ABC. Thus:

$$\sin 30° = \frac{d}{5} \quad \text{and} \quad d = 5 \sin 30° = 2.50 \text{ ft}$$

This is the perpendicular distance from *A* to the 200-lb force. Then, by Equation 4.1,

$$M = F \times d = 200 \text{ lb} \times 2.50 \text{ ft}$$

$$\mathbf{M = 500 \text{ ft-lb}}$$

Now place your right hand at *A* with your thumb pointing out of the paper. Point your fingers in the direction of the 200-lb force and gradually curl them up. The flow from your knuckles to the tip of your fingers will represent a counterclockwise flow, which is the direction of this moment of force. This may be represented by a vector perpendicular to the plane in the direction of your thumb. This vector representation of a moment of force is important in three-dimensional problems but unnecessary in two-dimensional problems. For the latter we need merely to note whether the moment is clockwise or counterclockwise. We will call counterclockwise *positive* and clockwise *negative*. This, by the way, is in agreement with the standard sign system for angular measurement you learned in trigonometry. Thus the moment above is:

$$\mathbf{M = +500 \text{ ft-lb}}$$

Sometimes to be certain, or for emphasis, we will write:

$$\mathbf{M = 500 \text{ ft-lb}\circlearrowleft}$$

Example Problem 4.2

Find the moment of the 200-lb force in Fig. 4.3 about the point *D*.

Solution

Notice that point *D* is on the opposite side of the force from point *A*. We construct *DE* perpendicular to *BE* and find:

$$\sin 30° = \frac{d}{4} \quad \text{and} \quad d = 4 \sin 30° = 2.00 \text{ ft}$$

Then:

$$M = F \times d = 200 \text{ lb} \times 2 \text{ ft} = 400 \text{ ft-lb}$$

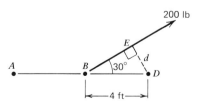

FIG. 4.3 Example Problem 4.2.

The 200-lb force produces a tendency to rotate *clockwise* around D, thus this moment of force is *negative*, and we write:

$$M = -400 \text{ ft-lb}$$

or

$$M = 400 \text{ ft-lb} \circlearrowleft$$

If you place your right hand at D, it will be necessary to point your thumb *into* the paper to get your fingers to agree with the tendency to rotate clockwise. The moment vector represented by the sense of your thumb, into the paper, is a negative vector.

4.2 MOMENT OF SEVERAL FORCES ABOUT A POINT

We have seen how to calculate the tendency of a force to cause rotation about a point—the moment of the force. If we have more than one force acting, each force will have its own moment of force about a given point. The total moment of force will simply be the sum of the individual moments of force, arrived at using the sign system we have established. This will be referred to as the *resultant moment of force*. In equation form it is:

$$M = M_1 + M_2 + \cdots + M_n \tag{4.2}$$

This equation says the resultant moment M about a point is equal to the sum of the individual moments (M_1, M_2, etc.) about the same point. It is important to pay attention to the last phrase. If we want to add moments of force, they must be moments *about the same point*. We can abbreviate Eq. 4.2 by writing:

$$M = \sum M_i \tag{4.3}$$

Example Problem 4.3

Find the moment of the force system in Fig. 4.4 about point A.

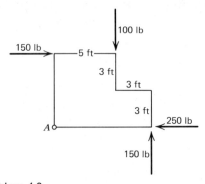

FIG. 4.4 Example Problem 4.3.

Solution

We sum the moments of force about point A, noting forces that tend to produce a counterclockwise rotation about point A as positive and those tending to a clockwise rotation as negative.

$$M_A = \sum M_i = -6(150) - 5(100) + 8(150) + (0)250$$
$$M_A = -1400 + 1200$$
$$\mathbf{M_A = -200 \ ft\text{-}lb}$$

The negative sign means that the resultant moment of force is in the clockwise direction. Thus we write:

$$\mathbf{M_A = 200 \ ft\text{-}lb \circlearrowright}$$

Observe that the 250-lb force acted through point A and had zero moment arm. Hence it had a zero moment. This will always be the case when a force acts through a point about which we are taking moments.

4.3   THE MOMENT OF A FORCE IS EQUAL TO THE SUM OF THE MOMENTS OF ITS COMPONENTS

We could proceed from the title of this section to the next one. The title of this section contains all that we will try to convey here. Read it again. Once more. Now close your eyes and visualize the words. Got it? Then let's see what it means.

Example Problem 4.4

Find the moment of the 200-lb force in Fig. 4.2 about the point A.

Solution

In Example Problem 4.1 we found the moment of the 200-lb force in Fig. 4.2 by finding the perpendicular distance AC. This figure is redrawn in Fig. 4.5, where the force is replaced by horizontal and vertical components as follows.

$$F_x = 200 \cos 30° = 173 \ lb$$
$$F_y = 200 \sin 30° = 100 \ lb$$

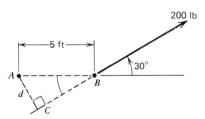

FIG. 4.2   Example Problem 4.1 Figure repeated from page 76.

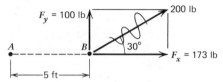

FIG. 4.5   Example Problem 4.4.

The perpendicular distances from A to each component are now obvious, and we find the moment of each component as follows.

$$M_1 = 5(100) = +500 \text{ ft-lb}$$
$$M_2 = 0(173) = 0$$

Note once more that when a force (F_x) acts through a point, it has no moment about that point. The resultant moment is

$$M_A = M_1 + M_2 = 500 + 0 = \textbf{500 ft-lb}$$

This answer, of course, agrees with the preceding result and confirms the title of this section.

Example Problem 4.5

Find the moment of the force system shown in Fig. 4.6 about point A.

Solution

From Section 4.2 we know that the total moment will be the sum of the moments of each force. From this section we know that the moment of each force is the sum of the moments of the components. We observe the components by proportion and replace the forces with their components as shown in Fig. 4.7. Observing the perpendicular distances and the proper sign for the moments (with counterclockwise positive), we write the moment equation as follows:

$$M_A = \sum M_i = +4(80) + 2(60) - 2(240) + 3(100)$$
$$M_A = 320 + 160 - 480 + 300 = \textbf{+300 N·m}$$

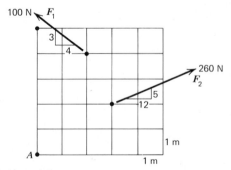

FIG. 4.6   Example Problem 4.5.

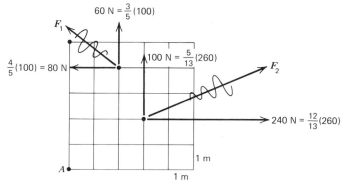

FIG. 4.7 Example Problem 4.5: amplification of Fig. 4.6.

The resultant moment about A is 300 N·m counterclockwise. As the number of forces increases in a problem, the advantage of this approach grows.

This principle is known as Varignon's theorem, after the French mathematician Pierre Varignon.

4.4 COUPLES

A common tire tool is shown in Fig. 4.8. There is a 30-lb downward force on one handle and a 30-lb upward force on the other. A plane projection of the handle is shown in Fig. 4.9. If we sum forces horizontally and vertically we find:

$$\sum F_x = 0 = R_x$$
$$\sum F_y = +30 - 30 = 0 = R_y$$

Thus the resultant force is zero; that is, this force system has no tendency to translate the tire tool. Now we sum the moment of the forces about O in Fig. 4.9.

$$\sum M_0 = -10(30) - 10(30) = -600 \text{ in.-lb}$$

The resultant moment is 600 in.-lb clockwise, and there is a tendency to rotate the tire tool clockwise. The applied force system can be represented by the following.

$$R = 0$$
$$\sum M_0 = -600 \text{ in.-lb}$$

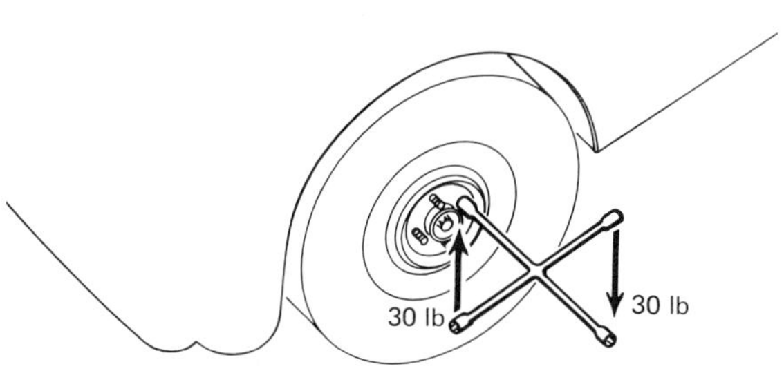

FIG. 4.8 A tire tool transfers a couple.

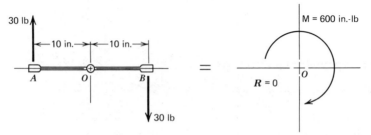

FIG. 4.9 Moment applied to the tire tool is a couple.

Such a force system, which has a tendency to rotate the body but no tendency to translate it, is called a *couple*. Couples are very common in mechanics and are very important, although they are a little difficult to master. This is unfortunate because they are not inherently complex. Difficulties can be minimized by attempting to thoroughly understand them from the beginning, so pay attention!

Figure 4.9 also shows the alternate representation of a couple, namely, a curved vector of the proper sense (clockwise in this case). This symbol represents a tendency to rotate but no tendency to translate the body it acts on.

Other examples of couples occur when we turn a key, a television knob, or a water faucet, or twist a screw driver. In each of these it is our intent to produce a rotation without a translation—thus a couple is appropriate.

There are several characteristics of a couple worth noting. The first can be observed by returning to Fig. 4.9. We sum the moments about point A and get:

$$\sum M_A = -20(30) = -600 \text{ in.-lb}$$

Then we sum the moments about B and get:

$$\sum M_B = -20(30) = -600 \text{ in.-lb}$$

Thus we observe that *the moment of a couple is the same regardless of the point about which moments are taken.*

In Fig. 4.10 we show several equivalent couples. The first three are composed of vertical forces of different magnitudes. For each,

$$R = \sum F = 0$$
$$\sum M_{\text{any point}} = -600 \text{ in.-lb}$$

Thus each has a tendency to rotate equal to -600 in.-lb, but no tendency to translate. These couples are *statically equivalent*. The next three couples in Fig. 4.10 are composed of different horizontal forces. However each of them also results in:

$$R = \sum F = 0$$
$$\sum M_{\text{any point}} = -600 \text{ in.-lb}$$

Thus each of these is statically equivalent to any of the other three. Finally we have this couple shown as a concentrated moment acting about three different points. Again the static result is the same, so each of these is statically equivalent to each of the preceding six force systems and to each other. Statically, it does

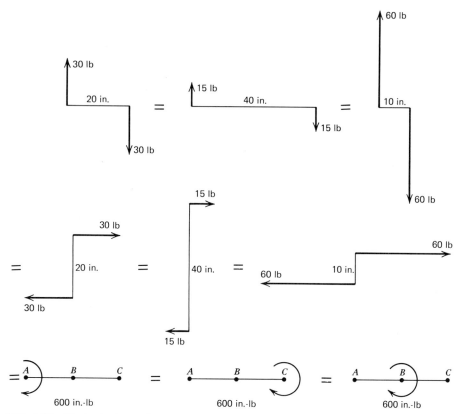

FIG. 4.10 Equivalent couples.

not matter where the couple is applied. Because of this, a couple is sometimes referred to as a *free vector*, meaning that it does not matter where it is attached to the body. We also observe that the magnitude of a couple is always

$$M = F \times d \tag{4.4}$$

where F is the magnitude of one of the forces and d is the perpendicular distance between them. This is independent of the reference point.

Note that a couple may be applied to any point on a rigid body with the same *static* effect. However internal loads, stresses, and deflections *do* depend on where a couple is applied. This is illustrated in Fig. 4.11, where the same couple M produces entirely different bending patterns in the beam as it is moved from one end of the beam to the other.

FIG. 4.11 Statically equivalent couples produce different deflections in a beam.

To summarize, we note:

1. A force system that has a resultant moment but no resultant force is called a *couple*.
2. Force systems that are couples and produce the same resultant moment of force are *equivalent couples*; that is, they produce the same tendency to rotate.
3. A couple produces the same moment of force on a rigid body regardless of where it is applied and is therefore said to be *free*. It may be moved to any location without changing its static effect.

Example Problem 4.6

Find the moment of the force system shown in Fig. 4.12 about points A, D, and C.

Solution

Summing moments about various points, we have the following:

About A:

$$\sum M_A = -2 \text{ m}(100 \text{ N}) = -200 \text{ N} \cdot \text{m}$$

About D:

$$\sum M_D = -4(100) - 2(100) = -200 \text{ N} \cdot \text{m}$$

About C:

$$\sum M_C = +1(100) - 3(100) = -200 \text{ N} \cdot \text{m}$$

Note that the moment *is the same* in every case. This could have been found directly from Eq. 4.4:

$$M = F \times d = -100(2) = -200 \text{ N} \cdot \text{m}$$

Example Problem 4.7

Find a "couple" of vertical forces applied at points C and E in Fig. 4.12 that will give a negative 200-N·m moment.

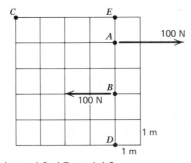

FIG. 4.12 Example Problems 4.6, 4.7, and 4.8.

Solution

Using Eq. 4.4,

$$M = F \times d$$

$$F = \frac{M}{d} = \frac{200 \text{ N} \cdot \text{m}}{4 \text{ m}} = \textbf{50.0 N}$$

The pair of forces need a sense that will produce a clockwise (negative) moment. Thus the 50-N force at C is up and that at E is down, as shown in Fig. 4.13. The distance d used was 4 m. This distance is perpendicular to the 50-N forces. If the distance CE were not perpendicular to the desired forces, it would not be the correct distance.

Example Problem 4.8

Find the magnitude of two forces acting through points C and D (Fig. 4.12) and perpendicular to the line CD that will produce a -200-N$\cdot$m couple.

Solution

First we find the distance between C and D using the Pythagorean theorem as illustrated in Fig. 4.14.

$$d = \sqrt{5^2 + 4^2} = 6.40 \text{ m}$$

Then by Eq. 4.4,

$$M = F \times d$$

$$F = \frac{M}{d} = \frac{200 \text{ N} \cdot \text{m}}{6.40 \text{ m}} = \textbf{31.2 N}$$

The sense of the forces is chosen to give a clockwise moment.

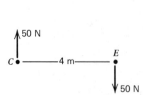

FIG. 4.13 Solution to Example Problem 4.7.

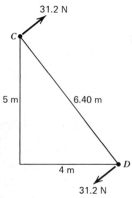

FIG. 4.14 Solution to Example Problem 4.8.

4.5 ADDING COUPLES

In Section 4.2 we found that the moment of several forces about a point is simply the sum of the moments of each force about that point. This applies to couples as well. The resultant moment of several couples is the algebraic sum of the couples.

Remember that the moment of a couple is independent of the point about which the moment is taken, so the resultant moment is independent of the reference point used in summing moments. We emphasize that this applies *only* to force systems that are purely *couples*. The resultant moment of other force systems *does depend* on the point about which moments are taken.

Finally, couples may be freely added to moments of force.

Example Problem 4.9

For the force system shown in Fig. 4.15, find the resultant force and the resultant moment about point A.

Solution

We recognize the 60-lb force pair at A and F and the horizontal 150-lb force pair to be couples. Furthermore, the 1200-in.-lb couple at C has no force component. Hence:

$$R = 0$$

Alternately, we sum forces:

$$R_x = \sum F_x = +60 \cos 30° - 60 \cos 30° + 150 - 150$$
$$R_x = 0$$
$$R_y = \sum F_y = 60 \sin 30° - 60 \sin 30° = 0$$
$$R = 0$$

Note that the 1200-in.-lb couple makes *no* contribution to the force equations. In either case we recognize there are three couples acting on the body.

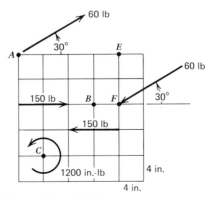

FIG. 4.15 Example Problems 4.9 and 4.10.

Now we sum moments about A by resolving the 60-lb force into its components and picking up the perpendicular distances to A.

$$M_A = \sum M_A = -16(60 \sin 30°) - 8(60 \cos 30°) + 8(150) - 12(150) + 1200$$
$$M_A = -296 \text{ in.-lb}$$

Note that there is no transfer distance associated with the 1200-in.-lb couple. It is merely added into the moment equation with the appropriate sign.

Example Problem 4.10

Find the resultant moment of the force system in Fig. 4.15 about point B.

Solution

$$M_B = \sum M_B = -12(60 \sin 30°) - 8(60 \cos 30°) - 4(60 \sin 30°)$$
$$+ 0(60 \cos 30°) + 0(150) - 4(150) + 1200$$
$$M_B = -296 \text{ in.-lb}$$

This is, of course, exactly the same as the moment about point A, because this force system is, in fact, just three couples. The two 60-lb forces oppose each other and give a clockwise couple of 60 lb times 14.9 in. (derived below), or -895 in.-lb. The two 150-lb forces oppose each other and give a clockwise couple of 150 lb times 4 in. or -600 in.-lb. The concentrated couple is $+1200$ in.-lb. Recognizing this as a system of couples, we could have written:

$$M_B = \sum M = -895 - 600 + 1200$$
$$M_B = -295 \text{ in.-lb}$$

with a slight difference due to round-off error. This is also the moment about point A or any other point. We should also note these couples will produce the same result regardless of where they are attached to the body. The three couples produce a net result that is a tendency to rotate the body clockwise. The measure of this tendency is 296 in.-lb.

Getting the 14.9-in. perpendicular distance between the two 60-lb forces can be a bit difficult. A practical method that should not be overlooked is to draw the figure to scale and *measure* the distance. In any case results should be checked by making an approximate measurement. The geometry is constructed in Fig. 4.16, where FG

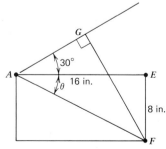

FIG. 4.16 Geometric solution to Example Problem 4.10.

is constructed perpendicular to AG, the direction of the 60-lb force. Note that the distances AE and EF are 16 and 8 in., respectively, and form the sides of the right triangle AEF, from which:

$$\tan \theta = \frac{8}{16} = 0.5$$

$$\theta = 26.6°$$

$$AF = \frac{8}{\sin 26.6°} = 17.9$$

Then for the right triangle AGF we have:

$$\angle FAG = \theta + 30° = 26.6° + 30° = 56.6°$$
$$FG = AF \sin (FAG) = 17.9 \sin 56.6°$$
$$FG = 14.9 \text{ in.}$$

This is the perpendicular distance between the two 60-lb forces.

   This problem illustrates a fairly common occurrence in statics where the geometry is more difficult than the statics problem. Such problems illustrate the importance of geometry and trigonometry. As such problems reveal weakness in your own background, get out your trigonometry text and work a few review problems! A well-made, accurately drawn sketch provides an easy graphical verification of the results. It is well worth the effort.

4.6   REPLACING A FORCE WITH A FORCE AND A COUPLE

Two-force systems are said to be statically equivalent if they satisfy two conditions:

$$\sum F_1 = \sum F_2 = R \tag{4.5}$$
$$\sum M_1 = \sum M_2 = M_R \tag{4.6}$$

The first condition requires that the systems have the same resultant force. This means that each will have the same tendency to translate a body. The second condition requires that the systems have the same resultant moment about any common point. This means that each will have the same tendency to rotate a body about the common point.

   Consider the 10-in. wrench handle in Fig. 4.17a with a 20-lb force applied to the end of the handle, point A. In Fig. 4.17b we add the two opposing 20-lb forces F_2 and F_3 at the center of the wrench head, point O. These two forces are equal and opposite and clearly cancel each other. Their addition will have no effect on the body, since their resultant is zero. However, once they are present, we may regroup them to aid our thinking, and thus we observe that F_1 and F_3 constitute a couple with a magnitude of 200 in.-lb (20×10). The remaining force F_2 acts at point O as a resultant force. In Fig. 4.17c we have replaced F_1 and F_3 with the 200-in.-lb couple, leaving F_2 at the wrench center, O.

   The three force systems in Fig. 4.17 are equivalent to each other. It will frequently be convenient to replace a system such as Fig. 4.17a with one like Fig.

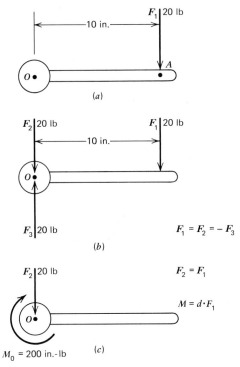

FIG. 4.17   Replacing a force with a force and a couple.

4.17c. It is also occasionally convenient to do the reverse, that is, to replace a force and couple with a single resultant force. The same principles, Eqs. 4.5 and 4.6, apply.

Example Problem 4.11

A gear with all but one tooth cut away is shown in Fig. 4.18. The load on the tooth is 500 N. Replace this load with an equivalent load and couple at the center of the gear.

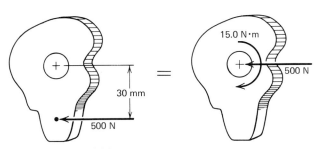

FIG. 4.18   Example Problem 4.11.

Solution

By Eq. 4.5, the equivalent force will be

$$R = \sum F = 500 \text{ N}$$

In the case of a single force, the resultant is always the same as the given force. We find the couple by summing the moments about the center of the gear using Eq. 4.6.

$$M_0 = \sum M_0 = -500 \text{ N} \times 30 \text{ mm} = -15{,}000 \text{ N} \times \text{mm}$$
$$M_0 = -15.0 \text{ N} \cdot \text{m}$$

Thus, as pictured in Fig. 4.18, the 500-N force 30 mm below the center is equivalent to the 500-N force at the center and the accompanying 15.0-N·m clockwise couple. This means that the two force systems produce the same tendency to translate and rotate the gear. The load must be expressed in this form to design the shaft carrying the gear.

Example Problem 4.12

Replace the force system shown in Fig. 4.19a with an equivalent force and couple at point A.

Solution

By Eq. 4.5:

$$R = \sum F = 70.0 \text{ lb}$$

And by Eq. 4.6.

$$M_A = \sum M_A = -6(70) + 560 = 140 \text{ in.-lb}$$

The resultant is as shown in Fig. 4.19b. Once again these two force systems have the same tendency to produce motion.

Example Problem 4.13

Replace the force system in Fig. 4.20 with an equivalent force system where the accompanying couple is zero.

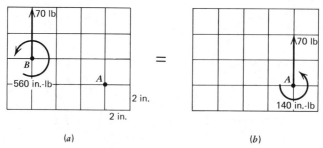

(a)   (b)

FIG. 4.19 Example Problem 4.12.

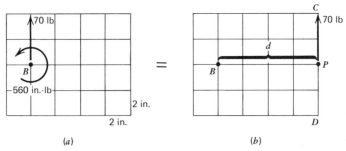

FIG. 4.20 Example Problem 4.13.

Solution

We know what the force system is, a 70-lb upward force. What we don't know is where it acts. We assume an as-yet unidentified point P such that

$$M_P = 0$$

Then

$$M_P = \sum M_P = +560 - 70 \times d = 0$$

where d is the distance from point B to point P measured perpendicular to the 70-lb vertical force and assumed to be positive to the right of B. Solving for d, we have:

$$d = \frac{560}{70} = \textbf{8.00 in.}$$

The point P is 8.00 in. to the right of B. Actually it can be anywhere along the line of action of the 70-lb force through point P (i.e., anywhere along the line CPD). The force system of Fig. 4.20b is statically equivalent to the force system of Fig. 4.20a. These systems are also statically equivalent to the force systems of Fig. 4.19. The property of static equivalence means that these systems have the same resultant force and the same resultant moment of force about any point as expressed by Eqs. 4.5 and 4.6. This further implies the same tendency to cause motion.

4.7 RESULTANT OF A SYSTEM OF FORCES

We repeat two important equations:

$$R = \sum F_1 = \sum F_2 \tag{4.5}$$
$$M_R = \sum M_1 = \sum M_2 \tag{4.6}$$

In Section 4.6 the equations were applied to a single force and couple. However they may be generalized to a *system* of forces and couples. Equation 4.5 says that two force systems are equivalent in their tendency to translate a body if they produce the same resultant force. Equation 4.6 says that two force systems are equivalent in their tendency to rotate a body if the resultant moment of the forces about a point is the same. Two force systems are said to be equivalent if both equations are satisfied.

The direct application of the above is that any system of forces may be reduced to a *single* resultant force and couple at any desired point. In cases of a resultant force that is not zero, a location may also be found for the resultant for which the accompanying couple is zero. If the resultant loading is a pure couple (zero resultant force), such a point cannot be found.

The idea of a resultant force and couple is an important concept. When either of these is nonzero the pair will produce an acceleration on the body that will result in its motion. In *dynamics* we learn that the acceleration produced is proportional to the resultant force and couple. If the resultant force and couple are both zero, we have no acceleration and a body at rest will remain at rest. This condition is known as *static equilibrium*, the primary subject of this text.

Example Problem 4.14

Reduce the force system shown in Fig. 4.21a to a single force and couple at point A.

Solution

Summing forces, we have:

$$R_x = \sum F_x = +40.0 \text{ N}$$
$$R_y = \sum F_y = +30 \text{ N} - 65 \text{ N} = -35.0 \text{ N}$$

Combining these two components, we get:

$$R = 53.2 \text{ N at } -41.2°$$

To get the accompanying couple, we sum moments about A:

$$M_A = \sum M_A = -225 + 350 + 3(65) - 2(40)$$
$$M_A = +240 \text{ N·m}$$

The result is shown in Fig. 4.21b.

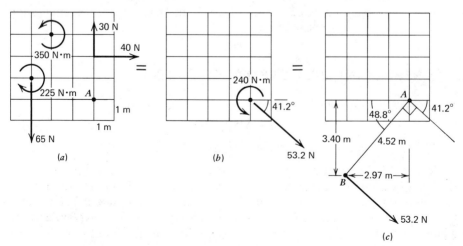

(a)   (b)   (c)

FIG. 4.21   Example Problems 4.14 and 4.15.

Example Problem 4.15

Reduce the force system in Fig. 4.21a to a single resultant force, if possible.

Solution

In Example Problem 4.14 the force system was reduced to a single force and couple at point A. We eliminate the couple by moving the 53.2-N force along a line perpendicular to the force such that:

$$M_A = 240 \text{ N·m} = 53.2 \times d$$

$$d = \frac{240}{53.2} = 4.52 \text{ m}$$

The force will have to be below and to the left of point A to produce the counterclockwise 240 N·m moment. Thus the force acts at point B as shown in Fig. 4.21c. We find the coordinates of point B with respect to point A by noting the indicated 48.8° angle. Then:

$$d_x = -4.52 \cos 48.8° = -2.97 \text{ m}$$
$$d_y = -4.52 \sin 48.8° = -3.40 \text{ m}$$

Thus the resultant force is

$$R = \textbf{53.2 N at } -\textbf{41.2°}$$

acting *2.97 m to the left* and *3.40 m below* point A.

Also note that the force systems in Fig. 4.21a–c are equivalent. All have exactly the same resultant force and moment of force about any point and exactly the same tendency to cause motion.

Example Problem 4.16

The I beam shown in Fig. 4.22a weighs 150 lb/ft and is loaded as shown. Find an equivalent force system at the support A.

Solution

The weight of the beam is 1500 lb and may be treated as acting at the center of the beam as shown in Fig. 4.22a. The resultant force is:

$$R_y = \sum F_y = -1500 - 5000 = -\textbf{6500 lb}$$

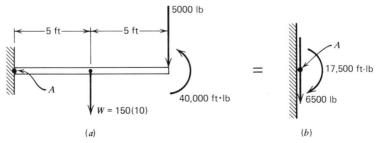

(a)

(b)

FIG. 4.22 Example Problem 4.16.

The negative sign means the resultant is down. Summing moments about point A, we get:

$$M_A = \sum M_A = -5(1500) - 10(5000) + 40,000$$
$$M_A = -17,500 \text{ ft-lb}$$

The negative sign means that the resultant moment is clockwise. The resultant system is shown in Fig. 4.22b and tends to translate the beam downward and rotate it clockwise about point A.

4.8 SUMMARY

The moment of a force is a measure of its tendency to rotate a body. It is calculated by the equation:

$$M = F \times d$$

with counterclockwise positive. The resultant of a force system is:

$$R = \sum F_i$$

The resultant moment of a force system is:

$$M = \sum M_i$$

The resultant moment will depend on the point about which moments are being taken, except for a system of couples. Force systems are equivalent if they produce the same resultant force and moment.

A couple is a pair of equal and opposite forces that have a resultant moment and a zero resultant force. A couple may be considered to be free; that is, it does not matter in statics where on a body the couple acts. Furthermore, the same resultant moment is obtained regardless of the point about which moments are taken.

PROBLEMS

4.1 For each of the following figures, calculate the moment of force about point A by finding the distance from the point to the force. Explicitly state whether the moment is clockwise or counterclockwise.

    (a) Fig. 4.23   (b) Fig. 4.24   (c) Fig. 4.25   (d) Fig. 4.26

4.2 For each of the following figures, calculate the moment of force about point B by finding the distance from the point to the force. Explicitly state whether the moment is clockwise or counterclockwise.

    (a) Fig. 4.23   (b) Fig. 4.24   (c) Fig. 4.25   (d) Fig. 4.26

4.3 If a mechanic can exert 20 lb of force by hand and a bolt needs to be torqued (moment of force applied) to 110 in.-lb, what minimum length of wrench is needed?

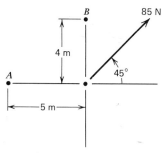

FIG. 4.23 Problems 4.1a, 4.2a, 4.7a, 4.8a.

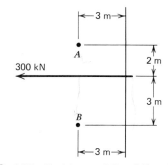

FIG. 4.24 Problems 4.1b, 4.2b, 4.7b, 4.8b, 4.32.

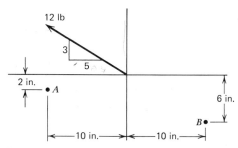

FIG. 4.25 Problems 4.1c, 4.2c, 4.7c, 4.8c, 4.33.

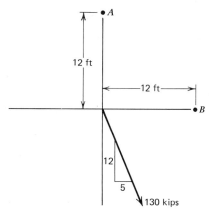

FIG. 4.26 Problems 4.1d, 4.2d, 4.7d, 4.8d.

4.4 An electric winch can produce a torque (moment of force) of 20 N·m. It is attached to a cable drum having a diameter of 240 mm. What is the maximum force the cable can exert? How could you increase the force? Explain.

4.5 Find the moment of the force system in Fig. 4.27 about the following points.

(a) A   (b) B   (c) C   (d) D

(e) E   (f) F   (g) G   (h) H

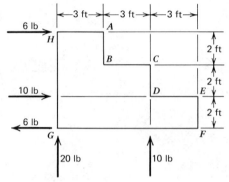

FIG. 4.27   Problems 4.5, 4.40, 4.41.

4.6   Find the moment of the force system in Fig. 4.28 about the following points.

(a)   *A*   (b)   *B*   (c)   *C*   (d)   *D*

(e)   *E*   (f)   *F*   (g)   *G*   (h)   *H*

4.7   Do the assigned part of Problem 4.1 using the theorem of Varignon (Section 4.3).

4.8   Do the assigned part of Problem 4.2 using the theorem of Varignon.

4.9   (a)   Find the moment of the 60-lb vertical force about the center of the winch in Fig. 4.29.

(b)   Find a horizontal force that will produce the same moment.

(c)   Find the smallest force that will produce the same moment.

4.10   Find the moment of the force system shown in Fig. 4.30 about the indicated point.

(a)   *A*   (b)   *B*   (c)   *C*   (d)   *D*   (e)   *E*

4.11   Find the moment of the force system shown in Fig. 4.31 about the indicated point.

(a)   *A*   (b)   *B*   (c)   *C*   (d)   *D*   (e)   *E*

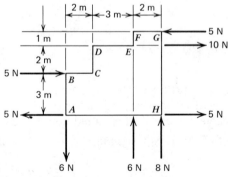

FIG. 4.28   Problems 4.6, 4.42, 4.43.

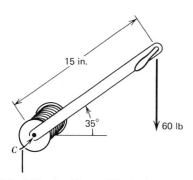

FIG. 4.29   Problems 4.9, 4.34

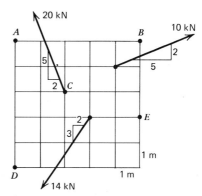

FIG. 4.30   Problems 4.10, 4.44, 4.45.

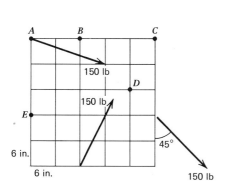

FIG. 4.31   Problems 4.11, 4.46, 4.47.

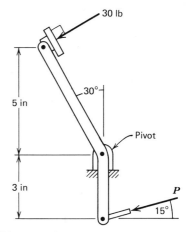

FIG. 4.32   Problems 4.12, 4.35, 4.48.

4.12 The 30-lb force on the brake pedal is perpendicular to the arm in Fig. 4.32. Find the moment of this force about the pivot. Find the force P exerted by the connecting rod on the lower arm required to resist this moment.

4.13 For the wheelbarrow in Fig. 4.33, find the moment of the 1.20-kN weight about the center of the wheel. Also find the force P required to resist this moment.

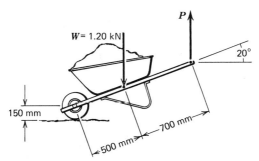

FIG. 4.33   Problem 4.13.

4.14 The clamp shown in Fig. 4.34 is used to hold a workpiece while it is being machined. A clamping force (equal to *P*) is exerted on the workpiece by tightening the bolt. If the bolt has a tension of 250 lb, what moment is produced about the pivot point? What force *P* is required to resist this moment?

4.15 Find the resultant of the force system shown in Fig. 4.35 and the moment of the force system about the indicated points by calculating the moment of each force. Compare the answers from several points.

   (a) *A*   (b) *B*   (c) *C*   (d) *D*
   (e) *E*   (f) *F*   (g) *G*

4.16 In Fig. 4.35 move the 20-N force at *E* to *F*. How does the moment of this new force system about point *A* compare to the moment of the original force system about point *A*? What principle does this result demonstrate?

4.17 In Fig. 4.35 move the 20-N force at *D* to *B*. How does the moment of this new force system about point *A* compare to the moment of the original force system about *A*? What does this tell you about changing the distance between forces forming a couple?

4.18 Find the resultant of the force system shown in Fig. 4.36 and the moment of the force system about the indicated point by calculating the moment of each force. Compare the answers from several points.

   (a) *A*   (b) *B*   (c) *C*   (d) *D*
   (e) *E*   (f) *F*   (g) *G*

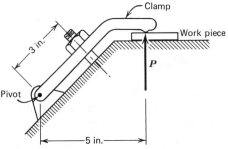

FIG. 4.34 Problem 4.14.

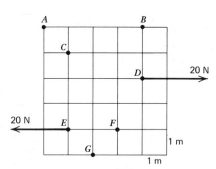

FIG. 4.35 Problems 4.15, 4.16, 4.17.

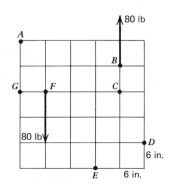

FIG. 4.36 Problems 4.18, 4.19, 4.20.

4.19 In Fig. 4.36 move the 80-lb force at *B* to *C*. How does the moment of this new force system about point *A* compare to the moment of the original force system about point *A*? What principle does this result demonstrate?

4.20 In Fig. 4.36 move the 80-lb force at *F* to *G*. How does the moment of this new force system about point *A* compare to the moment of the original force system about *A*? What does this tell you about changing the distance between forces forming a couple?

4.21 A double-ended tire tool provides a moment arm of 15 in. (end to end). What minimum force on each end of the handle is required to produce a moment of 300 in.-lb? What is the direction of this force relative to the handle?

4.22 Often a mechanic will pull on a wrench with a primary force F_1 (Fig. 4.37) and support the wrench with a secondary force F_2. If F_1 equals F_2, what is the effect of this secondary force?

4.23 The wrench shown in Fig. 4.37 is approximately 250 mm long. Assuming F_1 equal to F_2, what minimum force is required to produce a 15-N·m couple? What direction must F_1 and F_2 have with respect to the wrench handle in order to be a minimum?

4.24 The cross section of a large missile (Fig. 4.38) is 4.5 m in diameter. The missile has two small rockets, called roll thrusters, on its sides to cause the missile to roll about its longitudinal axis. What moment is produced by these thrusters when each exerts a 4-kN force on the missile? What moment will be produced if the thrust is tangent to the cross section of the missile?

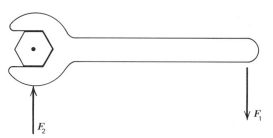

FIG. 4.37   Problems 4.22, 4.23.

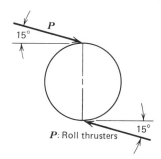

FIG. 4.38   Problem 4.24.

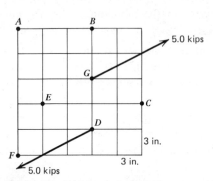

FIG. 4.39 Problems 4.25, 4.26.

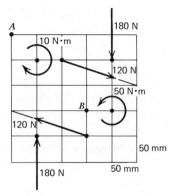

FIG. 4.40 Problem 4.27.

4.25 Find the resultant of the force system shown in Fig. 4.39 and the moment of the force system about the indicated point.

(a) *A*   (b) *B*   (c) *C*   (d) *D*

(e) *E*   (f) *F*   (g) *G*

4.26 For Fig. 4.39 move the 5.0-kip force at point *G* to point *B*. Calculate the moment of the force about the indicated point.

(a) *A*   (b) *B*   (c) *C*   (d) *D*

(e) *E*   (f) *F*   (g) *G*

4.27 Find the moment of the force system in Fig. 4.40:

(a)   By summing moments about point *A*

(b)   By summing moments about point *B*

(c)   By adding the couples

4.28 Find the moment of the force system in Fig. 4.41:

(a)   By summing moments about point *A*

(b)   By summing moments about point *B*

(c)   By adding the couples

4.29 A screwdriver blade contacts the edge of a screw slot as shown by points *A* and *B* in Fig. 4.42. If the screw head has a $\frac{1}{4}$-in. diameter and a couple of

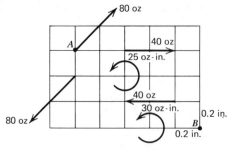

FIG. 4.41 Problem 4.28.

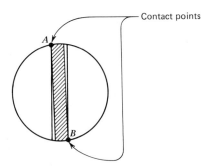

FIG. 4.42 Problems 4.29, 4.30.

10 in.-lb is applied to the screwdriver handle, what approximate force is exerted on the screw at points A and B?

4.30 A screwdriver blade contacts the edge of a screw slot as shown by points A and B in Fig. 4.42. If the screw head is 8 mm in diameter and a couple of 1.2 N·m is applied to the screwdriver handle, what approximate force is exerted on the screw at points A and B?

4.31 Explain the mechanical advantage of a screwdriver in terms of the couple applied to the handle and the couple applied to the screw.

4.32 Replace the 300-kN force in Fig. 4.24 with an equivalent force and couple at:

(a) Point A (b) Point B

4.33 Replace the 12-lb force in Fig. 4.25 with an equivalent force and couple at:

(a) Point A (b) Point B

4.34 Replace the 60-lb force on the crank arm in Fig. 4.29 with an equivalent force and couple at C.

4.35 Replace the 30-lb force on the brake pedal in Fig. 4.32 with an equivalent force and couple at the pivot.

4.36 Replace the force and couple given in Fig. 4.43 with an equivalent system at:

(a) Point A (b) Point B

4.37 For the force and couple given in Fig. 4.43 locate an equivalent force and a zero couple with respect to point C.

4.38 Replace the force and couple given in Fig. 4.44 with an equivalent system at:

(a) Point A (b) Point B

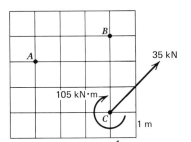

FIG. 4.43 Problems 4.36, 4.37.

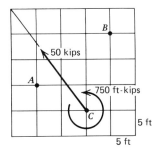

FIG. 4.44 Problems 4.38, 4.39.

4.39 For the force and couple given in Fig. 4.44 locate an equivalent force and a zero couple with respect to point *C*.

4.40 Replace the force system shown in Fig. 4.27 with a single resultant force and couple acting at each of the following points.

(a) *A*   (b) *B*   (c) *C*   (d) *D*

4.41 Find a resultant force and its location with respect to point *A* in Fig. 4.27 such that the accompanying moment is zero.

4.42 Replace the force system shown in Fig. 4.28 with a single resultant force and couple acting at each of the following points.

(a) *A*   (b) *B*   (c) *C*   (d) *D*

4.43 Find a resultant force and its location with respect to point *A* in Fig. 4.28 such that the accompanying moment is zero.

4.44 Replace the force system shown in Fig. 4.30 with a resultant force and couple acting at each of the following points.

(a) *A*   (b) *B*   (c) *C*   (d) *D*

4.45 Find the resultant force and its location with respect to point *A* in Fig. 4.30 such that the accompanying moment is zero.

4.46 Replace the force system shown in Fig. 4.31 with a resultant force and couple acting at each of the following points.

(a) *A*   (b) *B*   (c) *C*   (d) *D*

4.47 Find the resultant force and its location with respect to point *A* in Fig. 4.31 such that the accompanying moment is zero.

4.48 Let the force *P* in Fig. 4.32 be 85 lb. Find the resultant force and moment of the two forces at the pivot.

4.49 For the beam shown in Fig. 4.45, find the resultant force and couple at:

(a)   Point *A*   (b)   Point *B*

4.50 For the beam shown in Fig. 4.45, find the resultant force and its location such that the accompanying couple is zero.

4.51 For the beam shown in Fig. 4.46, find the resultant force and couple at:

(a)   Point *A*   (b)   Point *B*

4.52 For the beam shown in Fig. 4.46, find the resultant force and its location such that the accompanying couple is zero.

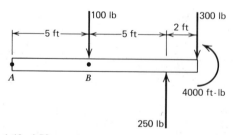

FIG. 4.45   Problems 4.49, 4.50.

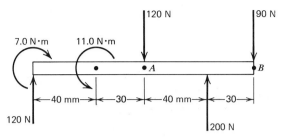

FIG. 4.46 Problems 4.51, 4.52.

4.53 A mechanic exerts a 40-lb downward force P on the 14-in., single-ended tire tool shown in Fig. 4.47. Find the equivalent force and couple on the bolt where it is applied. The bolt circle has a 6-in. diameter. Find the force and moment equivalent to this at the center of the hub of the 24-in. wheel.

4.54 A mechanic exerts a 200-N downward force P on the 340-mm, single-ended tire tool shown in Fig. 4.47. The bolt circle has a 150-mm diameter. Find the force and couple on the bolt. Find an equivalent force and couple at the center of the hub of the 600-mm wheel.

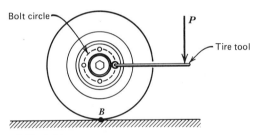

FIG. 4.47 Problems 4.53, 4.54.

5

Statics of Rigid
Bodies in a Plane

In this chapter we extend to rigid bodies the principle governing the statics of a particle. It turns out that the same principle introduced in Chapter 3—Newton's first law—must be satisfied. However, satisfying the force equation alone does not ensure static equilibrium. In cases like this we say that a condition is necessary but not sufficient. We will learn what is necessary and sufficient for rigid bodies and see how it is applied in a number of different situations.

5.1 WHEN A 40-TON LOCOMOTIVE IS A RIGID BODY

In Section 3.1 we discussed when one may treat a 40-ton locomotive as a particle. We could somewhat facetiously say that a 40-ton locomotive is a rigid body when it is not a particle. Actually this is a very good statement, although some elaboration may be appropriate. A particle problem is inherently simpler than a rigid body problem. When a rigid body problem can be reduced to a particle problem without destroying the validity of the answers, it should be—because it is simpler, and simpler means fewer errors. But alas, in some situations such simplification distorts the problems excessively and cannot be justified. The following examples illustrate the point.

A simplified 40-ton locomotive is shown in Fig. 5.1. To determine the forces on each set of wheels (Fig. 5.2), it is necessary to recognize that these forces are parallel and separated by an appreciable distance. Treating the forces as collinear and through the center of gravity as though the locomotive were a particle will not do. Or, consider lifting the rear of the locomotive with a jack (Fig. 5.3). This presents a similar problem where the locomotive cannot be treated as a particle. If the locomotive pulls a load at the rear hitch (Fig. 5.4), tipping is possible. Or, if the locomotive goes around a curve at a high speed (Fig. 5.5), it might roll over. (This is not strictly a statics problem, since the centrifugal force F_c depends on the dynamics. The problem can be analyzed as a statics problem, however, once the centrifugal force is known.)

For the foregoing examples we feel intuitively that the distances between the forces are important because they determine the moment of each force about any given point. We can illustrate this importance by reconsidering Fig. 5.2. In this figure let R_1 equal W and R_2 equal zero, in which case:

$$\sum F = 0$$

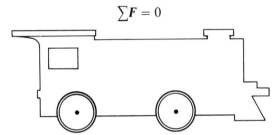

FIG. 5.1 Forty-ton locomotive.

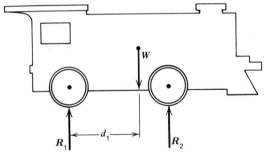

FIG. 5.2 Wheel reaction forces.

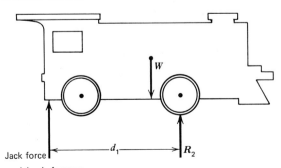

FIG. 5.3 Wheel and jack forces.

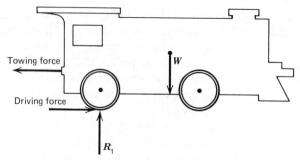

FIG. 5.4   Excessive towing force.

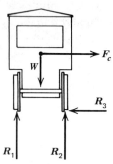

FIG. 5.5   A locomotive going around a curve.

and Newton's first law for particles is satisfied. However, further study reveals that there is an unbalanced clockwise moment on the locomotive equal to W times d_1. Its value depends on *where* the forces act. Whenever the answer we are seeking depends on where the forces act, we cannot reduce a rigid body problem to a particle problem. The unbalanced moment also produces a tendency for the body to rotate clockwise, and unless this tendency to rotate is sufficiently resisted, the body will rotate. This suggests that for rigid bodies there is more to equilibrium than the equation:

$$\sum F = 0$$

It is a valid suggestion, which is pursued in the next section. Meanwhile we observe that the discussion above would similarly apply to Figs. 5.3. through 5.5 as well, and we cannot handle them as particles.

5.2   NEWTON'S FIRST LAW APPLIED TO RIGID BODIES

In Chapter 3 we learned, and learned to use, Newton's first law, namely:

$$\sum F = 0 \tag{5.1}$$

or in component form:

$$\sum F_x = 0 \tag{5.2}$$

$$\sum F_y = 0 \tag{5.3}$$

We show a simple lever system and its free body diagram in Figs. 5.6 and 5.7, respectively. We ask what force P is required to hold the 200-N weight in place. Your intuition may tell you that P will have to be 100 N because its lever arm (10 m) is twice that of the 200 N weight (5 m). If so, your intuition happens to be correct, but what if it is not? Not to worry; the purpose of this course is to develop the ability to solve problems such as this, and much more complicated than this, without relying on intuition. Accepting the intuitive conclusion that P is 100 N we apply Eq. 5.3:

$$\sum F_y = 0 = +A - 200 + 100$$

Solving for A, we have:

$$A = 100 \text{ N}$$

We recall now from Chapter 4 that the moment of a force about a point is a measure of the force system's tendency to rotate the body it acts on about the point. We ask what is the tendency of this force system to rotate the lever about the pivot at A and answer it by summing the moments of force about point A in Fig. 5.7.

$$\sum M_A = -5(200) + 10(100) = 0$$

The moment is zero, and there is no tendency to rotate about point A! This illustrates an important extension of Newton's first law. *For a rigid body to be in equilibrium, the sum of the moments of force on it must be zero.* Since that means there is a zero tendency to rotate the body, it is a pretty straightforward principle. We write:

$$\sum M_A = 0 \tag{5.4}$$

Two additional items: (1) point A can be any point, and (2) this is an "if and only if" proposition. If the body is at rest rotationally, the sum of the moments is zero, and if the sum of the moments is zero, the body is at rest rotationally (or rotating at constant velocity.)

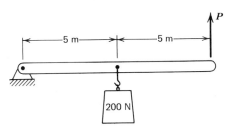

FIG. 5.6 Simple lever system.

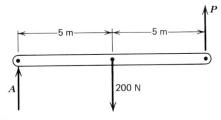

FIG. 5.7 Free body diagram.

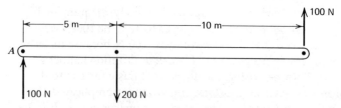

FIG. 5.8   Altered free body diagram.

Return again to the free body diagram of Fig. 5.7. Let the lever be 15 m long instead of 10 m, with the loads remaining the same, as shown in Fig. 5.8. We sum the forces.

$$\sum F_y = +100 - 200 + 100 = 0$$

The resultant force is zero; there is no tendency to translate the body, and Eq. 5.3, a condition for equilibrium, is satisfied. Next sum the moments of force about point A.

$$\sum M_A = -5(200) + 15(100) = +500 \; \text{N} \cdot \text{m}$$

There is a resultant counterclockwise moment of 500 N·m tending to rotate the body counterclockwise, and the equilibrium condition of Eq. 5.4 is not satisfied. The body would undergo angular acceleration. *It is not in equilibrium.*

There are three equations (Eqs. 5.2, 5.3, and 5.4) that must be satisfied for a rigid body to be in equilibrium. Together they constitute Newton's first law in two dimensions. Since we may impose these three equations on any rigid body at rest, it means that we can solve this type of problem for three unknowns in general. We should note that Eq. 5.4 is valid for any point, and thus an infinite number of equations may be written. However, only three of these will be "linearly independent"; that is, no one of the three equations can be obtained from some combination of the other two.

5.3   WRITE "FREE BODY DIAGRAM" 100 TIMES

Once again it is time for the drumroll and trumpet fanfare. You should also reread Section 3.3. (If you skipped over it before, read it twice now). And once again, we emphasize that drawing free body diagrams is essential. We repeat the four steps from Section 3.3:

1. Select a body.
2. Show all externally applied forces.
3. Remove each support and replace it with an appropriate force.
4. Label all forces and important dimensions.

Figure 5.9 shows a frame holding a 100-lb weight. A free body diagram of the entire structure is shown in Fig. 5.10. The externally applied load of 100 lb is shown at E. To make the body free, we cut the support at A. Since this is a fixed support, three components of reaction R_x, R_y, and M are required. *A reaction is*

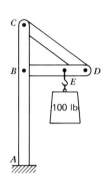

FIG. 5.9 Rigid frame.

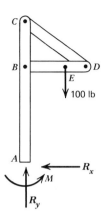

FIG. 5.10 Free body diagram of rigid frame.

required for each type of motion that is prevented by the support. The fixed support resists motion horizontally, giving R_x; vertically, giving R_y; and rotationally, giving M. The only way motion can be resisted is by a force (or moment of force).

Figure 5.11 indicates several supports, the motions they prevent, and the reactions they consequently produce. In the first case we have a rod or leg on a smooth surface, which can slip along parallel to the rigid surface. It can also rotate. Since neither of these motions is prevented, there is no accompanying force or moment of force. However, the leg cannot penetrate the rigid surface, as indicated by the vertical dashed line in the second column. Note that this line is *perpendicular* to the surface, and the force that prevents this motion, shown in the third column, is *perpendicular* to the surface. The roller on the second row behaves in a similar manner. In both cases the sense of the force is shown pushing upward on the leg, as it must if the supports are constructed as shown. We can, however, invert the support or use a track and have a reaction with a downward sense. Either of these presents a more complex sketch, so we will use those shown in Fig. 5.11 to mean either. If the force needs a downward sense, that will be OK, just make a note of it.

The leg on the friction surface (row 3) prevents motion perpendicular to the surface and parallel to it (unless it slips); hence the horizontal and vertical components. If the leg slips, we still have a resisting horizontal component of force. No rotation is resisted, and there is no moment of force. The pinned support or hinge (row 4) behaves in a similar manner. The last support, called a *fixed* support, is obtained when members are rigidly attached by bolting, welding, riveting, nailing, gluing, and so on. The schematic represents a timber embedded in concrete, preventing motion parallel and perpendicular to the beam and preventing rotation; thus the reactions shown.

In general we will not know the sense of the unknown reactions R_x, R_y, and M. Not to worry—guess! If we guess correctly, we will get positive answers from the mathematics. If we guess incorrectly, we will get negative answers.

The first step in the solution of any statics problem is an accurate and complete free body diagram. Given such a free body diagram, equations satisfying Newton's first law are written in agreement with the free body diagram. The rest is algebra.

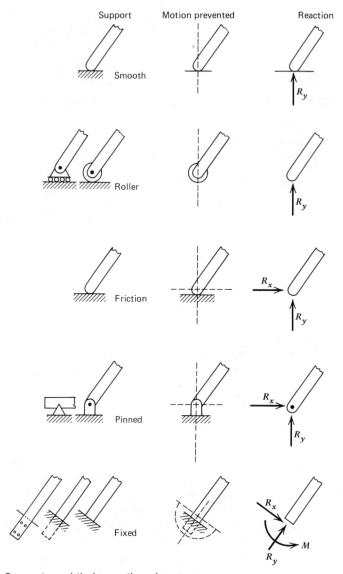

FIG. 5.11 Supports and their reactions in free body diagrams.

5.4 PARALLEL FORCE PROBLEMS

Chapter 3 dealt with concurrent force problems, a class of problems for which only two unknowns can be found. That is because only two equations give relevant independent information:

$$\sum F_x = 0$$

and

$$\sum F_y = 0$$

Another special case is presented when all the forces acting on a body are parallel. In such cases the only relevant equations are:

$$\sum M = 0$$

and

$$\sum F_y = 0$$

where Y is the coordinate parallel to the forces. Once more there are only two equations, so only two unknowns may be found. Beams are an important class of problems that fit into this category as illustrated below.

Example Problem 5.1

Find the reactions at A and B for the simply supported beam shown in Fig. 5.12.

Solution

A free body diagram is constructed in Fig. 5.13. First the applied loads of 10 kN, 15 kN, and 25 kN·m are drawn. Then the support at A is cut loose and the reactions A_x and A_y are supplied, since this pinned connection will not allow motion in either of these directions. (If this is not intuitively clear, refer to Fig. 5.11, row 4.) Because all the applied forces are vertical, the horizontal component A_x is zero. As you mature in your ability to do statics, you will recognize that and leave it out of the free body diagram. Until then it's OK to put it in. Always supply the force if there is any doubt. Moving to

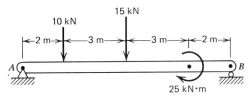

FIG. 5.12 Example Problem 5.1.

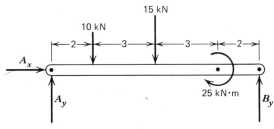

FIG. 5.13 Free body diagram for Example Problem 5.1.

point B we see that this roller resists vertical motion but not horizontal or rotational motion; thus the only reaction is vertical B_y, as shown. The body is now free from all support, and we should have an accurate and complete free body diagram. If so, all is well; *if not, we cannot possibly solve the problem correctly.*

We now apply Newton's first law by summing the moments of the forces about point A. We can sum the moments about any point, but if we use point A or B we isolate a single unknown in the moment equation and avoid solving simultaneous equations. We write:

$$\sum M_A = 0 = -2(10) - 5(15) - 25 + 10B_y$$

Note that each of the clockwise moments is listed as negative and the counterclockwise moment of B_y is positive. Also note that there is no transfer distance associated with the couple of 25 kN·m. Solving the equation above for B_y, we have:

$$B_y = \frac{20 + 75 + 25}{10} = \frac{120}{10}$$

$$B_y = 12.0 \text{ kN}$$

The positive sign means the assumed upward sense was correct. Now summing forces vertically

$$\sum F_y = 0 = A_y - 10 - 15 + B_y$$

The 25-kN·m moment does not affect the force equation. Solving for A_y,

$$A_y = 25 - B_y = 25 - 12$$
$$A_y = 13.0 \text{ kN}$$

Once again the positive sign means the assumed upward sense was correct.

EVALUATION   Looking only at the vertical loads of 10 and 15 kN, we would expect the reaction at A to be greater than the reaction at B, since these loads are shifted toward A. The effect of the clockwise couple is to shift the load toward B. It does not matter where the couple acts. Its sense and magnitude determine its effect. With the couple, the reactions at A and B are nearly equal.

Example Problem 5.2

Find the reactions at A for the cantilever beam shown in Fig. 5.14.

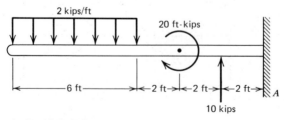

FIG. 5.14   Example Problem 5.2.

Solution

As before we proceed by drawing a free body diagram. This problem presents a distributed load of 2 kips/ft over a 6-ft span. In this case the load is uniformly distributed. This load is equivalent to

$$2 \text{ kips/ft} \times 6 \text{ ft} = 12 \text{ kips}$$

acting at the center (or "center of gravity") of the distributed load. This is 3 ft from the free end as shown in Fig. 5.15. In Chapter 6 we will deal with distributed loads in general and show why the foregoing is true. In the meantime it gives us a more interesting array of problems. Besides, it is probably intuitively obvious and most have seen it before. We proceed with the free body diagram by adding the 20-ft-kip couple and the 10-kip upward force.

Last we come to the fixed support, giving A_y and M_A in agreement with Fig. 5.11, which indicates that a horizontal force A_x is also called for. We observe that all the loading is vertical and $A_x = 0$; we therefore choose to leave it off the diagram. This is a common practice with beams having only vertical load, and one you will want to adopt; but use it only when you are sure. With the free body diagram complete, we can proceed to apply Newton's first law. We sum forces vertically, obtaining:

$$\sum F_y = 0 = -12 + 10 + A_y$$

from which:

$$A_y = 12 - 10 = \textbf{2.00 kips}$$

Then summing the moments about point A:

$$\sum M_A = +9(12) - 20 - 2(10) + M_A = 0$$

from which:

$$M_A = 20 + 20 - 108 = -68.0 \text{ ft-kip}$$
$$M_A = \textbf{68.0 ft-kips} \curvearrowright$$

The negative sign we obtained means that the assumed counterclockwise sense for M_A was incorrect; it is in fact 68.0 ft-kips clockwise.

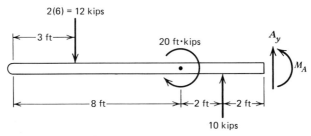

FIG. 5.15 Free body diagram for Example Problem 5.2.

EVALUATION   The distributed load of 12 kips is well out on the beam and produces a counterclockwise moment about A. The upward load of 10 kips and the couple oppose this, but do not override it, since the reaction at A is clockwise. The net applied force is downward, and so we get the upward reaction of 2 kips. Everything appears to be in order.

5.5 SOME PROBLEMS

In Section 5.2 we expressed the conditions for equilibrium and then emphasized the need for the free body diagram. Now we will show additional applications of these principles to general two-dimensional problems.

Example Problem 5.3

Find the external loads at A and B for Fig. 5.16.

Solution

Draw a free body diagram of the entire structure and resolve A into components as in Fig. 5.17. We are now ready for Eqs. 5.2, 5.3, and 5.4. If we arbitrarily apply them, the worst that we can get is three equations in three unknowns. Then the algebra will yield a solution, but "that ain't exactly no picnic." We can reduce the work substantially if we are more clever in writing equations, especially moment equations. We note, for instance, that the unknowns B_x, B_y, and the component A_x of the unknown A all pass through point B. If we sum moments about B, these terms will not appear in the equation (their moment arms being zero). This leaves only A_y, and the equation may be solved quickly and directly for it. Thus we have:

$$\sum M_B = 0 = 6A_y - 4(200)$$

$$A_y = \frac{4(200)}{6} = 133 \text{ lb}\downarrow$$

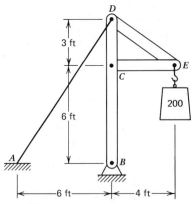

FIG. 5.16 Example Problem 5.3.

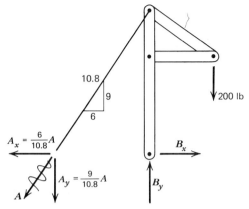

FIG. 5.17 Free body diagram for Example Problem 5.3.

By proportion:

$$\frac{A_x}{6} = \frac{A_y}{9}$$

$$A_x = \frac{6}{9} A_y = \frac{6}{9} \left(\frac{4(200)}{6} \right)$$

$$A_x = \frac{800}{9} = \textbf{88.9 lb} \leftarrow$$

Resolving the components A_x and A_y gives:

$$A = \textbf{160 lb at } \diagup_{6}^{9}$$

We now need to find B_x and B_y. Applying the principle used in obtaining our first equation, we would sum the moments about point D yielding B_x or about point A yielding B_y. That is fine, and some will prefer these steps. In taking these steps we are replacing Eqs. 5.2 and 5.3 with additional versions of Eq. 5.4, which is legitimate. However, in this case even simpler equations may be obtained by writing 5.2 and 5.3 directly. These equations are always preferred when they contain a single unknown (because they will be simpler). Thus:

$$\sum F_x = 0 = -88.9 + B_x$$
$$B_x = \textbf{88.9 lb}$$

and

$$\sum F_y = 0 = -133 + B_y - 200$$
$$B_y = 200 + 133 = \textbf{333 lb}$$

The positive signs for A and B_x and B_y mean that all the assumed senses were correct.

EVALUATION   If we consider the frame pinned at *B*, we recognize that we must have the cable in tension to balance the moment of the weight of 200 lb. We found a tensile load of 160 lb. This magnitude also looks reasonable. With a tensile load in the cable, B_x will have to be to the right. With both A_y and the weight acting downward, B_y must act upward.

Example Problem 5.4

A brake pedal is modeled as shown in Fig. 5.18. In an actual system the cable activates a brake cylinder. Find the force in the cable and the reaction at the pin.

Solution

A free body diagram is drawn in Fig. 5.19. The cable will have the force **P** along it. Two components B_y and B_x occur at the pivot. For this free body diagram we have selected a coordinate system along and perpendicular to the

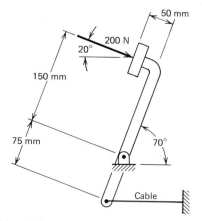

FIG. 5.18   Example Problem 5.4.

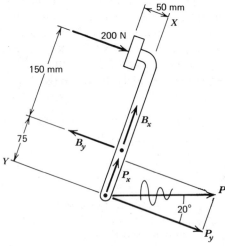

FIG. 5.19   Free body diagram for Example Problem 5.4.

brake arm. We are free to use any we like. This coordinate system will make the geometry easier. Often the mathematics of a problem can be simplified by judicious selection of a coordinate system. The idea is to make the coordinate system fit the problem. In using this coordinate system, B_x and B_y are parallel and perpendicular, respectively, to the brake arm. We also resolve the cable force P into X and Y components. Now we sum the moments about B.

$$\sum M_B = 0 = -150(200) + 75P_y$$

$$P_y = \frac{200(150)}{75} = 400 \text{ N}$$

$$P_y = P \cos 20°$$

$$P = \frac{P_y}{\cos 20°} = \frac{400}{\cos 20°} = \textbf{426 N}$$

Then summing the forces in the Y direction:

$$\sum F_y = -200 + B_y - P_y = 0$$
$$B_y = 200 + 400 = \textbf{600 N}$$

and for the X direction:

$$\sum F_x = 0 = +B_x + P_x$$
$$B_x = -P_x$$
$$P_x = P \sin 20°$$
$$B_x = -426 \sin 20° = \textbf{-146 N}$$

Of course the minus sign means that B_x is opposite the sense shown in Fig. 5.19.

EVALUATION   You want to start developing your own evaluation. We'll ask a few questions to help you.

Was the sense of the force P as expected? Can the cable handle a force of this sense, or will a rigid rod be required? Is the magnitude of P reasonable? Are the reactions at B appropriate?

Example Problem 5.5

The pipe wrench shown in Fig. 5.20 is used on a pipe perpendicular to the length AB, producing the 20-lb force and 180-in.-lb couple. Find the reaction on this pipe at the support A.

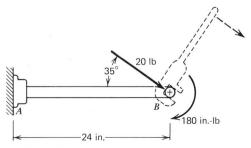

FIG. 5.20 Example Problem 5.5.

Solution

The 20-lb force is resolved into components and the free body diagram is drawn in Fig. 5.21. The support at A is fixed. Horizontal, vertical, and rotational motions are all resisted by R_x, R_y, and M, respectively. Summing forces gives:

$$\sum F_x = -R_x + 20 \cos 35° = 0$$
$$R_x = \textbf{16.4 lb}$$
$$\sum F_y = R_y - 20 \sin 35° = 0$$
$$R_y = \textbf{11.5 lb}$$

Then summing the moments of forces about point A gives:

$$\sum M_A = +M - 180 - 24(20 \sin 35°) = 0$$
$$M = 180 + 24(11.5) = \textbf{455 in.-lb}$$

EVALUATION   Do the horizontal and vertical components of the reaction at A oppose the applied loads? Is the sense of M proper? Is its magnitude reasonable?

5.6   HOW TO HANDLE PULLEYS AND *WHY*

In Section 3.5 we said that the tension in a cable around a pulley is the same everywhere. We will now see why this is so. In Fig. 5.22 we have a cable supporting an 80-N weight over a pulley of radius r. We wish to know the force in the cable and the pin reaction forces on the pulley. We draw the appropriate free body diagram in Fig. 5.23. Summing moments about the pin we get:

$$\sum M_p = -r(80) + rT_2 = 0$$
$$T_2 = \textbf{80.0 N}$$

We find the tension to be the same on either side of the pulley. This is because the moment must be balanced, and the moment arm for both forces is the radius of the pulley. If there is friction in the pulley, the tension will be less on one side of the pulley than on the other. To continue our study of the pulley, we sum forces horizontally.

$$\sum F_x = 0 = R_x - T_2$$
$$R_x = T_2 = \textbf{80.0 N}$$

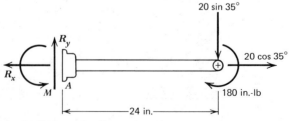

FIG. 5.21   Free body diagram for Example Problem 5.5.

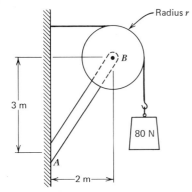

FIG. 5.22 Pulley problem.

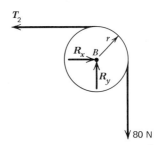

FIG. 5.23 Free body diagram of pulley.

and then vertically

$$\sum F_y = 0 = R_y - 80$$
$$R_y = \textbf{80.0 N}$$

We see that the pin reaction exactly equals the tension in the cables. Applying Newton's third law, we draw the forces acting on the pin in Fig. 5.24, which is a free body diagram of the support shaft. This analysis leads us to the same two conclusions we presented in Chapter 3, namely:

1. *The tension in a cable acting on a frictionless pulley is everywhere the same.*
2. *These tension forces are transferred undiminished to the pulley pin.*

Now we see that these conclusions are based on drawing a free body diagram of the pulley and applying Newton's first law.

Example Problem 5.6

Find the reactions at the wall support *A* in Fig. 5.22.

Solution

In the free body diagram for this shaft (Fig. 5.24), the tension in the cable, 80 N, has been transferred to the center of the pulley. The support at *A* is fixed. It does not allow motion in the vertical or horizontal direction, nor does it allow rotation. Thus we have the components A_x, A_y, and M_A. There are these three unknowns, and we may proceed with the solution:

$$\sum F_x = 0 = -A_x - 80$$
$$A_x = \textbf{-80.0 N} \rightarrow$$

$$\sum F_y = 0 = +A_y - 80$$
$$A_y = \textbf{80.0 N} \uparrow$$

$$\sum M_A = +3(80) - 2(80) - M_A = 0$$
$$M_A = \textbf{80.0 N} \cdot \textbf{m}$$

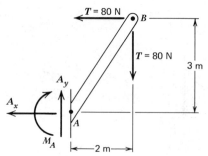

FIG. 5.24 Free body diagram of support shaft.

EVALUATION You are on your own, but note that the diameter of the pulley has no bearing on the problem.

5.7 HOW TO HANDLE TWO-FORCE MEMBERS AND *WHY*

A great number of members in building and machine structures may be classified as *two-force members*. Developing the ability to readily recognize these members will greatly aid in the analysis of such structures. By seeing why two-force members behave as they do, you should gain a better understanding and recognize them more readily. In Fig. 5.25 we draw a rather nondescript two-force member with the force P at B and the force Q at A. It is called a two-force member because there are only two forces acting on it. A better definition however is that *forces act at only two locations*, since multiple forces at B can be resolved into single force P. The same is also true at A.

We wish now to apply Newton's first law to this free body diagram by summing moments of force about point A:

$$\sum M_A = 0 = -d \cdot P$$

There are two ways the product $d \cdot P$ can be zero; either d must be zero or P must be zero. If P is zero, we have no problem. The only way d can be zero is for the force P to pass through the point A. Since P is applied at the point B and must pass through point A, we conclude that it must be along the line AB. If we sum moments of force about point B, we find that the force Q must also act along the

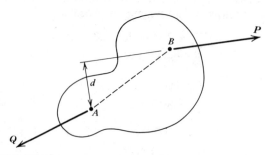

FIG. 5.25 Two-force member.

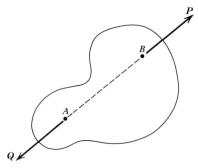

FIG. 5.26 Corrected free body diagram for a two-force member.

line AB. In Fig. 5.26 we draw a corrected free body diagram with the forces P and Q acting along the line AB. We emphasize that this is the *only possible* configuration for equilibrium. Any other will have unbalanced moments of force. If we sum forces along the line AB we also find

$$P = Q$$

Thus the forces must act along the line AB, be equal in magnitude, and be opposite in sense.

Example Problem 5.7

Find the reactions at A and B in Fig. 5.27.

Solution

A free body diagram is drawn in Fig. 5.28. The tension in the cable is 190 lb on either side of the pulley. This in turn is transferred to the center of the

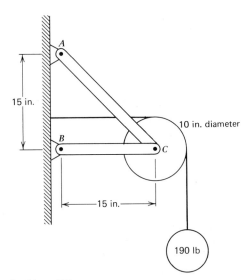

FIG. 5.27 Example Problem 5.7.

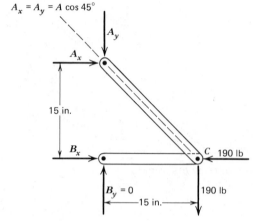

FIG. 5.28 Free body diagram for Example Problem 5.7.

pulley C as shown. Make sure that the proper sense is used. It might be more natural to think of the horizontal 190-lb force at C as pulling on the pin at C. We have shown it as pushing so that we can illustrate it clearly on the figure. It does not matter whether it is shown as pushing or pulling, but it is essential that it be shown as acting to the left, its proper sense. Also notice once more that the diameter of the frictionless pulley is not important.

Proceeding to the pin at point B, we recognize that two components B_x and B_y are possible. We also recognize that forces come into member BC only at points B and C and therefore this is a *two-force member*. This requires the resultant force at B and C to be along a line from B to C and therefore the vertical component B_y must be zero as indicated in Fig. 5.28.

Moving to point A, we also recognize member AC to be a *two-force member* and the reaction at A must be along the line AC as indicated. Since this line makes an angle of $45°$ with the horizontal, we have:

$$A_x = A_y = A \cos 45°$$

as indicated in the figure. There are then only two unknowns on this free body diagram and the problem is solvable. Before proceeding, we note that we have assumed the sense of A_x to be to the right. We are free to do that. However *we are not* then free to assume the sense of A_y to be up. Assuming the sense of A_x to the left fixes the sense of A_y to be up. Other combinations will *not* produce a reaction along the line AC and are therefore incorrect. Writing the force equations, we have:

$$\sum M_A = 0 = +15B_x - 190(15) - 190(15)$$

$$B_x = \frac{5700}{15} = 380 \text{ lb}$$

$$\sum F_x = 0 = B_x + A_x - 190$$
$$A_x = 190 - B_x = 190 - 380$$
$$A_x = -190 \text{ lb} \leftarrow$$

$$\sum F_y = 0 = -A_y - 190$$

$$A_y = -190 \text{ lb} \uparrow$$

$$A_x = -190 \text{ lb} = A_y \qquad \textbf{Check}$$

In this case the reaction at A is up and to the left.

If we had failed to recognize members BC and AC as two-force members, we would have had four unknowns in this problem (A_x, A_y, B_x, and B_y) and could not solve it at this point. Later (Chapter 8) we will see that we can solve it without recognizing the two-force members. So it is not necessary to recognize them, but it sure makes for shorter nights.

5.8 THREE-FORCE MEMBERS

We will consider one last special case, that of a *three-force member*. A free body diagram of a three-force member is shown in Fig. 5.29 with the forces P at B, Q at A, and S at C. The concept of a *three-force member* may be expanded to mean that *forces are applied at only three locations*, A, B, and C. The force P at B may actually be the resultant of any number of forces acting at B, and the same is true for Q and S at A and C. Nonetheless, the term *three-force member* is well established, and we will stick with it for its literal meaning or its expanded meaning. Returning to Fig. 5.29 we extend the lines of action of forces P and Q and find their intercept, point D. For this body to be in equilibrium, the sum of the moments of force about any point must equal zero. We pick point D as this reference point. Since the forces P and Q pass through point D, they will have no moment and we have:

$$\sum M_D = 0 = d \cdot S$$

where d is the perpendicular distance from the line of action of force S to point D.

The equation above can be satisfied only when d or S or both equal zero. If S equals zero there is no force at C and we have a two-force member—return to Section 5.7. But if d equals zero, then the force S acts through point D. A corrected free body diagram is shown in Fig. 5.30 and we draw the following

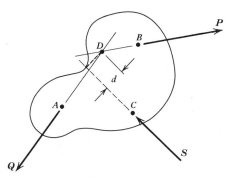

FIG. 5.29 Three-force member.

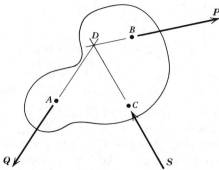

FIG. 5.30 Corrected free body diagram for a three-force member.

conclusion:

> For a three-force member to be in equilibrium, all three forces must act through a common point unless the forces are parallel.

This principle can be very useful in determining the direction of an unknown force, as illustrated in the example problem that follows. One word of caution: since the principle is based on the moment equation from Newton's first law, using it uses the moment equation, and only two equations remain for plane problems.

Example Problem 5.8

Find the reactions at *A* and *B* for the structure shown in Fig. 5.31.

Solution

Member *AC* is a cable, and the force on it must be along it. If it were a rigid link, the same would be true, because it is a two-force member. We draw a free body diagram of the structure *BDCE* (Fig. 5.32).

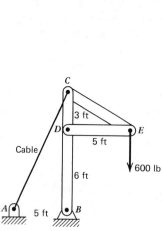

FIG. 5.31 Example Problem 5.8.

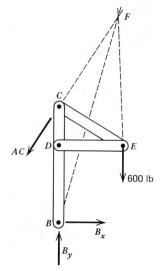

FIG. 5.32 Free body diagram for Example Problem 5.8.

To solve this problem, sum moments about *B*, solving for *AC*, or better, sum moment about *C*, solving for B_x. Then sum forces horizontally and vertically, solving for the remaining unknowns.

However, we can take a different approach by recognizing the frame to be a three-force member; that is, forces are applied only at *B*, *C*, and *E*. This requires the three forces to be concurrent—to come together at a common point. This point, labeled *F*, is found by extending the lines of action for the 600-lb vertical force and the force *AC*, as shown in Fig. 5.32.

This can be done analytically but is much simpler graphically. The force at *B* must also pass through *F*. Its direction is determined by the line *BF* as shown. The force polygon is then drawn by laying out the 600-lb vertical force to scale (Fig. 5.33). The vectors *AC* and **B** are drawn by constructing them parallel to Fig. 5.32. We then scale their values, yielding

$$AC = 700 \text{ lb}$$

$$B = 1280 \text{ lb}$$

The angle *B* makes with the horizontal is measured and found to be 73.8°. Thus

$$B = 1280 \text{ lb at } 73.8°$$

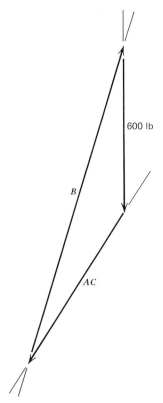

FIG. 5.33 Force polygon for Example Problem 5.8.

5.9 SOME MORE PROBLEMS

In this section we further illustrate the principles of statics by several problems. You should start to observe a sameness in the solutions. In each case we draw a free body diagram, write the equations for Newton's first law, and finally solve them for the appropriate unknowns.

Example Problem 5.9

Find the reactions at A and D for the mechanical arm in Fig. 5.34.

Solution

A free body diagram is drawn in Fig. 5.35. The pin at A yields two components, A_x and A_y. The roller at D yields a single force perpendicular to the wall. As shown in Fig. 5.35, the force D will make an angle of 20° with the horizontal. We observe there are three unknowns in the free body diagram and we may proceed with the solution. We sum moments about A yielding:

$$\sum M_A = 0 = -6(30) - 420 + 6(D \cos 20°) + 20(D \sin 20°)$$

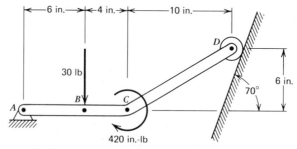

FIG. 5.34 Example Problem 5.9.

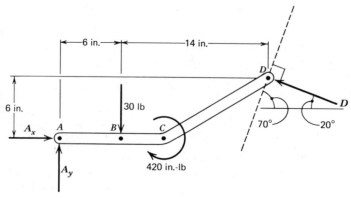

FIG. 5.35 Free body diagram for Example Problem 5.9.

Note there is *no* moment arm associated with the 420-in.-lb couple. Solving for *D*, we have:

$$D(6 \cos 20° + 20 \sin 20°) = 180 + 420$$

$$D = \frac{600}{12.48} = \textbf{48.1 lb}$$

Summing forces horizontally:

$$\sum F_x = 0 = A_x - D \cos 20°$$
$$A_x = \textbf{45.2 lb}$$

And vertically:

$$\sum F_y = 0 = A_y - 30 + D \sin 20$$
$$A_y = 30 - 48.1 \sin 20°$$
$$A_y = \textbf{13.6 lb}$$

Also note that the 420-in.-lb couple makes *no* contribution to the force equations.

We might think that this is a three-force member because forces are applied only at *A*, *B*, and *D*. If it were, we could extend the lines of action of the 30-lb force at *B* and the force *D* to find their intersection and the direction of the force *A*. Force *A* would have to be along the line from point *A* to this intersection. However the couple at *C* invalidates the conclusion that this is a three-force member, and the reaction at *A* is not through this intersection. *Members with couples or distributed loads cannot be classified as two- or three-force members.*

Example Problem 5.10

Find the reactions at *C* and *D* for the structure shown in Fig. 5.36.

Solution

A free body diagram is drawn in Fig. 5.37. First the cable is cut, giving 80 N on each side of the pulley, which in turn is transferred undiminished to the pulley center. Member *AC* is not a two-force member, since forces are applied at *A*, *B*, and *C*. Therefore when the pin at *C* is cut we get two components, C_x and C_y, not just C_x along the line *AC*. Member *BD* is a two-force member, and the reaction at *D* will be along the line from *B* to *D*, which is not along the member in this case. The free body diagram is now complete, and with three unknowns the problem is solvable. We proceed by calculating the third side of the 60–100 triangle to be 116.6. Then summing moments about *C* yields:

$$\sum M_c = 0 = +200(80) - 200(80 \sin 45°) - 40 \frac{100}{116.6} D - 100 \frac{60}{116.6} D$$

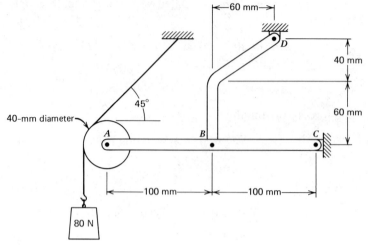

FIG. 5.36   Example Problem 5.10.

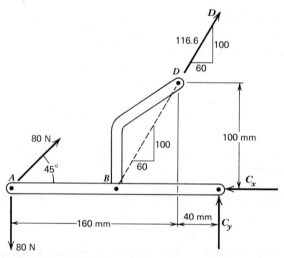

FIG. 5.37   Free body diagram for Example Problem 5.10.

Solving for D, we have:

$$D\left[\frac{40(100)}{116.6} + \frac{100(60)}{116.6}\right] = +16,000 - 11,310$$

$$D\left[\frac{10,000}{116.6}\right] = 4686$$

$$\boldsymbol{D = 54.7 \text{ N}}$$

Summing forces horizontally

$$\sum F_x = 0 = 80 \cos 45° + \frac{60}{116.6} D + C_x$$

$$C_x = \textbf{84.7 N}$$

And

$$\sum F_y = 0 = -80 + 80 \sin 45° + \frac{100}{116.6} D + C_y$$

$$C_y = 80 - 80 \sin 45° - \frac{100D}{116.6}$$

$$C_y = \textbf{-23.4 N}$$

The negative sign for C_y means this reaction is down rather than up, as indicated in the free body diagram.

Example Problem 5.11

Find the reactions at C and D for the structure shown in Fig. 5.38.

Solution

This problem is very similar to Example Problem 5.10. The differences are quite subtle but, as we shall see, their importance is overriding. As before, a free body diagram is drawn (Fig. 5.39a). The cable is cut on both sides of the pulley, yielding forces of 80 N, which are transferred undiminished to the center of the pulley and parallel to the original directions. In this case, however, the cable is anchored to the structure at E and this force must also be shown. Note that the two tension forces between A and E oppose each other. The reaction at C is two unknowns, C_x and C_y. We come now to point D. With the force at

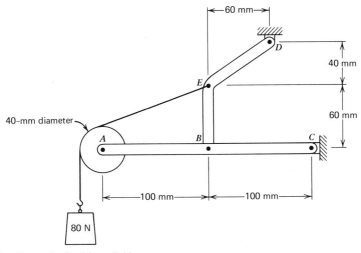

FIG. 5.38 Example Problem 5.11.

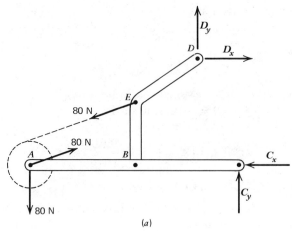

FIG. 5.39a Free body diagram for Example Problem 5.11.

E, member BD is no longer a two-force member and the force at D is *not* along a line from B to D. There are two unknowns at D, D_x and D_y. This completes the free body diagram.

We observe that there are four unknowns, C_x, C_y, D_x, and D_y. Although this particular problem can be solved by the methods of Chapter 8, it is unsolvable at this point because we have only three equations available. In general, this is what is meant by statically indeterminate. This problem is not truly statically indeterminate, but it still illustrates the need to determine whether a problem is solvable before jumping into the force equations.

An alternate free body diagram, (Fig. 5.39b) is obtained if we choose not to cut the cable from A to E. In this figure BD is still not a two-force member and there are still four unknowns.

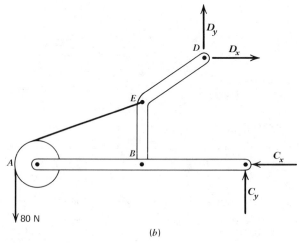

FIG. 5.39b Alternate free body diagram for Example Problem 5.11.

Example Problem 5.12

An industrial garbage container has a lid weighing 60 lb. The weight is represented by the 1.2 lb/in. distributed load in Fig. 5.40. Find the reactions at *A* and *D*.

Solution

This problem is typical of many real problems in that it has a lot of tacky detail. That is very common in the real world and presents a barrier that is hard to penetrate even when one has a pretty good grasp of the basics. Pushing ahead in such problems requires the development of confidence in one's ability to solve geometric problems, and that generally comes from practice. So we'll practice.

A line sketch of the problem is made in Fig. 5.41. All known information is shown and desired unknowns are labeled. We recognize member *BD* to be a two-force member, and the reaction at *D* will be along *BD*. Hence we need to know the angle *BD* makes with the horizontal, angle $\theta + \phi$ in Fig. 5.41.

We observe that θ may be found from the right triangle *AED* by:

$$\tan \theta = \frac{10}{40} = 0.250$$

$$\theta = 14.0°$$

Then:

$$\sin \theta = \frac{10}{l}$$

$$l = \frac{10}{\sin 14.0°} = 41.2$$

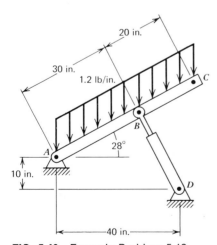

FIG. 5.40 Example Problem 5.12.

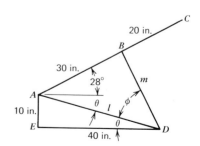

FIG. 5.41 Geometry for Example Problem 5.12.

We find ϕ by solving for the parts of the nonright triangle ABD. We observe:

$$\measuredangle BAD = \theta + 28° = 42.0°$$

Then by the law of cosines:

$$m^2 = 30^2 + 41.2^2 - 2(30)(41.2) \cos 42.0°$$
$$m = 27.6$$

And by the law of sines:

$$\frac{30}{\sin \phi} = \frac{m}{\sin 42.0°}$$

$$\sin \phi = \frac{30}{27.6} \sin 42° = 0.727$$

$$\phi = 46.7°$$

And finally:

$$\theta + \phi = 14.0° + 46.7° = \mathbf{60.7°}$$

Solving the problem analytically is fine and often needed. We should note, however, that a solution can be found much quicker by laying the problem out graphically. Graphics is a very easy way to solve many complex geometric problems and should not be overlooked. At the least an approximate sketch should be made, to make it easier to generate the analytical solution and finally to confirm it.

Now that the geometry is solved, a free body diagram is drawn in Fig. 5.42, observing the components at D required for this force to be along BD. We also replace the distributed load (weight) with a concentrated 60 lb at the center of

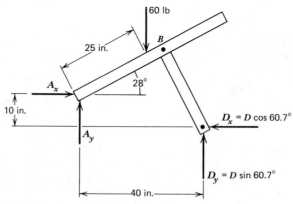

FIG. 5.42 Free body diagram for Example Problem 5.12.

gravity. Summing the moment of forces about A gives:

$$\sum M_A = 0 = -(25 \cos 28°)60 - 10(D \cos 60.7°) + 40(D \sin 60.7°)$$

$$D = \frac{1324}{30.0} = \textbf{44.2 lb}$$

$$\sum F_x = 0 = A_x - D \cos 60.7°$$
$$A_x = \textbf{21.6 lb}$$

$$\sum F_y = 0 = A_y - 60 + D \sin 60.7°$$
$$A_y = 60 - 38.5 = \textbf{21.5 lb}$$

The solution was almost too easy after the tacky geometry was solved!

5.10 SUMMARY

In general, statics problems are solved by the following steps.

1. Draw a free body diagram.
2. Write the force equations.

$$\sum M = 0$$
$$\sum F_x = 0$$
$$\sum F_y = 0$$

3. Solve for the unknowns.

Only three unknowns may be found in simple plane statics problems.
    Recognizing two- and three-force members and handling them and pulleys correctly can reduce the effort required.

PROBLEMS

5.1 For Fig. 5.43 find the reactions at A and B when:

	a	b	P
(a)	6 in.	4 in.	80 lb
(b)	5 in.	3 in.	120 lb
(c)	80 mm	40 mm	20.0 N
(d)	2 m	1 m	40 kN

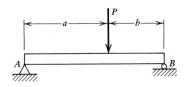

FIG. 5.43 Problem 5.1.

5.2 For Fig. 5.44 find the reactions at *A* and *B* when:

	a	*b*	*P*
(a)	6 in.	4 in.	80 lb
(b)	5 in.	3 in.	120 lb
(c)	80 mm	40 mm	200 N
(d)	2 m	1 m	40 kN

For each of the following problems (5.3–5.15), find the reactions at the supports.

5.3 Fig. 5.45	**5.4** Fig. 5.46	**5.5** Fig. 5.47
5.6 Fig. 5.48	**5.7** Fig. 5.49	**5.8** Fig. 5.50
5.9 Fig. 5.51	**5.10** Fig. 5.52	**5.11** Fig. 5.53
5.12 Fig. 5.54	**5.13** Fig. 5.55	**5.14** Fig. 5.56
5.15 Fig. 5.57		

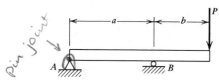

FIG. 5.44   Problem 5.2.

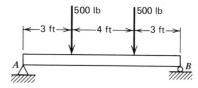

FIG. 5.45   Problem 5.3.

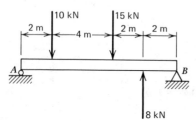

FIG. 5.46   Problem 5.4.

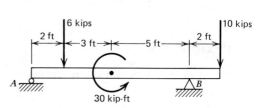

FIG. 5.47   Problem 5.5.

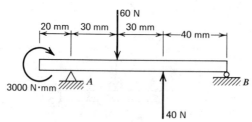

FIG. 5.48   Problem 5.6.

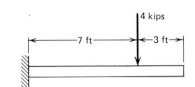

FIG. 5.49   Problem 5.7.

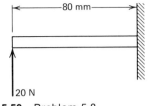

FIG. 5.50   Problem 5.8.

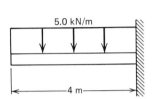

FIG. 5.51   Problem 5.9.

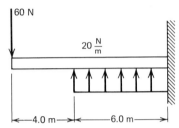

FIG. 5.52   Problem 5.10.

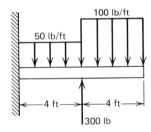

FIG. 5.53   Problem 5.11.

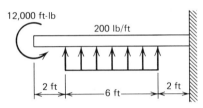

FIG. 5.54   Problem 5.12.

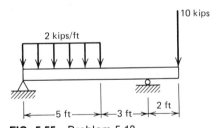

FIG. 5.55   Problem 5.13.

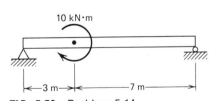

FIG. 5.56   Problem 5.14.

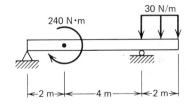

FIG. 5.57   Problem 5.15.

For each of the following problems (5.16–5.23), find the reactions at the supports.

5.16 Fig. 5.58   **5.17** Fig. 5.59   **5.18** Fig. 5.60

5.19 Fig. 5.61   **5.20** Fig. 5.62   **5.21** Fig. 5.63

5.22 Fig. 5.64   **5.23** Fig. 5.65

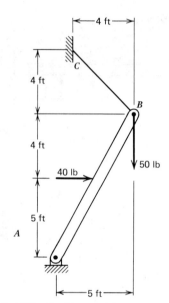

FIG. 5.58   Problem 5.16.

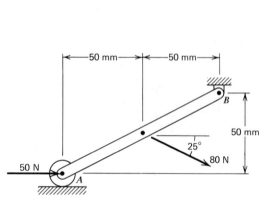

FIG. 5.59   Problem 5.17.

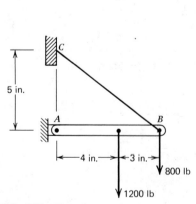

FIG. 5.60   Problem 5.18.

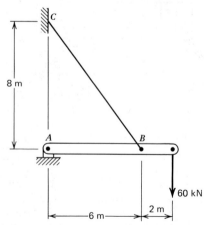

FIG. 5.61   Problems 5.19, 5.51a.

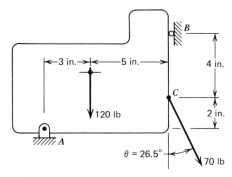

FIG. 5.62   Problem 5.20.

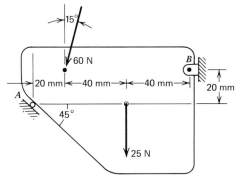

FIG. 5.63   Problem 5.21.

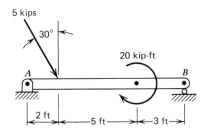

FIG. 5.64   Problem 5.22.

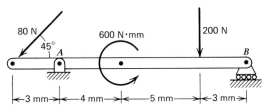

FIG. 5.65   Problem 5.23.

For each of the following problems (5.24–5.28), find the reactions at the supports.

5.24 Fig. 5.66   **5.25** Fig. 5.67   **5.26** Fig. 5.68

5.27 Fig. 5.69   **5.28** Fig. 5.70

5.29 A diver jumps on the end of a 6-ft-long diving board, exerting a dynamic force equal to three times her weight of 150 lb. Find the reaction at the rigidly supported end of the board.

5.30 A large wrench is 300 mm long. A mechanic exerts a force of 150 N perpendicular to the wrench handle to turn a bolt. Find the reaction in the bolt.

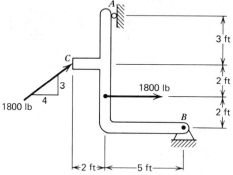

FIG. 5.66   Problem 5.24.

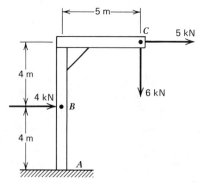

FIG. 5.67   Problem 5.25.

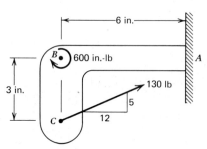

FIG. 5.68   Problem 5.26.

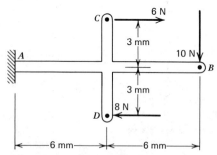

FIG. 5.69   Problem 5.27.

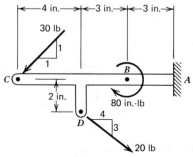

FIG. 5.70   Problem 5.28.

5.31 The race car shown in Fig. 5.71 goes around a sharp curve at a high speed and is on the verge of rolling to the right. The tendency to roll is caused by the "inertia force," which is the mass m times the normal acceleration a_n. Under these conditions there is no force on the left wheels. There is an upward force from the road and a friction force to the left acting at the lower right-hand corner of the right wheels. Assuming this to be a static equilibrium condition, and treating the front and rear wheels as one, find the forces on the right . Find the normal acceleration a_n of the vehicle. Explain why it is important for a race car to have a low center of gravity.

(a) $W = 2000$ lb, $h = 20$ in., $w = 70$ in.

(b) $W = 10$ kN, $h = 500$ mm, $w = 1800$ mm

5.32 Find the resultant force on the pin at B from the pulley and the reaction at the fixed support A in Fig. 5.72.

5.33 Find the resultant force on the pin at B from the pulley and the reaction at the fixed support A in Fig. 5.73.

5.34 For Fig. 5.74:

(a)   Find the reaction at A.

(b)   Find the resultant force on the pin from the pulley at points B, C, and D.

5.35 For Fig. 5.75:

(a)   Find the reaction at A.

(b)   Find the resultant force on the pin from the pulley at points B, C, and D.

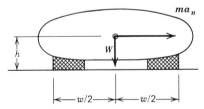

FIG. 5.71   Problem 5.31.

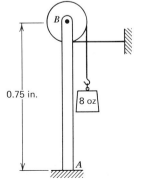

FIG. 5.72   Problem 5.32.

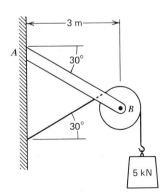

FIG. 5.73   Problem 5.33.

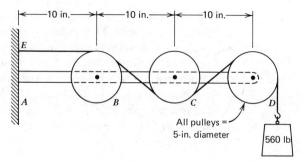

FIG. 5.74   Problem 5.34.

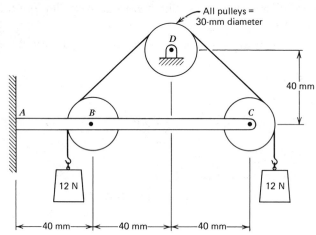

FIG. 5.75   Problem 5.35.

5.36 For Fig. 5.76:

(a)   Find the reaction at *A*.

(b)   Find the resultant force on the pin from the pulley at points *B* and *C*.

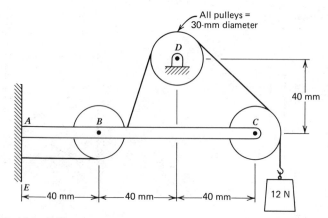

FIG. 5.76   Problem 5.36.

5.37 Find the reactions at A and D in Fig. 5.77.

5.38 Find the reactions at A and D in Fig. 5.78.

5.39 Find the reactions at A and E in Fig. 5.79. (*Hint:* Treat the frame $BCDE$ as a rigid body.)

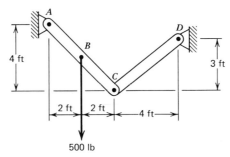

FIG. 5.77 Problems 5.37, 5.51b.

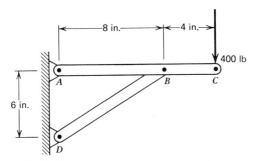

FIG. 5.78 Problems 5.38, 5.51c.

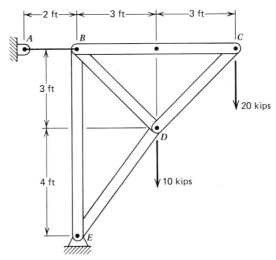

FIG. 5.79 Problem 5.39.

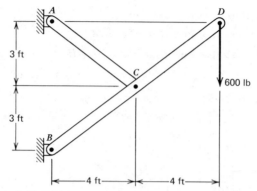

FIG. 5.80   Problems 5.40, 5.51d.

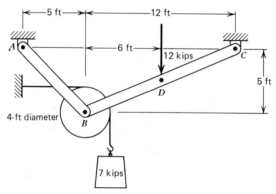

FIG. 5.81   Problem 5.41.

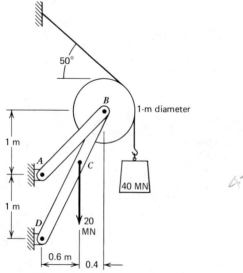

FIG. 5.82   Problem 5.42.

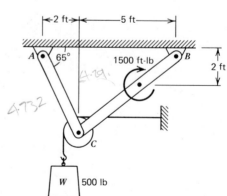

FIG. 5.83   Problem 5.43.

5.40 Find the reactions at points A and B in Fig. 5.80.

5.41 Find the reactions at points A and C in Fig. 5.81.

5.42 Find the reactions at points A and D in Fig. 5.82.

5.43 Find the reactions at points A and B in Fig. 5.83. (*Hint: BC* is not a two-force member.)

5.44 Find the reactions at A and B in Fig. 5.84. (*Hint: BC* is not a two-force member.)

5.45 Find the reactions at A and C in Fig. 5.85.

5.46 Find the reactions at E and D in Fig. 5.86.

5.47 Find the reactions at B and E in Fig. 5.87. (*Hint:* The line drawing is schematic of a rigid truss similar to Fig. 5.86.)

5.48 Find the reactions at A and D in Fig. 5.88.

5.49 Find the reactions at A and B in Fig. 5.89.

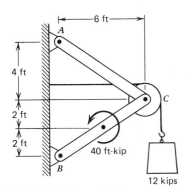

FIG. 5.84   Problem 5.44.

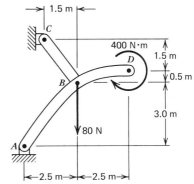

FIG. 5.85   Problem 5.45.

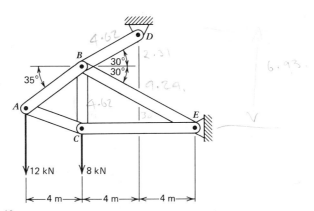

FIG. 5.86   Problem 5.46.

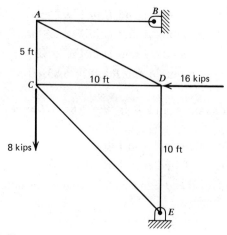

FIG. 5.87   Problem 5.47.

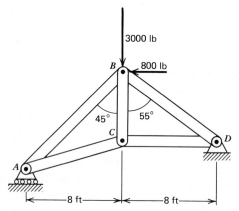

FIG. 5.88   Problem 5.48.

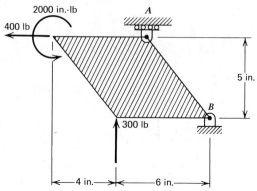

FIG. 5.89   Problem 5.49.

5.50 Find the reactions at *A* and *B* in Fig. 5.90.

5.51 Using the principle of a three-force member, graphically determine the direction of the indicated force. Then graphically solve for the force using the force polygon.

(a) Fig. 5.61, *A*   (b) Fig. 5.77, *A*

(c) Fig. 5.78, *A*   (d) Fig. 5.80, *B*

5.52 Find the reactions at *A* and *D* in Fig. 5.91.

5.53 Find the reactions at *A* and *C* in Fig. 5.92.

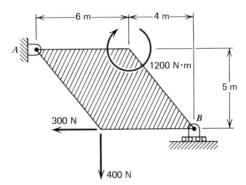

FIG. 5.90 Problem 5.50.

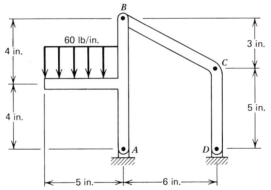

FIG. 5.91 Problem 5.52.

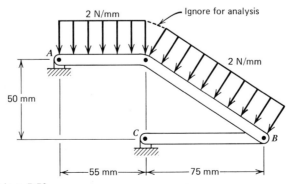

FIG. 5.92 Problem 5.53.

5.54 An irrigation gate is to be lifted by the counterbalance W (Fig. 5.93). The force due to fluid pressure is shown as linearly distributed force. Find the minimum weight W required to lift the gate and the reaction at A.

5.55 The push rod at B (Fig. 5.94) activates the connecting rod at C by pushing on the arm AC. Consider the 10-lb arm AC to be uniform and include its weight in finding the force P and the reaction at A.

5.56 Solve Problem 5.55 without including the weight of the arm. What is the percentage difference in the force P?

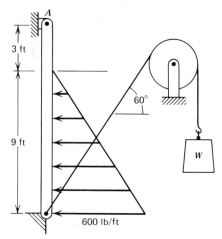

FIG. 5.93   Problem 5.54.

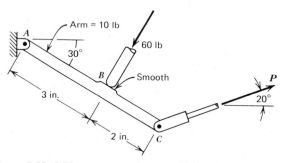

FIG. 5.94   Problems 5.55, 5.56.

6

Distributed Forces

Our emphasis has been on concentrated loads, which is another concept that fits into a neat, well-defined package but really does not exist. All loads are *distributed* to some extent; that is, they act over *some* area. The area may be relatively small, and if it is, little is lost and much is gained by treating the load as though it acted at a point; but loads do not really act at just *one point*.

In Section 3.7 we discussed the fact that weight, a *distributed load*, may be treated as a concentrated load acting through the *center of gravity*. In this chapter we see why that is so and develop the ability to find the center of gravity for more complicated loading. Finally, we examine pressure or stress as another type of distributed load.

6.1   AN APPROXIMATE SOLUTION AND A MEANING FOR THE INTEGRAL

In one fairly simple form of loading (Fig. 6.1), a uniformly varying distributed load acts on a simply supported beam. We wish to find the reactions on each end of the beam. To do this, we must find the resultant force of the distributed load and its moment about a given point.

We approximate this loading by the three uniformly distributed loads shown in Fig. 6.2. This approximation is obtained by dividing the beam into three 2-ft sections. For each section, a uniform load is chosen that will approximate the actual load. For the first 2 ft the distributed load rate goes from 0 to 200 lb/ft. This is approximated by a constant load rate of 100 lb/ft, as shown in Fig. 6.2. The error of this approximation is indicated in the figure by broken lines (vertical when

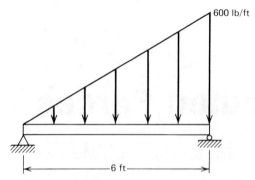

FIG. 6.1 Uniformly varying distributed load.

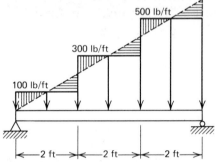

FIG. 6.2 Approximation of a distributed load using three intervals.

over; horizontal when under). In the middle 2 ft, the load rate goes from 200 to 400 lb/ft. It is approximated by a constant 300-lb/ft load rate. The final section is approximated by a constant 500 lb/ft as it goes from 400 to 600 lb/ft. Next each uniformly distributed load is replaced with an equivalent load acting through its center of gravity. This is shown in Fig. 6.3, where we have a load of 100 lb/ft times 2 ft, or 200 lb replacing the 100-lb/ft constant load rate acting over the first 2 ft. The 200-lb force acts through the center of gravity of the uniformly distributed load, which is 1 ft from the left-hand end of the beam. The middle section is replaced by a 600-lb load 3 ft from the left-hand end, and the last section is replaced by 1000 lb, 5 ft from the left. We then find the total load by summing these forces:

$$W' = (100)(2) + (300)(2) + (500)(2) = \mathbf{1800\ lb} \tag{6.1}$$

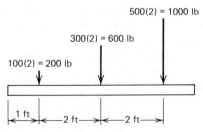

FIG. 6.3 Statically equivalent load to load in Fig. 6.2.

where the prime (W') means we are approximating W. We know the actual total load to be the area under the load rate curve

$$W = \frac{(6)(600)}{2} = \textbf{1800 lb}$$

In this case the approximate solution is exact for calculating the load. That will always be so for a linearly distributed load if we take the midpoint value for each rectangular interval. However, in general, this will be an approximation that does not give the exact answer. Recall now that an equivalent load must have the same magnitude *and* the same moment about any point. We calculate the moment about the left-hand end of Fig. 6.3 by the following.

$$M'_L = -(1)(100)(2) - (3)(300)(2) - (5)(500)(2) = \textbf{-7000 ft-lb} \qquad (6.2)$$

where the prime denotes an approximation. You may know from previous work, or we could demonstrate experimentally, that the actual center of gravity is one-third of the length from the right-hand end or 2 ft. Thus the actual moment about the left-hand end is

$$M_L = -4(1800) = \textbf{-7200 ft-lb}$$

And we see that although our approximation gives the exact total force, the moment of force is 3% (200 out of 7200) low.

A reasonable question is, How may this approximation be improved? In Fig. 6.4 we approximate this loading using six equal intervals. We calculate the total load as follows:

$$W'' = (50)(1) + (150)(1) + (250)(1) + (350)(1) + (450)(1) + (550)(1) = \textbf{1800 lb}$$

This approximation is exact, as before. Now calculating the moment of force about the left-hand end, we get:

$$M''_L = -(0.5)(50)(1) - (1.5)(150)(1) - (2.5)(250)(1) - (3.5)(350)(1)$$
$$-(4.5)(450)(1) - (5.5)(550)(1) = \textbf{-7150 ft-lb}$$

The error has been reduced from 3% to less than 1% (50 out of 7200).

We conclude from this exercise that if we increase the number of intervals we will improve the accuracy of the approximation. So let the number of intervals

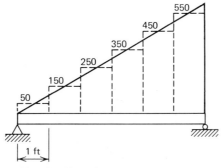

FIG. 6.4 Approximation of a distributed load using six intervals.

get very large. Note that with three intervals, each was 2.0 ft wide. With six, each was 1.0 ft wide. If there are 100 intervals, each will be 0.06 ft wide. As the number of intervals increases, the size decreases and the accuracy of the approximation improves.

In Fig. 6.5 we draw a very small interval. The load rate is w_i, which is any value between 0 and 600 lb/ft. The width of the interval is Δx_i, which is very small. The location of the interval is x_i from the left-hand end, which is any distance from 0 to 6 ft. The load due to this interval is:

$$W_i = w_i \cdot \Delta x_i$$

The total load is the sum of the W_i:

$$W' = w_1 \cdot \Delta x_1 + w_2 \cdot \Delta x_2 + \cdots + w_n \cdot \Delta x_n$$

or

$$W' = \sum W_i = \sum w_i \cdot \Delta x_i \tag{6.3}$$

We rewrite Eq. 6.1 along with Eq. 6.3 and see that Eq. 6.1 is an expression of Eq. 6.3:

$$W' = (100)(2) + (300)(2) + (500)(2) \tag{6.1}$$

$$W' = w_1 \cdot \Delta x_1 + w_2 \cdot \Delta x_2 + w_3 \cdot \Delta x_3 \tag{6.3}$$

Equation 6.3 is an approximation that approaches the exact value as the number of intervals increases.

Since we can approximate the force as closely as we would like by increasing the number of elements, why not do so? Well, it's a lot of work! However, using the magic of advanced mathematics we can avoid the increased work *and* get an *exact* answer. That sounds like too good a deal to pass. It is and we won't. We make a slight transformation of Eq. 6.3 by letting:

$$\Delta x_i = dx.$$

But now dx is infinitesimally small. Guess how small it is. Come on, guess! Wrong— it's smaller than that. No matter what you say, it is smaller. Now let's replace our summation sign $\sum$ with another summation sign $\int$. The first is a Greek capital S,

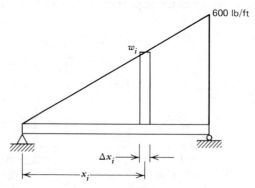

FIG. 6.5 Approximation of a distributed load using an infinitesimal interval.

the second is an old English S. Both mean *summation*. We use $\sum$ when we are talking about finite things, things we can measure. We use $\int$ when we are talking about infinitesimal things, things that are too small to measure, such as dx. Using both transformations, Eq. 6.3 becomes:

$$W = \sum w_i \cdot \Delta x_i = \int w\, dx$$

It is more accurate mathematically to say:

$$W = \lim_{\Delta x \to 0} \sum w_i \cdot \Delta x_i = \int w\, dx \tag{6.4}$$

which says that as we let Δx become smaller and smaller, there is a natural limit, an upper boundary, to the approximation:

$$\sum w_i \cdot \Delta x_i$$

This limit is:

$$\int w\, dx$$

which is the summation of the infinitesimal areas $w\, dx$ but more commonly called the *integral* of $w\, dx$. In calculus we learn to evaluate the integral.

This summation (or integration) will produce the area of the triangular loading in Fig. 6.5. That is one meaning of the integral—it is an area. We will not formally evaluate the integral at this point but will approximate it.

Returning to Fig. 6.5, we calculate the moment of force of the infinitesimal load about the left-hand end as follows:

$$M_i = x_i(w_i \cdot \Delta x_i)$$

Summing these, we get the moment of force of the entire load as follows:

$$M'_L = \sum M_i = \sum x_i(w_i \cdot \Delta x_i) \tag{6.5}$$

The accuracy of this estimate will improve, as we have illustrated, as Δx_i becomes small. Proceeding as we did above in discussing the total force, we take the limit of Eq. 6.5 and get:

$$M_L = \lim_{\Delta x_i \to 0} \sum x_i(w_i \cdot \Delta x_i) = \int xw\, dx \tag{6.6}$$

Evaluation of this integral requires us to know the relation between w and x, but it gives an exact result. We will also approximate this integral for the time being.

Example Problem 6.1

Approximate the total force and moment of force for the distributed load in Fig. 6.6 using five intervals. Where would a single statically equivalent load have to act?

Solution

The five intervals and their values are shown in Fig. 6.7. The tops of the intervals should be selected so that the excessive area (vertical cross-hatching) approximately equals the deficient area (horizontal cross-hatching). It is not necessary

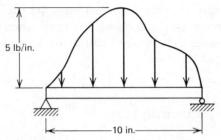

FIG. 6.6   Distributed load of Example
Problem 6.1.

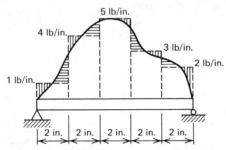

FIG. 6.7   Approximating a distributed load
by five discrete, uniform loads.

to draw in the cross-hatching, but do pay attention to balancing the areas. Applying Eq. 6.3, we write:

$$W' = \sum w_i \cdot \Delta x_i$$
$$W' = 1(2) + 4(2) + 5(2) + 3(2) + 2(2) = \textbf{30.0 lb}$$

One shortcoming of approximate methods is that they do not always produce the same answer. Your neighbor may get a slightly different answer to the same problem. To find the moment about the left-hand end, we apply Eq. 6.5.

$$M'_L = \sum x_i w_i \cdot \Delta x_i$$
$$M'_L = -1(1)2 - 3(4)2 - 5(5)2 - 7(3)2 - 9(2)2$$
$$M'_L = -\textbf{154 in.-lb}$$

A statically equivalent force will have the same magnitude and produce the same moment. So:

$$M'_L = \bar{x}'W' \tag{6.7}$$

Solving for the location $\bar{x}'$, we have:

$$\bar{x}' = \frac{M'_L}{W'} = \frac{\sum x_i w_i \cdot \Delta x_i}{\sum w_i \cdot \Delta x_i} \tag{6.8}$$

This location is also the *approximate* center of gravity for this distributed load. To get the exact location, we replace the numerator and denominator with

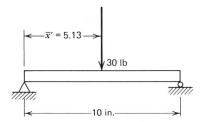

FIG. 6.8 A single equivalent force.

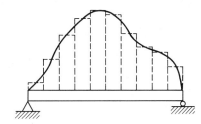

FIG. 6.9 Approximating a distributed load with 10 discrete, uniform loads.

their equivalent integral expressions:

$$\bar{x} = \frac{\int xw\,dx}{\int w\,dx} \tag{6.9}$$

But back to Eq. 6.8, we have:

$$\bar{x}' = \frac{154 \text{ in.-lb}}{30.0 \text{ lb}} = \mathbf{5.13 \text{ in.}}$$

Figure 6.8 shows a load that is approximately statically equivalent to the distributed load in Fig. 6.6.

In Fig. 6.9 we show a better approximation of the load using 10 intervals. As you contemplate the work in that calculation, the advantages of an *exact* solution by integration may start to emerge. By the way, our solution to this problem has in fact been a numerical integration.

6.2 REPLACING A DISTRIBUTED LOAD WITH A STATICALLY EQUIVALENT CONCENTRATED LOAD

In the preceding section we saw how to approximate a distributed load by breaking the load into several uniformly distributed loads. To do that we recognized that the weight of a uniformly distributed load is equal to the area under the load rate curve and acts through the center of gravity, which is at the geometric center of the area. This is illustrated in Fig. 6.10. A linearly distributed load and

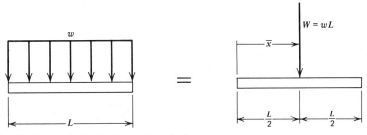

FIG. 6.10 Static equivalent of a uniformly distributed load.

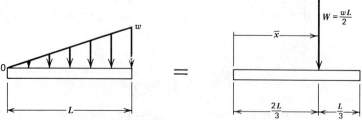

FIG. 6.11 Static equivalent of a linearly distributed load.

its equivalent are shown in Fig. 6.11. You probably already have some impression of both these loadings. They can be easily demonstrated experimentally. Their mathematical verification requires calculus, specifically evaluating Eqs. 6.4, 6.6, and 6.9. These two cases will cover most of the problems we wish to tackle.

Example Problem 6.2

Replace the distributed loads of Fig. 6.12 with statically equivalent loads and find the reactions at the supports.

Solution

The uniformly distributed (rectangular) load is the area under the curve:

$$W_1 = 20(4) = 80 \text{ N}$$

and acts at the center of the rectangular area or 2 m from A as shown in Fig. 6.13. The linearly distributed (triangular) load is also the area under the curve:

$$W_2 = \frac{30(6)}{2} = 90 \text{ N}$$

It acts through the center of gravity of the load which according to Fig. 6.11 is two-thirds the base length from the zero value. That is, 4 m from B in this case, as shown in Fig. 6.13.

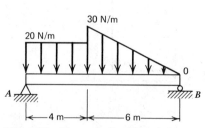

FIG. 6.12 Example Problem 6.2.

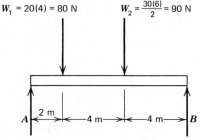

FIG. 6.13 Equivalent free body diagram for Example Problem 6.2.

With the distributed loads reduced to statically equivalent concentrated loads, the problem is completed as a routine statics problem.

$$\sum M_A = 0 = -2(80) - 6(90) + 10B$$

$$B = \frac{700}{10} = \textbf{70.0 N}$$

$$\sum F_y = 0 = A + B - 80 - 90$$
$$A = \textbf{100 N}$$

EVALUATION   Looking at Fig. 6.13 we can see that the load is shifted toward *A* and we expect it to be larger than *B*. It is a little harder to detect this load shift when observing the distributed load in Fig. 6.12. Two things need to be emphasized.

1. The solution above, using Figs. 6.10 and 6.11, is exact. Solutions of Section 6.1 were approximate.
2. Figure 6.13 is *statically* equivalent to Fig. 6.12. It is not equivalent. Later you will probably get into trouble by treating such cases as though they were identical. They are not. "Statically equivalent" means they give the same reactions at *A* and *B*. They are not equivalent in most other senses.

Example Problem 6.3

Find the reactions at the supports in Fig. 6.14.

Solution

We don't find the distributed load of Fig. 6.14 in Figs. 6.10 or 6.11. However, as shown in Fig. 6.15 we can break this into two loads that do fit the given information. We break the load into a rectangular portion of 20 lb/in. and a triangular portion with a maximum load rate of 30 lb/in. The sum of the two is 50 and 20 lb/in. on the right- and left-hand ends, respectively. We proceed to draw the equivalent free body diagram in Fig. 6.16 by replacing the rectangular area W_1 with 120 lb acting 3 in. from the right-hand end. The triangular area W_2 is 90 lb acting 2 in. from the same end. The concentrated 150-lb load is also shown on the diagram. It is unaffected by the distributed load. We show the reactions of *A* and *B*.

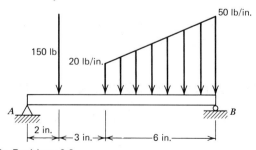

FIG. 6.14 Example Problem 6.3.

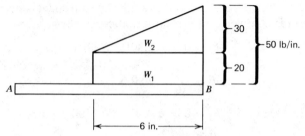

FIG. 6.15 Partitioning the distributed load
into triangular and rectangular portions.

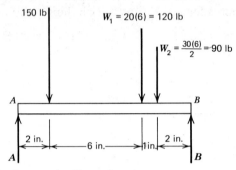

FIG. 6.16 Free body diagram for Example
Problem 6.3.

Proceeding by summing the moments of force about point A, we get:

$$\sum M_A = 0 = -2(150) - 8(120) - 9(90) + 11B$$

$$B = \frac{2070}{11} = \mathbf{188 \ lb}$$

Summing the forces:

$$\sum F_y = 0 = A + B - 150 - 120 - 90$$
$$A = \mathbf{172 \ lb}$$

Distributed loads that cannot be reduced to some combination of Figs. 6.10
and 6.11 can be handled by one of the following measures:

1. Direct integration.
2. Numerical integration (an approximation) as in Section 6.1.
3. Using the properties of areas, as developed later.

6.3   PRESSURE OR STRESS ACTING OVER AN AREA

Fig. 6.17 shows a uniform wind load acting over a sign or billboard. We characterize the wind load as a force per unit area or pressure. Since the pressure is
uniform, we may obtain the total force-F by

$$F = pA \qquad\qquad (6.10)$$

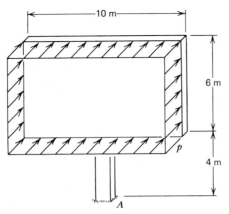

FIG. 6.17 Wind load on a sign.

where p is the pressure and A is the area. This applies to any shape of area as long as the pressure is uniform. We need to know the magnitude of a force and its location. The location is at the *centroid* of the area the force acts over. Possession of a centroid is a property of areas that is analogous to the center of gravity. We will deal with the centroid in detail in a later chapter, and you will probably end up knowing a good deal more about it than you really wanted to. In the meantime, we determine the location of the force by either of the following:

1. Consider the uniformly distributed load as a weight (by rotating it in your mind—or on paper, if necessary). The force will act through the center of gravity of the "weight."
2. If an area over which the pressure acts has two axes of symmetry, its centroid is at the intersection of the two axes. The force acts there. We are used to calling this point the "center."

Another type of loading that is very similar to pressure is *stress*. It is also expressed as load per unit area, and when uniform can be evaluated as above. Of course not all stresses, or pressures for that matter, are uniform. In Section 6.4 we will see how to handle one case of nonuniform stresses. A more detailed treatment is postponed until we have developed additional tools.

Example Problem 6.4

If the wind load p in Fig. 6.17 is 2.0 kN/m², find the equivalent load and tell where it acts. [The preferred unit of pressure is pascal (Pa) in the SI. For simplicity, we use N/m² in this chapter.] Find the reaction at the ground, point A, on the supporting pole.

Solution

From Eq. 6.10 the force is:

$$F = pA$$

$$F = 20 \frac{kN}{m^2} (10 \text{ m})(6 \text{ m}) = \textbf{1200 kN}$$

The rectangular sign has two axes of symmetry as shown in Fig. 6.18, and the centroid is at their intersection, or 3.00 m above the bottom edge and 5.00 m to the left of the right-hand edge. Since the load acts in line with the pole, we may draw the planar free body diagram in Fig. 6.19. If the resultant wind load was not centered on the pole, we would have a three-dimensional statics problem. The wind load is shown as 1200 kN acting 7.00 m above the ground. At the ground the connection is rigid. The vertical reaction P is zero if we ignore the weight of the sign and pole. Summing moments about A, we have:

$$\sum M_A = 0 = -7(1200) + M$$
$$M = \textbf{84.0 MN}\cdot\textbf{m}$$

and

$$\sum F_x = 0 = 1200 - V$$
$$V = \textbf{1200 kN}$$

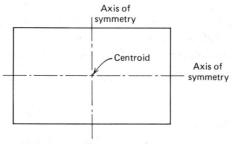

FIG. 6.18   Location of the centroid by the intersection of axes of symmetry.

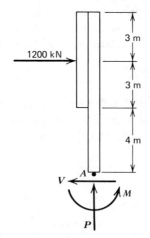

FIG. 6.19   Free body diagram for Example Problem 6.4.

6.4 FORCES ON SUBMERGED SURFACES

The preceding section dealt with pressure distributions that were uniform or constant over the area they acted on. Pressure in a liquid varies with depth as indicated by the formula:

$$p = \gamma h \tag{6.11}$$

where γ = specific weight (lb/ft^3 or N/m^3)

h = depth below the free surface (ft or m)

Therefore, Section 6.3 will apply only to a surface at a uniform depth such as the rectangular gate *PQRS* on the bottom of the tank in Fig. 6.20. The gate *ABCD* has a pressure distribution that varies linearly with depth as predicted by Eq. 6.11 and shown in Fig. 6.21, which gives the profile of the gate. The pressure is zero at *AB* if the tank is filled to *AB*. The gate has a uniform dimension, *AB* or *CD*, into the paper. If this dimension is not constant, the problem is more complicated and cannot be handled by the method given here. Perhaps the load distribution in Fig. 6.21 looks familiar. It should, since it is the same as shown in Fig. 6.11. In fact, if we multiply the pressure by the width *b* (*AB* in Fig. 6.20) into the paper we get

$$w = pb \tag{6.12}$$

which is the load per unit length acting on the gate. We may treat the problem exactly as those in Section 6.2.

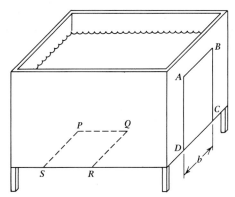

FIG. 6.20 Gates in a tank.

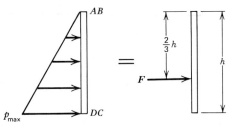

FIG. 6.21 Pressure distribution in a liquid.

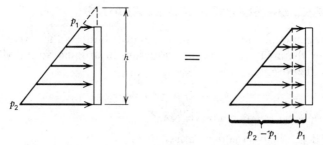

FIG. 6.22 Pressure distribution in a liquid on a plate below the surface.

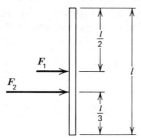

FIG. 6.23 Equivalent forces for Fig. 6.22.

The total load will equal the area under the loading, and it will act at the "center of gravity" of the loading area as shown in Fig. 6.21. If the tank in Fig. 6.20 is filled to the top, the pressure at *AB* is no longer zero. The new pressure distribution is shown in Fig. 6.22. In this figure the distributed load is broken into rectangular and triangular portions, which are in turn replaced by the concentrated loads F_1 and F_2 in Fig. 6.23 in the manner of Section 6.2.

Example Problem 6.5

The tank in Fig. 6.20 is filled to the top with water. A hinge at *AB* is 0.40 m below the surface. Water has a specific weight of 9.81 kN/m³. The tank has a total depth of 2.4 m and the gate is 0.30 m wide. Find:

(a) The pressure at *AB* and *DC*.
(b) The force on the hinge at *AB* and the force applied at *DC* necessary to hold the gate shut.

Solution

From Eq. 6.11:

$$p_{AB} = \gamma h$$

$$p_{AB} = 9.81 \ \frac{kN}{m^3} \ (0.4 \ m) = \textbf{3.92 kN/m}^2$$

$$p_{DC} = 9.81 \ \frac{kN}{m^3} \ (2.4 \ m) = \textbf{23.5 kN/m}^2$$

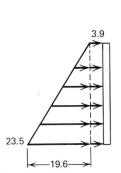

FIG. 6.24 Pressure distribution for Example Problem 6.5.

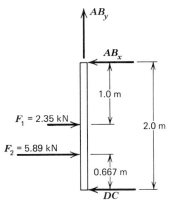

FIG. 6.25 Free body diagram for Example Problem 6.5.

The pressure distribution is shown in Fig. 6.24, broken into rectangular and triangular portions. For the rectangular portion we have

$$F_1 = p \cdot b \cdot l$$

$$F_1 = 3.92 \frac{\text{kN}}{\text{m}^2} (0.3 \text{ m})2.0 \text{ m} = 2.35 \text{ kN}$$

acting at the middle of the gate. For the triangular portion we have:

$$F_2 = \tfrac{1}{2} p \cdot b \cdot l$$

$$F_2 = \tfrac{1}{2}(23.5 - 3.92) \frac{\text{kN}}{\text{m}^2} (0.3 \text{ m})(2.0 \text{ m})$$

$$F_2 = 5.89 \text{ kN}$$

acting one-third of the gate height from the bottom. These forces are shown in Fig. 6.25, where the free body diagram of the gate is completed by showing the reaction at the hinge AB and the applied force to hold the gate closed at DC. The reactions are found by the following equations:

$$\sum M_{AB} = 0 = 1(2.35) + 1.33(5.89) - 2DC$$
$$DC = \textbf{5.09 kN}$$
$$\sum F_x = 0 = 2.35 + 5.89 - DC - AB_x$$
$$AB_x = \textbf{3.15 kN}$$
$$\sum F_y = \textbf{0} = AB_y$$

6.5 SUMMARY

Distributed loads may be approximated by a series of small, uniformly distributed loads. Summing their forces and their moments gives:

$$W' = \sum w_i \cdot \Delta x_i \qquad (6.13)$$

and

$$M'_L = \sum x_i (w_i \cdot \Delta x_i) \qquad (6.14)$$

The approximation increases in accuracy as the number of intervals increases and Δx_i decreases. Obtaining the exact value requires integration:

$$W = \int w \, dx \qquad (6.15)$$

and

$$M_L = \int x \, w \, dx \qquad (6.16)$$

A distributed load may be replaced by a concentrated load whose magnitude is given by Eq. 6.13 or 6.15. The location of the concentrated load is at the *center of gravity* given by:

$$\bar{x}' = \frac{\sum x_i (w_i \cdot \Delta x_i)}{\sum w_i \cdot \Delta x_i} \qquad (6.17)$$

or

$$\bar{x} = \frac{\int x w \, dx}{\int w \, dx} \qquad (6.18)$$

The results of Eq. 6.18 are shown in Figs. 6.10 and 6.11 for rectangular and triangular loads. We will limit our attention to these loads or combinations of them.

A uniformly distributed load or pressure may be replaced by a concentrated load of:

$$F = pA \qquad (6.19)$$

at the *centroid* of the surface over which the pressure acts.

The pressure on a submerged plate is given by:

$$p = \gamma h \qquad (6.20)$$

Forces acting on a submerged plate of constant width may be found by multiplying the pressure by the width of the plate, to transform the pressure distribution into a distributed load.

PROBLEMS

6.1   Approximate the total force, the moment of force about the left-hand end, and the location of a single statically equivalent force in Fig. 6.26 using:

    (a)   4 intervals   (b)   8 intervals

6.2   Approximate the reactions at the supports in Fig. 6.26 using:

    (a)   4 intervals   (b)   8 intervals

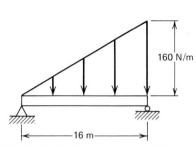

160 N/m

16 m

FIG. 6.26 Problems 6.1, 6.2, 6.11.

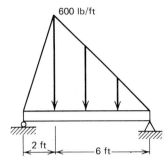

600 lb/ft

2 ft   6 ft

FIG. 6.27 Problems 6.3, 6.4, 6.12.

6.3 Approximate the total force, the moment of force about the left-hand end, and the location of a single statically equivalent force in Fig. 6.27 using:

(a)   4 intervals   (b)   8 intervals

6.4 Approximate the reactions at the supports in Fig. 6.27 using:

(a)   4 intervals   (b)   8 intervals

6.5 Approximate the total force, the moment of force about the left-hand end, and the location of a single statically equivalent force in Fig. 6.28 using:

(a)   3 intervals   (b)   6 intervals

6.6 Approximate the reactions at the supports in Fig. 6.28 using:

(a)   3 intervals   (b)   6 intervals

6.7 Find the equivalent load (magnitude and location) for the loading shown in Fig. 6.29 by dividing it into:

(a)   3 uniform sections   (b)   6 uniform sections

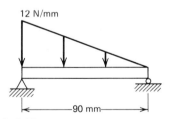

12 N/mm

90 mm

FIG. 6.28 Problems 6.5, 6.6, 6.13.

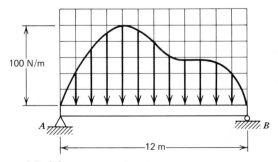

100 N/m

A   B

12 m

FIG. 6.29 Problems 6.7, 6.8.

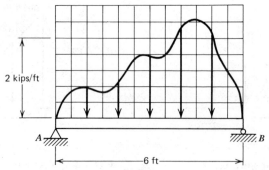

FIG. 6.30   Problems 6.9, 6.10.

6.8   Find the reactions at *A* and *B* for the beam in Fig. 6.29 by dividing the loading into:

(a)   3 uniform sections   (b)   6 uniform sections

6.9   Find the equivalent load (magnitude and location) for the loading in Fig. 6.30 by dividing it into:

(a)   3 uniform sections   (b)   6 uniform sections

6.10   Find the reactions at *A* and *B* for the beam in Fig. 6.30 by dividing the load into:

(a)   3 uniform sections   (b)   6 uniform sections

6.11   Find the exact reaction at the supports for Fig. 6.26 using Fig. 6.11.

6.12   Find the exact reaction at the supports for Fig. 6.27 using Fig. 6.11.

6.13   Find the exact reaction at the supports for Fig. 6.28 using Fig. 6.11.

6.14   Find the reactions at *A* and *B* in Fig. 6.31.

6.15   Find the reactions at *A* and *B* in Fig. 6.32.

6.16   Find the reactions at *A* and *B* in Fig. 6.33.

6.17   Find the reactions at *A* and *B* in Fig. 6.34.

6.18   Find the reactions at *A* and *B* in Fig. 6.35.

6.19   Find the reaction at *A* in Fig. 6.36.

6.20   Find the reaction at *A* in Fig. 6.37.

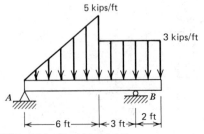

FIG. 6.31   Problem 6.14.

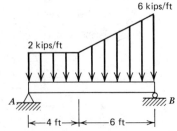

FIG. 6.32   Problem 6.15.

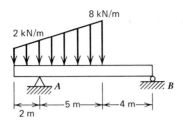

FIG. 6.33   Problem 6.16.

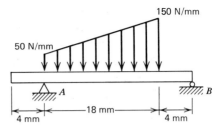

FIG. 6.34   Problem 6.17.

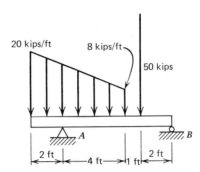

FIG. 6.35   Problem 6.18.

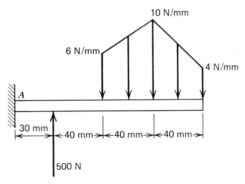

FIG. 6.36   Problem 6.19.

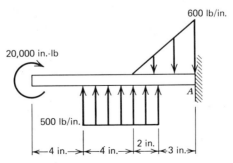

FIG. 6.37   Problem 6.20.

6.21 A uniform wind pressure of 80 N/m² acts over a sign that is 1 m high and 2 m long. It is simply supported along its vertical edges. Find the total force reaction on each edge.

6.22 A uniform wind pressure of 20 lb/ft² acts over a sign that is 3 ft high and 6 ft long. It is simply supported along its vertical edges. Find the total force reaction on each edge.

6.23 A large circular highway sign is 3 m in diameter and is mounted on a pole so that its top is 14 m off the ground. For a uniform wind load of 3.0 kN/m², find the reaction at the bottom of the pole if its base is fixed.

6.24 A large circular highway sign is 10 ft in diameter and is mounted on a pole so that its top is 40 ft off the ground. For a uniform wind load of 70 lb/ft², find the reaction at the bottom of the pole if its base is fixed.

6.25 A hexagonal stop sign is 0.30 m on a side and mounted on a pole with its bottom 2.0 m off the ground. Find the reaction on the pole at the ground where it is fixed if the uniform wind pressure is 2.0 kN/m².

6.26 A hexagonal stop sign is 1.0 ft on a side and mounted on a pole with its bottom 7 ft off the ground. Find the reaction on the pole at the ground where it is fixed if the uniform wind pressure is 80 lb/ft².

6.27 The cross section of a column carries a uniform stress of 40 N/mm². Find the total load on this column and tell where it acts for:

(a) Fig. 6.38

(b) A circular cross section 60 mm in diameter

6.28 The cross section of a column carries a uniform stress of 80,000 lb/in². Find the total load on this column and tell where it acts for:

(a) Fig. 6.39

(b) A circular cross section 4.0 in. in diameter

6.29 Find the force **R** needed to hold the gate in Fig. 6.40 and the reaction on the hinge at A. The gate is 0.80 m wide and water has a specific weight of 9.81 kN/m³.

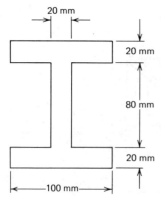

FIG. 6.38 Problem 6.27a.

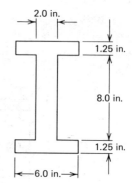

FIG. 6.39 Problem 6.28a.

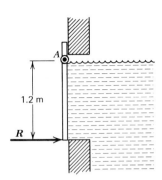

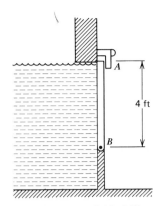

FIG. 6.40   Problems 6.29, 6.30.   **FIG. 6.41**   Problems 6.31, 6.32.

6.30 Solve Problem 6.29 if the water level is:

(a)   0.5 m above the hinge at A (b)   0.5 m below the hinge at A

6.31 Find the force at A and the reaction at the hinge at B in Fig. 6.41. The gate is 2 ft wide and water has a specific weight of 62.4 lb/ft³.

6.32 Solve Problem 6.31 if the water level is:

(a)   2 ft above point A (b)   2 ft below point A

6.33 Two liquid chemicals, A and B, are separated by the gate shown in Fig. 6.42. Chemical A has a specific weight of 12.0 kN/m³. Chemical B has a specific weight of 8.0 kN/m³. Find the moment M_0 that must be applied at the hinge to hold the gate in place if it is 1 m wide and

(a) h_A is 2 m and h_B is 3 m   (b) h_A is 3 m and h_B is 4 m

6.34 Two liquid chemicals, A and B, are separated by the gate shown in Fig. 6.42. Chemical A has a specific weight of 80 lb/ft³. Chemical B has a specific weight of 50 lb/ft³. Find the moment M_0 that must be applied at the hinge to hold the gate in place if it is 3 ft wide and:

(a) h_A is 6 ft and h_B is 10 ft   (b) h_A is 10 ft and h_B is 13 ft

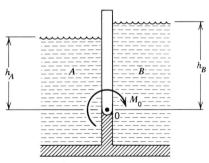

FIG. 6.42   Problems 6.33, 6.34.

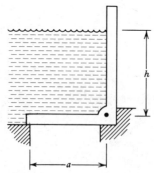

FIG. 6.43   Problems 6.35, 6.36.

6.35 A level control valve is made as shown in Fig. 6.43. If the valve is 0.4 m wide and a is 0.6 m, what must h be for the valve to open? Assume a specific weight for the liquid and then discuss its significance.

6.36 A level control valve is made as shown in Fig. 6.43. If the valve is 18 in. wide and a is 24 in., what must h be for the valve to open? Assume a specific weight for the liquid and then discuss its significance.

6.37 A level control valve for a tank is shown in Fig. 6.44. The gate is 200 mm wide and the tank contains water at 9.81 kN/m³. Neglect the weight of the valve.

(a)   Find the weight W of the ballast so that the valve will open when h is 3.0 m.

(b)   If the ballast had the weight found in part (a) and the tank were filled with alcohol at 8.0 kN/m³ instead of water, what would happen?

6.38 If the ballast in Fig. 6.44 weighs 1.0 kN, and the valve is supposed to open when h is 2.0 m, how wide must the valve be? The liquid is oil at 9.0 kN/m³. Neglect the weight of the valve.

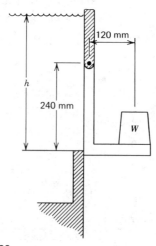

FIG. 6.44   Problems 6.37, 6.38.

7

Analysis of Trusses

Chapters 7 and 8 give two applications of the principles of statics. They do not present new theory. A study of this material will produce a better understanding of what has·been developed thus far. Beyond that, the topics—trusses, and frames and machines—are important in their own right. Trusses occur everywhere: in houses, bridges, machines, airplanes, stadia—the list goes on. This chapter on trusses is an introduction to structural analysis. In the next chapter we will analyze frames and machines.

7.1 TRUSSES AND TWO-FORCE MEMBERS

Ideally a truss consists of a structure composed of long, slender members pinned at each end. A truss is generated by starting with a single triangular shape and adding pairs of members, producing a more complex truss as shown in Fig. 7.1. A symbolic representation of a truss appears in Fig. 7.2. Although the detail is not shown in the figure, *each point is considered to be pinned.* Moreover, no member

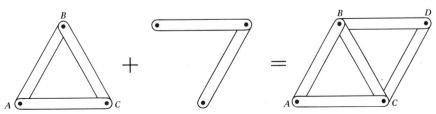

FIG. 7.1 Generation of a truss.

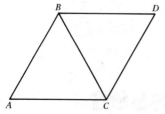

FIG. 7.2 Symbolic representation of a truss.

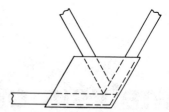

FIG. 7.3 Truss joint with gusset plate connection.

continues through a joint. In our analysis we will always treat the structure as though it were pinned. On occasion that is true in the field, but most of the time joints are not *pinned*. I have never seen a house constructed without a truss. Nor have I ever seen a house that had the joints pinned! The gusset plate structure of Fig. 7.3, with the joints nailed and/or glued, is common. Bolted, riveted, and welded joints are also common for metal structures. Why, if joints are usually not pinned, do we treat them as though they were? There are two reasons. It works, and it's relatively easy. Joints *are* sometimes pinned, although frequently the purpose of the pin is to assist in transporting or assembling the truss. It's fun to look for and spot pinned trusses in structures. (We old fuddy-duddies have an unusual sense of fun.) Amaze your friends as you spot one. Old bridges are a good bet.

Another characteristic of a truss is that loads must come into it through the joints only. Supports must also be at the joints, as illustrated in Fig. 7.4. Since the members are usually long and slender, they are not designed to take loads elsewhere.

The requirements just stated—pinned joints, and loads only at pins—lead us to an extremely important conclusion for trusses. If we examine member *BD* in Fig. 7.4, for example, we see that loads come into this member only at joint *B* and at joint *D*. Thus member *BD* is a *two-force member*. This requires that the reactions on member *BD* at *B* and *D* be along the member *BD*. If we examine member *BC* we reach a similar conclusion, and so it is with members *AB*, *AD*, and *CD*. Thus *a truss is made up entirely of two-force members*, and therefore *the resultant force in each member will be along the member*.

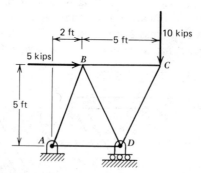

FIG. 7.4 Loads and reactions must enter a truss at the joints.

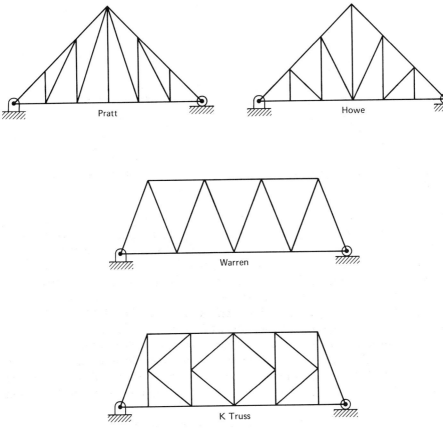

FIG. 7.5 Common trusses.

Trusses come in many sizes, shapes, and forms. Some common trusses are shown in Fig. 7.5. We have represented trusses as plane structures. They are usually loaded and analyzed as such. In some applications they are linked together to form three-dimensional structures.

7.2 INTERNAL FORCES AND NEWTON'S THIRD LAW

We have been primarily concerned with finding forces external to a structure or body. We have done this by cutting a body free from all its supports (in our own minds), drawing a free body diagram, and applying Newton's first law. To find the force in a member such as BC (Fig. 7.4), we proceed in a similar manner. We choose a portion of a structure (joint C in this case) supported by the member of interest, and cut the member BC. To obtain a *free body*, we must cut all other supports until the body is totally free. Thus we must also cut member CD (Fig. 7.4) for joint C to be free. We may now draw a free body diagram of joint C as shown in Fig. 7.6. In Section 7.1 we established that members BC and CD are

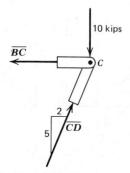

FIG. 7.6 Free body diagram of joint *C*.

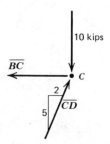

FIG. 7.7 Simplified free body diagram of joint *C*.

two-force members; therefore the forces $\overline{BC}$ and $\overline{CD}$ will be along each member, respectively. This being the case (i.e., forces along the members), it is unnecessary to show a portion of each member cut as in Fig. 7.6. In the future we will use diagrams like Fig. 7.7, which are easier to draw.

We assumed the force $\overline{BC}$ to be to the left. If our assumption is correct, the analysis will give us a positive value; and if wrong, a negative value, as previously. The force $\overline{BC}$ (Fig. 7.6) pulls on joint *C* and attempts to stretch the member *BC*. Such action is called *tension*. We assumed that force $\overline{CD}$ pushes on joint *C* and compresses member *CD*. This action is called *compression*. When finding the force acting in a member, it is important to indicate whether the force acts in tension or in compression. Compression members are subject to buckling and require considerably more attention than tension members. On the other hand, a tension member can be a cable or rope.

In cutting members *BC* and *CD*, we chose to draw a free body diagram of joint *C*. We could just as well have drawn a free body diagram of the remaining part of the structure as shown in Fig. 7.8, where the reactions at *A* and *D* have also been supplied. Notice that $\overline{BC}$ is shown to the right in Fig. 7.8, opposite its direction in Fig. 7.7. This is in agreement with Newton's third law. It should also be clear that if member *BC* in Fig. 7.4 is in tension, it pulls both on joint *B* and on joint *C*. Conversely, joints *B* and *C* pull on member *BC*. Also note that the force $\overline{CD}$ in Fig. 7.8 has the opposite sense of the force $\overline{CD}$ in Fig. 7.7. Finally, if

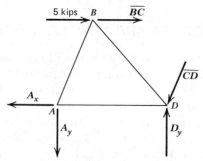

FIG. 7.8 Free body diagram of remaining portion of the structure *ABCD*.

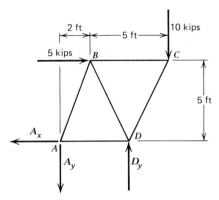

FIG. 7.9 Overall free body diagram.

we superimpose Fig. 7.7 on Fig. 7.8, we get the overall free body diagram for the truss *ABCD* as shown in Fig. 7.9. The equal and opposite pairs of forces, $\overline{BC}$ and $\overline{CD}$, cancel each other and *do not* appear in the overall free body diagram. They are *internal* to it, and forces internal to the free body diagram are not shown.

7.3 METHOD OF JOINTS: COMPONENTS

We will develop two methods of finding the forces in a truss—the method of joints and the method of sections. The method of joints reduces to a concurrent force problem, and any of the methods of solving concurrent force problems from Chapter 3 (components, graphical, or analytical) may be used with it. Also recall that in a concurrent force problem the moment equation is not functional, and therefore we can solve for only *two* unknowns at each step. The method of joints using components is illustrated in the following example.

Example Problem 7.1

Find the internal forces in each member of the truss in Fig. 7.4 using the method of joints by components.

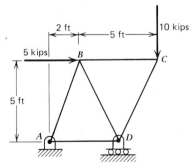

FIG. 7.4 Loads and reactions must enter a truss at the joints. Figure repeated from page 170.

Solution

Step 1   Draw a free body diagram of the entire truss and solve for the external supports. When solving for the entire truss this step *should* be taken even though it is not always necessary. The free body diagram was drawn in Fig. 7.9. Summing the moments about point A gives:

$$\sum M_A = 0 = -5(5) - 7(10) + 5D_y$$
$$D_y = 19.0 \text{ kips}$$

and

$$\sum F_y = 0 = D_y - 10 - A_y$$
$$A_y = 9.00 \text{ kips}$$

and finally

$$\sum F_x = 0 = -A_x + 5$$
$$A_x = 5.00 \text{ kips}$$

Step 2   Select a joint with no more than two unknowns and find the forces acting on it. We could go to joint C where we cut BC and CD, or having found A_x and A_y, we could go to joint A, where we cut AB and AD. We could not go to joint B or D. We choose C, cut members BC and CD, and get the free body diagram of Fig. 7.7. Note that the problem is a concurrent force problem and only two unknowns can be handled. (The method employed at this point is that of Section 3.8. If you experience difficulty in following the solution, return to that section for a general review.) We sum forces, getting:

$$\sum F_y = 0 = \frac{5}{5.39} \overline{CD} - 10$$

$$\overline{CD} = 10.8 \text{ kips compression}$$

The positive sign means the sense of the force is as assumed, namely, compressive. Then:

$$\sum F_x = 0 = -\overline{BC} + \frac{2}{5.39} \overline{CD}$$

$$\overline{BC} = 4.00 \text{ kips tension}$$

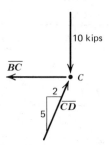

FIG. 7.7 Simplified free body diagram of joint C. Figure repeated from page 172.

Step 3   Proceed to additional joints, with two or fewer unknowns, until all the members have been found.   We can go to any of the remaining joints. Although going to joint B or D will require cutting three members, only two of them are unknown at this point. We arbitrarily choose B and draw the free body diagram in Fig. 7.10. Since $\overline{BC}$ was found to be a tensile force, it will pull on joint B, and be to the right, opposite of its sense at joint C. The forces in members AB and BD are along the members. Their senses are assumed as shown. Summing the forces gives:

$$\sum F_y = 0 = \frac{-5}{5.39}\,\overline{AB} + \frac{5}{5.83}\,\overline{BD}$$

or

$$\overline{AB} = \frac{5.39}{5.83}\,\overline{BD} \tag{7.1}$$

and

$$\sum F_x = 0 = -\frac{2}{5.39}\,\overline{AB} - \frac{3}{5.83}\,\overline{BD} + 5 + 4$$

$$\frac{2}{5.39}\,\overline{AB} + \frac{3}{5.83}\,\overline{BD} = 9$$

Substituting for $\overline{AB}$ from above:

$$\frac{2}{5.39}\left(\frac{5.39}{5.83}\,\overline{BD}\right) + \frac{3}{5.83}\,\overline{BD} = 9$$

$$\frac{5}{5.83}\,\overline{BD} = 9$$

$$\overline{BD} = \textbf{10.5 kips compression}$$

Substituting this into Eq. 7.1 gives:

$$\overline{AB} = \frac{5.39}{5.83}\,(10.5)$$

$$\overline{AB} = \textbf{9.69 kips tension}$$

This joint required the solving of simultaneous equations. Often that will be the case.

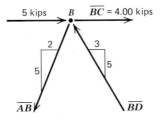

FIG. 7.10   Free body diagram of joint B.

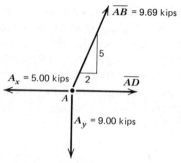

FIG. 7.11   Free body diagram of joint A.

We can now proceed to joint A or D. We select A because of its simpler geometry and draw its free body diagram in Fig. 7.11. The force $\overline{AB}$ is known to be in tension and the sense of $\overline{AD}$ is guessed. Summing forces gives:

$$\sum F_x = 0 = -5 + \frac{2}{5.39}(9.69) + \overline{AD}$$

$$\overline{AD} = 1.40 \text{ kips tension}$$

This completes the analysis, even though we have an equation remaining. We use it as a check:

$$\sum F_y = 0 = \frac{+5}{5.39}(9.69) - 9$$

$$0 = 0 \quad \text{check}$$

We could also proceed to joint D for a comprehensive check. That step is recommended for homework and especially fieldwork.

7.4   METHOD OF JOINTS: GRAPHICALLY

The graphic method follows that of the preceding section until after the free body diagram has been drawn. In Chapter 3 we learned that we can also solve concurrent force problems by drawing a force polygon and solving for its parts analytically or graphically. Frequently in truss problems four or more members or loads act on a joint. In such cases an analytical solution is very tedious and rarely used. However, the graphical method works quite well, as illustrated in the following problem.

Example Problem 7.2

Graphically find the force in each member in the truss shown in Fig. 7.12.

   Solution

   Step 1   Draw a free body diagram of the entire truss and solve for the external supports.   The free body diagram is drawn in Fig. 7.13. Summing moments

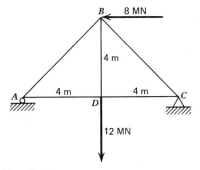

FIG. 7.12 Example Problem 7.2.

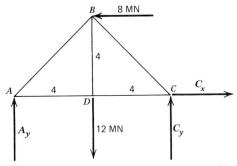

FIG. 7.13 Free body diagram for Example Problem 7.2.

about point C gives:

$$\sum M_C = 0 = +4(8) + 4(12) - 8A_y$$
$$A_y = \textbf{10.0 MN}$$

Summing forces:

$$\sum F_x = 0 = -8 + C_x$$
$$C_x = \textbf{8.00 MN}$$

and

$$\sum F_y = 0 = A_y - 12 + C_y$$
$$C_y = \textbf{2.00 MN}$$

It is worthwhile to check the solution by summing moments about B.

$$\sum M_B = 0 = -4A_y + 4C_x + 4C_y$$
$$0 = -4(10) + 4(8) + 4(2) = 0 \qquad \textbf{Check}$$

Step 2 Select a joint with no more than two unknowns and find the forces acting on it. Joints A and C are candidates; A is chosen because it has fewer forces acting. Draw its free body diagram in Fig. 7.14. Solve for the two unknowns $\overline{AB}$ and $\overline{AD}$ graphically by drawing the force polygon in Fig. 7.15.

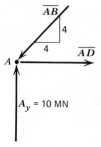

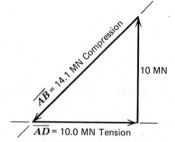

FIG. 7.14 Free body diagram for joint A.

FIG. 7.15 Force polygon for joint A.

(The method employed here is that of Section 3.8. If you experience difficulty in following the solution, return to that section for a general review.) From this figure we get:

$$\overline{AB} = 14.1 \text{ MN compression}$$

and

$$\overline{AD} = 10.0 \text{ MN tension}$$

Step 3   Proceed to additional joints, with two or fewer unknowns, until all the members have been found.   Any of the remaining joints B, C, or D qualifies. Taking D, we draw the free body diagram and force polygon in Fig. 7.16. Note that $\overline{AD}$ is shown in tension. From the polygon we get:

$$\overline{DC} = 10.0 \text{ MN tension}$$

and

$$\overline{BD} = 12.0 \text{ MN tension}$$

We then proceed to joint C, constructing its free body diagram and force polygon in Fig. 7.17. The polygon is constructed by starting at point O and

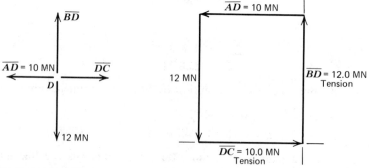

FIG. 7.16 Free body diagram and force polygon for joint D.

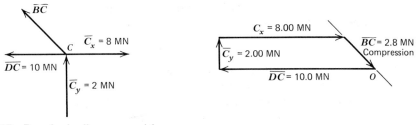

FIG. 7.17 Free body diagram and force polygon for joint C.

laying the vectors $\overline{DC}$, C_y, and C_x tip to tail. The closing vector $\overline{BC}$ is drawn from the end of C_x in the proper direction and the polygon is closed as it crosses the line of action of $\overline{DC}$. It should pass through point O, but if error has been accumulated (and usually it has), there will be a slight failure to close. Of course, if the failure to close is more than "slight," we have made an error in logic or execution. This built-in check should not be ignored. A comprehensive check may be had by drawing the force polygon for joint B. From Fig. 7.17 we get:

$$\overline{BC} = \textbf{2.8 MN compression}$$

Last of all we present the results by drawing the truss and showing the load in each member including whether it is in tension (T) or compression (C) as in Fig. 7.18. This is called a *load diagram* and is a very useful way of presenting results when solving truss problems.

An alternate method of graphical solution uses a Maxwell diagram, in which the force polygons are superimposed on each other. It is not necessary to draw the free body diagram, and the method is very efficient. It is the preferred method when solving trusses by hand. However, widespread availability of computer methods is replacing the Maxwell diagram as a design tool.

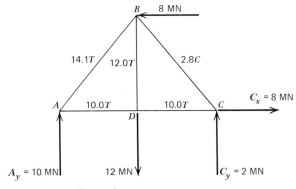

FIG. 7.18 Load diagram for Example Problem 7.2.

7.5 ZERO MEMBERS AND OTHER UNIQUE LOADING CONDITIONS

There are a couple of unique loading conditions that merit special attention. Recognition of these situations can be used to speed up analysis or to check work as it progresses. In the first situation a member called a *zero-force member*, carries no load. (I never cease to be amazed at the clever terminology we've generated!) A zero-force member is illustrated in Example Problem 7.3.

Example Problem 7.3

Find the force in member BD in Fig. 7.19 using the method of joints.

Solution

A free body diagram is drawn in Fig. 7.20. Finding the reactions shown is left to the student. Next a free body diagram of joint A is drawn in Fig. 7.21 and we sum the forces.

$$\sum F_y = 0 = 2 - \overline{AB}_y$$
$$\overline{AB}_y = 2.00 \text{ kips}$$

$$\overline{AB} = \frac{\sqrt{20}}{2}\overline{AB}_y = \textbf{4.47 kips compression}$$

and

$$\sum F_x = 0 = -\frac{4}{\sqrt{20}}\overline{AB} + \overline{AD}$$

$$\overline{AD} = \textbf{4.00 kips tension}$$

Proceeding to joint D, we draw the free body diagram in Fig. 7.22. To emphasize the results we are about to reach, we show the force $\overline{BD}$ broken into components $\overline{BD}_x$ and $\overline{BD}_y$. Summing the forces in the vertical direction, we have

$$\sum F_y = 0 = \overline{BD}_y$$

and

$$\overline{BD} = \textbf{0}$$

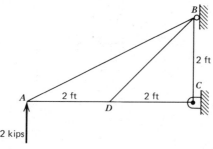

FIG. 7.19 Example Problem 7.3.

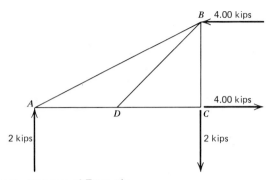

FIG. 7.20 Free body diagram of Example Problem 7.3.

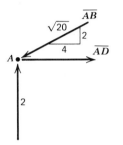

FIG. 7.21 Free body diagram of joint,A.

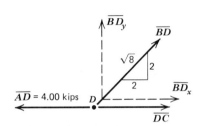

FIG. 7.22 Free body diagram of joint D.

Notice that we reached this conclusion without getting into the direction of $\overline{BD}$. That means the conclusion is valid regardless of the direction of $\overline{BD}$. From this we generalize the rule:

> When only three members (or forces) come together at a joint AND two of the members are collinear, then the third member is a zero-force member.

Summing the forces in the horizontal direction gives:

$$\sum F_x = -\overline{AD} + \overline{DC}$$
$$\overline{DC} = \overline{AC} = \textbf{4.00 kips tension}$$

From this we complete the rule:

> The remaining two members carry forces of the same magnitude.

The second special loading condition we wish to examine is illustrated by joint D in Example Problem 7.2 (Fig. 7.12). The free body diagram for this joint is shown in Fig. 7.16. It is clear that summing forces vertically gives:

$$\overline{BD} = 12 \text{ MN}$$

FIG. 7.23 Forces pass through a joint with pairs of collinear members.

and summing the forces horizontally gives:

$$\overline{AD} = \overline{DC}$$

We see the forces being passed through the joint when we have pairs of collinear members or forces meeting at a joint. It is not necessary that the pairs be horizontal and vertical or even perpendicular. The general case is illustrated in Fig. 7.23. From this we reach the rule:

> When only four members (or forces) come together at a joint in two collinear pairs, then each member will have the same magnitude of force as the opposing member.

As indicated previously, these two principles can be used to speed up the analysis or to verify results as they are independently obtained.

7.6 METHOD OF SECTIONS

The method of joints is adequate for the *total* analysis of any truss and is the method most frequently used when an entire truss must be analyzed or designed. We proceed joint by joint, and a great deal of work is done before we find the load in interior members of a large truss. A more efficient method of obtaining the forces in one or a few interior members is the *method of sections*. Like the method of joints, it also relies on the basic concepts of statics without expanding them. We simply apply those tried and true procedures of:

1. Passing a cutting plane through the members of interest.
2. Drawing a free body diagram.
3. Applying Newton's first law.

In contrast to the method of joints, however, we will be able to use the moment equation allowing us to solve for three unknowns for each free body diagram.

Example Problem 7.4

Find the load in members *CD*, *DH*, and *HG* in the truss in Fig. 7.24.

   Solution

   Step 1   Draw a free body diagram of the entire truss and find the external reactions. This is shown in Fig. 7.25, with the analysis left to the reader.

   Step 2   Pass a cutting plane *completely* through the truss, cutting one or more of the members of interest. No more than three unknown members should be

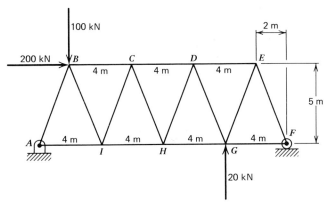

FIG. 7.24 Example Problem 7.4.

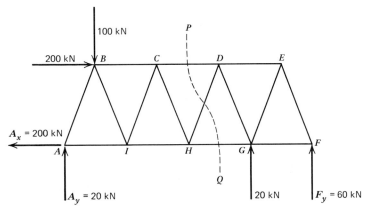

FIG. 7.25 Free body diagram and
reactions for Example Problem 7.4.

cut. The desired cut is shown as the broken line PQ in Fig. 7.25. We can draw
a free body diagram of either portion. We choose the simpler right-hand
portion.

Step 3 Draw a free body diagram of the selected portion of the truss, as in
Fig. 7.26. Remember we know the directions of the forces $\overline{CD}$, $\overline{DH}$, and $\overline{GH}$
because they are two-force members. We assume each to be in tension; nega-
tive values mean compression.

Step 4 Apply Newton's first law to solve for up to three unknowns. By carefully choosing the reference point for summing moments, we can simplify the
algebra. Accordingly we choose point D, the intersection of CD and DH, and
get:

$$\sum M_D = 0 = +6(60) + 2(20) - 5\overline{GH}$$

$$\overline{GH} = \frac{400}{5} = +80.0 \text{ kN tension}$$

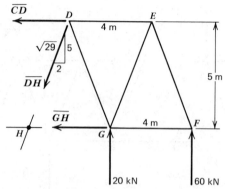

FIG. 7.26   Free body diagram of right portion of truss.

Summing forces vertically gives:

$$\sum F_y = 0 = 20 + 60 - \frac{5}{\sqrt{29}} \overline{DH}$$

$$\overline{DH} = \frac{80\sqrt{29}}{5} = +86.2 \text{ kN tension}$$

Then horizontally:

$$\sum F_x = 0 = -\overline{CD} - \frac{2}{\sqrt{29}} \overline{DH} - \overline{GH}$$

$$\overline{CD} = -80 - \frac{2(86.2)}{\sqrt{29}} = -112 \text{ kN compression}$$

In some problems the force equations result in simultaneous equations. That can be avoided sometimes by a cleverly chosen second moment equation. In the present problem a simple equation is obtained by summing moments about point H. It does not matter that the point H is off the free body diagram.

Example Problem 7.5

For the truss in Fig. 7.27 find the load in members CD, CF, CG, and HG.

Solution

Step 1 is carried out in Fig. 7.28. The reactions may be calculated from the force equations or simply observed, since we have symmetry of the truss *and* the loading. If we cut through all the desired members, we will cut four members and have four unknowns. Since we can solve for only three at a time, we will have to solve the problem in two phases. For the first phase we pass the cutting plane PQ for **step 2**. The free body diagram of the right-hand portion is drawn in Fig. 7.29, completing **step 3**. Again tension is assumed.

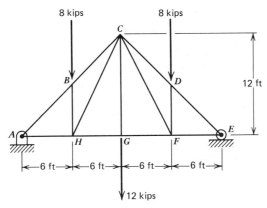

FIG. 7.27 Example Problem 7.5.

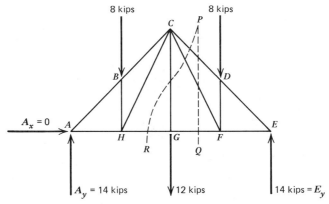

FIG. 7.28 Free body diagram for Example Problem 7.5.

There are several options for **step 4**. We will sum moments about point C (off the body) and isolate $\overline{GF}$.

$$\sum M_C = 0 = -6(8) + 12(14) - 12\overline{GF}$$

$$\overline{GF} = \frac{120}{12} = +10.0 \text{ kips tension}$$

Ordinarily we would next sum the forces horizontally or vertically. Each equation would contain two unknowns, and the two equations would have to be solved simultaneously. This is a perfectly acceptable procedure, although it may be avoided by summing moments about point F:

$$\sum M_F = 0 = 6(14) + 6(\overline{CD}_x)$$

$$\overline{CD}_x = \frac{-6(14)}{6} = -14.0 \text{ kips}$$

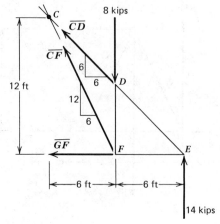

FIG. 7.29 Free body diagram of the right-hand portion of the truss.

and

$$\overline{CD} = \frac{\sqrt{72}}{6} \overline{CD}_x = \frac{\sqrt{72}}{6}(-14)$$

$$\overline{CD} = -19.8 \text{ kips compression}$$

Finally:

$$\sum F_y = 0 = -8 + 14 + \overline{CF}_y + \overline{CD}_y$$

$$\overline{CF}_y = -14 + 8 - \frac{6}{\sqrt{72}}(-19.8) = +8.00$$

$$\overline{CF} = \frac{\sqrt{180}}{12} \overline{CF}_y = \frac{\sqrt{180}(8)}{12} = \textbf{8.94 kips tension}$$

We recycle through steps 2 through 4 to determine $\overline{CG}$ and $\overline{GH}$. For **step 2** we pass the cutting plane *PR* (Fig. 7.28). It cuts four members, but two of these, *CD* and *CF*, are known. Thus, only two unknowns are involved. The free body diagram in Fig. 7.30 satisfies **step 3**. Moving to **step 4**, we sum moments about *C*:

$$\sum M_C = 0 = -6(8) + 12(14) - 12\overline{HG}$$

$$\overline{HG} = \textbf{10.0 kips tension}$$

Since we know $\overline{CD}$ and $\overline{CF}$, we may sum forces vertically.

$$\sum F_y = 0 = -8 + 14 - 12 + \overline{CD}_y + \overline{CF}_y + \overline{CG}$$

$$\overline{CG} = 6 - \frac{6}{\sqrt{72}}(-19.8) - (8.00)$$

$$\overline{CG} = \textbf{12.0 kips tension}$$

The procedure we have just completed illustrates the method of sections when multiple cuts must be made. However, easier ways of handling this particular

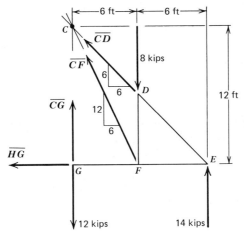

FIG. 7.30 Free body diagram from cutting plane *PR*.

problem are available and should be used when they will work. After solving for the free body diagram in Fig. 7.29, we knew $\overline{GF}$. We could use the isolated joint G and solve for $\overline{HG}$ and $\overline{CG}$. Easier still is to observe that joint G consists of two collinear pairs of members, and therefore according to Section 7.5:

$$\overline{CG} = 12 \text{ kips tension}$$

and

$$\overline{\mathbf{HG}} = \overline{\mathbf{GF}}$$

7.7 SUMMARY

Trusses may be analyzed by applying previously learned principles; no additional theory is needed. All joints in a truss are pinned, and loads may enter the truss only through the joints. This results in all members being two-force members, which means that the forces in the members act along the members. Trusses are solved by:

1. Cutting the members of interest, isolating a portion of the truss.
2. Drawing a free body diagram of the isolated portion.
3. Applying Newton's first law to determine the desired forces.

There are two methods of applying these three steps.

METHOD OF JOINTS

The isolated portion is a joint, and the resulting free body diagram is a concurrent force problem. Only two unknowns can be found, so no more than two unknowns should be cut in isolating the joint. The concurrent force problem can be solved by components or graphically. The method of joints is commonly used when a complete analysis or design is required.

METHOD OF SECTIONS

The isolated portion will not in general reduce to a concurrent force problem, and all three equations from Newton's first law are used for solution. No more than three unknowns should be cut. This method is preferred when the load in one or more members in the interior of a large truss is desired.

Carefully determine whether a member is in tension or compression and label the results clearly. It is convenient to present the results in a load diagram, which is a sketch of the truss that shows the load on each member and tells whether the member is in tension or compression.

PROBLEMS

For Problems 7.1 through 7.11 find the force in each member (or the members specified by your instructor) *by components* using the method of joints for the indicated figure. Be sure and indicate whether the member is in tension or compression.

7.1 Fig. 7.31   **7.2** Fig. 7.32

7.3 Fig. 7.33   **7.4** Fig. 7.34

7.5 Fig. 7.35   **7.6** Fig. 7.36

7.7 Fig. 7.37   **7.8** Fig. 7.38

7.9 Fig. 7.39   **7.10** Fig. 7.40

7.11 Fig. 7.41

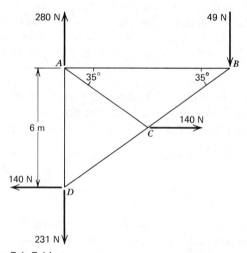

FIG. 7.31 Problems 7.1, 7.14.

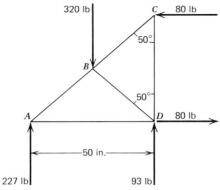

FIG. 7.32 Problems 7.2, 7.15.

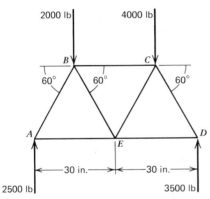

FIG. 7.33 Problems 7.3, 7.16, 7.28.

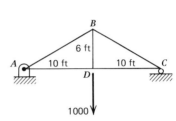

FIG. 7.34 Problems 7.4, 7.17.

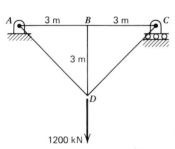

FIG. 7.35 Problems 7.5, 7.18.

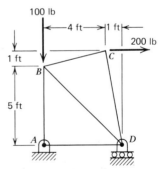

FIG. 7.36 Problems 7.6, 7.19.

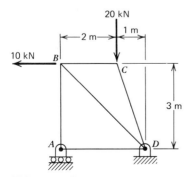

FIG. 7.37 Problems 7.7, 7.20.

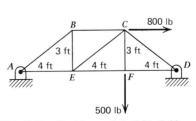

FIG. 7.38 Problems 7.8, 7.21, 7.29.

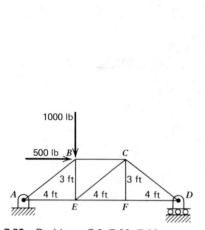

FIG. 7.39   Problems 7.9, 7.22, 7.30.

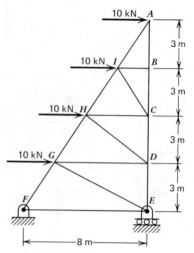

FIG. 7.40   Problems 7.10, 7.23, 7.31, 7.32.

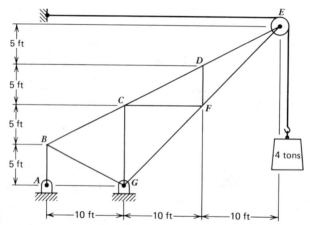

FIG. 7.41   Problems 7.11, 7.24, 7.33.

7.12 Solve Example Problem 7.2 using the method of joints with *components.*

7.13 Solve Example Problem 7.1 *graphically* using the method of joints.

For Problems 7.14 through 7.24, *graphically* find the force in each member (or the members specified by your instructor) using the method of joints. Be sure to indicate whether the member is in tension or compression.

7.14 Fig. 7.31   **7.15** Fig. 7.32
7.16 Fig. 7.33   **7.17** Fig. 7.34
7.18 Fig. 7.35   **7.19** Fig. 7.36
7.20 Fig. 7.37   **7.21** Fig. 7.38
7.22 Fig. 7.39   **7.23** Fig. 7.40
7.24 Fig. 7.41

7.25 By observation, identify the zero-force members in the trusses in Figs. 7.31 through 7.41. Not every truss has one.

7.26 By observation, identify all joints in Figs. 7.31 through 7.41 in which forces are passed through the joints in collinear pairs as discussed in Section 7.5. Not every truss has such a joint.

7.27 Using the *method of sections*, find the force in the indicated members in Example Problem 7.4, Fig. 7.24.

   (a) Members *CD*, *CH*, and *HI*   (b) Members *BC*, *CI*, and *HI*

7.28 Using the *method of sections*, find the force in the indicated members in the truss in Fig. 7.33.

   (a) Members *BC*, *BE*, and *AE*   (b) Members *BC*, *CE*, and *DE*

7.29 Using the *method of sections*, find the force in the indicated members in the truss in Fig. 7.38.

   (a) Members *BC*, *BE*, and *AE*   (b) Members *BC*, *CE*, and *EF*

7.30 Using the *method of sections*, find the force in the indicated members in the truss in Fig. 7.39.

   (a) Members *BC*, *CE*, and *EF*   (b) Members *CD*, *CF*, and *EF*

7.31 Using the *method of sections*, find the force in the indicated members in the truss in Fig. 7.40.

   (a) Members *IH*, *IC*, and *BC*   (b) Members *HG*, *HD*, and *CD*

   (c) Members *IH*, *HC*, and *CD*   (d) Members *HG*, *GD*, and *DE*

7.32 Using the *method of sections*, find the force in the indicated members in the truss in Fig. 7.40.

   (a) Members *AB*, *BI*, *IC*, and *IH*

   (b) Members *HG*, *GD*, *GE*, and *FE*

7.33 Using the *method of sections*, find the force in the indicated members in the truss in Fig. 7.41.

   (a) Members *CD*, *CF*, and *FG*.

   (b) Members *CD*, *CF*, *CG*, and *BG*.

   (c) Members *DE*, *DF*, *CF*, and *FG*.

8

Frames and Machines

In the chapter on trusses we applied the principles we had learned earlier. No new theory was developed. In this chapter likewise, we systematically and carefully apply principles we already know to a new class of problems. If you find that you can readily solve the problems of this chapter, you are well along the way of mastering the concepts of statics. But if statics appears to be mastering you, return to the fundamental concepts that are giving you difficulty. Work additional problems in Chapters 3, 4, and 5 and then proceed.

Trusses consist of pin-connected structures composed entirely of two-force members. Frames are not limited to pin connections or two-force members. Machines are similar to frames, but since they amplify force or motion, they are designed to move. Frames and machines are analyzed in the same way.

8.1 ANATOMY OF A FRAME

A typical frame carrying a load of 20 kN is shown for our inspection in Fig. 8.1. We observe pin connections at points A, B, C, and E, which includes all the joints. This is a pin-connected structure, which is the first requirement for being a truss. We examine the horizontal member $ABCD$, which is a *continuous* member; that is, it does not break at joints B or C. We observe that loads come into this member at points A, B, and C from the supporting structure and that an external load is applied at D. It is a *four-force* member; its load does not act along it, and this structure is *not* a truss. Next we examine member CEF, noting again that it

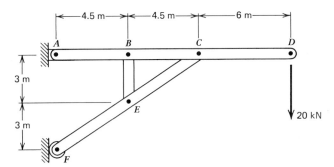

FIG. 8.1 A loaded frame.

is *continuous* past point E, and observing that loads come into it at three locations, C, E, and F. It is a three-force member. Last, we examine the vertical strut BE and see that only it is a two-force member.

The structure shown is not a truss, and in general neither the method of joints nor the method of sections will provide useful results. To illustrate the point, consider isolating joint B by cutting first the vertical member between B and E. The vertical member is a two-force member, and the reaction $\overline{BE}$ will be along it as shown in Fig. 8.2. Cutting next between A and B, we would have only $\overline{BA}_x$ between A and B if the horizontal member were a two-force member. However, since it is rigid and continues past B, the additional components of $\overline{BA}_y$ and M_{BA} must also be included. A similar situation exists to the right of joint B. We have a total of seven unknowns on this free body diagram; and with only three equations available, the prospects of analyzing this structure by the method of joints are growing exceedingly dim.

Sparks's first principle states, "If it ain't broke, don't fix it!" Our present approach to this problem is, however, definitely "broke" and in need of "fixin'." By now you should have developed a gut instinct for drawing a free body diagram when stumped or bewildered, and, occasionally, just for the fun of it. Following that instinct, we draw the free body diagram shown in Fig. 8.3. If $ABCD$ were a two-force member, the reaction at A would be A_x only. That not being the case, A_y is also required. Because of the roller at F, only F_x is required at F. We have anticipated the sense of the reactions, but it is not important. Careful checking shows that we now have three unknowns and three equations, and the reactions at A and F may be found. This will not always be the case, and at

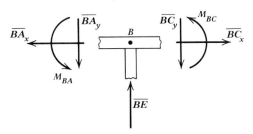

FIG. 8.2 Free body diagram of joint B.

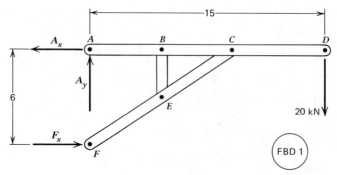

FIG. 8.3 Free body diagram of frame.

times we may be tempted to invoke Sparks's corollary. "If it's still broke, the heck with it!" On the dimmer side, some frames are statically indeterminate and may not be completely solved by the methods of this chapter. If the roller at F were a pin, that would be true for this structure.

8.2   MEMBERS ONLY

In contrast to the methods of joints and sections used with trusses, for frames (and machines) we will use the method of *members*. This consists of simply isolating each member and drawing a free body diagram of it. Before beginning, identify all two-force members in the structure. Only these will have their forces along them. As noted previously, member BE is the only two-force member in our frame in Fig. 8.1.

We begin in Fig. 8.4a by isolating member $ABCD$. We show the external load of 20 kN at point D. Cutting pin A, we have A_x and A_y. If an overall free body diagram has been drawn as in Fig. 8.3, the labels and assumed senses for these reactions must be *identical*. Next we cut the pin at B. Since BE is a two-force member, the reaction is along BE as shown. At C we have the multi-force member FEC. The direction of the reaction at C is *not* known. Observe that there are five unknowns on this free body diagram.

In Fig. 8.4b we draw the free body diagram for BE. Frequently such simple free body diagrams are left out of the analysis. We include one here to emphasize how it functions and for completeness. The force at B is, of course, along the member BE. In Fig. 8.4a we showed the force B as acting up on member $ABCD$. According to Newton's third law, the reaction between these members will be equal and opposite, and thus B is shown as acting *down* on member BE, *opposite* of its sense on member $ABCD$. It must also carry the same symbol, B in this case, not $-B$. At E we also get a reaction E along BE. It is obvious from Fig. 8.4b that:

$$B = -E$$

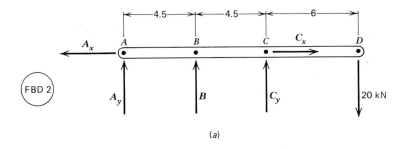

(a)

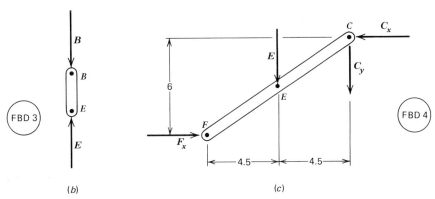

(b)   (c)

FIG. 8.4 Free body diagrams of the
members of the frame.

Finally we come to member FEC, which is shown in Fig. 8.4c, where F_x carries the same sense and label as in Fig. 8.3; E carries the same label but opposite sense from that in Fig. 8.4b; C_x and C_y have the same label but opposite senses from those in Fig. 8.4a. This free body diagram has four unknowns.

Observe that if member BE (Fig. 8.4b) is superimposed on member $ABCD$ (Fig. 8.4a). The up-and-down forces labeled B cancel each other. If member FEC (Fig. 8.4c) is now superimposed on this combination, the two forces at E will cancel, and the two pairs of forces, C_x and C_y, at C will also cancel. The result is the overall free body diagram shown in Fig. 8.3. Notice that there are no forces in this diagram at B, C, or E. Forces at these points are *internal* to the frame. Internal forces should never be shown on a free body diagram.

8.3   WHAT TO DO WHEN THREE EQUATIONS WON'T

We've mentioned that some of the free body diagrams we have drawn have excessive unknowns (i.e., more than three). We have also observed that several of the unknowns are common to two free body diagrams. In fact, all are, and therein lies the solution to this problem. Although in Fig. 8.4 there are five unknowns on member *ABCD*, four on *FEC*, and two on *BE*, there are only seven distinct unknowns, not eleven. Since we have three equations for each free body diagram, the result is seven unknowns and nine equations—a solvable problem. We may and frequently do, write equations for the overall free body diagram, but these equations are redundant to the nine just mentioned, since the overall free body diagram may be obtained by superimposing the individual free body diagrams.

The point of all this is that if the first free body diagram produces more unknowns than equations, simply draw another. Be sure to show previously identified reactions correctly. Continue this process until enough equations have been generated to solve the problem. The problem we have been discussing is one of the more complex ones we will solve.

Example Problem 8.1

Find the reactions at *A* and *F* and the pin forces at *B*, *E*, and *C* for the frame in Fig. 8.1.

Solution

The free body diagrams have been drawn in Figs. 8.3 and 8.4 and discussed previously. We label Fig. 8.3 as FBD 1 and sum moments for it about point *A*. The use of the free body diagram label (FBD 1) will help keep the work organized. So:

(FBD 1)

$$\sum M_A = 0 = -15(20) + 6F_x$$
$$F_x = 50.0 \text{ kN} \rightarrow$$
$$\sum F_x = 0 = -A_x + F_x$$
$$A_x = 50.0 \text{ kN} \leftarrow$$
$$\sum F_y = 0 = A_y - 20$$
$$A_y = 20.0 \text{ kN} \uparrow$$

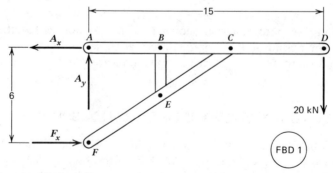

FIG. 8.3 Free body diagram of frame.
Figure repeated from page 194.

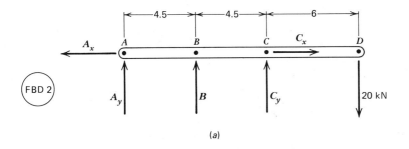

FBD 2

(a)

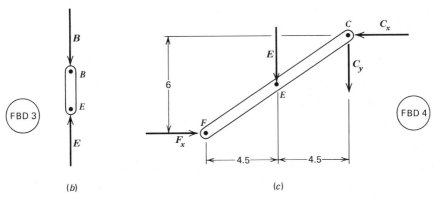

FBD 3   FBD 4

(b)   (c)

FIG. 8.4   Free body diagrams of the members of the frame. Figure repeated from page 195.

Moving to Fig. 8.4*a* (FBD 2):

FBD 2

$$\sum M_C = 0 = -9A_y - 4.5B - 6(20)$$
$$B = -66.7 \text{ kN} \downarrow$$
$$\sum F_x = 0 = -A_x + C_x$$
$$C_x = 50.0 \text{ kN} \rightarrow$$
$$\sum F_y = 0 = A_y + B + C_y - 20$$
$$C_y = 66.7 \text{ kN} \uparrow$$

The senses of the forces indicated in these answers are those acting on member *ABCD*. For Fig. 8.4*b* we have:

FBD 3

$$\sum F_y = 0 = -B + E$$
$$E = -66.7 \text{ kN} \downarrow$$

Example Problem 8.2

Find the external reactions at *A* and *D* and the pin force at *B* for the frame in Fig. 8.5.

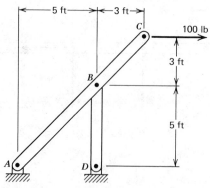

FIG. 8.5 Example Problem 8.2.

Solution

An overall free body diagram is drawn in Fig. 8.6. Since *BD* is identified as a two-force member, the reaction at *D* is along the member *BD*. Member *ABC* is not a two-force member, and the reaction at *A* has two components. Summing moments about *A* yields:

$$\sum M_A = 0 = +5D - 8(100)$$
$$D = 160 \text{ lb}\uparrow$$
$$\sum F_x = 0 = A_x + 100$$
$$A_x = -100 \text{ lb}\leftarrow$$
$$\sum F_y = 0 = A_y + D$$
$$A_y = -160 \text{ lb}\downarrow$$

We may draw the free body diagram for member *ABC* or *BD* to find *B* or simply observe that the reaction at *D* is transmitted to *B*. In either case:

$$B = 160 \text{ lb}$$

The force **B** will act up on member *ABC* but down on member *BD*.

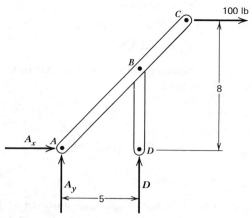

FIG. 8.6 Free body diagram for Example Problem 8.2.

Example Problem 8.3

Find the reactions at A, C, and E for the frame shown in Fig. 8.7.

Solution

The first step is to identify any two-force members. Member CDE is obviously not one. The couple at B also prevents ABC from being one; so, there are no two-force members in this structure. An overall free body diagram is drawn in Fig. 8.8. The directions of the reactions at A and E are not known. There are four unknowns here, so an additional free body diagram must be drawn. Ultimately it does not matter which member is taken, although some choices will sometimes result in easier mathematics than others. We arbitrarily choose member ABC, and the free body diagram is shown in Fig. 8.9. The reaction at A must be exactly as shown in Fig. 8.8, and, of course, the couple at B is included.

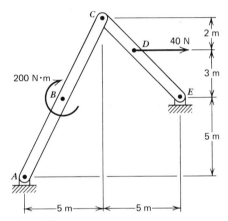

FIG. 8.7   Example Problem 8.3.

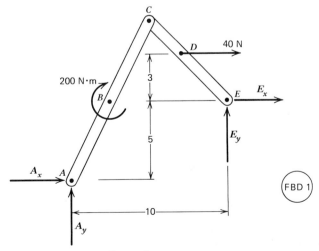

FIG. 8.8   Free body diagram for Example Problem 8.3.

The reaction at C has not been previously designated, so we are free to assign the senses. Note that C_x and C_y are external to member ABC and are shown in Fig. 8.9. However, they are internal to the entire frame and *should not* be shown in Fig. 8.8. There are also four unknowns in Fig. 8.9, but between Fig. 8.8 and Fig. 8.9 there are only six unknowns, A_x and A_y being common. Since we can write three equations for each free body diagram, there are a total of six unknowns and six equations—a solvable, albeit still substantial, problem. Clever selection of equations, especially moment equations, can greatly simplify the algebra.

For this case we sum moments about point E in Fig. 8.8, isolating A_x and A_y.

FBD 1

$$\sum M_E = 0 = -3(40) - 200 - 10A_y + 5A_x$$
$$5A_x - 10A_y = 320$$

Then, summing moments about point C in Fig. 8.9, we also isolate A_x and A_y.

FBD 2

$$\sum M_C = 0 = -200 - 5A_y + 10A_x$$
$$10A_x - 5A_y = 200$$

Solving the two equations simultaneously yields:

$$A_x = 5.33 \text{ N} \rightarrow$$
$$A_y = -29.3 \text{ N} \downarrow$$

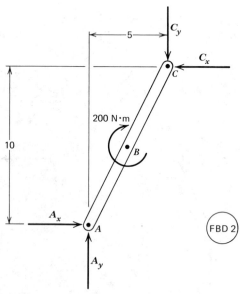

FIG. 8.9   Free body diagram of member *ABC*.

Then summing forces for Fig. 8.8:

(FBD 1)

$$\sum F_x = 0 = A_x + 40 + E_x$$
$$E_x = -40 + (5.33)$$
$$\boldsymbol{E_x = -34.7\ N\leftarrow}$$
$$\sum F_y = 0 = A_y + E_y$$
$$E_y = -A_y = -(-29.3)$$
$$\boldsymbol{E_y = 29.3\ N\uparrow}$$

And for Fig. 8.9:

(FBD 2)

$$\sum F_x = 0 = A_x - C_x$$
$$\boldsymbol{C_x = 5.33\ N\leftarrow}$$
$$\sum F_y = 0 = A_y - C_y$$
$$\boldsymbol{C_y = -29.3\ N\uparrow}$$

The senses shown for C_x and C_y are for the forces on member ABC.

8.4 LOADS AT A JOINT AND PIN FORCES

Up to this point we have not considered a load occurring on the pin, and we have avoided problems in which a load occurred at a joint. We have treated the pin as though part of one of the members. That is the simplest treatment, and it is recommended when it will do. *It will do* unless the pin must be designed or analyzed. In such cases we must have the details of the joint.

In an "exploded" view of a simple pin joint (Fig. 8.10), members A and B and the pin are shown as separate pieces. The forces acting on each of the members

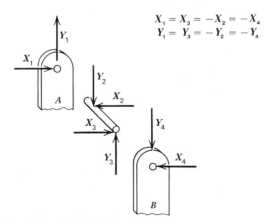

$$X_1 = X_3 = -X_2 = -X_4$$
$$Y_1 = Y_3 = -Y_2 = -Y_4$$

FIG. 8.10 Interactive forces between a member and a pin with no external load.

are also shown: X_1 and Y_1 are the forces exerted by the pin on member A, X_2 and Y_2 are the forces exerted by member A on the pin—these have to be equal and opposite. In addition, X_3 and Y_3 are the forces exerted by member B on the pin, and X_4 and Y_4 are the forces exerted by the pin on member B—these are also opposing and equal pairs. Since the pin must also be in equilibrium, it follows that X_2 and Y_2 are also equal and opposite X_3 and Y_3, respectively. Thus:

$$X_1 = X_3 = -X_2 = -X_4$$

and

$$Y_1 = Y_3 = -Y_2 = -Y_4$$

Since all these components are respectively equal, it does not matter whether we are talking about the force between members or between the pin and the member. If you attach the pin to member A, X_1 cancels X_2, Y_1 cancels Y_2, and the force exerted by the pin on member B is still X_4 and Y_4, as shown in Fig. 8.11. So in this case it is immaterial how we see the joint. The simplest approach is to *assume that the pin is attached to one member*, and it will not matter which member.

If there is a load at the joint, the situation is more troublesome. Figure 8.12 shows the analysis of a loaded joint in which the force P *is assumed* to act on the pin. Since the pin must be in equilibrium:

$$X_2 = -X_3 + P_x$$

In this case X_2 is the force member A exerts on the pin, but it is not equal to $-X_3$ the force member B exerts on the pin. If the pin is attached to member A, X_1 and Y_1 cancel X_2 and Y_2, and X_4 and Y_4, the forces exerted by the pin on member B, will show up as the joint forces. This is illustrated in Fig. 8.13. For simplicity of analysis, we will *assume a load at a joint acts on one of the members*. As demonstrated in Example Problem 8.4, the reactions at all other joints will not be affected by our choice. The reaction at the joint in question will depend on which member the load has been attached to. The two possible answers will differ by the load at the joint (P in Figs. 8.12 and 8.13). If we wish to analyze or design the joint, it is important to work out these details which we will leave to texts on machine design and structural analysis.

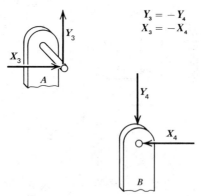

FIG. 8.11   Forces between members with pin attached.

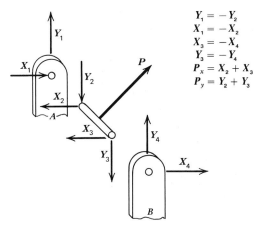

$$Y_1 = -Y_2$$
$$X_1 = -X_2$$
$$X_3 = -X_4$$
$$Y_3 = -Y_4$$
$$P_x = X_2 + X_3$$
$$P_y = Y_2 + Y_3$$

FIG. 8.12   Interactive forces between a member and a pin with an external load P on the pin.

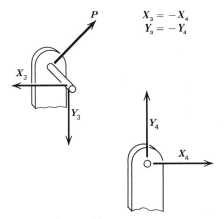

$$X_3 = -X_4$$
$$Y_3 = -Y_4$$

FIG. 8.13   Forces between members with pin attached and external load on the member.

Example Problem 8.4

Find the reactions at A and C for the frame in Fig. 8.14. Also find the interacting force at B.

Solution

A free body diagram of the entire structure is drawn in Fig. 8.15a. We see that there are four unknowns, and so we draw a second free body diagram of member AB in Fig. 8.15b. We can include the 10-lb external force at B or leave it off, as we choose. It's easier to leave it off, so we do. This diagram also has four unknowns, but two are common with the first diagram, so we

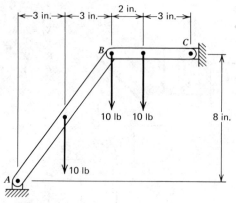

FIG. 8.14 Example Problem 8.4.

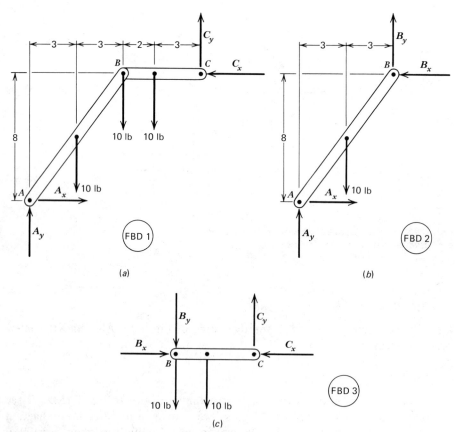

FIG. 8.15 Free body diagrams for Example
Problem 8.4.

204

have six unknowns and six equations, which are solvable. By carefully select-ing moment equations, we can minimize the algebra.

(FBD 1)

$$\sum M_C = 0 = +3(10) + 5(10) + 8(10) + 8A_x - 11A_y$$
$$8A_x - 11A_y = -160$$

(FBD 2)

$$\sum M_B = 0 = +3(10) + 8(A_x) - 6A_y$$
$$8A_x - 6A_y = -30$$

Solving the two equations simultaneously gives:

$$A_y = \textbf{26.0 lb}$$
$$A_x = \textbf{15.8 lb}$$

Then:

(FBD 1)

$$\sum F_x = 0 = A_x - C_x$$
$$C_x = \textbf{15.8 lb}$$
$$\sum F_y = 0 = A_y - 10 - 10 - 10 + C_y$$
$$C_y = \textbf{4.0 lb}$$

To find the interacting forces at B:

(FBD 2)

$$\sum F_x = 0 = A_x - B_x$$
$$B_x = \textbf{15.8 lb}$$
$$\sum F_y = 0 = A_y - 10 + B_y$$
$$B_y = \textbf{-16.0 lb}\downarrow$$

For completeness, member BC is shown in Fig. 8.15c. Since we put the 10-lb load at B on this member, the load for B obtained here is the force exerted by the pin at B on member AB. Superimposing Fig. 8.15c on Fig. 8.15b gives Fig. 8.15a.

If we put the 10-lb load at B on member AB, we will obtain the same forces at A and C. The forces at B will be different because they will then represent the interaction between the pin and member BC.

Example Problem 8.5

Find the reactions at A and E, the pin forces at B and D, and the interaction at C for the frame in Fig. 8.16.

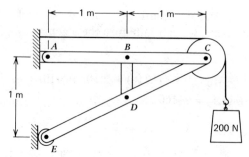

FIG. 8.16 Example Problem 8.5.

Solution

The overall free body diagram is drawn in Fig. 8.17. The forces in the pulley cables are transmitted undiminished to the center of the pulley as shown at point C. Then:

(FBD 1)

$$\sum M_A = 0 = -2(200) + 1E_x$$
$$E_x = \textbf{400 N}$$
$$\sum F_x = 0 = A_x + E_x - 200$$
$$A_x = \textbf{-200 N}\leftarrow$$
$$\sum F_y = 0 = A_y - 200$$
$$A_y = \textbf{200 N}$$

We then draw a free body diagram for member ABC (Fig. 8.18a). We can attach the pulley forces to member ABC or member EDC and choose the latter. We show the reaction at A we have just found: A_x is labeled -200 because it actually acts to the left. (You may prefer to simply show it that way.) Since BD is recognized as a two-force member, B_y is the only component at B. The forces C_x and C_y are the ones exerted by the pin at C on member

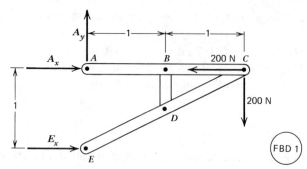

FIG. 8.17 Free body diagram for Example Problem 8.5.

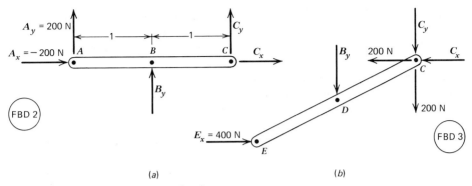

FIG. 8.18 Free body diagrams for the members in Example Problem 8.5.

ABC. The pulley forces are left to member *CDE.* Then:

(FBD 2)

$$\sum M_c = 0 = -1B_y - 2(200)$$
$$B_y = -400 \text{ N}\downarrow$$
$$\sum F_x = 0 = -200 + C_x$$
$$C_x = 200 \text{ N}$$
$$\sum F_y = 0 = +200 + B_y + C_y$$
$$C_y = -200 - (-400)$$
$$C_y = 200 \text{ N}$$

Since *BD* is a two-force member, the force at *D* is:

$$B_y = -400 \text{ N}\uparrow$$

It acts down on member *BD* and up on member *EDC.* The free body diagram for member *EDC* is shown in Fig. 8.18*b*, although it is not needed for this solution. It is useful for checking results. It also illustrates that if we superimpose the free body diagram for all the members (including member *BD*, which is not shown), Fig. 8.18 reduces to Fig. 8.17.

If we wish to know more about the joint at *C*, such as the pin force on member *EDC* (it is not C_x and C_y), we need additional free body diagrams and ultimately more details on the joint.

8.5 MACHINES

Machines are designed to amplify force or motion. They permit relative motion of their parts, although many machines are used with their parts locked in position like a pair of pliers. Other machines operate with their parts in motion. If a body is in motion at constant velocity, it is in equilibrium, and it should be analyzed statically. This statement is based on the fine print in Newton's first law. If a body is being accelerated, additional forces are present that depend on the mass and acceleration involved. These forces, called inertia forces, are determined using the methods of *dynamics*. Generally, they may be disregarded for slow moving machines, and such machines are analyzed by the methods of statics. Finally, even when inertia forces are important, after they have been accounted for, the process of analysis follows that presented here.

Although machines represent a class of problems different from frames, we analyze them using the same procedure. Often a machine is designed to produce a certain motion, as in the feeder mechanism on a paper duplicating machine. The study of such motion is called *kinematics* and is another topic in dynamics.

Example Problem 8.6

The piston at C in Fig. 8.19 is 2 in. in diameter and has a pressure of 400 psi acting over it. Find the resisting moment M at A and the pin reactions at A, B, and C. Assume that the cylinder wall is frictionless. This is known as a *slider–crank mechanism*.

Solution

The force at C due to the pressure on the piston is:

$$P = pA$$

$$P = \frac{400 \text{ lb}}{\text{in.}^2} \frac{\pi(2 \text{ in.})^2}{4} = 1260 \text{ lb}$$

A free body diagram of the entire mechanism is shown in Fig. 8.20. A pin reaction occurs at A. Forces at B are internal to this free body diagram. A

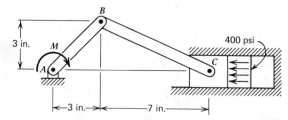

FIG. 8.19 Example Problem 8.6.

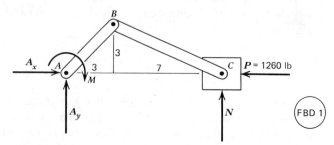

FIG. 8.20 Free body diagram for Example Problem 8.6.

normal force N also acts on the piston from the cylinder wall. There are four unknowns here, A_x, A_y, N, and the moment M. (The moment M at A prevents AB from being a two-force member.) Another free body diagram is needed, so we draw the connecting rod (member BC) and the piston in Fig. 8.21a, from which we get:

(FBD 2)

$$\sum M_B = 0 = 7N - 3(1260)$$
$$N = \textbf{539 lb}$$
$$\sum F_x = 0 = B_x - 1260$$
$$B_x = \textbf{1260 lb}$$
$$\sum F_y = 0 = -B_y + N$$
$$B_y = \textbf{539 lb}$$

Returning to Fig. 8.20:

(FBD 1)

$$\sum M_A = 0 = -M + 10N$$
$$M = \textbf{5390 in.-lb}$$
$$\sum F_x = 0 = A_x - 1260$$
$$A_x = \textbf{1260 lb}$$
$$\sum F_y = 0 = A_y + N$$
$$A_y = \textbf{-539 lb}\downarrow$$

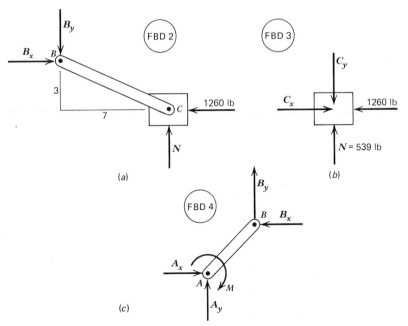

FIG. 8.21 Free body diagrams for the members in Example Problem 8.6.

To find the forces at C, a free body diagram of the piston is drawn yielding:

$$C_x = 1260 \text{ lb}$$
$$C_y = 539 \text{ lb}$$

For completeness, a free body diagram of member AB is drawn in Fig. 8.21c. Again observe that if the free body diagrams of members AB and BC are superimposed, they yield the free body diagram for the whole structure in Fig. 8.20. If you observed BC to be a two-force member, you are correct. The components B_x and B_y result in a force at B acting along member BC.

8.6 SHEAR AND AXIAL COMPONENTS OF FORCE

Forces perpendicular to a straight member are called *shear* forces. Those parallel to a straight member are called *axial* forces. (Actually they must be along the axis of the member.) In order for us to analyze or design a structural member, the forces acting on it must be given in terms of axial and shear components. If the member is horizontal or vertical, the components we have found will be shear and axial forces. For example, in Fig. 8.18 member ABC is horizontal and A_x and C_x are axial loads; A_y, B_y, and C_y are shear loads. Member CDE, however, is at an incline; and the horizontal and vertical components are not shear and axial components. Forces are resolved into shear and axial components in Example Problem 8.7.

Example Problem 8.7

Member AB in Fig. 8.15 is redrawn in Fig. 8.22. Resolve the forces on this member into axial and shear components.

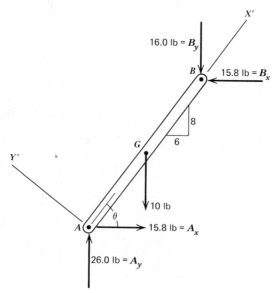

FIG. 8.22 Example Problem 8.7.

Solution

Horizontal and vertical components are as shown. A new set of axes X' and Y' are shown parallel and perpendicular to the member. These will correspond to axial and shear components, respectively. The midpoint is labeled G. The angle between the X' axis and horizontal is found by:

$$\tan \theta = \frac{8}{6} \quad \text{and} \quad \theta = 53.1°$$

The components at A, A_x, and A_y are redrawn in Fig. 8.23, where each is further resolved into X' and Y' components and it is seen that:

$$(A_y)_{X'} = A_y \sin 53.1°$$
$$(A_y)_{X'} = 26.0 \sin 53.1°$$
$$(A_y)_{X'} = +20.8 \text{ lb}$$

Similarly:

$$(A_y)_{Y'} = 26.0 \cos 53.1°$$
$$(A_y)_{Y'} = +15.6 \text{ lb}$$

and

$$(A_x)_{X'} = 15.8 \cos 53.1°$$
$$(A_x)_{X'} = +9.5 \text{ lb}$$
$$(A_x)_{Y'} = -15.8 \sin 53.1°$$
$$(A_x)_{Y'} = -12.6 \text{ lb}$$

The resultant at A is then:

$$A_{x'} = (A_y)_{X'} + (A_x)_{X'}$$
$$A_{x'} = +20.8 + 9.5$$
$$A_{x'} = \textbf{30.3 lb}$$

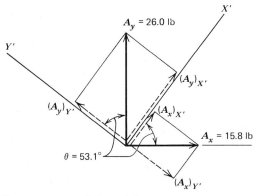

FIG. 8.23 X' and Y' components of $\mathbf{A}_x$ and $\mathbf{A}_y$.

which is the axial load at A. And:

$$A_{y'} = (A_y)_{Y'} + (A_x)_{Y'}$$
$$A_{y'} = +15.6 - 12.6$$
$$A_{y'} = +3.0 \text{ lb}$$

which is the shear load at A.

The results above are summarized by the following equations.

Axial component:

$$F_{x'} = F_x \cos \theta + F_y \sin \theta \qquad (8.2)$$

Shear component:

$$F_{y'} = -F_x \sin \theta + F_y \cos \theta \qquad (8.3)$$

where θ is the angle between the member and the positive horizontal axis and F_x and F_y are positive to the right and up respectively. Applying Eqs. 8.2 and 8.3 to point G (Fig. 8.22) gives:

$$G_{x'} = 0 + (-10) \sin 53.1°$$
$$G_{x'} = -8.0 \text{ lb}$$

for the axial component, and

$$G_{y'} = 0 + (-10) \cos 53.1°$$
$$G_{y'} = -6.0 \text{ lb}$$

for the shear component.

Applying the equations to point B gives:

$$B_{x'} = -15.8 \cos 53.1° - 16 \sin 53.1°$$
$$B_{x'} = -22.3 \text{ lb}$$

which is the axial component, and

$$B_{y'} = -(-15.8) \sin 53.1° + (-16.0) \cos 53.1°$$
$$B_{y'} = +3.0 \text{ lb}$$

which is the shear component. The results for all three points are shown in Fig. 8.24. The analysis can be checked by applying Newton's first law to the X' and Y' axes. The loads on a member must be expressed in this format before proceeding with its analysis or design.

8.7 SUMMARY

Frames and machines contain members that are not two-force members, and therefore these structures may not be solved by the methods used for trusses. Such problems are solved using the method of members. Key points are as follows.

1. Draw an overall free body diagram.
2. Identify all two-force members.

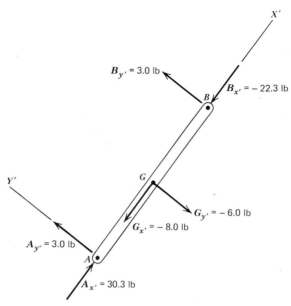

FIG. 8.24 Shear and axial components on member *AB*.

3. Draw additional free body diagrams of individual members until the problem is solvable.
4. Show paired internal forces at a joint with a common label and opposite senses.
5. Attach an external load at a joint to either of the members where it acts.
6. Apply Newton's first law to obtain a solution.

PROBLEMS

For the indicated figure, find the loads at the supports and at each joint.

8.1 Fig. 8.25   **8.2** Fig. 8.26

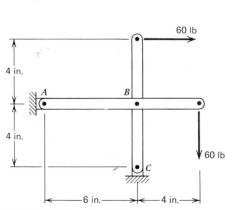

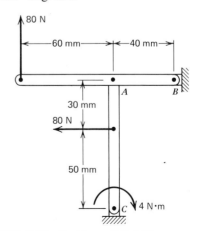

FIG. 8.25 Problem 8.1.   **FIG. 8.26** Problems 8.2, 8.14.

For the indicated figure, find the loads at the supports and at each joint.

✓ 8.3	Fig. 8.27	8.4	Fig. 8.28
✓ 8.5	Fig. 8.29	✓ 8.6	Fig. 8.30
✓ 8.7	Fig. 8.31	✓ 8.8	Fig. 8.32

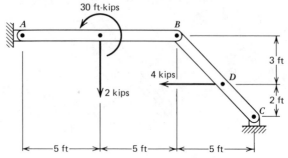

FIG. 8.27   Problems 8.3, 8.15, 8.30.

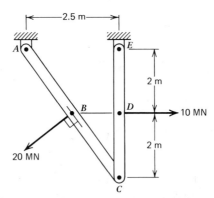

FIG. 8.28   Problems 8.4, 8.16, 8.31.

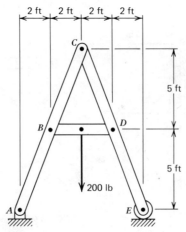

FIG. 8.29   Problems 8.5, 8.17, 8.32.

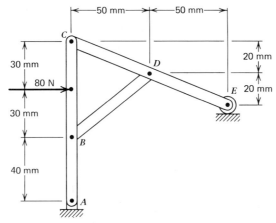

FIG. 8.30 Problems 8.6, 8.18, 8.33.

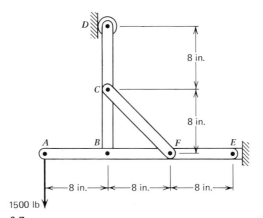

FIG. 8.31 Problem 8.7.

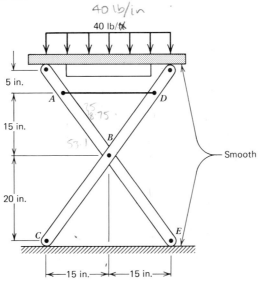

FIG. 8.32 Problem 8.8.

215

For the indicated figure, find the loads at the supports and at the joints.

8.9 Fig. 8.33   **8.10** Fig. 8.34

8.11 Fig. 8.35   **8.12** Fig. 8.36

8.13 Fig. 8.37

8.14 For Fig. 8.26 what will be the reactions at points B and C if an upward 80-N vertical-load is added to point A?

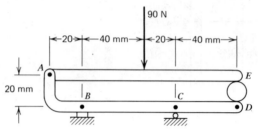

FIG. 8.33 Problem 8.9.

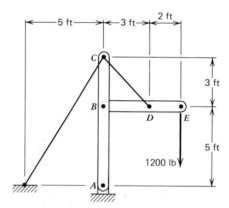

FIG. 8.34 Problem 8.10.

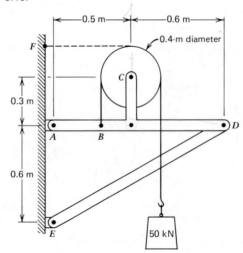

FIG. 8.35 Problems 8.11, 8.19, 8.34.

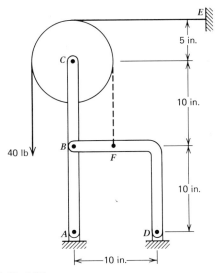

FIG. 8.36 Problems 8.12, 8.20.

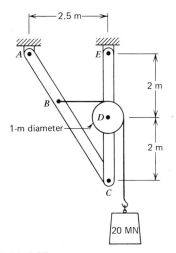

FIG. 8.37 Problems 8.13, 8.21, 8.35.

8.15 Add an upward vertical load of 2 kips to point *B* in Fig. 8.27 and find the reactions at points *A* and *C*.

8.16 Add a horizontal load of 10 MN to the right to point *C* in Fig. 8.28 and find the reactions at points *A* and *E*.

8.17 Add a horizontal load of 100 lb to the right at point *C* in Fig. 8.29. Find the reactions at points *A*, *B*, *D*, and *E*.

8.18 Add a vertical downward force of 80 N to point *D* in Fig. 8.30. Find the reactions at *A*, *B*, *C*, and *E*.

8.19 For Fig. 8.35, move the cable connection at point B to point F on the wall as shown by the broken line. Also add a vertical downward force of 20 kN at point D. Find the reactions at A, C, and E.

8.20 For Fig. 8.36 move the cable connection from point E to point F as shown by the broken line. Also add a horizontal force of 80 lb to the left at point B. Find the reactions at A and D.

8.21 For Fig. 8.37 add a horizontal force to the left of 10 MN at point C. Find the reactions at A and E.

8.22 For Fig. 8.38 the applied moment M is 2000 in.-lb. The crank arm AB is 2.8 in. long and the connecting rod BC is 5.6 in. long. Find the resisting force P for equilibrium and the force at each pin when:

(a) $\theta = 60°$ (b) $\theta = 45°$ (c) $\theta = 30°$ (d) $\theta = 15°$

8.23 For Fig. 8.38 the applied force P is 20 kN. The crank arm AB is 80 mm long and the connecting rod BC is 180 mm long. Find the resisting moment M for equilibrium and the force on each pin when:

(a) $\theta = 35°$ (b) $\theta = 70°$ (c) $\theta = 105°$ (d) $\theta = 140°$

8.24 For the pliers shown in Fig. 8.39 the applied force P is 10 lb, and the dimensions are: $a = 8.0$ in., $b = 1.75$ in. Find the clamping force on the bolt and the reaction at the pivot.

8.25 The pliers in Fig. 8.39 have the following dimensions: $a = 180$ mm, $b = 30$ mm. Find the force P required to produce a clamping force of 300 N and the reaction at the pivot.

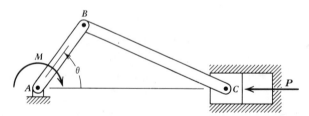

FIG. 8.38 Problems 8.22, 8.23.

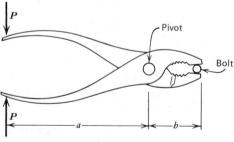

FIG. 8.39 Problems 8.24, 8.25.

8.26 The hand press shown in Fig. 8.40 has the following dimensions: $AB = 10$ in., $BC = 10$ in., $BD = 12$ in. If the activating force Q is 20 lb, find the resisting force P and the reaction at the pins A and B when:

(a) $\theta = 30°$ (b) $\theta = 60°$ (c) $\theta = 80°$

8.27 Work Problem 8.26 if Q is horizontal and to the right.

8.28 A portable lift is shown in Fig. 8.41. The engine being lifted weighs 1400 N. Find the reactions at the wheels and at the pins A, B, and E.

8.29 Work Problem 8.28 if point C is 0.2 m to the right of B and the engine weighs 2000 N.

8.30 Resolve the forces on member BDC (Fig. 8.27, Problem 8.3) into shear and axial components.

8.31 Resolve the forces on member ABC (Fig. 8.28, Problem 8.4) into shear and axial components.

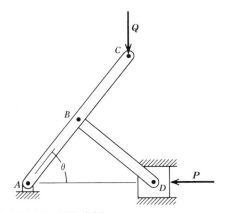

FIG. 8.40   Problems 8.26, 8.27, 8.36, 8.37.

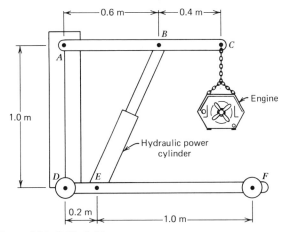

FIG. 8.41   Problems 8.28, 8.29, 8.39.

8.32 Resolve the forces on member *ABC* (Fig. 8.29, Problem 8.5) into shear and axial components.

8.33 Resolve the forces on member *CDE* (Fig. 8.30, Problem 8.6) into shear and axial components.

8.34 Resolve the forces on member *DE* (Fig. 8.35, Problem 8.11) into shear and axial components.

8.35 Resolve the forces on member *ABC* (Fig. 8.37, Problem 8.13) into shear and axial components.

8.36 Resolve the forces on member *ABC* into shear and axial components from Problem 8.26a, Fig. 8.40.

8.37 Resolve the forces on member *ABC* into shear and axial components from Problem 8.26b, Fig. 8.40.

8.38 A simplified drawing of an oil pumping rig is shown in Fig. 8.42. A moment *M* is applied to arm *AB* by a motor. This ultimately produces a tension *T* in the cable *EF*. For the values given below, find *M* or *T* and the force at each pin.

	a	*b*	*c*	*d*	*e*	*f*	*M*	*T*
(a)	2 ft	3 ft	5 ft	5 ft	5 ft	7 ft	—	2000 lb
(b)	1.5 ft	3 ft	4 ft	5 ft	4 ft	6 ft	10,000 ft-lb	—
(c)	0.7 m	1 m	1.5 m	2 m	1.5 m	2 m	—	10 kN
(d)	1 m	1.2 m	2 m	2 m	2.5 m	3 m	30 kN·m	—

8.39 The hydraulic power cylinder in Fig. 8.41 has a pressure of 2.00 N/mm² (2.00 MPa) acting over a cylinder with a diameter of 50 mm. Find the weight of the engine this will support. Also find the pin reaction at A and the reactions at the wheels.

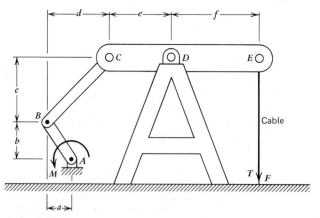

FIG. 8.42   Problem 8.38.

9

Friction

I have a little fantasy. It has to do with four defensive linemen from the Dallas Cowboys professional football team. (In Texas, cowpersons have not yet replaced cowboys.) For the sake of nonfootball fans I should mention that defensive linemen are very large, weighing 250–280 lb, extremely strong, and except when they are doing commercials for Coca-Cola, mean. I am none of these things. My size and disposition resemble that of a field-goal kicker. The fantasy takes place at half time at next year's Super Bowl. I challenge these four linemen to a tug-of-war with the provision that if they have not moved me after 5 minutes, I win. Obviously there's a catch, which is this: I wrap the tug-of-war rope around the goalpost several times as shown in Fig. 9.1. Try as they may, the four linemen will not move me, and after 300 ticks of the clock I'll go into my victory dance, spike my calculator, and welcome the congratulations of the Dallas Cheerleaders.

Let's say I've been working out regularly and can resist the linemen with a force of 50 lb. If I wrap the rope around the goalpost only twice, the linemen will have to pull with a combined force of 2170 lb, or 542 lb per man, to move me. If I am feeling a little puny and exert only 25 lb, they will still need 271 lb apiece. If I happen to be in a really tough frame of mind and wrap the rope around the goalpost three times, they will need to pull with a combined force of 7140 lb to overcome my 25-lb pull. If I am up to 50 lb—well, it's mind boggling. Of course, my ally in this tug-of-war is friction. In Section 9.7 on belt friction we will see how these numbers are obtained. For the moment we simply observe that friction can greatly affect equilibrium conditions.

In this chapter we examine several aspects of friction. We will see that even though friction is not understood very well, we can deal with it effectively in many

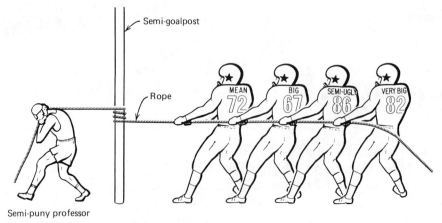

FIG. 9.1 The defensive linemen of the
Dallas Cowboys are unable to win a
tug-of-war.

cases. We will see further that while it is essential for productive work, it is also
a constant opponent to progress. Whole industries exist based on a desire to exploit
friction (brakes, belts, clutches, tires), and others are based on a need to overcome
it (ball bearings, lubricating oils, greases, low friction plastics).

9.1 STATIC AND DYNAMIC FRICTION

We begin our investigation of friction by considering a block weighing 100 N as
it sits on a flat horizontal table as shown in Fig. 9.2. Initially at rest, the weight
of 100 N would push down, and a reaction of 100 N pushes up normal to the
surface. We now apply a small horizontal force P as shown in the figure. At first
it is 1 N, then 5, then 10, but still the force P is too small to move the block. The
force P is being resisted by a friction force F, which is parallel to the surface, opposite
the applied force P, and perpendicular to the normal force N, as shown in Fig. 9.3.
In this free body diagram of the block, W and P are the applied loads. The force
N is the normal reaction (perpendicular to the table surface), and the friction force

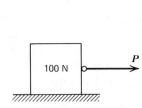

FIG. 9.2 A block at rest.

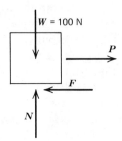

FIG. 9.3 Free body diagram of block
at rest.

is F. If the body is at rest, these forces must satisfy Newton's first law; hence:

$$\sum F_y = 0 = -100 + N$$
$$N = \mathbf{100\ N}$$

In this case the normal force is equal to the weight. Don't jump to the conclusion that that is always so; it's not. Proceeding, we write:

$$\sum F_x = 0 = P - F$$
$$\mathbf{F = P}$$

The friction force is equal to the applied force P, which is also a special case. The friction force is at first 1 N, then 5 then 10, going up with P, with the block just sitting there the whole time.

We continue to increase the force P until we reach 40 N, at which time the block is on the verge of moving. The slightest increase in force will cause it to move. However, the free body diagram in Fig. 9.3 and the preceding analysis are still valid. Thus:

$$N = 100\ N$$

and

$$F = P = 40\ N$$

This is a critical point in the life of a block on a plane. We call it *motion impending*. At this point there is a special relationship between the friction force F and the normal force N–namely, the ratio of F to N is a fixed value depending on the two materials involved and the condition of the contacting surfaces. This principle is expressed as follows:

$$\mu_s = \frac{F}{N} \qquad (9.1)$$

where μ (the Greek letter mu—equivalent to an English m) stands for the *coefficient of friction*. The subscript s that indicates we are talking about the *static coefficient of friction*, implying that the body is still at rest. It is important to note that Eq. 9.1 applies only when motion is impending. Before that the friction force was *less* than $\mu_s N$. A broader principle is that for a body at rest force F is always *less than or equal to* $\mu_s N$.

$$F \leq \mu_s N \qquad (9.2)$$

In other words, the friction force is limited by $\mu_s N$. As the applied load P exceeds $\mu_s N$, the "friction connection" breaks loose and the block starts to move.

Once the block starts moving, an interesting thing happens: The force required to keep it moving at a constant velocity goes down. The free body diagram of Fig. 9.3 still applies, as does the analysis above, and there is still a fixed relation between F and N, namely:

$$\mu_D = \frac{F}{N} \qquad (9.3)$$

TABLE 9.1   TYPICAL DRY
COEFFICIENTS OF FRICTION

Materials	μ_s	μ_D
Brake pad on cast iron	0.5	0.4
Steel on brass	0.6	0.4
Steel on steel	0.4	0.3
Tire on pavement	0.9	0.8
Wood on steel	0.4	0.3
Leather on steel	0.5	0.4

where the subscript D refers to the dynamic coefficient of friction. Thus we have three cases of interest.

1. Motion not impending:

$$F < \mu_s N \qquad (9.4)$$

2. Motion impending:

$$F = \mu_s N \qquad (9.5)$$

3. Motion:

$$F = \mu_D N \qquad (9.6)$$

In all three cases Newton's first law must be satisfied; but in the last two, and *only* in the last two, an additional friction equation must also be satisfied. Equation 9.6 also applies to accelerated motion, but only constant velocity motion is governed by Newton's first law.

Reliable values for μ_s and μ_D can be pretty hard to obtain, although handbook values are readily available. Table 9.1 gives some handbook values; note that it is labeled "typical." Values for a specific application are best obtained by testing. Table 9.1 will serve primarily as a source of values for the problems in this text and can be used for preliminary estimates of forces. It should not be relied on for final calculations because of the many factors that can affect the values. These coefficients are for dry friction. When surfaces are lubricated, the coefficients are reduced dramatically. Although some of the same concepts are applicable to the study of lubrication, this topic is considerably more complicated. Lubrication is treated in courses in fluid mechanics and machine design. Another more complex form of friction is the rolling resistance of wheels, which we will reserve for dynamics.

9.2   MORE CONCURRENT FORCE PROBLEMS

A careful inspection of Fig. 9.3 will reveal an unbalanced clockwise couple caused by F and P; its magnitude is P times the distance between the two forces. It was ignored in the preceding analysis, and we will ignore it when it is relatively small.

This, in effect, reduces the problem to one of concurrent forces. Judgment and experience will guide one in knowing when a problem may be safely reduced. When in doubt, treat it as a rigid body until you know otherwise. For the problems in this chapter, treat the body as a particle unless necessary dimensions are implied.

Remember that there are three cases to be considered in friction problems.

1. Motion not impending.
2. Motion impending.
3. Motion.

Example Problem 9.1

Determine the normal and friction forces acting on the block in Fig. 9.4 and state whether the block will move under this loading.

Solution

It is not obvious into which of the three friction categories this problem falls. We will assume category 1 (motion not impending), and we will verify the correctness of this assumption. A free body diagram is constructed in Fig. 9.5 with the friction force F opposing motion. Since we have assumed case 1, Eq. 9.4 applies and F is *not* equal to $\mu_s N$. Summing the forces vertically we get

$$\sum F_y = 0 = -180 + N + 30 \sin 20°$$
$$N = 180 - 30 \sin 20° = \mathbf{170\ N}$$

The normal force N is not equal to the weight. Summing the forces horizontally, we find:

$$\sum F_x = 0 = -F + 30 \cos 20°$$
$$F = \mathbf{28.2\ N}$$

We check our assumption by calculating the maximum friction force possible:

$$F_{max} = \mu_s N$$
$$F_{max} = 0.30(170) = 50.9\ N$$

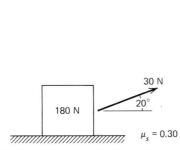

FIG. 9.4 Example Problem 9.1.

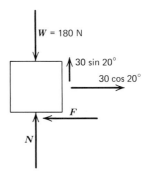

FIG. 9.5 Free body diagram for Example Problem 9.1.

Since

$$F = 28.2 < F_{max} = 50.9$$

the assumption is valid and the solution stands. The block will not move, the normal force is 170 N, and the friction force is 28.2 N. Note that in particular

$$F \neq \mu_s N \quad \text{and} \quad N \neq W$$

Example Problem 9.2

Find the force **P**, parallel to the plane, required to move the block down the plane in Fig. 9.6.

Solution

The problem statement places the problem in category 2 (motion impending). No assumption is needed. The free body diagram in Fig. 9.7 shows the applied forces **W** and **P**. The normal force **N** is drawn perpendicular to the plane, not vertical. Before drawing the friction force, it is worthwhile to indicate the sense of the impending motion (by the broken arrow). The friction force will oppose this sense. Thus **F** is drawn as shown and is equal to $\mu_s N$, since motion is impending. Summing the forces vertically, we get:

$$\sum F_y = 0 = -140 - P \sin 15° + F \sin 15° + N \cos 15°$$

and horizontally:

$$\sum F_x = 0 = P \cos 15° - F \cos 15° + N \sin 15°$$

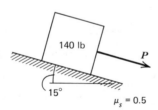

140 lb

P

15°

$\mu_s = 0.5$

FIG. 9.6   Example Problem 9.2.

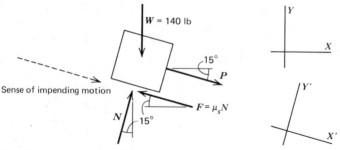

W = 140 lb

15°

P

Sense of impending motion

N

15°

$F = \mu_s N$

Y

X

Y'

X'

FIG. 9.7   Free body diagram for Example Problem 9.2.

With three unknowns, P, F, and N, things are not looking very good. However, a third equation is obtained from Eq. 9.5, namely:

$$F = \mu_s N$$

and we have three equations with three unknowns—a difficult but solvable problem. Substituting the last equation into the first two and reducing them, we have:

$$-P \sin 15° + (\cos 15° + \mu_s \sin 15°)N = 140 \qquad (9.7)$$

and

$$P \cos 15° + (\sin 15° - \mu_s \cos 15°)N = 0 \qquad (9.8)$$

Solving Eq. 9.8 for P gives

$$P = -\left(\frac{\sin 15° - 0.5 \cos 15°}{\cos 15°}\right)N$$

$$P = 0.232N \qquad (9.9)$$

Substituting this into Eq. 9.7 gives:

$$-(0.232N) \sin 15° + (\cos 15° + \mu_s \sin 15°)N = 140$$

and

$$N = \frac{140}{-0.0600 + 0.966 + 0.129} = \textbf{135 lb}$$

Substituting this into Eq. 9.9 gives:

$$P = 0.232 \, N = \textbf{31.4 lb}$$

Thus a 31.4 lb force is required to pull the block down the plane. The normal force is 135 lb. Once again it is not equal to the weight. This solution is conceptually very straightforward: sum the forces, use the friction equation, and solve for the unknowns. However, it is tacky algebraically. We can avoid the tackiness in this problem, and in many others, by rotating the coordinate system to fit the problem. This algebraic simplification is illustrated in the following alternate solution.

Alternate Solution

The free body diagram is as before (Fig. 9.7). Noting that three of the four forces are parallel or perpendicular to the inclined plane suggests that summing the forces in these directions, X' and Y', is desirable. We proceed by summing forces in the Y' direction, perpendicular to the plane:

$$\sum F_{Y'} = 0 = -140 \cos 15° + N$$
$$N = \textbf{135 lb}$$

Then summing in the X' direction:

$$\sum F_{X'} = 0 = +140 \sin 15° + P - F$$
$$P = F - 36.2$$

Adding the friction equation

$$F = 0.5 \text{ N}$$

and substituting into the equation above gives:

$$P = 0.5(135) - 36.2$$
$$\mathbf{P = 31.4 \text{ lb}}$$

Technically this alternate solution is no better than the original. Practically it is preferred because it is less work, and therefore less likely to be wrong.

9.3   THE ANGLE OF FRICTION

Return now to the initial problem of Fig. 9.2 where the 100-N block is on the verge of moving. The free body diagram is drawn in Fig. 9.3 and when motion is impending,

$$F = \mu_s N$$

The free body diagram is redrawn in Fig. 9.8, where we also show the resultant R of the friction force F and the normal force N. For a true concurrent force problem, W, P, and R should come together at a point. As we have mentioned, the dimensions are considered negligible, and we will not bother with this detail. The angle between R and N is labeled ϕ_f, and we observe:

$$\tan \phi_f = \frac{F}{N} \tag{9.10}$$

But

$$\mu_s = \frac{F}{N} \tag{9.1}$$

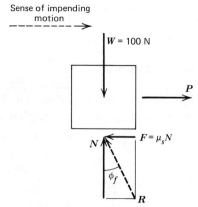

FIG. 9.8   Free body diagram applicable when motion is impending.

also; so we come to the following conclusion:

$$\tan \phi_f = \mu_s \tag{9.11}$$

The angle of ϕ_f is known as the *friction angle*, and we observe that when slipping is impending, the tangent of the friction angle equals the coefficient of friction. Before slipping is impending, the tangent of the friction angle is less than the coefficient of friction. Be sure to rotate the resultant R so that the friction component F opposes motion.

This concept is useful in obtaining graphical solutions to friction problems and in quickly determining whether a body will slip on an inclined plane.

Example Problem 9.3

Graphically find the force P required to move the block in Fig. 9.8 using the friction angle. $\mu_s = 0.4$. Also find the normal and friction forces.

Solution

The necessary free body diagram has been constructed in Fig. 9.8, where we consider the resultant force R to replace F and N. This gives us three concurrent forces, and we proceed to draw the force polygon in Fig. 9.9 after noting:

$$\tan \phi_f = \mu_s = 0.4$$
$$\phi_f = 21.8°$$

The weight is drawn vertically for 100 N, the horizontal P through its tail, and R at 21.8° from the vertical (N) through its head, giving the triangle shown. Finally P and R are scaled, giving:

$$P = 40 \text{ N} \rightarrow$$
$$R = 108 \text{ N at } 111.8°$$

Example Problem 9.4

Solve Example Problem 9.2 graphically, using the friction angle.

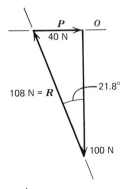

FIG. 9.9 Force polygon for Example Problem 9.3.

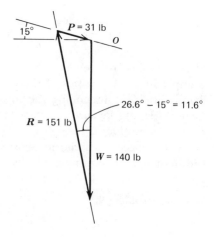

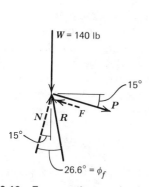

FIG. 9.10 Force acting on the free body in Example Problem 9.4.

FIG. 9.11 Force polygon for Example Problem 9.4.

Solution

The problem is shown in Fig. 9.6 and the free body diagram in Fig. 9.7. From Eq. 9.11, we have:

$$\tan \phi_f = \mu_s = 0.5$$
$$\phi_f = 26.6°$$

The forces from the free body diagram are redrawn in Fig. 9.10 showing the relationship of R with the other forces. The normal force N is 15° clockwise from the vertical. The resultant R is 26.6° counterclockwise from N or 11.6° counterclockwise from the vertical. The weight of 140 lb is drawn vertically in Fig. 9.11; then lines parallel to P and R are drawn through tail and head, respectively, completing the force triangle. Finally, the forces are scaled, giving:

$$P = 31 \text{ lb at } -15.0°$$
$$R = 151 \text{ lb at } 101.6°$$

The concept of the friction angle is also very useful in determining the coefficient of friction. A block on a plane is shown in Fig. 9.12. The plane is tilted very slowly until the block moves. At the instant motion begins, the plane will be tilted to the friction angle ϕ_f and the coefficient of friction can be calculated from Eq. 9.11. Proof of this is left for a student problem.

9.4   INCLINED PLANES AND WEDGES

One of the simplest and earliest of all machines is the inclined plane. Remember, a machine amplifies force or motion. The inclined plane in Fig. 9.6 can be used as such if we reverse the force P. We can determine the force P required to push the block up this plane by reversing the sense of P and the friction force F in the free body diagram in Fig. 9.7. The analysis is similar to Example Problem 9.2, and we get a force of 104 lb required to lift the 140-lb block. This illustrates the

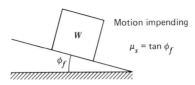

FIG. 9.12 Inclined plane method of determining the coefficient of friction.

inclined plane's machine characteristic, although in this case, because of the high coefficient of friction, the machine is not a very good one. If the plane were friction-less, the 140-lb block could be lifted with 36.2 lb.

A second simple machine is the wedge, an inclined plane that moves (i.e., in-stead of the block). There is really no difference mechanically between an inclined plane and a wedge, although in actual problems wedges turn out to be a little more complicated, because frequently more than one surface has friction acting on it. Wedges are still used to obtain a mechanical advantage when moving large loads. The analysis of wedges does not require additional theory. It does require that we use the theory we have very carefully and systematically. The solution of wedge problems often calls for two free body diagrams and simultaneous equations, as illustrated in Example Problems 9.5 and 9.6.

Example Problem 9.5

Find the force P required to lift the block A in Fig. 9.13, and find the reaction on block A at the wall. On all surfaces except the roller on the vertical wall, which is frictionless, $\mu_s = 0.15$.

Solution

We have a choice of three free body diagrams: block A, block B, and blocks A and B combined. We will draw block A first. It is very important to recognize that for motion to occur, block A must go up and block B must go to the right. These motions will occur simultaneously. Block A cannot go up unless B goes right, and vice versa. In Fig. 9.14 we show block A with its weight. The reaction

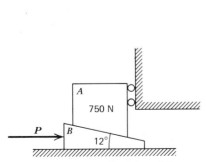

FIG. 9.13 Example Problem 9.5.

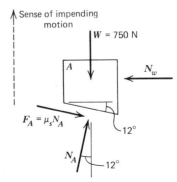

FIG. 9.14 Free body diagram for block A, Example Problem 9.5.

at the wall is normal to it and labeled N_w. Because of the roller there is no friction force. If there were, it would be down, opposing the *relative* motion seen by an observer on the wall. We proceed to the interaction between the two blocks. The sense of the normal force N_A is easily obtained; and since motion is impending, we know that

$$F_A = \mu_s N_A$$

The sense of F_A is another matter, and it requires careful analysis. Previously when we were unsure of the sense of a force, we learned to guess and let the sign system and algebra take care of it. *That is not a valid approach* for friction forces when motion is impending. Assuming the sense of impending motion fixes the sense of the friction force, that is, it opposes the relative motion. Arbitrarily assigning an incorrect sense to the friction force will change the problem or introduce a contradiction. So the sense of the friction force must be accurately determined.

Now friction resists relative motion. The absolute motion is A slipping up vertically, while B slides past it to the right. But what will be the *relative* motion of A with respect to B? That is, how would an observer on B view the motion of A? Would he not see A slide off to his left? He would! And the force F_A exerted by B on A will *oppose* this relative motion and is therefore down and to the right as shown. Alternately, one can think of the block B slipping to the right and attempting to pull block A to the right by friction. Get the sense of F_A any way you choose, but you must get it right.

We now have a concurrent force problem with three unknowns: F_A, N_A, and N_W. We have the two force equations and the friction equation, so the problem is solvable at this point. However, in many other problems the solution must be postponed until a second free body diagram has been drawn. We proceed with:

$$\sum F_x = 0 = -N_W + F_A \cos 12° + N_A \sin 12° \qquad (9.12)$$
$$\sum F_y = 0 = -750 - F_A \sin 12° + N_A \cos 12° \qquad (9.13)$$

and

$$F_A = \mu_s N_A = 0.15 N_A \qquad (9.14)$$

Substituting Eq. 9.14 into Eq. 9.13 yields:

$$-0.15 N_A \sin 12° + N_A \cos 12° = 750$$
$$0.947 N_A = 750$$
$$N_A = 792 \text{ N}$$
$$F_A = 0.15(792) = 119 \text{ N}$$

Substituting these into Eq. 9.12 gives:

$$N_W = 119 \cos 12° + 792 \sin 12°$$
$$\mathbf{N_W = 281 \text{ N}}$$

We need a second free body diagram (block B, Fig. 9.15). A sense of impending motion must be chosen consistent with that used for the free body diagram for block A. Inconsistency will lead to contradictions. The senses of the applied force P and the normals N_A and N_B are easily obtained. The friction forces F_A and F_B are chosen to oppose motion. Note that impending motion simultaneously occurs on both surfaces, so Eq. 9.1 applies at both surfaces. An independent check of the sign of F_A can be obtained by comparing the two free body diagrams. Recalling Newton's third law, F_A and N_A should be equal and opposite in the two diagrams (Figs. 9.14 and 9.15), as they are.

For this free body diagram we have originally five unknowns. Since we obtained F_A and N_A above, that leaves three, and we have the two force equations and the friction equations:

$$\sum F_x = 0 = P - N_A \sin 12° - F_A \cos 12° - F_B \qquad (9.15)$$
$$\sum F_y = 0 = N_B - N_A \cos 12° + F_A \sin 12°$$
$$N_B = 792 \cos 12° - 119 \sin 12°$$
$$N_B = 750 \text{ N}$$

and

$$F_B = 0.15 N_B$$

Substituting into Eq. 9.15:

$$P = +792 \sin 12° + 119 \cos 12° + 0.15(750)$$
$$P = 393 \text{ N}$$

It should be observed that a wedge is really just a form of inclined plane. In Fig. 9.13 the plane (wedge B) is moved rather than the block (A). If the block A were to be pushed up the plane B (think of the wedge B as being fixed), the force N_W found in Example Problem 9.5 would be the force required to push it, and the normal and friction forces, N_A and F_A, would also be as found. It should also be observed that graphical solutions are frequently easier for this type of problem, as will be shown now.

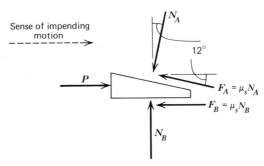

FIG. 9.15 Free body diagram for wedge B, Example Problem 9.5.

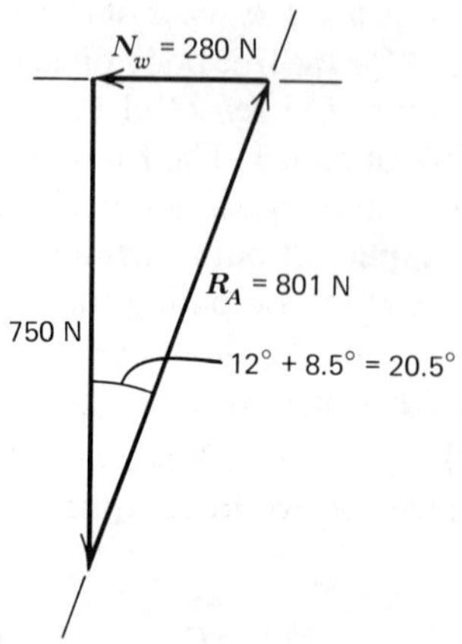

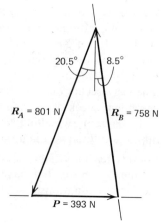

$N_w = 280$ N

$R_A = 801$ N

750 N

$12° + 8.5° = 20.5°$

FIG. 9.16 Force polygon for block A, Example Problem 9.6.

20.5°   8.5°

$R_A = 801$ N $R_B = 758$ N

$P = 393$ N

FIG. 9.17 Force polygon for wedge B, Example Problem 9.6.

Example Problem 9.6

Graphically find the force P required to push the block A in Fig. 9.13 up the wall. The conditions are the same as in Example Problem 9.5.

Solution

The free body diagram of block A in Fig. 9.14 is modified by replacing F_A and N_A with their resultant R_A, which is 8.5° clockwise from N_A or 20.5° clockwise from the vertical. (Remember $\mu_s = \tan \phi_f$.) The resulting force triangle is shown in Fig. 9.16 where the scaled values are given. Proceeding to the free body diagram of the wedge B (Fig. 9.15), R_A replaces N_A and F_A, and R_B replaces N_B and F_B, making an angle of 8.5° counterclockwise to N_B. The force triangle is drawn in Fig. 9.17, using R_A from Fig. 9.16, and P is scaled to be:

$$P = 393 \text{ N}$$

9.5 INCLINED PLANES AND SQUARE THREADED SCREWS

We have just considered the inclined plane as a wedge. Now we observe that if an inclined plane is wrapped about an axis as in Fig. 9.18, it becomes a screw. In this figure the length of the plane is equal to the circumference of the screw, πD. Its rise is labeled L. The angle of incline for the plane is θ_L, where:

$$\tan \theta_L = \frac{L}{\pi D} \tag{9.16}$$

The advance from one thread to the next on a screw is referred to as the *lead* (or pitch), and thus the label L. The angle θ_L is called the *lead angle* (or pitch angle). Threads are used for mechanical advantage on various types of screws and

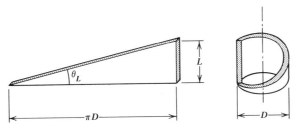

FIG. 9.18 An inclined plane wrapped around an axis becomes a screw.

fasteners. On fasteners the threads are usually not square. Threads are still square on many force and power transmission devices such as a jack or power screws. We will limit our attention to square threads; conventional threads are discussed in texts on machine design.

Lifting a load with a screw (pushing it up the plane) is modeled in Fig. 9.19 by an inclined plane. A free body diagram of this problem is drawn in Fig. 9.20, where P is the load required to move the load up the plane, and W is the load to be moved or force to be exerted. The friction force resists relative motion. We have replaced the normal force N and the friction force F with the resultant force R, which makes an angle of ϕ_f, the friction angle, with the normal force. Summing the forces vertically gives:

$$\sum F_y = 0 = -W + R\cos(\phi_f + \theta_L)$$

from which we have:

$$R = \frac{W}{\cos(\phi_f + \theta_L)}$$

Summing forces horizontally gives:

$$\sum F_x = 0 = P - R(\sin\phi_f + \theta_L)$$

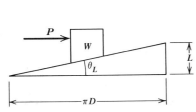

FIG. 9.19 Analyzing a screw as an inclined plane.

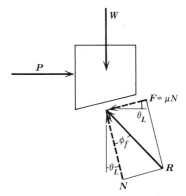

FIG. 9.20 Free body diagram for lifting a load with a screw.

Substituting R from above and solving for P gives:

$$P = \frac{W \sin(\phi_f + \theta_L)}{\cos(\phi_f + \theta_L)}$$

from which

$$P = W \tan(\phi_f + \theta_L) \tag{9.17}$$

This gives the force P required to *lift* a load. Often we need to know the torque T required to turn this screw. Figure 9.21 shows a typical jack handle arrangement, from which:

$$T = P\frac{D}{2}$$

Substituting for P from Eq. 9.17, we have:

$$T = \frac{WD}{2} \tan(\phi_f + \theta_L) \tag{9.18}$$

as the torque required to lift a load.

The force Q required to turn the jack handle in Fig. 9.21 is applied at a distance r from the center of the jack.

For equilibrium, we have

$$Qr = \frac{PD}{2} = T$$

and from Eq. 9.18:

$$Q = \frac{WD}{2r} \tan(\phi_f + \theta_L) \tag{9.19}$$

If a similar analysis is made for pushing the load down the incline in Fig. 9.19, we get:

$$P = W \tan(\phi_f - \theta_L) \tag{9.20}$$

and

$$T = \frac{WD}{2} \tan(\phi_f - \theta_L) \tag{9.21}$$

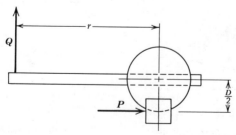

FIG. 9.21   Top view of screw.

In Eq. 9.20 P will be positive if ϕ_f exceeds θ_L; that is, a force is required to lower the load. Such screws are called *self-locking*. On the other hand if θ_L exceeds ϕ_f, the load will come down on its own. In such cases Eq. 9.20 gives a negative value for P, meaning that a load is required to hold the weight in place. Note that to lift a load, the weight and friction force must be overcome. In lowering a load the friction force still must be overcome, but the weight works for us.

Example Problem 9.7

The jackscrew shown in Fig. 9.22 is to lift the building resting on it by exerting 3500 lb. The screw is 1.50 in. in diameter, and the jack handle is 18.0 in. long (from the jack centerline). Find the force required to turn the handle if the house is lifted 0.250 in. for each complete turn of the screw. The coefficient of friction is 0.20.

Solution

From Eq. 9.16 the lead angle is:

$$\tan \phi_L = \frac{L}{\pi D} = \frac{0.250}{\pi(1.50)} = 0.0531$$

$$\phi_L = 3.04°$$

The friction angle is:

$$\phi_f = \tan^{-1} 0.2$$
$$\phi_f = 11.3°$$

and

$$\phi_f + \theta_L = 11.3° + 3.04° = 14.3°$$

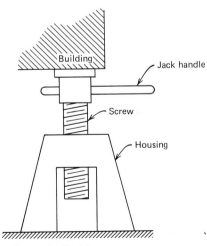

FIG. 9.22   Jackscrew for Example Problem 9.7.

By Eq. 9.19, the required force is:

$$Q = \frac{WD}{2r} \tan(\phi_f + \theta_L)$$

$$Q = \frac{3500 \text{ lb } (1.5 \text{ in.})}{2(18 \text{ in.})} \tan 14.3°$$

$$Q = 37.3 \text{ lb}$$

This is a very small force, and most of it is to overcome friction. If the screw were frictionless, only 7.74 lb would be required! Since we are lifting 3500 lb with a force of 37.3 lb, the mechanical advantage is nearly 100. By reducing the friction, we can increase this to nearly 500, and we see that the screwjack is a very effective machine.

Example Problem 9.8

Is the screw in Example Problem 9.7 self-locking?

Solution

$$\phi_f = 11.3°$$
$$\theta_L = 3.04°$$

Therefore

$$\phi_f > \theta_L$$

and *yes*, the screw is self-locking. A force must be applied to lower the building.

9.6 RIGID BODY PROBLEMS

Thus far, our analysis has involved bodies that can be treated as particles. This covers a large class of problems, but not all. To extend our discussion to plane rigid bodies, we need no additional theory. Once again we use the tools we have developed to solve a new class of problem. These tools are:

1. Drawing a complete and accurate free body diagram.
2. Applying Newton's first law. We'll have a moment equation now.
3. Applying the friction law when motion occurs or is impending.
4. Solving for the unknowns.

In carrying out step 3, it will still be useful to show the sense of the assumed motion. Be certain that the friction forces oppose this motion. Also remember that when a rigid body moves, it moves everywhere. Last, there may be more than one friction equation, so we may be solving for four or more unknowns.

Example Problem 9.9

The book shown in Fig. 9.23 weighs 3 lb and is 12 in. long. Find the reactions at the wall and shelf and the angle θ at which the book will slip if the coefficient of friction is zero at the wall and 0.20 at the shelf.

Solution

A free body diagram is drawn in Fig. 9.24 with the sense of impending motion down and to the left as indicated. The friction force F_B opposes the impending

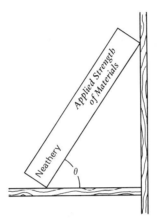

FIG. 9.23 Example Problem 9.9.

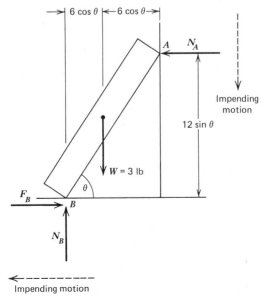

FIG. 9.24 Free body diagram for Example Problem 9.9.

motion. There are four unknowns on the free body diagram, F_B, N_B, N_A, and θ; and four equations including the friction equation. So solution is possible. Proceeding, we write:

$$\sum F_y = 0 = -3 + N_B$$
$$N_B = 3.00 \text{ lb}$$

Since motion is impending, we have:

$$F_B = \mu N_B = 0.2(3.00) = 0.60 \text{ lb}$$
$$\sum F_x = 0 = F_B - N_A$$
$$N_A = 0.60 \text{ lb}$$

Now using the moment equation and neglecting the thickness of the book:

$$\sum M_B = 0 = N_A(12 \sin \theta) - 3(6 \cos \theta)$$
$$12 N_A \sin \theta = 18 \cos \theta$$

$$\frac{\sin \theta}{\cos \theta} = \frac{18}{12 N_A}$$

$$\tan \theta = \frac{18}{12(0.60)} = 2.5$$

$$\theta = 68.2°$$

Motion is impending at this angle. When θ is greater than 68.2° the book will not slip. The normal force N_B will still be 3.00 lb. Because of a shorter moment arm for the weight (6 cos θ), N_A will be less than 0.60 lb, and F_B will be less than μN_B.

Example Problem 9.10

A race car weighing 10 kN (Fig. 9.25) goes around a corner so fast that a centrifugal force of 6 kN is generated as shown. Will this car roll? If it does not roll, find the reactions at the wheels. The coefficient of friction at the wheels is 0.80.

Solution

In this problem, and many similar problems, the body may tip (roll), slip, or do neither. We assume one of the three, work the problem, and confirm or

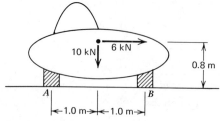

FIG. 9.25 Example Problem 9.10.

reject the assumption. If an assumption must be rejected, we proceed to the next one. We assume tipping first. The free body diagram is shown in Fig. 9.26. Since the vehicle is on the verge of tipping to the right, there will be no normal force (and, therefore, no friction force) at A. The friction force at B is not μN_B generally. Summing moments about B gives

$$\sum M_B = -0.8(6) + 1(10) = +5.20 \text{ kN·m}$$

There is a resultant counterclockwise moment of the vehicle and a reaction at A will be required to balance it.

The car does not roll.

If the resultant moment were clockwise, rolling or tipping would occur.

The free body diagram for no tipping is drawn in Fig. 9.27, which is valid regardless of whether slipping occurs. We assume that slipping is impending, in which case:

$$F_B = \mu_s N_B \qquad (9.22)$$

and

$$F_A = \mu_s N_A \qquad (9.23)$$

Summing moments about A gives:

$$\sum M_A = 0 = +2(N_B) - 0.8(6) - 1(10) \qquad (9.24)$$

$$N_B = \frac{14.8}{2} = \textbf{7.40 kN}$$

$$\sum F_y = 0 = N_A - 10 + N_B \qquad (9.25)$$
$$N_A = 10 - 7.40 = \textbf{2.60 kN}$$

and

$$F_B = \mu_s N_B = 0.8(7.4) = 5.92 \text{ kN}$$
$$F_A = 0.8(2.60) = 2.08 \text{ kN}$$

However, if we now sum forces horizontally, we get:

$$\sum F_x = 6 - F_A - F_B = -2.0 \neq 0$$

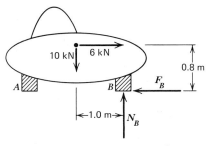

FIG. 9.26 Free body diagram for Example Problem 9.10, assuming tipping.

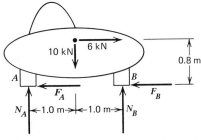

FIG. 9.27 Free body diagram for Example Problem 9.10 without tipping.

Since the resultant friction force available is 8 kN (5.92 + 2.08), and the applied horizontal force is only 6.0 kN, slipping does not occur and Eqs. 9.22 and 9.23 are not valid. The second assumption is also rejected.

Last, we assume (the logic should not be overwhelming) that slipping does not occur. The free body diagram of Fig. 9.27 is valid, as are Eqs. 9.24 and 9.25, and the results are:

$$N_B = 7.40 \text{ kN}$$
$$N_A = 2.60 \text{ kN}$$

Summing the forces horizontally gives:

$$F_x = 0 = -F_A - F_B + 6$$

and

$$F_A + F_B = 6$$

which is the best we can do, since

$$F_A \neq \mu N_A$$

and

$$F_B \neq \mu N_B$$

This portion of the problem is actually statically indeterminate. We cannot determine F_A and F_B.

To recap, we started with assumption of tipping with the free body diagram of Fig. 9.26, which was rejected because the unbalanced moment was counter-clockwise, opposite the assumed sense of tipping. We then assumed slipping with the free body diagram of Fig. 9.27 and let the friction forces equal the coefficient of friction times the normal force. This resulted in an unbalanced force to the left, opposite the assumed sense of slipping, which contradicted this assumption. Finally (Eureka!) we assumed no slipping and found the normal forces but could not find F_A and F_B because the problem is statically indeterminate.

9.7   BELT FRICTION

In the introduction to this chapter I revealed my plan to defeat the Dallas Cowboys' defensive line in a tug-of-war. Now we will see how the plan works. Belt friction is very common in industry. It is a cheap way to transmit mechanical power that tolerates considerable misalignment and shock loading. Generally V-belts are used today. We will limit our attention to flat belts, ropes, and cables, leaving V-belts and others to texts on machine design. (The principles are the same.)

Figure 9.28 shows a rope or belt wrapped over a horizontal post. The angle subtended by the arc from P_1 to P_2 is called the angle of contact, and we label it β (beta, the Greek equivalent to B). T_2 is the tension in the belt pulling counter-clockwise, and T_1 is the tension opposing it. Both T_1 and T_2 are tangent to the

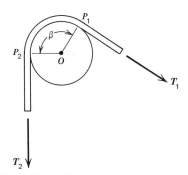

FIG. 9.28 Belt friction.

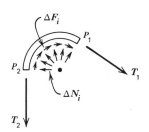

FIG. 9.29 Free body diagram for belt over the angle of contact.

post at their respective points of contact, P_1 and P_2. We examine the condition when the post is stationary, and the belt is on the verge of slipping counterclockwise. In this case friction works against motion and T_2 is greater than T_1.

In Fig. 9.29 we draw a free body diagram of the belt from point P_1 to point P_2. The post will exert a normal force ΔN_i, which will push out on the belt. The direction of these forces is normal to the curve, so they change continually from P_1 to P_2 as shown in Fig. 9.29. Similarly the friction forces ΔF_i are tangent to the curve from P_1 to P_2. The friction forces oppose the impending motion of the belt. Looking at the free body diagram it should be clear that T_2 is greater than T_1. Having a completed free body diagram, we next apply Newton's first law. However, you may have difficulty in handling the ever-changing direction of ΔF_i and ΔN_i. I certainly do, and will avoid the problem by drawing a free body diagram of an elemental piece of the belt as shown in Fig. 9.30. Here the normal direction is designated Y and the tangential X. We have a very short length of belt Δs spanning the arc $\Delta \theta$. The tension to the right is T and to the left some incrementally greater value T', where

$$T' = T + \Delta T$$

The normal force is ΔN_i and the friction force is ΔF_i. These forces act in the Y and X directions, respectively.

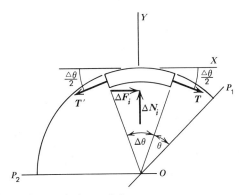

FIG. 9.30 Free body diagram of elemental piece of belt.

We can apply Newton's first law to this elemental piece of belt by summing forces in the X and Y directions. After some algebraic manipulation and allowing $\Delta\theta$ to approach zero, we end up with a differential equation for this problem:

$$\frac{dT}{T} = \mu\, d\theta \tag{9.26}$$

Readers unfamiliar with integration may drop down to Eq. 9.29 and accept this development on faith. The effect of putting all the elements from P_1 to P_2 together may be obtained by integrating Eq. 9.26 as θ goes from 0 to β. This gives:

$$\int_{T_1}^{T_2} \frac{dT}{T} = \int_0^\beta \mu\, d\theta \tag{9.27}$$

The tension T_1 and the angle 0 correspond to the conditions at P_1 and constitute the lower limits of integration. Similarly T_2 and β correspond to P_2 and the upper limits. Integrating both sides yields:

$$\ln T \Big|_{T_1}^{T_2} = \mu\theta \Big|_0^\beta$$

which becomes:

$$\ln T_2 - \ln T_1 = \mu(\beta - 0) \tag{9.28}$$

Remember that:

$$\ln\left(\frac{a}{b}\right) = \ln a - \ln b$$

so Eq. 9.28 becomes:

$$\ln\left(\frac{T_2}{T_1}\right) = \mu\beta \tag{9.29}$$

Also remember that:

$$\ln(e^a) = a$$

and

$$e^{\ln a} = a$$

So Eq. 9.29 is transformed by taking the antilog to:

$$\frac{T_2}{T_1} = e^{\mu\beta} \tag{9.30}$$

Equations 9.29 and 9.30 are two forms of the same principle: Taking the logarithm of Eq. 9.30 brings us back to Eq. 9.29. Use whichever form is convenient.

These equations state the basic principle of belt friction. They apply whether we are talking about a rope wrapped around a post or power being transmitted by a pulley and a flat belt at high speed. They say that the ratio of the tensions in a belt (T_2/T_1) equals e raised to the $\mu\beta$ power. Since μ and β are both greater than 0, $e^{\mu\beta}$ must be greater than one, and once again, T_2 must be greater than T_1. The ratio T_2/T_1 is dimensionless, and so is the right-hand side of Eq. 9.30.

The exponent must also be dimensionless, and $\mu\beta$ is. The angle is dimensionless when measured in radians, so β in Eqs. 9.29 and 9.30 must be in radians. Also keep in mind that this equation is valid only if slipping is impending.

Example Problem 9.11

The puny professor in Fig. 9.1 pulls on the rope with a force of 25 lb. What force must the four football players exert to overcome him? The coefficient of friction is 0.3.

Solution

Since the rope is wrapped around the post three times, we have:

$$\beta = 3(2\pi) = 6\pi \text{ rad}$$

and

$$\mu\beta = 0.3(6\pi) = 5.655$$

(For greater *repeatability* of answers, you may want to carry exponents to four significant figures). Then:

$$e^{\mu\beta} = e^{5.655} = 286$$

If your calculator does not have an e^x key, then with 5.655 displayed, punch the inverse key (INV) and the natural logarithm (ln x) key. The calculator should now display 286. From Eq. 9.30, we get:

$$T_2 = e^{\mu\beta} T_1$$
$$T_2 = 286(25 \text{ lb}) = \textbf{7140 lb}$$

and I win the tug-of-war! Be sure to use T_1 for the smaller force.

Example Problem 9.12

Pulley A in Fig. 9.31 drives pulley B with a moment of 3.0 kN·m. Both pulleys rotate clockwise. For a coefficient of friction of 0.25, find the tension between points 1 and 2 and between points 3 and 4. The pulley is 200 mm in diameter.

Solution

A free body diagram is drawn in Fig. 9.32. The main purpose of this diagram is to establish which portion of the belt is to be labeled T_1 and which is T_2.

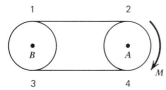

FIG. 9.31 Example Problem 9.12.

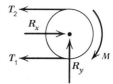

FIG. 9.32 Free body diagram for Example Problem 9.12.

The moment M will be transmitted by friction acting in the same clockwise direction. Thus the upper belt will have greater tension and will be labeled T_2. Summing moments about the center of the pulley, we have:

$$\sum M_0 = 0 = +rT_2 - M - rT_1$$

from which:

$$T_2 - T_1 = \frac{M}{r}$$

$$T_2 - T_1 = \frac{3.0 \text{ kN} \cdot \text{m}}{0.100 \text{ m}} = 30.0 \text{ kN} \qquad (9.31)$$

From Eq. 9.30:

$$\frac{T_2}{T_1} = e^{\mu\beta}$$

The angle of contact β is $180°$ or π rad. Thus:

$$T_2 = e^{\mu\beta} T_1 = e^{0.25(\pi)} T_1$$
$$T_2 = e^{0.7854} T_1 = 2.19 T_1$$

Substituting into Eq. 9.31 gives:

$$2.19 T_1 - T_1 = 30.0$$

$$T_1 = \frac{30.0}{1.19} = 25.1 \text{ kN}$$

This is the tension from point 3 to 4, so:

$$T_{3-4} = T_1 = 25.1 \text{ kN}$$

Then:

$$T_2 = 2.19(25.1) = 55.1 \text{ kN}$$
$$\mathbf{T_{1-2} = T_2 = 55.1 \text{ kN}}$$

9.8 SUMMARY

We have seen a number of applications of friction. There are many more, and a number may be found in standard texts on machine design. Our approach to friction problems is a straightforward application of previous principles (i.e., drawing a free body diagram and summing the forces). There are three possibilities to consider.

1. Slipping not impending:

$$F < \mu_s N$$

2. Slipping impending:

$$F = \mu_s N$$

3. Slipping:

$$F = \mu_D N$$

In the last two cases the sense of F must be accurately determined and shown on the free body diagram (i.e., opposing relative motion). Cases 2 and 3 provide additional equations that allow us to solve for additional unknowns. Sometimes the algebra may be simplified by using a coordinate system parallel to the plane of possible motion.

Problems may also be simplified by using the angle of friction and a graphical solution. The angle of friction ϕ_f is defined by:

$$\tan \phi_f = \mu$$

It is the angle the resultant of the normal and friction forces makes with the normal. It may be used only when slipping occurs or is impending.

Wedges are another form of inclined plane. The difference lies in whether the workpiece or the plane is moved. When the plane is moved, it is called a wedge. Wedge problems usually involve multiple friction surfaces and are typically more complicated, requiring multiple free body diagrams and simultaneous equations. In drawing free body diagrams, care must be taken to show the proper sense for friction forces. A screw also is a form of inclined plane. The torque required to lift a load on a screw was found to be:

$$T = \frac{WD}{2} \tan(\phi_f + \theta_L)$$

where ϕ_f is the friction angle and θ_L is the lead angle. We also found that screws were self-locking when the friction angle exceeds the lead angle.

For rigid bodies we have the three equations for Newton's first law plus one or more friction equations. If slipping is impending, it is impending at all contact surfaces.

Last, we applied friction principles to belt drives or friction wraps using ropes or cables. The equation governing this situation is:

$$\frac{T_2}{T_1} = e^{\mu\beta}$$

or alternately:

$$\ln\left(\frac{T_2}{T_1}\right) = \mu\beta$$

PROBLEMS

Many of the following problems may be solved analytically or graphically. Solve the problems analytically unless your instructor or the problem specifies a graphical solution.

9.1 For each figure shown find the normal and frictional force assuming no motion takes place. Check this assumption.

    (a) Fig. 9.33   (b) Fig. 9.34   (c) Fig. 9.35   (d) Fig. 9.36

9.2 Find the additional force parallel to the plane required to move the block to the left in the indicated figure.

    (a) Fig. 9.33   (b) Fig. 9.34

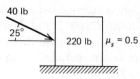

FIG. 9.33 Problems 9.1a, 9.2a, 9.10a.

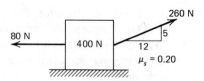

FIG. 9.34 Problems 9.1b, 9.2b, 9.10b.

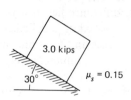

FIG. 9.35 Problems 9.1c, 9.3a, 9.11a.

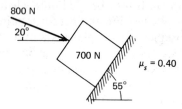

FIG. 9.36 Problems 9.1d, 9.3b, 9.11b.

9.3 Find the additional force parallel to the plane required to move the block up the plane in the indicated figure.

(a) Fig. 9.35   (b) Fig. 9.36

9.4 Find the force P in Fig. 9.37 required to:

(a) Hold the block in place

(b) Push the block up the plane (if possible)

9.5 Find the weight W in Fig. 9.38 required to:

(a) Hold the block in place

(b) Move the block up the plane

9.6 Let $P = 0$ in Fig. 9.39 and assume no motion occurs. Find the tension in the cable and verify the assumption.

9.7 Find the tension in the cable and the force P required to move the block to the left in Fig. 9.39 when:

(a) $\theta = 0°$ (b) $\theta = 30°$ (c) $\theta = -30°$

9.8 The plane shown in Fig. 9.40 is tilted slowly. The block begins to slip when θ reaches the indicated value. Find the normal and friction forces and find the coefficient of friction.

(a) $W = 40$ kN, $\theta = 25°$ (b) $W = 80$ N, $\theta = 32°$

(c) $W = 20$ tons, $\theta = 18°$ (d) $W = 12.5$ oz., $\theta = 10°$

9.9 For Problem 9.8, show the effect of the weight and the angle θ on the coefficient of friction.

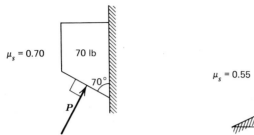

FIG. 9.37 Problems 9.4, 9.12.

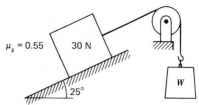

FIG. 9.38 Problems 9.5, 9.13.

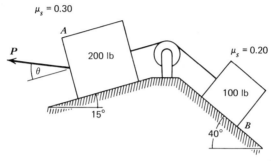

FIG. 9.39 Problems 9.6, 9.7.

9.10 Using the friction angle, graphically find the additional force parallel to the plane required to move the block to the left in the indicated figure.

    (a) Fig. 9.33   (b) Fig. 9.34

9.11 Using the friction angle, graphically find the additional force parallel to the plane required to move the block up the plane in the indicated figure.

    (a) Fig. 9.35   (b) Fig. 9.36

9.12 Using the friction angle, graphically find the force P in Fig. 9.37 required to:

    (a) Hold the block in place

    (b) Push the block up the plane (if possible)

9.13 Using the friction angle, graphically find the weight W in Fig. 9.38 required to:

    (a) Hold the block in place   (b) Move the block up the plane

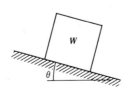

FIG. 9.40 Problems 9.8, 9.9.

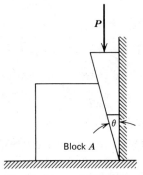

Block A

FIG. 9.41 Problems 9.14, 9.15.

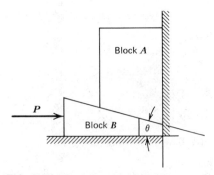

Block A

P

Block B

θ

FIG. 9.42 Problems 9.16, 9.17.

9.14 For Fig. 9.41, find the force *P* required to move block *A*. If the weight of the wedge is negligible, the vertical wall is frictionless, and the remaining surfaces have the same coefficient of friction. The following conditions apply.

	Weight *A*	Coefficient of Friction	θ
(a)	800 lb	0.20	10°
(b)	6.00 N	0.08	8.0°
(c)	120 MN	0.35	20°

9.15 Work the assigned part of Problem 9.14 if the vertical wall has the same coefficient of friction as the other surfaces.

9.16 Find the force *P* required to lift block *A* if the vertical wall is frictionless and all other surfaces have the same coefficient of friction in Fig. 9.42. The following conditions apply.

	Weight *A*	Weight *B*	Coefficient of Friction	θ
(a)	2000 lb	0	0.20	12°
(b)	400 N	0	0.30	10°
(c)	1200 kN	500 kN	0.40	25°

9.17 Solve the assigned part of Problem 9.16 if the vertical wall has the same coefficient of friction as the other surfaces.

9.18 A building (Fig. 9.43) is to be lifted by driving the wedge with force *P*. Find this force if the load from the building is 8 tons, the angle of the wedge is 12°, and the coefficient of friction for all surfaces is 0.17. Neglect the weight of the wedges.

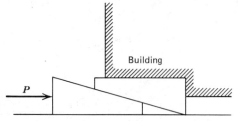

Building

P

FIG. 9.43 Problems 9.18, 9.19, 9.20, 9.21.

9.19 A building (Fig. 9.43) is to be lifted by driving the wedge with force P. Find the force if the load from the building is 70 kN, the angle of the wedge is 10°, and the coefficient of friction for all surfaces is 0.22. Neglect the weight of the wedges.

9.20 If the building in Fig. 9.43 exerts a downward force of 12.0 tons and the wedge angle is 12°, find the minimum coefficient of friction so that the building will stay in place without a holding force (i.e., $P = 0$).

9.21 If the building in Fig. 9.43 exerts a downward force of 70 kN and the wedge angle is 10°, find the minimum coefficient of friction so that the building will stay in place without a holding force (i.e., $P = 0$).

9.22 A jackscrew has a diameter of 50 mm. It supports a load of 400 kN. It has a lead of 20 mm and a coefficient of friction of 0.15.

(a) Find the torque required to raise the load.

(b) Is the screw self-locking? If not, find the torque required to hold the load in place. If so, find the torque required to lower it.

9.23 A jackscrew has a diameter of 100 mm. It supports a load of 1500 kN. It has a lead of 20 mm and a coefficient of friction of 0.15.

(a) Find the torque required to raise the load.

(b) Is the screw self-locking? If not, find the torque required to hold the load in place. If so, find the torque required to lower it.

9.24 A jackscrew has a diameter of 0.50 in. It supports a load of 600 lb. It has a lead of 0.125 in. and a coefficient of friction of 0.15.

(a) Find the torque required to raise the load.

(b) Is the screw self-locking? If not, find the torque required to hold the load in place. If so, find the torque required to lower it.

9.25 A jackscrew has a diameter of 4.00 in. It supports a load of 10 tons. It has a lead of 0.50 in. and a coefficient of friction of 0.20.

(a) Find the torque required to raise the load.

(b) Is the screw self-locking? If not, find the torque required to hold the load in place. If so, find the torque required to lower it.

9.26 The food press shown in Fig. 9.44 has a 6-in. handle (to the centerline of the screw) and a screw 0.75 in. in diameter. If the screw must be turned six times to advance 1.00 in., and the coefficient of friction is 0.20, find the compression force that can be delivered by a 10-lb force on the handle. How much is the force increased if the coefficient of friction is reduced to 0.05?

9.27 The food press shown in Fig. 9.44 has a 200-mm handle (to the centerline of the screw) and a screw 30 mm in diameter. If the screw must be turned six times to advance 30 mm, and the coefficient of friction is 0.30, find the compression force that can be delivered by a 50-N force on the handle. How much is the force increased if the coefficient of friction is reduced to 0.03?

9.28 The automobile shown in Fig. 9.45 weighs 2200 lb. The wheelbase $(a+b+c)$ is 120 in. A screw jack like the one in Fig. 9.22 is placed 20 in. in front of the rear wheel (c) and the vehicle's center of gravity is 30 in. in front of the rear

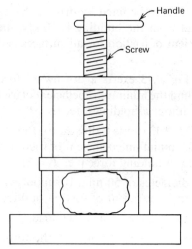

FIG. 9.44   Problems 9.26, 9.27.

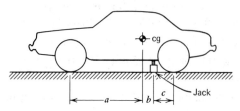

FIG. 9.45   Problems 9.28, 9.29.

wheel $(b + c)$. Assuming a person can exert 40 lb on an 18-in. jack handle and a coefficient of friction of 0.15, determine the maximum lead for each of the following screw diameters in order to lift the automobile.

(a)   0.500 in.   (b)   1.25 in.

9.29   The automobile shown in Fig. 9.45 weighs 12 kN. The wheelbase $(a + b + c)$ is 4.2 m. A screw jack like the one in Fig. 9.22 is placed 0.75 m in front of the rear wheel (c) and the vehicle's center of gravity is 1.00 m in front of the rear wheel $(b + c)$. Assuming a person can exert 200 N on an 0.50-m jack handle and a coefficient of friction 0.18, determine the maximum lead for each of the following screw diameters in order to lift the automobile.

(a)   20 mm   (b)   45 mm

9.30   Find the reactions at the wall and floor for the 30-lb board in Fig. 9.46. The coefficient of friction is zero at the wall and 0.40 at the floor $(P = 0)$.

9.31   A force P equal to 50 lb is applied to the 30-lb board in Fig. 9.46. Find the location y of this force to push the board up the frictionless wall. The coefficient of friction at the floor is 0.45.

9.32   The flywheel in Fig. 9.47 has a clockwise moment of 20 N·m applied $\mu = 0.80$.

(a)   Find the friction force at the brake pad, the activating force P, and the reaction at A when no motion is allowed.

(b)   Solve part (a) if the moment is counterclockwise.

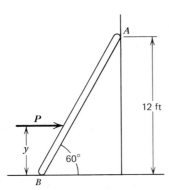

FIG. 9.46 Problems 9.30, 9.31.

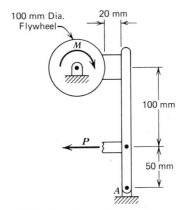

FIG. 9.47 Problems 9.32, 9.33.

9.33 An activating force P of 130 N is applied to the brake lever in Fig. 9.47 $\mu = 0.90$. Find the braking torque on the wheel if it is rotating:

(a) Clockwise (b) Counterclockwise

9.34 A mover pushes on the cabinet in Fig. 9.48 with a force of 15 lb (P), 50 in. (h) above the floor. What will happen if:

(a) $\mu_s = 0.40$ (b) $\mu_s = 0.20$

9.35 A mover pushes on the cabinet in Fig. 9.48 with a force of 50 lb. Find the maximum value of h so that the cabinet will not tip. The coefficient of friction is 0.60.

9.36 A hanging cabinet door weighing 20 N slides on a rail supported by sliders at A and B as shown in Fig. 9.49. Find the maximum coefficient of friction so that the door can be moved with a force P of 6.0 N. Find the value of h so that it will be impossible to tilt the door with a horizontal force.

9.37 The hanging door in Fig. 9.49 weighs 30 N. The slider at A jams, and the coefficient of friction becomes 0.40. At B it is 0.1, and h is 125 mm. Find the force P required to move the door to the left. Will the door tip?

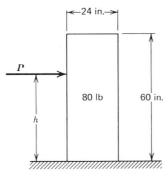

FIG. 9.48 Problems 9.34, 9.35.

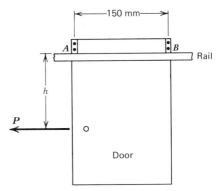

FIG. 9.49 Problems 9.36, 9.37.

PROBLEMS 253

For the next four problems, using the data given, find the force **P** required to tow the vehicle shown in Fig. 9.50 when:

    (a) The front wheels are locked in problem 9.38.

    (b) The rear wheels are locked in problems 9.39, 9.40.

    (c) The front and rear wheels are locked in problem 9.41.

	W	a	b	c	d	e	θ	μ
9.38	3000 lb	12 in.	24 in.	36 in.	84 in.	30 in.	5.0°	0.8
9.39	2000 lb	10 in.	18 in.	30 in.	70 in.	24 in.	10°	0.9
9.40	10 kg	300 mm	600 mm	900 mm	2000 mm	750 mm	15°	0.9
9.41	7.2 kg	250 mm	450 mm	750 mm	1500 mm	600 mm	0°	0.8

9.42 For $x = 6$ in. and $\mu = 0.30$, determine whether the bracket in Fig. 9.51 will slip and the reactions at A and B, if possible, when:

    (a) The wheel at A is free to roll (no friction) and the wheel at B is locked.

    (b) The wheel at B is free to roll (no friction) and the wheel at A is locked.

9.43 Find the minimum value of x for the bracket in Fig. 9.51 to hold when the coefficient of friction is 0.35 and both wheels are locked.

9.44 The coefficient of friction between the rope and post in Fig. 9.52 is 0.35. If the weight is 10 kN, find:

    (a) The force required to *hold* the weight.

    (b) The force required to *lift* the weight.

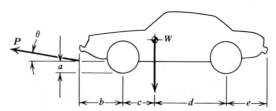

FIG. 9.50   Problems 9.38, 9.39, 9.40, 9.41.

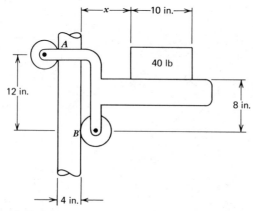

FIG. 9.51   Problems 9.42, 9.43.

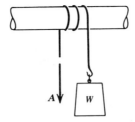

FIG. 9.52 Problems 9.44, 9.45, 9.46.

9.45 The weight in Fig. 9.52 is 750 lb. For a coefficient of friction of 0.20 find the force *A* required to:

(a) *Hold* the weight   (b) *Lift* the weight

9.46 The weight in Fig. 9.52 is 500 kN, and it is held in place by a force *A* of 20 kN. Find the minimum coefficient of friction.

9.47 A large ship is anchored by wrapping a line around an anchor post. Find the number of turns required to resist the ship's 4000-lb force with a 20-lb force if:

(a) $\mu = 0.40$ (b) $\mu = 0.20$

9.48 Two 10-in.-diameter pulleys are connected by a belt. The tension in the tight side is 500 lb. For a coefficient of friction of 0.23, find the tension in the slack side if slipping is about to occur. Also find the torque (moment) that can be transmitted by this system.

9.49 Power is transmitted by a belt–pulley system as shown in Fig. 9.53 as the small pulley drives the large one clockwise. The maximum tension allowed in the belt is 25 kN. For the properties given below, find the maximum torque (moment) that can be transmitted.

	r_1	r_2	D	μ
(a)	200 mm	400 mm	800 mm	0.70
(b)	1.5 m	2.5 m	5.0 m	0.60

Hint: From the sketch:

$$\sin \theta = \frac{r_2 - r_1}{D}$$

Draw the pulley system to scale and verify this result.

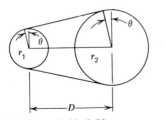
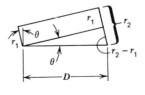

FIG. 9.53 Problems 9.49, 9.50.

9.50 Power is transmitted by a belt–pulley system as shown in Fig. 9.53 as the small pulley drives the large one counterclockwise. The maximum tension allowed in the belt is 800 lb. For the properties given below, find the maximum torque (moment) that can be transmitted.

	r_1	r_2	D	μ
(a)	6 in.	10 in.	20 in.	0.90
(b)	24 in.	36 in.	75 in.	0.75

Hint: From the sketch:

$$\sin \theta = \frac{r_1 - r_2}{D}$$

Draw the pulley system to scale and verify this result.

9.51 The drum shown in Fig. 9.54 rotates clockwise. Find the tension on each side of the band brake under the following conditions.

Drum Diameter	a	P	μ
300 mm	600 mm	80 kN	0.70

9.52 Work Problem 9.51 if the drum rotates counterclockwise.

9.53 The drum shown in Fig. 9.54 rotates clockwise. Find the tension on each side of the band brake under the following conditions.

Drum Diameter	a	P	μ
10 in.	14 in.	35 lb	0.80

9.54 Work Problem 9.53 if the drum rotates counterclockwise.

9.55 Determine the tension in the band brake in Fig. 9.55 at points A and B for $\mu = 0.50$.

9.56 Work Problem 9.55 if the rotation of the drum is clockwise.

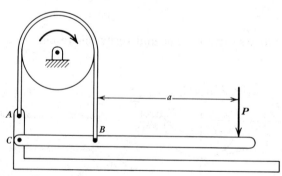

FIG. 9.54   Problems 9.51, 9.52, 9.53, 9.54.

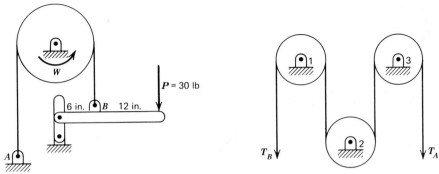

FIG. 9.55 Problems 9.55, 9.56.   **FIG. 9.56** Problem 9.57.

9.57 A portion of a film transport mechanism is shown in Fig. 9.56. All three rollers are intended to roll freely (no friction) as film is pulled through to the right. If the tension T_A is 3.0 lb and $\mu = 0.15$ when a roller is stuck, find T_B when:

(a) Roller 2 is stuck   (b) Rollers 2 and 3 are stuck.

(c) Rollers 1 and 3 are stuck.   (d) All three rollers are stuck.

9.58 For Fig. 9.57 let $B = 5.0$ N, $\theta = 60°$, and $\mu = 0.32$. Find the weight of block A required to hold block B in place if:

(a) The pulley is free.   (b) The pulley is fixed.

9.59 For Fig. 9.57 let $B = 5.0$ lb, $\theta = 40°$, and $\mu = 0.48$. Find the weight of block A required to lift block B if:

(a) The pulley is free.   (b) The pulley is fixed.

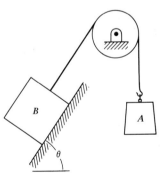

FIG. 9.57 Problems 9.58, 9.59.

10

Introduction To
Strength of Materials

10.1   BASEBALL, HOTDOGS, APPLE PIE, AND CHEVROLET

Once upon a time there were three little pigs, . . . Oh well, you know the story of these poor, misguided creatures. Of course, they were excellent and hard-working craftsmen. (Not unlike your everyday, average technology student.) And, my, such efficiency has seldom been seen. But, alas, they had failed to recognize the intricacies of statically indeterminate structures and temperamentally indeterminate wolves. This text can be of great assistance in designing wolf-resistant structures. It won't be much help with the wolf. (Similarities between the wolf and your instructor are purely coincidental.)

The topic at hand, strength of materials, is fundamental to the design of houses—straw, hay, or brick—airplanes, spaceships, pool rooms, football stadia, beer cans, elevators, dirt bikes, lawn mowers, ferris wheels, freeways, toilet booths, vending machines, skyscrapers, tug boats, nuclear missiles, nuclear reactors, canal locks, casket handles, voting machines, snuff cans, bar stools, batting helmets, artificial limbs, seat belts, speedometer cables, paper clips, electric power cables, hospital beds, socket wrenches, screwdrivers, paint scrapers, eyeglass frames, and one or two other items. It is an applied subject!

In the Bible in the tenth chapter of Ecclesiastes, it is recorded of King Solomon, "Through indolence the rafters sag, and through slackness the house leaks." Thus we find that the wisest of men from antiquity appreciated hard work *and* the deflection of beams. It has always been so! The successful student in this subject will likewise come to appreciate hard work and the deflection of beams.

There are several points which we will emphasize in this introductory chapter. The first is that this text is written for the student. (This statement is commonly used in the introduction to textbooks. It often is the last thing you understand.) That is a bit of a problem, because although you, the student, buy the book, your instructor selects it. So, you'll forgive me if from time to time I include a paragraph or two for your instructor's benefit. In writing for the student I'll use a personal style. That is not the usual style for technical writing. However, I have found that the student who benefits most from a text is the one who reads it. I want to make that pleasant—even enjoyable. I'll try to lighten the load with a touch of humor.

You should understand from the outset that although this subject is extremely important, your passing or failing will do little to change the course of the world. Pass or fail, God will still be in His heaven. Most successful people in the world live rewarding lives without having ever heard of it. Why, some of my best friends don't even know Poisson had a ratio! So it is important—but not the meaning of life.

Second, we must recognize that although the name *strength of materials* is traditional, we will be concerned with strengths only in an incidental way. It is not a very descriptive name. "Mechanics of materials" is a better title, and the one I prefer. Engineering schools might use "statics of deformable bodies" or even "continuum mechanics."

Most students find the subject very demanding. You can take it one of two ways—seriously or again. It will lean heavily on the mathematics and statics you have learned previously. Weaknesses in these subjects will cause severe problems. Substantial deficiencies will be very hard to overcome and should be remedied before proceeding with this study. I have taught this subject many times and have discussed it at length with others who have also. The three most common difficulties students seem to have are (1) algebra, (2) trigonometry, and (3) statics. All three are prerequisites for this course. A distant recognition of these topics is inadequate. You must have a working command of them.

In addition, as noted earlier, this material requires an understanding of the basics of differential and integral calculus. Few problems actually require the manipulation of calculus equations. However, since calculus is universally required in engineering technology programs and since the differential and the integral are so powerful in explaining and developing the concepts of the subject, it seems negligent not to use them. The brief review in Sections 10.3 and 10.4 will allow the uninitiated to read the text and handle practically all the problems (most of the problems do not require calculus). There will be a few problems that the uninitiated will find excessively difficult.

This will be the second course in mechanics for most students. As in the first nine chapters, on statics, a proper approach to problems is very important. An orderly approach to problem solution cannot be overemphasized. Significant problems cannot be worked three to a page. Nor can they often be worked without error. Hence the objective of the neat and orderly format is not only to make it easier to arrive at the correct answer, but to make it easier to find the errors you are sure to make. An appropriate format is emphasized throughout. Again, an "engineer's pad" or some similar form of grid paper will be very helpful.

10.2   UNITY ON UNITS?

In the United States engineering calculations have traditionally been made using English units, especially in the mechanical and civil fields. Undoubtedly this system will be around for years to come. Most technical literature available today continues to be in English units in these fields. Nonetheless the switch is on, and the switch is to metric, or more correctly Système International d'Unités (SI), as introduced in Chapter 1. This switch is already complete in some industries, while meeting significant resistance in others. There is no doubt that the switch is expensive—and inconvenient—so continued resistance by industry is understandable and predictable. However, the greatest resistance appears to be in the public sector.

Now, the focus on problems is not always the sharpest in the public sector. Political organizations have already been formed to oppose the adoption of the SI. Some antagonists see the SI as a communist plot, others only as part of a takeover by the international oil cartel. Still others believe it results in sterility to left-handed people. I have access to a suppressed report showing that Canadian rats kept in metric cages develop intestinal cancer 37.3% more frequently than rats kept in cages with English measurements. (This paper was to be presented at the 1979 Annual Meeting of the Flat Earth Society but was stricken from the program due to pressure from the International Committee for a True Two-by-Four.)

In spite of the pressure and reluctance, the cold, hard reality is that today's technologists will function with a dual measurement system for much of their professional lives. Thus in this text we present both. The real crunch comes in going from one system to the other.

The methods of unit transformation presented in Section 1.4 are totally adequate for transforming between different English units and SI units. Because our purpose here is to gain understanding and skill in the use of the concepts of strength of materials, we are reluctant to confound the issue and burden the student further with the transformation of units. Hence we generally keep them separate, which makes it a whole lot easier. However, our reluctance to tackle the problem of transformation will not make it go away. Sooner or later, it's going to get you!

10.3   THE DERIVATIVE IN A CHANGING WORLD

There are two principal ideas in calculus—the derivative and the integral. Both these concepts can be best understood by their geometric interpretations. Figure 10.1 plots the function $y = 2(x)^{1/2}$. In the language of the mathematician—or as Charlie Brown would say, for those who speak algebra—we can express this in the general form as $y = f(x)$. What this says is that y is a function of x, and it represents the function above, or for that matter, most any other function. Now let's suppose we wish to know the slope of the curve at the point (1, 2). It escapes me for the moment just why we want to know the slope at this point, but please bear with me. We construct a line through the point and tangent to the curve at the point (Fig. 10.1). The slope of this line is the slope of the curve at this point, and it is equal to the tangent of the angle θ, which is the angle the line makes with a horizontal. This slope is approximated by the value $\Delta y/\Delta x$.

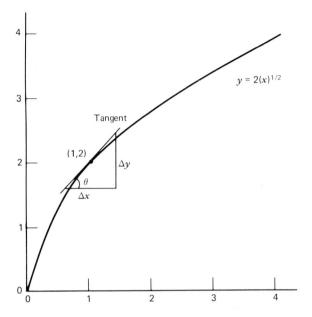

FIG. 10.1

This approximation becomes more and more accurate as Δy and Δx become smaller. This idea is expressed mathematically as:

$$\lim_{\Delta x \to 0} \frac{\Delta y}{\Delta x} = \frac{dy}{dx}$$

This expression dy/dx is known as the derivative. Geometrically it is the slope of the curve at the point in question. Physically it has many other interpretations. Rules for taking the derivative are given in calculus texts, and a summation of these is given in Table A-6. From this table we take Eq. 6, which reduces to

$$\frac{d}{dx}(x^n) = nx^{n-1}$$

Applying this to the equation:

$$y = 2(x)^{1/2}$$

we get:

$$\frac{d}{dx}(2x^{1/2}) = 2(\tfrac{1}{2})x^{-1/2}$$

and thus:

$$\frac{dy}{dx} = \frac{1}{x^{1/2}} = y'$$

where y' (say "y prime") is a shorthand notation for the first derivative. Now evaluating this for the point (1, 2) gives:

$$\frac{dy}{dx} = \frac{1}{(1)^{1/2}} = 1.00$$

$$\tan \theta = \frac{dy}{dx} = 1.00$$

and

$$\theta = 45° = \frac{\pi}{4} \text{ rad}$$

The angle θ is the angle the tangent makes with the horizontal. We have specifically found the slope at the point (1, 2). However, in doing so, we also found the equation of the derivative in general form, namely:

$$y' = \frac{1}{x^{1/2}}$$

This equation is the equation of the slope of the curve $y = 2x^{1/2}$ for all values of x. To find the slope at any point, one need only substitute the appropriate value of x into equation $y' = 1/\sqrt{x}$. This relatively insignificant problem illustrates the power of using the appropriate mathematical tool to solve an entire class of problems in a single step.

The application above is a geometric one and is illustrative of many cases in which geometry can be applied directly or by analogy to physical problems. To illustrate the idea further, consider an object in free-fall motion, say a gravity drop-type pile driver. It has been determined that the motion of the pile driver can be described by the equation:

$$s = 16.1t^2$$

where s is the displacement of the driver (in feet) at any time t (in seconds). We wish to know its velocity after it has fallen for one-half second. The velocity can be defined as the first derivative of displacement with respect to time.

$$v = \frac{ds}{dt}$$

Again using Eq. 6 from Table A-6, we have:

$$v = \frac{ds}{dt} = 2(16.1)t = 32.2t$$

Substituting in $t = 0.5$ s we have:

$$v = 32.2(0.5) = 16.1 \text{ ft/s}$$

We have found the velocity to be 16.1 ft/s after free falling for 0.5 s. Notice that in the process we have again solved a more general problem and have found an equation for velocity as a function of time.

10.4 SUMMING UP ON INTEGRATION

Integration is essentially a summation process. If we wish to know the total area bounded by the curve in Fig. 10.2, we find it by summing up the small areas ΔA, shown thus:

$$A = \Delta A_1 + \Delta A_2 + \Delta A_3 + \cdots + \Delta A_n$$
$$= \sum \Delta A_i$$

where $\sum$ is the capital Greek letter sigma (English s) and stands for summation. The subscript i takes on the values of 1 to n as the summation is executed. If we now let the ΔAs become smaller, the ΔAs at the border such as ΔA_n fit the border better, and we approximate the total area more closely. In fact, if we could let the ΔAs become small enough, the total would approach the exact area to whatever degree of precision we desired. Mathematically we can let ΔA decrease without bound, and if we do, the total area is exactly equal to the summation. We express this as follows:

$$A = \lim_{\Delta A \to 0} \left(\sum \Delta A_i \right) = \int dA$$

This geometric interpretation of the integral is a very important one. You should remember that integration is a summation process. Again as before, the symbol for summation $\sum$ is the Greek equivalent to a capital S while the integral sign $\int$ is an old English script S. Both are indicating summation. We use the symbol dA for the infinitesimal limit of ΔA. This is known as the differential of A. The integrals for several common expressions are given in Table A-7.

There are, of course, other interpretations of the integral as well as various applications. We will see some of these as we continue. An additional important one can be observed if we consider the differential equation:

$$\frac{dy}{dx} = x$$

This equation is solved by separating the variables:

$$dy = x \, dx$$

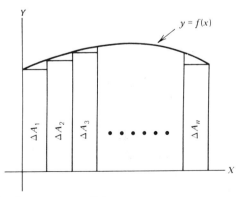

FIG. 10.2 Area under the curve $y = f(x)$.

and integrating using Eq. 4 from Table A-7:

$$y = \int x \, dx$$

$$y = \frac{x^2}{2} + C$$

The C is for a constant of integration. It is called an *arbitrary constant*, since it identifies a specific curve out of a family of curves. In physical problems it is not "arbitrary" at all but has a specific value based on the initial or boundary conditions of the particular problem. If we differentiate the equation above we get:

$$\frac{dy}{dx} = x$$

which is what we started with. Thus the integral is the inverse of the differential, and vice versa. Because of this, the integral is often called the antiderivative.

Table A-7 lists some common integral forms. Note the similarity between these forms and the differential forms in Table A-6. The arbitrary constant, which must be added when the integration is indefinite, is not included in Table A-7. The forms are used without the arbitrary constant for definite integration (or integration with limits). Indefinite integration (with an arbitrary constant) is frequently used to find a functional relation between variables. Definite integration is more often used to find the specific numerical answer to a problem, although these roles are reversible. (Examples of definite integration are given in the problems that follow.)

Example Problem 10.1

By integration, find the area bounded on the top by the curve:

$$y = 2 + 2x$$

on the bottom by the X axis, on the left by the Y axis, and on the right by the line $x = 6$, as shown in Fig. 10.3.

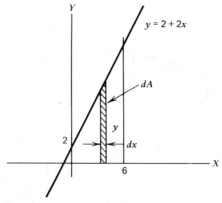

FIG. 10.3 Example Problem 10.1.

Solution

A rectangular element of area is identified as follows:

$$dA = y\,dx$$

The total area is the summation of all the elements of area between $x = 0$ and $x = 6$. Mathematically we say:

$$A = \int dA = \int_0^6 y\,dx$$

Before this equation can be evaluated we must know y as a function of x. This is the equation of the bounding curve, namely,

$$y = 2 + 2x$$

By substitution,

$$A = \int_0^6 (2 + 2x)\,dx$$

Because integration is a summation process, we may split this into parts:

$$A = \int_0^6 2\,dx + \int_0^6 2x\,dx$$

These integrals can be evaluated by Eqs. 2, 3, and 4 from Table A-7. Thus we have:

$$A = 2\int_0^6 dx + 2\int_0^6 x\,dx$$

$$= 2x\Big|_0^6 + 2\left(\frac{x^2}{2}\right)\Big|_0^6$$

$$= 2[(6) - (0)] + [(6)^2 - (0)^2]$$

$$A = \mathbf{48}$$

We have worked this problem without units. Dimensionally the area will be length squared.

Example Problem 10.2

The deceleration of a car during a crash is as shown in Fig. 10.4. This deceleration pulse is approximated by the function:

$$a = -644 \sin\left(\frac{\pi}{0.12}\right)t$$

where t is given in seconds, the angle is evaluated in radians, and a will be in feet per second squared. The change in velocity of the car during the crash will be the area under the acceleration curve, or the integral:

$$\Delta v = \int a\,dt$$

Find the change in velocity.

Solution

$$\Delta v = \int a\, dt$$

$$\Delta v = -644 \int_0^{0.12} \sin\left(\frac{\pi}{0.12}\right) t\, dt$$

where the constant has been factored outside the integral and the limits of integration are set from 0 to 0.12 s. Equation 7, Table A-7, is:

$$\int \sin x\, dx = -\cos x$$

To make our problem fit this form, we observe:

$$x = \frac{\pi}{0.12}\, t$$

So

$$dx = d\left(\frac{\pi t}{0.12}\right) = \frac{\pi\, dt}{0.12}$$

Thus we rewrite our problem as follows:

$$-644 \left(\frac{0.12}{\pi}\right) \int_0^{0.12} \sin \frac{\pi}{0.12} t \left(\frac{\pi\, dt}{0.12}\right)$$

And on integration we get:

$$\Delta v = \frac{-644(0.12)}{\pi} \left[-\cos \frac{\pi t}{0.12} \right]_0^{0.12}$$

$$\Delta v = +\frac{644}{\pi}(0.12)\left[\cos \frac{\pi}{0.12}(0.12) - \cos \frac{\pi}{0.12}(0) \right]$$

$$\Delta v = +24.6(\cos \pi - \cos 0)$$

The cosine is evaluated for the angle in radians.

$$\Delta v = 24.6[(-1) - (+1)]$$

$$\mathbf{\Delta v = -49.2\ ft/s = -33.5\ mph}$$

Incidentally, this value is also the area under the curve in Fig. 10.4.

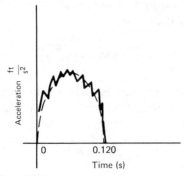

FIG. 10.4 Example Problem 10.2.

PROBLEMS

10.1 Differentiate each of the following expressions with respect to x.

(a) $y = 6x^3$ (b) $y = 8x^2 + 2x + 3$ (c) $y = 2 \sin (2x)$

(d) $y = 3 \ln x$ (e) $y = x \sin (x/2)$

10.2 Find the slope of the following curves at the indicated values of x.

(a) $y = 4x - 3$ at 2, 4, and 6   (b) $y = 6x^2 + 4$ at 2, 4, and 6

(c) $y = \sin 2x$ at 0, 45°, and 90°   (d) $y = x$ at 0, 4, and 9

(e) $y = 3 \ln x$ at 1, 4, and 9

10.3 Integrate the following expressions:

(a) $\int 2x^3 \, dx$ (b) $\int \left(\dfrac{x^2}{3} + 2x + 4 \right) dx$ (c) $\int \sin 2x \, dx$

(d) $\int \sqrt{3x} \, dx$ (e) $\int 4 \cos 3\theta \, d\theta$

10.4 Evaluate each of the integrals in Problem 10.3 for the indicated limits:

(a) 0 to 6   (b) 2 to 4   (c) 0 to 20°

(d) 2 to 8   (e) 0 to 45°

10.5 Find the area bounded by the x and y axes, the vertical line $x = 8$, and the curve:

(a) $y = 4 + 10x$ (b) $y = 6 + 8x^2$ (c) $y = x^2 + 2x + 2$

10.6 An automobile is accelerated at 12 m/s^2. If its initial velocity is zero, what will its speed be after 5 s? How far will it have traveled? *Hint:* $v = \int a \, dt$, $s = \int v \, dt$

10.7 An automobile crashes into a rigid barrier and comes to rest. It is decelerated at a constant $20 \, g$ ($1 \, g = 32.2 \text{ ft/s}^2$) for 200 ms. What was its initial velocity? *Hint:* $v = \int a \, dt$

11

Stress and Strain

11.1 NORMAL STRESS

Previously we found the internal loads in members of trusses. Unknowingly, the first step was taken in determining the stress in the member. The force found in a member was the load necessary to maintain equilibrium. The force was found by passing a cutting plane through the member and is, therefore, an *internal force* or internal load. This is the first step in any stress analysis problem—to find the internal load. The second step is to find the stress produced by that load, and that is the principal subject of this part of the book, but the first and necessary step is always to find the load causing the stress.

Consider a 2-in.-square member that is found to carry say a 1170-lb tensile load as shown in Fig. 11.1a. Now, given the load in the member, the question is raised, How is that load carried? For the moment it is assumed that it is uniformly carried, as shown in Fig. 11.1b. If the load is equally shared by all the 2 in.^{2} of cross-sectional area, then the stress in the member is the load divided by the area, or:

$$\text{stress} = \frac{\text{load}}{\text{area}} = \frac{P}{A} = \frac{1170\ \text{lb}}{2\ \text{in.}^2}$$

$$\sigma = \frac{585\ \text{lb}}{\text{in.}^2} = 585\ \text{psi}$$

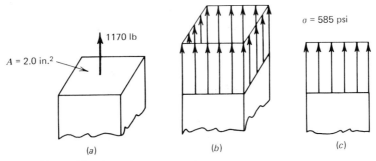

FIG. 11.1a–c   Normal load produces normal stress.

There are several things to be observed regarding this exercise. The first is the symbol for stress, σ. This is the lowercase Greek letter sigma, the equivalent to the English s. Some texts use the English s, but σ is much more common, and so we will use it. Becoming used to it now will make later work more convenient. In structural design it is common to use f for stress.

The second point is the equation we now label:

$$\sigma = \frac{P}{A} \tag{11.1}$$

This equation, fundamental to the subject at hand, should be learned by the student, and normally it will be, from repeated use. In obtaining the equation it was *assumed* the stress is uniform, that is, equally distributed. That turns out to have been a very good assumption, which is approximately true in a very large number of cases. Even when it is patently untrue, the design stress is frequently based on the average stress, so Eq. 11.1 has very wide application.

The direction of this stress should also be noted. It is perpendicular or normal to the surface over which it acts and is, therefore, called a *normal stress*. "Normal" means perpendicular to the surface. In addition to these two properties (direction and magnitude), a third characteristic of stress is its distribution—uniform in this case. It is often convenient to sketch the stress distribution. When it is not sketched, the student should always visualize a mental picture. A three-dimensional representation of this stress distribution is shown in Fig. 11.1b. The more common two-dimensional representation is shown in Fig. 11.1c.

The sense of the stress is also important. It cannot be determined from the sign of the force vector. It depends instead on the action of the stress on the body. If the stress is tending to stretch the body or pull it apart, it is called *tension*. Normally, stress-producing tension is considered positive. If the stress is compressing or squashing the body, it is called *compression* and carries a negative sign.

The last aspect considered here is that of the units for stress. These follow from Eq. 11.1:

$$\sigma = \frac{P}{A} \triangleq \frac{\text{force}}{\text{area}} = \frac{\text{lb}}{\text{in.}^2} = \text{psi}$$

These are the most common units for stress in the English system. Students who have studied topics in fluid mechanics will recognize these units as those for pressure. This follows from the fact that pressure is nothing more than normal stress. Because of the properties of many engineering materials, it is common to think in terms of thousands of pounds, or kilopounds, per square inch (abbreviated as kpsi or simply ksi). Kilopounds force is also abbreviated as kips (say "kips" and spell out "k-s-i"). There are, of course, other units, and any unit of force divided by any unit of area is legitimate.

In the SI the unit of force is the newton and the unit of area is the meter squared. Thus the unit of stress is the newton per meter squared. This is a derived unit in the SI and carries the name pascal, abbreviated Pa,

$$1 \text{ Pa} = \frac{1 \text{ N}}{\text{m}^2}$$

A newton is a bit more than a fifth of a pound, and a square meter is a relatively large area. The pascal is, therefore, a relatively small unit of stress. More precisely:

$$1 \text{ Pa} = 1.450E - 4 \text{ psi}$$

or

$$1 \text{ psi} = 6.895 \, E3 \text{ Pa}$$

Because this unit is so small, it is commonly used with the multiplying prefixes:

mega (MPa = 1,000,000 Pa)   and   giga (GPa = 1,000,000,000 Pa)

when referring to stresses and other properties of engineering interest.

A special type of normal stress called a bearing stress occurs when two objects come into contact or bear on each other. The stress that a table leg exerts on the floor is an example. Of course, bearing stresses are always compressive. Otherwise they are just normal "Normal stresses . . ." normally.

Example Problem 11.1

A short column (Fig. 11.2) has a 2 in. × 2 in. cross section. It is used to carry a 9000-lb load. Find the normal stress in the member.

Solution

$$\sigma = \frac{P}{A} = \frac{9 \text{ kips}}{2 \text{ in.} \times 2 \text{ in.}}$$

$$\sigma = \frac{9}{(2)(2)} \frac{\text{kips}}{\text{in.}^2} = 2.25 \text{ ksi compression}$$

The stress distribution is uniform. The two-dimensional sketch is Fig. 11.3. Note that the stress is perpendicular (or normal) to the surface it acts over.

Example Problem 11.2

If in Example Problem 11.1 the applied load is 15 kN and the cross section is 2 cm × 3 cm, find the bearing stress of the block on the table it sits on.

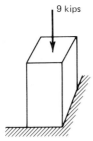

9 kips

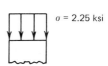

σ = 2.25 ksi

FIG. 11.2 Example Problem 11.1.

FIG. 11.3 Stress distribution for Example Problem 11.1.

Solution

The stress due to the 15-kN load will be transmitted to the table as a bearing stress. Thus

$$\sigma = \frac{P}{A} = \frac{15 \text{ kN}}{(0.02 \text{ m})(0.03 \text{ m})} = 25,000 \frac{\text{kN}}{\text{m}^2}$$

$$\sigma = 25,000 \text{ kPa} = \mathbf{25.0 \text{ MPa}}$$

11.2 SHEAR STRESS

In Example Problem 11.1 the applied force was normal, that is, perpendicular to the cross section. Figure 11.4a represents a section in which the internal load is not normal. In Fig. 11.4b this force P, a vector, has been resolved into a normal component P_y and a tangential component P_x. The normal component P_y can be related to a normal stress, as in Fig. 11.5. Thus $\sigma = P_y/A$ gives the average normal stress, which approximates the true situation very closely. The effect of tangential component P_x is to shear the member, as indicated in Fig. 11.6. An average shear stress may be calculated:

$$\tau_{AV} = \frac{P_x}{A} \tag{11.2}$$

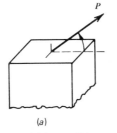

P

(a)

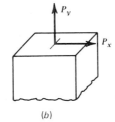

P_y

P_x

(b)

FIG. 11.4a–b Non-normal force **P** is resolved into normal and shear components.

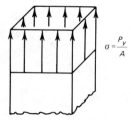

FIG. 11.5 Normal load P_y produces normal stress.

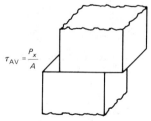

FIG. 11.6 Shear load tends to shear the member.

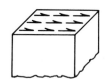

FIG. 11.7 Shear load P_x produces average shear stress.

This equation, however, differs considerably from the true stress situation. Nonetheless, for many practical reasons Eq. 11.2 is widely used in many engineering applications. The subscript AV indicates that an *average* stress, not the true stress, is being calculated.

The Greek letter tau (τ) (equivalent to t) is most frequently used for shear stress, although s_s is not uncommon. Since this is also a load divided by an area, it also has units of psi, ksi, Pa, MPa, and so on.

The preceding section noted the importance of the magnitude, direction, and distribution of the stress represented by Eq. 11.1. This is important for the shear stress as well. The magnitude is, of course, given by Eq. 11.2. The direction is parallel to the surface, tending to shear, and thus is called *shear stress*. The stress distribution is assumed to be uniform, as shown in Fig. 11.7.

A common application of Eq. 11.2 is in the analysis of bolted or riveted connections. Example Problems 11.3 and 11.4 illustrate its application.

Example Problem 11.3

A 400-lb load is carried by a 1.00-in. diameter rivet as shown in Fig. 11.8. Find the average shear stress in the rivet.

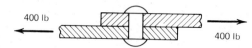

FIG. 11.8 Example Problem 11.3.

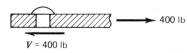

400 lb

V = 400 lb

FIG. 11.9 Free body diagram for
Example Problem 11.3.

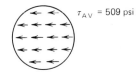

τ_{AV} = 509 psi

FIG. 11.10 Shear stress distribution.

Solution

A free body diagram of the top plate is drawn (Fig. 11.9) and the load is
determined:

$$\sum F_x = 0$$
$$400 - V = 0$$
$$V = 400 \text{ lb}$$

The shear load is 400 lb. Now calculate the average shear stress:

$$\tau_{AV} = \frac{P}{A} = \frac{P}{\dfrac{\pi D^2}{4}} = \frac{4P}{\pi D^2}$$

Again, we usually use a single division bar:

$$\tau_{AV} = \frac{400 \text{ lb } (4)}{\pi (1 \text{ in.})^2}$$

$$\tau_{AV} = \textbf{509 psi}$$

The stress distribution is uniform, as shown in Fig. 11.10. This is known as
single shear. In single shear the rivet carries the full load on the joint.

Example Problem 11.4

A 1-kN load is carried by a 2-cm-diameter rivet, as shown in Fig. 11.11. Find
the average shear stress in the rivet.

Solution

A free body diagram of the top plate is drawn (Fig. 11.12) and the shear load
is determined.

$$\sum F_x = 0$$
$$0.5 - V_T = 0$$
$$V_T = 0.500 \text{ kN}$$

0.5 kN

1 kN

0.5 kN

FIG. 11.11 Example Problem 11.4.

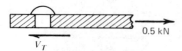

FIG. 11.12 Free body diagram for Example Problem 11.4.

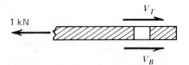

FIG. 11.13 Alternate free body diagram.

A free body diagram of the middle plate is then drawn (Fig. 11.13).

$$\Sigma F_x = 0$$
$$-1.0 + V_T + V_B = 0$$
$$V_B = 1.0 - 0.5 = 0.500 \text{ kN}$$

Thus we see the shear load on either side of the middle plate is 0.500 kN. This condition is known as *double shear*, and in it the rivet carries only half the total load. In single shear it carries the total load. To calculate the stress we have:

$$\tau_{AV} = \frac{P}{A} = \frac{P}{\dfrac{\pi D^2}{4}} = \frac{4P}{\pi D^2} = \frac{4(0.500 \text{ kN})}{\pi(0.02 \text{ m})^2} = 1590 \text{ kPa}$$

$$\tau_{AV} = \mathbf{1.59 \text{ MPa}}$$

11.3   NORMAL STRAIN

Consider now a member of uniform cross section whose length is L (Fig. 11.14). An axial tensile load P is applied to the member, and it stretches in the direction of the applied load. This *elongation*, labeled δ (lowercase Greek delta—English d) is called total strain or *deformation*. Unit strain is then defined as the deformation

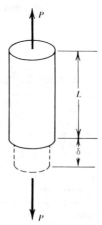

FIG. 11.14 Deformation under axial load.

per unit length or:

$$\text{unit strain} = \frac{\text{deformation}}{\text{original length}}$$

or symbolically:

$$\varepsilon = \frac{\delta}{L} \tag{11.3}$$

The symbol for unit strain is ε, the lowercase Greek epsilon (equivalent to the English e). Most often we refer to unit strain simply as *strain*, and that will be our practice throughout.

Note the units for strain:

$$\varepsilon = \frac{\delta}{L} \underset{=}{\scriptstyle D} \frac{\text{in.}}{\text{in.}}$$

So the units are inch per inch, which really is dimensionless. When working with metals the strains that are allowed are usually very small. In Example Problem 11.5, a strain of 0.00165 in./in. will be found. Because the magnitude of the number is so small, it is convenient to write it as 1650 (10^{-6} in./in.). The value inside the parentheses is called microstrain (micro represents the metric prefix 10^{-6} or, in "computerese," E-6). The Greek letter mu (μ) is used to represent it, so we write

$$\varepsilon = 1650 \; \mu$$

This terminology is common in the experimental stress analysis field. Of course, since strain is dimensionless, it makes absolutely no difference which unit system we are in.

Example Problem 11.5

A test piece (Fig. 11.15) has a diameter of 0.505 in. and a gage length of 2.00 in. (Gage length is the active length of the test piece.) Under a tensile load of 10,000 lb it elongates 0.00330 in. Find the stress and strain in the member.

Solution

From Eq. 11.1:

$$\sigma = \frac{P}{A}$$

$$A = \frac{\pi d^2}{4} = 0.200 \text{ in.}^2$$

and

$$\sigma = \frac{P}{A} = \frac{P}{0.200} = 5P = 5(10{,}000) = \mathbf{50{,}000 \; psi}$$

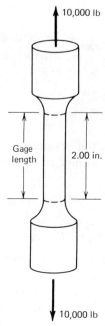

10,000 lb

Gage length

2.00 in.

10,000 lb

FIG. 11.15   Example Problem 11.5.

The 0.505-in.-diameter test piece gives an area of 0.200 in.^{2} and the stress in psi may be calculated as 5 times the load in pounds. Because of this convenience, the 0.505-in. diameter is a standard for tensile tests. From Eq. 11.3, we have:

$$\varepsilon = \frac{\delta}{L} = \frac{0.00330 \text{ in.}}{2 \text{ in.}} = \mathbf{0.00165} \frac{\mathbf{in.}}{\mathbf{in.}}$$

Since strain is dimensionless, we may leave the units off. We can also write the answer as 1650 μ, meaning microstrain.

11.4   HOOKE'S LAW

In 1676 Robert Hooke postulated the principle that now bears his name. He arrived at this principle from studying springs. The original, which was in Latin, can be roughly translated as "The force varies with deflection." Today we are more likely to say that "Stress is proportional to strain." We write:

$$\sigma = E\varepsilon \tag{11.4}$$

In this equation E, the constant of proportionality, turns out to be a property of the material. It is called the *modulus of elasticity* or Young's modulus. It can be determined from the experiment described in Example Problem 11.5 as follows.

Solving for E in Eq. 11.4, we have:

$$E = \frac{\sigma}{\varepsilon}$$

Substituting from the example problem:

$$E = \frac{50,000\ \text{lb}}{\text{in.}^2 \left(0.00165\ \dfrac{\text{in.}}{\text{in.}} \right)} = 30.3 \times 10^6\ \frac{\text{lb}}{\text{in.}^2}$$

$$E = 30.3 \times 10^6\ \textbf{psi}$$

This is a very large number. Numbers of this magnitude are common for metals. Note that the units are the same as those for stress—psi. This can be clearly seen in the algebraic manipulation above, where E is equal to the stress—psi—divided by the strain—dimensionless; thus the units for E are the same as for stress. Values of the modulus of elasticity for various metals are given in Table A-8. This number is a measure of the *stiffness* of a material. The greater the modulus, the stiffer the material. Thus if identical parts are made, one of steel ($E = 30\ E6$ psi) and the other of aluminum ($E = 10.3\ E6$ psi), the stiffer steel part will deflect only one-third as much as the aluminum part under identical loading.

In the SI we have for this example:

$$E = 30.3 \times 10^6\ \text{psi} \left(\frac{6895\ \text{Pa}}{1\ \text{psi}} \right)$$

$$= 209,000 \times 10^6\ \text{Pa} = 209 \times 10^9\ \text{Pa} = 209\ \text{GPa}$$

Because of the very large value of the modulus of elasticity in SI units for common engineering materials, the unit GPa (gigapascals) is normally used.

A geometric interpretation of E may also be made. Figure 11.16 is a *stress–strain diagram* for a mild steel. This diagram is obtained by plotting the stress against the strain during a tensile test of a material. Modern testing machines are equipped with instrumentation that automatically produce this diagram during a tensile test. A straight line is drawn between the origin and point A. The slope of this line can be calculated as $\Delta\sigma/\Delta\varepsilon$, which is the modulus of elasticity—E. The behavior of the material is described by Hooke's law between 0 and A. The relation between σ and ε is linear over this range. Point A is called the *proportional limit*. If the material is loaded beyond A, Eq. 11.4 no longer holds. This, however, does not seriously limit the equation, because for many engineering structures loading beyond point A would be considered a failure.

Many materials do not have a truly linear range on a stress–strain diagram. Equation 11.4 is widely applied to such materials by approximating the value of E. This amounts to linearizing the stress–strain curve.

While discussing the stress–strain curve (Fig. 11.16), we should note a few other properties of materials that can be obtained from it. This particular stress–strain curve does not characterize engineering materials in general. A given material may not exhibit all the properties discussed here. However, defining the properties for Fig. 11.16 will assist us in learning the terms.

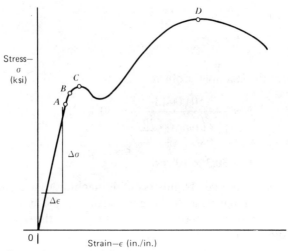

FIG. 11.16   Stress–strain diagram for a ductile material.

ELASTIC LIMIT: POINT *B*

If the load is increased to any value less than *B* and then removed, the stress–strain diagram will retrace its path, returning to 0. If the load exceeds *B*, as shown in Fig. 11.17, the plot will return to the zero stress level parallel to the initial line. It will not return to zero strain, and a permanent set in the material results. Point *B* is known as the *elastic limit*.

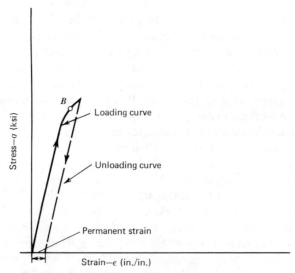

FIG. 11.17   Exceeding the elastic limit.

YIELD POINT: POINT C (ALSO CALLED YIELD STRENGTH)

If the load reaches the *yield point* (point C), there will be additional deflection without additional load. For ductile steels the yield point is easily identified. Therefore, and because of the close proximity of A, B, and C, its value is normally used as a design value, even though the failure theory is based on A or B. Consequently, material property tables like Table A-8 often give this value.

We use the term "stress" to mean the actual load on a material. "*Strength*" refers to the property of the material. In a material's property test, the stress at failure becomes the strength.

ULTIMATE STRENGTH: POINT D (ALSO CALLED TENSILE STRENGTH)

The *ultimate strength* (point D) is the maximum stress the material can experience without separation. This stress is calculated using the original area, although for many materials the actual area at this time is considerably reduced. The design stress is often based on the ultimate strength, which is also commonly included in tables like Table A-8. The strength based on the true area at failure is called the *true tensile strength*. It is of interest to metallurgists but is rarely used in design.

Returning again to the experiment described in Example Problem 11.5, we can now develop a direct relation between the load and deformation. From our definitions:

$$\sigma = \frac{P}{A}$$

$$\varepsilon = \frac{\delta}{L}$$

and Hooke's law is:

$$\sigma = E\varepsilon$$

Then by the appropriate substitution we have:

$$\frac{P}{A} = \frac{E\delta}{L}$$

Solving for δ yields:

$$\delta = \frac{PL}{AE} \tag{11.5}$$

This significant equation need not be memorized, because it is so easily obtained from the definitions of stress, strain, and Hooke's law. It is, however, worthwhile to carefully observe what it says and thereby reinforce or correct our intuition. Equation 11.5 says that the deformation is directly proportional to two things: load and length. Double the load and you double the deformation. Double the length and you double the deformation. It further says that the deformation is inversely proportional to two things: area and modulus of elasticity. Double the area and you cut the deformation in half. Double the modulus of elasticity—use a "stiffer" material—and you cut the deformation in half.

This relationship emphasizes that every structural member is really a spring—usually very stiff, but nonetheless a spring. Springs are normally described by the relation:

$$F = k\delta \tag{11.6}$$

where k is known as the spring constant whose units are pounds per inch. Evaluating Eq. 11.6 in terms of Eq. 11.5 yields:

$$k = \frac{AE}{L} \tag{11.7}$$

Example Problem 11.6

A member whose cross section is 2×4 (actual size) is loaded as shown in Fig. 11.18. The deformation is 0.120 in. Calculate the stress, strain, and modulus of elasticity.

Solution

We calculate the stress:

$$\sigma = \frac{P}{A} = \frac{500 \text{ lb}}{2 \text{ in. } (4 \text{ in.})} = \frac{500 \text{ lb}}{8 \text{ in.}^2}$$

$$\sigma = 62.5 \text{ psi}$$

and then the strain:

$$\varepsilon = \frac{\delta}{L} = \frac{0.120 \text{ in.}}{18 \text{ in.}} = 0.00667 \frac{\text{in.}}{\text{in.}}$$

and finally the modulus of elasticity:

$$E = \frac{\sigma}{\varepsilon} = \frac{62.5 \text{ lb}}{\text{in.}^2} \frac{\text{in.}}{(0.00667) \text{ in.}} = 9380 \text{ psi}$$

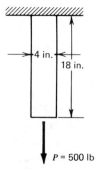

FIG. 11.18 Example Problem 11.6.

We could have calculated E directly from the given data and Eq. 11.5 as follows:

$$\delta = \frac{PL}{AE}$$

$$E = \frac{PL}{A\delta} = \frac{(500 \text{ lb}) (18 \text{ in.})}{(2 \text{ in.}) (4 \text{ in.}) (0.120 \text{ in.})} = \textbf{9380 psi}$$

Example Problem 11.7

Solve Example Problem 11.6 if the load is 2 kN, the length 0.5 m, the cross section 50 mm $\times$ 100 mm, and the deformation 3.00 mm.

Solution

Similar to the above:

$$\sigma = \frac{P}{A} = \frac{2 \text{ kN}}{(50 \text{ mm}) (100 \text{ mm})} = 4.00 \times 10^{-4} \frac{\text{kN}}{(\text{mm})^2} \left(\frac{1000 \text{ mm}}{\text{m}} \right)^2$$

$$\sigma = 4.00 \times 10^2 \frac{\text{kN}}{\text{m}^2} = \textbf{400 kPa}$$

$$\varepsilon = \frac{\delta}{L} = \frac{3.00 \text{ mm}}{0.5 \text{ m}} = 6.00 \frac{\text{mm}}{\text{m}} = \textbf{6.00} \times \textbf{10}^{-3} \frac{\textbf{m}}{\textbf{m}}$$

$$E = \frac{\sigma}{\varepsilon} = \frac{400 \text{ kPa}}{6.00 \times 10^{-3}} = 6.67 \times 10^4 \text{ kPa}$$

$$E = \textbf{66.7 MPa}$$

Example Problem 11.8

Determine the spring constant for the 2×4 described in Example Problem 11.6.

Solution

Since $F = k\delta$, we can write:

$$k = \frac{F}{\delta} = \frac{500 \text{ lb}}{0.120 \text{ in.}} = \textbf{4170} \frac{\textbf{lb}}{\textbf{in.}}$$

Alternately, by Eq. 11.7, we have:

$$k = \frac{AE}{L}$$

$$= \frac{(2 \times 4) \text{ in.}^2}{18 \text{ in.}} \frac{9380 \text{ lb}}{\text{in.}^2} = \textbf{4170} \frac{\textbf{lb}}{\textbf{in.}}$$

11.5   CHARACTERISTICS OF OTHER MATERIALS

Figure 11.16 is a typical stress–strain diagram for a ductile material, such as a mild steel. Certain material properties such as yield point are vividly illustrated by this diagram. Of course, not all materials are ductile, and not all ductile materials are described by this diagram. For instance, Fig. 11.19 is a typical stress–strain diagram for a brittle material. This material may have a fairly linear stress–strain curve up to the proportional limit, labeled *P*. (It may not, too.) However, it does not exhibit a definite yield point, as the ductile material does—point *C* in Fig. 11.16. In such cases we sometimes estimate a yield strength using the offset method. Typical offsets for metals are strains of 0.001 and 0.002. Much smaller offsets are suggested for materials such as wood or concrete. To determine the yield strength using the offset method, draw a line parallel to the linear portion of the stress–strain curve from a point of zero stress and the offset strain, point *A* in Fig. 11.19, to where it intersects the stress–strain curve, point *Y*. The stress corresponding to this point is taken as the yield strength.

This method of determining the yield strength can be used for any material that does not exhibit a definite yield point such as bronze or less ductile steels. In the case of very brittle materials such as cast iron or concrete it is used in only special circumstances. Accordingly, Table A-8 does not list yield strengths for these materials. Designs using such materials are more often based on the ultimate strength.

Another characteristic demonstrated in Fig. 11.16 that is not possessed by all materials is a linear stress–strain relationship in the initial stages. Figure 11.20 is a typical stress–strain curve for a material that does not exhibit this linearity. For

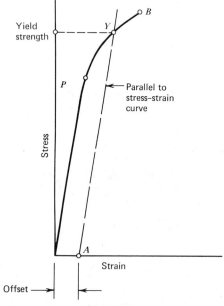

FIG. 11.19   Typical stress–strain curve for a brittle material.

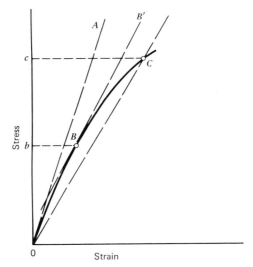

FIG. 11.20 Non-linear stress–strain curve.

such materials, special definitions of modulus of elasticity are necessary, and several are common. Recall that the modulus of elasticity is the slope of the stress–strain curve. One way of handling curves like those in Fig. 11.20 is to take the slope of the initial portion of the curve. Accordingly, the line OA is the *initial tangent modulus*. Second, we might find the slope at some intermediate point B. The line BB' then represents this modulus. It is called the *tangent modulus at stress b*, the stress associated with this point. The third concept is sort of an average modulus, where the line is not drawn tangent to the curve but from the origin to the point being referenced. The line OC represents this in Fig. 11.20. It is referred to as the *secant modulus at stress c*.

It is emphasized that the properties given in Table A-8 are typical of the materials indicated. Some of these vary very little, such as the density of the metals or the modulus of elasticity of steels. Others vary widely, such as the strength of steels or the modulus of elasticity of bronze. We use these properties as though they were the property of the material. You should realize that such is generally not the case. More detailed specifications, which are usually available from material suppliers, should be consulted for specific values for particular applications. However, the values from Table A-8 represent typical values and are appropriate for many non-critical applications.

11.6 POISSON'S RATIO

Again we return to Example Problem 11.5 concerning the tensile test of a metal specimen. The preceding section discussed the change in length in the axial direction δ_A the direction of the applied load. If we were to measure the diameter as the load is applied, we would find it to be decreasing, as shown in Fig. 11.21. In fact, it would decrease in a very orderly manner. This phenomenon is known as the

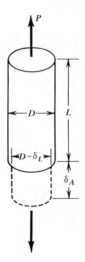

FIG. 11.21 Poisson effect.

Poisson effect. It can be described mathematically as follows:

$$\mu = -\frac{\varepsilon_{\text{lateral}}}{\varepsilon_{\text{axial}}} = -\frac{\varepsilon_L}{\varepsilon_A} \tag{11.8}$$

where

$$\varepsilon_A = \frac{\delta_{\text{axial}}}{\text{length}} = \frac{\delta_A}{L}$$

$$\varepsilon_L = \frac{\delta_{\text{lateral}}}{\text{diameter}} = \frac{\delta_L}{D}$$

and

$$\mu = \text{Poisson's ratio}$$

Since strain is dimensionless, the ratio of two strains is likewise dimensionless, and thus Poisson's ratio is also dimensionless.

We previously used μ for E-6 referring to microstrain. The Greek letters are used to provide additional symbols so that duplication is minimized—minimized but not eliminated. Usually, the context of the usage will clarify what is intended.

Frequently Eq. 11.8 is given without the negative sign. The negative sign takes into account the fact that the lateral strain is always of opposite sign of the axial strain. If the length is extended, the diameter will be reduced. If the length is compressed, the diameter will be extended. Later equations using μ always treat it as a positive value, so the negative sign in Eq. 11.8 is really needed.

The Poisson effect describes the strain in the lateral direction if the piece is free to move. If the piece is restrained from moving, a stress will be generated in the lateral direction. This stress can be calculated using Hooke's law.

Poisson's ratio is a property of the material. Since it is a ratio of strains, which are dimensionless quantities, it is also dimensionless. Theoretically, it can range in value from 0 to 0.5. Most metals have a value near 0.3, as can be seen in Table A-8.

Example Problem 11.9

A plate is loaded as shown in Fig. 11.22.
(a) Find the stress, axial strain, and lateral strain.
(b) If the plate were fixed in the lateral (4-in.) direction, what stress would be generated in this direction? The material is an aluminum for which:

$$E = 11 \times 10^6 \text{ psi} \quad \text{and} \quad \mu = 0.30$$

Solution

(a) $\sigma = \dfrac{P}{A} = \dfrac{10{,}000 \text{ lb}}{4(1) \text{ in.}^2} = \mathbf{2500 \text{ psi}}$

Rearranging Eq. 11.4 we have:

$$\varepsilon_A = \frac{\sigma}{E} = \frac{2500 \text{ lb-in.}^2}{\text{in.}^2\; 11 \times 10^6 \text{ lb}} = 0.000227 \frac{\text{in.}}{\text{in.}}$$

$$\varepsilon_A = \mathbf{227 \text{ E-6}}$$

This is the *axial* strain, or the strain in the direction of the load. The lateral strain or strain perpendicular to the load is, by Eq. 11.8,

$$\varepsilon_L = -\mu\varepsilon_A$$
$$= -0.3(0.000227) = -0.0000682$$
$$\varepsilon_L = \mathbf{-68.2 \text{ E-6}}$$

The minus sign means that there is a reduction in the lateral dimension.
(b) If the side is restrained, ε_L will not be allowed to take place. Hence a stress large enough to produce this strain will be generated:

$$\sigma_L = E\varepsilon_L = 11 \times 10^6 \text{ psi}(0.0000682)$$
$$\sigma_L = \mathbf{750 \text{ psi tension}}$$

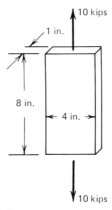

FIG. 11.22 Example Problem 11.9.

11.7   THERMAL STRAIN

A common assembly procedure in manufacturing metal components is a shrink fit: one part is heated, thereby expanding, and its mating part is cooled, thereby contracting. After sufficient heating and cooling, the two parts can be assembled without interference. As they come back to room temperature, the two parts are locked together. Dealing quantitatively with this situation involves thermal strains. We define a thermal strain in the same manner as we define other strains:

$$\varepsilon_T = \frac{\delta_T}{L}$$

where δ_T is the change in length due to a change in temperature (ΔT) and L is the original length.

The thermal strain is proportional to the change in temperature:

$$\varepsilon_T = \alpha(\Delta T) \tag{11.9}$$

where α (lowercase Greek alpha, English a) is the coefficient of thermal expansion. Table A-8 gives values of α for various materials; α will have the units per degree Fahrenheit (°F) or per degree Celsius (°C) in SI.

If thermal strain is not allowed to occur, a stress will be generated that may be calculated from Hooke's law. The thermal strain is equal in every direction.

Example Problem 11.10

A steel rod 1.25 in. in diameter and 2.0 ft long is heated 200°F. Find the thermal strain and the change in its diameter and length.

Solution

From Table A-8 we read the coefficient of thermal expansion

$$\alpha \times E6 = 6.5/°F.$$

Thus

$$\alpha = \frac{6.5 \times 10^{-6}}{°F}$$

We calculate the thermal strain as follows:

$$\varepsilon_T = \alpha(\Delta T) = \frac{6.5 \times 10^{-6} \times (200°F)}{°F}$$

$$\varepsilon_T = \mathbf{1.30 \times 10^{-3}}$$

The thermal strain is the same in every direction, so the change in diameter is:

$$\delta_{\text{diam}} = \varepsilon_T D = 1.30 \times 10^{-3}(1.25 \text{ in.}) = \mathbf{0.00165 \text{ in.}}$$

And the change in length is:

$$\delta_{\text{length}} = \varepsilon_T L = 1.30 \times 10^{-3}(2 \text{ ft})12 \text{ in./ft}$$

$$\delta_{\text{length}} = \mathbf{0.0312 \text{ in.}}$$

Example Problem 11.11

A steel plate $\frac{1}{4}$ in. × 2 in. is 12 in. long (Fig. 11.23). It is placed into a 12-in. opening where it exactly fits. Assuming that the opening does not change in size with temperature, find the stress in the plate when the temperature is increased 120°F.

Solution

From Table A-8:

$$\alpha = \frac{6.5 \times 10^{-6}}{°F} \quad \text{and} \quad E = 30 \times 10^6 \text{ psi}$$

If the plate were unrestrained, it would experience a thermal strain of:

$$\varepsilon_T = \alpha(\Delta T) = \frac{6.5 \times 10^{-6}}{°F} \times (120°F) = 7.80 \times 10^{-4}$$

or an extension of

$$\delta = \varepsilon L = 7.80 \times 10^{-4}(12 \text{ in.}) = \mathbf{9.36 \times 10^{-3} \text{ in.}}$$

This extension would occur if the plate were unrestrained. Since the extension does not take place, a load must be applied that would produce an equal compression of the plate.

$$\delta = \frac{PL}{AE}$$

$$P = \frac{\delta AE}{L} = \frac{9.36 \times 10^{-3} \text{ in. } (2 \text{ in.} \times 0.25 \text{ in.})}{12 \text{ in.}} \left(\frac{30 \times 10^6 \text{ lb}}{\text{in.}^2}\right)$$

$$P = 11,700 \text{ lb}$$

This load would produce a stress:

$$\sigma = \frac{P}{A} = \frac{11,700 \text{ lb}}{(2 \times 0.25) \text{ in.}^2} = \mathbf{23,400 \text{ psi}}$$

Alternately, the stress could have been calculated directly from the strain.

$$\sigma = E\varepsilon = 30 \times 10^6 \text{ psi } (7.8 \times 10^{-4}) = \mathbf{23,400 \text{ psi}}$$

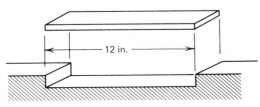

12 in.

FIG. 11.23 Example Problem 11.11.

11.8   SHEAR STRESS AND STRAIN

Consider now a square element of a material in an undisturbed state as shown in Fig. 11.24a. To this element a shear stress τ is applied to each face in the directions shown. By associating the stresses with the respective areas, it can be shown that equilibrium conditions are met. This is left to the student. The application of the shear stresses will produce the deformation shown in Fig. 11.24b. Fig 11.24c shows the element rotated clockwise through the angle $\gamma/2$ so that the entire deformation can be easily seen as the angle γ (lowercase Greek gamma—English g). This angle is defined as shear strain—measured in radians, which is a dimensionless term.

We calculate γ as follows:

$$\tan \gamma = \frac{\delta}{L} = \gamma \tag{11.10}$$

remembering that for very small angles:

$$\gamma = \tan \gamma$$

This equation for shear strain looks very similar to Eq. 11.3 for normal strain. There is, however, a very important difference. In Eq. 11.3 δ and L are in the same direction. In Eq. 11.10 they are perpendicular. In both cases the deformation δ is in the direction of the applied stress.

How is the shear stress τ, related to the shear strain γ? By Hooke's law, for shear which is:

$$\tau = G\gamma \tag{11.11}$$

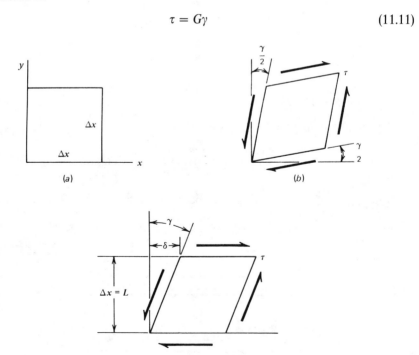

FIG. 11.24a–c   Shear strain.

where G is the *shear modulus of elasticity*, sometimes called the *modulus of rigidity*. Since γ is dimensionless, G must have the units of τ (psi or Pa). Note that this expression is parallel to Hooke's law for normal stress and strain:

$$\sigma = E\varepsilon$$

It is also very similar in words: the shear stress is proportional to shear strain.

The shear modulus of elasticity is determined experimentally. The method of doing this is discussed in Chapter 13. Like the modulus of elasticity, it is a property of the material. In addition to these two elastic properties, E and G, we also have Poisson's ratio μ. From the theory of elasticity—an advanced subject in engineering mechanics requiring considerable mathematical agility—it can be shown:

$$E = 2G(1 + \mu) \tag{11.12}$$

Not aspiring in this text to such agility, we accept the point at face value and go on to evaluate its implications, namely, that the three elastic constants, E, G, and μ, are not independent. If any two are known, the third may be determined.

Example Problem 11.12

A vibration isolation mounting is 20 mm wide (Fig. 11.25). It is made of rubber that has a shear modulus of elasticity of 50 MPa. Find the shear stress, shear strain, and angle of displacement in the direction of the load. Assume that Hooke's law for shear applies.

Solution

The 800-N load acts over the 50 mm × 20 mm plate, so:

$$\tau_{AV} = \frac{P}{A} = \frac{800 \text{ N}}{20 \text{ mm (50 mm)}} = \textbf{0.800 MPa}$$

Then by Eq. 11.11:

$$\gamma = \frac{\tau}{G} = \frac{0.800 \text{ MPa}}{5.0 \text{ MPa}} = 0.160$$

This is the shear strain, but it is also the angle of deformation in radians, and:

$$\delta = \gamma L = 0.16(10 \text{ mm}) = \textbf{1.60 mm}$$

which is the displacement of the plate in the direction of the 800-N load.

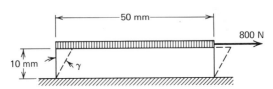

FIG. 11.25 Example Problem 11.12.

11.9 ALLOWABLE STRESS

In the first two sections of this chapter equations were developed for finding the normal stress and average shear stress in a structural member. These equations can also be used to select the size of a member if the member's *strength* is known. The strength of a material can be defined in several ways, depending on the material and the environment in which it is to be used. One definition is the ultimate strength or stress. Ultimate strength is the stress at which a material will rupture when subjected to a purely axial load. This property is determined from a tensile test of the material. This is a laboratory test of an accurately prepared specimen which usually is conducted on a universal testing machine. The load is applied slowly and is continuously monitored. The ultimate stress or strength is the maximum load divided by the original cross-sectional area. The ultimate strength for most engineering materials has been accurately determined and is readily available. Appendix Table A-8 gives some typical values for common materials.

If a member is loaded beyond its ultimate strength it will fail—rupture. In most engineering structures it is desirable that the structure not fail. Thus design is based on some lower value called *allowable stress* or *design stress*. If, for example, a certain steel is known to have an ultimate strength of 110,000 psi, a lower allowable stress would be used for design, say 55,000 psi. This allowable stress would allow only half the load the ultimate strength would allow. The ratio of the ultimate strength to the allowable stress is known as the *factor of safety*:

$$\text{factor of safety} = \frac{\text{ultimate strength}}{\text{allowable stress}}$$

$$N = \frac{S_u}{S_A} \tag{11.13}$$

We use S for strength or allowable stress and σ for the actual stress in a material. In a design:

$$\sigma \leq S_A$$

This so-called factor of safety covers a multitude of sins. It includes such factors as the uncertainty of the load, the uncertainty of the material properties, and the inaccuracy of the stress analysis. It could more accurately be called a factor of ignorance! In general, the more accurate, extensive, and expensive the analysis, the lower the factor of safety necessary.

In many cases failure is predicated on the material's yielding. When this is the case the yield strength replaces the ultimate strength in Eq. 11.13. And, of course, if failure is by shear, then shear strength goes into Eq. 11.13.

In some areas, primarily the aircraft industry, the idea of *margin of safety* (M) is used. It may be defined as follows:

$$M = N - 1 \tag{11.14}$$

In Chapter 21 two concepts that limit the direct application of this material

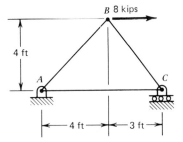

FIG. 11.26a Example Problem 11.13.

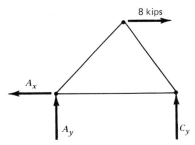

FIG. 11.26b Free body diagram for Example Problem 11.13.

are presented: *stress concentrations* and *fatigue*. These are very important restrictions, especially as it is applied to machine design. Stress concentration and fatigue are sometimes handled by very large factors of safety. Advancements in our understanding of these phenomena and the need to design effectively and efficiently are making the use of these very large factors of safety less and less desirable.

Example Problem 11.13

The truss in Fig. 11.26a is to be made of circular steel rods whose ultimate strength is 64,000 psi. Using a factor of safety of 4, find the size of member *AB*.

Solution

Draw a free body diagram (Fig. 11.26b) of the structure and find the reactions.

$$\sum M_A = 0 = -4(8) + 7(C_y)$$
$$C_y = \tfrac{32}{7} = 4.57 \text{ kips}\uparrow$$
$$\sum F_y = 0 = A_y + C_y$$
$$A_y = -4.57 \text{ kips}\downarrow$$
$$\sum F_x = 0 = -A_x + 8$$
$$A_x = 8.00 \text{ kips}\leftarrow$$

Draw a free body diagram (Fig. 11.27) of joint *B* and find the load in *AB*.

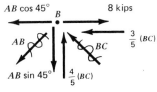

FIG. 11.27 Free body diagram of joint *B*.

Resolve forces into components:

$$\sum F_y = 0 = -AB \sin 45° + \tfrac{4}{5}BC$$

$$-0.707AB + 0.800BC = 0 \tag{1}$$

$$\sum F_x = 0 = -AB \cos 45° - \tfrac{3}{5}BC + 8$$

$$0.707AB + 0.600BC = 8.00 \tag{2}$$

Adding Eq. 2 to Eq. 1, we have:

$$(-0.707 + 0.707)AB + (0.800 + 0.600)BC = 8.00$$

$$1.40BC = 8.00$$

$$BC = \frac{8.00}{1.40} = 5.71 \text{ kips} \nwarrow \text{ compression}$$

Substituting back into Eq. 1:

$$-0.707AB + 0.800(5.71) = 0$$

$$AB = \frac{-0.800(5.71)}{-0.707} = 6.46 \text{ kips} \nearrow \text{ tension}$$

This is the load we must design for. The allowable stress S_A is found by Eq. 11.13:

$$S_A = \frac{S}{N} = \frac{64,00 \text{ psi}}{4} = 16,000 \text{ psi}$$

which we set equal to the actual stress σ in the member.

$$\sigma = S_A = \frac{P}{A}$$

Solving for A:

$$A = \frac{P}{S_A} = \frac{\pi D^2}{4}$$

And then D:

$$D^2 = \frac{4P}{\pi S_A} = \frac{4(6460 \text{ lb}) \text{ in.}^2}{\pi(16,000 \text{ lb})} = 0.514 \text{ in.}^2$$

$$D = \sqrt{0.514 \text{ in.}^2} = 0.717 \text{ in. minimum diameter}$$

11.10   SUMMARY

A number of new terms and equations are presented in this chapter. The student can minimize the confusion by concentrating on five definitions. Knowing the definition in words allows the equation to be written and vice versa. These terms and their equations are:

Normal stress:

$$\sigma = \frac{P}{A}$$

Strain:

$$\varepsilon = \frac{\delta}{L}$$

Hooke's law and modulus of elasticity:

$$\sigma = E\varepsilon$$

Coefficient of thermal expansion:

$$\alpha = \frac{\varepsilon_T}{\Delta T}$$

Poisson's ratio:

$$\mu = -\frac{\varepsilon_L}{\varepsilon_A}$$

The first three terms have parallel expressions in shear. Namely,

Average shear stress:

$$\tau_{AV} = \frac{P}{A}$$

Shear strain:

$$\gamma = \frac{\delta}{L}$$

Hooke's law for shear and the shear modulus of elasticity:

$$\tau = G_\gamma$$

Finally we have the concepts of allowable stress and factor of safety given by the equation:

$$N = \frac{S_u}{S_A}$$

We continue to provide summaries of essential information at the end of each chapter. As before, you will find it more helpful to make your own summary as you go through the chapter. Give particular emphasis to the topics your instructor emphasizes. Add details and clarifying notes that are meaningful to you. A good exercise to enhance your mastery of the subject is to start with a clean sheet of paper and reproduce your summary as you think your way through the chapter.

PROBLEMS

11.1 The block shown in Fig. 11.28 weighs 150 lb. What bearing stress due to its weight does it exert on the table it is resting on? If it is tipped to the left, where it rests on its side, what bearing stress will it exert?

11.2 A steel block has the dimensions 2 in. × 4 in. × 12 in. It rests on a table. What force does it exert on the table? If it is lying flat on one side, what is the maximum bearing stress it can exert? The minimum?

11.3 A steel block has the dimensions 50 mm × 100 mm × 300 mm. It rests on a table. What force does it exert on the table? If it is lying flat, what is the maximum bearing stress it can exert? The minimum?

11.4 For Fig. 11.29 the load P is 400 lb and the diameter of the shaft is 2 in. Find the normal stress.

11.5 For Fig. 11.29 the load is 2.50 kN and the diameter of the shaft is 5 mm. Find the normal stress.

11.6 What diameter rod is required to carry 1200-lb axial load if the stress is not to exceed 15,000 psi?

11.7 What diameter rod is required to carry 5.00-kN axial load if the stress is not to exceed 100 MPa?

11.8 The two rivets (in Fig. 11.30) carry a total load of 8000 lb. They are $\frac{1}{2}$ in. in diameter. Find the shear stress if the rivets are:

(a) As shown

(b) In double shear

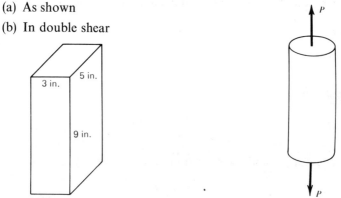

FIG. 11.28 Problem 11.1.   **FIG. 11.29** Problems 11.4, 11.5.

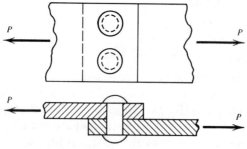

FIG. 11.30 Problems 11.8, 11.9.

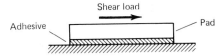

FIG. 11.31   Problems 11.10, 11.11, 11.47.

11.9   The two rivets (in Fig. 11.30) carry a total load of 40 kN. They are 12 mm in diameter. Find the shear stress if the rivets are:

(a) As shown   (b) In double shear

11.10   A brake pad carries a 650-lb shear load (Fig. 11.31). Its dimensions are 2 in. $\times$ $3\frac{1}{2}$ in. $\times$ $\frac{1}{4}$ in. thick. Find the average shear stress the adhesive must withstand.

11.11   A brake pad carries a 3-kN shear load (Fig. 11.31). Its dimensions are 50 mm $\times$ 100 mm $\times$ 6 mm thick. Find the average shear stress the adhesive must withstand.

11.12   A punch press is to punch $\frac{3}{4}$-in.-diameter slugs out of $\frac{1}{4}$-in.-thick aluminum sheet. Assuming an average shear strength of 14,000 psi, what capacity press is required?

11.13   A punch press is to punch 20-mm-diameter slugs out of 8.0-mm-thick aluminum sheet. Assuming an average shear strength of 96 MPa, what capacity press is required?

11.14   The truss shown (Fig. 11.32) is constructed of $\frac{1}{4}$-in. thick 2 $\times$ 2 angle iron (carbon steel) which has a cross-sectional area of 0.94 in.^{2} Find the stress in members:

(a)   *AB, AE*   (b)   *AE, BE, CE, EF*   (c)   *BC, CE, EF*

(d)   *EF, CF, CD*   (e)   *CD, DF*   (f)   All members

11.15   The steel truss shown in Fig. 11.33 is constructed of circular rods with a cross section of 2.00 cm^2. Find the stress in members:

(a)   *AB, BC*

(b)   *AD, CD*

(c)   *AB, AC, AD*

(d)   All members

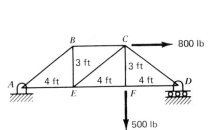

FIG. 11.32   Problems 11.14, 11.16.

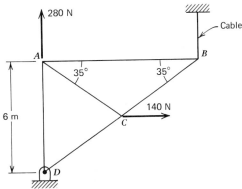

FIG. 11.33   Problems 11.15, 11.17.

11.16 For Problem 11.14, find the axial strain and deformation in the members indicated in each part.

11.17 For Problem 11.15, find the axial strain and deformation in the members indicated in each part.

11.18 A 1.0-in.-diameter rod is loaded with 50,000 lb. Its length is 15 in., and its modulus of elasticity is 11,000,000 psi. Find the stress, the strain, and the total elongation.

11.19 A 25-mm-diameter rod is loaded with 200 kN. Its length is 400 mm, and its modulus of elasticity is 71 GPa. Find the stress, the strain, and the total elongation.

11.20 A 0.50-in.-diameter rod is loaded with 10,000 lb. It is 12 in. long and deflects 0.003 in. under this load. Find the stress, the strain, and the modulus of elasticity.

11.21 A 0.50-in.-diameter rod is loaded in tension ($P = 15,000$ lb). The total deformation resulting from this load is measured to be 0.008 in. If the rod is 2 ft long, determine the stress, strain, and modulus of elasticity.

11.22 A 12-mm-diameter rod is loaded in tension (70 kN). The total deformation resulting from this load is measured to be 600 mm. If the rod is 6000 mm long, determine the stress, strain, and modulus of elasticity.

11.23 A 0.75-in.-diameter rod is loaded in tension ($P = 12,000$ lb). The total deformation is measured to be 0.005 in. under this load. If the rod is 1.5 ft long, determine the stress, the strain, and modulus of elasticity.

11.24 A tensile test is made of a steel specimen cut from a pressure cylinder. The gage length is 2.00 in., the width 0.500 in., and the thickness 0.230 in. From the following data, plot a stress–strain curve and determine the yield strength, the ultimate strength, and the percentage of elongation at failure.

Load (lb)	Elongation (in.)	Load (lb)	Elongation (in.)
1000	0.00062	10,000	0.01200
2000	0.00120	9900	0.02400
3000	0.00183	9900	0.03620
4000	0.00244	12,000	0.06050
5000	0.00305	14,000	0.10072
6000	0.00360	14,200	0.15065
7000	0.00421	14,000	0.20016
8000	0.00478	10,000	0.25005
9000	0.00535	8250	0.31612
10,000	0.00605		

11.25 For the data in Problem 11.24, plot the stress–strain diagram up to the proportional limit (load = 10,000 lb) and calculate the modulus of elasticity.

11.26 A tensile test is made of an aluminum specimen that has a gage length of 50.8 mm and a diameter of 12.8 mm. Plot the stress–strain diagram and determine the approximate yield strength, the ultimate strength, and the percentage elongation at failure.

Load (kN)	Elongation (μm)
4.0	22
8.0	44
12.0	66
16.0	89
20.0	111
24.0	133
28.0	155
32.0	178
36.0	200
40.0	500
44.0	1120
48.0	2390
52.0	4060
54.2	8130
48.2	10,200

11.27 For the data in Problem 11.26, plot the stress–strain diagram up to the proportional limit (load = 36.0 kN) and calculate the modulus of elasticity.

11.28 A $\frac{1}{8}$-in.-diameter steel bolt is 6 in. long. Find its spring constant.

11.29 A 30-mm-diameter steel bolt is 150 mm long. Find its spring constant.

11.30 A tensile test specimen has a circular cross section of 0.505-in. diameter and a gage length of 4.00 in. It is loaded to 18,000 lb and stretches 0.0240 in. Its diameter shrinks 0.0010 in. Under these conditions find the normal stress, axial strain, modulus of elasticity, and Poisson's ratio.

11.31 A tensile test specimen has a circular cross section of 13-mm diameter and a gage length of 100 mm. It is loaded to 80 kN and stretches 0.61 mm. Its diameter shrinks 25.4 μm. Under these conditions find the normal stress, axial strain, modulus of elasticity, and Poisson's ratio.

11.32 A tensile test specimen has a gage length of 8 in. Its circular cross section is 0.505 in. in diameter. It stretches 0.0240 in. when loaded to 32,000 lb. Under these conditions find the axial strain, the normal stress, and the modulus of elasticity. For a Poisson's ratio of 0.30, find the change in diameter.

11.33 A magnesium test bar with a $\frac{1}{2}$ in. $\times$ $1\frac{1}{2}$ in. cross section is loaded in compression parallel to its 10-in. length by an 8000-lb load.

(a) Find the change in length of this bar.

(b) Find the change in cross-sectional area.

11.34 A magnesium test bar with a 12 mm $\times$ 38 mm cross section is loaded in compression parallel to its 250-mm length by a 35.0-kN load.

(a) Find the change in length of this bar.

(b) Find the change in cross-sectional area.

11.35 A bar of aluminum has a cross-sectional area of 3.00 in.^{2}. It is 12.0 in. long. Find its change in length when it is heated 150°F. What load would be developed in the bar if its ends had been totally restrained during the heating?

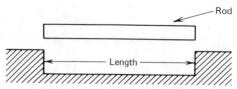

FIG. 11.34   Problems 11.38, 11.39.

11.36 A bar of aluminum has a cross-sectional area of 20 cm². It is 300 mm long. Find its change in length when it is heated 85°C. What load would be developed in the bar if its ends had been totally restrained during the heating?

11.37 A bar of bronze has a cross-sectional area of 2.00 in.². It is 20.0 in. long. It is heated 100°F. Find its change in length. What load would be developed in the bar if its ends had been totally restrained during the heating?

11.38 A ¾-in.-diameter steel rod exactly 6.0 in. long is placed between two rigid plates that are fixed exactly 6.0 in. apart (Fig. 11.34). The rod is heated 400°F in an attempt to force the plates apart. What force is developed in the rod?

11.39 A 20-mm-diameter steel rod, exactly 150 mm long, is placed between two rigid plates that are fixed exactly 150 mm apart (Fig. 11.34). The rod is heated 250°C in an attempt to force the plates apart. What force is developed in the rod?

11.40 A 2-in.-diameter steel shaft is to fit into a 2-in.-diameter hole in an aluminum housing. There is an interference of 0.003 in. between the two parts.

(a)   If the housing is held at room temperature, how much must the shaft be cooled for assembly?

(b)   If the shaft is held at room temperature, how much must the housing be heated for assembly?

(c)   If both are heated, how much must they be heated for assembly?

11.41 An aluminum electric power cable is strung between two towers on a summer day in Stillwater when it is 100°F. The towers are 300 yd apart, and the 1-in.-diameter cable is pulled to a tension of 1200 lb. Treating the cable as a solid rod, find the tension in it on a January day when the temperature drops to 10°F. Assume the towers to be immovable and the cable length to be exactly 300 yd.

11.42 An aluminum electric power cable is strung between two towers on a summer day in Stillwater when it is 38°C. The towers are 300 m apart and the 25-mm-diameter cable is pulled to a tension of 5.4 kN. Treating the cable as a solid rod, find the tension in it on a January day when the temperature

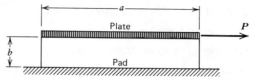

FIG. 11.35   Problems 11.43, 11.44, 11.45, 11.46.

drops to $-12°C$. Assume the towers to be immovable and the cable length to be exactly 300 m.

11.43 A plate is attached to rubber isolation pad as shown in Fig. 11.35. Find the magnitude of the force **P** required to deflect the plate 1.0 mm for the following properties.

	Width (mm)	a (mm)	b (mm)	G (MPa)
(a)	10	60	12	7.0
(b)	20	100	20	4.0
(c)	20	50	30	10.0

11.44 A plate is attached to a rubber isolation pad as shown in Fig. 11.35. The plate moves 0.0500 in. in the direction of the load **P** under the conditions indicated below. Find the shear modulus of elasticity.

	Width (in.)	a (in.)	b (in.)	P (lb)
(a)	1.00	0.40	2.00	300
(b)	0.50	1.00	3.00	600
(c)	2.00	0.80	6.00	600

11.45 The plate shown in Fig. 11.35 is found to deflect 1.5 mm in the direction of a 1.0-kN load (**P**) when the pad is 12 mm thick. What will be the deflection if the pad's thickness b is increased to 30 mm and all other conditions remain the same?

11.46 The plate shown in Fig. 11.35 is found to deflect 0.12 in. in the direction of an 80 lb load (**P**) when the plate is 10.0 in. long. What will be the deflection if the plate length (a) is reduced to 4.0 in. and all other conditions remain the same?

11.47 For Problem 11.10 and Fig. 11.31, assume the adhesive is $\frac{1}{16}$ in. thick and has a shear modulus of elasticity of 1.0×10^6 psi. What shear strain would be developed in the adhesive? How far would the brake pad translate in the direction of the load due to the shear strain?

11.48 From a tensile test, an aluminum alloy is found to have a modulus of elasticity of 12.0×10^6 psi and a Poisson's ratio of 0.33. Find the shear modulus of elasticity.

11.49 From a tensile test an aluminum alloy is found to have a modulus of elasticity of 83 GPa and a Poisson's ratio of 0.33. Find the shear modulus of elasticity.

11.50 Using Eq. 11.12, verify the Poisson's ratio given in Table A-8, assuming E and G to be correct.

(a) Using SI units, check bronze and stainless steel.

(b) Using English units, check cast iron and magnesium.

11.51 Determine the diameter of the rivets in Fig. 11.36 if the ultimate strength in shear is 60,000 psi and a safety factor of 3 is desired for a load $P = 1500$ lb.

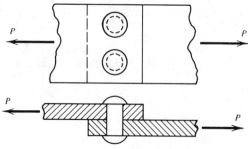

FIG. 11.36   Problems 11.51, 11.52.

11.52 Determine the diameter of the rivets in Fig. 11.36 if the ultimate strength in shear is 400 MPa and a safety factor of 3 is desired for a load $P = 7.0$ kN.

11.53 Determine the diameter of the steel rivets in Fig. 11.37 if the ultimate strength in shear is 80,000 psi and a safety factor of 4 is desired for a load $P = 2500$ lb.

11.54 Determine the diameter of the steel rivets in Fig. 11.37 if the ultimate strength in shear is 550 MPa and a safety factor of 4 is desired for a load $P = 11.0$ kN.

11.55 Define and if appropriate, write an equation for the following terms:

(a)   Normal stress (b)   Normal strain
(c)   Deformation (d)   Thermal strain
(e)   Shear modulus of elasticity (f)   Poisson's ratio
(g)   Young's modulus (h)   Hooke's law

11.56 For the truss of Fig. 11.38; based on an ultimate strength of 6000 psi and a factor of safety of 4, find the minimum cross-sectional area of the following members. (Members loaded in compression may buckle, but you may neglect that consideration for the present.)

(a)   *AB, AE* (b)   *AE, BE, CE, EF* (c)   *BC, CE, EF*
(d)   *EF, CF, CD* (e)   *CD, DF* (f)   All members

11.57 For Fig. 11.38, what size pin is required for joint *A* based on an allowable shear stress of 20,000 psi?

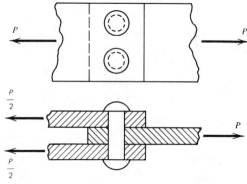

FIG. 11.37   Problems 11.53, 11.54.

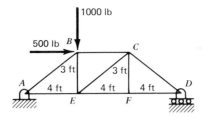

FIG. 11.38 Problems 11.56, 11.57.

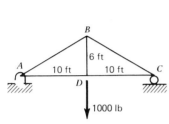

FIG. 11.39 Problem 11.58.

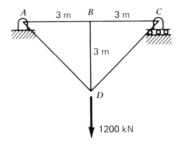

FIG. 11.40 Problem 11.59.

11.58 For the truss shown in Fig. 11.39, find the axial stress, strain, and deformation for member BC. Its cross section is 2 in. × 2 in. square. The members are steel.

11.59 For the truss shown in Fig. 11.40, find the axial stress, strain, and deformation for BC, which is an aluminum member having a rectangular cross section of 100 mm × 30 mm.

11.60 For Fig. 11.41, find the force Q required to compress the 1.5-in.-diameter block 0.002 in. What is the change in diameter of this block under this load? The block is aluminum.

11.61 The support bracket at B in Fig. 11.41 is shown in detail in Fig. 11.42. Based on a shear strength of 45 ksi and a factor of safety of 3, what size pin is needed if the force Q is 500 lb?

11.62 For Fig. 11.43, the bronze link CD is 80 mm long and 20 mm × 10 mm in cross section. Find the strains in link CD in the 20-mm and 80-mm directions under the loading shown.

11.63 The support bracket at point B in Fig. 11.43 is shown in detail in Fig. 11.42. Based on a shear strength of 360 MPa and a factor of safety of 4, what size pin is needed?

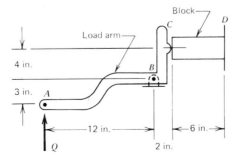

FIG. 11.41 Problems 11.60, 11.61.

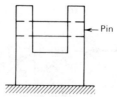

FIG. 11.42 Support bracket *B* for Figs. 11.41 and 11.43.

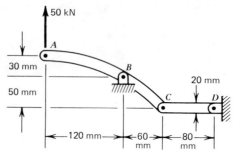

FIG. 11.43 Problems 11.62, 11.63.

11.64 Find the load, stress, strain, and deformation in the member *AB*, Fig. 11.44. Its cross section is 13 mm × 25 mm and it is aluminum.

11.65 Find the load, stress, strain, and deformation in member *AB*, Fig. 11.45. It is a solid rod with a $\frac{3}{4}$-in. diameter and is steel.

11.66 Find the diameter of connecting pin needed at *B* for the linkage shown in Fig. 11.46, based on shear strength of 15 ksi and a safety factor of 3.

11.67 Find the diameter of the pin needed at *C* for the pump handle shown in Fig. 11.47. Use a shear strength of 80 MPa and a factor of safety of 4.

11.68 Member *BD* (Fig. 11.48) is a steel pipe, 80 mm O.D. and 70 mm I.D. From the loading shown find its:

(a) Stress   (b) Change in length

(c) Change in diameter

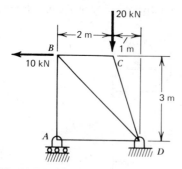

FIG. 11.44 Problem 11.64.

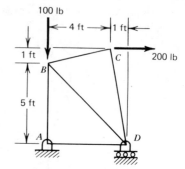

FIG. 11.45 Problem 11.65.

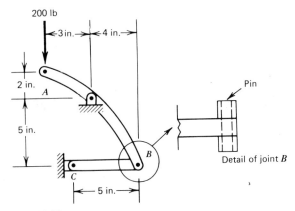

FIG. 11.46   Problem 11.66.

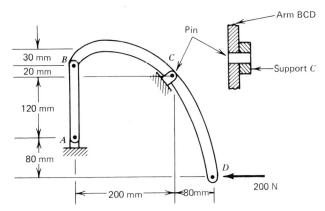

FIG. 11.47   Problem 11.67.

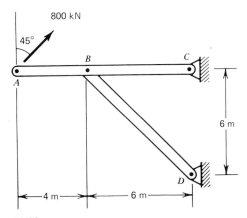

FIG. 11.48   Problem 11.68.

12

Properties of Areas

There are two approaches to the topic at hand. One is to treat it as a mathematical curiosity. The other is the totally utilitarian one of finding needed values in tables when necessary. Neither approach is adequate for our needs. The first neglects the simplicity with which detailed data may be had and used. The second fails to consider how these phenomena—centroid, moment of area, and moment of inertia—behave, and therefore it fails to promote an understanding of how they affect stress and deflection. There are also numerous occasions when handbook data are not available. We will strike a middle path—we seek maximum under-standing *and* computational ease. We demonstrate the importance of these con-cepts by the following example. Say we take a 2 × 12 that is 20 ft long. We wish to support it on each end and walk across it. In the first case we turn it edgewise, that is, 2 in. wide and 12 in. deep. We walk to the center. The deflection is hardly noticeable. Second, we turn the same 2 × 12 flat, that is, 12 in. wide and 2 in. deep. Now we walk toward the center. The deflection is substantial indeed, and we may even break the board before we reach the center. Same board, same load, and same span, but something is drastically different! The drastic difference is that the stress has been increased by a factor of 6 and the deflection by a factor of 36. This behavior is perfectly predictable, based on an understanding of the moment of inertia of the cross section of the board. In this chapter we will learn to compute this and associated properties, and we will see how these properties vary with the geometry of the cross section.

12.1 DISTRIBUTED LOAD AND CENTER OF GRAVITY

We have classified loads as being distributed or concentrated. We treat concentrated loads as though they act at a point, when in fact all loads are distributed to some degree. The most common distributed load is an object's weight.

Consider the rather general distributed load on the simply supported beam in Fig. 12.1. We characterize this general shape mathematically by writing:

$$w = f(x)$$

That is, w is a function of x, or in still plainer terms, the load rate w (i.e., load per unit length of the beam) depends on the position x. We pick a small element of the beam—dx. The load on this element is:

$$dW = w\,dx$$

The total load on the beam is the sum of all these elements from the left-hand end to the right:

$$W = \int dW = \int_0^L w\,dx$$

If $w = f(x)$ is known, this integral can be evaluated mathematically. A more useful form to us is to recognize that this integral is simply the area under the curve w. These areas are normally those we recognize—rectangular, triangular, and the

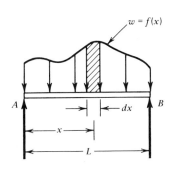

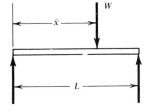

FIG. 12.1 Equivalent loads.

like—and we can easily compute their areas from standard formulas. Thus we write:

$$W = \int_0^L w\,dx = \text{area under load rate curve} \qquad (12.1)$$

The moment of the element of dW about A is the magnitude of the force times the distance to it, or:

$$dM = x\,dW = x(w\,dx)$$

Then the total moment is:

$$M = \int dM = \int x\,dW = \int_0^L x(w\,dx) \qquad$$

Again if $w = f(x)$ were known, the equation above could be evaluated. Since we can evaluate the total load by recognizing the area of loading, we ask the question: Where would this load W have to act to give the same moment about A? We designate this position as $\bar{x}$, then:

$$\bar{x}W = \bar{x}\int dW = \int x\,dW \qquad (12.2)$$

In other words, the moment of the sum of the forces is equal to the sum of the moments of the forces. We solve for $\bar{x}$, the location in question:

$$\bar{x} = \frac{\int x\,dW}{\int dW} \qquad (12.3)$$

We call this point the center of gravity and reach the following important conclusion. For the purposes of statics—finding the reactions at A and B (Fig. 12.1)—the distributed load is equivalent to the total load concentrated at the center of gravity. This is because they both give the same moment of force about any point, and they both give the same resultant force. Thus they are said to be *statically equivalent*.

12.2   AREA, MOMENT OF AREA, AND THE CENTROID

Equation 12.1 allows us to find total load for a distributed load. Looking at the Fig. 12.1, we observe that $w\,dx$ is really just the area of this infinitesimal rectangular element, and summing all such areas will simply give the total area under the load rate curve. Thus, for Fig. 12.2 we generate an analogous expression for the area bounded by the arbitrary curve $y = f(x)$, the X and Y axes, and the vertical line $x = x_0$:

$$A = \int y\,dx \qquad (12.4)$$

where the height of the curve is y instead of w.

Equation 12.2 gives values for the moment of force. Again going to Fig. 12.2, we obtain an analogous equation for *moment of area*:

$$M_y = \int x(y\,dx) = \int x\,dA \qquad (12.5)$$

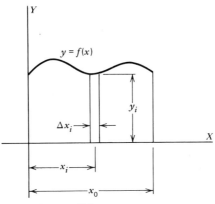

FIG. 12.2   Area under the curve $y = f(x)$.

The moment of area is a new concept to many, and sometimes it causes a good deal of difficulty. It shouldn't. It is really very straightforward. Just take it as a mathematical expression until you develop a good feel for it. Like other moments it must have a reference axis, the Y axis in this case. Its units will be length times area (ft^3, m^3, etc.).

Finally we take Eq. 12.3 and apply it to the area in Fig. 12.2 and get:

$$\bar{x} = \frac{\int x \, dA}{\int dA} \tag{12.6}$$

For a distributed load $\bar{x}$ refers to the center of gravity. For an area it locates the *centroid*. Dimensionally we have:

$$\bar{x} \overset{D}{=} \frac{ft^3}{ft^2} = ft$$

Evaluation Eqs. 12.4, 12.5, and 12.6 for various areas give the results shown in Table A-9. The centroid is located in these figures by the intersection of axes or a dot. Later we will introduce the other properties given in the table. At this point, note that if an area has an axis of symmetry, the centroid will be on it. If it has two axes of symmetry, the centroid must be the intersection of those axes.

Tables A-10 through A-15 give the properties of structural steel shapes including pipes. These tables are for steel members, although aluminum beams are manufactured with many of the same specifications. The center section of the standard I beam is known as the web (see illustration in Table A-10). The top and bottom portions are called flanges. The first column gives the beam's official designation. The first one listed is S 24 × 120. The "S" means that this is a *standard* beam. The 24 is the *nominal* (not necessarily exact) *depth* of the beam. The last number refers to the *weight per foot* of the beam. Thus a 10-ft length of this beam would weigh 1200 lb. The second column gives the cross-sectional area A. If the beam is treated as three rectangular areas of the dimensions given, this number will be approximated. Small differences exist because of fillets at the corners and tapering of the flanges. The third column gives the actual depth d. Sometimes this is the same as the nominal depth, but frequently it is not. Because of symmetry, the centroid will be at the $X-X$ axis half the depth from the base. For this beam it will be 12.00 in. The next two columns refer to the flange. The first is the width and the second is the average thickness; the flanges are actually tapered. Again because of symmetry the vertical centroidal axis is the $Y-Y$ axis, which is half the width from either side, 4.024 in. in this case. And finally we have the thickness of the web. The remaining six columns will be considered later.

Table A-11 is for wide flange beams (W). Table A-12 is for channels (C), sometimes called "channel iron," although the term really refers to structural steel. The first six columns have the same meaning as for the standard beams. The designation "C 12 × 25" means that a channel (C), is nominally 12 in. in depth (12) and weighs 25 lb/ft (25). The $X-X$ axis is a centroidal axis by symmetry and is half the depth from the base, 6.00 in. in this case. There is no vertical axis of symmetry, and the vertical centroidal axis is located by $\bar{x}$ from the left side of the web, 0.674 in. for this channel.

Tables A-13 through A-15 follow a similar pattern for other shapes. These tables are provided by the American Institute of Steel Construction and other trade organizations.

It is worthwhile to examine Eq. 12.6 further. We multiply both sides of the equation by the area and get:

$$\bar{x} \int dA = \int x \, dA = \bar{x} A \tag{12.7}$$

The expression is now one for moment of area and tells us that it is equal to the distance from the reference axis to the centroid of the area, $\bar{x}$, times the total area, $\int dA$. This concept will prove to be very useful.

These equations give properties with respect to a Y axis. Similar equations may be written with respect to the X axis, namely:

$$M_x = \int y \, dA = \bar{y} \int dA = \bar{y} A \tag{12.8}$$

$$\bar{y} = \frac{\int y \, dA}{\int dA} \tag{12.9}$$

Example Problem 12.1

Using Table A-9, find the centroid and the moment of the area shown in Fig. 12.3 with respect to the X and Y axes.

Solution

From the table (or general knowledge) the area of the semicircle is

$$A = \frac{\pi D^2}{8} = \frac{\pi (12 \text{ in.})^2}{8} = 56.5 \text{ in.}^2$$

We observe the vertical axis of symmetry to be the centroidal axis for the

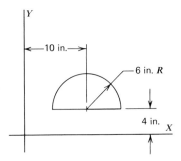

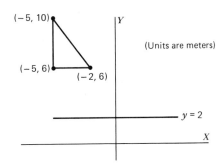

FIG. 12.3   Example Problem 12.1.   **FIG. 12.4**   Example Problem 12.2.

semicircle and by observation:

$$\bar{x} = 10.0 \text{ in.}$$

From Table A-9 we see the centroid is $2D/3\pi$ above the base. So:

$$\bar{y} = 4 + \frac{2(12)}{3\pi} = 6.55 \text{ in.}$$

From Eq. 12.7 the moment of area about the Y axis is the distance from the axis to the centroid times the area, or:

$$M_y = \bar{x}A = 10 \text{ in.}(56.5 \text{ in.}^2) = 565 \text{ in.}^3$$

and

$$M_x = \bar{y}A = 6.55(56.5) = 370 \text{ in.}^3$$

Both these moments of area are positive because the distances from the reference axes are positive and of course real areas are always positive. We have *negative* moments of area when the distance to the centroid is negative.

EVALUATION   The centroid is closer to the X axis than it is to the Y axis; therefore M_x is less than M_y. We observe that the further an area is from a reference point, the greater its moment about that axis will be.

Example Problem 12.2

(a) Locate the centroid of the triangular area shown in Fig. 12.4 with respect to the X and Y axes.
(b) Find the moment of area with respect to the X and Y axes.
(c) Also find the moment of area with respect to the axis $y = 2$.

Solution

(a) Looking at Table A-9 we see that the centroid is one-third of the height away from the base or two-thirds from the apex. Thus:

$$\bar{y} = 6 + \tfrac{1}{3}(4) = 7.33 \text{ m}$$

and

$$\bar{x} = -2 - \tfrac{2}{3}(3) = -4.00 \text{ m}$$

Since the distance is to the left of the Y axis, its proper sign is negative.

(b) The area is:

$$A = \frac{bh}{2} = \frac{3(4)}{2} = 6.00 \ m^2$$

The moments of area are:

$$M_x = \bar{y}A = 7.33 \ m(6.00 \ m^2) = \textbf{44.0 m}^3$$
$$M_y = \bar{x}A = -4.00(6.00) = \textbf{-24.0 m}^3$$

The moment of area with respect to the Y axis is negative because the moment arm is negative.

(c) Finally the moment about the axis, $y = 2$, is the distance from this axis to the centroid $(7.33 - 2)$ times the area:

$$M_{y=2} = (7.33 - 2)(6.00) = \textbf{32.0 m}^3$$

12.3 MOMENT OF AREA AND CENTROID OF COMPOSITE AREAS

Tables such as Table A-9 can be generated by evaluating Eqs. 12.5 through 12.9. In practice, this manipulation is rarely made. Most areas for which the centroid must be evaluated may be handled by using tabular information and a finite form of Eqs. 12.6 and 12.9, namely:

$$\bar{x} = \frac{\sum \bar{x}_i A_i}{\sum A_i} \tag{12.10}$$

$$\bar{y} = \frac{\sum \bar{y}_i A_i}{\sum A_i} \tag{12.11}$$

These equations restate the concept that the moment of the sum of the areas is equal to the sum of the moments of the areas. We apply them to most problems by recognizing those areas to be the sum of elementary areas whose properties, that is, area and centroid location, are known.

If the areas in Table A-9 are thought of as solids of uniform thickness, the centroids will coincide with the centers of gravity. Note that a body may be balanced by supporting it at its center of gravity. On this basis we see that the centers of gravity are about where we would expect them to be.

Example Problem 12.3

Find the moment of area and the centroid of the area shown in Fig. 12.5 with respect to the Y axis.

Solution

We break the area into components whose properties are known and calculate the total area.

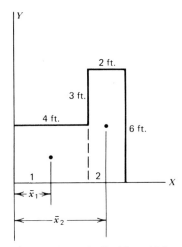

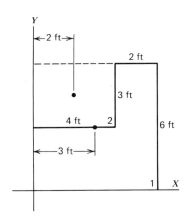

FIG. 12.5 Example Problem 12.3.

FIG. 12.6 Alternate solution for Example Problem 12.3.

$$A_T = A_1 + A_2$$
$$= 4(3) + 2(6) = 24.0 \text{ ft}^2$$

Next, we compute the moment of area about the Y axis.

$$\bar{x}A_T = \sum \bar{x}_i A_i$$
$$= 2[4(3)] + (4 + 1)[2(6)]$$
$$\bar{x}A_T = 24 + 60 = \mathbf{84.0 \text{ ft}^3}$$

Then the centroid with respect to the Y axis is

$$\bar{x} = \frac{\sum \bar{x}_i A_i}{\sum A_i} = \frac{84.0 \text{ ft}^3}{24.0 \text{ ft}^2} = \mathbf{3.50 \text{ ft}}$$

Note that the centroid at 3.50 ft is between the centroids of the two component areas, as we would expect. This quick check of calculations is always available and should be routinely used.

Alternate Solution

A second way to approach this problem is to view the area as a 6 ft × 6 ft square (area 1) with a 4 × 3 (area 2) corner (hole) cut off as shown in Fig. 12.6. The total area is:

$$A_T = A_1 + A_2$$
$$A_T = 6(6) + -4(3) = 24.0 \text{ ft}^2$$

The 4 × 3 hole is treated as a negative area, and since the area is a hole, it will also have a negative moment of area.

$$\bar{x}A_T = \sum \bar{x}_i A_i$$
$$\bar{x}A_T = 3[6(6)] + 2[-4(3)] = \mathbf{84.0 \text{ ft}}$$

We note at this point that the moment arms $\bar{x}_i$ can also be negative. A negative moment arm times a positive area gives a negative moment of area. A negative moment arm times a negative area (hole) gives a positive moment of area. Continuing with the solution, we find the centroid to be:

$$\bar{x} = \frac{84.0 \text{ ft}^3}{24.0 \text{ ft}^3} = \textbf{3.50 ft}$$

Example Problem 12.4

Find the area, moments of area about the X and Y axes, and horizontal and vertical centroidal axes for the triangular area in Fig. 12.7. The circular hole has a diameter of 30 mm.

Solution

The area is found by subtracting the area of the hole A_2 from the area of the triangle A_1.

$$A = A_1 - A_2$$

$$A = \frac{bh}{2} - \frac{\pi D^2}{4}$$

$$A = \frac{60(90)}{2} - \frac{\pi(30)^2}{4}$$

$$A = 2700 - 707 = \textbf{1990 mm}^2$$

The hole is considered to be a negative area in calculating the area. It also is considered to be a negative area in calculating the moment of area about the X axis. Thus:

$$M_x = \bar{y}_1 A_1 - \bar{y}_2 A_2$$

$$M_x = \frac{90}{3}(2700) - 20(707) = \textbf{66,900 mm}^3$$

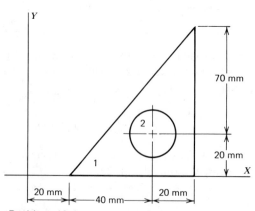

FIG. 12.7 Example Problem 12.4.

And similarly:

$$M_y = \bar{x}_1 A_1 - \bar{x}_2 A_2$$

$$M_y = \left(20 + \frac{2(60)}{3}\right) 2700 - 60(707)$$

$$M_y = \textbf{120,000 mm}^3$$

The centroidal axes are found by dividing the moments of area by the area according to Eqs. 12.10 and 12.11. The *horizontal* centroidal axis is located by:

$$\bar{y} = \frac{M_x}{A} = \frac{66,900 \text{ mm}^3}{1990 \text{ mm}^2}$$

$$\bar{y} = \textbf{33.6 mm}$$

And for the *vertical*:

$$\bar{x} = \frac{M_y}{A} = \frac{120,000 \text{ mm}^3}{1990 \text{ mm}^2} = \textbf{60.0 mm}$$

Since the vertical centroidal axis of the triangle coincides with the axis of the circular hole, we could have simply observed this result.

Example Problem 12.5

A beam has the cross section shown in Fig. 12.8. Find its centroid with respect to a horizontal axis.

Solution

A horizontal axis $X-X$ is drawn at the bottom of the member.

Geometric properties of the members are found from Tables A-11 and A-12. The W 14 × 61 is a wide flange beam (W), nominally 14 in. deep (14), but actually 13.91 in. (column 3), and weighs 61 lb/ft (61). It has an area of 17.9 in.^{2}

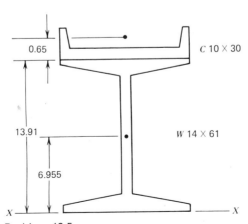

FIG. 12.8 Example Problem 12.5.

(column 2). Its centroid is at its midpoint, so:

$$\bar{y}_1 = \frac{13.91}{2} = 6.955 \text{ in.}$$

The C 10 × 30 is a channel (C), nominally 10 in. deep and actually 10.00 in. deep (column 3). It weighs 30 lb/ft (30). Its area is 8.82 in.^{2} (column 2). Its centroid is 0.649 in. above its base (the last column, "$\bar{x}$"). Then:

$$\bar{y}_2 = 13.91 + 0.649 = 14.56 \text{ in.}$$

The total area is:

$$A = \sum A_i = A_1 + A_2 = 17.9 + 8.82 = 26.72 \text{ in.}^2$$

The total moment of area is:

$$\bar{y}A = \sum y_i A_i = 6.955(17.9) + 14.56(8.82)$$
$$\bar{y}A = 252.9 \text{ in.}^3$$

And the centroid is found by:

$$\bar{y} = \frac{\sum y_i A_i}{\sum A_i} = \frac{252.9}{26.72} = \textbf{9.47 in.}$$

Note that this centroid is bounded by the centroids of the component parts.

12.4   CENTROIDS BY INTEGRATION

The area, moment of area, and centroid of common areas given in Table A-9 are derived by integration of Eqs. 12.4, 12.5, and 12.6. With such tables available, it is unusual to evaluate these equations by integration—unusual, but not unknown. Although you can have considerable success in dealing with the material at hand without calculus, there are several reasons for actually evaluating the integral.

1. It is necessary to solve some problems this way.
2. Evaluating integrals will help you understand how moment of area and the centroid behave and will give a better grasp of these elusive concepts.
3. Some areas must be evaluated by numerical integration. In such cases the problem is set up as though the integral were going to be evaluated analytically.

Example Problem 12.6

Find the centroid of the triangle shown in Fig. 12.9 with respect to the Y axis.

Solution

Since the centroid is the moment of area divided by the area, we must find these two quantities. Start with the incremental area:

$$dA = y\,dx$$

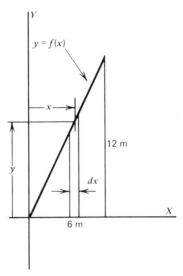

FIG. 12.9 Example Problem 12.6.

You should pick an area with its finite dimension y parallel to the reference axis. Then:

$$A = \int y\,dx$$

To evaluate this equation requires knowledge of y as a function of x. Evaluating the general equation for a straight line:

$$y = mx + b$$

we get:

$$y = 2x + 0$$

for the line shown. Then integrating in the X direction and setting the limits from 0 to 6 gives:

$$A = \int_0^6 (2x)\,dx = \left.\frac{2x^2}{2}\right|_0^6$$

$$A = 6^2 - 0^2 = 36 \text{ m}^2$$

The moment of area of the element about the Y axis will be the distance from the axis to the element, x in this case.

$$dM_y = x\,dA$$

$$M_y = \int x(y\,dx)$$

Substituting for y from the equation of the line and setting limits as before, we have:

$$M_y = \int x(2x)\,dx = \int_0^6 2x^2\,dx$$

$$M_y = \frac{2x^3}{3}\Big|_0^6 = \frac{2}{3}(6^3 - 0^3)$$

$$M_y = 144 \text{ m}^3$$

Then:

$$\bar{x} = \frac{M_y}{A} = \frac{144 \text{ m}^3}{36 \text{ m}^2} = \textbf{4.00 m}$$

12.5 SECOND MOMENT OF AREA OR MOMENT OF INERTIA

We have examined the expression, $\int y\,dA$, the moment of area. This expression and the related concept of centroid occur frequently as we analyze the mechanics of materials. A second set of expressions that also occurs commonly is:

$$I_x = \int y^2\,dA \tag{12.12}$$

and

$$I_y = \int x^2\,dA \tag{12.13}$$

Since the distance to the element of area is squared in these expressions, they are properly called the second moment of area equations, but more commonly, the term *moment of inertia* is used.

We started this chapter by discussing a 2×12 and noting the differences in its deflection and stress, depending on orientation. The factor that changes with orientation is the moment of inertia. This property is also pivotal in predicting the buckling of columns and the stress and deflection that occur in torsional loading. So it is a most important concept for the study of strength of materials.

Most often we are interested in the moment of inertia about a centroidal axis. Table A-9 gives the moment of inertia of various common shapes about a centroidal axis. These were obtained by evaluating Eqs. 12.12 and 12.13. Tables A-10 through A-17 give similar properties about centroidal axes for various structural shapes. Only rarely do we actually evaluate Eqs. 12.12 and 12.13. Analytically, however, an understanding of their behavior is very useful.

Note the following regarding these equations:

1. The equations are for the second *moment* of area. A moment requires a reference point or axis, so any time we talk about a moment of inertia we must talk about it with respect to some axis.
2. The components are an area (dA) times a distance squared (y^2). If we are talking about real areas, the area will be a positive value. (We use negative values for

holes.) The distance y may be positive or negative, but y^2 will be positive regardless. Hence the $\int y^2\, dA$ will be the product of two positive quantities and will always be positive. On the other hand, the first moment of area may be positive, negative, or zero. We should also note that as material is placed farther and farther from the centroid, its influence on the moment of inertia will be greatly increased, because it varies with the distance squared.

3. The equations are evaluated dimensionally as follows:

$$\int y^2\, dA \stackrel{D}{=} \text{in.}^2(\text{in.}^2) \stackrel{D}{=} \textbf{in.}^4$$

Hence moment of inertia has the units of in.^{4} or its equivalent.

Example Problem 12.7

Find the moment of inertia of the semicircle shown in Fig. 12.10 about its own horizontal and vertical centroidal axes using Table A-9.

Solution

Table A-9 gives moment of inertia formulas about the centroidal axes, so all we need to do is read the table carefully and plug in the values. For the horizontal axis:

$$I_x = (6.86\ E\text{-}3)D^4$$
$$I_x = (6.86\ E\text{-}3)(12\ \text{in.})^4 = \textbf{142 in.}^4$$

For the vertical axis:

$$I_y = \frac{\pi D^4}{128} = \frac{(12\ \text{in.})^4}{128} = \textbf{509 in.}^4$$

Because the area on average is closer to the horizontal axis, it has the lower value.

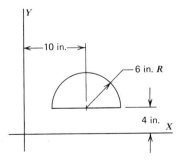

FIG. 12.10   Example Problem 12.7. Figure repeated from page 309.

12.6   MOMENT OF INERTIA BY INTEGRATION

For the same reasons given in Section 12.4, we will also find moment of inertia by integration. As with centroid, moment of inertia can also be handled with some success without integration. However, it is a very elusive but very important concept. Anything that will assist the student in understanding the concept is worthwhile. Most of the equations for stress and deflection of members involve this important quantity. If we understand moment of inertia, it will be much easier to understand the stress and deflection equations that depend on it.

Example Problem 12.8

Find the moment of inertia of the triangle shown in Fig. 12.11 about the Y axis by integration.

Solution

Since we are taking the moment about the Y axis, we need Eq. 12.13:

$$I_y = \int x^2 \, dA$$

The element of area is:

$$dA = y \, dx$$

Note that for moment of inertia we must select an element of area with an infinitesimal dimension (dx) in the direction of the moment arm (x). A hori-

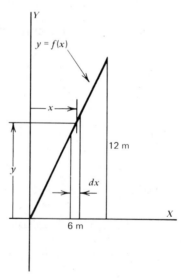

FIG. 12.11   Example Problem 12.8.

zontal element $(x\,dy)$ will not do in this case. Evaluating y in terms of x,

$$y = 2x$$
$$dA = 2x\,dx$$

$$I_y = \int_0^6 x^2(2x\,dx) = \frac{2x^4}{4}\bigg|_0^6 = \frac{2 \cdot 6^4}{4} = \textbf{648 m}^4$$

12.7 PARALLEL AXIS THEOREM

We now consider the moment of inertia of the area about the X axis in Fig. 12.12. The axis X_{cg} is a centroidal axis parallel to X, an arbitrary coordinate axis. We write:

$$I_x = \int y^2\,dA$$

and note from Fig. 12.12:

$$y = y_1 + d$$

where d is the distance from X to the centroidal axis X_{cg}, and y_1 is the distance from the centroidal axis to the element of area.

By substitution, we get:

$$I_x = \int (y_1 + d)^2\,dA = \int (y_1^2 + 2d \cdot y_1 + d^2)\,dA$$
$$I_x = \int y_1^2\,dA + \int 2d \cdot y_1\,dA + \int d^2\,dA$$

Now we examine each of these three integrals. The first is the moment of inertia of the area about the X_{cg} or centroidal axis:

$$\bar{I} = I_{x_{cg}} = \int y_1^2\,dA$$

(We commonly use $\bar{I}$ to denote the moment of inertia about a centroidal axis.)

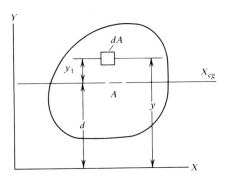

FIG. 12.12 Parallel axes.

For the second integral, 2 and d are constants, so we can bring them outside the integral:

$$\int 2d \cdot y_1 \, dA = 2d \int y_1 \, dA$$

The remaining integral represents the moment of area about X_{cg} or the centroidal axis. The moment of area about a centroid is always zero, so:

$$2d \cdot \int y_1 \, dA = 0$$

For the third integral d^2 is constant, so:

$$\int d^2 \, dA = d^2 \int dA = d^2 \cdot A$$

since the remaining integral is simply the area. Returning to the original expression, we have:

$$I_x = \int y_1^2 \, dA + \int 2d \cdot (y_1 \, dA) + \int d^2 \cdot dA$$
$$I_x = \bar{I} + Ad^2 \qquad\qquad (12.14)$$

This is known as the *parallel axis theorem*. It says that the moment of inertia about any axis is equal to the moment of inertia about a parallel axis through the centroid plus the area times the distance between the two axes squared. This relationship is widely applied in calculating moment of inertia.

Example Problem 12.9

Find the moment of inertia of the semicircular area shown in Fig. 12.13 about the X axis.

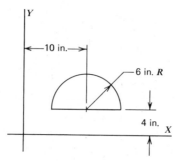

FIG. 12.13 Example Problem 12.9. Figure repeated from page 309.

Solution

From Table A-9 the distance from the base of the semicircle to the centroid is:

$$\bar{y} = \frac{2D}{3\pi} = \frac{2(12 \text{ in.})}{3\pi}$$

$$\bar{y} = 2.55 \text{ in.}$$

Then:

$$d = \bar{y} + 4 = 6.55 \text{ in.}$$

In Example Problem 12.7 we found:

$$I_x = 142 \text{ in.}^4$$

This is the moment of inertia about the horizontal centroidal axes, which is $\bar{I}$ in Eq. 12.14. Then:

$$I_x = \bar{I} + Ad^2$$

$$I_x = 142 \text{ in.}^4 + \frac{\pi(12 \text{ in.})^2}{8}(6.55 \text{ in.})^2$$

$$I_x = 142 + 2423 = \textbf{2570 in.}^4$$

Notice that the second term, Ad^2, provides the biggest part of I_x. This will always be the case when the transfer distance d is large compared to the size of the object. Also notice that I_x goes up with d^2.

Example Problem 12.10

Find the moment of inertia about the Y axis of the triangle in Fig. 12.14 using Table A-9 and the parallel axis theorem.

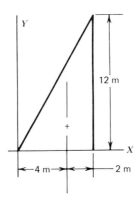

FIG. 12.14 Example Problem 12.10.

Solution

From Table A-9 we have the centroid 4 m to the right of y as shown in Fig. 12.14 and:

$$\bar{I} = \frac{bh^3}{36}$$

We have to orient the table to fit our particular problem. In this case h is 6 m and b is 12 m. The *base b* is always *parallel to the axis* about which we are taking the moment. The moment of inertia about the vertical centroidal axis is:

$$\bar{I} = \frac{12(6)^3}{36} = 72.0 \text{ m}^4$$

The area is:

$$A = \tfrac{1}{2}bh = \tfrac{1}{2}(12)(6) = 36 \text{ m}^2$$

The distance between the Y axis and the parallel centroidal axis (transfer distance) is:

$$d = 4 \text{ m}$$

Then by applying Eq. 12.14 to a vertical axis, we get:

$$I_y = \bar{I} + Ad^2$$
$$= 72 + (36)(4)^2$$
$$\mathbf{I_y = 648 \text{ m}^4}$$

This of course agrees with the answer of Example Problem 12.8. We are much more likely to use this simpler, algebra-based method than the integration method.

12.8   MOMENT OF INERTIA OF COMPOSITE AREAS

We have observed that the moment of inertia is an integral function—a summation. In summation we may break the problem into parts and add them in any order. We may do the same thing in integration, and we conclude:

> The moment of inertia of a whole is equal to the sum of the moments of inertia of the parts.

Second, we reemphasize that we are adding the *moments* of inertia, and for moments to be added, the moment must be about the same axis. We, therefore, have the following general procedure for computing the moment of inertia of composite bodies

1. Break the body into parts whose centroidal moments of inertia may be found.
2. Using tables like A-9 through A-17, compute or look up the centroidal moment of inertia for each part.

3. Using the parallel axis theorem, compute the moment of inertia of each part about the desired *common* axis.
4. Sum the moments of inertia of the parts to get the total moment of inertia.

Normally, it is the centroidal moment of inertia that is desired. The following problems illustrate the method. The second and third problems present a tabular form that is very useful in practice for determining all the properties of a cross-sectional area.

Example Problem 12.11

Find the moment of inertia about a vertical centroidal axis for Fig. 12.15.

Solution

The area is broken into two areas as in Example Problem 12.3, from which $\bar{x} = 3.50$ ft.

From Table A-9, we have:

$$\bar{I} = \frac{bh^3}{12}$$

Note that in this equation b is the base or side parallel to the axis under consideration.

Then for area 1:

$$I_1 = \frac{bh^3}{12} + Ad^2 = \frac{3(4)^3}{12} + (3)4(3.5 - 2)^2$$

The transfer distance d is the distance between the centroids of area 1 and the composite area; thus $(3.5 - 2)$:

$$I_1 = 16.0 + 27 = 43.0 \text{ ft}^4$$

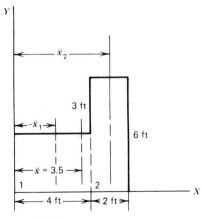

FIG. 12.15   Example Problem 12.11.

This is the moment of inertia of area 1 about the vertical axis through the composite centroid. For area 2, we write:

$$I_2 = \frac{bh^3}{12} + Ad^2 = \frac{6(2)^3}{12} + (6)2(5 - 3.5)^2$$

The transfer distance is the distance between the centroids of area 2 and the composite area; thus $(5 - 3.5)$:

$$I_2 = 4.0 + 27 = 31.0 \text{ ft}^4$$

This is the moment of inertia of area 2 about the vertical axis through the composite centroid. The total moment of inertia about this axis is the sum of I_1 and I_2.

$$\bar{I} = I_1 + I_2 = 43.0 + 31.0 = \mathbf{74.0 \text{ ft}^4}$$

Example Problem 12.12

Find the centroid and centroidal moment of inertia with respect to the x axis for Fig. 12.16.

Solution

The area is broken into three components. Area 3 is a negative area to be subtracted from area 2, a 6 in. × 6 in. square. We now introduce a table that is convenient for centroidal and moment of inertia calculations. The components are identified in the initial column.

		1	2	3	4	5	6
Components		A_i	$\bar{y}_i$	$\bar{y}_i A_i$	$\bar{I}_i$	$d_i = \bar{y}_i - \bar{y}$	$A_i d_i^2$
1		$6(8)$ $= 48$	$+4$	192	$\dfrac{(6)(8)^3}{12}$ $= 256$	$4 - 3.76$ $= 0.24$	2.76
2		$6(6)$ $= 36$	$+3$	108	$\dfrac{(6)(6)^3}{12}$ $= 108$	$3 - 3.76$ $= -0.76$	20.8
3		$\dfrac{-(6)(3)}{2}$ $= -9$	$+2$	-18	$\dfrac{-(3)(6)^3}{36}$ $= -18$	$2 - 3.76$ $= -1.76$	-27.9
Σ		75.0		282	346		-4.32

Columns **1, 2,** and **3** are filled in first. It is good to write the factors down and perform the calculations, even when they are done mentally. This makes it easier to locate errors, which are inevitable. Column **1** is the area of each component. Notice that area 3 is negative. Column **2** is the distance from the

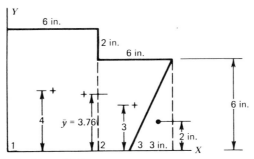

FIG. 12.16 Example Problem 12.12.

reference axis X to the centroid of the component areas. The distance $\bar{y}_i$ may be positive or negative. Column **3**, $\bar{y}_i A_i$, is simply the product of the elements in the first two columns with the appropriate algebraic sign. We are now ready to compute the centroid location using the sums of columns **1** and **3**.

$$\bar{y} = \frac{\sum y_i A_i}{\sum A_i} = \frac{282}{75.0} = \textbf{3.76 in.}$$

Column **4** is the moment of inertia of each component area about its *own* centroidal axis. We proceed to fill in column **4** using Table A-9. For structural shapes these values may be found directly from tables. Notice the negative area 3 will have a negative value of $\bar{I}$. Note that in every case b, the base, is the side parallel to the axis about which we are taking moments. Column **5** is the distance between the centroid of the component area and the centroid of the composite or whole area. To apply the parallel axis theorem, the transfer distances d_i are computed. They may be positive or negative. These can be computed by examining the geometry or by the equation $d_i = \bar{y}_i - \bar{y}$. Calculating by one method and checking by the second is recommended. Column **6** is the second term in the parallel axis theorem, Ad^2. Since d is squared, its sign is not significant. The sign of the area will determine the sign of Ad^2. Since area 3 is negative, the corresponding value of Ad^2 will also be negative.

To apply the parallel axis theorem we could add the elements of columns **4** and **6**, that is,

$$I_i = \bar{I}_i + A_i d_i^2$$

The total $\bar{I}$ would then be the sum of the I_i. Evaluating this we have:

$$\bar{I} = \sum I_i = \sum (\bar{I}_i + A_i d_i^2)$$
$$\bar{I} = \sum \bar{I}_i + \sum A_i d_i^2$$

The two summations on the right-hand side of the equation represent the sums of columns **4** and **6**. Hence it is not necessary to add the elements of columns **4** to **6**.

$$\bar{I} = \sum \bar{I}_i + \sum A_i d_i^2$$
$$= 346 - 4.32 = \textbf{342 in.}^{4}$$

In this problem the Ad^2 term plays a minor role. That is not characteristic; Ad^2 often provides the major portion of the resultant moment of inertia.

Example Problem 12.13

Find the moment of inertia of the cross section in Fig. 12.17 about its horizontal centroidal axis.

Solution

The centroid was found in Example Problem 12.5. It is recomputed here using the table. The values for columns **1**, **2**, and **3** are found from Tables A-11 and A-12 as before.

Components	1 A_i	2 $\bar{y}_i$	3 $\bar{y}_iA_i$	4 $\bar{I}_i$	5 $d_i = \bar{y}_i - \bar{y}$	6 $A_id_i^2$
I	17.9	$\dfrac{13.91}{2}$ $= 6.955$	124.8	641	$6.955 - 9.47$ $= 2.52$	113.2
⌐	8.82	$13.91 + 0.65$ $= 14.56$	128.1	3.94	$14.56 - 9.47$ $= 5.09$	228.5
Σ	26.72		252.9	644.9		341.7

We compute $\bar{y}$ by dividing the sum of column **3** by the sum of column **1**.

$$\bar{y} = \frac{\sum y_i A_i}{\sum A_i} = \frac{252.9}{26.72} = \textbf{9.47 in.}$$

Column **4** lists the moment of inertia of each component about its *own* centroidal axis. Be sure to orient the part properly in reading these tables. For

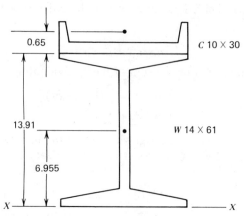

FIG. 12.17 Example Problem 12.13.

the W 14 × 61 we need 641 from column **7** of Table A-11, not 107 from column **10**. From Table A-12 we need for the C 10 × 30, 3.94 from column **10**, not 103 from column **7**.

Our column **5** is the difference between the component centroids and the composite centroid and these are calculated as shown. Column **6** is column **5** squared times column **1**.

The resultant moment of inertia of the composite area is the sum of column **4** plus the sum of column **5**.

$$\bar{I} = \sum(\bar{I}_i + A_i d_i^2)$$
$$= \sum\bar{I}_i + \sum A_i d_i^2$$
$$\bar{I} = 644.9 + 341.7 = \textbf{987 in.}^4$$

12.9 RADIUS OF GYRATION

For the purpose of calculating the moment of area, the entire area may be considered as concentrated at the centroid:

$$\text{moment of area} = \bar{y}A$$

An analogous idea for the second moment of area, or moment of inertia, is called the *radius of gyration*. We define a k such that:

$$I = k^2 A$$

That is, the moment of inertia may be calculated by considering the entire area A as being concentrated at a distance k from the axis. Solving for k:

$$k = \sqrt{\frac{I}{A}} \tag{12.15}$$

where k is the *radius of gyration*.

The concept of radius of gyration has a number of applications in mechanics. When we study columns we find that the load that can be carried by a column depends on it. Tables A-10 through A-15 give the values of the radius of gyration, which is labeled r in these tables. Of course, there is enough information in the table to calculate k (or r), but it is used frequently enough to justify the separate listing.

12.10 POLAR MOMENT OF INERTIA

Consider the area shown in Fig. 12.18. We have examined the moments of inertia about the X and Y axes. These are called the rectangular moments of inertia defined by Eqs. 12.12 and 12.13 as follows:

$$I_x = \int y^2\, dA \tag{12.12}$$

$$I_y = \int x^2\, dA \tag{12.13}$$

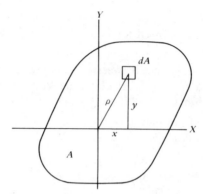

FIG. 12.18 Polar moment of inertia.

The moment of inertia about a third axis may also be considered, namely, the Z axis or the axis perpendicular to the paper passing through the intersection of the X and Y axes. This moment is also the distance ρ (lowercase Greek rho) to an element of area squared times the area. It is called the *polar moment of inertia*. We designate it as J. In differential form it is:

$$dJ = \rho^2 \, dA$$

and in integral form:

$$J = \int \rho^2 \, dA \qquad (12.16)$$

The polar moment of inertia is conceptually similar to the rectangular moment of inertia. The concepts of radius of gyration and the parallel axis theorem are applicable. Thus we write:

$$k = \sqrt{\frac{J}{A}} \qquad (12.17)$$

and

$$J = \bar{J} + Ad^2 \qquad (12.18)$$

There are a couple of special relationships worth observing. Referring to Fig. 12.18, we note:

$$\rho^2 = x^2 + y^2$$

Then:

$$J = \int \rho^2 \, dA = \int (x^2 + y^2) \, dA$$
$$= \int x^2 \, dA + \int y^2 \, dA$$
$$J = I_x + I_y \qquad (12.19)$$

Thus we see that the polar moment of inertia is the sum of the rectangular moments of inertia where the three axes in question intersect at a point.

We now evaluate Eq. 12.16 for the important case of a solid circular cross section. This is an important property for determining the stress and deflection in shafts, which we consider in the next chapter. Figure 12.19 is a circle of radius R. At a distance ρ from the origin a circular element of area of width $d\rho$ has been drawn. Its area is its circumference times its width—$d\rho$, which is small compared to the radius:

$$dA = 2\pi\rho\, d\rho$$

Then:

$$J = \int \rho^2\, dA = \int \rho^2 2\pi\rho\, d\rho$$

We factor out the constant 2π and integrate from 0 to R.

$$J = 2\pi \int_0^R \rho^3\, d\rho = 2\pi\, \frac{\rho^4}{4}\bigg|_0^R$$

$$J = \frac{\pi}{2}\,[R^4 - 0^4] = \frac{\pi R^4}{2} \tag{12.20a}$$

Or in terms of the diameter D:

$$J = \frac{\pi}{2}\left(\frac{D}{2}\right)^4 = \frac{\pi D^4}{32} \tag{12.20b}$$

Polar moment of inertia has the same units as rectangular moment of inertia, that is, in.^{4}.

Example Problem 12.14

Find the centroidal polar moment of inertia of a 3-in.-diameter circular cross section. Also find the polar radius of gyration.

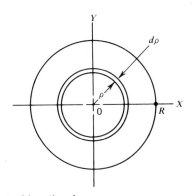

FIG. 12.19 Polar moment of inertia of a circular cross section.

Solution

. From Eq. 12.20b:

$$J = \frac{\pi D^4}{32} = \frac{\pi (3)^4}{32} = 7.95 \text{ in.}^4$$

We can find k directly from Eq. 12.17. Here we solve it algebraically first:

$$k = \sqrt{\frac{J}{A}} = \sqrt{\frac{\pi D^4}{32} \cdot \frac{4}{\pi D^2}} = \sqrt{\frac{D^2}{8}}$$

$$k = \frac{\sqrt{2}}{4} \cdot D$$

Then substituting the value for D:

$$k = \frac{\sqrt{2}}{4} \cdot (3) = 1.06 \text{ in.}$$

12.11 SUMMARY

Each of the equations associated with this chapter, is generally best understood as a concept or definition rather than merely an equation or formula.

Moment of area:

$$M_x = \int y \, dA$$

Centroid:

$$\bar{y} = \frac{\int y \, dA}{\int dA} = \frac{\sum \bar{y}_i A_i}{\sum A_i}$$

Moment of inertia:

$$I_x = \int y^2 \, dA$$

Parallel axis theorem:

$$I_x = \bar{I} + Ad^2$$

Radius of gyration:

$$k = \sqrt{\frac{I}{A}}$$

Polar moment of inertia:

$$J = \int \rho^2 \, dA$$

$$k = \sqrt{\frac{J}{A}}$$

$$J = \bar{J} + Ad^2$$

$$J = I_x + I_y$$

Many students find the tables in Example Problems 12.12 and 12.13 easier to work with. Whichever approach is used, it should be exercised until the student is comfortable and confident with it. *Every* topic that follows depends on understanding the moment of inertia.

PROBLEMS

12.1 Using Table A-9, find the centroid and moment of area with respect to the X and Y axes for the indicated figure.

    (a) Fig. 12.20   (b) Fig. 12.21   (c) Fig. 12.22   (d) Fig. 12.23

12.2 Using Table A-9, find the moment of area about the given axis for each figure.

    (a) Fig. 12.20, $y = 4$ (b) Fig. 12.20, $x = -2$

    (c) Fig. 12.20, $y = 6$ (d) Fig. 12.21, $y = 9$

    (e) Fig. 12.21, $x = 6$ (f) Fig. 12.21, $x = 2$

    (g) Fig. 12.22, $y = 4$ (h) Fig. 12.22, $x = 4$

    (i) Fig. 12.22, $y = -4$ (j) Fig. 12.23, $y = 80$

    (k) Fig. 12.23, $y = 90$ (l) Fig. 12.23, $x = -70$

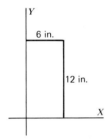

FIG. 12.20 Problems 12.1a, 12.2a, 12.2b, 12.2c, 12.23, 12.35a, 12.36a, 12.37a, 12.38a.

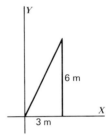

FIG. 12.21 Problems 12.1b, 12.2d, 12.2e, 12.2f, 12.24, 12.35b, 12.36b, 12.37b, 12.38b

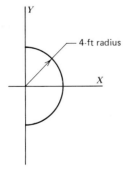

FIG. 12.22 Problems 12.1c, 12.2g, 12.2h, 12.2i, 12.25, 12.35c, 12.36c, 12.37c, 12.38c.

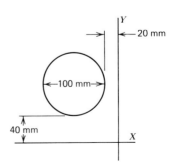

FIG. 12.23 Problems 12.1d, 12.2j, 12.2k, 12.2l, 12.26, 12.35d, 12.36d, 12.37d, 12.38d.

12.3 Find the centroid of Fig. 12.24 with respect to the X axis.

12.4 Find the centroid of Fig. 12.24 with respect to the Y axis.

12.5 Find the centroid of Fig. 12.25 with respect to the X axis.

12.6 Find the centroid of Fig. 12.25 with respect to the Y axis.

12.7 Locate the horizontal centroidal axis for the plane area in Fig. 12.26.

12.8 Locate the vertical centroidal axis for the plane area in Fig. 12.26.

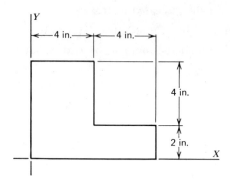

FIG. 12.24 Problems 12.3, 12.4, 12.39.

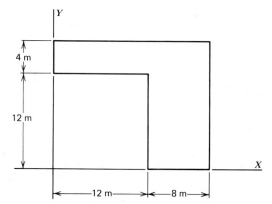

FIG. 12.25 Problems 12.5, 12.6, 12.40.

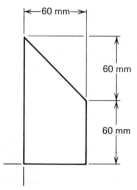

FIG. 12.26 Problems 12.7, 12.8, 12.41.

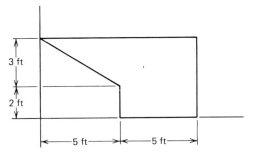

FIG. 12.27 Problems 12.9, 12.10, 12.42.

12.9 Locate the horizontal centroidal axis for the plane area in Fig. 12.27.

12.10 Locate the vertical centroidal axis for the plane area in Fig. 12.27.

12.11 Locate the horizontal centroidal axis for the plane area in Fig. 12.28.

12.12 Locate the vertical centroidal axis for the plane area in Fig. 12.28.

Locate the centroid for the plane area shown in the indicated figure.

12.13 Fig. 12.29   **12.14** Fig. 12.30

12.15 Fig. 12.31   **12.16** Fig. 12.32

12.17 Fig. 12.33   **12.18** Fig. 12.34

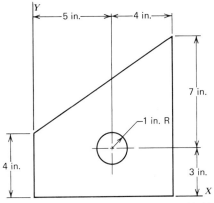

FIG. 12.28 Problems 12.11, 12.12, 12.43.

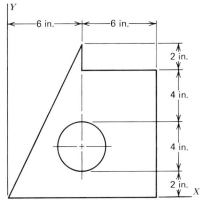

FIG. 12.29 Problems 12.13, 12.44.

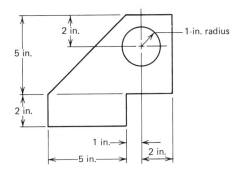

FIG. 12.30 Problems 12.14, 12.45.

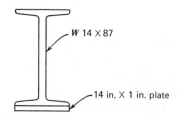

FIG. 12.31 Problems 12.15, 12.46.

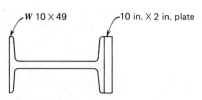

FIG. 12.32 Problems 12.16, 12.47.

12.19 For the triangle shown in Fig. 12.35, *by integration* find the area, the moment of area, and the centroid location with respect to the Y axis.

12.20 For the triangle shown in Fig. 12.35, *by integration* find the area, the moment of area, and the centroid location with respect to the X axis. *Hint:* Use a horizontal element.

12.21 For the area shown in Fig. 12.36, *by integration* find the area, the moment of area, and the centroid location with respect to the Y axis.

12.22 For the area shown in Fig. 12.37, *by integration* find the area, the moment of area, and the centroid location with respect to the X axis. *Hint:* Use the horizontal element.

12.23 Find the moment of inertia for Fig. 12.20 about the horizontal and vertical centroidal axes using Table A-9.

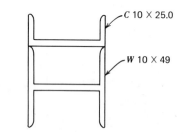

FIG. 12.33 Problems 12.17, 12.48.

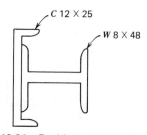

FIG. 12.34 Problems 12.18, 12.49.

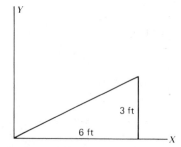

FIG. 12.35 Problems 12.19, 12.20, 12.27, 12.28.

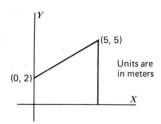

FIG. 12.36 Problems 12.21, 12.31, 12.33.

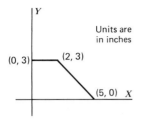

FIG. 12.37   Problems 12.22, 12.32, 12.34.

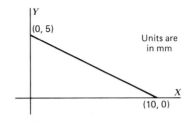

FIG. 12.38   Problems 12.29, 12.30.

12.24 Find the moment of inertia for Fig. 12.21 about the horizontal and vertical centroidal axes using Table A-9.

12.25 Find the moment of inertia for Fig. 12.22 about the horizontal and vertical centroidal axes using Table A-9.

12.26 Find the moment of inertia for Fig. 12.23 about the horizontal and vertical centroidal axes using Table A-9.

12.27 *By integration* find the moment of inertia of the triangle in Fig. 12.35 about the *Y* axis.

12.28 *By integration* find the moment of inertia of the triangle in Fig. 12.35 about the *X* axis. *Hint:* Use a horizontal element.

12.29 *By integration* find the moment of inertia of Fig. 12.38 about the *Y* axis.

12.30 *By integration* find the moment of inertia of Fig. 12.38 about the *X* axis. *Hint:* Use a horizontal element.

12.31 *By integration* find the moment of inertia of the area shown in Fig. 12.36 about the *Y* axis.

12.32 *By integration* find the moment of inertia of the area shown in Fig. 12.37 about the *X* axis. *Hint:* Use a horizontal element.

12.33 *By integration* find the moment of inertia of the area shown in Fig. 12.36 about the axis $x = -2$.

12.34 *By integration* find the moment of inertia of the area shown in Fig. 12.37 about the axis $y = 5$. *Hint:* Use a horizontal element.

12.35 Using Table A-9 and the parallel axis theorem, find the moment of inertia about the *X* axis for:
(a) Fig. 12.20   (b) Fig. 12.21   (c) Fig. 12.22   (d) Fig. 12.23

12.36 Using Table A-9 and the parallel axis theorem, find the moment of inertia about the *Y* axis for:
(a) Fig. 12.20   (b) Fig. 12.21   (c) Fig. 12.22   (d) Fig. 12.23

12.37 Using Table A-9 and the parallel axis theorem, find the moment of inertia about the indicated axis.
(a) Fig. 12.20, $x = 4$ (b) Fig. 12.21, $y = 10$
(c) Fig. 12.22, $x = -2$ (d) Fig. 12.23, $y = 6$

12.38 Using Table A-9 and the parallel axis theorem, find the moment of inertia about the indicated axis.

(a)   Fig. 12.20, $y = 4$ (b)   Fig. 12.21, $x = 4$

(c)   Fig. 12.22, $y = 40$ (d)   Fig. 12.23, $x = -20$

For the following figures, find the moment of inertia about the horizontal and vertical centroidal axes.

12.39 Fig. 12.24   **12.40** Fig. 12.25

12.41 Fig. 12.26   **12.42** Fig. 12.27

12.43 Fig. 12.28   **12.44** Fig. 12.29

12.45 Fig. 12.30   **12.46** Fig. 12.31

12.47 Fig. 12.32   **12.48** Fig. 12.33

12.49 Fig. 12.34

12.50 Find the polar moment of inertia and radius of gyration for a 5-cm-diameter circular cross section.

12.51 A 4-in.-diameter shaft is hollowed out with a 3-in. diameter. Find the polar moment of inertia and radius of gyration. Treat the hole as a negative area.

12.52 Solve for J in Problem 12.51 by evaluating Eq. 12.16.

12.53 Find $\bar{I}_x$, $\bar{I}_y$, and $\bar{J}_0$ for the Fig. 12.39.

12.54 Find J_A and the polar radius of gyration about A for Fig. 12.39.

12.55 Find the moment of inertia and radius of gyration about the X axis for Fig. 12.40.

12.56 Find the moment of inertia and radius of gyration about the Y axis for Fig. 12.40.

12.57 Find the polar moment of inertia and radius of gyration about the centroid for Fig. 12.40.

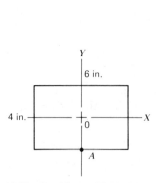

FIG. 12.39 Problems 12.53, 12.54.

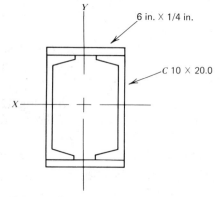

FIG. 12.40 Problems 12.55, 12.56, 12.57.

12.58 For the cross section shown in Fig. 12.41 find:

   (a) The horizontal centroidal axis and the moment of inertia and radius of gyration about it.

   (b) The vertical centroidal axis and the moment of inertia and radius of gyration about it.

12.59 For the cross section shown in Fig. 12.42 find:

   (a) The horizontal centroidal axis and the moment of inertia and radius of gyration about it.

   (b) The vertical centroidal axis and the moment of inertia and radius of gyration about it.

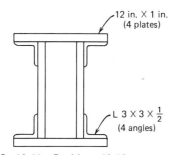

FIG. 12.41 Problem 12.58.

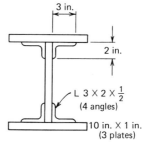

FIG. 12.42 Problem 12.59.

13

Torsional Loads

Many modern machines involve a transmission of mechanical energy. The trail of man's technical advances is well marked by the development of mechanical power transmission devices. Many of these date from antiquity, but for others the ink on the patent is hardly dry. The family automobile contains many, such as gears, V-belts and pulleys, geared belts, clutches, rigid shafts, flexible shafts, and U-joints. All these devices are connected to a shaft. Thus a shaft is extremely common in transmitting power.

When power is transmitted by a shaft, a torque is applied to the shaft. A torque is merely a moment of force. If this moment tends to twist the shaft about its longitudinal axis, we call it a *torque* (see Fig. 13.1). If it tends to bend the shaft about an axis perpendicular to the longitudinal axis, we call it a *bending moment*. Both, however, are simply moments of force.

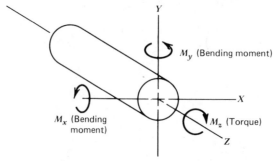

FIG. 13.1   Torque and bending moment.

338

13.1 POWER TRANSMISSION

If 500 hp is to be transmitted at 3600 rpm, what size shaft is to be used? Can the same shaft transmit 1000 hp? Why are so many transmission shafts hollow? In this chapter we answer these and similar questions. Before doing this, however, it is necessary to understand thoroughly the terms and concepts we are going to use. These are all basic physics concepts, but it is worthwhile to review them.

Let's start with the idea of *work*. In mechanics, work is defined as a force (F) acting through a distance (s) where both have the same direction. So:

$$W = F \cdot s \tag{13.1}$$

The units are foot-pounds. What if the force is moving in a circular path, as in Fig. 13.2, driving a wrench around a bolt? If the force is everywhere tangent to the path, we have:

$$dW = F(ds)$$

for the work done as the force F moves the incremental distance ds. Then:

$$ds = r(d\theta)$$

and

$$dW = F(r \, d\theta)$$

or, regrouping,

$$dW = (F \cdot r)(d\theta)$$

where $F \cdot r$ is the moment of force (or torque) of F about 0, and $d\theta$ is the incremental angular displacement. We see, then, that the work done by a torque ($T = F \cdot r$) is the product of the torque times its angular displacement:

$$dW = T \, d\theta$$

Integrated through a finite angle, this yields:

$$W = T\theta \tag{13.2}$$

The units are foot-pounds for torque and none for the angle—if radian measure is used—resulting in foot-pounds for work.

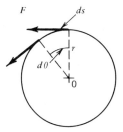

FIG. 13.2 A force acting along a circular path.

In the SI the units for torque are newton-meters (N·m). The angular measurement in radians is the same, so for work we have simply the newton-meter or its recognized equivalent, the joule (J).

Power is defined as the time rate of doing work. This may be found by taking the derivative of Eq. 13.2 with respect to time:

$$P = \frac{dW}{dt} = \frac{d}{dt}(T\theta)$$

$$P = T\frac{d\theta}{dt} \qquad \text{if } T \text{ is constant}$$

Here $d\theta/dt$ is the rate of change of angular position with time or angular velocity. Normally, the lowercase Greek letter ω (omega) is used for angular velocity. We write:

$$P = T\omega \qquad\qquad (13.3)$$

and say that power equals torque times angular velocity. This equation, like Eqs. 13.1 and 13.2, is a basic physical equation—in a sense, a definition—and is valid for any set of units. Typical units would be:

$$P = T\omega \overset{D}{=} \text{ft-lb}\,\frac{\text{rad}}{\text{s}} = \frac{\text{ft-lb}}{\text{s}}$$

Remember that radian is a dimensionless quantity—a ratio of lengths—and all basic physical equations involving angles require radian measure.

Now we have power in foot-pounds per second—or any other consistent set of units you wish to use, though these units are often used. In the English-speaking world, the term horsepower (hp) is also commonly used, especially if mechanical power is involved. It is an artificial unit defined simply as follows:

$$1 \text{ hp} = 550 \text{ ft-lb/s} \qquad\qquad (13.4a)$$

If we multiply the right-hand side by 60 s/min, we have:

$$1 \text{ hp} = 33,000 \text{ ft-lb/min} \qquad\qquad (13.4b)$$

There are many special equations, useful in special situations, for horsepower in various textbooks. However, all the student *needs* to deal with power in English units is Eq. 13.3—a definition of power—and either Eq. 13.4a or 13.4b—a definition of the unit horsepower. Other forms can be had by dimensional algebra. Note that when using the special formulas, not only must the formula be known, but also the units that go with each term. Of course, if one routinely solves a particular type problem, an appropriate special form is certainly in order.

Evaluating Eq. 13.3 dimensionally for the SI gives:

$$P = T\omega \overset{D}{=} (\text{N}\cdot\text{m})\left(\frac{\text{rad}}{\text{s}}\right)$$

$$P \overset{D}{=} \frac{\text{N}\cdot\text{m}}{\text{s}} = \frac{\text{J}}{\text{s}} = \text{W}$$

That is, the units for power are newton-meters per second, or using the equivalent for work, joules per second. This, of course, yields the watt (W), the unit for power so common in the electrical industries, even where the English system of units is dominant. In fact, this unit of power is so widely used that we frequently invert these relations and speak of work or energy as watts times time. For example, in paying my electric bill I buy a quantity of energy described as kilowatt-hours (kW·h). Although the relation is easily derived, it is convenient to note:

$$745.7 \text{ W} = 1 \text{ hp}$$

At this juncture, the advantages of a scientifically developed units system like the SI strongly emerge. In fact, those of us who cut our "dimensional teeth" by finding how many stone-furlongs per fortnight were required to raise 400 barrels of olive oil a day to a height of 12 fathoms find the simplicity of the SI—well, dull.

A power shaft from a lawn tractor is shown in Fig. 13.3. Consider 8 hp coming into the shaft from the engine, 3 hp taken off at the second pulley for the mower, and 5 hp taken off at the third pulley to drive the tractor. To size the shafts for this system, the power transmitted by each section must be known. This can be determined by applying the principle of conservation of power—a corollary to the principle of conservation of energy. (This, of course, neglects energy losses in the system.) If a section is passed at A and we apply the principle—power in equals power out—we find that the shaft carries 8 hp between pulleys 1 and 2.

Applying the principle to section B, we get 5 hp transmitted by the shaft between pulleys 2 and 3. By the methods covered earlier in this section, the power

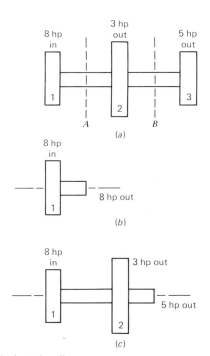

FIG. 13.3a–c   Power shaft and pulleys.

transmitted can be related to torque if the shaft speed is known. Presently we will relate torque in the shaft to stress and angular deflection.

Figures 13.3b and 13.3c are thinly veiled free body diagrams. If first of all, the input torque is found, then Figs. 13.3b and 13.3c are free body diagrams and the torque in each shaft can be found by summing the moment of force about the axis of the shaft.

Example Problem 13.1

The following equation is often used:

$$T = \frac{63,000P}{N}$$

where T is in inch-pounds, P is in horsepower, and N is in revolutions per minute. Prove that this formula is valid from basic equations.

Solution

From Eq. 13.3:

$$P = T\omega$$

$$T = \frac{P}{\omega}$$

Substituting the desired units and doing the dimensional algebra:

$$T = \frac{P(\text{hp})(\text{min})}{N(\text{rev})} \frac{\text{rev}}{2\pi\text{ rad}} \frac{550\text{ ft-lb}}{\text{s-hp}} \frac{60\text{ s}}{\text{min}} \frac{12\text{ in.}}{\text{ft}}$$

$$= \frac{550(60)(12)P}{2\pi N} \text{ in.-lb}$$

$$T = \frac{63,000\ P}{N} \text{ (in.-lb)}$$

Example Problem 13.2

The power shaft illustrated in Fig. 13.3 is rotating at 2400 rpm. Find the torque in each portion of the shaft.

Solution

First find the input torque.

$$T_1 = \frac{P_1}{\omega} = \frac{8\text{ hp}}{} \frac{550\text{ ft-lb}}{\text{s-hp}} \cdot \frac{\text{min}}{2400\text{ rev}} \cdot \frac{\text{rev}}{2\pi\text{ rad}} \cdot \frac{60\text{ s}}{\text{min}}$$

$$= \frac{8(550)(60)}{2400(2\pi)} \frac{\text{ft-lb}}{\text{rad}} = \textbf{17.5 ft-lb}$$

We assume clockwise as viewed from the right-hand end.

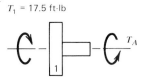

FIG. 13.4   Free body diagram for Example
Problem 13.2.

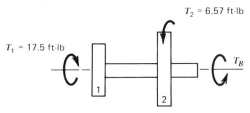

FIG. 13.5   Free body diagram for pulleys
1 and 2.

Ignoring the power analysis of Fig. 13.3 (which would give identical results),
we draw a free body diagram (Fig. 13.4) with the shaft cut between pulleys 1
and 2.

$$\sum M_{\text{axis}} = -17.5 + T_A$$
$$T_A = \textbf{17.5 ft-lb}$$

To find the torque taken out at pulley 2, we calculate:

$$T_2 = \frac{P_2}{\omega} = \frac{(3)(550)(60)}{2400(2\pi)} = \textbf{6.57 ft-lb}$$

Notice that only the 3 hp replaces the 8 hp from above. Alternately, with 17.5
stored in the calculator, we write:

$$T_2 = T_1(\tfrac{3}{8}) = \textbf{6.57 ft-lb}$$

Now drawing a second free body diagram (Fig. 13.5) with the shaft cut between
pulleys 2 and 3, we get:

$$\sum M_{\text{axis}} = 0 = -17.5 + 6.57 + T_B$$
$$T_B = \textbf{10.9 ft-lb}$$

13.2   SHEAR STRESS

We now come to the important development of the relationship between shear
stress and torsional load. It is developed using the calculus—because the development is exact (a good application of basic mathematics) and because it helps the
student understand shear stress, especially the all-important stress distribution.
There are a number of assumptions the reader should note carefully, even if
unimpressed by the mathematical development. These assumptions constitute
limitations on the resulting equation.

We consider a shaft loaded in pure torsion as shown in Fig. 13.6. The assumptions are:

1. The cross section is circular—so the equation will not apply to rectangular or other noncircular cross sections.
2. The member is straight.
3. On twisting, plane sections do not warp. This rules out "large" deflections.
4. Hooke's law is obeyed; that is, stress is proportional to strain. This rules out stresses beyond the proportional limit.

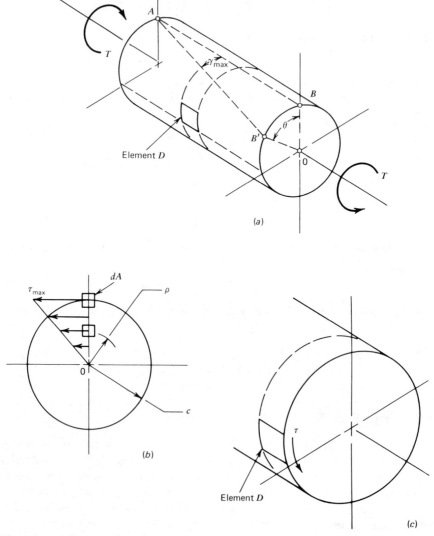

FIG. 13.6a–c   Pure torsion.

The torque T applied to the body results in the twisting of the cylinder rotating point B to B'. This motion results in the shear strain being proportional to the distance from the center 0. Following Hooke's law, the stress must also be proportional to the distance from the center. The resulting distribution is illustrated in Fig. 13.6b. Note that the stress is zero at the center and maximum at the surface. We may express this in equation form as follows:

$$\tau = \frac{\rho}{c}\,\tau_{max} \tag{13.5}$$

where ρ is the distance from the center to an element and c is the radius of the shaft. We wish to relate this stress τ (the Greek tau, English t) to the applied torque T. Considering each element of area (dA) to have a stress τ acting on it, we have an element of force:

$$dF = \tau\,dA$$

which produces an element of moment of force (or torque) about 0 as follows:

$$dT = \rho\,dF = \rho\tau\,dA$$

Since this is the torque of τ acting over dA about 0, the total torque may be found by summing these elements of torque over the entire area. Hence:

$$T = \int dT = \int_{area} \rho\tau\,dA$$

We previously indicated the stress distribution of Eq. 13.5. Substituting this for τ in the equation above yields:

$$T = \int_{area} \rho\left(\frac{\rho}{c}\,\tau_{max}\right)dA$$

$$T = \frac{\tau_{max}}{c}\int_{area}\rho^2\,dA$$

Since τ_{max} and c are constants, they may be factored outside the integral. The integral contains the distance to an element (ρ) squared times the area of the element (dA). This is the second moment of area or the moment of inertia—in this case, the polar moment of inertia. It was shown in Chapter 12 that for a circular section this is:

$$J = \int \rho^2\,dA = \frac{\pi D^4}{32} \tag{13.6}$$

where D is the diameter of the shaft. Hence we have:

$$T = \frac{\tau_{max}}{c}\,J$$

or solving for τ_{max}:

$$\tau_{max} = \frac{Tc}{J} \tag{13.7}$$

This is the fundamental relation for shear stress due to torsion in circular members. Combining this with Eq. 13.5 yields a similar equation for the shear stress at any distance from the center:

$$\tau = \frac{T\rho}{J} \qquad (13.8)$$

Check the units of the equation:

$$\tau = \frac{Tc}{J} \underset{\text{D}}{=} \frac{\text{in.-lb} \times \text{in.}}{\text{in.}^4} \underset{\text{D}}{=} \frac{\text{lb}}{\text{in.}^2}$$

So psi, Pa, or any other previous unit of stress is acceptable. Note the relationship being described. If torque is doubled—shear stress will be doubled. As the diameter varies, we consider:

$$\tau_{\text{max}} = \frac{T\left(\dfrac{D}{2}\right)(32)}{\pi D^4}$$

$$\tau_{\text{max}} = \frac{16T}{\pi D^3} \qquad (13.9)$$

which shows that the shear stress varies inversely as the diameter cubed. Hence doubling the shaft diameter reduces the shear stress by a factor of 8. Also, review what load is causing this stress condition—a torque about the axis of the shaft. And note the stress pattern produced—that shown in Fig. 13.6b with zero shear stress at the axis and a maximum on the surface.

Example Problem 13.3

A 50-mm-diameter shaft carries a torque of 700 N·m. Find the maximum shear stress in the shaft.

Solution

Mostly we are interested in the maximum shear stress τ_{max} and tend to omit the subscript. Thus

$$\tau = \frac{Tc}{J} \qquad (13.7)$$

First we evaluate J using Eq. 12.20b:

$$J = \frac{\pi D^4}{32} = \frac{\pi (50 \text{ mm})^4}{32} = 614,000 \text{ mm}^4$$

Then:

$$\tau = \frac{Tc}{J} = \frac{700 \text{ N·m}(25 \text{ mm})}{614,000 \text{ mm}^4} \left(\frac{1000 \text{ mm}}{\text{m}}\right)^3$$

$$\tau = 28.5 \text{ } E6 \text{ N/m}^2 = \textbf{28.5 MPa}$$

By now it is worthwhile to note the convenience of working in newtons and millimeters for typical stress problems. For this example we have:

$$\tau = \frac{700,000 \text{ N}\cdot\text{mm}(25 \text{ mm})}{614,000 \text{ mm}^4} = 28.5 \frac{\text{N}}{\text{mm}^2}$$

and we recognize:

$$1 \text{ MPa} = 1 \frac{\text{N}}{\text{mm}^2}$$

Thus:

$$\tau = \textbf{28.5 MPa}$$

13.3 LONGITUDINAL SHEAR STRESS

Refer once again to Fig. 13.6a and examine element D on the surface. This area of the shaft is shown enlarged in Fig. 13.6c with stress τ acting on it. If another section is made to the left of the element D, we isolate an element shown in Fig. 13.7a. This left-hand face would have the same shear stress acting on it as acts on the right-hand face, namely τ.

We have extracted a square element Δx by Δx. Assuming a depth of unity, we examine the equilibrium of this element. Summing the forces vertically yields zero, as indicated in Fig. 13.7a. We then sum the moments of force about the lower left-hand corner, point P. The force due to the shear stress is:

$$F = \tau \Delta x$$

and the moment of force is:

$$M = (\Delta x)F = \Delta x(\tau \Delta x)$$

At this point this moment appears to be unbalanced and would cause the element to rotate clockwise. What counteracts this rotation? A shear stress on the top horizontal surface. Since the moment arms and areas are equal, Δx, the magnitude of this stress, must also be τ. However, it must provide a counterclockwise moment and thus must act to the left, as shown in Fig. 13.7b.

Finally, we sum forces horizontally. This requires that there also be a shear stress to the right on the bottom surface. Its magnitude is also τ.

Figure 13.7c indicates that when a shear stress acts on one face of an element of area, it must act on all four faces.

Figure 13.7d shows the distortion generated in the element by these stresses. Note that the stresses must meet at the corners for equilibrium. The only other possible condition for shear stress that satisfies equilibrium is shown in Fig. 13.7e. It also has the stresses meeting at the corners.

The significance of this is that although shear stresses are generated on the face of a transverse plane by an applied torque, they are simultaneously generated

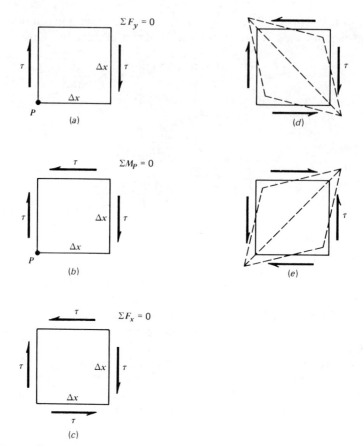

FIG. 13.7a–e Shear stress element.

longitudinally as well. This is illustrated in Fig. 13.8. This longitudinal stress was very evident when wooden shafts were commonly used to transmit power. These shafts were constructed with the grain parallel to the longitudinal axis. Of course, the wood was very weak in shear parallel to the grain, and so failure of wooden shafts was often due to longitudinal shear.

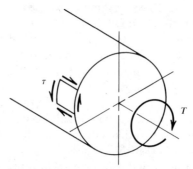

FIG. 13.8 Transverse and longitudinal shear stresses.

Example Problem 13.4

A wooden shaft can carry 1000 psi in shear stress perpendicular to the grain and 150 psi in shear stress parallel to the grain. What torque can a 3-in.-diameter shaft carry?

Solution

$$\tau = \frac{Tc}{J}$$

Solving for T and doing the algebra:

$$T = \frac{\tau J}{c} = \tau\left(\frac{\pi D^4}{32}\right)\left(\frac{2}{D}\right) = \frac{\pi \tau D^3}{16}$$

Then, substituting for τ and D, we have:

$$T = \pi\left(1000\,\frac{\text{lb}}{\text{in.}^2}\right)\frac{(3\text{ in.})^3}{16} = \frac{\pi(1000)(3)^3}{16}\text{ lb-in.}$$

$$T_{\text{trans}} = \textbf{5300 in.-lb}$$

This is the load that can be carried without shearing perpendicular to the grain. To find the load that can be carried without shearing parallel to the grain, we use 150 psi instead of 1000 psi for τ.

$$T_{\text{long}} = \frac{\pi(150)}{16}(3)^3 \text{ lb-in.} = \textbf{795 in.-lb}$$

The smaller of the two will limit the load, so the allowable torque is:

$$T = \textbf{795 in.-lb}$$

13.4 HOLLOW SHAFTS

In the developing Eq. 13.7 it was assumed that the cross section of the shaft was circular. It was *not* assumed that it was solid. Hence Eq. 13.7 applies equally well to hollow shafts. In fact, a hollow shaft is a preferred shape for a shaft for economical use of the material.

Figure 13.9a shows the stress distribution accompanying Eq. 13.7. We have already referred to the fact that this stress is zero at the center and varies linearly to a maximum at the surface. Careful observation reveals that material near the center of the shaft is not highly stressed, but near the surface of the shaft it is. Efficient use of the material requires the removal of lower stressed areas. This is illustrated in Fig. 13.9b, where only the more highly stressed material remains.

Applying Eq. 13.7 to a hollow shaft requires the evaluation of J for a hollow shaft (the value c is unchanged). Recall that J, the polar moment of inertia, is:

$$J = \int \rho^2 \, dA$$

and that an integral is simply a summation.

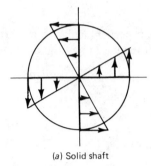

(a) Solid shaft   (b) Hollow shaft

FIG. 13.9a–b Stress distribution.

Hence:

$$J_{\text{hollow}} = J_{\text{solid}} - J_{\text{hole}}$$

This treats the hole as negative area.
Carrying out the above, we have:

$$J = \frac{\pi D_s^4}{32} - \frac{\pi D_H^4}{32}$$

$$J_{\text{hollow}} = \frac{\pi}{32}(D_s^4 - D_H^4) \tag{13.10}$$

Note the following:

$$D_s^4 - D_H^4 \neq (D_s - D_H)^4$$

Because the hollow shaft uses the material very efficiently, it is usually found where the weight of the shaft is critical, the material is expensive, or the production volume is high. In the last case, savings in materials may be offset by higher production costs. The optimum shape, according to this theory, is one with a maximum J, which is obtained by a very thin film at an infinite radius. Other modes of failure—as well as certain impracticalities—preclude this optimized shape. This theory would suggest that a tin can with the ends removed would make an excellent shaft. You've probably never observed such a shaft in use. The reason is that failure will occur in a mode not predicted by this theory—namely, surface buckling. The study of surface buckling is beyond the scope of this text.

Example Problem 13.5

A 3-in.-diameter shaft is made lighter by taking 1.5 in. out of the center. What material savings is achieved by removing half of the diameter? What reduction in strength follows?

Solution

First we calculate the volume of a solid shaft of diameter D_2:

$$V_s = \frac{\pi D_2^2}{4} \cdot L$$

Then we find the volume of a hollow shaft, where the hole diameter is D_1 is:

$$V_H = \frac{\pi D_2^2}{4} \cdot L - \frac{\pi D_1^2}{4} \cdot L = \frac{\pi L}{4}(D_2^2 - D_1^2)$$

For the shaft in this problem:

$$D_1 = \frac{D_2}{2}$$

and

$$V_H = \frac{\pi L}{4}\left[D_2^2 - \left(\frac{D_2}{2}\right)^2\right] = \frac{\pi L}{4}\left(D_2^2 - \frac{D_2^2}{4}\right)$$

$$V_H = \frac{3}{4}\left(\frac{\pi D_2^2}{4} \cdot L\right) = \frac{3}{4}V_s$$

This is three-quarters of the volume of the solid shaft; hence 25% of the weight is saved. We describe strength in terms of the torque that can be carried, assuming constant material properties. From Eq. 13.7:

$$\tau = \frac{Tc}{J}$$

(again writing τ for τ_{max} without misunderstanding). For a solid shaft:

$$T_s = \frac{\tau J}{c} = \frac{\tau \pi D_2^4}{32\left(\frac{D_2}{2}\right)} = \frac{\tau \pi D_2^3}{16}$$

And for a hollow one, where c is still $D_2/2$:

$$T_H = \frac{\tau J_H}{c} = \frac{\tau(2)}{D_2}\left[\frac{\pi}{32} \cdot (D_2^4 - D_1^4)\right]$$

Again:

$$D_1 = \frac{D_2}{2}$$

$$T_H = \frac{\pi \tau}{16 D_2}\left[D_2^4 - \left(\frac{D_2}{2}\right)^4\right]$$

$$= \frac{\pi \tau}{16 D_2}\left(D_2^4 - \frac{D_2^4}{16}\right) = \frac{\pi \tau}{16 D_2}\left(\frac{15}{16}D_2^4\right)$$

$$T_H = \frac{15}{16}\left(\frac{\tau \pi D_2^3}{16}\right)$$

The term inside the brackets is T_s, the torque that can be carried by a solid shaft, so:

$$T_H = \tfrac{15}{16}\, T_s$$

Hence the strength is reduced by $\frac{1}{16}$ or 6%, and the weight is reduced 25%. Note that we have solved the problem in general for any shaft with the center half of its diameter removed.

Example Problem 13.6

An oil well drill pipe is assembled by applying a torque of 6000 ft-lb to twist a section of the pipe into its coupling. If the drill pipe is a 3-in. standard weight steel pipe, find the maximum shear stress in the pipe and the shear stress on the inner surface.

Solution

The properties of this pipe are found in Table A-15, from which:

$$D_o = 3.500 \text{ in.}$$
$$D_i = 3.068 \text{ in.}$$

Then:

$$J = \frac{\pi}{32}(D_o^4 - D_i^4)$$

$$J = \frac{\pi}{32}[(3.500)^4 - (3.068)^4] \text{ in.}^4 = 6.03 \text{ in.}^4$$

This could have been obtained from Table A-15 by observing:

$$J = I_x + I_z = 2I = 2(3.02)$$
$$J = 6.04 \text{ in.}^4$$

The maximum shear stress will be at the outer surface, where:

$$c = \frac{3.500}{2} = 1.750 \text{ in.}$$

$$\tau = \frac{Tc}{J} = \frac{60,000 \text{ ft-lb}(1.75 \text{ in.})}{6.04 \text{ in.}^4}\left(\frac{12 \text{ in.}}{\text{lb}}\right) = \textbf{20,900 psi}$$

At the inner surface:

$$\tau_i = \frac{6000\left(\dfrac{3.068}{2}\right)}{6.04}(12) = \textbf{18,300 psi}$$

Or we could use proportion to get:

$$\tau_i = \frac{r_i}{c}\tau_{max}$$

$$\tau_{max} = \frac{1.534}{1.750}(20,900) = \textbf{18,300 psi}$$

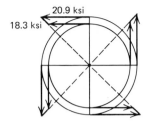

FIG. 13.10 Stress distribution on drill pipe.

The stress distribution is shown in Fig. 13.10. The stress at any intermediate point may be found by proportion. Note that the stress on the inner surface is nearly 90% of that on the outer surface. This small variation in stress indicates that the material is being used efficiently to carry the torque. Remember that the same stresses act longitudinally as well.

13.5 ANGULAR TWIST

Return once more to Fig. 13.6a. Because of the applied torque T, B will rotate to point B' representing the twist of the member. Line $0B$ rotates to $0B'$, forming the angle θ, and line AB to AB', forming the angle $\gamma_{\max}$. For clarity, the section $0BB'A$ is redrawn as a rotated segment from the shaft in Fig. 13.11. With this figure we can also examine some of our assumptions. Additional points D, D', E, and F are added to aid our discussion. The D' represents the rotation of D due to the applied load. There is no rotation of AEF. We label the maximum rotation $\delta_{\max}$, which is the arc length BB' at a radius c from the center 0. The displacement of any arbitrary point D to D' at a distance of ρ from 0 may be described as follows:

$$\delta = \delta_{\max} \frac{\rho}{c}$$

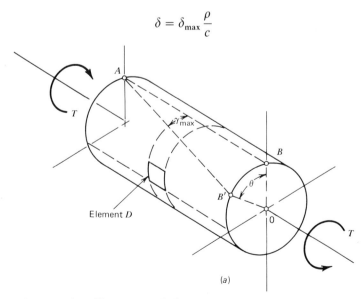

(a)

FIG. 13.6a Pure torsion. Figure repeated from page 344.

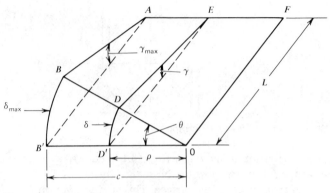

FIG. 13.11   Distortion of shaft segment due to torque.

This displacement is proportional to the distance from the center. We now calculate the angle of rotation from the definition of an angle, namely, arc length divided by radius:

$$\theta = \frac{\delta_{max}}{c} \quad \text{and} \quad \theta = \frac{\delta}{\rho}$$

The angle θ, the angle of twist, does not vary with the distance ρ. We get the same value for θ regardless of the distance from the center used.

Notice, again, that the line segment AEF does not rotate. Hence the angle θ will vary from zero at the far end of the segment to some maximum value at the section we are considering—and the variation is linear. In summary, θ, the angle of twist, depends on the position along the length of the shaft but not on the position along the radius.

Next, we turn our attention to the angle γ. This angle is the shear strain in the shaft. This angle can be calculated by dividing the arc length δ, by the length L, since we are only considering very small angles of γ. Thus:

$$\gamma = \frac{\delta}{L}$$

Recalling from above:

$$\delta = \delta_{max} \frac{\rho}{c}$$

we get:

$$\gamma = \frac{\delta_{max}}{L} \frac{\rho}{c}$$

Defining:

$$\gamma_{max} = \frac{\delta_{max}}{L}$$

then:

$$\gamma = \gamma_{max} \frac{\rho}{c}$$

This says that the shear strain is proportional to the distance from the center, which was one of our original assumptions. This can be seen from Fig. 13.11 by observing that while δ changes with ρ, the length of the element L does not. We now have:

$$\gamma_{max} = \frac{\delta_{max}}{L}$$

or

$$\delta_{max} = \gamma_{max} L$$

and

$$\theta = \frac{\delta_{max}}{c}$$

or

$$\delta_{max} = \theta c$$

Thus, by equating the two values of δ_{max},

$$\gamma_{max} L = \theta c$$

and solving for θ gives:

$$\theta = \frac{\gamma_{max} L}{c}$$

Hooke's law for shear is:

$$\gamma = \frac{\tau}{G}$$

where G is the shear modulus of elasticity—a material property. Substituting into the above gives:

$$\theta = \frac{\tau_{max} L}{cG}$$

From Eq. 13.7

$$\tau_{max} = \frac{Tc}{J}$$

so

$$\theta = \frac{Tc}{J} \frac{L}{cG}$$

$$\theta = \frac{TL}{JG} \tag{13.11}$$

KNOW THIS OK?!

This is the equation for the twist in a circular member. We examine the units:

$$\theta \stackrel{\mathrm{D}}{=} \frac{(\text{in.-lb})(\text{in.})(\text{in.}^2)}{\text{in.}^4(\text{lb})} \stackrel{\mathrm{D}}{=} \text{dimensionless} = \text{radians}$$

As always, naturally occurring angular measurements are in radians—a dimensionless ratio of lengths.

Now let's see what the equation says. The twist varies directly with the applied torque; double the load—double the twist. It varies directly with the length; double the length—double the twist. It varies inversely with the shear modulus of elasticity; doubling G cuts θ in half. It varies inversely with the polar moment of inertia J, which varies with the diameter to the fourth power. Double the diameter and reduce the twist by a factor of 16!

It is beneficial to our understanding and recollection of Eq. 13.11 to compare it with Eq. 11.5:

$$\delta = \frac{PL}{AE} \tag{11.5}$$

$$\theta = \frac{TL}{JG} \tag{13.11}$$

The following analogies are noted.

Deflection:

δ (in.)

θ (rad)

Load:

P—axial (lb)

T—torque (in.-lb)

Length:

L (in.)

L (in.)

Geometric property:

$A = $ area (in.^{2})

$J = $ polar moment of inertia (in.^{4})

This analogy illustrates how moment of inertia for rotational problems is similar to area for linear ones.

Material property:

$E = $ modulus of elasticity (psi)

$G = $ shear modulus of elasticity (psi)

Equation 13.11 is for a uniform member. If we go through the same argument with a length of dL instead of L and $d\theta$ instead of θ we obtain:

$$d\theta = \frac{T\,dL}{JG} \tag{13.12}$$

which is Eq. 13.11 in differential form.

This equation must be integrated along L to obtain the twist. This integration can take into account variations in T, J, and G with L.

$$\theta = \int \frac{T\,dL}{JG} \tag{13.13}$$

These equations allow us to handle problems such as a tapered shaft. In finite form Eq. 13.13 becomes:

$$\theta = \sum \frac{T_i L_i}{J_i G_i} \tag{13.14}$$

This can be used to calculate the total angle of twist in a shaft composed of multiple uniform sections and/or several discretely applied torques. As before, this development is based on a circular cross section. It does not apply directly to noncircular ones. It does apply to circular cross sections that are hollow.

Example Problem 13.7

A 3-in.-diameter shaft is 18 in. long. It transmits a torque of 200 ft-lb. Find its deflection.

$$G = 12 \times 10^6 \text{ psi}$$

Solution

From Eq. 13.11:

$$\theta = \frac{TL}{JG} = \frac{(200 \text{ ft-lb})(18 \text{ in.})}{\left(\dfrac{\pi(3 \text{ in.})^4}{32}\right)\left(12\,E6\,\dfrac{\text{lb}}{\text{in.}^2}\right)} \times \frac{12 \text{ in.}}{\text{ft}}$$

$$\theta = \textbf{4.53 E-4 rad}$$

or in degrees

$$\theta = 4.53\,E\text{-}4 \text{ rad}\left(\frac{180°}{\pi \text{ rad}}\right) = \textbf{(2.59 E-2)}°$$

Example Problem 13.8

The shaft shown in Fig. 13.12 is aluminum. Find the rotation of the left-hand end.

$$G = 4.0\,E6 \text{ psi}$$

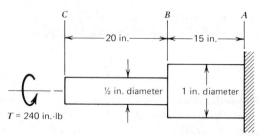

FIG. 13.12   Example Problem 13.8.

Solution

From Eq. 13.13:

$$\theta = \int \frac{T\,dL}{JG} = \int_B^A \frac{T\,dL}{J_{AB}G} + \int_C^B \frac{T\,dL}{J_{CB}G}$$

breaking the integral into parts. Carrying out the integration would give:

$$\theta = \frac{TL_{AB}}{GJ_{AB}} + \frac{TL_{BC}}{GJ_{BC}}$$

Since T and G are common, they are factored out:

$$\theta = \frac{240 \text{ in.-lb}}{4 \times 10^6\, \dfrac{\text{lb}}{\text{in.}^2}} \left\{ \frac{15 \text{ in.}}{\left(\dfrac{\pi(1 \text{ in.})^4}{32}\right)} + \frac{20 \text{ in.}}{\left(\dfrac{\pi(0.5 \text{ in.})^4}{32}\right)} \right\}$$

$$\theta = \mathbf{0.205 \text{ rad}}$$

$$\theta = 0.205 \text{ rad} \times \frac{180°}{\pi \text{ rad}} = \mathbf{11.7° = \theta}$$

13.6   SHAFT COUPLINGS

Shaft couplings occur in two forms—rigid and nonrigid. The nonrigid allow for nonalignment of the shafts. A common coupling of this type is the universal joint found in many automobile drive shafts. The analysis of flexible couplings is beyond the scope of this text. They are properly covered in texts on machine design. Rigid couplings are not only within our scope but also offer the opportunity to extend the present concepts.

A rigid coupling can consist of a flange with bolt holes, as shown in Fig. 13.13. Our analysis of this coupling makes use of two assumptions made previously. One, we assume that the stress on the bolt is proportional to its distance from the center, as we did in developing the shear stress equation for torsional loading. Also, we assume that the shear stress on each bolt is uniform, as we did in Chapter 11 when discussing average shear stress. Because the bolt diameter is typically small compared to the bolt circle diameter, this assumption produces little error.

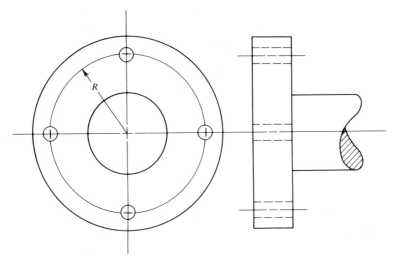

FIG. 13.13 Bolted flange coupling.

These assumptions would allow us to say:

$$\tau_{max} = \frac{Tc'}{J}$$

where c' is the distance to the center of the bolts in the largest bolt circle in the coupling and J is the polar moment of inertia of all the bolt areas about their collective centroid—which coincides with the center of the shaft. This, however, is not as functional as the following. A single bolt at radius R_i is shown in Fig. 13.14 where A_i is the area of the bolt, τ_i is the average stress on the bolt, and F_i is the force on it giving:

$$F_i = \tau_i A_i$$

Then:

$$T_i = R_i F_i = R_i \tau_i A_i$$

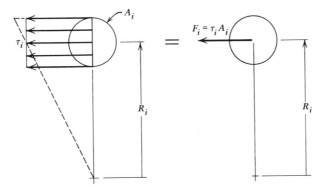

FIG. 13.14 Shear force acting on a bolt at radius R_i.

where T_i is the torque resisted by an individual bolt at a distance R_i from the centroid of the coupling. For a coupling with N bolts of the same size A on a single bolt circle of radius R, we have:

$$T = \sum R_i \tau_i A_i = NRA\tau \tag{13.15}$$

where T is the total applied torque.

For two bolt circles we have:

$$T = N_1 R_1 A_1 \tau_1 + N_2 R_2 A_2 \tau_2 \tag{13.16}$$

and

$$\frac{\tau_1}{R_1} = \frac{\tau_2}{R_2} \tag{13.17}$$

Combining Eqs. 13.16 and 13.17 allows this type of problem to be solved.

This analysis assumes that the entire torque is carried in shear. Since the bolts are tightened, there will be a friction force between the flange plates, reducing the torque carried by the bolts. In fact, high tensile strength bolts may be tightened until the entire load is carried by friction and the bolts are not in shear at all.

Example Problem 13.9

There are four 1.5-in.-diameter bolts on an 8-in.-diameter bolt circle, as shown in Fig. 13.13. Each bolt has an allowable shear stress of 5000 psi. What torque can the coupling carry?

Solution

Using Eq. 13.15:

$$T = NRA\tau$$

$$T = 4(4 \text{ in.})\left(\frac{\pi(1.5)^2 \text{ in.}^2}{4}\right)\frac{5000 \text{ lb}}{\text{in.}^2}$$

T = 141,000 in.-lb

Note that the shank area of the bolt is used, since it is in shear—not the threads. The area could have been obtained from Table A-16, where it is identified as the gross area.

13.7 SUMMARY

Preliminary concepts and equivalencies are:

$$P = T\omega$$

$$1 \text{ hp} = \frac{550 \text{ ft-lb}}{\text{s}} = \frac{33,000 \text{ ft-lb}}{\text{min}}$$

$$1 \text{ W} = \frac{1 \text{ J}}{\text{s}} = 1\frac{\text{N}\cdot\text{m}}{\text{s}}$$

Shear stress distribution is linear, as seen in Fig. 13.9. It is zero at the center and maximum at the surface and may be found by:

$$\tau = \frac{Tc}{J}$$

This acts transversely and longitudinally.

For a circular cross section:

$$J = \frac{\pi D^4}{32}$$

The twist is given by:

$$\theta = \frac{TL}{JG}$$

For bolted couplings:

$$T = N_1 R_1 A_1 \tau_1 + N_2 R_2 A_2 \tau_2$$

$$\frac{\tau_1}{R_1} = \frac{\tau_2}{R_2}$$

PROBLEMS

13.1 An automobile engine delivers 120 hp at 4000 rpm. What is the torque?

13.2 A motor delivers 90 kW at 4000 rpm. What is the torque?

13.3 A crank arm 10 in. long requires a 35-lb force perpendicular to it to turn it. It must go through five full turns every second. What is the minimum horsepower of a motor driving it?

13.4 A crank arm 25 mm long requires a 150-N force perpendicular to it to turn it. It must go through five full turns every second. What is the minimum power of a motor driving it?

13.5 A $\frac{1}{8}$-horsepower drill motor drives a 4-in.-diameter disk sander at 1800 rpm. What is the maximum tangential force it can exert at the edge of the disk?

13.6 A 100-W drill motor drives a 100-mm-diameter disk sander at 1800 rpm. What is the maximum tangential force it can exert at the edge of the disk?

13.7 The allowable shear stress in a 1-in.-diameter shaft is 12,000 psi. What torque can this shaft transmit?

13.8 The allowable shear stress in a 25-mm-diameter shaft is 80 MPa. What torque can this shaft transmit?

13.9 Find the maximum shear stress in a $\frac{1}{2}$-in.-diameter bolt when a 50-lb force is applied to the end of an 8-in. wrench.

13.10 Find the maximum shear stress in a 12-mm-diameter bolt when a 200-N force is applied to the end of a 200-mm wrench.

13.11 A 2-in.-diameter shaft rotates at 300 rpm and has an allowable stress of 10,000 psi. What horsepower can be transmitted?

13.12 A 50-mm-diameter shaft rotates at 300 rpm and has an allowable stress of 70 MPa. What power can be transmitted?

13.13 Design a solid shaft to transmit 80 hp at 200 rpm using an allowable stress of 8000 psi.

13.14 Design a solid shaft to transmit 60 kW at 200 rpm using an allowable stress of 50 MPa.

13.15 The wooden shaft shown in Fig. 13.15 can carry 1200 psi perpendicular to the grain and 200 psi parallel to the grain in shear stress. Considering only torsional loading, what load P can be carried?

13.16 Find the shear stress parallel to the grain in Fig. 13.15 if the load P is 2000 lb.

13.17 Find the transverse and longitudinal shear stresses on element A in Fig. 13.16 if P is 200 N. Sketch the element A, showing these stresses.

13.18 The shaft in Fig. 13.16 is Douglas fir. Its shear strength perpendicular to its grain is 50% of its ultimate strength. Parallel to the grain the shear strength is 10% of the ultimate. The grain runs parallel to the line a–a. Find the load P that can be supported by this shaft.

13.19 Solve Problem 13.7 if the shaft has a $\frac{3}{4}$-in.-diameter longitudinal hole in it.

13.20 Solve Problem 13.8 if the shaft has a 20-mm-diameter longitudinal hole in it.

13.21 Solve Problem 13.9 if the bolt is hollow with a $\frac{1}{8}$-in. wall thickness.

13.22 Solve Problem 13.10 if the bolt is hollow with a 3-mm wall thickness.

13.23 Solve Problem 13.11 for a hollow shaft with an inside diameter of a 1.5 in.

13.24 Solve Problem 13.12 for a hollow shaft with an inside diameter of 38 mm.

13.25 Design a hollow shaft to transmit 80 hp at 200 rpm using an allowable stress of 8000 psi and $D_i = 0.90D_o$.

13.26 Design a hollow shaft to transmit 60 kW at 200 rpm using an allowable stress of 55 MPa and $D_i = 0.90D_o$.

13.27 An 8-ft shaft with a diameter of 1.5 in. is twisted 5°. What torque is required? What stress would this torque produce ($G = 10,000,000$ psi)?

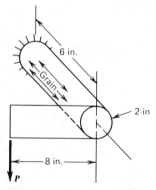

FIG. 13.15 Problems 13.15, 13.16.

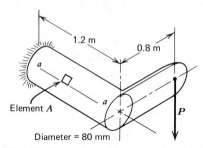

FIG. 13.16 Problems 13.17, 13.18.

13.28 A 2.5-m long aluminum shaft with a diameter of 40 mm is twisted 5°. What torque is required? What stress would this torque produce?

13.29 Solve Problem 13.27 if the shaft is hollow with $D_i = 1.0$ in.

13.30 Solve Problem 13.28 if the shaft is hollow with $D_i = 25$ mm.

13.31 A 10-ft shaft has a diameter of 2 in. The allowable stress is 8000 psi, and the shear modulus of elasticity is 12,000,000 psi. Find the allowable torque. Find the angle of twist if this load is applied.

13.32 A 3.0-m shaft has a diameter of 60 mm. The allowable stress is 55 MPa, and the shear modulus of elasticity is 85 GPa. Find the allowable torque. Find the angle of twist if this load is applied.

13.33 Solve Problem 13.31 for a hollow shaft with $D_i = 1.5$ in.

13.34 Solve Problem 13.32 for a hollow shaft with $D_i = 40$ mm.

13.35 A 2-in.-diameter solid steel shaft that is 5 ft long must withstand a torque of 20,000 in.-lb at an angular velocity of 1570 rad/min. Determine the horsepower transmitted, the stress produced in the shaft, and the angle of twist of the shaft.

13.36 A 50-mm-diameter solid steel shaft that is 1.5 m long must withstand a torque of 2.3 kN·m at an angular velocity of 1570 rad/min. Determine the power transmitted, the stress produced in the shaft, and the angle of twist of the shaft.

13.37 A solid aluminum shaft 3 in. in diameter and 6 ft long must transmit 60 hp at an angular velocity of 1520 rad/min. Determine the required torque, the stress produced in the shaft, and the angle of twist of the shaft.

13.38 A solid bronze shaft 75 mm in diameter and 2.0 m long must transmit 45 kW at an angular velocity of 1520 rad/min. Determine the required torque, the stress produced in the shaft, and the angle of twist of the shaft.

13.39 Solve Problem 13.35 if the shaft is hollow with a 1.75-in. I.D.

13.40 Solve Problem 13.36 if the shaft is hollow with a 40-mm I.D.

13.41 Solve Problem 13.37 if the shaft is hollow with a 2.5-in. I.D.

13.42 Solve Problem 13.38 if the shaft is hollow with a 60-mm I.D.

13.43 A flange coupling similar to Fig. 13.13 has four $\frac{1}{2}$-in.-diameter bolts on a 6-in.-diameter bolt circle. For an allowable shear stress of 6000 psi, what torque can be transmitted by the connection?

13.44 If the flange in Problem 13.43, Fig. 13.13 also has four $\frac{1}{2}$-in. bolts at a 4-in.-diameter bolt circle, what torque can be transmitted?

13.45 The coupling shown in Fig. 13.17 has six bolts of $\frac{3}{8}$-in. diameter. The bolt circle has a 3-in. diameter. The hollow shaft is 3 ft long and 2 in. in diameter with a wall thickness of $\frac{1}{4}$ in.; 200 hp is transmitted at 3000 rpm. Find the maximum stress in the bolts, the maximum stress in the shaft, and the twist of the steel shaft.

13.46 The coupling shown in Fig. 13.17 has six bolts of 10-mm diameter. The bolt circle has an 80-mm diameter. The hollow shaft is 1.0 m long and 60 mm in diameter with a wall thickness of 8 mm; 120 kW is transmitted at 3600 rpm.

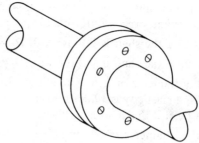

FIG. 13.17   Problems 13.45, 13.46.

Find the maximum stress in the bolts, the maximum stress in the shaft, and the twist of the stainless steel shaft.

13.47 A 3.0-in. shaft has a torque of 20,000 in.-lb applied. Calculate the shear stress at the center of the shaft and every 0.25 in. along the radius. Make a plot of shear stress versus radius.

13.48 A 60-mm shaft has a torque of 2.0 kN·m applied. Calculate the shear stress at the center of the shaft and every 5 mm along the radius. Make a plot of shear stress versus radius.

13.49 A hollow shaft, 4.0 in. O.D. and 3.5 in. I.D., has a shear stress of 9000 psi on the inside surface. Find the maximum shear stress on this shaft.

13.50 A hollow shaft, 100 mm O.D. and 80 mm I.D., has a shear stress of 60 MPa on the inside surface. Find the maximum shear stress on this shaft.

13.51 For the structure shown in Fig. 13.18 find the torque in section *BC*. Find the twist of the arm at *B* with respect to the fixed end at *C*. The aluminum shaft has a 3-in. diameter.

13.52 Find the twist of the arm at *A* in Problem 13.51.

13.53 A 3-in.-diameter hollow magnesium shaft (Fig. 13.19) is 8 ft long and is to be rotated 2° clockwise at the end connected to the linkage. Find the force

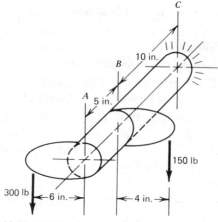

FIG. 13.18   Problems 13.51, 13.52.

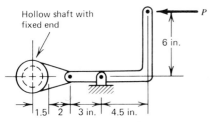

FIG. 13.19   Problem 13.53.

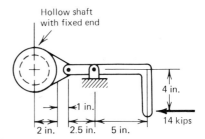

FIG. 13.20   Problem 13.54.

P, applied as shown, necessary to cause this rotation and find the maximum shear stress produced in the shaft. The shaft has a wall thickness of $\frac{1}{4}$ in.

13.54 A 4-in.-diameter hollow shaft (Fig. 13.20) with a wall thickness of $\frac{1}{4}$ in. and a length of 6 ft is connected to the lever shown. Assuming the far end of the shaft to be fixed, find the rotation of the aluminum shaft and the maximum shear stress produced in it.

13.55 An oil well drilling string is a 4-in. standard weight steel pipe, 500 ft long. What will be the angle of twist of the string when an applied torque of 3000 ft-lb is used for drilling? What will the stress in the pipe be?

13.56 A speed reduction transmission is shown schematically in Fig. 13.21. The power in (which is equal to the power out) is 10 horsepower. The input shaft rotates at 1800 rpm. Find the speed of each shaft, the torque carried by each shaft and the minimum diameter of each shaft based on an allowable shear stress of 8000 psi. The gear diameters are:

$$D_1 = D_3 = 2.0 \text{ in.}$$
$$D_2 = 6.0 \text{ in.}$$
$$D_4 = 4.0 \text{ in.}$$

Hint: shaft speeds are related by the equation

$$\frac{N_1}{N_2} = \frac{D_2}{D_1}$$

where *N* is the shaft speed.

13.57 A speed reduction transmission is shown schematically in Fig. 13.21. An output torque of 1200 N·m is desired at 600 rpm. Find the required input power, and the speed, torque and maximum shear stress in each shaft. All shafts are 40.0 mm in diameter. The gear diameters are:

$$D_1 = D_3 = 30 \text{ mm}$$
$$D_2 = 120 \text{ mm}$$
$$D_4 = 90 \text{ mm}$$

Hint: shaft speeds are related by the equation

$$\frac{N_1}{N_2} = \frac{D_2}{D_1}$$

where *N* is the shaft speed.

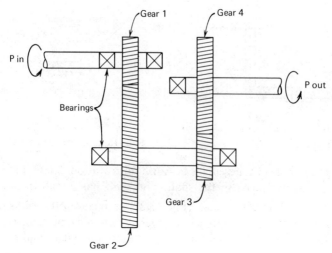

FIG. 13.21 Schematic of transmission. Problems 13.56, 13.57.

14

Internal Forces

The methods of statics have been primarily used to determine external reactions. However, in the analysis of trusses and other structures the loads carried by members and the loads at joints have been determined. These loads are *internal* loads. In this chapter internal loads are examined more generally. In selecting members for a machine or structure, a stress analysis must be made. Finding the internal load is the necessary first step in any stress analysis. In strength of materials the relation of the stress to the internal load is determined, but first the internal load must be determined.

Three principles, examined previously, are relied on in determining the internal loads. The first is an extension of Newton's first law.

1. If a body is at rest and therefore in equilibrium, all its parts—real or imagined—are at rest and in equilibrium.
2. An imaginary cutting plane may be passed through any body in equilibrium without disturbing its equilibrium. Passing the cutting plane will result in two sections, each of which is independently in equilibrium.
3. When a cutting plane is passed through a member, additional forces and moments of forces may be necessary for equilibrium. These forces, which are internal forces, occur in equal but opposite pairs according to Newton's third law. One set will act on each of the pair of free bodies created by the section.

These principles are illustrated in the sections that follow.

14.1   AXIAL LOADS

The loads on the structure in Fig. 14.1 can be solved from statics, from which the loads on member *CE* are as shown in Fig. 14.2*a*. A common design problem is to select a member (i.e., its size and shape) that will function as member *CE*. Ultimately, stresses must be calculated. However, as indicated, the first step in that analysis is to find the internal loads. Notice that the 267-lb loads are external to the member *CE* but they are internal to the entire structure.

The steps for finding the internal load are as follows:

1. Draw a free body diagram for the entire structure.
2. Solve for all external reactions, if possible.
3. Draw free body diagrams of the members.
4. Solve for all reactions external to the members.

The first four steps are left to the reader.

5. Pass a cutting plane through the member at the section of interest and draw a free body diagram of the simpler portion (Figs. 14.2*a*, 14.2*b*).

In this case, where the axial load is uniform, any location is satisfactory.

6. Apply Newton's first law to determine the internal loads.

$$\sum F_x = 0 = P - 267$$
$$P = 267 \text{ lb}$$

Thus it is found that the internal load is 267-lb compression. In strength of materials this load is related to stress, which provides a basis for selecting a member adequate to carry the load. Fig. 14.2*c* shows the alternate segment of the member. Note that this force *P* is in the opposite direction on this body. This is in accordance with Newton's third law. Note further that although the force *P* acts in opposite directions on the two parts, in both cases it is a compressive load.

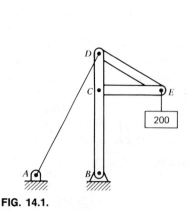

FIG. 14.1.

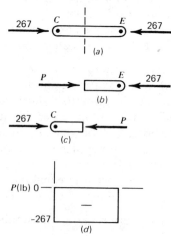

FIG. 14.2*a–d*   Axial loads in member *CE*.

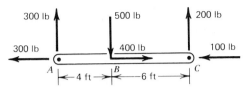

FIG. 14.3 Example Problem 14.1.

Sometimes it is desirable to make a plot of the internal load along the member. This is shown in Fig. 14.2d. When the loading is very simple, as in this case, it is unnecessary, but in more complex load situations it can be desirable, as shown in Example Problem 14.1.

Example Problem 14.1

Construct an axial load diagram for member ABC with the loading as shown in Fig. 14.3.

Solution

A cutting plane is passed between A and B resulting in the free body diagram of Fig. 14.4a. Alternately the right-hand end may be used as shown in Fig. 14.4b. Notice, the internal reactions (P_1, V_1, M_1) differ only by sense in the two diagrams.

The internal reactions V_1 and M_1 are ignored for the present, since we are only interested in the axial load. Summing the forces on the left-hand free

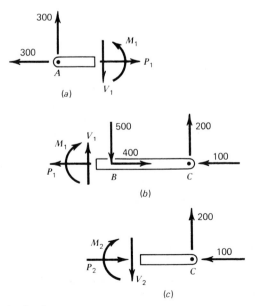

FIG. 14.4a–c Free body diagrams.

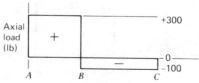

FIG. 14.5   Axial load diagram.

body diagram yields:

$$\sum F_x = 0 = -300 + P_1$$
$$P_1 = 300 \text{ lb tension}$$

Since this section is typical of any location between A and B, this will be the axial load for all points between A and B.

Moving to a section between B and C and drawing the free body diagram (Fig. 14.4c), we write:

$$\sum F_x = 0 = +P_2 - 100$$
$$P_2 = 100 \text{ lb compression}$$

This value is typical of the section from B to C.

Plotting these values yields the result shown in Fig. 14.5—a picture of the axial loads in the member—from which the maximum load and its location are easily identified.

14.2   BEAMS

When referring to beams, one normally pictures the cross members in a building structure, and that is a correct picture. However, the analysis of beams has a much broader application. Beam analysis is used when the dominant loads are perpendicular to the longitudinal axis of a member. For example, the leaf spring–axle assembly for a trailer (Fig. 14.6a) is pin supported at each end, where it is connected to the trailer frame. The load from the axle comes into the middle of the spring. These loads are perpendicular to the length of the spring (Fig. 14.6b), and the spring is analyzed as a beam. The axle is also analyzed as a beam. Figure 14.6c shows that the loads from the wheels and the springs are perpendicular to the axle.

Loading in beams is treated as concentrated or distributed. Figure 14.7 shows examples of both. The distributed loads of Figs. 14.7b and 14.7c are uniform. Nonuniform distributed loads are also common in beams. Figure 14.7e shows such a load.

Beams are often classified according to the method of support. Types of support and their classifications are shown in Fig. 14.7. Only the beams in Figs. 14.7a, 14.7b, and 14.7d are statically determinate; that is, their reactions may be found from the methods of statics. The others are called statically indeterminate. They require an understanding of the beam deflection characteristics to determine the

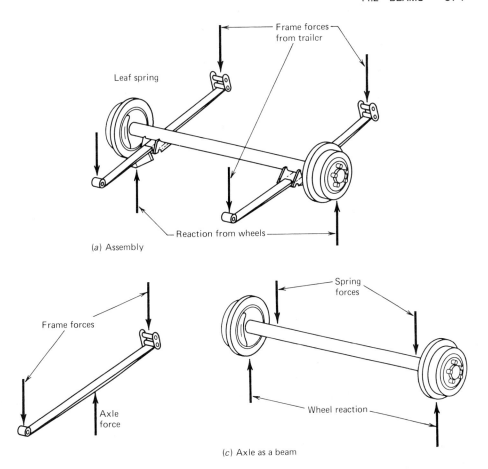

Leaf spring

Frame forces
from trailer

Reaction from wheels

(a) Assembly

Frame forces

Spring
forces

Axle
force

Wheel reaction

(c) Axle as a beam

(b) Spring as a beam

FIG. 14.6a–c Axle–spring assembly for a
trailer.

reactions. Methods of handling statically indeterminate beams are taken up in Chapter 22.

Figure 14.7a shows a simply supported beam with a concentrated load. It is statically determinate. Figure 14.7b shows a simply supported, overhanging beam with a concentrated load and a uniformly distributed load. It, too, is statically determinate. Figure 14.7c shows a beam with redundant simple supports. This beam is called *continuous*. It is not statically determinate. It has two concentrated loads and a uniformly distributed load. The beam in Fig. 14.7d is rigidly supported on one end and free on the other. It is called a *cantilever beam*, and it is statically determinate. The load is concentrated. The next beam, Fig. 14.7e, is fixed on one end and simply supported on the other. It is not statically determinate. It has a concentrated load and a uniformly varying distributed load. Figure 14.7f shows a beam with both ends fixed. It is not statically determinate, and the two loads are concentrated.

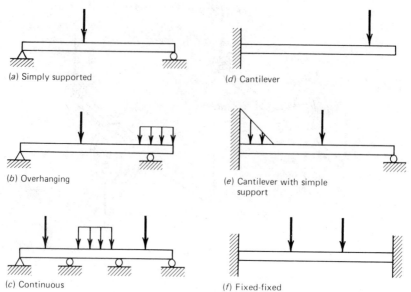

(a) Simply supported

(d) Cantilever

(b) Overhanging

(e) Cantilever with simple support

(c) Continuous

(f) Fixed-fixed

FIG. 14.7a–f Beams classified by supports.

14.3 INTERNAL SHEAR AND BENDING MOMENT

A simply supported beam whose reactions have been found is shown in Fig. 14.8a. Thus the first four steps outlined in Section 14.1 have been completed. It is desired to find the internal load at D. Step 5 is carried out by passing a cutting plane perpendicular to the member at point D and drawing a free body diagram of the right-hand portion, as in Fig. 14.8b. Step 6 requires the application of Newton's first law, yielding:

$$\sum F_y = 0 = -V + 200$$
$$V = 200 \text{ N}\downarrow$$

and

$$\sum M_D = 0 = -M + 4(200)$$
$$M = 800 \text{ N}\cdot\text{m}$$

Thus the *internal* shear load and the *internal* bending moment (moment of force) have been found.

The left-hand portion of the beam could also have been drawn. The right-hand part was used because it was simpler. However, it can be instructive to examine the left-hand side, which is shown in Fig. 14.8c. Applying Newton's first law to this free body diagram yields:

$$\sum F_y = 0 = 300 - 500 + V$$
$$V = 200 \text{ N}\uparrow$$
$$\sum M_D = 0 = -6(300) + 2(500) + M$$
$$M = 800 \text{ N}\cdot\text{m}$$

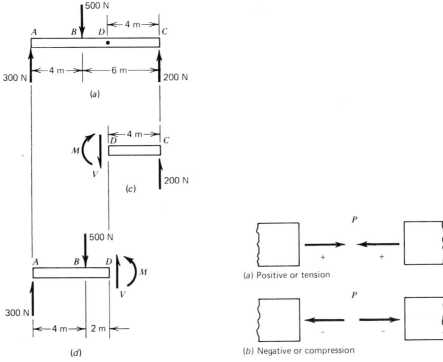

FIG. 14.8a–c Internal shear and bending moment.

FIG. 14.9a–b Axial forces.

As expected, analysis of the left-hand portion produces the same values for shear and bending moment. However, there is an important difference—the signs are opposite, even though there is a single state of shear and a single state of bending in the beam. This leads to the conclusion that the vector sign system used to describe forces and bending moments up to this point is inadequate to describe internal forces. The following sign system is arbitrarily but widely used.

Figure 14.9a shows an axial force pulling on the surface of a member. This is called *tension* or a *positive axial force*. Note that it may act either to the left or right—positive or negative vectors—but if it acts away from the surface it is a tensile, or positive, internal force. Alternately, if it acts into the surface, it is a compressive, or negative, internal force.

Figures 14.10 and 14.11 give two ways of thinking about internal shear load. The first shows the force acting on a face. A downward shear on a right-hand face or an upward shear on a left-hand face is considered positive. We can also think of positive shear as that combination of forces which tends to move the left-hand portion of the beam up with respect to the right-hand portion, as shown in Fig. 14.11. The opposite of these conditions is negative shear. Notice that once again the vector sign of a force is inadequate for characterizing the sign of an internal force.

Two ways of thinking of the bending moment sign are given in Figs. 14.12 and 14.13. We may think of a positive bending moment as counterclockwise on a

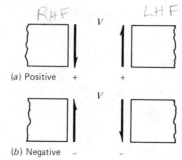

(a) Positive   +   +

(b) Negative   –   –

FIG. 14.10a–b Shear forces.

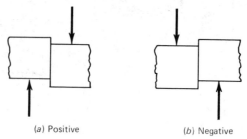

(a) Positive   (b) Negative

FIG. 14.11a–b Tendency to shear.

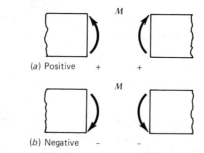

(a) Positive   +   +

(b) Negative   –   –

FIG. 14.12a–b Bending moment.

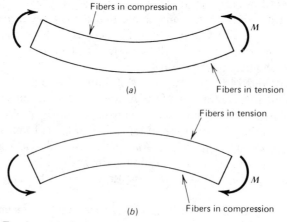

Fibers in compression

(a)

Fibers in tension

Fibers in tension

(b)

Fibers in compression

FIG. 14.13a–b Tendency to bend.

374

right-hand face or clockwise on a left-hand face. Or we may think of the sign in terms of what it tends to do to the geometry of the beam. If the beam were bent concave upward such that it would hold water, it would be positive bending. You may remember this more easily if you think of a smiling, happy face—therefore, "positive." Contrary to this we have a frowning, sad face—therefore, "negative." Still another way of thinking about the sign of bending is based on the stresses produced in the beam. Positive bending compresses the uppermost fibers and stretches the bottom ones. Negative bending produces just the reverse.

Most students remember the sign convention for axial loads and bending moments quite easily. The shear force sign system usually requires rote memorization.

Based on this sign convention, the shear in Fig. 14.8 is negative regardless of which portion of the beam is used. The bending moment, on the other hand, is positive. In this case the internal shear and bending moment at a single point, D, have been found. In a similar manner other points on the beam may be examined, as is illustrated in Example Problem 14.2.

Example Problem 14.2

Find the shear and bending moment every 2 ft across the beam in Fig. 14.14.

Solution

Pass a cutting plane 2 ft from the left-hand end and draw the free body diagram (Fig. 14.15a).

We can learn the internal sign system more quickly if we use it to show the unknown internal shear (V) and bending moment (M) as positive. These are positive *internal* signs but not necessarily positive *vectors*. When we write the force and moment equations, we are writing *vector* equations and accordingly should use *vector* signs. Thus summing the forces gives:

$$\sum F_y = 0 = 300 - V_2$$
$$V_2 = +300 \text{ lb}$$

The positive sign resulting from the equation means that the assumed direction for the vector was correct (i.e., downward), hence a negative *vector*. However, based on the sign system for shear (Fig. 14.10), a downward force on a right-hand face is positive internal *shear*.

$$V_2 = 300 \text{ lb positive shear}$$

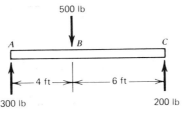

FIG. 14.14 Example Problem 14.2.

Summing the moments about the right-hand end:

$$\sum M_2 = 0 = -2(300) + M_2$$
$$M_2 = +600 \text{ ft-lb}$$

Again the positive sign means the assumed direction was correct. The sign system in Fig. 14.12 indicates that this is also a positive bending moment.

$M = 600$ ft-lb positive bending

At 4 ft the downward load of 500 lb occurs. The shear cannot be examined at this point; therefore, it will be examined slightly to the left of the load and then slightly to the right. Just to the left of the load excludes the 500-lb load from the free body diagram (Fig. 14.15b):

$$\sum F_y = 0 = 300 - V_{4L}$$
$$V_{4L} = 300 \text{ lb positive shear}$$
$$\sum M_4 = 0 = -4(300) + M_{4L}$$
$$M_{4L} = 1200 \text{ ft-lb positive bending}$$

Just to the right of the load includes the 500-lb load, Fig. 14.15c:

$$\sum F_y = 0 = +300 - 500 - V_{4R}$$
$$V_{4R} = -200 \text{ lb negative shear}$$
$$\sum M_4 = 0 = -4(300) + M_{4R}$$
$$M_{4R} = 1200 \text{ ft-lb positive bending}$$

The shear change is from 300-lb positive to 200-lb negative shear—a change of 500 lb, which exactly equals the load applied at the point. The bending moment did not change from one side of the 500-lb load to the other.

At 6 ft, Fig. 14.15d, we have:

$$\sum F = 0 = +300 - 500 - V_6$$
$$V_6 = -200 \text{ lb negative shear}$$
$$\sum M_6 = 0 = -6(300) + 2(500) + M_6$$
$$M_6 = 800 \text{ ft-lb positive bending}$$

The left-hand free body diagram is shown (Fig. 14.15e) for a cutting plane at 8 ft. Alternately, we may draw and analyze the simpler, right-hand free body diagram (Fig. 14.15f). Notice that force and moment are in equal but opposite pairs.

$$\sum F_y = +V_8 + 200 = 0$$
$$V_8 = -200 \text{ lb negative shear}$$
$$\sum M_8 = 0 = -M_8 + 2(200)$$
$$M_8 = 400 \text{ ft-lb positive bending}$$

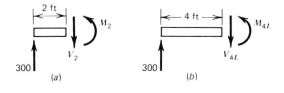

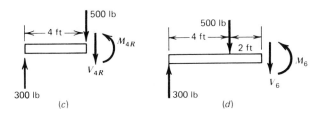

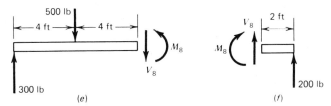

FIG. 14.15a–f   Free body diagrams for Example Problem 14.2.

Example Problem 14.3

Find the shear and bending moment every 2 m for the beam shown in Fig. 14.16.

Solution

In the free body diagram of Fig. 14.17, the distributed load has been replaced with a statically equivalent concentrated load of 160 N at 4 m from the support. Finding the indicated reactions is left to the reader.

A cutting plane is passed 2 m to the right of the *original* loading (Fig. 14.16), not the equivalent loading (Fig. 14.17). The internal shear V and internal bending moment M are shown in the positive sense in Fig. 14.18. The distributed load on

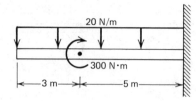

FIG. 14.16 Example Problem 14.3.

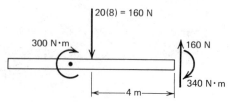

FIG. 14.17 Free body diagram showing equivalent load.

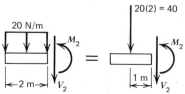

FIG. 14.18 Free body diagrams at 2 m.

this free body diagram is replaced in the equivalent diagram to the right. This step is not necessary, but many will find it helpful. Summing forces gives:

$$\sum F_y = 0 = -40 - V_2$$
$$V_2 = -40.0 \text{ N negative shear}$$

and

$$\sum M_2 = 0 = +(1)(40) + M_2$$
$$M_2 = -40.0 \text{ N} \cdot \text{m negative bending}$$

The negative signs mean the senses of the vectors are opposite those shown in Fig. 14.18, and the internal loads are negative. Proceeding to 4 m gives the free body diagram of Fig. 14.19. Summing forces gives:

$$\sum F_y = 0 = -80 - V_4$$
$$V_4 = -80.0 \text{ N negative shear}$$
$$\sum M_4 = 0 = +2(80) - 300 + M_4$$
$$M_4 = +140 \text{ N} \cdot \text{m positive bending}$$

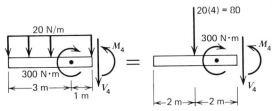

FIG. 14.19 Free body diagrams at 4 m.

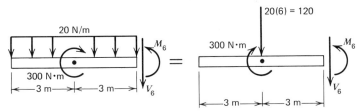

FIG. 14.20 Free body diagrams at 6 m.

For 6 m we have Fig. 14.20, and:

$$\sum F_y = 0 = -120 - V_6$$
$$V_6 = -120 \text{ N negative shear}$$
$$\sum M_6 = 0 = +3(120) - 300 + M_6$$
$$M_6 = -60.0 \text{ N} \cdot \text{m negative moment}$$

At 8 m the results are the same as in the overall free body diagram in Fig. 14.17. Using the established sign system we have:

$$V_8 = 160 \text{ N negative shear}$$
$$M_8 = 340 \text{ N} \cdot \text{m negative moment}$$

14.4 EQUATIONS FOR SHEAR AND BENDING MOMENT

In Example 14.2 the shear and bending moment were found at five different locations. Additional locations could, of course, be found. One way to represent the pattern of shear and bending moment being developed is to graph them, as in Fig. 14.21. If additional points were sampled, the points would be found on the graph matching the broken lines. These graphs are very valuable aids in the design and analysis of beams, and they are examined further in this chapter.

In Example Problem 14.2 the shear and bending moment were examined every 2 ft. By applying algebraic principles, this process can be simplified. A general section is examined at some position x for each portion of the beam bounded by discrete loads. Example Problem 14.4 illustrates this method. This analysis yields *equations* for the shear and bending moment for each section of the beam. The equations can be evaluated for any location for a number; they can be substituted into more detailed analysis; they can be programmed into a computer; they can

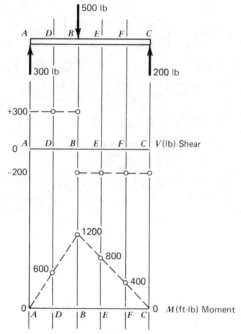

FIG. 14.21 Graph of shear and bending moment.

be examined functionally to determine how the shear and bending moment behave in the beam (such as where do maximums or minimums occur?); and finally, they can be plotted as in Fig. 14.21.

Example Problem 14.4

Find the necessary equations for the shear and bending moment for the beam shown in Fig 14.22.

Solution

Note that the sections are bounded by discrete loads. A cutting plane is passed at a distance x to the right of A. The free body diagram is drawn (Fig. 14.23), and we write:

$$\sum F_y = 0 = 300 - V_1$$
$$V_1 = 300 \text{ lb positive shear}$$

This says the shear is constant, independent of position, between A and B.

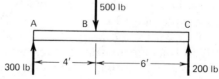

FIG. 14.22 Example Problem 14.4.

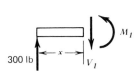

FIG. 14.23 Free body diagram for $0 < x < 14$.

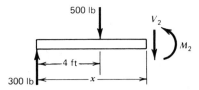

FIG. 14.24 Free body diagram for $4 < x < 10$.

To find the moment M_1 we may sum the moments of force about any point. However, it is usually desirable to sum moments about a point at the section in question. This eliminates V_1, the shear at the section, from the expression for the moment. Thus:

$$\sum M_x = 0 = -300x + M_1$$
$$M_1 = 300x \text{ positive bending moment}$$

This equation is limited to values of x between 0 and 4, that is, $0 < x < 4$. The equations above allow the shear and bending moment to be evaluated for any position between A and B substituting the appropriate value of x. Referring to Fig. 14.21, these two equations are those for the curves plotted as shear and bending moment between A and B. At this point showing V and M as positive internal values becomes almost essential. By making this assumption, it will be easy to interpret the meaning of values obtained from the equations.

Now pass a cutting plane between B and C and proceed (Fig. 14.24):

$$\sum F_y = 0 = +300 - 500 - V_2$$
$$V_2 = -200 \text{ lb negative shear}$$
$$\sum M_x = 0 = -300x + 500(x - 4) + M_2$$
$$M_2 = 300x - 500x + 2000$$
$$M_2 = 2000 - 200x \text{ positive bending}$$

These two equations are valid for

$$4 < x < 10$$

and are those for the curves plotted in Fig. 14.21 between B and C.

Shear is constant for the section and the bending moment varies as follows:

At $x = 4$ ft
$$M_4 = 200 - 200(4) = 1200 \text{ ft-lb}$$

At $x = 10$ ft
$$M_{10} = 2000 - 200(10) = 0$$

Remember, x is zero at the left end and measured positively to the right. Choose vectors representing positive internal shear and bending moment, as in Figs. 14.10a and 14.12a. Use the left-hand free body diagram. Then the sign from the equation for shear or bending will correspond to the physical sense given in Figs. 14.10 to 14.13.

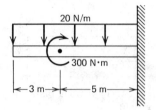

FIG. 14.25   Example Problem 14.5.

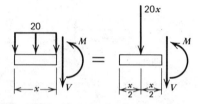

FIG. 14.26   Free body diagram for $0 < x < 3$.

Example Problem 14.5

Write the necessary equations to describe the internal shear and moment equations for the beam shown in Fig. 14.25. Make a graph of these equations.

Solution

The reaction at the support is shown in Example Problem 14.3, Fig. 14.17. Because of the concentrated moment at 3 m, two sections will be required. The first free body diagram, for $0 < x < 3$, is drawn in Fig. 14.26. We assume positive internal V and M. For some, the analysis will be easier if the distributed load is replaced with a statically equivalent load as shown in the right-hand diagram. Then:

$$\sum F_y = 0 = -20x - V$$
$$V = -20x \tag{1}$$

As positive values of x are substituted into Eq. 1, negative shear is obtained.

$$\sum M_x = 0 = +20x\left(\frac{x}{2}\right) + M$$

$$M = -10x^2 \tag{2}$$

Positives values of x will give negative moments. These two equations are valid for $0 < x < 3$.

The free body diagram is then drawn for $3 < x < 8$ in Fig. 14.27. Again the equivalent free body diagram is also shown. Then:

$$\sum F_y = 0 = -20x - V$$
$$V = -20x \tag{3}$$

$$\sum M_x = 0 = +20x\left(\frac{x}{2}\right) - 300 + M$$

$$M = 300 - 10x^2 \tag{4}$$

The shear equation is the same as before and will give negative values for $3 < x < 8$. The moment will be positive initially $(x = 3)$ and then becomes negative again.

The two pairs of equations are plotted in Fig. 14.28. Equation 1 is evaluated at $x = 0$ and $x = 3$. Since it is a *straight line*, these two points are all that are necessary to define the line. The graph also shows $x = 2$, which illustrates that the values obtained in Example Problem 14.3 agree with Eq. 1. Equations

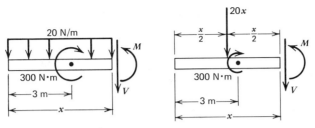

FIG. 14.27 Free body diagram for $3 < x < 8$.

for shear will not be valid *at* the end points (0 and 3) if a concentrated vertical load is applied there. However they will be valid just to the right of $(0+)$ and just to the left of $(3-)$ and can be used to obtain the graph in either case. Equation 3 is evaluated at $x = 3$ and $x = 8$. It is unusual to have the same equation for both portions of the beam. The values from Example Problem 14.3 for $x = 4$ and $x = 6$ are also shown in Fig. 14.28.

It is worth noting that the final point on this graph is -160 N. The vertical load at this support is an upward load of 160 N, which would bring this graph back to zero, as indicated by the vertical straight line on the graph. This is more than a coincidence.

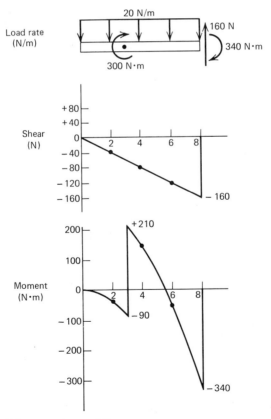

FIG. 14.28 Plot of shear and moment.

Equation 2 is evaluated at $x = 0$ and $x = 3$. A third point is required to accurately plot this *second-degree* equation. The value for $x = 2$ is calculated to be -40, which agrees with that obtained in Example Problem 14.3. Equation 4 is evaluated at $x = 3$, $x = 6$, and $x = 8$, and a plot is made. We observe the last point from Eq. 2 to be -90 and the first point from Eq. 4 to be $+210$. Thus there is a jump of 300 at the point $x = 3$, which exactly equals the applied moment at the point. This also is no coincidence. Finally we note the final value of the moment is -340, and this agrees with the moment reaction at the support of the beam. These jumps in the moment are caused by the applied couples and are represented by vertical lines in the graphs. Equation 2 is not valid for the point $x = 3$, and Eq. 4 is not valid for either $x = 3$ or $x = 8$, because a moment is applied at each point. But these equations are valid just before and just after these points, and the points may be used for plotting.

14.5   RELATION BETWEEN LOAD, SHEAR, AND BENDING MOMENT

The graphs plotted in Figs. 14.21 and 14.28 are more formally known as *shear* and *bending moment diagrams*. These diagrams greatly aid in the analysis and design of beams—which include a very large portion of the members in buildings, machines, and the like. Students often have great difficulty with these diagrams. It is true that considerable detail is involved, but the fundamental principle is quite simple. In our study we will eventually apply this principle in four successive steps. It is, therefore, worthwhile to master it early.

The plotting of the graphs in Figs. 14.21 and 14.28 was tedious and required many calculations. We will come to obtain graphs of this type very simply and quickly. As a basis for doing so we first develop fundamental relationships that exist between the load rate, shear, and bending moment. By "*load rate*" we mean the load per unit length of the beam.

Consider a beam under some general loading as in Fig. 14.29. The loading is shown upward, positive, to establish a sign system. Furthermore, the supports shown are schematic, so don't worry about the beam's lifting up. A very small element of length dx is cut from the beam, and a free body diagram is drawn (Fig. 14.30). The load on the left-hand end is a shear V and a bending moment M. Over the distance dx the shear changes an infinitesimal amount dV and the bending

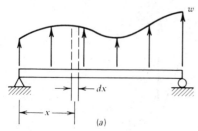

(a)

FIG. 14.29   A simply supported beam with a general distributed load.

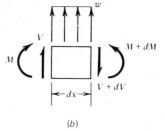

(b)

FIG. 14.30   An infinitesimal element from the beam in Fig. 14.29

moment dM. The distance dx is sufficiently short that w may be treated as constant over the interval. Applying equilibrium conditions to the element yields:

$$\Sigma F_y = 0 = +V + w\,dx - (V + dV)$$
$$w\,dx = dV$$

Then:

$$w = \frac{dV}{dx} \qquad\qquad (14.1)$$

which is the slope of the shear (V) curve. This says that the slope of the shear curve is equal to the instantaneous value of the load rate. Alternately, this may be stated as follows:

$$dV = w\,dx$$

and then integrated to give:

$$\Delta V = \int w\,dx = \text{area under } w \text{ curve} \qquad\qquad (14.2)$$

This says that the change in shear is equal to the area under the load rate diagram. The principles above are illustrated by the graphs in Fig. 14.21, hereafter called *load rate*, *shear*, and *bending moment diagrams*. There is no loading between A and B in Fig. 14.21; that is, $w = 0$. According to Eq. 14.1 the slope of the shear diagram for the segment $A-B$ should also be zero, which, of course, is the case. Equation 14.2 indicates that the change in the shear is equal to the area under the load rate curve. Since the load rate between A and B is zero, this area, and thus the change in shear, is also zero.

Referring again to the free body diagram of the element dx (Fig. 14.30), we sum the moment of the forces about the right end, giving:

$$\Sigma M_R = 0 = -M - V\,dx - (w\,dx)\frac{dx}{2} + (M + dM)$$

$$-V\,dx - \frac{w(dx)^2}{2} + dM = 0$$

The term $w(dx/2)^2$ is an order of magnitude smaller than $V\,dx$, so it is disregarded, giving:

$$V = \frac{dM}{dx} = \text{slope of the } M \text{ curve} \qquad\qquad (14.3)$$

This says that the slope of the bending moment curve is equal to the instantaneous value of the shear. Alternately, it may be stated as follows:

$$dM = V\,dx$$

Integrating gives:

$$\Delta M = \int V\,dx = \text{area under } V \text{ curve} \qquad\qquad (14.4)$$

This says that the change in bending moment equals the area under the shear curve. If we refer again to Fig. 14.21, it is observed that the area under the shear curve between A and D is $300\,\text{lb} \times 2\,\text{ft} = 600\,\text{ft-lb}$. According to Eq. 14.4, the change in the bending moment should then be 600 ft-lb, as it is. A similar area and a corresponding similar change in M is found from D to B, and so across the beam. Equation 14.3 indicates that the slope of the bending moment diagram at any point equals the corresponding value of the shear. The shear is constant and positive from A to B, and accordingly, the slope of the bending moment is also constant and positive.

A very important relationship is established here between load rate (w), shear (V), and bending moment (M); that is, each curve is the integral of the previous one. Alternately, each curve is the derivative of the following one. The integral of $x^n\,dx$ is as follows:

$$\int x^n\,dx = \frac{x^{n+1}}{n+1} + C$$

The degree (n) of a curve increases by one with each integration. Thus if the load rate is constant—zero degree—the shear will be first degree, linear, and the bending moment will be second degree, parabolic. The complexity here is considerably reduced when it is realized that the bending moment has the same relationship to the shear as the shear has to the load rate. These relationships are also illustrated in Fig. 14.28. The load rate is a constant -20, so the shear is a first-degree curve with a constant negative slope of -20. The moment curve in turn has an increasingly negative slope and is a second-degree curve.

These principles allow the shear and moment diagrams to be plotted directly from the solved free body diagram of the entire beam. This method quickly and efficiently gives a picture of the shear and bending moment in the entire beam, which is essential in comprehensive design problems. The method is detailed in Section 14.6.

The derivative and integral define the geometric relationships. In practice, we do not normally exercise the calculus at this point. However, if the concepts of the derivative and integral are well understood, they will be of great assistance in obtaining shear and moment diagrams. On the other hand, as the concepts of these diagrams are mastered, they can enhance our understanding of the derivative and integral.

14.6 GENERAL PROCEDURE FOR BEAM DIAGRAMS

The steps in constructing shear and bending moment diagrams are as follows:
   Step 1   Draw a free body diagram of the beam.
   Step 2   Solve for the support reactions using Newton's first law.

SHEAR DIAGRAM

   Step 3   Starting at the left-hand end of the beam, reproduce vertical loads as they occur. Upward forces make a positive change in shear; downward forces make a negative change.
   Step 4   Apply Eq. 14.2 to determine the change in shear between discrete forces. Note that $\int w\,dx$ equals the area under the load rate curve. (We use the word

"curve" in its general sense. The "curve" may be a straight line, zero valued, or any other function.) Downward load rates are negative; upward ones are positive.

Step 5   The shear curve will be one degree higher than the load rate curve. Its specific shape is determined by applying Eq. 14.1. Note that dV/dx is the slope of the shear curve. The curve will close at the right end.

(The next three steps are merely repetitions of steps 3 through 5.)

BENDING MOMENT DIAGRAM

Step 6   Starting at the left-hand end, reproduce discrete bending moments as they occur. The sign of the bending moment is determined by the effect it would have on the beam to its right; that is, if it will produce positive bending in the beam to its right, it will cause a positive change in the bending moment diagram. (Students hardly ever get this right the first time—better read it again.)

Step 7   Apply Eq. 14.4 to determine the change in bending moments between discrete forces or bending moments. The integral $\int V\,dx$ is the area under the shear curve.

Step 8   The bending moment curve will be one degree higher than the shear curve. Its specific shape is determined by applying Eq. 14.3. The derivative dM/dx is the slope of the moment curve. The curve will close at the right end.

Example Problem 14.6

Construct the shear and bending moment diagrams for the cantilever beam shown in Fig. 14.31.

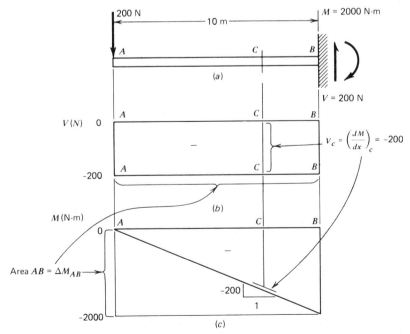

FIG. 14.31a–c   Example Problem 14.6.

Solution

Steps 1 and 2 are left to the student.

Executing step 3, we start at the left end. The 200-N downward force is reproduced on the shear diagram, as shown in Fig. 14.31b.

Applying step 4, we note that between A and B the load rate is zero ($w = 0$); thus there is no area under the load rate curve and therefore no change in shear. Alternately, the value of the load rate is the slope of the shear curve, both being zero in this case. This is step 5.

The 200-N concentrated reaction at B is reproduced, closing the diagram.

The shear diagram must always close. If it does not close, either you have made an error in its construction, or the beam was not in equilibrium to start with.

The shear is negative 200 N throughout the beam.

In step 6 (Fig. 14.31c), there is no bending moment at A, so this starts at zero. The change between A and B equals the area under the shear curve:

$$\Delta M_{A-B} = -200(10) = -2000 \text{ N}\cdot\text{m}$$

Notice the area and change are negative.

Since the shear is constant, according to Eq. 14.3, the slope of M is constant; hence the straight line. The slope at C, dM/dx, is equal to the value of shear at C.

The concentrated moment at B, 2000 N·m, would bend the beam to the right of it (if it existed) positively; thus it is treated as a positive 2000-N·m load, which closes the diagram.

The bending moment diagram must always close. If it does not close, either you have made an error in its construction, or the beam was not in equilibrium to start with.

Example Problem 14.7

Construct the shear and bending moment diagram for the uniformly loaded, simply supported overhanging beam shown in Fig. 14.32a.

Solution

1. We draw the free body diagram (Fig. 14.32b) of a statically equivalent beam by replacing the distributed 20-kip/ft load with a concentrated load of 200 kips at the center of the beam. This free body diagram is statically equivalent, but not equivalent!

2. $\sum M_A = 0 = -5(200) + 8(B)$

$$B = \frac{5(200)}{8} = \textbf{125 kips}$$

$$\sum F_y = 0 = A + B - 200$$
$$A = 200 - B = 200 - 125 = \textbf{75.0 kips}$$

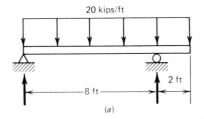

(a)

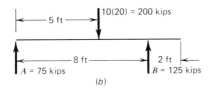

(b)

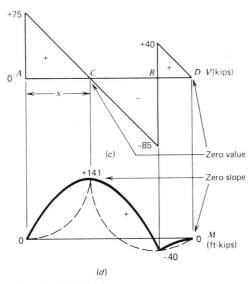

(d)

FIG. 14.32a–d Example Problem 14.7.

We proceed to step 3, reverting back to the original load diagram. We do not use the statically equivalent beam with the concentrated 200-kip load.

The shear diagram goes up 75 units at A (Fig. 14.32c). Between A and B the area under the load curve is:

$$\Delta V = 8(-20) = -160 \text{ kip}$$

Thus the shear just left of B is:

$$\Delta V_{BL} = +75 - 160 = -85 \text{ kip}$$

Since the load rate is constant—a zero-degree curve—the shear will be a first-degree or linear curve. Thus we draw a straight line from $+75$ to -85.

Another way of arriving at the same conclusion is to note:

$$w = \frac{dV}{dx} = \text{slope of shear}$$

That is, the instantaneous value of the load rate is the slope of the shear diagram. Since the load rate is constant and negative, the slope of the shear must also be constant and negative.

Applying step 3 again, at B the shear changes $+125$ kips. So:

$$V_{BR} = -85 + 125 = +40.0 \text{ kips}$$

This is a step change.

From B to the right end of the beam we find:

$$\Delta V = (2)(-20) = -40 \text{ kip}$$

This brings us back to 0 at the right-hand end, and the diagram closes as it always should. Applying Eq. 14.1 gives us a straight line for this portion of the curve. The diagram should be labeled as shown, indicating peak values, units, and positive and negative areas.

We proceed to the moment diagram and steps 6, 7, and 8. There is no concentrated moment at the left-hand end, so we start at zero. We notice that the shear curve changes from positive to negative between A and B. We must find this crossover point. We call the point C and say it is x ft to the right of A. The shear starts at $+75$ and must drop to zero over the distance x, so we write:

$$\Delta V = wx$$
$$-75 = (-20)x$$

The constant load rate of 20 kips/ft is downward, which we call negative; therefore, we write "-20" in the equation above. Then we have:

$$x = \frac{-75}{-20} = \textbf{3.75 ft}$$

Locating this point, we proceed with the moment diagram from A to C (Fig. 14.32d):

$$\Delta M = \text{area of triangle} = \tfrac{1}{2}bh$$
$$\Delta M = \tfrac{1}{2}(3.75)(+75) = 140.6 = +141 \text{ ft-kips}$$

The shear curve is first degree, so the moment curve will be second degree. Two possibilities of second-degree curves are shown, one solid and one broken. The solid is chosen by applying Eq. 14.3, which says:

$$V = \frac{dM}{dx}$$

So the slope must go from a highly positive value ($+75$) to zero. When a zero is included, this selection is much easier.

From C to B we have

$$\Delta M = \tfrac{1}{2}bh = \tfrac{1}{2}(8 - 3.75)(-85)$$
$$\Delta M = -180.6 \text{ ft-kips}$$

and

$$M_B = +141 - 181 = -40.0 \text{ ft-kips}$$

The curve required to connect +141, and −40 is again second degree. We select the solid one, zero slope at C, because of the zero value of shear at C. Finally, from B to the right end, D:

$$\Delta M = \tfrac{1}{2}bh = \tfrac{1}{2}(2)(+40)$$
$$= +40.0 \text{ ft-kips}$$

and

$$M_D = -40 + 40 = 0$$

The final value is zero, and once again the curve closes. The solid is chosen because of the zero shear at the right-hand end—zero shear gives zero slope on the moment curve.

With these diagrams at a glance we see the maximum shear load is −85 kip and the maximum bending moment is +141 ft-kips. We also know where these values occur. These and other values in the diagram are necessary to design (select) the beam.

Example Problem 14.8

For the beam shown in Fig. 14.33, construct the shear and moment diagrams.

Solution

An equivalent free body diagram is drawn (Fig. 14.33b), and the reactions are found.

$$V = 600 \text{ N}$$
$$M = 2400 \text{ N·m} \qquad \text{clockwise}$$

Returning to the original loading, note that the initial shear is zero. Thus the shear diagram (Fig. 14.33c), starts at zero. The change from the left-hand end to the right equals the area under the load rate curve:

$$\Delta V = \tfrac{1}{2}(-200 \text{ N/m})6 \text{ m}$$
$$\Delta V = -600 \text{ N}$$

The load rate curve is first degree, so the shear curve will be second degree—parabolic. The load rate goes from −200 to 0 so the slope of the shear curve must do the same, since:

$$w = \frac{dV}{dx}$$

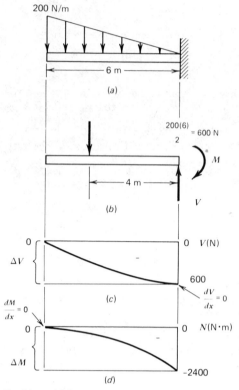

FIG. 14.33   Example Problem 14.8.

Of the two options available, we pick the one with zero slope at the right-hand end. Also note the shear curve has a negative slope everywhere. The 600-N reaction at the right-hand end closes the shear diagram.

For the moment diagram we start at zero on the left-hand end (Fig. 14.33*d*). The change in the moment from the left- to the right-hand end is equal to the area under the shear curve. The shear curve is second degree with a zero slope at the right-hand end, and the area under it is negative. We can find this area from the information in Table A-9 for a parabola. Note that to use this table we must include a vertex (point with zero slope for our purposes). The table gives:

$$A = \tfrac{1}{3}bh$$

for the smaller area within the *bh* rectangle. We have the larger or complimentary part, thus:

$$A = \tfrac{2}{3}bh$$

and

$$\Delta M = \tfrac{2}{3}(6 \text{ m})(-600 \text{ N})$$
$$\Delta M = -2400 \text{ N} \cdot \text{m}$$

This means that the change from the left- to the right-hand end is $-2400 \text{ N}\cdot\text{m}$. Since the shear is a second-degree curve, the moment, which is its integral, is a third-degree curve—which looks like a second-degree curve. We pick from our two options by noting that the shear is zero on the left-hand end, hence the slope of the moment curve must be zero on the left-hand end:

$$V = 0 = \frac{dM}{dx}$$

Finally, the concentrated moment, the reaction at the right-hand end, produces positive bending on a beam to its right (if it existed) and consequently produces a positive change of $2400 \text{ N}\cdot\text{m}$, closing the moment diagram. Notice that the bending moment is everywhere negative, as we would intuitively anticipate from the beam loading.

14.7 SUMMARY

Using the methods of statics, the *value* of internal loads at a specific point may be found; or we may find *equations* for internal loads at an arbitrary point. The vector sign system used up to now is not adequate to describe internal loading, and a new sign system is given in Figs. 14.9 through 14.13. A final method of determining internal loads is by beam diagrams.

Relations between load rate, shear, and bending moment are:

$$w = \frac{dV}{dx} = \text{slope of } V$$

$$V = \frac{dM}{dx} = \text{slope of } M$$

In integral form:

$$V = \int w\, dx = \text{area under } w$$

$$M = \int V\, dx = \text{area under } V$$

Beam diagrams are graphical interpretations of the above.

The step-by-step procedure of Section 14.6 gives a method for constructing beam diagrams. The efficient and rapid construction of shear and moment diagrams is necessary for the analysis and design of beams.

PROBLEMS

For the indicated figure, calculate the shear and bending moment every 2 ft or 2 m as appropriate (in the manner of Example Problem 14.2). Indicate whether each moment is positive or negative.

14.1 Fig. 14.34   **14.2** Fig. 14.35

14.3 Fig. 14.36   **14.4** Fig. 14.37

14.5 Fig. 14.38   **14.6** Fig. 14.39
14.7 Fig. 14.40   **14.8** Fig. 14.41

Obscure!

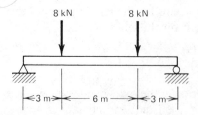

FIG. 14.34   Problems 14.1, 14.9, 14.17, 14.25.

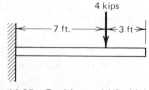

FIG. 14.35   Problems 14.2, 14.10, 14.18, 14.26.

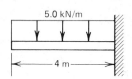

FIG. 14.36   Problems 14.3, 14.11, 14.19, 14.27.

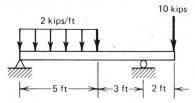

FIG. 14.37   Problems 14.4, 14.12, 14.20, 14.28.

Plot the shear and bending moment at 2-ft or 2-m intervals as appropriate in the indicated figure (as obtained in Problems 14.1–14.8).

14.9 Fig. 14.34   **14.10** Fig. 14.35
14.11 Fig. 14.36   **14.12** Fig. 14.37
14.13 Fig. 14.38   **14.14** Fig. 14.39
14.15 Fig. 14.40   **14.16** Fig. 14.41

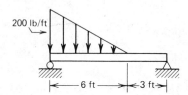

FIG. 14.38   Problems 14.5, 14.13, 14.21, 14.29.

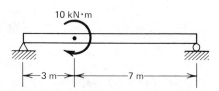

FIG. 14.39   Problems 14.6, 14.14, 14.22, 14.30.

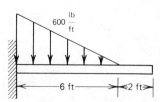

FIG. 14.40   Problems 14.7, 14.15, 14.23, 14.31.

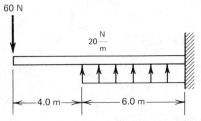

FIG. 14.41   Problems 14.8, 14.16, 14.24, 14.32.

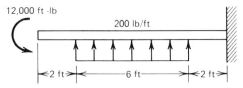

FIG. 14.42   Problem 14.33.

Write the necessary algebraic expressions for shear and bending moment to completely describe the beam in the indicated figure (as in Example Problem 14.4).

14.17 Fig. 14.34   **14.18** Fig. 14.35
14.19 Fig. 14.36   **14.20** Fig. 14.37
14.21 Fig. 14.38   **14.22** Fig. 14.39
14.23 Fig. 14.40   **14.24** Fig. 14.41

Directly plot the shear and bending moment diagrams for the indicated figure by the method of Section 14.6.

14.25 Fig. 14.34   **14.26** Fig. 14.35
14.27 Fig. 14.36   **14.28** Fig. 14.37
14.29 Fig. 14.38   **14.30** Fig. 14.39
14.31 Fig. 14.40   **14.32** Fig. 14.41

14.33 For the beam shown in Fig. 14.42 construct the shear and moment diagrams.

14.34 Construct the shear and moment diagrams for the beam shown in Fig. 14.43.

14.35 Construct the shear and moment diagrams for the beam shown in Fig. 14.44.

Construct the shear and bending moment diagrams for the beam in the indicated figures. Indicate the magnitude and location of the maximum shear and maximum bending moment.

14.36 Fig. 14.45

14.37 Fig. 14.46 *Hint:* Assume that the ground reaction is uniformly distributed.

14.38 Fig. 14.47

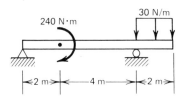

FIG. 14.43   Problem 14.34.

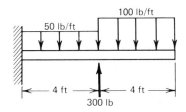

FIG. 14.44   Problem 14.35.

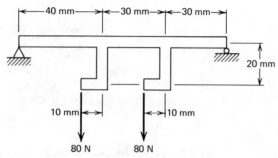

FIG. 14.45   Problem 14.36.

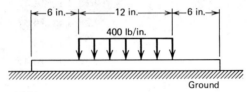

FIG. 14.46   Problem 14.37.

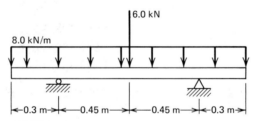

FIG. 14.47   Problem 14.38.

15

Stress and Strain from Bending Loads

15.1   Stress and Strain Distribution
15.2   Flexure Formula
15.3   Beam Design Using the Flexure Formula
15.4   Summary

In Chapter 11 we examined the relationship between an axial load and the stresses it produces; in Chapter 13 it was torque and its resultant stresses. In this chapter we examine the relationship between the bending moment and the stresses it produces. This relationship, called the flexure formula, may well be the most important of the three, because it so often governs the design in structures. At the risk of boring the reader, we once again emphasize that stress equations are of little value until the load causing the stress has been found—a statics problem. In the case of bending moment, it can be a rather involved statics problem, as illustrated in Chapter 14.

In this chapter we spend considerable effort in developing the governing equation. The arguments are about as exciting as tomato soup for lunch. However—like tomato soup—they are nourishing. The understanding of the bending phenomenon, the generation of the flexure formula, and most important, the stress distribution described by this equation, are essential for the intelligent application of this principle. It is tempting to forego the development, proceeding directly to Eq. 15.5 to "plug it in" to problems. And indeed that will work for many of the problems of this chapter. However, it will be totally inadequate when we get to Chapter 18.

Your soup's getting cold!

15.1   STRESS AND STRAIN DISTRIBUTION

To develop the flexure formula we consider an initially straight beam under pure bending (Fig. 15.1a). This requirement of pure bending does not prove restrictive, since we will be able to apply the results to most loading situations by the method of superposition. We show the cross section of the beam as rectangular, although

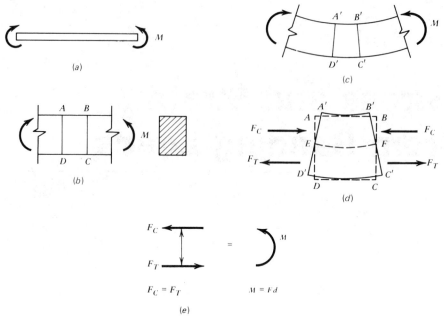

FIG. 15.1a–e Beam in pure bending.

the result is not restricted to that. A smaller section of the beam and its cross section are shown in its initially straight condition in Fig. 15.1b. Figure 15.1c shows the deformation that results from the applied bending moment M. If this deformation is not intuitively obvious, load a ruler in a similar manner until the point is clear. Notice that for this deformation to take place, the initial line element BC must rotate to a new position $B'C'$. We assume that it remains straight. This rotation is emphasized in Fig. 15.1d by superimposing the element $A'B'C'D'$ on its original shape $ABCD$ and further enlarging the figure.

Notice that the fiber AB has shortened to $A'B'$ while the fiber DC has been lengthened to $D'C'$. Thus the top portion of the element is shortened or compressed, but the bottom portion is stretched or placed in tension. Also note that some transition element, labeled EF in Fig. 15.1d, does not change length at all. This element is known as the *neutral axis*. All the fibers above the neutral axis are shortened. All the fibers below it are stretched.

The shortening of the fibers above EF requires a compressive force shown as F_C in Fig. 15.1d. The stretching of fibers below EF requires a tensile force, labeled F_T in Fig. 15.1d. The force F_C is equal to the force F_T, and they combine to form a couple equal to the applied bending moment M as illustrated in Fig. 15.1e. Recall that a couple is a system of forces having a resultant moment but no resultant force.

We have assumed that the line element BC remains straight and rotates to $B'C'$ as shown in Figs. 15.1b–15.1d. In Fig. 15.2 the element is rotated so that AD is in line with $A'D'$. This conveniently allows us to examine the total elongation of each fiber. Thus BB' is the change in length of fiber AB, and CC' is the change in length of fiber DC. We denote by δ the elongation of any fiber at any distance y

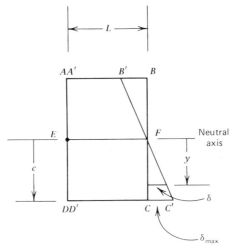

FIG. 15.2 Deformation is linearly distributed.

from the neutral axis. The maximum elongation δ_{max} of any fiber is equal to CC' and occurs on the extreme fiber at a distance c from the neutral axis. We observe that the elongation of any fiber is proportional to its distance from the neutral axis, and thus we can write:

$$\delta = \frac{y}{c}\,\delta_{max} \qquad (15.1)$$

This simply says that the deformation of fibers is a linear function of position, being zero at the neutral axis and a maximum at the extreme fiber.

The strain of any fiber can be found from the definition of strain, namely:

$$\varepsilon = \frac{\delta}{L}$$

Since all the fibers have the same original length L, we divide Eq. 15.1 by L to get:

$$\frac{\delta}{L} = \frac{y}{c}\frac{\delta_{max}}{L}$$

which yields:

$$\varepsilon = \frac{y}{c}\,\varepsilon_{max} \qquad (15.2)$$

Thus we see that the strain is also linearly distributed, being zero at the neutral axis and a maximum at the extreme fiber.

We decide now to limit our discussion to linearly elastic materials stressed below their proportional limits, so we may apply Hooke's law:

$$\sigma = E\varepsilon$$

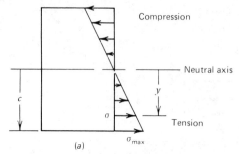 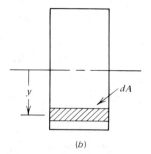

FIG. 15.3a–b Stress distribution.

or

$$\varepsilon = \frac{\sigma}{E}$$

And for Eq. 15.2, we have:

$$\frac{\sigma}{E} = \frac{y}{c} \frac{\sigma_{max}}{E}$$

giving:

$$\sigma = \frac{y}{c} \sigma_{max} \qquad (15.3)$$

This important relationship says that stress, like deflection and strain, is linearly distributed. It is zero at the neutral axis; that is, the neutral axis is unstressed and unstrained. It is a maximum at the extreme fiber. This stress distribution is shown in Fig. 15.3. Notice that it is compressive above the neutral axis and tensile below. The resultant force from the compressive stress is equal to F_C (Fig. 15.1d), and the force from the tensile stress is equal to F_T. The resultant of the two together is zero force and a couple equal to the applied moment M.

We have seen that pure bending results in linear distributions for total elongation, strain, and stress. All are zero at the neutral axis and maximum at the extreme fiber.

Example Problem 15.1

A beam with the cross section shown in Fig. 15.4 has a maximum stress of 120 MPa compression due to pure bending at fiber A. Its modulus of elasticity is 76 GPa. Calculate the stress and strain 30 mm below and 20 mm above the neutral axis.

Solution

The stress distribution is as shown in Fig. 15.5. At 30 mm below the neutral axis, we have:

$$\sigma_{-30} = \frac{y}{c} \sigma_{max}$$

$$\sigma_{-30} = \tfrac{30}{40}(120) = \textbf{90.0 MPa } C$$

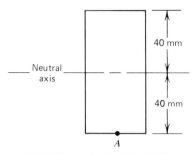

FIG. 15.4 Example Problem 7.1.

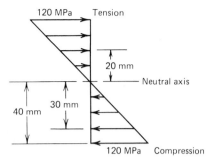

FIG. 15.5 Stress distribution.

where C designates compression. From Hooke's law the strain is:

$$\varepsilon_{-30} = \frac{\sigma}{E} = \frac{90.0\ \text{MPa}}{76\ \text{GPa}} = \textbf{1.18 E-3}$$

Similarly, for 20 mm:

$$\sigma_{+20} = \tfrac{20}{40}(120) = \textbf{60.0 MPa } \textbf{\textit{T}}$$

Note that on opposite sides of the neutral axis the signs of the stresses are also opposite:

$$\varepsilon_{+20} = \frac{\sigma}{E} = \frac{60.0\ \text{MPa}}{76\ \text{GPa}} = \textbf{0.789 E-3}$$

15.2 FLEXURE FORMULA

Our goal in this section is to develop a relationship between the applied bending moment and the stress it produces. First, however, the location of the neutral axis must be determined. We accomplish this by observing that the resultant force on the cross section of the beam is zero. Referring to Fig. 15.3a, we note that the stress on an element of area dA at a distance y from the neutral axis is σ. The element of force dF acting on the area is:

$$dF = \sigma\,dA$$

This is illustrated further in Fig. 15.6.

The total force can be found by summing these elements of force over the entire cross section. Thus:

$$F = \int dF = \int \sigma\,dA$$

As we said, the resultant force is zero. Then substituting Eq. 15.3, we have:

$$\int \sigma\,dA = \int \left(\frac{y}{c}\right) \sigma_{\max}\,dA = 0$$

For a given cross section, $\sigma_{\max}$ and c are constants and may be brought outside the integral:

$$\frac{\sigma_{\max}}{c} \int y\,dA = 0 \tag{15.4}$$

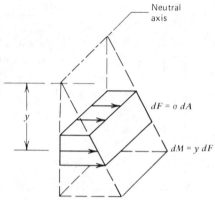

FIG. 15.6 Element of force.

Since σ_{max} and c are constant, Eq. 15.4 can be satisfied only if:

$$\int y\,dA = 0$$

Referring back to Fig. 15.3b, we see that this integral is y, the distance from the neutral axis to the element dA times dA. Thus this integral is simply the first moment of area—one of those exciting but abstract concepts from Chapter 12. (I promised it would be useful!) Now, when is the moment of area equal to zero? "When it's about a centroidal axis!" said the class in one accord. This leads to the very important (and convenient) conclusion that the neutral axis and our old friend the centroidal axis are one and the same.

Returning to Fig. 15.6, we note that the moment of the element of force dF about the neutral axis is:

$$dM = y\,dF$$

The total moment is the summation or integral of these moments over the cross section. This total moment equals the applied moment M.

$$M = \int dM = \int y\,dF$$

Using two equalities previously established, as follows:

$$dF = \sigma\,dA$$

$$\sigma = \frac{y}{c}\,\sigma_{max}$$

we have:

$$M = \int y\left(\frac{y}{c}\,\sigma_{max}\right)dA$$

Again factoring out the constants σ_{max} and c, we write:

$$M = \frac{\sigma_{max}}{c}\int y^2\,dA$$

Examining the integral, we see it to be the distance squared from the neutral (or centroidal) axis to the element dA. This expression is the second moment of area or moment of inertia of the cross section about its own centroid. This was designated I (or $\bar{I}$) in Chapter 12. Hence:

$$M = \frac{\sigma_{max}}{c}I$$

Solving for σ_{max} yields:

$$\sigma_{max} = \frac{Mc}{I} \tag{15.5}$$

This is known as the *flexure formula*. Combining it with Eq. 15.3 gives:

$$\sigma = \frac{My}{I} \tag{15.6}$$

which gives the stress on any fiber at a distance y from the neutral axis and once again shows this stress distribution to be linear.

Let's sum up what we have learned. Pure bending produces a linear stress distribution that is tension on one surface and compression on the other. There is an unstressed fiber called the neutral axis that coincides with the centroid of the cross section (for beams that are initially straight). The maximum stress occurs on the fiber furthest from the neutral axis and can be determined by Eq. 15.5. Note the it varies directly with the applied load M and with the distance to the extreme fiber c. It varies inversely with the moment of inertia I.

Also note that for Eq. 15.5, M is the moment about the centroidal axis, c is the distance to the extreme fiber from the centroidal axis, and I is the moment of inertia about the centroidal axis. That is, all the terms on the right-hand side of Eq. 15.5 refer to the same axis, namely, *the centroidal axis* of the cross section about which the bending moment acts. The equation is valid only for materials that are homogeneous, isotropic, and loaded below their proportional limit.

Example Problem 15.2

A 2×6 (actual size) turned on edge must carry a bending moment of 1200 ft-lb. (a) What is the maximum stress produced in the beam (Fig. 15.7)? (b) Solve part (a) for a finished 2×6 (S4S).

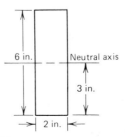

FIG. 15.7 Example Problem 15.2.

Solution

(a) We use our new friend, the flexure formula:

$$\sigma = \frac{Mc}{I}$$
(15.5)

It is common to leave off the subscript "max" when writing "σ_{max}." The distance c tells us we are talking about an extreme fiber, and now we know that implies maximum stress. We will write σ_{max} only when it is necessary to avoid confusion.

In Eq. 15.5, M, c, and I all are referenced to the same axis. If the bending moment M is about a horizontal axis, c will be the distance from that same axis to the extreme fiber, and I will be the moment of inertia about that same axis. Thus:

$$I = \frac{bh^3}{12} = \frac{2(6)^3}{12} = 36.0 \text{ in.}^4$$

Note that in this formula b, the base, is the side parallel to the axis about which we are finding the moment of inertia. Therefore, b is parallel to the axis about which the bending moment is acting. The centroid (hence the neutral) axis is at the middle of the cross section. The distance from the neutral axis to the extreme fiber, c, is 3 in. Then applying the flexure formula:

$$\sigma = \frac{1200 \text{ ft-lb}(3 \text{ in.})}{36.0 \text{ in.}^4}\left(\frac{12 \text{ in.}}{\text{ft}}\right)$$

$$\sigma = \mathbf{1200 \text{ psi}}$$

The stress distribution produced by this moment is that shown in Fig. 15.8, or just the opposite, depending on the direction of the applied moment. When the cross section is symmetric, the magnitude of the stresses will be equal at the top and bottom surfaces.

(b) The designation (S4S) means we are talking about the dressed size of finished lumber. Actual dimensions and properties are found in Table A-17.

$$h = 5.5 \text{ in.}$$
$$I = 20.8 \text{ in.}^4$$

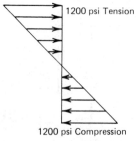

1200 psi Tension

1200 psi Compression

FIG. 15.8 Stress distribution for Example Problem 15.2.

Note that I for the finished size is only a little more than half of the full size:

$$\sigma = \frac{Mc}{I} = \frac{1200 \text{ ft-lb}(5.5 \text{ in.})}{20.8 \text{ in.}^4 \, 2} \frac{12 \text{ in.}}{\text{ft}}$$

$$\sigma = \mathbf{1900 \text{ psi}}$$

Note further that the stress in the finished size is more than 50% more than in the full cut.

Example Problem 15.3

The beam shown in Fig. 15.9a is an S 10 × 35. Find the maximum bending stress.

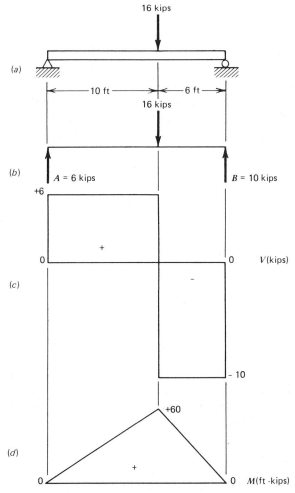

FIG. 15.9a–d Example Problem 15.3.

Solution

This problem well illustrates the general stress analysis problem.

Step 1. *Solve the statics problem.* Draw a free body diagram and find the reactions (Fig. 15.9b):

$$\sum M_A = 0 = -10(16) + 16(B)$$

$$B = \frac{16(10)}{16} = \textbf{10.0 kips}$$

$$\sum F_y = 0 = A - 16 + B$$
$$A = 16 - (10) = \textbf{6.00 kips}$$

Step 2. *Find the internal loads.* This can best be done in this case by drawing shear and bending moment diagrams (Figs. 15.9c, 15.9d).

We observe from the moment diagram that the maximum moment is 60.0 ft-kips.

Step 3. *Find the geometric properties of the cross section.* This beam is symmetric, and the centroid can be found by inspection. In other cases it must be calculated.

The moment of inertia can also be easily determined in this case from Table A-10. Note that two values of I are available, I_x and I_y. We must use the one that corresponds to the axis of the bending moment. Our problem does not state how this beam is oriented. We assume it is turned so that it will carry the greatest load, that is, so that it presents the greatest I. The result will be as good as the assumption.

$$I = \textbf{147 in.}^4 \qquad c = \textbf{5.00 in.}$$

Step 4. *Find the stress.* From Eq. 15.5:

$$\sigma = \frac{Mc}{I}$$

$$\sigma = \frac{60.0 \text{ ft-kips}(5.00 \text{ in.})}{147 \text{ in.}^4} \cdot \frac{12 \text{ in.}}{\text{ft}}$$

$$\sigma = \textbf{24.5 ksi}$$

The bending moment was positive 60 ft-kips. This will produce compression in the top fiber and tension in the bottom. Thus 24.5 ksi compression is produced in the top of the beam and 24.5 ksi tension in the bottom at the section 10 ft from the left support.

Example Problem 15.4

The cross section shown in Fig. 15.10 carries a positive bending moment of 200 ft-lb. Find the stress on the top and bottom fibers.

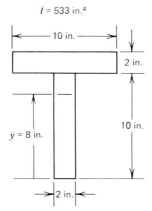

$I = 533$ in.^{4}

10 in.

2 in.

10 in.

$\bar{y} = 8$ in.

2 in.

FIG. 15.10   Example Problem 15.4.

Solution

By Eq. 15.6 the stress on the top fiber is:

$$\sigma_T = \frac{My}{I} = \frac{200 \text{ ft-lb}(4 \text{ in.})}{533 \text{ in.}^4} \cdot \frac{12 \text{ in.}}{\text{ft}}$$

$$\sigma_T = 18.0 \text{ psi compression}$$

Since the bending is positive, the top fiber is in compression. The stress on the bottom fiber is:

$$\sigma_B = \frac{My}{I} = \frac{200 \text{ ft-lb}(8 \text{ in.})}{533} \cdot \frac{12 \text{ in.}}{\text{ft}}$$

$$\sigma_B = 36.0 \text{ psi tension}$$

The resulting stress distribution is shown in Fig. 15.11. Note that the stress at the neutral axis is zero and that the stress is greatest on the fiber most distant from the neutral axis.

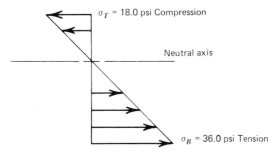

$\sigma_T = 18.0$ psi Compression

Neutral axis

$\sigma_B = 36.0$ psi Tension

FIG. 15.11   Stress distribution for Example Problem 15.4.

15.3 BEAM DESIGN USING THE FLEXURE FORMULA

When we speak of designing a beam we usually mean selecting the "most appropriate" beam that will satisfactorily carry the required load. This selection is normally from a finite number of choices, since we will normally use commonly available materials such as those given in Tables A-10 through A-17. "Most appropriate" usually means the most economical, which means the beam that uses the least material. For uniform beams of a given material, the amount of material used is directly proportional to the cross-sectional area. Thus our problem boils down to finding the beam of least cross-sectional area that can carry the required load. This is indicated by the area itself, or by the weight per unit length of the beam.

To select a beam for a given load situation, a full static analysis must be made and critical internal loads determined, as in steps 1 and 2 in Example Problem 15.3. Given these loads, we must now select a member that will have the appropriate geometric properties to keep the stress below some predetermined value—the design stress. Structural steel often carries a design stress of 24,000 psi (165 MPa) for static loads.

As we seek to apply Eq. 15.5 in design, we notice that it contains two geometric factors, c and I. Lumping these two together and solving for them, we have:

$$\frac{I}{c} = \frac{M}{\sigma}$$

If, for instance, the moment is 720 in.-kips and the allowable stress is 24 ksi, we would have:

$$\frac{I}{c} = \frac{720 \text{ in.-kips in.}^2}{24 \text{ kips}} = 30.0 \text{ in.}^3$$

Actually, I/c should be greater than 30.0 in.^{3} to keep the stress below 24 ksi. The I is available from Tables A-10 through A-17, and c may be easily calculated from the other geometric data—usually half the depth. Hence we may seek a combination of I divided by c that would be greater than 30 in.^{3}. Obviously, it would require a number of trials to arrive at a satisfactory number, and then we would not be sure we had the best beam unless we had exhausted the tables. This rather tedious and frustrating exercise is avoided by including in the tables an additional column that gives the quotient I divided by c.

We give this quotient the name *section modulus* and designate it thus:

$$Z = \frac{I}{c} \tag{15.7}$$

Although this is designated S in Tables A-10 through A-17, we will stick with Z to avoid confusing it with the beam shape or the material's strength. Equation 15.5 may then be written as follows:

$$\sigma = \frac{M}{Z} \tag{15.8}$$

This equation is essential for design and convenient for analysis.

In our design problem we now look in the tables for a section modulus Z greater than 30.0 in.^{3} for beams that can satisfactorily carry the load. After finding several candidates, we make a final choice based on the one that has the least area or weight per foot.

Example Problem 15.5

Find the best (lightest) S or W beam to carry a 720-in.-kip bending load if the allowable stress is 24 ksi.

Solution

For Eq. 15.8:

$$\sigma = \frac{M}{Z}$$

Solving for the section modulus Z:

$$Z = \frac{M}{\sigma} = \frac{720 \text{ in.-kip in.}^2}{24 \text{ kip}} = 30.0 \text{ in.}^3$$

From Table A-10, reading in the S ($S = Z$) column:

$$\text{S } 12 \times 31.8 \text{ has } Z = 36.4 \qquad \text{so it is satisfactory}$$

From Table A-11,

$$\text{W } 14 \times 26 \text{ has } Z = 35.1 \qquad \text{which is more than satisfactory}$$

Either of these beams would carry the load, but the W 14 × 26 is preferred because it uses less material.

Note that in this problem optimizing the solution involves a different parameter (weight per foot) from the one used to control the load-carrying capability (section modulus).

Example Problem 15.6

Select a standard or wide flange beam to carry 2000 lb/ft over a 12-ft length when supported as a cantilever (Fig. 15.12a). The yield strength is 36 ksi, and a safety factor of 4 is intended.

Solution

To select this beam we must know the load (maximum bending moment) it is to carry. Once again, a statics problem must be solved first. We make a sketch of the problem and then draw a free body diagram (Fig. 15.12b) of a statically equivalent beam for the purpose of finding the reactions V and M.

Applying Newton's first law yields the results indicated.

Having these reactions, we sketch shear and moment diagrams for the beam, remembering to return to the original loading. These are as shown in Figs. 15.12c and 15.12d. Their development is left to the student.

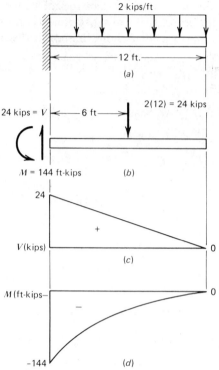

FIG. 15.12a–d   Example Problem 15.6.

Having solved a fairly substantial statics problem, we are now ready to apply the solution to a fairly simple strength of materials problem.

We examine the moment diagram to find the maximum moment on the beam. It is 144 ft-kips and occurs at the support. It turns out that the maximum moment will always be at the support on a cantilever beam when all the loading is perpendicular to the beam and in the same sense. However, in general, the moment diagram is needed, and this shortcut should not be taken until the student is very sure that the proper load has been obtained. We have a yield strength of 36 ksi and a factor of safety of 4, so:

$$S_A = \frac{S_y}{N} = \frac{36}{4} = 9.00 \text{ ksi}$$

Using Eq. 15.8,

$$\sigma = \frac{M}{Z}$$

$$Z = \frac{M}{\sigma} = \frac{144 \text{ ft-kips}}{9.0 \text{ kips}} \frac{12 \text{ in.}}{\text{ft}} = 192 \text{ in.}^3$$

This is the required section modulus. We go to Tables A-10 and A-11, seeking members with values of Z greater than this. For a standard we select S 24 × 100, having a section modulus of 199 in.^{3} For a wide flange there are several choices. The best is W 27 × 84 having a section modulus of 212 in.^{3}. Since it is 16% lighter than the standard beam, it is the one we specify.

15.4 SUMMARY

The neutral axis is an unstressed fiber at the centroid. The flexure formula states:

$$\sigma = \frac{Mc}{I}$$

giving a linear stress distribution that is zero at the centroid and maximum at the extreme fiber. Note that this bending stress is a normal stress.

The moment M, the distance c, and the moment of inertia I are all with respect to the same centroidal axis.

For design purposes it is often more convenient to use the section modulus:

$$Z = \frac{I}{c}$$

Remember that Tables A-10 through A-17 use S for Z. The design equation becomes:

$$\sigma = \frac{M}{Z}$$

PROBLEMS

15.1 The beam shown in Fig. 15.13 has the cross section indicated. Find the bending moment at B and the maximum stress due to bending on this cross section.

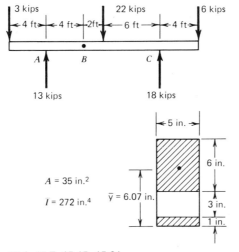

FIG. 15.13 Problems 15.1, 15.7, 15.15, 15.21.

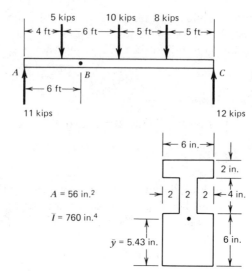

$A = 56$ in.²

$\bar{I} = 760$ in.⁴

$\bar{y} = 5.43$ in.

FIG. 15.14   Problems 15.2, 15.8, 15.16, 15.22.

15.2   The beam shown in Fig. 15.14 has the cross section indicated. Find the bending moment at B and the maximum stress due to bending on this cross section.

15.3   Find the maximum stress due to bending on a cross section at A if the beam is a W 8 × 40 (Fig. 15.15).

15.4   Find the maximum stress on a cross section at A due to bending if the beam is a W 12 × 36 (Fig. 15.16).

15.5   The beam shown in Fig. 15.17 is a W 14 × 38. Find the maximum bending stress on a cross section at A.

15.6   The beam shown in Fig. 15.18 is a W 4 × 13. Find the maximum bending stress on a cross section at A.

15.7   For a bending moment of 80 in.-kips and the cross section of Fig. 15.13, find the stress on the bottom fiber, 1 in. above the bottom fiber, 4 in. above the bottom fiber, at the centroid, 2 in. below the top fiber, and on the top fiber. Plot this stress distribution.

15.8   For a bending moment of 96 in.-kips and the cross section of Fig. 15.14, find the stress on the top fiber, 2 and 4 in. below the top fiber, at the centroid,

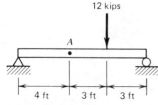

FIG. 15.15   Problems 15.3, 15.17, 15.23.

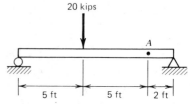

FIG. 15.16   Problems 15.4, 15.18, 15.24.

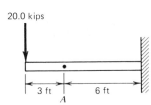

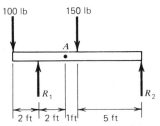

FIG. 15.17 Problems 15.5, 15.19, 15.25.

FIG. 15.18 Problems 15.6, 15.20, 15.26.

2 and 4 in. above the bottom fiber, and at the bottom fiber. Plot this stress distribution.

15.9 A 2 × 4 (actual size) turned on edge has a bending load of 60 ft-lb on it.

(a) Find the maximum stress due to bending.

(b) Find the stress if the beam is finish cut (S4S).

15.10 A 30 mm × 90 mm beam turned on edge has a bending load of 90 N·m on it. Find the maximum stress due to bending.

15.11 For each beam loading and cross section indicated, find the maximum stress due to bending on a cross section at point A.

	Cross Section	Beam
(a)	Fig. 15.19	Fig. 15.23
(b)	Fig. 15.20	Fig. 15.23
(c)	Fig. 15.21	Fig. 15.23
(d)	Fig. 15.22	Fig. 15.23

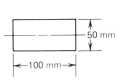

FIG. 15.19.

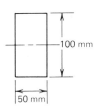

FIG. 15.20.

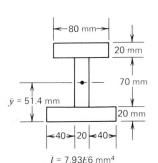

$\bar{y} = 51.4$ mm

$I = 7.93E6$ mm^4

FIG. 15.21.

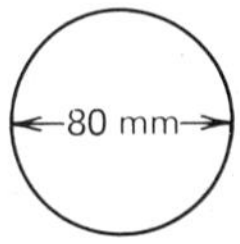

FIG. 15.22.

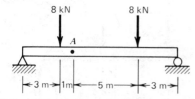

FIG. 15.23.

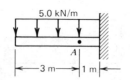

FIG. 15.24.

(e)	Fig. 15.19	Fig. 15.24
(f)	Fig. 15.20	Fig. 15.24
(g)	Fig. 15.21	Fig. 15.24
(h)	Fig. 15.22	Fig. 15.24
(i)	Fig. 15.19	Fig. 15.25
(j)	Fig. 15.20	Fig. 15.25
(k)	Fig. 15.21	Fig. 15.25
(l)	Fig. 15.22	Fig. 15.25
(m)	Fig. 15.19	Fig. 15.26
(n)	Fig. 15.20	Fig. 15.26
(o)	Fig. 15.21	Fig. 15.26
(p)	Fig. 15.22	Fig. 15.26

15.12 For each beam loading and cross section indicated, find the maximum stress due to bending that occurs anywhere in the beam.

	Cross Section	Beam
(a)	Fig. 15.19	Fig. 15.23
(b)	Fig. 15.20	Fig. 15.23
(c)	Fig. 15.21	Fig. 15.23
(d)	Fig. 15.22	Fig. 15.23
(e)	Fig. 15.19	Fig. 15.24
(f)	Fig. 15.20	Fig. 15.24
(g)	Fig. 15.21	Fig. 15.24
(h)	Fig. 15.22	Fig. 15.24
(i)	Fig. 15.19	Fig. 15.25
(j)	Fig. 15.20	Fig. 15.25

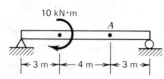

FIG. 15.25.

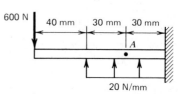

FIG. 15.26.

(k)	Fig. 15.21	Fig. 15.25
(l)	Fig. 15.22	Fig. 15.25
(m)	Fig. 15.19	Fig. 15.26
(n)	Fig. 15.20	Fig. 15.26
(o)	Fig. 15.21	Fig. 15.26
(p)	Fig. 15.22	Fig. 15.26

15.13 For the indicated loading, select a beam with a square cross section based on an allowable stress of 140 MPa.

    (a) Fig. 15.23   (b) Fig. 15.24   (c) Fig. 15.25   (d) Fig. 15.26

15.14 For the indicated loading, select a beam that is twice as deep (*h*) as it is wide (*b*), based on an allowable stress of 140 MPa.

    (a) Fig. 15.23   (b) Fig. 15.24   (c) Fig. 15.25   (d) Fig. 15.26

For each of the following problems, calculate the maximum stress due to bending that occurs anywhere in the beam. The loading and cross section are as indicated.

15.15 Fig. 15.13	**15.16** Fig. 15.14
15.17 Fig. 15.15 with a W 8 × 40	**15.18** Fig. 15.16 with a W 12 × 36
15.19 Fig. 15.17 with a W 14 × 38	**15.20** Fig. 15.18 with a W 4 × 13

For each of the following problems select the best S or W beam using an allowable stress of 24,000 psi and loading as indicated in the figures listed.

15.21 Fig. 15.13	**15.22** Fig. 15.14
15.23 Fig. 15.15	**15.24** Fig. 15.16
15.25 Fig. 15.17	**15.26** Fig. 15.18

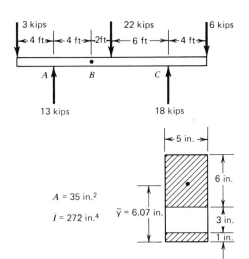

FIG. 15.13 Problems 15.1, 15.7, 15.15, 15.21. Figure repeated from page 411.

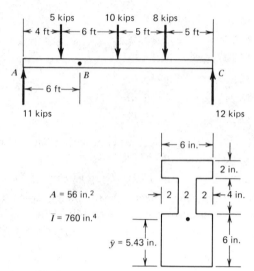

FIG. 15.14   Problems 15.2, 15.8, 15.16, 15.22.
Figure repeated from page 412.

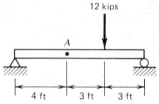

FIG. 15.15   Problems 15.3, 15.17,
15.23. Figure repeated from page 412.

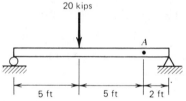

FIG. 15.16   Problems 15.4, 15.18,
15.24. Figure repeated from page 412.

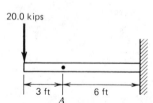

FIG. 15.17   Problems 15.5, 15.19,
15.25. Figure repeated from page 413.

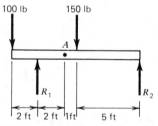

FIG. 15.18   Problems 15.6, 15.20,
15.26. Figure repeated from page 413.

15.27   The cross section of a 12-ft cantilever beam is 2 in. wide and 8 in. deep. The cantilever has a 200-lb load at the free end.
   (a)   Find the maximum bending stress.
   (b)   Find the maximum stress if the beam is finish cut (S4S).

15.28   A cross section of a 4-m cantilever beam is 60 mm wide and 180 mm deep. The cantilever has a 1.5-kN load at the free end. Find the maximum bending stress.

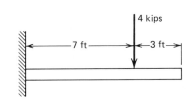

FIG. 15.27   Problem 15.30.

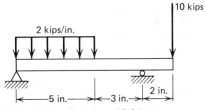

FIG. 15.28   Problem 15.31.

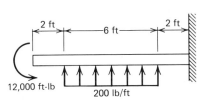

FIG. 15.29   Problem 15.32.

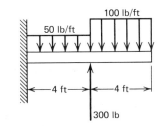

FIG. 15.30   Problem 15.33.

15.29 Compare the stress due to bending in a 2 × 4 (actual size) laid flat with the stress when it is laid on edge.

15.30 Select the best member as indicated to carry the load in Fig. 15.27. Use a yield strength of 24,000 psi and a factor of safety of 2.

(a)   A channel (Table A-12)

(b)   An unequal leg angle (Table A-14)

(c)   An equal leg angle (Table A-13)

(d)   A pipe (Table A-15)

15.31 Select the best member as indicated to carry the load in Fig. 15.28. Use a yield strength of 24,000 psi and a factor of safety of 6.

(a)   A channel (Table A-12)

(b)   An unequal leg angle (Table A-14)

(c)   An equal leg angle (Table A-13)

(d)   A pipe (Table A-15)

15.32 Select a finished timber (S4S) to carry the load in Fig. 15.29 using a strength of 9000 psi and a factor of safety of 3.

15.33 Select a finished timber (S4S) to carry the load in Fig. 15.30 using a strength of 8000 psi and a factor of safety of 4.

16

Beam Deflection

16.1 DEFLECTION IN DESIGN

In Chapter 15 we investigated the stresses that occur in a beam because of bending. A great number of design problems are governed by the stresses that are present. However, many design problems are governed by deflection rather than stress. For example, if a ceiling beam or joist deflects too much, the ceiling plaster will crack. In such cases deflection governs the design. In intricate, high speed machinery, excessive deflection of parts can interfere with and even prevent the desired motion. To avoid such negative effects, deflection must govern the design.

Since deflection of a beam sometimes governs a design, we must understand how deflection is related to load. There are, however, other reasons—which are equally important—for studying this relationship. Our attention in this book has been on statically determinate structures, that is, structures whose loads can be determined by the methods of statics. Many problems of concern to us can be adequately handled by such an analysis, but not all. Those that cannot be—called statically indeterminate structures—require load–deflection characteristics for solution. In Chapter 11 the relation between axial load and axial deflection was developed. In Chapter 13 the relation between torque and rotation was developed. These, along with the relations we will develop here, allow us to handle statically indeterminate problems.

418

A third reason for studying load–deflection relations is that they are necessary for the analysis of dynamic loading and vibration problems. Analysis of such
problems requires mathematics beyond that normally required in technology programs, so most technologists are not likely to solve such problems independently.
However, they are likely to be involved in these solutions.

16.2   RELATION BETWEEN BENDING MOMENT AND CURVATURE

We will examine several methods of finding the deflection of a beam. Fundamental to them all is the relationship between the applied bending moment and the
curvature of the beam. This extremely important relationship allows us to bridge
the gulf between the loads on a beam and its resulting geometry. An initially
straight beam with a constant bending moment is shown in Fig. 16.1a. Consider
an element of this beam whose length is Δx (Fig. 16.1b). The uniform bending
moment M results in the deformation shown in Fig. 16.1c. As discussed in Chapter 15, we assume that this bending takes place by the rotation of plane sections
that remain plane. Thus ABC and DEF rotate as shown, shortening the upper
fibers AD and stretching the lower fibers CF. The fiber BE, the neutral axis,
does not change length. We extend the rotated planes ABC and DEF until they
intersect. This point of intersection is the center of curvature, and we designate it
as O. The distance OB is the *radius of curvature*, which we designate as ρ (Greek
rho—say *row*—equivalent to *r*). This means that if we rotate a compass about O
with a radius of ρ we could trace out the path BE. That is, the arc BE is part of
the circle whose radius is ρ and whose center is O.

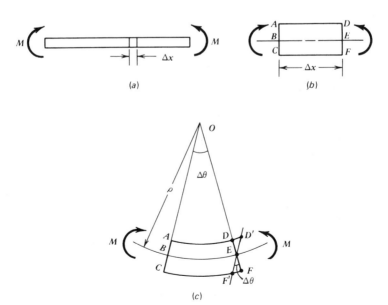

FIG. 16.1a–c Elements of a deflected
beam.

We now construct a line $D'EF'$ parallel to ABC. The segments AD', BE, and CF' all represent the original length of the fibers. Note that BE is unchanged, being the neutral axis. DD' represents the shortening of AD, and FF' represents the stretching of CF. Notice that the segment BOE is similar to the segment $F'EF$. (They have a common side OEF and parallel sides OB and EF'). Hence the included angles, which we label $\Delta\theta$, are equal. Recalling that an angle is defined as its arc length divided by its radius, we observe for the segment BOE:

$$\Delta\theta = \frac{BE}{OB} = \frac{BE}{\rho}$$

and for the segment $F'EF$:

$$\Delta\theta = \frac{FF'}{EF} = \frac{FF'}{c}$$

observing that EF is the distance from the neutral axis to the extreme fiber, labeled c. Setting the two equal, we get:

$$\frac{BE}{\rho} = \frac{FF'}{c}$$

or

$$\frac{1}{\rho} = \frac{FF'}{BE} \cdot \frac{1}{c}$$

Observe that FF' is the extension of the original element CF, and BE is equal to CF'. Hence this ratio (FF'/BE) is the deformation over the original length or the strain ε in the element CF. This yields:

$$\frac{1}{\rho} = \frac{\varepsilon}{c}$$

Applying Hooke's law:

$$\varepsilon = \frac{\sigma}{E}$$

we get:

$$\frac{1}{\rho} = \frac{\sigma}{E}\frac{1}{c}$$

and the flexure formula:

$$\sigma = \frac{Mc}{I}$$

gives:

$$\frac{1}{\rho} = \frac{Mc}{EI}\frac{1}{c}$$

giving finally:

$$\frac{1}{\rho} = \frac{M}{EI} \tag{16.1}$$

Recall that ρ is the radius of curvature. Its inverse, $1/\rho$, is called the *curvature*. We have, then, this most important relationship between the curvature and the bending moment. It has some applications of its own, which we will see in the problems that follow. More important, it serves as the basis for analyzing beam deflections, which we will explore in subsequent sections. Notice what the equation says—the curvature is proportional to the bending moment. The greater the bending moment, the greater the curvature. This means a tighter curve, that is, one with a smaller radius. The curvature is inversely proportional to the modulus of elasticity and moment of inertia. Using a stiffer material yields less curvature—greater radius. Using a greater moment of inertia yields less curvature.

Example Problem 16.1

A band saw turns over a 500-mm-diameter wheel. The steel saw is 0.800 mm thick and 10 mm wide. What stress is developed in the blade as it is bent over the wheel?

Solution

$$\frac{1}{\rho} = \frac{M}{EI} \tag{16.1}$$

Solving for M:

$$M = \frac{EI}{\rho}$$

then:

$$\sigma = \frac{Mc}{I} = \frac{EI}{\rho}\frac{c}{I}$$

$$\sigma = \frac{Ec}{\rho}$$

The modulus of elasticity E is 207 GPa for steel. The distance from the neutral axis to the extreme fiber c is half the thickness or 0.400 mm. The radius of curvature ρ is half the diameter of the pulley or 250 mm. Hence:

$$\sigma = \frac{207\ E9\ \text{Pa}(0.4\ E\text{-}3\ \text{m})}{0.250\ \text{m}}$$

$$= 3.31\ E8\ \text{Pa}$$

$$\sigma = \textbf{331 MPa}$$

16.3   LOAD RATE TO SHEAR TO BENDING MOMENT TO SLOPE TO DEFLECTION

In Chapter 14 the relationship between load rate and shear was developed:

$$w = \frac{dV}{dx} \tag{14.1}$$

Also developed was the relation between shear and bending moment:

$$V = \frac{dM}{dx} \tag{14.3}$$

and in Section 16.2 the moment was related to curvature:

$$\frac{1}{\rho} = \frac{M}{EI} \tag{16.1}$$

We extend this chain of relations a second step by noting the mathematical expression for curvature:

$$\frac{1}{\rho} = \frac{\dfrac{d^2y}{dx^2}}{\left[1 + \left(\dfrac{dy}{dx}\right)^2\right]^{3/2}} \tag{16.2}$$

This rather awful looking creature is the exact mathematical expression for curvature. For our purposes we simplify the expression by noting that for most engineering structures, large deflections are not acceptable. Accordingly,

$$\frac{dy}{dx} \simeq 0$$

Squaring the term will make it even smaller. Thus the denominator in Eq. 16.2 approaches 1.0, yielding:

$$\frac{1}{\rho} = \frac{d^2y}{dx^2} \tag{16.3}$$

We then observe by substitution of Eq. 16.1:

$$\frac{d^2y}{dx^2} = \frac{M}{EI} \tag{16.4}$$

A mathematician would say we *linearized* the equation. (As a general rule, one should never pass up the opportunity to linearize an equation.)

Equation 16.4 may also be written as follows:

$$\frac{d}{dx}\left(\frac{dy}{dx}\right) = \frac{M}{EI} \tag{16.5}$$

By definition,

$$\frac{dy}{dx} = \theta \tag{16.6}$$

which is the *slope* of the beam. Actually:

$$\frac{dy}{dx} = \tan \theta$$

But recall that for small angles:

$$\tan \theta = \theta$$

and thus Eq. 16.6. In linearizing the Eq. 16.2, we limited our discussion to small angle deflections, therefore Eq. 16.6 is appropriate. Equation 16.5 may be written, therefore, as follows:

$$\frac{d\theta}{dx} = \frac{M}{EI} \qquad (16.7)$$

For emphasis we recap, and for convenience we renumber:

   Load rate:

$$w = \frac{dV}{dx} \qquad (16.8)$$

Shear:

$$V = \frac{dM}{dx} \qquad (16.9)$$

Moment:

$$M = EI \frac{d\theta}{dx} \qquad (16.10)$$

Slope:

$$\theta = \frac{dy}{dx} \qquad (16.11)$$

The significance of this important chain of equations should not escape the student. Working from Eq. 16.11 to Eq. 16.8, we see that when we have the deflection, taking its derivative with respect to position x gives the slope of the beam. If the slope of the beam θ is known, taking its derivative gives the bending moment M (times $1/EI$). Given the bending moment, its derivative yields the shear V, and the derivative of the shear gives the load rate w. Hence starting with an equation of a beam's deflection and differentiating four times yields successively slope, bending moment, shear, and finally, load rate. This mathematical manipulation must occasionally be carried out. More important to the student, however, is the intimate relation between the variables expressed by these four equations.

   In Chapter 14 we noted the integral versions of Eqs. 16.8 and 16.9. Similar relations may be developed for Eqs. 16.10 and 16.11. Thus we may alternately write:

   Shear:

$$V = \int w \, dx \qquad (16.12)$$

Moment:

$$M = \int V \, dx \tag{16.13}$$

Slope:

$$\theta = \int \frac{M}{EI} \, dx \tag{16.14}$$

Deflection:

$$y = \int \theta \, dx \tag{16.15}$$

The order remains the same: load rate to shear to moment to slope to deflection. The integral of one variable yields the following one. Alternately, the derivative or slope of one variable is the instantaneous value of the previous one.

16.4 DEFLECTION BY MULTIPLE INTEGRATION

Equations 16.12 through 16.15 are the basis of the method of deflection by multiple integration. We know from the calculus that each time an integration is executed, an arbitrary constant is acquired. This arbitrary constant allows us to make a general mathematical solution fit our particular problem. The conditions that characterize our particular problem are called *boundary conditions*. For example, consider the deflection of a cantilever beam. At the support the beam has zero deflection. This is a boundary condition. Any equation that claims to be a solution to our problem must predict zero deflection at the support; that is, it must satisfy the boundary condition. Otherwise it is not a solution.

Boundary conditions, then, are constraints imposed on the solution by the physical characteristics of the problem. We need one boundary condition for each integration. That allows us to evaluate the one arbitrary constant that accrues at each integration. Example Problem 16.2 delineates the method.

Example Problem 16.2

Find an equation for the deflection of the beam shown in Fig. 16.2.

Solution

To determine the boundary conditions, it is necessary to draw a free body diagram and find the reactions at the support. A coordinate system is also established (Fig. 16.3).

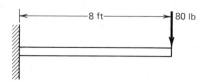

FIG. 16.2 Example Problem 16.2.

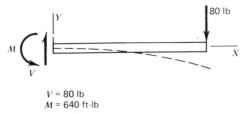

$$V = 80 \text{ lb}$$
$$M = 640 \text{ ft-lb}$$

FIG. 16.3 Free body diagram and coordinate system.

A mathematical expression for the load rate must be obtained. We note:

$$w = 0$$

Then by Eq. 16.12 we have:

$$V = \int w \, dx = \int 0 \, dx = 0 + C_1$$

where C_1 is the first constant. This equation simply says that for any value of x, V is a constant. We force this solution to fit our boundary condition to evaluate C_1. Since C_1 is in terms of shear, it follows that we need a boundary condition for shear; that is, we must determine the numerical value and appropriate sign for shear at some point in the beam. We note that just to the right of the support the shear will be $+80$ lb. It may be necessary to make a mental shear diagram to see this. Thus our first boundary condition is:

$$V_0 = C_1 = 80$$

and

$$V = 80$$

is the equation for shear anywhere in the beam.

Next we have:

$$M = \int V \, dx = \int 80 \, dx = 80x + C_2$$

This says that the bending moment is a linear function of x. We evaluate C_2 noting the boundary condition at $x = 0$:

$$M_0 = -640 \text{ ft-lb}$$

The negative sign is required because the reacting moment produces negative bending in the beam. We evaluate the equation above for $x = 0$:

$$M_0 = 80(0) + C_2 = -640$$
$$C_2 = -640$$

and

$$M = 80x - 640$$

From Eq. 16.14 we write:

$$\theta = \int \frac{M}{EI} \, dx = \frac{1}{EI} \int (80x - 640) \, dx$$

The terms in parentheses and the dx after the integral sign follow regular algebra rules. Thus:

$$\theta = \frac{1}{EI} \left\{ \int 80x\, dx - \int 640\, dx \right\}$$

$$\theta = \frac{1}{EI} \left\{ \frac{80x^2}{2} - 640x \right\} + C_3$$

To determine a boundary condition for θ, the slope of the beam, we must intuitively describe its shape. Thus we sketch the deflection shown in Fig. 16.3. Since the support is rigid and will not allow the beam to rotate at the support, we note the boundary condition:

$$\theta_0 = 0$$

Then evaluating the equation above at $x = 0$, we have:

$$\theta_0 = \frac{1}{EI} \left\{ \frac{80(0)^2}{2} - 640(0) \right\} + C_3 = 0$$

$$C_3 = 0$$

and

$$\theta = \frac{1}{EI} \left[40x^2 - 640x \right]$$

This equation may be evaluated for any value of x to find the corresponding value of θ, the slope of the beam. Maximum slope will occur at the free end of this beam where $x = 8$ ft. Substituting that, we get:

$$\theta = \frac{1}{EI} \left[40(8)^2 - 640(8) \right]$$

$$\theta = -\frac{2560}{EI} \text{ ft}^2\text{-lb}$$

Notice from Fig. 16.3 that the slope is negative at this point. The units used for x in deriving the equation must also be used in its evaluation. It is common to express slope (and deflection) in terms of EI. If these properties are specified, an exact value for θ may be obtained.

Finally we have:

$$y = \int \theta\, dx$$

$$= \frac{1}{EI} \int \left[40x^2 - 640x \right] dx$$

$$= \frac{1}{EI} \left\{ \int 40x^2\, dx - \int 640x\, dx \right\}$$

$$= \frac{1}{EI} \left\{ 40\frac{x^3}{3} - 640\frac{x^2}{2} \right\} + C_4$$

The constant C_4 is evaluated by noting that at $x = 0$, $y = 0$:

$$y_0 = \frac{1}{EI}\left\{\frac{40}{3}(0)^3 - 320(0)^2\right\} + C_4 = 0$$

$$C_4 = 0$$

$$y = \frac{1}{EI}\left\{\frac{40}{3}x^3 - 320x^2\right\}$$

The equation may be evaluated for any value of x to find the corresponding value of y, the beam deflection. For instance, at $x = 8$ ft:

$$y = \frac{1}{EI}\left\{\frac{40}{3}(8)^3 - 320(8)^2\right\} = \frac{-13{,}700}{EI}\text{ ft}^3\text{-lb}$$

which is the maximum deflection. Since the distance x was put in feet, E and I would have to be converted to feet as well. Substituting in the appropriate values of EI gives a numerical value for the deflection y. Notice that it has a negative sign—meaning that the deflection is down.

Example Problem 16.3

Find the maximum deflection and slope of the beam in Example Problem 16.2 if the beam is a 1.25-in.-diameter steel rod.

Solution

From Example Problem 16.2 we have:

$$y = \frac{-13{,}700}{EI}\text{ ft}^3\text{-lb}$$

Furthermore,

$$I = \frac{\pi D^4}{64} = \frac{\pi(1.25)^4}{64} = 0.120\text{ in.}^4$$

and

$$E = 30 \times 10^6\text{ psi}$$

Thus

$$y = \frac{-13{,}700\text{ ft}^3\text{-lb(in.}^2)}{30 \times 10^6\text{ lb(0.120 in.}^4)}$$

$$y = -3.80 \times 10^{-3}\frac{\text{ft}^3}{\text{in.}^2}\left(\frac{12\text{ in.}}{\text{ft}}\right)^2$$

$$y = -5.47 \times 10^{-1}\text{ ft} = -0.547\text{ ft}$$

$$y = -6.56\text{ in.}$$

Similarly from Example Problem 16.2:

$$\theta = -\frac{2560}{EI} \text{ ft}^2\text{-lb}$$

Substituting E and I gives:

$$\theta = \frac{-2560 \text{ ft}^2\text{-lb(in.}^2)}{30 \times 10^6 \text{ lb}(0.120 \text{ in.}^4)}$$

$$\theta = -7.11 \text{ } E\text{-4} \frac{\text{ft}^2}{\text{in.}^2} \left(\frac{12 \text{ in.}}{\text{ft}}\right)^2$$

$$\boldsymbol{\theta = -0.102 \text{ rad}}$$

Of course the dimensionless answer is in radians. Converting to degrees gives:

$$\boldsymbol{\theta = -5.87°}$$

Note that there will frequently be considerable conversion of units associated with evaluation of the deflection.

16.5   DEFLECTION BY GRAPHICAL INTEGRATION

In Section 16.4 we obtained beam deflection by integration. Recall that integration is a summation process. When we express Eq. 16.12 as follows:

$$V = \int w \, dx$$

we are saying that the change in shear V is equal to the area under the load rate curve. When Eq. 16.12 is evaluated with an arbitrary constant, it gives the value of shear. When it is evaluated without an arbitrary constant, it gives the change in shear. Thus we will also write:

$$\Delta V = \int w \, dx$$

as in Chapter 14. In Example Problems 14.4 through 14.6, we found the change in shear by finding the area under the load rate curve. This amounts to *graphical integration*. We call it graphical, although it would be more accurate to call it semigraphical. There are graphical methods that depend more on drawing lines and less on computation. We also evaluated Eq. 16.13,

$$M = \int V \, dx$$

by graphical integration. In the graphical integration, boundary conditions were accounted for by reproducing concentrated shear and bending moment loads as they occurred. In this section we will handle them in the same manner. In fact, the first two stages of graphical integration, load rate to shear and shear to bending moment, are exactly the same as in Section 14.6.

Evaluation of Eqs. 16.14 and 16.15 may also be done by graphical integration. However, for these two last stages we must identify boundary conditions, as we did for analytical integration. We then force the graphical integration to satisfy these boundary conditions. The following example problem illustrates the method.

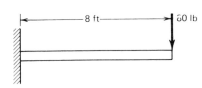

FIG. 16.4 Example Problem 16.4.

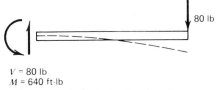

$V = 80$ lb
$M = 640$ ft-lb

FIG. 16.5 Free body diagram for
Example Problem 16.4.

Example Problem 16.4

Find the maximum deflection of the beam shown in Fig. 16.4 by graphical integration.

Solution

As in Example Problem 16.2 a free body diagram (Fig. 16.5) is drawn, and V and M are found. An approximate deflection curve is also drawn. Starting with the shear curve at 0, we reproduce the 80-lb upward load taking us to $V = +80$ lb (Fig. 16.6a). From the left to the right-hand end the load rate is zero, so the area under the load rate curve is zero, and thus there is no change in V.

At the right-hand end the 80-lb down load is reproduced, closing the shear curve. Shear is positive across the beam.

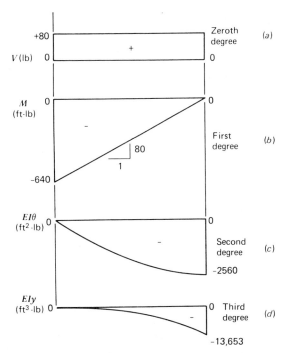

FIG. 16.6a–d Deflection by integration.
Example Problem 16.4.

The bending moment diagram starts at zero and reproduces the negative moment of 640 ft-lb (Fig. 16.6b). The change from the left-to the right-hand end is the area under the shear curve:

$$\Delta M = +80(8) = +640 \text{ ft-lb}$$

This takes us back to zero. Since the shear curve is the zeroth degree, the moment, its integral, will be first degree or linear. Its slope is $+80$, as indicated. The curve closes, and the bending is negative the entire length. At this point a qualitative check may be made by observing that the approximate shape of the beam, as originally drawn, calls for negative bending. We also recall that these first two curves must close to satisfy static equilibrium. As we proceed to the slope curve θ, it will be convenient to plot $EI\theta$ when the beam is uniform in EI. The boundary condition for slope needs to be noted at this point. We observe from the approximate shape that the slope of the beam at the left-hand end, the fixed end, is zero. Hence the $EI\theta$ diagram starts at zero (Fig. 16.6c). The change in θ is the area under the moment curve:

$$\Delta(EI\theta) = \tfrac{1}{2}bh = \tfrac{1}{2}(8 \text{ ft})(-640 \text{ ft-lb}) = -2650 \text{ ft}^2\text{-lb}$$

Thus the $EI\theta$ diagram goes from 0 to -2560 ft²-lb. The moment curve is first degree, so the slope curve is second degree, which may be concave upward or concave downward. By noting:

$$\frac{d}{dx}(EI\theta) = M$$

and that $M = 0$ at the right end (this is the slope of the slope curve), we conclude that the desired curve is concave up. The slope of the beam is negative. This can be qualitatively compared with the approximate beam curve. The figure shows a vertical line closing the curve. This is for consistency only. In general, there is no independent check that requires this curve to close.

For deflection when EI is constant, we also plot EIy. We observe that the deflection is zero at the left-hand end, which is the needed boundary condition. So EIy will start at zero (Fig. 16.6d). The change in deflection is the area under the slope curve. The slope is a second-degree curve or a parabola, which we find in Table A-9. Remember that to use this table we must have a *vertex*, which occurs at the right-hand end of the slope curve. We also note that we are after the complement of the area given in the table, thus:

$$\Delta(EIy) = \tfrac{2}{3}bh = \tfrac{2}{3}(8 \text{ ft})(-2560 \text{ ft}^2\text{-lb})$$
$$\Delta(EIy) = -13,700 \text{ ft}^2\text{-lb}$$

The deflection ends at $-13,700$ ft³-lb and is negative for the entire beam. Since the $EI\theta$ curve is second degree, the EIy curve will be third degree. The slope of the EIy curve will be zero at the left-hand end corresponding to a zero value for $EI\theta$. Thus the curve is concave downward and agrees with original intuitive approximation of the beam's shape.

We conclude

$$y_{max} = \frac{-13,700}{EI} \text{ ft}^3\text{-lb}$$

which agrees with Example Problem 16.2.

The equation for the area under an nth-degree curve in Table A-9 is exact. However, determining the presence of a vertex becomes more complicated for higher degree curves, and an exact solution will not always be obtained by using this table alone.

Graphical integration takes advantage of the skills we developed for moment diagrams. It gives a picture of the slope and deflection of the beam and provides the foundation for approximate graphical solutions. The method presented here is directly applicable only to a limited number of problems, however.

16.6 DEFLECTION BY DOUBLE INTEGRATION

In Section 16.4 we went from the load rate w to the deflection y by four successive integrations. The same process was graphically carried out in Section 16.5 and illustrates the relationship between the variables w, V, M, θ, and y. The first two integrations, which yield an equation for moment, can be replaced by a statics procedure. In Chapter 14 we found moment equations by passing a cutting plane at an arbitrary point, drawing a free body diagram, and summing the moments. We will do that here and then complete the deflection problem by integrating this equation twice.

Example Problem 16.5

Find the slope and deflection equations for the beam shown in Fig. 16.7 by double integration.

Solution

The overall free body diagram is drawn in Fig. 16.8. The reactions are as indicated. A free body diagram of the length x is drawn in Fig. 16.9. The unknown shear V and moment M *must* be drawn in the sense of *positive* internal loads.

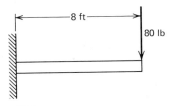

FIG. 16.7 Example Problem 16.5.

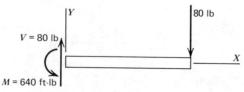

FIG. 16.8 Free body diagram for the entire beam.

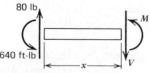

FIG. 16.9 Free diagram for length x.

It is instructive to sum forces vertically, although it is not required for the process. Doing so gives:

$$\sum F_y = 0 = +80 = V$$
$$V = +80$$

This agrees with the equation for shear found by integration in Example Problem 16.2. We find the equation for the bending moment by summing moments about x, giving:

$$\sum M_x = 0 = -80x + 640 + M$$
$$M = 80x - 640$$

This agrees with the moment equation found in Example Problem 16.2 and represents the starting point for integration. From this point forward the process is identical to Example Problem 16.2, giving:

$$\theta = \frac{1}{EI}\left[40x^2 - 640x\right]$$

$$y = \frac{1}{EI}\left[\frac{40}{3}x^3 - 320x^2\right]$$

Example Problem 16.6

Find the slope and deflection equation for the beam shown in Fig. 16.10 by double integration.

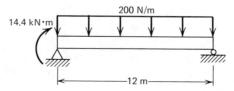

FIG. 16.10 Example Problem 16.6.

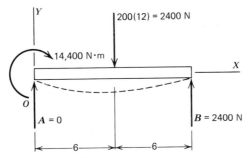

FIG. 16.11 Equivalent free body diagram.

Solution

An equivalent free body diagram is drawn and the reactions A and B found as shown in Fig. 16.11. We also sketch in the beam deflection and set the coordinate system to establish boundary conditions. A free body diagram of an arbitrary length x is then drawn in Fig. 16.12. Its equivalent is also shown. Remember it is essential to show V and M with positive signs. Summing moments about x gives:

$$\sum M_x = 0 = -14{,}400 + 200x\frac{x}{2} + M$$

$$M = 14{,}400 - 100x^2$$

Then by Eq. 16.14:

$$\theta = \frac{1}{EI}\int M\,dx$$

$$\theta = \frac{1}{EI}\int (14{,}400 - 100x^2)\,dx$$

$$\theta = \frac{1}{EI}\left[14{,}400x - \frac{100}{3}x^3\right] + C_1$$

For this simply supported beam, a boundary condition for slope is not available. Instead two boundary conditions for deflection are. Namely,

$$x = 0, y = 0 \quad \text{and} \quad x = 12, y = 0$$

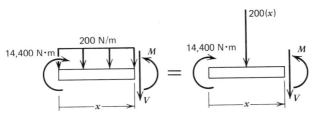

FIG. 16.12 Free body diagram and its equivalent of length x.

These will prove to be sufficient, but we must postpone evaluation of C_1 until the next step, which is by Eq. 16.15:

$$y = \int \theta \, dx$$

$$y = \frac{1}{EI} \int \left[14{,}400x - \frac{100}{3} x^3 + EIC_1 \right] dx$$

$$y = \frac{1}{EI} \left\{ \frac{14{,}400}{2} x^2 - \frac{100}{3 \cdot 4} x^4 + EIC_1 x \right\} + C_2$$

Using the first boundary condition gives:

$$y = 0 = \frac{1}{EI} \left\{ 7200(0)^2 - \frac{25}{3} (0)^4 + EIC_1(0) \right\} + C_2$$

$$C_2 = 0$$

And the second gives:

$$y = 0 = \frac{1}{EI} \left\{ 7200(12)^2 - \frac{25}{3} (12)^4 + EIC_1(12) \right\}$$

$$C_1 = \frac{-72{,}000}{EI}$$

and finally:

$$y = \frac{1}{EI} \left\{ -72{,}000x + 7200x^2 - \frac{25}{3} x^4 \right\}$$

The algebra may be checked by substituting in the boundary conditions to see if they are satisfied. Having solved for C_1, we may also write:

$$\theta = \frac{1}{EI} \left\{ -72{,}000 + 14{,}400x - \frac{100}{3} x^3 \right\}$$

Example Problem 16.7

Find the maximum deflection in the beam in Example Problem 16.6, assuming that it is a steel beam 30 mm wide and 60 mm high in cross section. Also tell where the maximum deflection occurs.

Solution

In general, the location of maximum deflection for simply supported beams cannot be determined by inspection. We observe that the maximum deflection will correspond to zero slope (Fig. 16.13). In Example Problem 16.6 we found the equation for slope, which we now set equal to zero:

$$\theta = 0 = \frac{1}{EI} \left\{ -72{,}000 + 14{,}400x - \frac{100}{3} x^3 \right\}$$

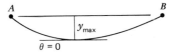

FIG. 16.13 Maximum deflection coincides with zero slope in simply supported beams.

We seek the roots of the cubic equation:

$$33.3x^3 - 14{,}400x + 72{,}000 = 0$$

The methods of finding these roots include the *graphical* and *trial-and-error* approaches. Since we know the approximate value of the root of interest (near but less than 6), we will use trial and error. We write:

$$R = 33.3x^3 - 14{,}400x + 72{,}000$$

where R is a remainder we wish to reduce to zero. Programming the equation on a programmable calculator makes the process very rapid. We enter the following values of x and get the indicated values of R.

x	R
5.00	4166
5.50	-1654
5.30	642
5.35	64
5.36	-51

Use 5.36 as the approximate location. Substituting this into the equation for deflection gives:

$$y = \frac{1}{EI}\left\{-72{,}000x + 7200x^2 - \frac{25}{3}x^4\right\}$$

$$y_{max} = \frac{1}{EI}\left\{-72{,}000(5.36) + 7200(5.36)^2 - \frac{25}{3}(5.36)^4\right\}$$

$$y_{max} = \frac{1}{EI}\{-186{,}000\}\ \text{N}\cdot\text{m}^3$$

Calculating I:

$$I = \frac{bh^3}{12} = \frac{0.030\ \text{m}(0.060\ \text{m})^3}{12}$$

$$I = 5.40(E\text{-}7)\ \text{m}^4$$

and from Table A-8:

$$E = 207\ \text{GPa}$$

Then

$$y_{max} = \frac{-186{,}000\ \text{N}\cdot\text{m}^3(\text{m}^2)}{207\ E9\ \text{N}(5.40\ E\text{-}7\ \text{m}^4)} = \mathbf{-1.66\ m}$$

at **5.36 m** from the left-hand end.

16.7   DEFLECTION BY FORMULAS

In Example Problem 16.2, we found the deflection in a beam 8 ft long with a load of 80 lb on the free end. If we replace this specific problem with a more general one—a beam of length L and load P—we would find the deflection to be:

$$y = -\frac{PL^3}{3EI}$$

Thus we may find the deflection for any cantilever beam of length L, end load P, modulus of elasticity E, and moment of inertia I simply by evaluating this formula. The type support and the type load must each be the same before this equation is used.

At this point it is worthwhile to look at the beam deflection formula and observe its behavior. First, we see that deflection is proportional to the load: the greater the load, the greater the deflection. It is proportional to length cubed. Doubling the length increases the deflection by a factor of 8! It is inversely proportional to the modulus of elasticity. A steel beam will deflect only one-third as much as an aluminum one under otherwise identical conditions. Finally, deflection is inversely proportional to the moment of inertia. Remember that the moment of inertia depends on the depth of the beam cubed; so double the depth and cut the deflection by a factor of 8!

The discussion above applies strictly to the cantilever beam under consideration. However, the tendencies indicated may be extrapolated to beams in general.

We can analyze other loading conditions in the manner of Example Problem 16.2. Table A-18 shows the results of this type of analysis for a number of loading conditions. This type of table is commonly available from a number of sources. The equations may be evaluated readily for a given set of conditions to obtain the deflection at any desired location. When available, equations of this form offer the easiest method of determining the deflection.

Example Problem 16.8

A simply supported beam carries a uniform load of 600 lb/ft over its 12-ft span. Find the deflection at the center of the beam if it is a steel W 12 × 65 oriented for minimum deflection.

Solution

From the tables in the Appendix

$$I = 533 \text{ in.}^4$$

$$E = 30 \times 10^6 \text{ psi}$$

And from Table A-18

$$y = \frac{-5wl^4}{384EI}$$

$$y = \frac{-5}{384}\frac{(600 \text{ lb})(12 \text{ ft})^4}{\text{ft}}\frac{\text{in.}^2}{30 \times 10^6 \text{ lb}}\frac{1}{(533 \text{ in.}^4)}\left(\frac{12 \text{ in.}}{\text{ft}}\right)^3$$

$$y = -0.0175 \text{ in.}$$

16.8 DEFLECTION BY THE METHOD OF SUPERPOSITION

One of the most important and broadly applicable principles in mechanics is superposition. This principle, as applied to deflection, says that the resultant deflection from a combination of loads is the sum of the deflections from each individual load. This is true when the individual deflections are linearly related to the individual loads—as they are in Table A-18. This principle presents a valuable method of determining beam deflection from a combination of loads.

Suppose we wish to know the maximum deflection of a beam loaded as shown in Fig. 16.14a. This combined loading is not available in Table A-18. If we separate the loading as shown in Figs. 16.14b and 16.14c, we have loading conditions that are available in the table. We can then find from cases 5 and 8, Table A-18:

$$y_1 = -\frac{P_1 L^3}{3EI}$$

and

$$y_2 = \frac{-Pb^2(3L - b)}{6EI}$$

The method of superposition says that the resultant deflection from these two individual loads is simply $y_1 + y_2$.

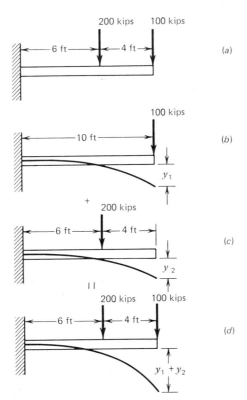

FIG. 16.14a–d Beam deflection by superposition.

We do not make the calculation at this point, but it is worth noting that in every sense the resultant beam in Fig. 16.14d is the sum of Figs. 16.14b and 16.14c. We can, for example, calculate the reactions at the beam support in b and c. Their sum is the reaction in Fig. 16.14d.

Example Problem 16.9

The beam shown in Fig. 16.14 is a W 14 × 78 of steel. Calculate the maximum deflection of the beam.

Solution

We replace the combined loading of Fig. 16.14a with the two separate loads of Figs. 16.14b and 16.14c. If we visualize superimposing Fig. 16.14c on Fig. 16.14b, we see that the result is Fig. 16.14d. We label the deflections in Figs. 16.14b and 16.14c as y_1 and y_2, respectively. From Table A-11, we get the beam properties, and from Table A-18 we get for y_1 (case 5):

$$y_1 = \frac{-PL^3}{3EI} = \frac{-100 \text{ kips}(10 \text{ ft})^3(\text{in.}^2)}{3(30 \times 10^6 \text{ lb})} \frac{1}{851 \text{ in.}^4} \times \frac{1000 \text{ lb}}{1 \text{ kips}} \frac{(12 \text{ in.})^3}{\text{ft}^3}$$

$$= \frac{-100(10)^3(1000)(12)^3 \text{ in.}}{3(30 \times 10^6)(851)}$$

$$y_1 = -2.26 \text{ in.}$$

Similarly for y_2 (case 8) we get

$$y_2 = \frac{-Pb^2(3L - b)}{6EI}$$

$$= \frac{-200 \text{ kips}(6 \text{ ft})^2(\text{in.}^2)}{(6)30 \times 10^3 \text{ kips}} \frac{(3(10)\text{ft} - 6 \text{ ft})}{851 \text{ in.}^4} \times \left(\frac{12 \text{ in.}}{\text{ft}}\right)^3$$

$$y_2 = -1.95 \text{ in.}$$

Then by superposition the total deflection is the sum of y_1 and y_2:

$$y_t = y_1 + y_2 = -2.26 - 1.95 = -4.20 \text{ in.}$$

16.9 THE MOMENT–AREA METHOD

The moment–area method of determining beam deflection is useful when deflection at a known point is desired. The loading can be of almost any pattern, and variation in beam cross section and properties can be routinely handled. The method can also be used for determining the equation of deflection, but it offers no significant advantages for such problems. Its greatest application, then, occurs when the deflection of one or more points is desired and deflection formula are not readily available.

There are two theorems on which the method is based. This first theorem is simply the application of Eq. 16.14:

$$\theta = \int \frac{M}{EI} \, dx \qquad (16.14)$$

As we previously indicated, when Eq. 16.14 is integrated between two specific points, the left-hand side of the equation is the change in the angle θ. This principle was used in finding the slope (θ) curve from the moment (M) curve in graphical integration. The theorem may be stated as follows:

Theorem 1. The change in slope between any two points on a beam is equal to the area under the M/EI curve between the same two points.

The theorem is illustrated in Fig. 16.15, where a general M/EI curve is on top and a plot of the deflection, or an elastic curve is on the bottom. (We have not included the slope diagram, which would be used for graphical integration.) As indicated in the figure, the change in slope of the elastic curve (the angle the tangent makes with the horizontal) between points A and B is equal to the area under the M/EI curve between points A and B.

We arrive at the second theorem by considering two points, C and D, that are separated by the infinitesimal distance dx (Fig. 16.16). Tangents to the elastic curve at these two points are drawn in the lower figure. By Theorem 1, the angle between the tangents is:

$$d\theta = \frac{M}{EI} \, dx$$

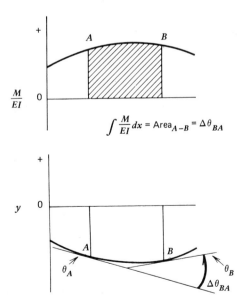

FIG. 16.15 The first moment–area theorem.

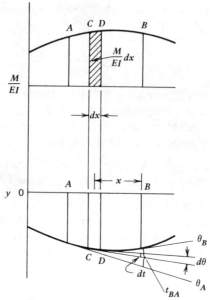

FIG. 16.16   The second moment–area theorem.

(This is also Eq. 16.10.) The vertical distance between the two tangents at position B is dt. Since the angles are very small, dt may be approximated by the arc length, that is,

$$dt = x \, d\theta$$

where x is the distance from B to the element. Substituting for $d\theta$ from above gives

$$dt = x \left(\frac{M}{EI} \right) dx$$

which is the *moment of area* of the element $(M/EI) \, dx$ about B. The deviation of the beam at B from a tangent at A is labeled t_{BA} and is the summation of the dt's from A to B, or:

$$t_{BA} = \int \frac{M}{EI} x \, dx \qquad (16.15)$$

Note that t_{BA} is the tangential deviation, *not* the deflection of the beam. The integral is the moment of area under the M/EI curve about B. Hence we may write:

$$t_{BA} = \bar{x} A_{A-B} \qquad (16.16)$$

where A_{A-B} is the area between A and B under the M/EI curve and $\bar{x}$ is the distance from the centroid of the area to B. In words we have:

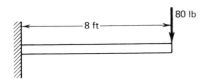

FIG. 16.17 Example Problem 16.10.

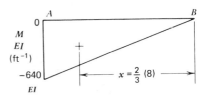

FIG. 16.18 Moment diagram for Example Problem 16.10.

Theorem 2.   The deviation of a point on a beam from the tangent drawn at a second point is the moment about the first point of the area under the M/EI curve between the two points.

The geometric properties of common areas given in Table A-9 will be useful in applying the moment area method. Its application is illustrated in the problems that follow.

Example Problem 16.10

Find the slope and deflection of the beam in Fig. 16.17 at its free end.

$$EI = 137,000 \text{ ft}^2\text{-lb}$$

Solution

The moment diagram was found for this loading in Example Problem 16.4. An M/EI curve may be found by dividing this curve by EI (Fig. 16.18). If EI is constant, the division is not necessary. Otherwise it is.

A sketch of the deflected beam is made noting the boundary conditions of zero deflection and zero slope at point A (Fig. 16.19).

We find the slope at the free end, point B, by applying Theorem 1. The change in slope between A and B is the area under the M/EI curve or:

$$\theta_{BA} = \frac{1}{2}\frac{M}{EI}(L)$$

$$\theta_{BA} = \frac{1}{2}\cdot\frac{-640(8)}{137,000} = -0.0187 \text{ rad}$$

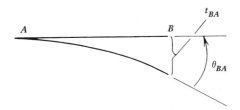

FIG. 16.19 Beam deflection for Example Problem 16.10.

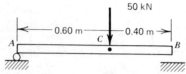

FIG. 16.20 Example Problem 16.11.

Since the slope at A is zero, this change in slope is the actual slope. Since the area is negative, the change in slope is negative. Also note that the angle involved is very small.

We find the deflection by applying Theorem 2. The tangential deviation is the moment of the area about B; thus:

$$t_{BA} = A\bar{x} = \frac{1}{2}\frac{(-640)(8)}{137,000}\left(\frac{2}{3}\right)(8)$$

$$t_{BA} = \mathbf{0.0997 \ ft}$$

This is the deviation of the beam at B from the tangent from A. In this case, since (1) the deflection at A is zero and (2) the slope at A is zero, this is also the deflection of the beam. Since cantilever beams have zero slope and deflection at the support, they are especially suitable for solution by the moment–area method.

Example Problem 16.11

Find the deflection at the point of loading, point C, for the beam shown in Fig. 16.20.

Solution

After solving the statics we arrive at the moment diagram (Fig. 16.21).

Next the deflected beam $AC'B$ is sketched (Fig. 16.22). The distance CC' is the desired dimension. We sketch a tangent at A and note that the deflection t_{CA} is the one governed by the second moment–area theorem. If we could find the slope of the beam at A, we could solve the problem from the geometry and the second theorem. We might look to the first theorem here, since it deals with slope. However, we lack a zero slope reference point and must seek elsewhere.

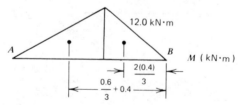

FIG. 16.21 Moment diagram for Example Problem 16.11.

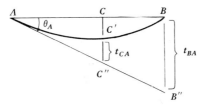

FIG. 16.22 Beam deflection for Example
Problem 16.11.

"Elsewhere" in this case is observing that t_{BA} may be found from the second theorem. Knowing t_{BA}, we can calculate θ_A. The second theorem says that t_{BA}, the deviation of B from the tangent from A, is the moment of the area under the M/EI curve between the two points about B. Thus t_{BA} is found by taking the moment of the two triangular areas in the moment diagram about B:

$$t_{BA} = \bar{x}_1 A_1 + \bar{x}_2 A_2$$

$$= \left[\frac{2(0.40)}{3} \frac{1}{2}(0.40)12 + \left(\frac{0.60}{3} + 0.4 \right) \frac{1}{2}(0.60)12 \right] \frac{1}{EI}$$

$$t_{BA} = \frac{2.80}{EI}$$

Since EI is constant, it is not necessary to find the M/EI diagram.

Knowing t_{BA}, we calculate θ_A as follows:

$$\theta_A = \frac{t_{BA}}{L} = \frac{2.80}{EI(1.0)} = \frac{2.80}{EI}$$

You may want to say $\tan \theta_A$; but remember, we are talking about very small angles, where

$$\tan \theta_A = \theta_A$$

Knowing θ_A, we can calculate CC'':

$$CC'' = \theta_A(AC) = 0.6 \frac{(2.80)}{EI} = \frac{1.68}{EI}$$

Now we apply the second moment–area theorem to find t_{CA}, which is the moment of the area between A and C about C:

$$t_{CA} = \frac{0.60}{3} \cdot \frac{1}{2} \cdot (0.60) \frac{(12.0)}{EI} = \frac{0.720}{EI}$$

The desired distance CC' is then computed as follows:

$$CC' = CC'' - t_{CA} = \frac{1.680}{EI} - \frac{0.720}{EI} = \mathbf{\frac{0.960}{EI}}$$

Finding deflection by the moment–area method usually involves combinations of the first and second theorems and geometric observations.

16.10 SUMMARY

Curvature:

$$\frac{1}{\rho} = \frac{M}{EI}$$

Beam equations:

Differential Form   **Integral Form**

SLOPE   AREA

$$w = \frac{dV}{dx}$$ $$V = \int w\,dx$$

$$V = \frac{dM}{dx}$$ $$M = \int V\,dx$$

$$\frac{M}{EI} = \frac{d\theta}{dx}$$ $$EI\theta = \int M\,dx$$

$$\theta = \frac{dy}{dx}$$ $$y = \int \theta\,dx$$

One boundary condition is needed for each integration. Beam deflections may be found by:

1. Multiple integration.
2. Graphical integration.
3. Double integration.
4. Formula.
5. Superposition.
6. The moment–area method.

The moment–area theorems are as follows:

Theorem 1.   The change in slope between any two points on a beam is equal to the area under the M/EI curve between the two points.

Theorem 2.   The tangential deviation of one point with respect to a second is the moment about the first point of the area under the M/EI curve between the two points.

PROBLEMS

16.1   Check the dimensions for Eq. 16.1.

16.2   A 1 in. thick × 6 in. deep southern pine board is to be bent and set into a curved member by a soaking process. The board is forced onto a form, soaked, and dried. The form has a radius of curvature of 8 ft (Fig. 16.23).

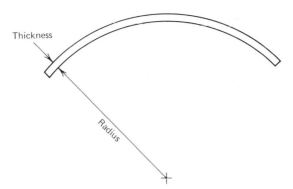

Thickness

Radius

FIG. 16.23 Problems 16.2, 16.3.

What bending moment will be required to set the board and what stress will be developed in it?

16.3 A 25 mm thick × 150 mm deep southern pine board is to be bent and set into a curved member by a soaking process. The board is forced onto a form, soaked, and dried. The form has a radius of curvature of 3 m (Fig. 16.23). What bending moment will be required to set the board and what stress will be developed in it?

16.4 A $\frac{3}{8}$-in.-diameter steel rod is to be bent into a circular ring of 400-in. diameter. Find the bending moment required to form the ring and the resultant stress.

16.5 A 10-mm-diameter steel rod is to be bent into a circular ring of 10-m diameter. Find the bending moment required to form the ring and the resultant stress.

16.6 A $\frac{1}{4}$-in.-diameter aluminum rod is bent into a circular ring until the maximum stress produced is 25,000 psi. What is the radius of the ring?

16.7 A 6-mm-diameter aluminum rod is bent into a circular ring until the maximum stress produced is 170 MPa. What is the radius of the ring?

16.8 The deflection of beams is given by the following equations. Successively differentiate the equations to find equations for slope, bending moment, shear, and load rate.

(a) $y = \dfrac{1}{EI}\left(100x^2 - 50x^3 + \dfrac{x^5}{20}\right)$

(b) $y = \dfrac{1}{EI}\left(64x^3 - \dfrac{x^6}{40} - \dfrac{32{,}678x}{10}\right)$

(c) $y = \dfrac{1}{EI}(-x^4 + 18x^3 - 180x^2 + 720x)$

For each indicated figure in the following problems:

(a) Write an equation for load rate as a function of beam position.

(b) Write boundary conditions for shear, bending moment, slope, and deflection.

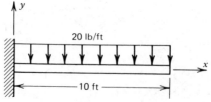

FIG. 16.24   Problems 16.9, 16.12, 16.15, 16.18, 16.25, 16.31, 16.36, 16.42a.

16.9   Fig. 16.24

16.10 Fig. 16.25

16.11 Fig. 16.26   *Hint:* Let w be the magnitude only.

For each beam shown in the following problems, find by successive integration equations for shear, bending moment, slope, and deflection *without* evaluating the constants of integration (C_1, C_2, etc.):

16.12 Fig. 16.24

16.13 Fig. 16.25

16.14 Fig. 16.26   *Hint:* Let w be the magnitude only.

For each beam shown, in the following problems:

(a)   Find the equation for shear, bending moment, slope, and deflection by successive integration, *including* the evaluation of the constants of integration.

(b)   Where the cross section and material are indicated, find the slope and deflection at the free end.

16.15 Fig. 16.24   2 × 12 (actual size), lying flat, southern pine.

16.16 Fig. 16.25   100 mm deep × 40 mm wide aluminum.

16.17 Fig. 16.26   *Hint:* Let w be the magnitude only.

For each beam shown in the following problems, find the maximum deflection by graphical integration:

16.18 Fig. 16.24

16.19 Fig. 16.25

16.20 Fig. 16.26   *Hint:* Let w be the magnitude only.

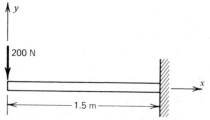

FIG. 16.25   Problems 16.10, 16.13, 16.16, 16.19, 16.26, 16.32, 16.37, 16.42b.

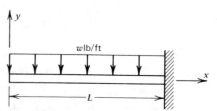

FIG. 16.26   Problems 16.11, 16.14, 16.17, 16.20, 16.27, 16.42c.

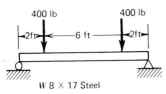

FIG. 16.27 Problems 16.21, 16.33, 16.43a, 16.44a, 16.45a, 16.54.

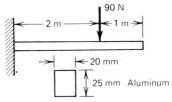

FIG. 16.28 Problems 16.22, 16.28, 16.34, 16.38, 16.42d.

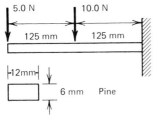

FIG. 16.29 Problems 16.23, 16.35, 16.42e.

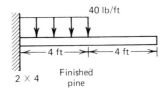

FIG. 16.30 Problems 16.24, 16.29.

In the following problems, draw shear, bending moment, slope, and deflection diagrams and calculate maximum deflection for the indicated figure:

16.21 Fig. 16.27   **16.22** Fig. 16.28

16.23 Fig. 16.29   **16.24** Fig. 16.30

Using statics write the equation for bending moment directly for the indicated beam. Then find the equations for slope and deflection using double integration. (Section 16.6)

16.25 Fig. 16.24   **16.26** Fig. 16.25

16.27 Fig. 16.26

Using statics, write the moment equation and find the equations of slope and deflection for the indicated portion of the indicated beam.

16.28 Fig. 16.28, 0 to 2 m   **16.29** Fig. 16.30, 0 to 4 ft

16.30 Fig. 16.31, full length

16.31 Find the maximum deflection of the beam in Fig. 16.24, by formula and superposition if necessary.

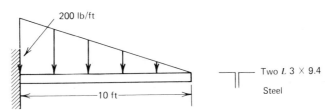

FIG. 16.31 Problems 16.30, 16.39, 16.42f.

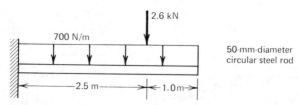

FIG. 16.32 Problem 16.40.

16.32 Find the maximum deflection of the beam in Fig. 16.25, by formula and superposition, if necessary.

16.33 Find the maximum deflection of the beam in Fig. 16.27, by formula and superposition, if necessary.

16.34 Find the maximum deflection of the beam in Fig. 16.28, by formula and superposition, if necessary.

16.35 Find the maximum deflection of the beam in Fig. 16.29, by formula and superposition, if necessary.

16.36 For the beam in Fig. 16.24 using Table A-18 find the deflection every foot along the beam. Make a plot of the beam deflection.

16.37 For the beam in Fig. 16.25 find the deflection every 0.3 m along the beam using Table A-18. Make a plot of the beam deflection.

16.38 For the beam in Fig. 16.28 find the deflection every 0.5 m along the beam using Table A-18. Make a plot of the beam deflection.

In the following problems, find the maximum deflection of the indicated beams by formula and superposition, if appropriate.

16.39 Fig. 16.31   **16.40** Fig. 16.32

16.41 Find the deflection at the center of the beam, by formula and superposition, for Fig. 16.33.

16.42 Using the moment–area method, find the slope and deflection of the free end of the cantilever beams in:

    (a)   Fig. 16.24

    (b)   Fig. 16.25

    (c)   Fig. 16.26

    (d)   Fig. 16.28

    (e)   Fig. 16.29

    (f)   Fig. 16.31

16.43 Using the moment–area method, find the deflection at the center of simply supported beams in:

    (a)   Fig. 16.27   (b)   Fig. 16.33

16.44 Using the moment–area method, find the slope and deflection at the left-hand load in:

    (a)   Fig. 16.27   (b)   Fig. 16.33

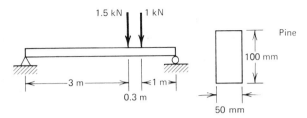

FIG. 16.33   Problems 16.41, 16.43b, 16.44b, 16.45b.

16.45 Using the moment–area method, find the slope and deflection at the right hand load in:

(a)   Fig. 16.27   (b)   Fig. 16.33

16.46 In analyzing a beam, the moment equation was found to be:

$$M = 30x^2 - 500$$

The following boundary conditions were also observed.

$$y(0) = 0 \quad \text{and} \quad \theta(10) = 0$$

Find the deflection equation for this beam.

16.47 After double integration, the following moment equation was found.

$$M = -200x^2 - 8000x$$

The slope of the beam is observed to be zero when x is zero and the deflection of the beam is zero when x is 8. Find the deflection equation for this beam.

16.48 Find the slope and deflection of the free end of the beam shown in Fig. 16.34 by the method of superposition.

$$E = 210 \text{ GPa} \quad \text{and} \quad I = 3.25 \text{ E6 mm}^4$$

16.49 Find the slope and deflection of the beam shown (by diagrams) if it is a standard steel I beam, 10×35.0 (Fig. 16.35).

16.50 A beam is observed to have a zero slope 4 m to the right of its left-hand support. The deflection is zero at the right support. Its moment diagram is given in Fig. 16.36. Draw the slope and deflection diagram for this beam, thoroughly labeling all relevant points. Indicate the maximum deflection.

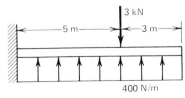

FIG. 16.34   Problem 16.48.

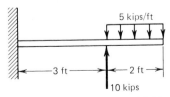

FIG. 16.35   Problems 16.49, 16.55.

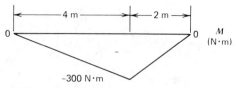

FIG. 16.36   Problem 16.50.

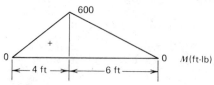

FIG. 16.37   Problem 16.51.

16.51 A moment curve for a beam is as shown in Fig. 16.37. Its slope and deflection are zero 4 ft to the right of the left-hand end. Draw the slope and deflection diagrams for this beam and find the maximum deflection. Thoroughly label all relevant points.

16.52 Using the information given in Table A-18, find the equation for the slope of the indicated beam.

   (a)   Case 1   (b)   Case 4   (c)   Case 5   (d)   Case 7

16.53 Using the information given in Table A-18, find the equation for the slope of the indicated beam over the designated portion.

   (a)   Case 2, 0 to a.   (b)   Case 3, 0 to a.
   (c)   Case 8, 0 to a.   (d)   Case 8, a to L.

16.54 Select a member as indicated which limits the deflection of the beam in Fig. 16.27 to 3 in. Also calculate the maximum bending stress in the beam selected.

   (a)   A steel angle

   (b)   A Douglas fir finished (S4S) timber

   (c)   An aluminum square cross section

16.55 Select a member as indicated that limits the deflection of the beam in Fig. 16.35 to 0.50 in. Also calculate the maximum bending stress in the beam selected.

   (a)   A steel angle

   (b)   A southern pine finished (S4S) timber

   (c)   A bronze rectangular cross section that is three times as deep as it is wide.

17

Shearing Stresses in Beams

We have seen that when a section is passed through a beam, there result three components of force: an axial load, a shear load, and a bending moment. In Chapter 15 we developed a relationship between the bending moment and the normal stress produced. Chapter 11 discussed the normal stress produced by an axial load and developed an equation for the average shear stress as a function of the shear load. We commented at that time that although the average shear stress concept is useful, it does not accurately represent the shear stress distribution. In this chapter we develop a more accurate relation between the shear load and the stress it produces. We also develop a relation between the shear load and a useful concept known as the shear flow.

The stress equation of this chapter is the most complex of all that we will consider. Thus you should pay particularly close attention to the development of this equation to ensure that you thoroughly understand each of its terms.

17.1   THE SHEAR STRESS FORMULA

Consider a beam as shown in Fig. 17.1. Also shown in the figure are the shear and moment diagrams. The element AB, which has a length dx, will be taken from the beam. Notice that the shear at A equals the shear at B, while the bending moment at B is greater than that at A. We designate the moment at A as M and that at B as $M + dM$. These moments produce the stress distribution shown in Fig. 17.2a. Of course, this results in the stresses at B, σ' being greater than the

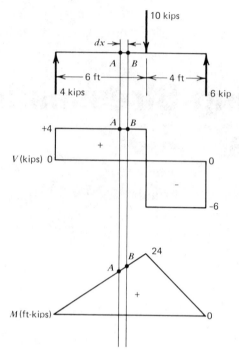

FIG. 17.1   A simply supported beam and its shear and moment diagrams.

stresses at A, σ, as shown in Fig. 17.2c. Figure 17.2b shows a rectangular cross section these stresses act over. (The method developed is applicable to other cross sections as well.) We examine the area bounded by c, the distance to the extreme fiber, and an arbitrary fiber y_0, designating this area as A'. The area A' contains the element of area dA over which the stresses σ (at section A) and σ' (at section B) act. Figure 17.2c shows the small element dx long, with a cross section A'. The stress at any location, y on the right end is σ'. It is due to $M + dM$ and will be greater than the corresponding stress at the same distance from the neutral axis

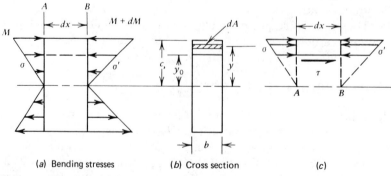

(a) Bending stresses   (b) Cross section   (c)

FIG. 17.2a–c   Development of shear stresses.

y on the left end. The stress on the left end is σ, and it is due to M, as shown in Fig. 17.2c. Since σ' is greater than σ, the resultant horizontal force to the left is greater than that to the right. For this element of the beam (Fig. 17.2c) to be in equilibrium, there must be an additional force to the right. This force is produced by the shear stress τ acting over the length dx as indicated in Fig. 17.2c.

To recap, the greater bending moment at B, $M + dM$, produces greater stresses, σ', on this section. The greater stresses produce an unbalanced resultant force to the left, which is ultimately balanced by the force due to shear stress, τ.

The relation between these variables is found by summing the forces horizontally:

$$\Sigma F_x = 0 = \int_{A'} \sigma \, dA - \int_{A'} \sigma' \, dA + \tau(b \cdot dx)$$

where b is the beam thickness (Fig. 17.2b) and the area $b \cdot dx$ is the area that τ acts over. From Eq. 15.6, we can write:

$$\sigma = \frac{My}{I}$$

and

$$\sigma' = \frac{(M + dM)y}{I}$$

Substituting these into the preceding force equation gives:

$$\int_{A'} \frac{My}{I} \, dA - \int_{A'} \frac{(M + dM)y}{I} \, dA + \tau(b \cdot dx) = 0$$

$$\int_{A'} \frac{My}{I} \, dA - \int_{A'} \frac{My}{I} \, dA - \int_{A'} \frac{(dM)y}{I} \, dA + \tau(b \cdot dx) = 0$$

The first two terms are identical and cancel each other. The third term calls for an integration over the area A'. Neither I nor dM varies as we integrate over the area A', so they may be factored out, giving:

$$\frac{-dM}{I} \int_{A'} y \, dA + \tau(b \cdot dx) = 0$$

Solving for τ, we get:

$$\tau = \frac{1}{Ib} \frac{dM}{dx} \int_{A'} y \, dA$$

From Eq. 14.3:

$$\frac{dM}{dx} = V$$

Thus:

$$\tau = \frac{V}{Ib} \int_{A'} y \, dA$$

We let:

$$Q = \int_{A'} y\, dA \qquad (17.1)$$

and then:

$$\tau = \frac{VQ}{Ib} \qquad (17.2)$$

Examining Eq. 17.1 and referring to Fig. 17.2b, we see that Q is the moment of area bounded by y_0 and c about the neutral axis. Equation 17.2 has the following terms:

τ The shear stress at y_0.

V The shear load at the cross section.

Q The moment of the *partial area* A' bounded by y_0 and c about the neutral axis.

I The moment of inertia of the entire cross-sectional area about the neutral axis.

b The thickness of the beam where the stress is being calculated, at y_0 in this case.

Since Q is the moment of area, Eq. 17.2 is often written as follows:

$$\tau = \frac{V(\bar{y}A')}{Ib} \qquad (17.3)$$

where A' is the partial area bounded by y_0 and c and $\bar{y}$ is the distance from the neutral axis to the centroid of the partial area A'.

The shear stress defined by Eq. 17.2 is longitudinal, although it is caused by a transverse shear load V. This can be reconciled by recalling that an element with shear stress on one face must have equal shear stress on all four faces, as shown in Fig. 17.3. Thus the shear load V produces transverse shear stresses resisting V and simultaneously produces longitudinal shear stress along the length of the beam.

It should be noted that although the development of Eq. 17.2 was based on a rectangular cross section, the results are not limited to that configuration. Of course substituting appropriate units for the variables will produce units for shear stress (in units of psi, Pa, etc.). We notice the shear stress varies directly with shear load: Double V and double τ. It varies inversely with the moment of inertia of the cross section and with the width b, where we are evaluating the stress. Last, it varies directly with Q, the moment of the partial area A' about the centroidal axis. As we shall see, the behavior of Q is a bit complicated.

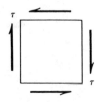

FIG. 17.3 Shear stress element.

Example Problem 17.1

For the beam shown in Fig. 17.1, which has a 2 in. × 8 in. (full size) cross section turned on edge, find the shear stress 2 in. below the top fiber and at the centroidal axis for the cross section 3 ft to the right of left-hand end.

Solution

From the shear diagram in Fig. 17.1, the shear is 4 kips, 3 ft to the right of the left-hand support:

$$V = 4 \text{ kips}$$

and I is the moment of inertia of the entire cross section about the neutral axis (Fig. 17.4):

$$I = \frac{bh^3}{12} = \frac{(2)(8)^3}{12} = 85.3 \text{ in.}^4$$

The width b, 2 in. below the top fiber, is also shown:

$$b = 2 \text{ in.}$$

and Q is the moment of area about the neutral axis of the area bounded by the extreme fiber and the fiber at which we are finding the shear stress. Thus from Fig. 17.4:

$$Q_2 = \bar{y}A' = 3(2 \times 2) = 12.0 \text{ in.}^3$$

Then by Eq. 17.2, the shear stress is:

$$\tau_2 = \frac{VQ}{Ib} = \frac{4 \text{ kips}(12.0 \text{ in.}^3)}{85.3 \text{ in.}^4(2 \text{ in.})} = \textbf{0.281 ksi}$$

At the centroidal axis only Q changes (Fig. 17.5):

$$Q_c = \bar{y}A' = 2(2 \times 4) = 16.0 \text{ in.}^3$$

$$\tau_c = \frac{4 \text{ kips}(16.0 \text{ in.}^3)}{85.3 \text{ in.}^4(2 \text{ in.})} = \textbf{0.375 ksi}$$

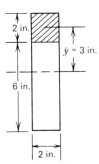

FIG. 17.4 Area A' bounded by extreme fiber and element 2 in. below it.

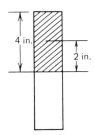

FIG. 17.5 Area A' bounded by extreme fiber and centroidal axis.

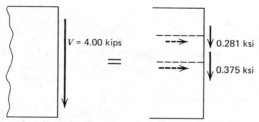

FIG. 17.6 Shear stress produced by shear load.

These shear stresses act transversely and down in agreement with the downward 4-kip shear load as shown in Fig. 17.6. They also act longitudinally, as indicated by the broken lines. Note that for this problem the shear stress at the centroid is greater than that 2 in. above it.

Example Problem 17.2

A W 10 × 60 beam carries a shear load of 30 kips. Find the shear stress just above and just below the web–flange junction and at the centroidal axis.

Solution

The cross section is shown in Fig. 17.7. Its properties are obtained from Table A-11. We wish to evaluate Eq. 17.2.

$$\tau = \frac{VQ}{Ib}$$

The V is given, and from Table A-11 we find:

$$I = 344 \text{ in.}^4$$

(We are assuming that the load is vertical in Fig. 17.7): V and I are always constant for the entire cross section, while Q and b depend on the particular point for which the equation is evaluated. The first point, just above the flange–web junction, is designated as A in Fig. 17.7. It is infinitesimally above

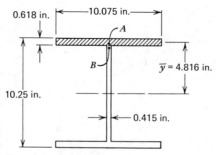

FIG. 17.7 Partial area bound by top fiber and A or B.

the junction, so that the partial area bounded by it and the top fiber (cross hatched in Fig. 17.7) is:

$$A' = 10.075(0.618) = 6.23 \text{ in.}^2$$

And the width b is the flange width:

$$b = 10.075 \text{ in.}$$

The moment of this area about the centroid is Q. The moment arm is the distance from the overall centroid to the centroid of this partial area:

$$\bar{y} = \frac{10.25}{2} - \frac{0.618}{2} = 4.816 \text{ in.}$$

Hence

$$Q = \bar{y}A' = 4.816(6.23) = 30.0 \text{ in.}^3$$

Then

$$\tau_A = \frac{VQ}{Ib} = \frac{30 \text{ kips}(30.0 \text{ in.}^3)}{344 \text{ in.}^4(10.075 \text{ in.})}$$

$$\tau_A = 0.260 \text{ ksi}$$

The second point, just below the web–flange junction, is designated B in Fig. 17.7. Since it is infinitesimally close to the junction, the area will remain the same (the cross-hatched area shown in Fig. 17.7). Neither A' nor $\bar{y}$ changes, hence the moment of area Q remains unchanged. The width becomes the web thickness, however. Thus:

$$\tau_B = \frac{VQ}{Ib} = \frac{30 \text{ kips}(30.0 \text{ in.}^3)}{344 \text{ in.}^4(0.415 \text{ in.})}$$

$$\tau_B = 6.30 \text{ ksi}$$

This reveals a step change in the shear stress τ due to the sudden reduction in the width b. In reality a small transition zone is required.

Last we find the shear stress at the centroid: V and I are constant for the cross section (any cross section); only Q and b are subject to change. At the centroid b is the web thickness. The partial area A' is bound by the top fiber and the centroid. This is shown as the cross-hatched area in Fig. 17.8, where it is broken into the flange area and the half-web area for the purpose of calculating the moment of area Q. Since we do not know where the centroid of this T-shaped area is, we break it in to the two rectangular areas shown. (Note that it is *not* necessary to find the centroid of this T shape.) Then the moment of area Q is found by:

$$Q = \bar{y}_1 A'_1 + \bar{y}_2 A'_2$$

The half-web height is found to be 4.507 in. Then:

$$\bar{y}_1 = \frac{4.507}{2} = 2.254 \text{ in.}$$

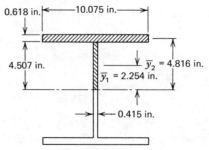

FIG. 17.8 Partial area bound by top fiber and centroid.

The values of $\bar{y}_2$ and A_2' are the same as $\bar{y}$ and A' in Fig. 17.7. Thus:

$$Q = 2.254[4.507(0.415)] + 4.816[10.075(0.618)]$$
$$Q = 34.2 \text{ in.}^3$$

and

$$\tau_c = \frac{VQ}{Ib} = \frac{30 \text{ kips}(34.2 \text{ in.}^3)}{344 \text{ in.}^4(0.415 \text{ in.})}$$

$$\tau_c = \textbf{7.19 ksi}$$

These three shear stresses will act transversely up or down in agreement with the shear load V. They will also act longitudinally. Note that once again the largest value was obtained at the centroid.

17.2 SHEAR STRESS DISTRIBUTION

In this section we examine Eq. 17.2 to determine how the shear stress varies over the cross section, where the maximum shear stress occurs and where zero values of shear stress occur. Again we examine a rectangular cross section, although the results may be extended in principle to other common shapes.

Figure 17.9 shows a rectangular cross section whose dimensions are b by h. We ask, What is the shear stress on an arbitrary fiber at a distance y from the centroidal axis? To answer the question, we evaluate Eq. 17.2 for this fiber:

$$\tau = \frac{VQ}{Ib} \tag{17.2}$$

Since V is the shear load on the section and I is the moment of inertia for the entire cross section, these will be constant for any position y. The width of the fiber under consideration is b. It would change with y for some cross sections, but for a rectangular one it is constant. Thus for this cross section V, I, and b are independent of y, leaving only Q, which is defined by:

$$Q = \int_{A'} y \, dA \tag{17.1}$$

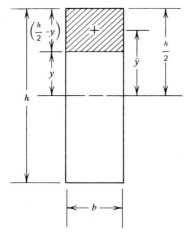

FIG. 17.9 Rectangular cross section.

This is simply the moment of the area bounded by y and $h/2$ about the centroidal axis. Hence:

$$Q = \int_{A'} y \, dA = \bar{y} A'$$

The distance from the overall centroidal axis to the centroid of this partial area is:

$$\bar{y} = \frac{1}{2}\left(\frac{h}{2} + y\right)$$

And the area of the shaded portion is its width times its height:

$$A' = b\left(\frac{h}{2} - y\right)$$

So

$$Q = \frac{1}{2}\left(\frac{h}{2} + y\right)(b)\left(\frac{h}{2} - y\right)$$

$$= \frac{b}{2}\left[\left(\frac{h}{2}\right)^2 - (y)^2\right]$$

Then

$$\tau = \frac{V}{Ib} \cdot \frac{b}{2}\left[\left(\frac{h}{2}\right)^2 - y^2\right]$$

We evaluate I for the entire rectangular cross section:

$$I = \frac{bh^3}{12}$$

$$\tau = \frac{V(12)}{bh^3} \cdot \frac{1}{2}\left[\left(\frac{h}{2}\right)^2 - y^2\right]$$

$$\tau = \frac{6V}{bh^3}\left[\left(\frac{h}{2}\right)^2 - y^2\right] \tag{17.4}$$

Equation 17.4 gives the shear stress for a rectangular cross section. It is of little use in and of itself. However, the conclusions to which it leads us are very important. For a given situation, V, b, and h are constant. Thus the only variable in the equation for the cross section under consideration is y, the distance from the centroidal axis to the element under consideration. Notice also that y is squared, and if we were to plot τ versus y we would get a second-degree curve, namely, a parabola. So we see that the shear stress distribution is parabolic. We could find the maximum shear stress by treating Eq. 17.4 as a classical maximum–minimum problem from the calculus—that is, set the derivative equal to zero, find the roots, and substitute them back into the original equation. It is simple enough, however, to find the maximum by inspection in Eq. 17.4. The distance y varies from 0 at the centroidal axis to $h/2$ at the extreme fiber. Equation 17.4 is maximum when y is 0, or at the centroidal axis. The location is more important than the value in the long run. The maximum value is found by substituting y equals 0 into the equation:

$$\tau_{max} = \frac{6V}{bh^3}\left[\left(\frac{h}{2}\right)^2 - (0)^2\right]$$

$$= \frac{6V}{bh^3}\left(\frac{h}{2}\right)^2$$

$$\tau_{max} = \frac{3}{2}\frac{V}{bh}$$

Note that bh is the area of the cross section, so:

$$\tau_{max} = \frac{3}{2}\frac{V}{A} \tag{17.5}$$

This result has been developed *for a rectangular area only*, but most shapes have the maximum shear stress at the centroidal axis.

We further observe that Eq. 17.4 yields zero when y equals $h/2$, that is, at the extreme fiber. We have, therefore, a shear stress distribution that is zero at the extreme fibers, maximum at the centroidal axis, and parabolic. This stress distribution is shown in Fig. 17.10. It acts vertically resisting the direct shear and horizontally as required for equilibrium of the element as shown in Fig. 17.3.

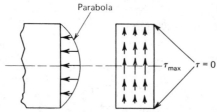

FIG. 17.10 Shear stress distribution for a rectangular cross section.

Example Problem 17.3

The cross section of a beam is shown in Fig. 17.11. Find the shear stress on the top surface and every 10 mm to the bottom surface. The shear load at the cross section is 12 kN.

Solution

We need to evaluate Eq. 17.2 for the locations A through G. We have the following fixed values:

$$V = 12 \text{ kN}$$
$$b = 30 \text{ mm}$$
$$I = \frac{bh^3}{12} = \frac{30 \text{ mm}(60 \text{ mm})^3}{12} = 5.40 \text{ E5 mm}^4$$

Since these are fixed, we need only evaluate Q at each location. First we seek the stress at level A; Q is the moment about the centroidal axis of the area bounded by A and the extreme fiber, which "ain't much." It is, in fact, zero. Thus:

$$\tau_A = \frac{VQ}{Ib} = \frac{12 \text{ kN}(0)}{5.40 \text{ E5 mm}^4(30 \text{ mm})} = 0$$

Next we seek the stress at level B; Q will be the moment about the centroidal axis of the area bounded by B and the extreme fiber, or the top rectangular area, as indicated in Fig. 17.12:

$$Q_B = \bar{y}A' = 25 \text{ mm}(10 \text{ mm})(30 \text{ mm})$$
$$Q_B = 7.50 \text{ E3 mm}^3$$

Then:

$$\tau_B = \frac{12 \text{ kN}(7.50 \text{ E3 mm}^3)}{5.40 \text{ E5 mm}^4(30 \text{ mm})} = 5.56 \frac{\text{N}}{\text{mm}^2} = \textbf{5.56 MPa}$$

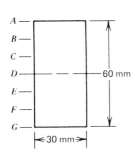

FIG. 17.11 Example Problem 17.3.

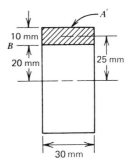

FIG. 17.12 Partial area above B.

Proceeding in this manner we get:

$$Q_C = \bar{y}A' = 20 \text{ mm}(20 \text{ mm})30 \text{ mm} = 1.20 \text{ } E4 \text{ mm}^3$$

$$\tau_C = \frac{12 \text{ kN}(1.20 \text{ } E4 \text{ mm}^3)}{5.40 \text{ } E5 \text{ mm}^4(30 \text{ mm})} = \textbf{8.89 MPa}$$

$$Q_D = 15 \text{ mm}(30 \text{ mm})(30 \text{ mm}) = 1.35 \text{ } E4 \text{ mm}^3$$

We save time by proportioning the previous answer:

$$\tau_D = \tau_C \frac{Q_D}{Q_C}$$

$$\tau_D = 8.89 \text{ MPa}\left(\frac{1.35}{1.20}\right) = \textbf{10.0 MPa}$$

We can move to point E proceeding as above and as shown in Fig. 17.13:

$$Q_E = 10 \text{ mm}(40 \text{ mm})(30 \text{ mm})$$
$$= 1.20 \text{ } E5 \text{ mm}^3$$

It might occur to someone to calculate Q for the area between E and the bottom extreme fiber, rather than the top. If it does, someone is being extremely perceptive and may move to the front of the class. Following someone's lead, we have:

$$Q_E = \bar{y}A' = 20 \text{ mm}(20 \text{ mm})(30 \text{ mm}) = 1.20 \text{ } E4 \text{ mm}^3$$

This is, of course, the same value as for point C before. This is because we are taking the moment of area about a centroidal axis. Technically the two moments are of opposite sign, which when added together yield zero, which is a property of centroids. The signs of the moments are of no consequence to us in calculating shear stress. Proceeding, we then get:

$$\tau_E = \textbf{8.89 MPa}$$

This is the same value we had for C and raises the question of symmetry. Symmetry does apply in this problem, and we also have by symmetry:

$$\tau_F = \tau_B = \textbf{5.56 MPa}$$
$$\tau_G = \tau_A = \textbf{0}$$

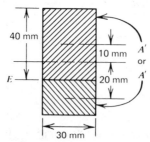

FIG. 17.13 Partial area above or below E.

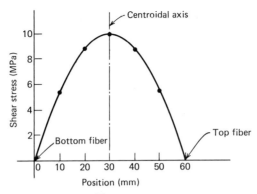

FIG. 17.14 Shear stress versus position.

These stresses are plotted against position across the cross section in Fig. 17.14. Note that the shear stress is zero at the extreme fibers and maximum at the centroidal axis as developed above. Also note the parabolic shape of the curve.

17.3 MAXIMUM SHEAR STRESS FOR COMMON CROSS SECTIONS

In Eq. 17.5 we found that for a rectangular cross section:

$$\tau_{max} = \frac{3}{2}\frac{V}{A} \tag{17.5}$$

In Chapter 11 we found the average shear stress to be

$$\tau_{AV} = \frac{V}{A} \tag{11.2}$$

Thus we see the actual shear stress varies from zero (at the surface) to maximum (at the centroidal axis) which is 50% greater than the average stress.

For a circular cross section we also find the shear stress to be zero at the extreme fiber and maximum at the neutral axis. Its development requires a straightforward (but messy) application of the calculus, yielding:

$$\tau_{max} = \frac{4}{3}\frac{V}{A} \tag{17.6}$$

For an I-beam (S or W shape) the maximum shear stress can be approximated by the equation:

$$\tau_{max} = \frac{V}{A_{web}} \tag{17.7}$$

Remember that the web is the vertical connecting center section in the figure in Tables A-10 and A-11. Since maximum stress usually governs design, Eqs. 17.5,

17.6, and 17.7 are frequently used for arriving at this value. These equations can be used only for the specific cross sections for which they were developed, however. For other cross sections or for stresses other than the maximum, Eq. 17.2 must be used.

17.4   SHEAR FLOW

Equation 17.2 gives the shear stress caused by a shear load. It has been indicated a number of times that this shear stress acts transversely and longitudinally. An additional useful concept called *shear flow* can be developed from the longitudinal shear stress:

$$\tau = \frac{VQ}{Ib} \qquad (17.2)$$

If we multiply by b, the width, we get:

$$\tau b = \frac{VQ}{I}$$

which is defined as the shear flow, using the symbol q:

$$q = \frac{VQ}{I} \qquad (17.8)$$

Dimensionally q is force per unit length. It can be thought of as the longitudinal shear load per unit length of beam. Define f and d as follows:

f = load per fastener

d = distance between fasteners

Alternately, we may say $1/d$ is the frequency of the fasteners (i.e., nails per foot, etc.) Then we can write:

$$f = q \cdot d \qquad (17.9)$$

This equation and its algebraic variations, along with Eq. 17.8, are useful in designing joints as illustrated below. The equation need not be memorized, since it may be obtained from logic or dimensional consistency.

Example Problem 17.4

A T section (Fig. 17.15) is made by nailing two 2 × 6s (full size) together as shown. The nails can carry an average shear load of 200 lb, $\bar{I} = 136$ in.^{4}, and $\bar{y} = 5$ in. For a vertical shear load of 120 lb, what is the maximum allowable spacing between the nails?

Solution

From Eq. 17.8:

$$q = \frac{VQ}{I}$$

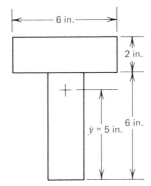

FIG. 17.15 Example Problem 17.4.

The nail will be in shear where the two boards come together; thus:

$$Q = \bar{y}A' = 2(2 \times 6) = 24 \text{ in.}^3$$

$$q = \frac{120 \text{ lb}(24 \text{ in.}^3)}{136 \text{ in.}^4} = 21.2 \text{ lb/in.}$$

This is the shear flow longitudinally, where the two boards come together. It means that as we move longitudinally along this joint, a longitudinal shear load is being accumulated at the rate of 21.2 lb/in. After 1 in. we have 21.2 lb to be resisted, after 2 in., 42.4 lb, and so forth. The nails that hold these two boards together must resist this shear load. If we have a nail every 1 in., it must resist a shear load of 21.2 lb; if every 2 in., 42.4 lb, and so forth. Thus we write:

$$\text{longitudinal shear load} = q \cdot d = f$$

where d is the distance between the nails. This is Eq. 17.9. Since our nails can carry 200 lb in shear, we have:

$$d = \frac{f}{q} = \frac{200 \text{ lb}}{21.2} \frac{\text{in.}}{\text{lb}}$$

$$d = 9.44 \text{ in.}$$

This is the maximum distance between nails for load per nail not to exceed 200 lb.

17.5 SUMMARY

The shear stress equation is:

$$\tau = \frac{VQ}{Ib}$$

where

$$Q = \int_{A'} y \, dA$$

and Q is the moment about the centroidal axis of the area bounded by an extreme fiber and the position at which shear stress is being determined.

This shear stress is zero at the extreme fibers and is usually maximum at the neutral axis. It acts transversely and longitudinally. For a rectangular cross section:

$$\tau_{max} = \frac{3V}{2A}$$

For circular:

$$\tau_{max} = \frac{4}{3}\frac{V}{A}$$

For an I beam the shear may be approximated by:

$$\tau_{max} = \frac{V}{A_{web}}$$

Shear flow:

$$q = \frac{VQ}{I}$$

The last expression is useful for spacing fasteners when making composite beams.

PROBLEMS

17.1 A rectangular 4 in. × 16 in. beam carries a shear load of 5 kips. Calculate the shear stress on the top and bottom surfaces and at 2-in. intervals across the cross section. Make a plot of stress versus position.

17.2 A rectangular 20 mm × 100 mm beam carries a shear load of 25 kN. Calculate the shear stress on the top and bottom surfaces and at 20 mm intervals across the cross section. Make a plot of stress versus position.

17.3 The cross section of Fig. 17.16 carries a 1000-lb shear load. Calculate the shear stress at:

(a) The bottom surface

(b) Just below 2.0 in. from the bottom (point A)

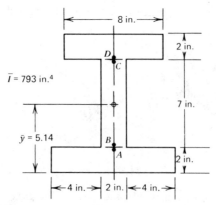

FIG. 17.16 Problem 17.3.

(c) Just above 2.0 in. from the bottom (point *B*)

(d) At the centroid

(e) Just below 9.0 in. from the bottom (point *C*)

(f) Just above 9.0 in. from the bottom (point *D*)

(g) At the top surface

Plot the stress distribution above.

17.4 A rectangular 100 mm × 400 mm beam carries a 4.0-MN shear load. Calculate the shear stress at 50-mm intervals from the centroidal axis to the extreme fiber. Make a plot of these stresses against their position across the cross section of the beam.

17.5 A rectangular 4 in. × 16 in. beam carries a 10,000-lb shear load. Calculate the shear stress at 1-in. intervals from the centroidal axis to the extreme fiber. Make a plot of these stresses against their position across the beam.

17.6 Using the cross section and load of Example Problem 17.4 (Fig. 17.15), calculate the shear stress on the top fiber and every inch to the bottom fiber. (Calculate for just above and just below the joint.) Make a plot of this stress distribution.

17.7 For Fig. 17.17, find the maximum shear and bending stresses in a section at point *B*.

17.8 For Fig. 17.17, find the maximum shear and bending stresses in the beam.

17.9 For Fig. 17.18, find the shear stress at the centroidal axis and 2 in. above it for a section at point *B*. Compare this with the maximum bending stress at *B*.

17.10 For Fig. 17.18, find the maximum shear and bending stress in the beam.

17.11 For Fig. 17.19, find the maximum shear and bending stresses in the W 8 × 40 beam.

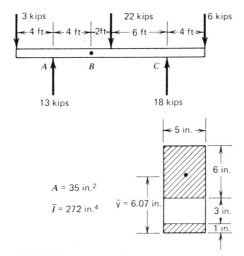

FIG. 17.17 Problems 17.7, 17.8.

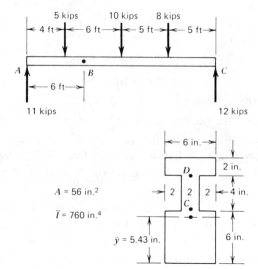

FIG. 17.18   Problems 17.9, 17.10, 17,20, 17.22.

17.12 Do Problem 17.11 if the cross section is:

(a)   4 × 12 timber (full size)

(b)   A 3-in.-diameter pipe (standard weight)

(c)   4 × 12 timber (finished S4S)

17.13 For Fig. 17.20, find the maximum shear stress in a section at point *A* and at any location in the W 12 × 36 beam.

17.14 For Fig. 17.21, find the maximum shear stress in a section at point *A* and at any location in the W 14 × 38 beam.

17.15 For Fig. 17.22, find the maximum shear stress in a section at point *A* and at any location in the W 16 × 50 beam.

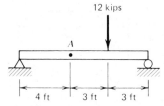

FIG. 17.19   Problems 17.11, 17.12.

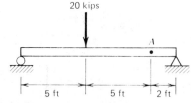

FIG. 17.20   Problem 17.13.

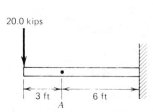

FIG. 17.21   Problems 17.14, 17.23.

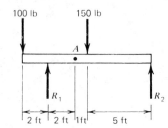

FIG. 17.22   Problem 17.15.

17.16 For the loading and cross section indicated find the maximum shear stress on a section at point A.

	Cross Section	Loading		Cross Section	Loading
(a)	Fig. 17.23	Fig. 17.27	(i)	Fig. 17.23	Fig. 17.29
(b)	Fig. 17.24	Fig. 17.27	(j)	Fig. 17.24	Fig. 17.29
(c)	Fig. 17.25	Fig. 17.27	(k)	Fig. 17.25	Fig. 17.29
(d)	Fig. 17.26	Fig. 17.27	(l)	Fig. 17.26	Fig. 17.29
(e)	Fig. 17.23	Fig. 17.28	(m)	Fig. 17.23	Fig. 17.30
(f)	Fig. 17.24	Fig. 17.28	(n)	Fig. 17.24	Fig. 17.30
(g)	Fig. 17.25	Fig. 17.28	(o)	Fig. 17.25	Fig. 17.30
(h)	Fig. 17.26	Fig. 17.28	(p)	Fig. 17.26	Fig. 17.30

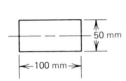

FIG. 17.23.

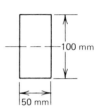

FIG. 17.24.

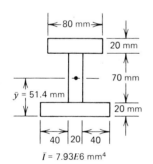

$\bar{y} = 51.4$ mm

$\bar{I} = 7.93E6$ mm^4

FIG. 17.25.

FIG. 17.26.

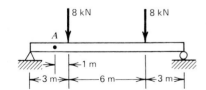

FIG. 17.27.

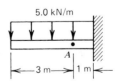

FIG. 17.28.

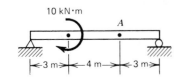

FIG. 17.29.

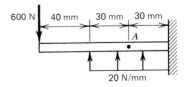

FIG. 17.30.

17.17 For the indicated loading and cross section find the maximum shear stress and maximum bending stress in the beam.

	Cross Section	Loading
(a)	Fig. 17.23	Fig. 17.27
(b)	Fig. 17.24	Fig. 17.27
(c)	Fig. 17.25	Fig. 17.27
(d)	Fig. 17.26	Fig. 17.27
(e)	Fig. 17.23	Fig. 17.28
(f)	Fig. 17.24	Fig. 17.28
(g)	Fig. 17.25	Fig. 17.28
(h)	Fig. 17.26	Fig. 17.28
(i)	Fig. 17.23	Fig. 17.29
(j)	Fig. 17.24	Fig. 17.29
(k)	Fig. 17.25	Fig. 17.29
(l)	Fig. 17.26	Fig. 17.29
(m)	Fig. 17.23	Fig. 17.30
(n)	Fig. 17.24	Fig. 17.30
(o)	Fig. 17.25	Fig. 17.30
(p)	Fig. 17.26	Fig. 17.30

17.18 For the indicated loading, select a beam with a square cross section based on a shear strength of 70 MPa and a factor of safety of 3.

(a) Fig. 17.27   (b) Fig. 17.28   (c) Fig. 17.29   (d) Fig. 17.30

17.19 The beam of Example Problem 17.3 is constructed by gluing three boards together, each having a 20 mm × 30 mm cross section.

(a) Find the shear flow at the two glued joints.

(b) If the boards are nailed together instead, and each nail can withstand 8-kN shear load, what is the minimum spacing of the nails?

17.20 Find the shear flow on a section at B in Fig. 17.18 where the top 2 × 6 joins the middle 2 × 4, point D.

17.21 Cross section of Fig. 17.25 has a shear load of 12 kN. Find the shear flow where the top and bottom flange boards join the web. Determine the minimum spacing on the top and bottom for screws that carry a shear load of 1200 N.

17.22 Find the shear flow on a section at B in Fig. 17.18 where the middle 2 × 4 joins the bottom 6 × 6, point C.

17.23 Find the shear flow where the web joins the flange for an S 7 × 20 beam carrying the load shown in Fig. 17.21.

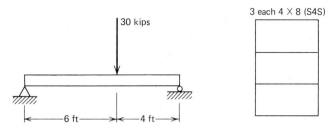

FIG. 17.31 Problem 17.26.

17.24 An I beam is to be made from plate steel to the dimensions of an S 15 × 50. It carries 20 kips. Using the flange and web dimensions of Table A-10, find the shear flow at the web–flange joint. The pieces are to be spot welded, and each spot weldment can resist 280 lb in shear. Find the spacing of these weldments.

17.25 An I beam is to be made from plate steel to the dimensions of a W 18 × 40. It carries 30 kips. Using the flange and web dimensions of Table A-11, find the shear flow at the web–flange joint. The pieces are to be spot welded, and each spot weldment can resist 350 lb in shear. Find the spacing of these weldments.

17.26 For the southern pine beam shown in Fig. 17.31:
  (a) Draw the shear and moment diagram.
  (b) Find the centroid and moment of inertia of the cross section.
  (c) Find the maximum bending stress.
  (d) Find the maximum shear stress.
  (e) Find the deflection of the beam at its center.
  (f) Find the shear flow where the 4 × 8s are joined.
  (g) Find the spacing for nails that can carry 800 lb in shear.
  (h) Identify any of the conditions above that would make this beam unsuitable.

17.27 For the southern pine beam shown in Fig. 17.32:
  (a) Draw the shear and moment diagram.
  (b) Find the centroid and moment of inertia of the cross section.

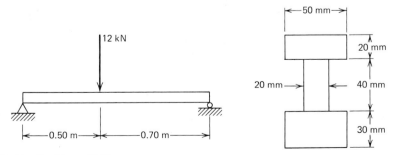

FIG. 17.32 Problem 17.27

(c) Find the maximum bending stress.

(d) Find the maximum shear stress.

(e) Find the deflection of the beam at its center.

(f) Find the shear flow where the members are joined.

(g) Find the spacing for nails which can carry 400 N in shear.

(h) Identify any of the conditions above that would make this beam unsuitable.

18

Putting It All Together: Compound Stress

Any loading in a member can be resolved into components of shear and axial load, moments of force that cause bending, and moments of force that cause twisting. In the preceding chapters we developed equations for the stresses produced by these loads. We have found those stresses as though they were the only ones present. In this chapter and the next we will examine the interaction of these stresses—a task requiring a firm understanding of the equations and the stress distributions described, and most of all an ability to visualize the stress patterns.

18.1 NORMAL STRESSES

Up to now we have learned to calculate and describe the stress distribution that results from a single cause, such as an axial load. But what if the load is not axial? (At this point you may want to examine the fine print on the guarantee that goes with this course.) In any case, it is necessary to examine the fine print that accompanied the stress equations that we have learned. For example, to return to the axial load, as shown in Fig. 18.1, if a load P acts on a straight member, along its longitudinal axis and through the centroid of its cross section, the resultant stress distribution will be as shown in Fig. 18.2. A small, infinitesimal element of area is shown as point B on the block in Fig. 18.2. The stresses acting at this point or *stress element* are shown in Fig. 18.3. The actual stresses are distributed as shown

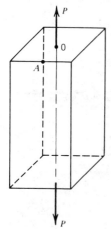

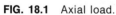

FIG. 18.1   Axial load.

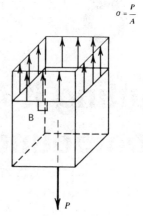

FIG. 18.2   Uniform stress distribution resulting from an axial load.

in Fig. 18.2, although we will show them schematically as single vectors. This element is as small as we would like, essentially $dx \times dy$. The maximum stress produced can be calculated from:

$$\sigma = \frac{P}{A} \tag{18.1}$$

As indicated in Chapter 11, four characteristics of this situation should be noted:

1. Condition of the load: axial.
2. Condition of the body: straight and homogeneous.
3. Stress equation: $\sigma = P/A$.
4. Stress distribution: uniform.

Our applications have emphasized point 3, and you may have gotten by with mechanically plugging into this stress equation. Bad news! "That ain't gonna work no more!" Successful application of the material in this chapter requires that you thoroughly appreciate all four points above for each stress equation developed

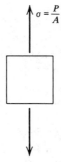

FIG. 18.3   Stresses on the stress element B due to an axial load.

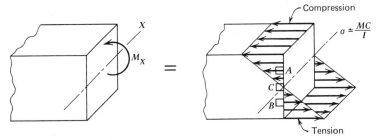

FIG. 18.4 Bending moment and resulting stress distribution.

thus far. We will postpone our query regarding a nonaxial load while we review these four points for our other normal stress.

The bending moment shown on the member in Fig. 18.4 produces the stress distribution represented. Stress elements A and B are shown in Figs. 18.5 and 18.6, respectively. The stress element at C, which is on the neutral axis, will be unstressed. The characteristics of the bending stress equation are:

1. Condition of the load: a bending moment about a centroidal or neutral axis of the cross section.
2. Condition of the body: straight, homogeneous, linearly elastic.
3. Stress equation:

$$\sigma = \frac{Mc}{I} \qquad (18.2)$$

4. Stress distribution: varies linearly with distance from the neutral axis, where it is zero; maximum tension on one surface and maximum compression on the opposite surface.

Note that the stresses described by Eqs. 18.1 and 18.2 are both normal; that is, they are perpendicular to the surface over which they act.

Suppose that instead of P acting through 0 as shown in Fig. 18.1, it acts through point A on the front surface. It no longer acts through the axis of the member and, therefore, is no longer an axial load. We very cleverly call it a *nonaxial load*. Since the load is not an axial load, condition 1 for Equation 18.1 is not satisfied; hence Equation 18.1 does not describe the stress produced by such loading. Equation 18.1 cannot be used directly!

Nonaxial loading (also called eccentric loading, meaning not at the center) is a common occurrence in real problems. In fact, pure axial loading is the ideal case and exists only in the heads of fuzzy-minded professors who write textbooks. A significant problem in materials testing is minimizing the degree of eccentricity

FIG. 18.5 Stress element A in compression.

FIG. 18.6 Stress element B in tension.

in the applied load. Eccentricity always exists to some degree, and you should become sensitive to it as a potential problem. Fortunately, it can be adequately dealt with in most situations, and it turns out the professor's fuzzy-minded ideal has very wide application.

18.2   NONAXIAL LOADS

The nonaxial load problem is solved by applying two principles that will be useful throughout the chapter. The first principle is one from statics. It is illustrated in Fig. 18.7, where a force acts parallel to the longitudinal axis but not along it. In Fig. 18.7b a section has been passed, a free body diagram drawn, and the internal force necessary for equilibrium found. This force does not act through the centroid of the section, and so Equation 18.1 does not apply. Figure 18.7c shows the same free body. This time, however, P is shown acting at 0. Now $\sum F = 0$ is satisfied, a necessary condition from Newton's first law. But $\sum M = 0$ is not satisfied. This is also a necessary condition; therefore, the free body, as shown (Fig. 18.7c), is not in equilibrium. If a moment $M_x = Pe$ is added as shown in Fig. 18.7d, the second

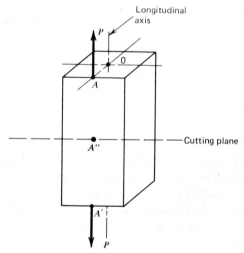

FIG. 18.7a   Nonaxial load.

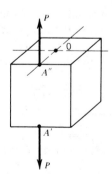

FIG. 18.7b   Equilibrium.

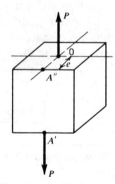

FIG. 18.7c   No equilibrium.

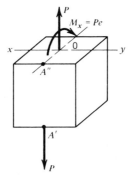

FIG. 18.7d Equilibrium (equivalent to 18.7b).

condition is also satisfied. So both Figs. 18.7b and 18.7d show free body diagrams that are in equilibrium. The two conditions are statically equivalent.

What advantage does the analysis in Fig. 18.7d have over that in Fig. 18.7b? In Fig. 18.7d the load P acts through the centroid. Condition 1 is satisfied, and we may apply Eq. 18.1. Furthermore, M_x is about a centroidal axis and satisfies condition 1 for Eq. 18.2; hence, it also may be applied. This leads us to our first rule, which is:

Rule 1.   Replace nonqualifying loads with statically equivalent loads that do satisfy condition 1.

We may alternately state the rule as follows:

Rule 1'.   When finding internal loads use components that satisfy condition 1.

To continue our discussion, loads have been found that satisfy condition 1. Therefore, the stress distribution and stress values from Eqs. 18.1 and 18.2 may be determined. This is illustrated for the axial load and the bending load in Figs. 18.8 and 18.9, respectively.

$$\sigma = \frac{P}{A} \tag{18.1}$$

$$\sigma = \frac{Mc}{I} \tag{18.2}$$

This gives us the stress distribution and values from each cause. Since the resultant applied load may be obtained by superimposing the bending load on

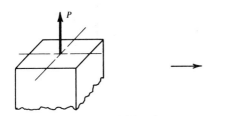
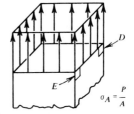

FIG. 18.8 Stress due to axial load.

FIG. 18.9   Stress due to bending moment.

the axial load, it follows that the resultant stress pattern may be obtained by superimposing the stress from the bending load on the stress from the axial load. Hence the bending load of Fig. 18.9 is superimposed on the axial load of Fig. 18.8, and the resultant stress is obtained by superimposing the bending stress on the axial stress as shown in Fig. 18.10. In this case the stresses may be added directly as though they were scalar quantities. This is because they are stresses of the same type, they have a common direction, and they act over the same area. In general, stresses cannot be combined in a scalar fashion or even as vectors. We will deal with that later. For the time being, note that *stresses may be added as though they were scalars when they are of the same type, have the same direction, and act over the same area.*

Thus our second rule as illustrated above is:

> **Rule 2.**   Find the stress distribution due to each load and superimpose them on each other. If the stresses are of the same type and direction acting over the same area, they may be added as scalars.

Figure 18.10 shows the overall stress field. If we wish to find the stress on a particular stress element, say point E, we may obtain it directly from the properties of this stress field. Alternatively, we could find the stress from each cause (axial load and bending) at point E and superimpose these as shown in Fig. 18.11. The resulting stress on the element at E is the same either way. A similar analysis for the stress element at point D is shown in Fig. 18.12. The resulting stress will be compressive when compression is the greater component.

Rules 1 and 2 are illustrated in Example Problem 18.1.

Example Problem 18.1

A 400-kip load is applied to the 2 in. × 6 in. cast iron machine support as shown in Fig. 18.13. Find the maximum tensile and compressive stresses. Sketch the stress elements, showing these stresses.

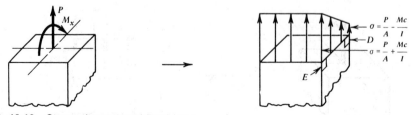

FIG. 18.10   Stress due to combined load.

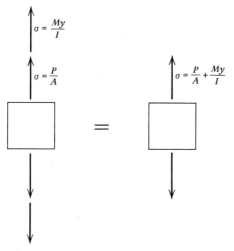

FIG. 18.11   Superimposing stresses on stress element *E*.

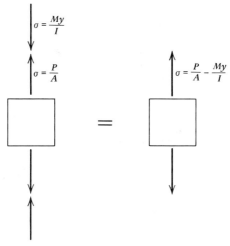

FIG. 18.12   Superimposing stresses on stress element *D*.

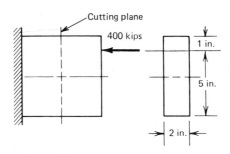

FIG. 18.13   Example Problem 18.1.

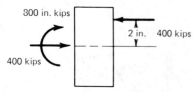

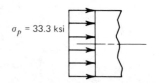

FIG. 18.14 Free body diagram for Example Problem 18.1.

FIG. 18.15 Stress due to axial load.

Solution

We seek a plane of maximum stress and, therefore, maximum loading. All vertical planes will see the same loading in this problem, so we arbitrarily select one and pass a cutting plane as indicated in Fig. 18.13.

We apply Rule 1 and find an equivalent load that satisfies the load conditions, namely, loads through and about the centroidal axis. Drawing the free body diagram (Fig. 18.14) and solving the statics, we get:

$$P = 400 \text{ kips}$$
$$M = Pe = 400 \text{ kips}(2 \text{ in.})$$
$$M = 800 \text{ in.-kips}$$

Next we find the stress distribution for each load and sketch the distribution. The stress due to axial load is (Fig. 18.15):

$$\sigma_P = \frac{P}{A} = \frac{400 \text{ kips}}{(6 \text{ in.})(2 \text{ in.})} = 33.3 \text{ ksi}$$

The maximum stress due to the bending load is (Fig. 18.16):

$$\sigma_M = \frac{Mc}{I} = \frac{800 \text{ in.-kips } (3 \text{ in.})(12)}{(2 \text{ in.})(6 \text{ in.}^3)} = 66.7 \text{ ksi}$$

The stress distributions are now imposed upon one another, resulting in the stress distribution shown in Fig. 18.17. The peak values are:

$$\sigma_A = -33.3 \text{ ksi} - 66.7 \text{ ksi} = -100 \text{ ksi compression}$$
$$\sigma_B = -33.3 \text{ ksi} + 66.7 \text{ ksi} = +33.3 \text{ ksi tension}$$

The stress elements A and B are taken directly from Fig. 18.17 and are shown in Fig. 18.18.

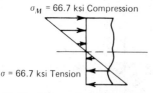

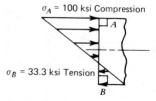

FIG. 18.16 Stress due to bending.

FIG. 18.17 Combined stress.

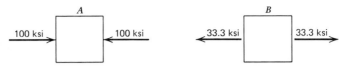

FIG. 18.18   Stress elements *A* and *B*.

18.3   A SPECIAL CASE: CONCRETE AND MASONRY STRUCTURES

Example Problem 18.1 indicates the danger of simply calculating the maximum stress by adding stresses. We illustrate this by asking the question, If this part were made of gray cast iron, could it carry this load? The largest stress found was 100 ksi in compression. Gray cast iron has a maximum compressive strength of 120 ksi, and based on this strength, the design appears safe. However, cast iron is much weaker in tension (as are most brittle materials), having an ultimate tensile strength of only 30 ksi. Hence, based on the tensile stress, the design is *unsafe*. This type of consideration must be given whenever the materials used have differing tensile and compressive properties.

Concrete and masonry structures present a special problem, in that without reinforcement, they can carry only very small tensile loads. Hence they must be designed so that no tensile stresses are produced. In Fig. 18.19 the shaded area shown is known as the *kern*. If a compressive load is applied within this area, the stress will be compressive everywhere. If a compressive load is applied outside this area, tension will be produced. For nonreinforced concrete or masonry structures the load must be applied within the kern.

Example Problem 18.2

From Example Problem 18.1 it is obvious that the 400-kip load is applied outside the kern, since a tensile stress of 33.3 ksi is produced on the lower surface. Find the location of *P* so that no tensile stress is produced—that is, find the upper boundary of the kern.

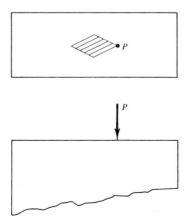

FIG. 18.19   Cross section showing the kern.

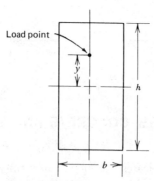

FIG. 18.20 Cross section for Example
Problem 18.2.

Solution

We assume that the force P acts at a distance y from the centroid (Fig. 18.20).
From the solution of Example Problem 18.1, the stress on the lower element
is the difference in the axial load stress and the bending stress, which should
be zero in the limiting case.

$$\sigma = -\frac{P}{A} + \frac{Mc}{I} = 0$$

Substituting general parameters of b and h for Fig. 18.20, we get:

$$\sigma = -\frac{P}{bh} + \frac{Py(12)h}{bh^3(2)} = 0$$

Dividing through by P/bh gives:

$$-1 + \frac{6y}{h} = 0$$

Solving for y gives:

$$y = \frac{h}{6}$$

This says when $y = h/6$ the stress on the bottom surface is zero. As we saw
in Example Problem 18.1, if the load is applied above this point, tension will
be produced. If the load is applied below this level, compressive stresses will be
produced on the bottom surface and everywhere else. This will be true as we
move down until $y = -h/6$. At this point the stress will be zero on the top
surface. As we move below, or outside the point, tension will be produced on
the top surface.

Thus if the load is applied on the middle third of the centerline, the stresses
will be compressive over the surface. If they are applied outside the middle
third, tensile stresses will be produced, and the structure will fail if it is un-
reinforced masonry. Because of this we very often find these structures with
steel reinforcing.

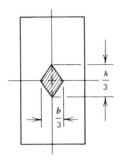

FIG. 18.21 Location of the kern.

If the same question were asked with regard to the X axis, a similar answer, that is, $x = b/6$, would be obtained. The four points obtained by moving $h/6$ from the center of the section in the y direction and $b/6$ in the x direction constitute boundary points of the kern (Fig. 18.21). Thus the old rule of thumb that the load should be in the middle third of the structure is supported by the theory. It should also be noted that the solution obtained is perfectly general for rectangular cross sections.

We could have solved Example Problem 18.2 numerically by moving the load toward the center a step at a time until the stresses were all compressive, then perhaps backing up until we had found the exact point where the stress on the lower boundary was zero. We avoided this tedious trial-and-error process by generalizing the problem and applying one of the mathematical tools at our disposal—namely, algebra. In doing so we solved not only the problem at hand, but an entire class of problems. We have found the kern for any rectangular cross section. This is another instance in which a general mathematical approach is a superior approach. This will not always be the case, but when it is, it should not be avoided.

18.4 LOADS NOT PARALLEL TO THE AXIS

Another important type of loading is shown in Fig. 18.22. In this situation the loading is not only not centric, but it also is not parallel to the axis of the member. In Fig. 18.23, we have replaced the inclined load P with vertical P_y and horizontal P_x, components that are statically equivalent to P. In a second step we transfer these components from point Q to point O, as shown in Fig. 18.24. As P_x is moved

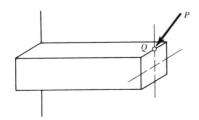

FIG. 18.22 Nonparallel loads.

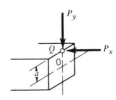

FIG. 18.23 Components.

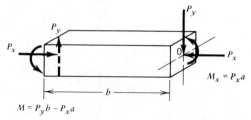

$$M_x = P_x a$$

$$M = P_y b - P_x a$$

FIG. 18.24 Equivalent loads in a free body diagram.

from Q to O it must be accompanied by the moment $M_x = P_x a$ to maintain static equivalency. No moment is developed in the transfer of P_y, since it is transferred along its line of action.

We have applied Rule 1, and all the loads developed at this section satisfy the conditions of previously developed stress equations. Therefore, we can calculate the stresses and determine the stress distribution from each load according to Rule 2. If this were a critical section—one that would likely govern the design—we would do just that. In this loading the supported left-hand end appears more likely to be the critical section. The loads at this section can be found by constructing a free body diagram of the beam and computing the reaction.

When this is done we find the shear and axial loads are of the same magnitude as they were, respectively, on the right-hand end of the beam. The bending moment has changed by the component developed by P_y, the shear load. Since the shear and axial loads are constant, the bending moment will determine the critical section. A bending moment diagram can aid in the determination of the critical section.

The stresses due to each load and their distributions may now be determined, as shown in Fig. 18.25. (The shear stress equation is reviewed in the next section.) The normal stresses due to the axial and bending loads can be combined by super-position, and the critical value is found by scalar addition, since we have the same type of stresses (normal) acting on a common area. The shear stress distribution may also be superimposed with the two normal stress distributions. However, its

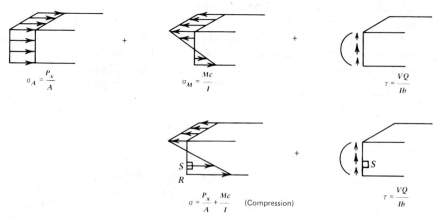

FIG. 18.25 Superposition of stresses.

combining effect cannot be determined by simple algebraic addition or even vector addition. The combination of normal and shear stresses is a very complex subject. Notice that the maximum normal stress occurs at the lower surface point. The shear stress is zero at this location. (Once more, knowing stress distribution is as important as knowing the maximum stress.) Therefore, the shear stress does not affect the maximum stress at this critical surface, and we can postpone the combination of shear and normal stresses until a later chapter.

To recap, we have found loads at a critical section meeting the requirements of relevant stress equations. We have calculated stresses and their distributions from those loads and superimposed them. We have found that the maximum normal stress was the algebraic summation of the normal stresses from the axial and bending loads. The shear stress at this extreme surface is zero and, therefore, will not affect the design. It is possible to have the dimensions such that the stress at point R, Fig. 18.25, does not govern the design; in such cases the shear stress at other locations plays an important role and the method developed in the next chapter is required. Usually, if the beam is long and slender, that is, if b (Fig. 18.24) is much greater than a (Fig. 18.23), the normal stresses govern the design.

A stress element at S (Fig. 18.25) will have compressive normal stress and a shear stress as shown in Fig. 18.26. The sense of the shear stress will agree with the sense of the shear load P_y.

Example Problem 18.3

A 20-kip load is applied to the edge of a 2 in. × 1 in. column as shown in Fig. 18.27. Find the maximum normal stress and sketch the stress distribution at the base.

Solution

Replace P with its components at A.

$$P_x = P \cos 45° = 20 \cos 45° = 14.14 \text{ kips}$$
$$P_y = P \sin 45° = 20 \sin 45° = 14.14 \text{ kips}$$

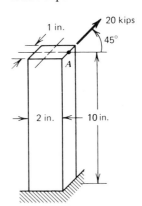

FIG. 18.27   Example Problem 18.3.

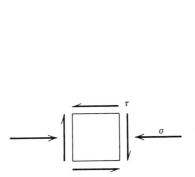

FIG. 18.26   Stress element S showing normal and shear stresses.

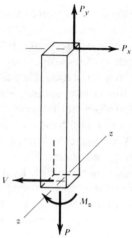

FIG. 18.28 Free body diagram for Example
Problem 18.3.

Complete a free body diagram (Fig. 18.28), passing a cutting plane through
the support.

$$\sum F_x = 0, \; V = P_x = \textbf{14.1 kips}$$
$$\sum F_y = 0, \; P = P_y = \textbf{14.1 kips}$$
$$\sum M_z = 0 = +P_y(1) - P_x(10) - M_z$$
$$M_z = -10P_x + 1P_y$$
$$= -10 \text{ in.}(14.14) + 1 \text{ in.}(14.14)$$
$$M_z = -\textbf{127 in.-kips}$$

Find the stress and stress distribution due to each load. The stress due to the
axial load is:

$$\sigma_P = \frac{P}{A} = \frac{14.14 \text{ kips}}{(2 \text{ in.})(1 \text{ in.})} = 7.07 \text{ ksi}$$

with the stress distribution of Fig. 18.29. The stress due to bending is:

$$\sigma_M = \frac{Mc}{I} = \frac{(127.3 \text{ in.-kips})(1 \text{ in.})(12)}{(1 \text{ in.})(2 \text{ in.})^3}$$

$$\sigma_M = 190.9 \text{ ksi}$$

with the stress distribution of Fig. 18.30.

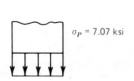

FIG. 18.29 Stress due to axial load.

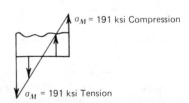

FIG. 18.30 Stress due to bending.

The stress due to the shear load V is not calculated, since it is zero where the normal stresses are maximum.

Superimpose the stress distributions and compute the maximum stress:

$$\sigma_{\max} = \sigma_P + \sigma_M$$
$$\sigma_{\max} = 7.07 + 190.9 = \textbf{198 ksi } T$$
$$\sigma = \sigma_P - \sigma_M$$
$$\sigma = 7.07 - 190.9 = \textbf{184 ksi } C$$

The resulting stress distribution is shown in Fig. 18.31.

18.5 SUPERPOSITION OF SHEARING STRESSES

The student will be relieved to know that shear stresses are handled in exactly the same manner as normal stresses—that is, observing Rules 1 and 2, which we review here.

Rule 1. Find load components that satisfy the conditions imposed by the stress equations (i.e., along or about a centroidal axis).

Rule 2. Find the stress magnitude and the distribution due to each load and superimpose them on the same cross section. If the stresses are of the same type acting over the same area, they may be added as scalars.

We also review the four characteristics of the two shear stress equations developed previously. From Chapter 17, we have for direct shear:

1. Condition of the load: through the centroid and perpendicular to the neutral plane (Fig. 18.32).
2. Condition of the body: straight, homogeneous, and linearly elastic.
3. Stress equation:

$$\tau = \frac{V}{It} \int y\, dA \qquad (18.3)$$

$$\tau_{\max} = \frac{3}{2}\frac{V}{A} \qquad \text{for rectangular cross sections} \qquad (18.4)$$

$$\tau_{\max} = \frac{4}{3}\frac{V}{A} \qquad \text{for circular cross sections} \qquad (18.5)$$

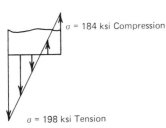

$\sigma = 184$ ksi Compression

$\sigma = 198$ ksi Tension

FIG. 18.31 Combined stress.

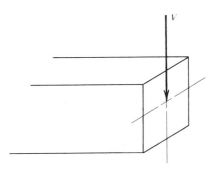

FIG. 18.32 Shear load.

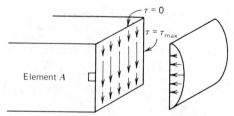

FIG. 18.33 Shear stress distribution.

4. Stress distribution: varies depending on the shape of the cross section but generally is second degree. The maximum value usually occurs at the centroid. Free surfaces have zero shear stress. The distribution shown in Fig. 18.33 is for rectangular cross sections only. Also, note that the shear described by the relation is simultaneously acting on the face of the cross section and longitudinally as shown on element A in Fig. 18.34.

From Chapter 13 we have the conditions for shear stress from torsional loading as follows and as shown in Figs. 18.35 through 18.37.

1. Condition of load: a moment of force (torque) about the longitudinal axis (Fig. 18.35).
2. Condition of the body: straight, circular cross section, homogeneous, and linearly elastic.
3. Stress equation:

$$\tau = \frac{Tc}{J} \tag{18.6}$$

4. Stress distribution: linear from zero at the center to a maximum value on the surface (Fig. 18.36). As with the shear stress from a direct shear load, the shear stress also acts longitudinally as well as on the face of the cross section as shown by the stress element A in Fig. 18.37.

Consider the everyday problem of tightening a bolt with a socket wrench, shown schematically in Fig. 18.38. A force P is applied at the end of the wrench. What stress does this action produce in the extension rod at a section through point A? We solve this problem, as previously, by applying the two rules we have

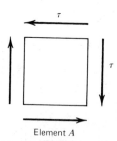

FIG. 18.34 Shear stress on element.

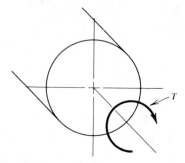

FIG. 18.35 Torsional load.

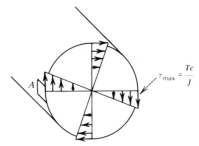

FIG. 18.36   Shear stress distribution.

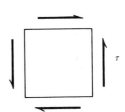

FIG. 18.37   Shear stress on element
A.

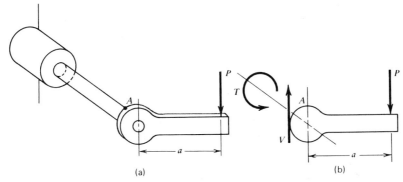

(a)

(b)

FIG. 18.38a–b   Socket wrench.

developed. By drawing a free body diagram of the handle with a section passed through point A we find the reactions according to Rule 1, Fig. 18.38b:

$$\sum F_y = 0: V = P \qquad \text{shear load}$$
$$\sum M = 0: T = Pa \qquad \text{torque}$$

For clarity in visualizing the sense of the stress produced, we show the matching piece at point A in Fig. 18.39a. According to Newton's third law, these forces are equal to and opposite those found in Fig. 18.38b. Applying rule 2 for the shear load V we get:

$$\tau_V = \frac{4}{3}\frac{V}{A}$$

and the distribution shown in Fig. 18.39b. For the torque T we get:

$$\tau_T = \frac{Tc}{J}$$

with the distribution shown in Fig. 18.39c. Then by the method of superposition:

$$\tau_{max} = \tau_V + \tau_T = \frac{4}{3}\frac{V}{A} + \frac{Tc}{J}$$

This maximum stress will occur on the right-hand side of the shaft as shown in Fig. 18.39d. The stress on the left will be $\tau_V - \tau_T$. Stresses can be obtained by

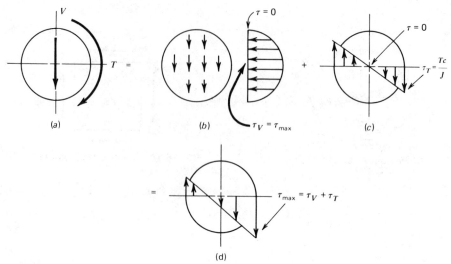

FIG. 18.39a–d Stresses in extension rod.

simple algebraic addition only along this axis and at the top and bottom elements. Fortunately that includes the maximum and minimum values.

Example Problem 18.4

A 3-in.-diameter gear transmits 5 hp to a short 1-in.-diameter shaft at 300 rpm. Find the maximum shear stress in the shaft.

Solution

The transmitted load is shown schematically in Fig. 18.40 and is found as follows:

$$P = T\omega$$

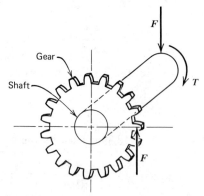

FIG. 18.40 Example Problem 18.4.

from which we solve for the torque T:

$$T = \frac{P}{\omega} = \frac{5 \text{ hp } 550 \text{ ft-lb}}{\text{s hp}} \left(\frac{\text{min}}{300 \text{ rev}}\right) \left(\frac{1 \text{ rev}}{2\pi \text{ rad}}\right) \left(\frac{60 \text{ s}}{\text{min}}\right) \left(\frac{12 \text{ in.}}{\text{ft}}\right)$$

$$= \frac{5(550)(60)(12)}{300(2\pi)} \text{ in.-lb} = \textbf{1050 in.-lb} = \textbf{\textit{T}}$$

Next we find the transmitted load F, which equals the shear load.

$$T = Fr$$

$$F = \frac{T}{r} = \frac{1050}{1.5} = \textbf{700 lb} = \textbf{\textit{F}}$$

In Fig. 18.40 the free body diagram is completed so that the reacting shear load is F and the reacting moment is T. The force and torque are shown with opposite senses on the matching section of the shaft in Fig. 18.41. This will make it easier to visualize the stresses. These loads satisfy the restrictions of the stress equations (18.5 and 18.6), so those stresses may now be calculated.

Applying Eq. 18.5 results in the stress distribution shown in Fig. 18.42 and a maximum shear stress of:

$$\tau_V = \frac{4}{3}\frac{V}{A} = \frac{4}{3}\frac{(700.3)(4)}{\pi(1)^2}$$

$$\tau_V = 1189 \text{ psi}$$

Applying Eq. 18.6 results in the stress distribution shown in Fig. 18.43, and the maximum stress is:

$$\tau_T = \frac{Tc}{J} = \frac{T\dfrac{d}{2}}{\dfrac{\pi d^4}{32}} = \frac{16T}{\pi d^3}$$

$$= \frac{16(1050)}{\pi(1)^3} = 5350 \text{ psi}$$

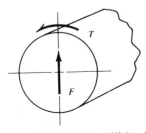

FIG. 18.41 Equivalent qualifying loads.

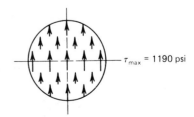

FIG. 18.42 Stress due to shear load.

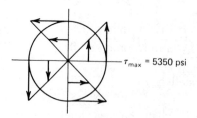

τ_{max} = 5350 psi

FIG. 18.43   Stress due to torque.

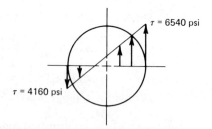

τ = 6540 psi

τ = 4160 psi

FIG. 18.44   Combined stress.

Superimposing these results gives:

$$\tau = \tau_V + \tau_T = 1189 + 5350$$
$$\tau_{max} = 6539$$
$$\boldsymbol{\tau_{max} = 6540 \text{ psi}}$$

The stress distribution along the midline is shown in Fig. 18.44, with the maximum shear stress occurring at the right-hand surface.

Example Problem 18.5

An 8-mm shaft is rigidly attached to a pinion gear. Figure 18.45 shows one tooth of the gear on the shaft. The tangential component of the load may be treated as acting at a radius of 30 mm. Find the maximum shear stress in the shaft due to the 500-N load and sketch the stress element A.

Solution

We find values of V and T by applying Newton's first law for Fig. 18.45.

$$V = \mathbf{500 \ N} \rightarrow$$
$$T = 500 \text{ N} (30 \text{ mm})$$
$$T = 15,000 \text{ N} \cdot \text{mm} = \mathbf{15.0 \ N \cdot m}$$

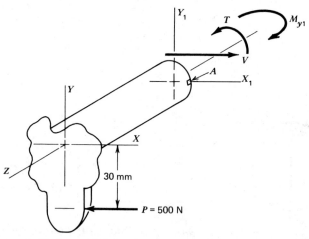

FIG. 18.45   Example Problem 18.5.

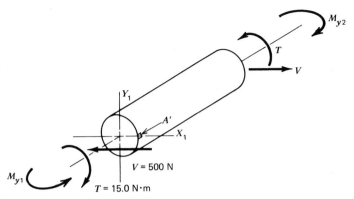

FIG. 18.46 Matching section.

(A bending moment M_{y1} would also occur at this section. We will ignore it for the present.) For convenience in visualization a facing section is shown in Fig. 18.46. We now calculate the stresses produced by each component of load. For the shear load V:

$$\tau_V = \frac{4}{3}\frac{V}{A} = \frac{4}{3}\frac{500 \text{ N}(4)}{\pi(0.008 \text{ m})^2}$$

$$\tau_V = \textbf{13.3 MPa}$$

This stress distribution is sketched in Fig. 18.47. For the torque T:

$$\tau_T = \frac{Tc}{J} = \frac{15.0 \text{ N}\cdot\text{m}(0.004 \text{ m})(32)}{\pi(0.008 \text{ m})^4}$$

$$\tau_T = \textbf{149 MPa}$$

as shown in Fig. 18.48. These are superimposed to give:

$$\tau_{\text{top}} = 149 - 13.3 = \textbf{136 MPa}$$
$$\tau_{\text{bottom}} = 149 + 13.3 = \textbf{162 MPa}$$

which is the maximum shear stress, as shown in Fig. 18.49.

Finding the bending stress on element A requires finding the moment M_{y1} in Fig. 18.45. Summing moments about the Y_1 axis gives:

$$M_{y1} = P \cdot d$$

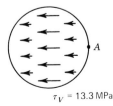

$\tau_V = 13.3 \text{ MPa}$

FIG. 18.47 Stress due to shear load.

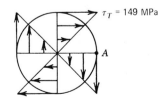

$\tau_T = 149 \text{ MPa}$

FIG. 18.48 Stress due to torque.

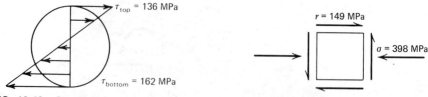

FIG. 18.49   Combined stress.   FIG. 18.50   Stress element A.

where d is the length of this section of shaft. This moment appears in the opposite sense in Fig. 18.46, where A', the matching element is shown. Since A represents a point, A and A' may be thought of as the same element. This moment produces compression at A and tension on the opposite side of the shaft from A. The Y_1 axis is the neutral axis. The compressive stress on A is found from:

$$\sigma = \frac{Mc}{I}$$

If the shaft is 40 mm long, the moment is 20 N·m; and the normal stress is 398 MPa. A different length, of course, gives a different moment and stress. The stress due to V at A is zero; due to T, it is 149 MPa. Superimposing these three gives the stress element in Fig. 18.50. The combination of these stresses is the subject of the next chapter.

18.6   COILED SPRINGS

Closely coiled helical springs are widely used for absorbing and storing energy. Many automobiles use a coiled spring suspension, especially for the front end. If you are taking notes with a ballpoint pen with a retractable point, chances are it contains a coil spring. Coil springs come in many sizes and are made of several materials. While many, perhaps most, are "off the shelf," custom-made coiled springs are also common. Thus the coiled spring represents a direct application of combining shear stresses.

The wire of the closely coiled helical spring in Fig. 18.51 is circular in cross section. Rectangular cross sections are also common but are not analyzed here. A vertical section is passed through one turn of the coil, resulting in the free body diagram shown in Fig. 18.52. Keeping Rule 1 in mind, we sum forces:

$$\sum F_y = 0: V = F$$

$$\sum M = 0: T = \frac{FD}{2}$$

The next step is to apply Rule 2. At this point we are going to assume something we know to be false! Namely, we assume that the shear stress due to the direct shear load V is uniform and may be calculated by:

$$\tau_v = \frac{V}{A} = \frac{4F}{\pi d^2} \tag{18.7}$$

This is illustrated in Fig. 18.53.

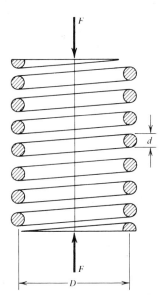

FIG. 18.51 Coiled spring.

We know from our previous analysis that $\tau_{v_{\max}} = \frac{4}{3}V/A$ and that the distribution is not uniform. So why do we assume a value known to be 33% low? Well, for several reasons. First, it is customary. An unpleasant fact of life is that we must interact with the world as it is, not as we think it should be. For years, I guess literally centuries, we have put up with the clumsy English units system. In this age of enlightenment we are rapidly moving to a metric system, more precisely, the SI. No matter how convinced we may be of the SI's superiority, we in America will continue to interact with the English system for some time. And today's student must be conversant in both. So, we do many things because they are customary. That doesn't mean we don't work for change when it's needed (we are changing to the SI). Although, in general, I have observed that things became customary because that was a good way to operate.

FIG. 18.52 Free body diagram.

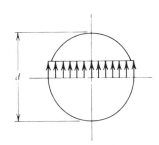

FIG. 18.53 "Uniform" stress due to shear load.

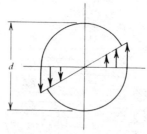

FIG. 18.54 Linearly distributed stress due to torque.

A second reason for making assumptions we know to be incorrect is to simplify the problem. In the engineering world we should always use the simplest analysis that produces an acceptable result. This leads to a consideration of the effect of the simplification. If a more rigorous analysis does not lead to significantly different results in the final answer, the rigor is not justified. Meanwhile back at the spring . . . .

Following our patently false assumption, we make a more accurate assumption concerning the shear stress due to the torque:

$$\tau = \frac{Tc}{J} = \frac{\left(\dfrac{FD}{2}\right)\left(\dfrac{d}{2}\right)}{\dfrac{\pi d^4}{32}} = \frac{8FD}{\pi d^3} \tag{18.8}$$

This stress distribution is illustrated in Fig. 18.54. Superimposing the stress of Eq. 18.7 on that of 18.6 gives a maximum stress of:

$$\tau = \frac{4F}{\pi d^2} + \frac{8FD}{\pi d^3}$$

$$\tau = \frac{8FD}{\pi d^3}\left(\frac{d}{2D} + 1\right) \tag{18.9}$$

as shown in Fig. 18.55. Note that if the wire size (d) is small compared to the spring diameter (D), then $d/2D$ is considerably smaller than 1.0 and the direct shear does not have a large effect. Hence we see that our simplifying assumption does not produce significant error in many cases.

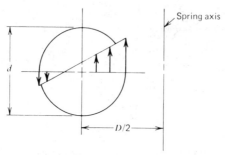

FIG. 18.55 Theoretical resultant stress.

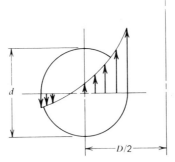

FIG. 18.56   Actual resultant stress.

We can simplify Eq. 18.9 by letting K represent $(d/2D) + 1$. This yields:

$$\tau_{max} = K\left(\frac{8FD}{\pi d^3}\right) \qquad (18.10)$$

The parentheses in Eq. 18.10 contain the stress due to torsion. Hence at this point the K factor modifies the torsional stress to include the effect of direct shear. Because of the curvature of the spring winding, there will be a further concentration of stress on the inside edge. This more accurate stress distribution is shown in Fig. 18.56. We now allow K to include this effect as well, so that we can calculate the maximum stress as the factor K times the stress due to simple torsion. In this form K is known as the Wahl correction factor. Figure 18.57 plots K versus (D/d), which is known as the spring index. These values of K come from a solution of the problem using the theory of elasticity—an advanced topic in mechanics.

For small spring indices—springs with a high relative curvature—the stress concentration is high. For larger spring indices it is only slightly greater than 1.

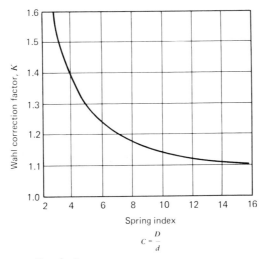

FIG. 18.57   Wahl correction factor.

Springs are highly stressed compared to other steel parts. Typical ultimate strengths of common steels are from 50 to 150 ksi. Spring steels have strengths up to 300 ksi.

Example Problem 18.6

A coil spring is made of 5-mm wire turned on a 40-mm diameter. Find the theoretical and the actual stress in this spring due to a 500-N load.

Solution

The theoretical load is found by evaluating Eq. 18.9:

$$\tau = \frac{8FD}{\pi d^3}\left(\frac{d}{2D} + 1\right) = \frac{8(500 \text{ N})(0.040 \text{ m})}{\pi (0.005 \text{ m})^3}\left(\frac{0.005 \text{ m}}{2(0.040 \text{ m})} + 1\right)$$

$$\tau = 407 \ E6(0.0625 + 1) = \textbf{433 MPa}$$

To calculate the actual stress, we need to find the spring index and use Eq. 18.10:

$$C = \frac{D}{d} = \frac{40 \text{ mm}}{5 \text{ mm}} = \textbf{8.00}$$

From Fig. 18.57 we read:

$$K = 1.17$$

and

$$\tau = K\left(\frac{8FD}{\pi d^3}\right) = 1.17(407 \ E6) = \textbf{477 MPa}$$

Thus we see the actual stress is 44 MPa, or about 10% greater than the theoretical stress. This higher value has two sources. First, we assumed average stress due to direct shear, but this value turned out to be higher. Second, we neglected stress concentrations.

18.7 SUMMARY

All the stress equations are summarized in the following four relations.
Normal stresses:

$$\sigma = \frac{P}{A}$$

$$\sigma = \frac{Mc}{I}$$

Shear stresses:

$$\tau = \frac{Tc}{J}$$

$$\tau = \frac{VQ}{Ib}$$

We also have the average shear stress equation, which is frequently used.

$$\tau_{AV} = \frac{V}{A}$$

By now these basic stress equations need to be thoroughly ingrained. If they are not, work at reproducing them on a blank sheet of paper until they are. Include the load causing the stress, where it must act , and the resulting stress distribution on this paper.

Rule 1.   Resolve loads into components that satisfy these equations at the cross section of interest.

Rule 2.   Find the stresses and their distributions. Then superimpose stress distributions to get resultant stress distributions. Stresses of the same type that are in the same direction and act over the same area may be added as scalars. Others cannot.

Coiled spring:

$$\tau_{max} = K\left(\frac{8FD}{\pi d^3}\right)$$

PROBLEMS

18.1   Find the stress at the top and bottom fibers for the cross section in Fig. 18.58 for the given load at the indicated point. Compressive loads are into the paper, perpendicular to the cross section.

(a)   A 12-kN compressive load at point A

(b)   A 20-kN tensile load at point B

18.2   Find the stress on the extreme left- and right-hand fibers for the cross section in Fig. 18.58 when a 15-kN compressive force (into the paper) is applied at C.

18.3   Find the stress at the top and bottom fibers for the cross section in Fig. 18.59 for the given load at the indicated point. Compressive loads are into the paper, perpendicular to the cross section.

(a)   A 30-kip compressive load at A

(b)   A 20-kip tensile load at B

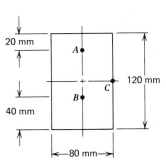

FIG. 18.58   Problems 18.1, 18.2, 18.5.

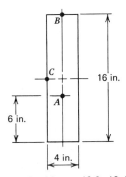

FIG. 18.59   Problems 18.3, 18.4, 18.6.

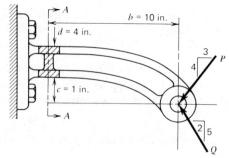

FIG. 18.60   Problems 18.7, 18.8, 18.9.

18.4   Find the stress on the extreme left- and right-hand fibers for the cross section in Fig. 18.59 when a 40-kip tensile load (out of the paper) is applied at point C.

18.5   Determine the kern for the cross section in Fig. 18.58. Will a tensile stress be produced by a compressive load applied at point A, B, or C?

18.6   Determine the kern for the cross section in Fig. 18.59. Will a tensile stress be produced by a compressive load acting at A, B, or C?

18.7   The bracket shown in Fig. 18.60 subjected to $P = 1000$ lb, $Q = 0$. Calculate the stresses at the top and bottom of the bracket at section A–A; $I = 10$ in.^{4}, $A = 8$ in.^{2}.

18.8   The bracket shown in Fig. 18.60 is subjected to $P = 0$, $Q = 500$ lb. Calculate the stress at the bottom of the bracket at section A–A; $I = 8$ in.^{4}, $A = 6$ in.^{2}.

18.9   The bracket shown in Fig. 18.60 has the following loads: $P = 1000$ lb, $Q = 500$ lb. Calculate the stresses at the top and bottom of section A–A; $I = 10$ in.^{4}, $A = 8$ in.^{2}. Sketch this stress distribution.

18.10   Find the stress at point A in Fig. 18.61.

18.11   Find the stress at point B in Fig. 18.61.

18.12   Sketch the stress distribution at the support and locate the fiber with zero stress for Fig. 18.61.

18.13   Find the stress at point A in Fig. 18.62.

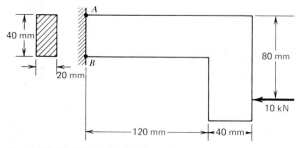

FIG. 18.61   Problems 18.10, 18.11, 18.12.

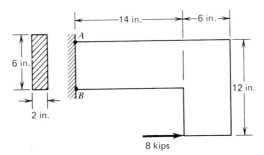

FIG. 18.62   Problems 18.13, 18.14, 18.15.

18.14 Find the stress at point B in Fig. 18.62.

18.15 Sketch the stress distribution at the support and locate the fiber with zero stress for Fig. 18.62.

18.16 For Fig. 18.63, determine the maximum stress produced in the 3-in.-diameter member when the tension in the rope is 500 lb and $\theta = 50°$.

18.17 In Problem 18.16 let θ vary from 0 to 90° in 30° steps. What is the maximum stress produced and what value of θ corresponds to it? Explain why.

18.18 For Fig. 18.64, determine the maximum stress produced in the 50-mm-diameter member when the tension in the rope is 1200 N and $\theta = 40°$.

18.19 In Problem 18.18, let θ vary from 0 to 90° in 30° steps. What is the maximum stress produced and what value of θ corresponds to it? Explain why.

18.20 Find the stress at point A on the 1 in. × 8 in. (actual size) cross section loaded as shown in Fig. 18.65. Also sketch the stress element at this point.

18.21 Find the stress at point B on the 1 in. × 8 in. (actual size) cross section loaded as shown in Fig. 18.65. Also sketch the stress element at this point.

18.22 A 150-mm-diameter post is loaded as shown in Fig. 18.66. Find the stress at point C.

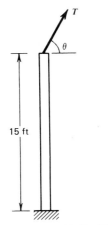

FIG. 18.63   Problems 18.16, 18.17.

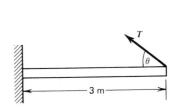

FIG. 18.64   Problems 18.18, 18.19.

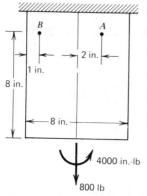

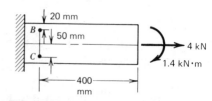

FIG. 18.65 Problems 18.20, 18.21.   **FIG. 18.66** Problems 18.22, 18.23.

18.23 A 150-mm-diameter post is loaded as shown in Fig. 18.66. Find the stress at point *B*.

18.24 The C-clamp shown in Fig. 18.67 is tightened until $P = 800$ N. Find the stress in cross section *A–A* at points *A* and *B*.

18.25 The C-clamp in Fig. 18.67 is made from a gray cast iron that has ultimate strength of 600 and 150 MPa in compression and in tension, respectively. Find the maximum load *P* that the clamp can exert.

18.26 The open-link chain shown in Fig. 18.68 carries a load *P* of 200 lb. Find the stress on the inner and outer surfaces of the straight portion. Sketch the stress element for these locations.

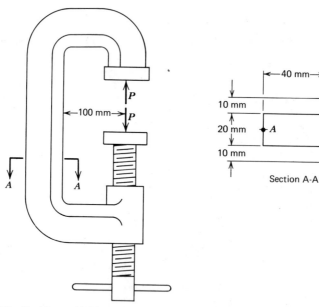

FIG. 18.67 Problems 18.24, 18.25.

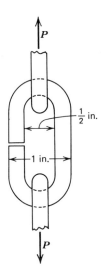

FIG. 18.68   Problem 18.27.

18.27 A torque wrench similar to Fig. 18.69 has an 8-in. handle (*a*). A load of 50 lb (*P*) is applied to the handle. The shaft has a $\frac{3}{8}$-in. diameter. Find the maximum shear stress in the shaft due to:

(a)   Direct shear

(b)   Torque

(c)   Both (a) and (b) combined

18.28 A torque wrench similar to Fig. 18.69 has a 150-mm handle (*a*). A load of 220 N (*P*) is applied to the handle. The shaft has a 10-mm diameter. Find the maximum shear stress in the shaft due to:

(a)   Direct shear

(b)   Torque

(c)   Both (a) and (b) combined

18.29 A torque wrench similar to Fig. 18.69 is made of steel with a shear strength of 18 ksi. If the shaft is $\frac{1}{2}$ in. in diameter and the handle 6 in. long, what load (*P*) can it carry? Consider only shear stress.

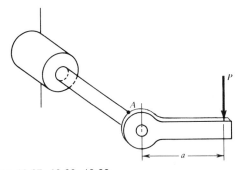

FIG. 18.69   Problems 18.27, 18.28, 18.29, 18.30.

18.30 A torque wrench similar to Fig. 18.69 is made of steel with a shear strength of 150 MPa. If the shaft is 15 mm in diameter and the handle 200 mm long, what load (P) can it carry? Consider only shear stress.

Problems 18.31–18.34 use the following values for Fig. 18.70.

$P_1 = 150$ lb $P_2 = 120$ lb
$R_1 = 6$ in. $R_2 = 8$ in.
$L_1 = 10$ in. $L_2 = 12$ in.

18.31 For the $\frac{3}{4}$-in.-diameter shaft shown in Fig. 18.70, between sections A and B, find the combined shear stress on:

  (a) A top element   (b) A right-hand element

  (c) A bottom element   (d) A left-hand element

18.32 For the $\frac{3}{4}$-in.-diameter shaft shown in Fig. 18.70, between sections B and C, find the combined shear stress on:

  (a) A top element   (b) A right-hand element

  (c) A bottom element   (d) A left-hand element

18.33 Based on a shear strength of 16 ksi and a factor of safety of 3, what size shaft is needed between sections A and B (Fig. 18.70)? (*Hint:* A trial-and-error solution may be necessary.)

18.34 Based on a shear strength of 16 ksi and a factor of safety of 3, what size shaft is needed between sections B and C (Fig. 18.70)? (*Hint:* A trial-and-error solution may be necessary.)

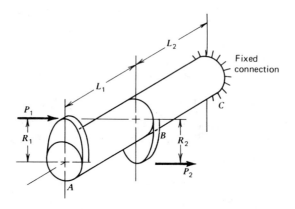

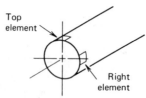

FIG. 18.70 Problems 18.31, 18.32, 18.33, 18.34, 18.35, 18.36, 18.37, 18.38.

Problems 18.35–18.38 use the following values for Fig. 18.70.

$P_1 = 80$ kN $\qquad$ $P_2 = 60$ kN
$R_1 = 300$ mm $\qquad$ $R_2 = 500$ mm
$L_1 = 250$ mm $\qquad$ $L_2 = 400$ mm

18.35 For the 80-mm-diameter shaft shown in Fig. 18.70, between sections A and B, find the combined shear stress on:

(a) A top element $\qquad\qquad$ (b) A right-hand element

(c) A bottom element $\qquad\qquad$ (d) A left-hand element

18.36 For the 80-mm-diameter shaft shown in Fig. 18.70, between sections B and C, find the combined shear stress on:

(a) A top element $\qquad\qquad$ (b) A right-hand element

(c) A bottom element $\qquad\qquad$ (d) A left-hand element

18.37 Based on a shear strength of 180 MPa and a factor of safety of 3, what size shaft is needed between sections A and B (Fig. 18.70)? (*Hint:* A trial-and-error solution may be necessary.)

18.38 Based on a shear strength of 180 MPa and a factor of safety of 3, what size shaft is needed between sections B and C (Fig. 18.70)? (*Hint:* A trial-and-error solution may be necessary.)

18.39 A $\frac{5}{8}$-in.-diameter shaft is keyed to a 2-in.-diameter gear. It is to transmit 3 hp at 1800 rpm. Find the maximum shear stress on the shaft.

18.40 A 14-mm-diameter shaft is keyed to a 60-mm-diameter gear. It is to transmit 2 kW at 1800 rpm. Find the maximum shear stress on the shaft.

18.41 A 5-in.-diameter gear accepts 10 hp at 3600 rpm. What size shaft is required for the gear based on a shear strength of 24 ksi?

18.42 A 125-mm-diameter gear accepts 6 kW at 2600 rpm. What size shaft is required for the gear based on a shear strength of 300 MPa?

18.43 A coil spring is wound from $\frac{1}{8}$-in.-diameter wire on a 1-in. radius. Find the spring index and stress produced in the spring by a 100-lb load.

18.44 A coil spring is wound from 4-mm-diameter wire on a 30-mm radius. Find the spring index and stress produced in the spring by a 100-N load.

18.45 A steel spring with a shear strength of 110 ksi has a wire diameter of 0.065 in. and spring diameter of $\frac{1}{2}$ in. What load can this spring carry?

18.46 A steel spring with a shear strength of 1.5 GPa has a wire diameter of 1.5 mm and spring diameter of 8 mm. What load can this spring carry?

19

Plane Stress Analysis

In Chapter 18 we looked at problems in which normal stresses from various causes were combined and shear stresses from various causes were combined. It was found that when stresses of the same type were acting over the same area, they could be simply added. Consideration of those problems should raise the question of what to do when both shear stresses and normal stresses are present on an element. Alas, they cannot be simply added! They cannot even be added as vectors. (Even though stresses have magnitude and direction, they are not vectors. Mathematically they are described as *tensors*, but use that term only when you need to sound especially precocious.)

In this chapter we develop methods of handling this important problem. It is necessary for a proper analysis of fairly simple items such as a power transmission shaft, which simultaneously has shear stresses produced by torque and a normal stress produced by bending moment. Beyond this problem and more complex ones, it is also necessary for the analysis of failure even in very simply loaded members.

19.1   STRESS ON AN INCLINED PLANE

Consider an axially loaded board as shown in Fig. 19.1 with a 1 in. × 0.5 in. cross section. The grain of the wood is at 30° to the direction of loading. The normal stress in the direction of loading is easily calculated as follows:

$$\sigma = \frac{P}{A} = \frac{500 \text{ lb}}{(1 \text{ in.})(0.5 \text{ in.})} = 1000 \text{ psi}$$

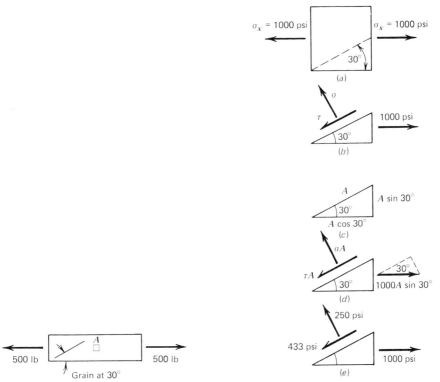

FIG. 19.1 Axially loaded board.

FIG. 19.2a–e Stresses on an inclined plane of a stress element.

In wood the grain represents a plane of weakness. The wood has a relatively low resistance to stresses perpendicular to the grain. Thus we need to know the normal stress in this direction. We develop three methods of handling this problem. The first requires only the application of principles established up to now. The second generalizes that analysis, resulting in equations that are broadly applicable. The last results from a graphical interpretation of the general equations. The graphical method will be most useful to us.

To analyze the stress at point A on the board we draw the stress element A, enlarged in Fig. 19.2a to show the stresses acting on it; also shown is the line of the grain, which makes an angle of 30° with the normal stress. We cut the stress element along this plane, as shown in Fig. 19.2b. On the cut plane there will be a normal stress σ and a shear stress τ, as shown. The original stress, 1000 psi, is also shown. There is no stress on the side parallel to the load.

We do not have a Newton's first law for stresses. So although this partial stress element is in equilibrium, Fig. 19.2b is not a free body diagram. To obtain a free body diagram, the stresses acting on the element must be replaced by the associated forces. If the element has a uniform depth (or unity if you prefer) and the inclined area is assigned the value A, the vertical area will be $A \sin 30°$ and the horizontal area will be $A \cos 30°$, as shown in Fig. 19.2c.

In Fig. 19.2d the stresses are associated with the areas they act over, yielding forces. *This is a free body diagram* and must satisfy Newton's first law. The force due to the normal stress σ is σA and due to the shear stress τ is τA. Since the vertical area is $A \sin 30°$, the normal force on it will be $(1000)A \sin 30°$. To determine the value of σ, the normal stress on the inclined plane, forces are summed in the normal direction, yielding:

$$\sum F_N = 0 = +\sigma A - [(1000)A \sin 30°] \sin 30°$$

The last $\sin 30°$ gives the component of the force due to the 1000-psi stress in the direction of the normal stress. The A's may be divided out, yielding:

$$\sigma = 1000 \sin^2 30° = \textbf{250 psi}$$

Thus we find a tensile stress of 250 psi perpendicular to the grain, attempting to pull the wood apart.

A similar analysis for τ, the shear stress, gives:

$$\sum F_T = 0 = -\tau A + [(1000)A \sin 30°] \cos 30°$$
$$\tau = 1000 \sin 30° \cos 30° = \textbf{433 psi}$$

There will also be a 433-psi shear stress attempting to shear along this grain. These stresses are shown on the element in Fig. 19.2e.

This method is further illustrated in Example Problem 19.1.

Example Problem 19.1

Find the normal and shear stresses on a plane making a 20° angle with the horizontal (Fig. 19.3).

Solution

The areas are as shown in Fig. 19.4. The resulting forces and the free body diagram are shown in Fig. 19.5. We now sum the forces in the direction of σ. Figure 19.6 shows the components in the normal direction of the forces acting on the right-hand face.

$$\sum F_N = 0 = \sigma A - (400A \sin 20°) \sin 20° - (100A \sin 20°) \cos 20°$$
$$- (100A \cos 20°) \sin 20° - (200A \cos 20°) \cos 20°$$

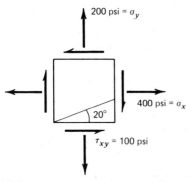

FIG. 19.3 Example Problem 19.1.

FIG. 19.4 Areas.

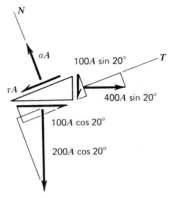

FIG. 19.5 Free body diagram.

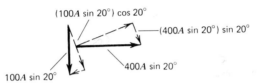

FIG. 19.6 Components of forces.

The last two terms are the components in the normal direction of the forces acting on the horizontal face.

Dividing out the A and solving for σ, we get:

$$\sigma = 400 \sin^2 20° + 100 \sin 20° \cos 20° + 100 \cos 20° \sin 20° + 200 \cos^2 20°$$

$\sigma = \mathbf{288\ psi}$

Similarly,

$$\sum F_T = 0 = -\tau A + (400A \sin 20°) \cos 20° - (100A \sin 20°) \sin 20°$$
$$+ (100A \cos 20°) \cos 20° - (200A \cos 20°) \sin 20°$$
$$\tau = 400 \sin 20° \cos 20° - 100 \sin^2 20° + 100 \cos^2 20°$$
$$- 200 \cos 20° \sin 20°$$

$\tau = \mathbf{141\ psi}$

The resultant stresses are shown in Fig. 19.7.

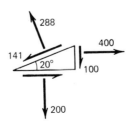

FIG. 19.7 Resultant stresses.

19.2   GENERAL STRESS FORMULAS

Without further work, the analysis of the preceding section must be carried out over and over. This situation suggests a need for a generalized analysis. Beyond eliminating the necessity for repeatedly carrying out the same analysis, the generalized form will allow us to examine the behavior of the stresses on an arbitrary plane—for example, to determine where maximums occur and what their values are.

Figure 19.8 shows a general stress element. All the stresses shown are in their *positive sense* for this analysis. Normal stresses are positive when in tension and negative when in compression. Shear stresses are considered to be positive when up on a right-hand face. This sign system for shear stress differs from the sign system for shear load used previously. An easy way to remember this sign system is by thinking of the *primary surfaces* as being the right-hand and top surfaces. The positive stresses on these surfaces will then have the sense of *positive vectors* perpendicular to these surfaces.

What would be the normal stress on a plane at an angle of θ from the vertical plane? Note that to arrive at the plane, the rotation is counterclockwise. This will continue to be called a positive rotation. Also note the reference plane is *a vertical plane*. We say *a* because it may be the left or right, at our convenience or preference. This is because the stress element represents the stress at a *point*. The element is infinitesimal in size, and the stress on the right-hand plane is identical to the stress on the left-hand plane. The stress on the top plane is identical to the stress on the bottom plane; and it follows that the stress is the same on the two parallel inclined planes, whether we reference from the left vertical or the right vertical. A portion of the stress element is drawn in Fig. 19.9, the new surface being formed at an angle θ from the left vertical plane. The direction of the normal stress on this plane makes an angle of θ with the original X direction. The normal and shear stresses on this new plane are σ and τ as before. The area of the inclined plane is A, giving $A \sin \theta$ and $A \cos \theta$ as the other two areas as indicated in Fig. 19.9. Forces may be summed in the directions of σ and τ, yielding explicit equations for each of

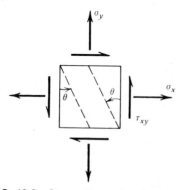

FIG. 19.8   Stress element showing positive sense of stresses and the angle θ.

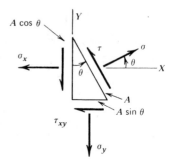

FIG. 19.9   Stress element cut at angle θ.

them. Simpler equations may be obtained by summing forces vertically and horizontally, though they will require algebraic manipulation before yielding explicit values for σ and τ. Also, remember that stresses are not forces, and Fig. 19.9 is not a free body diagram until the stresses are associated with their respective areas. However, after this has been done, summing the forces horizontally yields:

$$\sum F_x = 0 = -\sigma_x(A\cos\theta) - \tau_{xy}(A\sin\theta) - \tau A(\sin\theta) + \sigma A(\cos\theta) = 0$$

Dividing through by $A\cos\theta$, noting $\tan\theta = \sin\theta/\cos\theta$, and rearranging gives:

$$\sigma - \tau\tan\theta = \sigma_x + \tau_{xy}\tan\theta \tag{19.1}$$

Summing the forces in the vertical direction gives:

$$\sum F_y = 0 = -\sigma_y(A\sin\theta) - \tau_{xy}(A\cos\theta) + \tau A(\cos\theta) + \sigma A(\sin\theta)$$

After manipulating as above we get

$$\sigma\tan\theta + \tau = \sigma_y\tan\theta + \tau_{xy} \tag{19.2}$$

Equations 19.1 and 19.2 are two simultaneous equations in the unknowns σ and τ, in terms of the knowns, σ_x, σ_y, τ_{xy}, and θ. The two equations can be solved explicitly for σ and τ. Thus solving and then using numerous trigonometric identities, primarily those for double angles, and after considerable algebraic manipulation, we arrive at the following important results:

$$\sigma = \frac{\sigma_x + \sigma_y}{2} + \frac{\sigma_x - \sigma_y}{2}\cos 2\theta + \tau_{xy}\sin 2\theta \tag{19.3}$$

$$\tau = -\frac{\sigma_x - \sigma_y}{2}\sin 2\theta + \tau_{xy}\cos 2\theta \tag{19.4}$$

These equations allow us to find the normal and shear stresses acting on any plane, defined by the angle θ, given the original state of stresses σ_x, σ_y, and τ_{xy}. However, in using them we must be careful to assign the proper sign to the input variables. Particular care must be taken with τ_{xy} and θ. Review the sign system shown in Fig. 19.8. *Sketch this element from memory until the sign system is firmly in mind.*

Example Problem 19.2

Find the normal and shear stresses on a plane making a 20° angle with the horizontal for an element loaded as shown in Fig. 19.10, using Eqs. 19.3 and 19.4. This will be Example Problem 19.1 the easier way.

Solution

From Fig. 19.10 based on the sign system of Fig. 19.8:

$$\sigma_x = +400 \text{ psi}$$
$$\sigma_y = +200 \text{ psi}$$
$$\tau_{xy} = -100 \text{ psi}$$

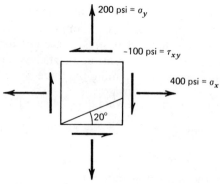

FIG. 19.10 Example Problem 19.2.

The desired plane makes an angle of 20° with the *horizontal* as shown in Fig. 19.11. But the reference plane in Fig. 19.8 is the vertical plane. Hence:

$$\theta \neq 20°$$

The desired plane is obtained by rotating 110° counterclockwise (positive) from the reference plane. Therefore:

$$\theta = +110°$$

Alternately, this angle may be described as $-70°$. It is emphasized that Eqs. 19.3 and 19.4 will not give correct results unless the sign system on which they are based is rigidly followed.

From Eq. 19.3:

$$\sigma = \frac{\sigma_x + \sigma_y}{2} + \frac{\sigma_x - \sigma_y}{2} \cos 2\theta + \tau_{xy} \sin 2\theta$$

$$= \frac{400 + 200}{2} + \frac{400 - 200}{2} \cos 220° + (-100 \sin 220°)$$

$$= 300 + 100(-0.766) - 100(-0.643)$$

$$\boldsymbol{\sigma = 288 \text{ psi}}$$

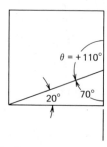

FIG. 19.11 Determining the angle θ.

And Eq. 19.4.

$$\tau = -\frac{\sigma_x - \sigma_y}{2} \sin 2\theta + \tau_{xy} \cos 2\theta$$

$$= -\frac{400 - 200}{2} \sin 220° + (-100 \cos 220°)$$

$$= -100(-0.643) - 100(-0.766)$$

$$\tau = +141 \text{ psi}$$

These answers, of course, agree with those of Example Problem 19.1 but are obtained with much less effort. The effort was expended in developing Eqs. 19.3 and 19.4, used here. We also note the positive sign associated with τ. This sign has significance concerning the sense of τ. We do not explore it in this text because it rarely matters.

Example Problem 19.3

For the stress element shown in Fig. 19.12, calculate the normal and shear stress every 15° using Eqs. 19.3 and 19.4. Plot σ versus θ and τ versus θ.

Solution

Based on the sign system of Fig. 19.8, we have:

$$\sigma_x = -80 \text{ MPa}$$
$$\sigma_y = +60 \text{ MPa}$$
$$\tau_{xy} = +30 \text{ MPa}$$

It is recommended that you deliberately write the sign + or −, to ensure that it is not neglected. For Eq. 19.3 we have:

$$\sigma = \frac{\sigma_x + \sigma_y}{2} + \frac{\sigma_x - \sigma_y}{2} \cos 2\theta + \tau_{xy} \sin 2\theta$$

$$\sigma = \frac{-80 + 60}{2} + \frac{-80 - (60)}{2} \cos 2\theta + 30 \sin 2\theta$$

$$\sigma = -10 - 70 \cos 2\theta + 30 \sin 2\theta$$

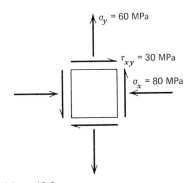

FIG. 19.12 Example Problem 19.3.

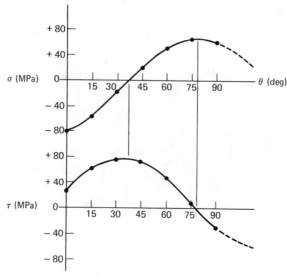

FIG. 19.13 Plots of stress versus angle.

Similarly, for Eq. 19.4 we get:

$$\tau = +70 \sin 2\theta + 30 \cos 2\theta$$

Evaluating these two equations for the indicated values of θ gives:

θ	σ (MPa)	τ (MPa)
0°	−80.0	+30.0
15°	−55.6	+61.0
30°	−19.0	+75.6
45°	+20.0	+70.0
60°	+51.0	+45.6
75°	+65.6	+9.0
90°	+60.0	−30.0

If you have a programmable calculator or home computer, Eqs. 19.3 and 19.4 offer an excellent opportunity to use the thing. The zero value of θ corresponds to the vertical face and the 90° value to the horizontal face. The values obtained are plotted in Fig. 19.13. If these curves are continued, sine waves will be generated. We might have suspected this by examining Eqs. 19.3 and 19.4 closely. Furthermore, the curves are 45° out of phase.

19.3   PRINCIPAL STRESSES

Equations 19.3 and 19.4 give the stresses as a function of the angle θ. To predict failure in a mechanical structure, we must be able to determine the maximum stress that exists anywhere in the structure. We could evaluate Eqs. 19.3 and 19.4 every few degrees, seeking the maximum values of σ and τ. However, the calculus gives us a more direct approach. In the calculus this is known as a maximum–minimum problem. It is based on viewing Eq. 19.3 as follows.

$$\sigma = f(\theta)$$

We could plot this equation on a graph, labeling the axes σ and θ (instead of X and Y). On a σ–θ graph the slope of the curve at any point would be:

$$\text{slope} = \frac{d\sigma}{d\theta}$$

That is, slope is the geometric meaning of the derivative. Now think about the slope of the curve when the curve reaches a maximum value. Will not the slope be zero?

To apply this to our problem, we take the derivative of σ with respect to θ and set it equal to zero (σ_x, σ_y, and τ_{xy} are constants in this equation).

$$\frac{d\sigma}{d\theta} = \frac{d}{d\theta}\left[\frac{\sigma_x + \sigma_y}{2} + \frac{\sigma_x - \sigma_y}{2}\cos 2\theta + \tau_{xy}\sin 2\theta \right]$$

$$= 0 + \frac{\sigma_x - \sigma_y}{2}(-\sin 2\theta)2 + \tau_{xy}(\cos 2\theta)2$$

$$\frac{d\sigma}{d\theta} = -(\sigma_x - \sigma_y)\sin 2\theta + 2\tau_{xy}\cos 2\theta = 0$$

The equation above contains the single unknown θ. If we solve for θ we will know where (what value of θ) the slope is zero, which is where the maximum stress occurs. We must add that minimum values of σ also occur where the slope is zero. So we are getting values of θ corresponding to a maximum or minimum value. At this point we don't know which. We proceed to solve for θ by rearranging:

$$(\sigma_x - \sigma_y)\sin 2\theta = 2\tau_{xy}\cos 2\theta$$

$$\frac{\sin 2\theta}{\cos 2\theta} = \frac{2\tau_{xy}}{\sigma_x - \sigma_y}$$

or

$$\tan 2\theta_p = \frac{2\tau_{xy}}{\sigma_x - \sigma_y} \tag{19.5a}$$

or

$$\tan 2\theta_p = \frac{\tau_{xy}}{\left(\dfrac{\sigma_x - \sigma_y}{2}\right)} \tag{19.5b}$$

If the values of τ_{xy}, σ_x, and σ_y are substituted into Eq. 19.5a, two values of 2θ, which are 180° apart, may be obtained. When these values of $2\theta_p$ are substituted into Eq. 19.3, one will give the maximum value of σ and the other will give the minimum. The resulting two values of σ are known as the *principal stresses*, and their directions are the *principal directions.* We use the subscript P to denote that this is the angle of the principal stresses. The principal directions θ_P will be 90° apart ($2\theta_P$ are 180° apart). The principal stresses are designated σ_1 and σ_2 for the maximum and minimum, respectively.

An equation yielding the principal stresses directly may be obtained by substituting $2\theta_P$ from Eqs. 19.5 into Eq. 19.3. In Fig. 19.14 the angle $2\theta_P$ is evaluated in terms of a triangle satisfying Eq. 19.5b. The hypotenuse of this triangle may be found by the Pythagorean theorem to be:

$$\left[\left(\frac{\sigma_x - \sigma_y}{2} \right)^2 + (\tau_{xy})^2 \right]^{1/2}$$

Thus we define:

$$\sin 2\theta_P = \frac{\tau_{xy}}{\left[\left(\frac{\sigma_x - \sigma_y}{2} \right)^2 + (\tau_{xy})^2 \right]^{1/2}}$$

and

$$\cos 2\theta_P = \frac{\left(\frac{\sigma_x - \sigma_y}{2} \right)}{\left[\left(\frac{\sigma_x - \sigma_y}{2} \right)^2 + (\tau_{xy})^2 \right]^{1/2}}$$

Then evaluating Eq. 19.3 gives:

$$\sigma = \frac{\sigma_x + \sigma_y}{2} + \frac{\sigma_x - \sigma_y}{2} \cos 2\theta + \tau_{xy} \sin 2\theta$$

$$= \frac{\sigma_x + \sigma_y}{2} + \frac{\sigma_x - \sigma_y}{2} \cdot \frac{\left(\frac{\sigma_x - \sigma_y}{2} \right)}{\left[\left(\frac{\sigma_x - \sigma_y}{2} \right)^2 + (\tau_{xy})^2 \right]^{1/2}}$$

$$+ \tau_{xy} \frac{\tau_{xy}}{\left[\left(\frac{\sigma_x - \sigma_y}{2} \right)^2 + (\tau_{xy})^2 \right]^{1/2}}$$

$$= \frac{\sigma_x + \sigma_y}{2} + \frac{\left(\frac{\sigma_x - \sigma_y}{2} \right)^2 + \tau_{xy}^2}{\left[\left(\frac{\sigma_x - \sigma_y}{2} \right)^2 + (\tau_{xy})^2 \right]^{1/2}}$$

$$\sigma_{1,2} = \frac{\sigma_x + \sigma_y}{2} + \sqrt{ \left(\frac{\sigma_x - \sigma_y}{2} \right)^2 + \tau_{xy}^2 } \qquad (19.6)$$

There are two roots to the second term on the right-hand side of Eq. 19.6. The larger one produces the maximum stress; the lesser, the minimum. Equation 19.6 may be used to directly calculate the principal stresses when σ_x, σ_y, and τ_{xy} are given.

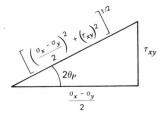

FIG. 19.14 Relation between angles of maximum stress and given variables.

What shear stresses accompany these principal stresses? That may be determined by substituting $2\theta_P$ from Eqs. 19.5 into Eq. 19.4. Thus:

$$\tau = -\frac{\sigma_x - \sigma_y}{2} \sin 2\theta + \tau_{xy} \cos 2\theta$$

$$= -\frac{\sigma_x - \sigma_y}{2} \cdot \frac{\tau_{xy}}{\left[\left(\frac{\sigma_x - \sigma_y}{2}\right)^2 + \tau_{xy}^2\right]^{1/2}} + \tau_{xy} \cdot \frac{\left(\frac{\sigma_x - \sigma_y}{2}\right)}{\left[\left(\frac{\sigma_x - \sigma_y}{2}\right)^2 + \tau_{xy}^2\right]^{1/2}}$$

$$\tau = 0 \tag{19.7}$$

This very important conclusion says that on the planes of principal stresses (maximum and minimum normal stresses) *the shear stress is zero.*

Example Problem 19.4

For the stresses on the element in Fig. 19.15, find the principal planes and the principal stresses.

Solution

From Fig. 19.15:

$$\sigma_x = +400 \text{ psi}$$
$$\sigma_y = +200 \text{ psi}$$
$$\tau_{xy} = -100 \text{ psi}$$

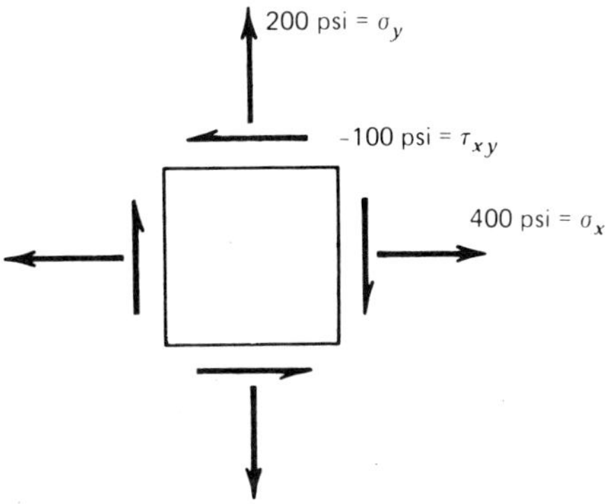

200 psi = σ_y

-100 psi = τ_{xy}

400 psi = σ_x

FIG. 19.15 Example Problem 19.4.

Equation 19.5:

$$\tan 2\theta_P = \frac{\tau_{xy}}{\dfrac{\sigma_x - \sigma_y}{2}} = \frac{-100}{\dfrac{400 - 200}{2}}$$

$$\tan 2\theta_P = -1.00$$
$$2\theta_P = -45°, 135°$$
$$\boldsymbol{\theta_P = -22.5°, 67.5°}$$

$$\sigma = \frac{\sigma_x + \sigma_y}{2} + \frac{\sigma_x - \sigma_y}{2}\cos 2\theta + \tau_{xy}\sin 2\theta$$

$$= \frac{400 + 200}{2} + \frac{400 - 200}{2}\cos(-45°) + (-100)\sin(-45°)$$

$$= 300 + 100(+0.707) - 100(-0.707)$$
$$\boldsymbol{\sigma_1 = 441 \text{ psi}}$$
$$\sigma_2 = 300 + 100\cos 135° - 100\sin 135°$$
$$\boldsymbol{\sigma_2 = 159 \text{ psi}}$$

Alternately, from Equation 19.6:

$$\sigma_{1,2} = \frac{\sigma_x + \sigma_y}{2} \mp \sqrt{\left(\frac{\sigma_x - \sigma_y}{2}\right)^2 + \tau_{xy}^2}$$

$$= \frac{400 + 200}{2} \mp \sqrt{\left(\frac{400 - 200}{2}\right)^2 + (-100)^2}$$

$$\sigma_{1,2} = 300 \mp 141 = \boldsymbol{441 \text{ psi}, 159 \text{ psi}}$$

Figure 19.16 shows the original state of stresses and the same state of stress defined in terms of the principal stresses. Note that the principal stresses are 90° apart and the accompanying shear stress is zero. In sketching the principal stress element, the angle θ_P is measured from a vertical surface as indicated by the sign system in Fig. 19.8. Either the left- or the right-hand surface may be used, and either value of θ_P may be used. An element of the same orientation will be produced regardless.

19.4   MAXIMUM SHEAR STRESS

In a manner similar to that used in finding the principal stresses, the maximum shear stress may be found, setting:

$$\frac{d\tau}{d\theta} = 0$$

When solved for 2θ, this yields:

$$\tan 2\theta_\tau = -\frac{\left(\dfrac{\sigma_x - \sigma_y}{2}\right)}{\tau_{xy}} \tag{19.8}$$

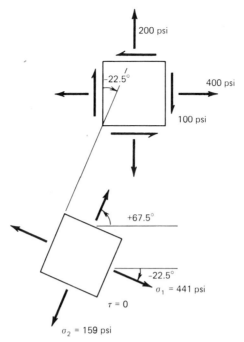

FIG. 19.16 Principal stresses for Fig. 19.15.

This equation may be evaluated for $2\theta_\tau$ and the value substituted into Eq. 19.4 to determine the maximum value of the shear stress. Or Eq. 19.4 may be evaluated in general, as in the preceding section, to give:

$$\tau_{max} = \sqrt{\left(\frac{\sigma_x - \sigma_y}{2}\right)^2 + \tau_{xy}^2} \tag{19.9}$$

Notice that this equation is the radical from Eq. 19.6. If the normal stress is evaluated by the value of $2\theta_\tau$ from Eq. 19.8, we get:

$$\sigma_\tau = \frac{\sigma_x + \sigma_y}{2} \tag{19.10}$$

which is the remaining portion of Eq. 19.6. Thus we find that the maximum shear stress (Eq. 19.9) is accompanied by a normal stress (Eq. 19.10), while the maximum normal stresses (principal) are associated with a zero shear stress. *The normal stress accompanying the maximum shear stress is equal on all four surfaces.*

Comparing Eqs. 19.8 and 19.5, we notice that the right-hand side of one is the negative reciprocal of the other. Noting the trigonometric identity:

$$\tan(90 + \phi) = -\frac{1}{\tan \phi}$$

we conclude that:

$$2\theta_\tau + 90 = 2\theta_P$$

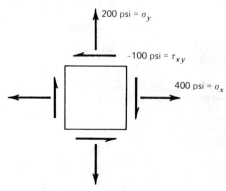

FIG. 19.17   Example Problem 19.5.

and

$$\theta_\tau + 45 = \theta_P$$

Hence *the plane of maximum shear stress is 45° from the plane of principal stress.*

Example Problem 19.5

Find the plane of maximum shear stress and the resulting maximum shear stress and associated normal stress for the stress element in Fig. 19.17.

Solution

Again from Fig. 19.17:

$$\sigma_x = 400 \text{ psi}$$
$$\sigma_y = 200 \text{ psi}$$
$$\tau_{xy} = -100 \text{ psi}$$

Equation 19.8:

$$\tan 2\theta_\tau = -\frac{\left(\dfrac{\sigma_x - \sigma_y}{2}\right)}{\tau_{xy}} = -\frac{\left(\dfrac{400 - 200}{2}\right)}{-100}$$

$$\tan 2\theta_\tau = +1.00$$
$$2\theta_\tau \doteq 45°, 225°$$
$$\boldsymbol{\theta_\tau = 22.5°, 112°}$$

Note that these planes are 90° apart and 45° from the principal planes found in Example Problem 19.4.

Equation 19.4:

$$\tau_{max} = \frac{\sigma_x - \sigma_y}{2} \sin 2\theta + \tau_{xy} \cos 2\theta$$

$$= -\left(\frac{400 - 200}{2}\right) \sin 45° + (-100) \cos 45°$$

$$\tau_{max} = -100(0.707) - 100(0.707) = \textbf{141 psi}$$

Note that the magnitude of the result is the same regardless of whether 45° or 225° is used.

To calculate the normal stress associated with the maximum shear stress use Eq. 19.3:

$$\sigma_{22.5} = \frac{\sigma_x + \sigma_y}{2} + \frac{\sigma_x - \sigma_y}{2} \cos 2\theta + \tau_{xy} \sin 2\theta$$

$$\sigma_{22.5} = \frac{400 + 200}{2} + \frac{400 - 200}{2} \cos 45° + (-100) \sin 45°$$

$$= 300 + 100(0.707) - 100(0.707)$$

$$\boldsymbol{\sigma_{22.5} = 300 \text{ psi}}$$

$$\sigma_{112} = \frac{400 + 200}{2} + \frac{400 - 200}{2} \cos 225° + (-100) \sin 225°$$

$$= 300 + 100(-0.707) - 100(-0.707)$$

$$\boldsymbol{\sigma_{112} = 300 \text{ psi}}$$

The normal stresses on the two planes are equal.

Alternately, Eqs. 19.9 and 19.10 could have been used:

$$\tau_{max} = \sqrt{\left(\frac{\sigma_x - \sigma_y}{2}\right)^2 + \tau_{xy}^2}$$

$$= \sqrt{\left(\frac{400 - 200}{2}\right)^2 + (-100)^2} = \sqrt{100^2 + 100^2}$$

$$\boldsymbol{\tau_{max} = 141 \text{ psi}}$$

$$\sigma_{22,112} = \frac{\sigma_x + \sigma_y}{2} = \frac{400 + 200}{2} = \boldsymbol{300 \text{ psi}}$$

Figure 19.18 shows the original stress element, the principal stresses, and the maximum shear stresses. These are three different descriptions of the same state of stress.

Note that the maximum shear stress is 45° from the principal stresses. Also, the shear stresses accompanying the principal stresses are zero. On the other hand, the normal stresses accompanying the maximum shear stress are not zero in general. However, they are equal on all four faces. The maximum shear stress element may be found directly from the given stress element using θ_τ as found in Eq. 19.8 or it may be found by rotating the principal stress element 45°.

19.5 MOHR'S CIRCLE

Equations 19.1 through 19.10 represent the normal and shear stresses on any plane and the locations and values of maximum shear and normal stresses. These equations are accurate, effective, and complete. However, they represent a large amount of detail and are not readily retained unless used frequently. The German engineer

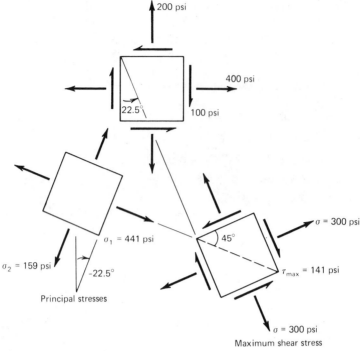

FIG. 19.18 Equivalent states of stress.

Otto Mohr discovered that the variables in these equations may be represented as parts on a circle. His method gives a graphical interpretation of these data, but more (or Mohr?) than that, they give us the capability to generate the information contained in Eqs. 19.1 through 19.10 without memorizing them.

Recalling Eqs. 19.3 and 19.4, we have:

$$\sigma = \frac{\sigma_x + \sigma_y}{2} + \frac{\sigma_x - \sigma_y}{2} \cos 2\theta + \tau_{xy} \sin 2\theta \qquad (19.3)$$

and

$$\tau = -\frac{\sigma_x - \sigma_y}{2} \sin 2\theta + \tau_{xy} \cos 2\theta \qquad (19.4)$$

For a given state of stress, σ_x, σ_y, and τ_{xy} are constants. The variables σ and τ are in terms of a third parameter θ. The parameter θ may be eliminated by combining the two equations. The resulting equation will be that of a circle, known as Mohr's circle. This circle will be extremely valuable in evaluating the stresses acting on an element.

The circle is obtained as follows. Positive signs for the stress element are as shown in Fig. 19.19. This is exactly the same sign system used in Fig. 19.8 and for Eqs. 19.1 through 19.10. Unfortunately, the sign system is not universal. When referring to other texts, check the sign system first. The vertical axis in Fig. 19.20 is for shear stress, and the horizontal axis is for normal stresses, positive being tensile and negative being compressive. Points on the circle represent the stresses,

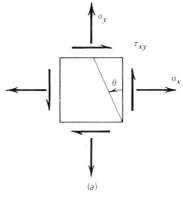

FIG. 19.19 Positive sign system for Mohr's circle.

normal and shear, on a plane. The first point plotted is $(\sigma_x, -\tau_{xy})$, which is point A in Fig. 19.20. The second is (σ_y, τ_{xy}), point B in Fig. 19.20. These two points define the circle whose center is on the horizontal or σ axis.

The circle may be analyzed graphically or semigraphically. Graphically the circle is obtained by drawing a straight line from B to A. The center of the circle is where this line intersects the σ axis, point C in Fig. 19.20. The radius is the distance CA or CB. The circle may easily be drawn now. Significant values, which are discussed below, can be scaled rather than calculated if a purely graphical method is used. In the semigraphical method the circle is sketched but its actual dimensions are calculated rather than measured, based on the properties of a circle and right triangles. Since we are already familiar with the properties of circles and right triangles, the method becomes very easy to use.

We observe that the center of the circle (C in Fig. 19.20) must be at $(\sigma_x + \sigma_y)/2$, that is, half-way between points B and A. The distance CD is $(\sigma_x - \sigma_y)/2$ and DA is τ_{xy}. Hence by noting ADC to be a right triangle, we may calculate the hypotenuse, which is the radius of the circle:

$$R = \sqrt{\left(\frac{\sigma_x - \sigma_y}{2}\right)^2 + \tau_{xy}^2}$$

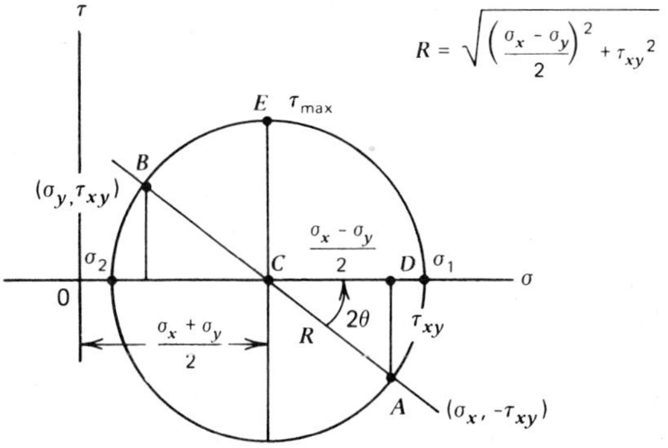

FIG. 19.20 Mohr's circle.

The maximum and minimum values of the normal stress, the principal stresses, are identified as σ_1 and σ_2 and are easily obtained. In fact, we may generate Eq. 19.6, noting that σ_1 is OC plus the radius:

$$\sigma_1 = OC + R$$

$$\sigma_1 = \frac{\sigma_x + \sigma_y}{2} + \sqrt{\left(\frac{\sigma_x - \sigma_y}{2}\right)^2 + \tau_{xy}^2} \qquad (19.6)$$

The difference in these two terms gives σ_2. Obviously, the shear stress accompanying the principal stresses is zero, since σ_1 and σ_2 are on the horizontal axis in Fig. 19.20.

Point E indicates the maximum shear stress, which is simply the radius of the circle:

$$\tau_{max} = \sqrt{\left(\frac{\sigma_x - \sigma_y}{2}\right)^2 + \tau_{xy}^2} \qquad (19.9)$$

The normal stress accompanying τ_{max} is:

$$\sigma_\tau = \frac{\sigma_x + \sigma_y}{2} \qquad (19.10)$$

There is a *double-angle relationship between Mohr's circle and real space*. However, both angles are positive in the counterclockwise direction. Angles may be calculated using trigonometric relations and the Mohr's circle. The angle θ (Fig. 19.19) in real space corresponds to 2θ in Mohr's circle space (Fig. 19.20). However, the directions of rotation are the same, counterclockwise, as we go from A to σ_1, for example. Point A represents the stresses on the right-hand face, σ_x and $-\tau_{xy}$. Point B represents the stresses on the top face, σ_y and τ_{xy}. Points A and B are 180° apart on Mohr's circle, while the faces they represent are 90° apart in real space, again illustrating the double-angle relationship.

The circle of Fig. 19.20 graphically illustrates several items we have discussed. Recall that each point on the circle represents the stresses, σ and τ, on some plane in space. An adjacent plane at 90°, the other side of a square element, will be 180° away on the circle because of the double-angle, 2θ relation. Thus points A and B are 180° apart on the circle, although they represent planes 90° apart in Fig. 19.19. Any pair of points 180° apart totally describes the stress on an element. Any other pair of points 180° apart totally describes *the same state of stress*, but in a *different* coordinate system. The circle consists of all possible descriptions. There is no equivalent description that is not represented by points on the circle.

Given the above, it is clear that the greatest σ coordinate for any point on the circle is σ_1. Thus this is the maximum normal or principal stress, and it is accompanied by zero shear stress. It is equally clear that σ_2 is the minimum normal (also principal) stress and that it, too, is accompanied by zero shear stress. We further observe that these two points are 180° apart on the circle, so they are 90° apart on perpendicular planes in real space.

The shear stress τ_{max} is 90° (45° in real space) from σ_1 or σ_2. The minimum shear stress is 180° away (90° in real space) and of equal magnitude. Both the maximum and the minimum shear stresses are accompanied by the same normal

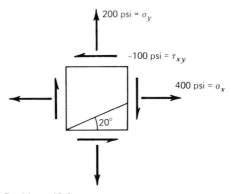

FIG. 19.21 Example Problem 19.6.

stress. The value of the normal is the same as the center of the circle, which is the average normal stress.

It may be helpful to reread the last two paragraphs after you have worked several problems.

Example Problem 19.6

For an element loaded as shown in Fig. 19.21, find the normal and shear stresses on a plane making an angle of 20° with the horizontal using Mohr's circle *graphically*. Also, find the principal stresses and the maximum shear stress.

Solution

From Fig. 19.21 we have $\sigma_x = +400$ psi, $\sigma_y = +200$ psi, and $\tau_{xy} = -100$ psi. The stresses on the right-hand face are plotted in Fig. 19.22 as (400, 100), since

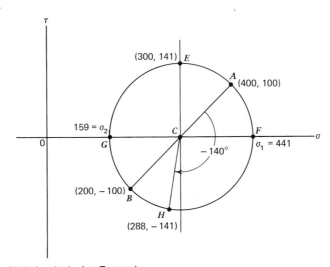

FIG. 19.22 Mohr's circle for Example Problem 19.6.

we plot $(\sigma_x, -\tau_{xy})$ $[-(-100) = +100]$, and are labeled point A. The stresses for the top face are plotted as $(200, -100)$ or (σ_y, τ_{xy}) and labeled B. The second point will always use the negative of the sign used for shear in the first point. A line AB connects these two points. As constructed, it intersects the σ axis at the center of the circle C. It breaks AB into two lengths, AC and BC, each of which is equal to the radius. Placing the compass at C with a radius AC the circle is drawn. The circle is now complete, fully describing the given state of stress at any orientation. It remains to be interpreted.

The stress on a plane at 20° with the horizontal is desired. This plane may also be described as −70° from the right-hand face (Fig. 19.23). In real space we rotate 70° clockwise (negative) to get the desired plane. For Mohr's circle we *double* the real space angle but maintain the direction. Thus from A, which represents the right-hand face of the element, we move around the circle clockwise the double angle, 140°.

Drawing this ray gives point H, which has the coordinates $(288, -141)$. Thus:

$$\sigma_{20°} = 288 \text{ psi}$$
$$\tau_{20°} = 141 \text{ psi}$$

A larger scale would enhance the accuracy of these values. Points G and F give the principal stresses and E the maximum shear stress. Thus:

$$\sigma_1 = 441 \text{ psi}$$
$$\sigma_2 = 159 \text{ psi}$$
$$\tau_{max} = 141 \text{ psi}$$
$$\sigma_{\tau_{max}} = 300 \text{ psi}$$

Example Problem 19.7

For the stress element of Fig. 19.21, use Mohr's circle to *calculate* the principal stresses, their location, the maximum shear stresses, and their location.

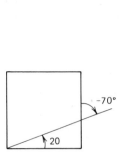

FIG. 19.23 Determining the reference angle θ from a vertical plane.

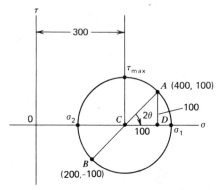

FIG. 19.24 Mohr's circle for Example Problem 19.7.

Solution

Points A and B are plotted (Fig. 19.24) as in Example Problem 19.6. Point C is observed to be halfway between the two, so:

$$OC = \frac{400 + 200}{2} = 300$$

CD is half the difference between A and B:

$$CD = \frac{400 - 200}{2} = 100$$

and AD is τ_{xy}; thus:

$$AD = 100$$

The radius of the circle is the hypotenuse of the triangle ADC:

$$R = \sqrt{100^2 + 100^2} = 141$$

The angle 2θ is formed by:

$$\tan 2\theta = \frac{100}{100} = 1.00$$

$$2\theta = 45°$$
$$\theta = 22.5° \qquad \text{clockwise to } \sigma_1$$

Here we are handling the sign of θ by observing the circle.
Thus

$$\tau_{max} = \text{radius} = \textbf{141 psi at 22.5°} \curvearrowright \text{from right-hand surface}$$
$$\sigma_{\tau_{max}} = \textbf{300 psi}$$
$$\sigma_1 = 300 + 141 = \textbf{441 psi at 22.5°} \curvearrowright \text{from right-hand surface}$$
$$\sigma_2 = 300 - 141 = \textbf{159 psi}$$

The sketches of these three descriptions of the same state of stress are given in Fig. 19.25. This figure should be studied and related to the circle in Fig. 19.24.

Example Problem 19.8

Plot Mohr's circle for the stress element in Fig. 19.26 and *graphically* find the principal stresses and their location. Also find the maximum shear stress, the accompanying normal stresses, and their location. Finally sketch stress elements, showing their orientation with respect to the original.

Solution

Using the sign system of Fig. 19.19, the initial stresses are:

$$\sigma_x = -2 \text{ MPa}$$
$$\sigma_y = -8 \text{ MPa}$$
$$\tau_{xy} = +10 \text{ MPa}$$

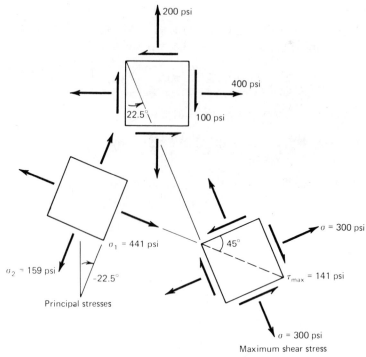

FIG. 19.25   Equivalent states of stress.

Point A has the coordinates $(-2, -10)$; point B has $(-8, +10)$. The two points are plotted in Fig. 19.27 and the line AB is drawn. Its intersection with the horizontal σ axis gives the center of the circle C. The length CA is the radius of the circle. Placing the compass point at C the circle is constructed. The angle 2θ is measured and found to be $73.3°$. Then θ is $36.7°$. Point A represents the stress or the vertical face of the original element in Fig. 19.26. If this plane is rotated $36.7°$ counterclockwise, we have the plane of the principal stress σ_1. This is illustrated in Fig. 19.28. From Fig. 19.27 we measure:

$$\sigma_1 = 5.4 \text{ MPa}$$
$$\sigma_2 = -15.4 \text{ MPa}$$

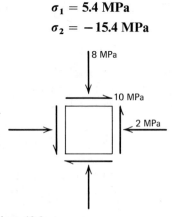

FIG. 19.26   Example Problem 19.8.

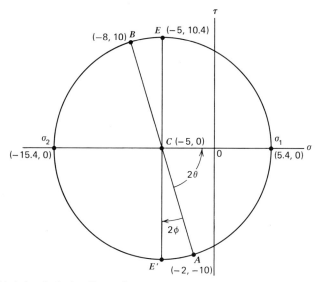

FIG. 19.27 Mohr's circle for Example Problem 19.8.

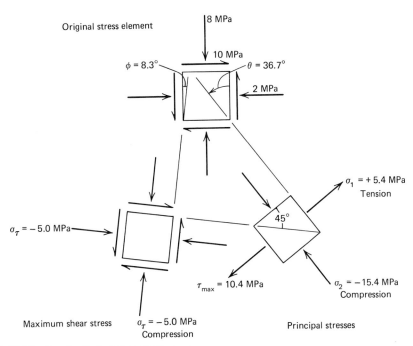

FIG. 19.28 Equivalent states of stress for Example Problem 19.8.

These stresses are 90° apart as shown in Fig. 19.28, and the accompanying shear stress is zero.

The maximum shear stress is found at point E or E' in Fig. 19.27. For convenience we go to E', which is measured to be 16.7° clockwise (2ϕ) from A. Thus in real space (Fig. 19.28), the plane of the maximum shear stress will be 8.3° clockwise (ϕ) from a vertical plane as shown. These planes are at 45° from the principal planes. Finally, we measure from the Mohr's circle:

$$\tau_{max} = 10.4 \text{ MPa}$$
$$\sigma_\tau = -5.0 \text{ MPa}$$

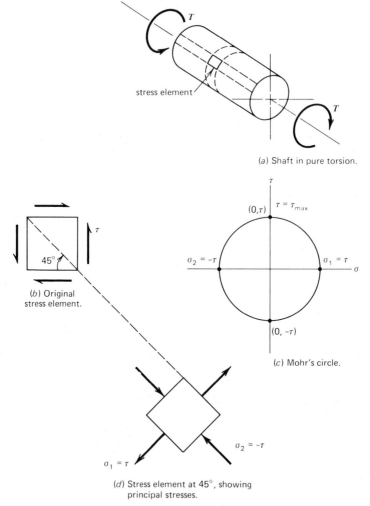

(a) Shaft in pure torsion.

(b) Original stress element.

(c) Mohr's circle.

(d) Stress element at 45°, showing principal stresses.

FIG. 19.29a–d   Maximum shear and principal stresses for pure torsion.

19.6 APPLICATIONS OF MOHR'S CIRCLE TO FAILURE ANALYSIS

Mohr's circle (or the other methods we have examined) can be very useful for finding the normal or shear stress on a particular plane from combined loading. It can be used to find principal stresses and the maximum shear stresses for complex loading situations. Beyond these applications it is also useful in understanding failure, even in very simple loading situations. Consider a circular shaft loaded in pure torsion to illustrate this application.

A shaft under pure torsional loading is shown in Fig. 19.29a. The stress on the surface element shown is as indicated in Fig. 19.29b. Its magnitude, found by Eq. 13.7, is:

$$\tau = \frac{Tc}{J} \tag{13.7}$$

The stress element is in pure shear, that is; there are no normal stresses acting on it in the orientation shown. Mohr's circle is drawn in Fig. 19.29c, using the points $(0, \tau)$ and $(0, -\tau)$. This circle has its center at the origin and its radius is τ. The maximum shear stress is the given stress τ. The principal stresses are also equal to τ in magnitude, σ_1 being $+\tau$ and σ_2 being $-\tau$. These stresses occur at 90° to either side of the given shear stresses on the Mohr's circle. Consequently, they occur 45° from the initial planes in real space, as indicated in Fig. 19.29d. Finally Fig. 19.30 shows the maximum shear stress on the shaft and Fig. 19.31 shows the principal stresses.

If the shaft is made of a ductile material, it will initially fail by yielding, which occurs because of the maximum shear stress. Thus a ductile shaft, such as mild steel, will fail in the direction of maximum shear stress or in a plane perpendicular to the axis of the shaft, as shown in Fig. 19.32. You can demonstrate this by taking a paper clip and twisting it to failure. (It may take 30 or more turns.) The failure plane will be as shown in Fig. 19.32.

If the shaft is made of a brittle material, it will be weakest in tension. The positive tensile stress σ_1 will initiate failure on a plane at 45° to the axis of the

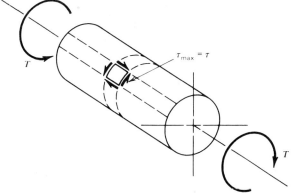

FIG. 19.30 Maximum shear stress due to pure torsion.

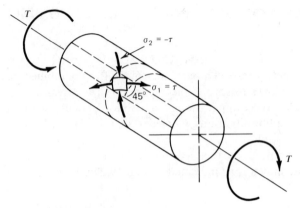

FIG. 19.31 Principal stresses due to pure torsion.

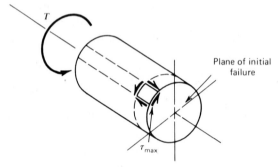

FIG. 19.32 Failure of a ductile shaft in pure torsion.

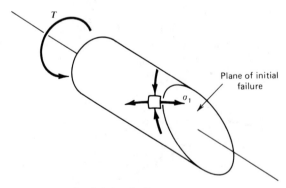

FIG. 19.33 Plane of failure of a brittle shaft in pure torsion.

shaft, as shown in Fig. 19.33. You can demonstrate this by twisting a piece of chalk to failure. Be careful not to bend it as you twist it. Note that Fig. 19.33 shows only the plane of failure, not the actual appearance of the failure.

Finally, if the shaft is hollow with a sufficiently thin wall and inadequate stiffness, failure will be by buckling due to the maximum compressive stress σ_2.

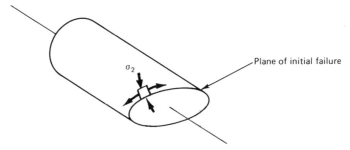

FIG. 19.34 Failure of a hollow tube in pure torsion.

(Buckling is treated in the next chapter.) This is initiated on a plane that also makes an angle of 45° to the axis of the shaft, but this plane is perpendicular to the plane of tensile failure. This plane is shown in Fig. 19.34. This failure can be observed by carefully twisting a soda straw or empty paper tube.

Most load situations are more complex than the pure torsion of this example. However, in many cases, the loading and resultant stresses are analyzed and related to the properties of the material in the manner illustrated here to predict failure.

19.7 SUMMARY

Stresses on an arbitrary plane may be found from the equations:

$$\sigma = \frac{\sigma_x + \sigma_y}{2} + \frac{\sigma_x - \sigma_y}{2} \cos 2\theta + \tau_{xy} \sin 2\theta$$

$$\tau = -\frac{\sigma_x - \sigma_y}{2} \sin 2\theta + \tau_{xy} \cos 2\theta$$

Refer to Fig. 19.8 for the sign system. Principal stresses may be found from:

$$\sigma_{1,2} = \frac{\sigma_x + \sigma_y}{2} \pm \sqrt{\left(\frac{\sigma_x - \sigma_y}{2}\right)^2 + \tau_{xy}^2}$$

These occur on the principal planes at:

$$\tan 2\theta_p = \frac{\tau_{xy}}{\left(\dfrac{\sigma_x - \sigma_y}{2}\right)}$$

where σ_1 and σ_2 are 90° apart. The accompanying shear stress is 0. The maximum shear stress may be found from:

$$\tau_{max} = \sqrt{\left(\frac{\sigma_x - \sigma_y}{2}\right)^2 + \tau_{xy}^2}$$

occurring at:

$$\tan 2\theta_\tau = -\frac{\left(\dfrac{\sigma_x - \sigma_y}{2}\right)}{\tau_{xy}}$$

which is 45° from the principal stresses. The accompanying normal stresses are:

$$\sigma_\tau = \frac{\sigma_x + \sigma_y}{2}$$

Mohr's circle contains all the information above in a simple graph. It is obtained as follows. Plot $(\sigma_x, -\tau_{xy})$ and (σ_y, τ_{xy}) on a τ (vertical) and σ (horizontal) space. Draw a line between these two points. It will intersect the horizontal axis (σ) at the center of the circle. The distance from the center to either point is the radius. Constructing the circle permits the determination of all important parameters by direct measurement or calculation. There is a double-angle relation between Mohr's circle and real space.

PROBLEMS

19.1 For the stress element shown in Fig. 19.35, find the normal and shear stresses by summation of forces on a plane:

    (a)   15° counterclockwise from the horizontal

    (b)   30° counterclockwise from the horizontal

    (c)   45° counterclockwise from the horizontal

19.2 For the stress element shown in Fig. 19.36, find the normal and shear stresses by summation of forces on a plane:

    (a)   15° counterclockwise from the horizontal

    (b)   30° counterclockwise from the horizontal

    (c)   45° counterclockwise from the horizontal

FIG. 19.35 Problems 19.1, 19.7, 19.13–19.24 (a part only).

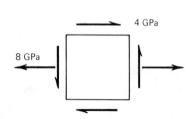

FIG. 19.36 Problems 19.2, 19.8, 19.13–19.24 (b part only).

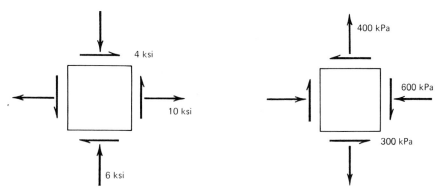

FIG. 19.37 Problems 19.3, 19.9, 19.13–19.24 (*c* part only).

FIG. 19.38 Problems 19.4, 19.10, 19.13–19.24 (*d* part only).

19.3 For the stress element shown in Fig. 19.37, find the normal and shear stresses by summation of forces on a plane:

(a) 15° counterclockwise from the horizontal

(b) 30° counterclockwise from the horizontal

(c) 45° counterclockwise from the horizontal

19.4 For the stress element shown in Fig. 19.38, find the normal and shear stresses by summation of forces on a plane:

(a) 20° counterclockwise from the horizontal

(b) 40° counterclockwise from the horizontal

(c) 60° counterclockwise from the horizontal

19.5 For the stress element shown in Fig. 19.39, find the normal and shear stresses by summation of forces on a plane:

(a) 20° counterclockwise from the horizontal

(b) 40° counterclockwise from the horizontal

(c) 60° counterclockwise from the horizontal

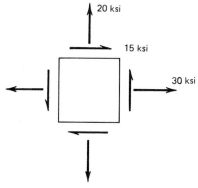

FIG. 19.39 Problems 19.5, 19.11, 19.13–19.24 (*e* part only).

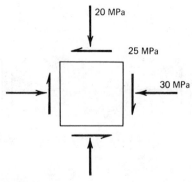

FIG. 19.40   Problems 19.6, 19.12, 19.13–19.24 (*f* part only).

19.6 For the stress element shown in Fig. 19.40, find the normal and shear stresses by summation of forces on a plane:

(a)   20° counterclockwise from the horizontal

(b)   40° counterclockwise from the horizontal

(c)   60° counterclockwise from the horizontal

19.7 For the stress element shown in Fig. 19.35, find the normal and shear stresses, using Eqs. 19.3 and 19.4, on a plane:

(a)   15° counterclockwise from the horizontal

(b)   30° counterclockwise from the horizontal

(c)   15° counterclockwise from the vertical

(d)   30° counterclockwise from the vertical

(e)   15° clockwise from the vertical

19.8 For the stress element shown in Fig. 19.36, find the normal and shear stress, using Eqs. 19.3 and 19.4, on a plane:

(a)   15° counterclockwise from the horizontal

(b)   30° counterclockwise from the horizontal

(c)   15° counterclockwise from the vertical

(d)   30° counterclockwise from the vertical

(e)   15° clockwise from the vertical

19.9 For the stress element shown in Fig. 19.37, find the normal and shear stress, using Eqs. 19.3 and 19.4, on a plane:

(a)   15° counterclockwise from the horizontal

(b)   30° counterclockwise from the horizontal

(c)   15° counterclockwise from the vertical

(d)   30° counterclockwise from the vertical

(e)   15° clockwise from the vertical

19.10 For the stress element shown in Fig. 19.38, find the normal and shear stress, using Eqs. 19.3 and 19.4, on a plane:

(a) 20° counterclockwise from the horizontal

(b) 40° counterclockwise from the horizontal

(c) 20° counterclockwise from the vertical

(d) 40° counterclockwise from the vertical

(e) 20° clockwise from the vertical

19.11 For the stress element shown in Fig. 19.39, find the normal and shear stress, using Eqs. 19.3 and 19.4, on a plane:

(a) 20° counterclockwise from the horizontal

(b) 40° counterclockwise from the horizontal

(c) 20° counterclockwise from the vertical

(d) 40° counterclockwise from the vertical

(e) 20° clockwise from the vertical

19.12 For the stress element shown in Fig. 19.40, find the normal and shear stress, using Eqs. 19.3 and 19.4, on a plane:

(a) 20° counterclockwise from the horizontal

(b) 40° counterclockwise from the horizontal

(c) 20° counterclockwise from the vertical

(d) 40° counterclockwise from the vertical

(e) 20° clockwise from the vertical

19.13 From Eq. 19.5, find the principal planes for the stress elements shown in the following figures:

(a) Fig. 19.35   (b) Fig. 19.36   (c) Fig. 19.37

(d) Fig. 19.38   (e) Fig. 19.39   (f) Fig. 19.40

19.14 From the results of Problem 19.13 and Eq. 19.3, calculate the principal stresses and sketch the element showing them for:

(a) Fig. 19.35   (b) Fig. 19.36   (c) Fig. 19.37

(d) Fig. 19.38   (e) Fig. 19.39   (f) Fig. 19.40

19.15 Using Eq. 19.6, calculate the principal stresses for:

(a) Fig. 19.35   (b) Fig. 19.36   (c) Fig. 19.37

(d) Fig. 19.38   (e) Fig. 19.39   (f) Fig. 19.40

19.16 For each indicated figure, calculate and plot the normal stresses every 15° from 0 to 180°. Calculate the principal stresses and their locations. Show these on the plot also.

(a) Fig. 19.35   (b) Fig. 19.36   (c) Fig. 19.37

(d) Fig. 19.38   (e) Fig. 19.39   (f) Fig. 19.40

19.17 Find the planes of maximum shear stress for the stress element shown in:

(a) Fig. 19.35   (b) Fig. 19.36   (c) Fig. 19.37

(d) Fig. 19.38   (e) Fig. 19.39   (f) Fig. 19.40

19.18 From the results of Problem 19.17 and Eqs. 19.3 and 19.4, calculate the maximum shear stress and the normal stress accompanying it for the stress element shown in:

(a) Fig. 19.35   (b) Fig. 19.36   (c) Fig. 19.37

(d) Fig. 19.38   (e) Fig. 19.39   (f) Fig. 19.40

19.19 Using Eqs. 19.9 and 19.10, find the maximum shear stress and the associated normal stress for:

(a) Fig. 19.35   (b) Fig. 19.36   (c) Fig. 19.37

(d) Fig. 19.38   (e) Fig. 19.39   (f) Fig. 19.40

19.20 Calculate and plot the shear stress every 15° from 0 to 180° for the following stress elements. Calculate the maximum shear stress and its location. Show this on the plot also.

(a) Fig. 19.35   (b) Fig. 19.36   (c) Fig. 19.37

(d) Fig. 19.38   (e) Fig. 19.39   (f) Fig. 19.40

19.21 Using Mohr's circle, *graphically* determine the principal stresses, the maximum shear stress, and the accompanying normal stress for the stress element shown in these figures:

(a) Fig. 19.35   (b) Fig. 19.36   (c) Fig. 19.37

(d) Fig. 19.38   (e) Fig. 19.39   (f) Fig. 19.40

19.22 Using Mohr's circle, *calculate* the maximum shear stress, the accompanying normal stress, the principal stresses, and all relevant angles, and sketch the appropriate stress elements showing these stresses and their orientation for the stress element in the following figures:

(a) Fig. 19.35   (b) Fig. 19.36   (c) Fig. 19.37

(d) Fig. 19.38   (e) Fig. 19.39   (f) Fig. 19.40

19.23 Using Mohr's circle, *graphically* find the stresses on the indicated plane for the indicated figure:

(a)   Fig. 19.35: 30° counterclockwise from the horizontal

(b)   Fig. 19.36: 30° clockwise from the horizontal

(c)   Fig. 19.37: 30° counterclockwise from the vertical

(d)   Fig. 19.38: 30° clockwise from the vertical

(e)   Fig. 19.39: 45° clockwise from the horizontal

(f)   Fig. 19.40: 45° clockwise from the vertical

19.24 Do Problem 19.23, *calculating* (using Mohr's circle) the indicated values.

19.25 Find the maximum shear stress and the principal stresses at point *A* in Fig. 19.41.

19.26 Find the maximum shear stress and the principal stresses at point *B* in Fig. 19.41.

19.27 Find the maximum shear stress and the principal stresses at point *A* in Fig. 19.42.

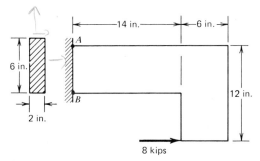

FIG. 19.41   Problems 19.25, 19.26.

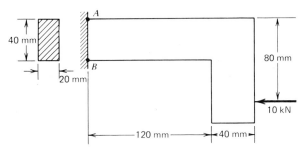

FIG. 19.42   Problems 19.27, 19.28.

19.28 Find the maximum shear stress and the principal stresses at point B in Fig. 19.42.

19.29 For the $\frac{3}{4}$-in.-diameter shaft in Fig. 19.43, find the maximum shear stress and the principal stresses on the element at:

(a) A (b) B (c) C

(d) D (e) E (f) F

(g) G

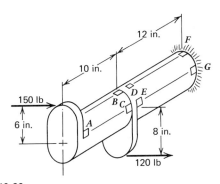

FIG. 19.43   Problem 19.29.

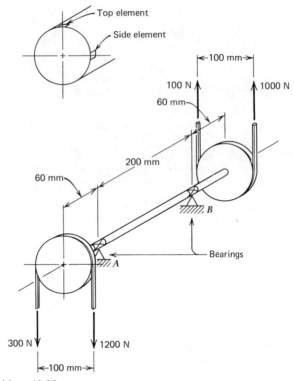

FIG. 19.44   Problem 19.30.

19.30 The transmission shaft in Fig. 19.44 is 20 mm in diameter. Treating the bearings as simple supports, find the maximum shear stress and the principal stresses on the indicated element. The length of the bearing is negligible.

(a) Just before bearing *A*, top element

(b) Just before bearing *A*, side element

(c) Just after bearing *A*, top element

(d) Just after bearing *A*, side element

(e) Just before bearing *B*, top element

(f) Just before bearing *B*, side element

(g) Just after bearing *B*, top element

(h) Just after bearing *B*, side element

20

Columns

20.1 BUCKLING

The buckling of structures is not something we observe every day. This is fortunate, because when buckling failures do occur, they are usually catastrophic. Catastrophic failures are unpleasant and limit one's opportunity to exercise one's design talent. We therefore expend considerable effort to prevent buckling.

While buckling is not observed frequently in structures, we are nonetheless quite familiar with the phenomenon. The futility of pushing on a rope is documented in legend, fairy tale, and even a few ethnic jokes. We know that the cable that can carry tons in tension cannot carry pounds in compression. That is a form of buckling. We can place a fairly large load perpendicular to the page you are reading—in excess of a hundred pounds. The paper will not be crushed. We can cut this page from the book and pull on it with 10 or 20 lb (if we grip it carefully). However, if we push on the same paper, we find that it folds quickly at the slightest load. We can dramatically change the capacity of this sheet of paper to carry a compressive load by rolling it into a cylinder. If we roll the same piece of paper into a cylinder, it will support its own weight (it would not before) and some small load besides.

These are examples of members that buckle under very low loads. For other members the load required for buckling can be more substantial. And we can have controlled buckling where catastrophic failure does not occur. Energy is simply stored elastically and then restored at the appropriate time. Large amounts of energy can be stored in this manner. A pole vaulter's pole is an example of such a device in which controlled buckling is a favorable event. Buckling can also be used to advantage by absorbing large amounts of energy as it occurs. The accordion-type buckling of the sheet metal and frame of an automobile takes much of the energy of a collision that otherwise would go to the vehicle occupant.

Thus we see that buckling can be elastic or plastic. It also can be catastrophic or advantageous. Buckling can occur in most types of loading, and it shows up in many forms. If we are addressing the compressive near-axial loading of members, we frequently call the members columns. In this book we are only concerned with the buckling of columns.

20.2 EULER'S EQUATION (THAT'S "OILERS," PADNUH!)

Consider a column as shown in Fig. 20.1a. This column is initially straight. It carries a compressive perfectly axial load P just sufficient to initiate buckling. This load is called the critical load. The end conditions are very important to this analysis. The column is pinned on both ends. We call it "*pinned-pinned*" (once again demonstrating our profound grasp of the language). In statics, "pinned" normally means that only rotations about the pin are allowed. We mean that here; plus, we will allow a small movement vertically at one of the supports. Otherwise we could not get the load to the member. Thus Fig. 20.1b represents the loaded and slightly buckled beam. As in statics, no motion to the left or right is allowed by these supports.

Establishing a coordinate system of positive y to the right and positive x downward, we move to any arbitrary distance x from the top support, pass a cutting plane, and draw a free body diagram of a portion of the column in equilibrium, as in Fig. 20.1c. In addition to the compressive load P, the cut section will have a moment equal to the force P times y, the distance the section has buckled away from its original centerline. If we sum the moments of force about the origin, we find that the moment at the section is equal to P times y:

$$M = Py$$

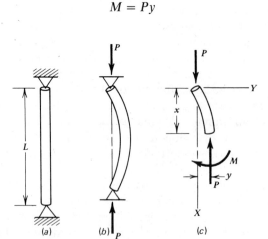

FIG. 20.1a–c Buckling of a simply supported column.

This is a vector equation, and as we have seen a vector sign system is not adequate to fully describe internal loads. In this case the bending moment is what we have called negative bending, in that it bends the beam "above" ($+y$) the x axis. Thus we write:

$$M = -Py$$

where P will carry the magnitude of the critical load. From Chapter 16 we learned that the bending moment was proportional to the curvature. The curvature is approximated by the second derivative for small deflections, and we have:

$$\frac{M}{EI} = \frac{d^2y}{dx^2} \qquad (16.4)$$

whose sign system fits the problem at hand. Making this substitution yields:

$$\frac{d^2y}{dx^2} = -\frac{P}{EI}\,y \qquad (20.1)$$

We transform the equation to the form:

$$\frac{d^2y}{dx^2} + \frac{P}{EI}\,y = 0 \qquad (20.2)$$

Our analysis of the problem has led us to an equation describing it. All that remains is to solve the equation. When studying beam deflections we were able to solve second-degree differential equations (heavy stuff) by integrating them twice. That won't work here because of the y on the right-hand side of Eq. 20.1. (We cannot integrate $\int y\,dx$ unless we know how y is related to x, which is, of course, what we are after to start with.) The solution of equations like this is formally studied in courses on differential equations. Without getting into that, we will simply state that it has a solution of the form:

$$y = A \sin \sqrt{\frac{P}{EI}}\,x + B \cos \sqrt{\frac{P}{EI}}\,x \qquad (20.3)$$

which is the general equation of a sine wave. Note that the deflected column in Fig. 20.1b resembles a portion of a sine wave. To show that Eq. (20.3) is *the* solution is quite an effort; however, it may be shown to be *a* solution quite easily. If we find its second derivative and substitute the appropriate values into Eq. 20.2, it will be satisfied. Any value or function for y that satisfies the equation is *a* solution to the equation. This exercise is left to the reader.

The proposed solution has two arbitrary constants, A and B. As we saw when we studied deflection, the values of arbitrary constants depend on the boundary conditions of the problem. They make the general solution fit the specific problem. In this case there is no deflection in the y direction at either end. Thus the boundary conditions are:

$$y_0 = 0$$
$$y_L = 0$$

Imposing these conditions leads to:

$$B = 0$$

and

$$A \sin \sqrt{\frac{P}{EI}}\,(L) = 0 \tag{20.4}$$

If $A = 0$, Eq. 20.4 becomes:

$$y = 0$$

for all values of x. This is a trivial solution, since it means there is no buckling. The alternate way of satisfying Eq. 20.4 is for:

$$\sin \sqrt{\frac{P}{EI}}\,(L) = 0$$

The sine is equal to zero when the argument (angle) is 0, 180°, 360°, ..., $n(180°)$ or in radian measure 0, π, 2π, ..., $n\pi$. Zero degrees (or radians) is a trivial solution (requiring a zero load, so no problem). The first nontrivial solution is:

$$\sqrt{\frac{P}{EI}}\,(L) = \pi$$

Solving this for P we have:

$$P_{CR} = \frac{\pi^2 EI}{L^2} \tag{20.5}$$

The subscript CR denotes *critical*, and we call P_{CR} the *critical load*, that is, the load at which buckling will be initiated. Loads below this value will not produce buckling in perfectly straight, axially loaded columns. The equation is known as *Euler's equation*. It is pronounced "oilers."

20.3   USING EULER'S EQUATION

Now that we've got it (Euler's equation), let's see what it is good for. First of all, what does it say about the critical or limiting load for buckling? It says that the critical load is proportional to the modulus of elasticity or stiffness of the material. That means that a steel column can carry three times the load of an identical aluminum column. Note that it is *stiffness*, not strength, that governs the load-carrying capability in buckling. By heat treating steel, the strength of the material can be greatly increased while its stiffness is unchanged. Thus although heat treating can increase a member's resistance to stress, it cannot increase a column's resistance to buckling. Next we see that the critical load is proportional to the moment of inertia. The smaller the moment of inertia, the smaller the load required for buckling. If the end conditions are the same in every direction, buckling will occur in the direction of minimum moment of inertia. Thus, a 2 × 4 buckles in the 2-in. direction, not the 4-in. one. If the cross section does not have symmetry, such as an angle iron, the buckling may not be parallel to a side but in

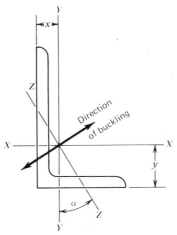

FIG. 20.2 The direction of buckling is perpendicular to the axis of minimum moment of inertia.

some third direction. Tables A-13 and A-14 give the cross-sectional properties of angle iron. As shown in Fig. 20.2 a third axis, Z–Z, is given, about which the moment of inertia is less than it is about either the X–X or Y–Y axes. When buckling occurs in these members its direction will be perpendicular to the Z–Z axis, the axis of minimum moment of inertia. Accordingly, Tables A-13 and A-14, give these properties as well.

Last, the Euler formula indicates that the critical load varies indirectly with the length squared. Thus doubling the length of a column will reduce the load it can carry without buckling by a factor of 4. Of course, changing the length has no effect on the direct stress.

Recall now that the radius of gyration is defined as the square root of the moment of inertia divided by the area. Or:

$$I = k^2 A$$

Substituting into Eq. 20.5 gives:

$$P_{CR} = \frac{\pi^2 E k^2 A}{L^2} \tag{20.6}$$

We divide both sides by A and move k^2 to the denominator, yielding:

$$\frac{P_{CR}}{A} = \frac{\pi^2 E}{\left(\dfrac{L}{k}\right)^2} \tag{20.7}$$

Equations 20.5 through 20.7 are all referred to as Euler's equation. The form of Eq. 20.7 is probably the most common. It gives the load over the area on the left-hand side, which may be thought of as the *critical stress*; that is, it is the value of normal stress at which buckling will occur. The denominator on the right-hand side, L/k, is known as the *slenderness ratio*. This is just the length divided by the radius of gyration (with the two having the same units). It is a governing parameter for columns, as we shall see.

Example Problem 20.1

An 8-ft-long 2 × 4 (actual size) is to be used as a column (Fig. 20.3). Calculate the slenderness ratio that will govern buckling if the supports are uniform in every direction.

Solution

We find the moment of inertia about the X and Y axes.

$$I_x = \frac{bh^3}{12} = \frac{2(4)^3}{12} = 10.7 \text{ in.}^4$$

$$I_y = \frac{bh^3}{12} = \frac{4(2)^3}{12} = 2.67 \text{ in.}^4$$

From Eq. 20.5 we see that the minimum moment of inertia will govern buckling. Thus we use:

$$I_y = 2.67 \text{ in.}^4$$

Then:

$$k_y = \sqrt{\frac{I_y}{A}} = \sqrt{\frac{2.67 \text{ in.}^4}{2 \text{ in.}(4 \text{ in.})}} = 0.577 \text{ in.}$$

Note that a minimum radius of gyration corresponds to a minimum moment of inertia. Finally,

$$\frac{L}{k_y} = \frac{8 \text{ ft}}{0.577 \text{ in.}} \left(\frac{12 \text{ in.}}{\text{ft}} \right) = 166$$

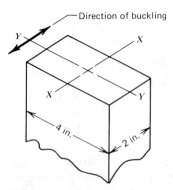

FIG. 20.3 Example Problem 20.1.

For comparison purposes, we calculate the alternate slenderness ratio:

$$k_x = \sqrt{\frac{10.7}{8}} = 1.15 \text{ in.}$$

$$\frac{L}{k_x} = \frac{8 \text{ ft}}{1.15 \text{ in.}}\left(\frac{12 \text{ in.}}{\text{ft}}\right) = 83.5$$

Thus we see that minimum moment of inertia, minimum radius of gyration, and maximum slenderness ratio all go together and correspond to the limit on the critical load.

Example Problem 20.2

Find the critical load for the column of Example Problem 20.1 if it is simply supported (pinned ends) and of southern pine. What compressive stress would the critical load produce?

Solution

From Eq. 20.7 we have:

$$P_{CR} = \frac{\pi^2 E A}{\left(\dfrac{L}{k}\right)^2}$$

From Example Problem 20.1, the slenderness ratio was found to be:

$$\frac{L}{k} = 166$$

From Table A-8 we get a modulus of elasticity of:

$$E = 1.6 \times 10^6 \text{ psi}$$

Then:

$$P_{CR} = \frac{\pi^2 (1.6 \times 10^6 \text{ lb})(8 \text{ in.}^2)}{\text{in.}^2 (166^2)} = 4580 \text{ lb}$$

The stress produced would be:

$$\sigma_{CR} = \frac{P_{CR}}{A} = \frac{4580 \text{ lb}}{8 \text{ in.}^2} = 573 \text{ psi}$$

This wood has a compressive strength of 8400 psi. In this case the load it can carry without buckling is much less than that required for a compressive failure. Under this loading the beam will buckle.

20.4 END CONDITIONS FOR COLUMNS

Equation 20.5 indicates that the critical load is a function of the modulus of elasticity, the length and the cross-sectional moment of inertia. A fourth factor, not revealed by this equation, consists of the *end conditions*. In Fig. 20.1 the column was pinned on each end. In Fig. 20.4 we show a similar column that is *fixed* on each end; that is, the ends will not be permitted to rotate. If we analyze this column as we did the pinned-pinned column in Section 20.2, we will find the following result:

$$P_{CR} = \frac{4\pi^2 EI}{L^2}$$

which says the critical load for a column with fixed ends is four times what it is for one with pinned ends. We can rewrite this as follows:

$$P_{CR} = \frac{\pi^2 EI}{(L/2)^2}$$

If we now introduce an *equivalent length* as:

$$L_E = \tfrac{1}{2}L \tag{20.8}$$

we can express the previous equation as follows:

$$P_{CR} = \frac{\pi^2 EI}{L_E^2} \tag{20.9}$$

This is the same form as Eq. 20.5.

We might have arrived at this conclusion intuitively by noticing that the middle portion of the column in Fig. 20.4b is similar in shape to the entire length of the column in Fig. 20.1b. Other end conditions are shown in Fig. 20.5. Their equivalent lengths are as indicated. Equation 20.8 is generalized as follows:

$$L_E = KL \tag{20.10}$$

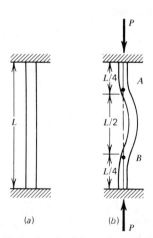

(a) (b)

FIG. 20.4a–b Buckling of a column with fixed ends.

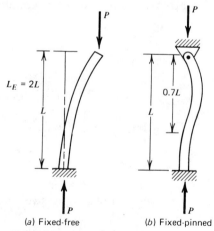

(a) Fixed-free (b) Fixed-pinned

FIG. 20.5a–b Additional buckling modes.

TABLE 20.1 EQUIVALENT LENGTH
FACTORS, $L_E = KL$

End Conditions	K
Fixed-fixed	0.5
Fixed-pinned	0.7
Pinned-pinned	1.0
Fixed-free	2.0

with values for K indicated in Figs. 20.1, 20.4, and 20.5 and Table 20.1. These values of K are theoretical. In practice, slightly larger, more conservative values are used. Also note that we are using a lowercase k for radius of gyration and a capital K for the *equivalent length factor*.

Noting that the critical load varies inversely with the square of the equivalent length, we see that a column with fixed-fixed end conditions can carry four times the load of pinned-pinned; fixed-pinned can carry twice as much, and fixed-free can carry only one-fourth as much.

Equation 20.7 is rewritten as follows:

$$\frac{P_{CR}}{A} = \frac{\pi^2 E}{\left(\dfrac{L_E}{k}\right)^2} \tag{20.11}$$

Example Problem 20.3

The 2 × 4 of Example Problem 20.2 has both ends fixed. What is its critical load?

Solution

From Example Problem 20.2:

$$k = 0.577 \text{ in.}$$
$$E = 1.6 \times 10^6 \text{ psi}$$
$$L = 96 \text{ in.}$$

From Table 20.1, $K = 0.5$. The equivalent length is:

$$L_E = KL = 0.5(96 \text{ in.}) = 48 \text{ in.}$$

And the equivalent slenderness ratio is:

$$\frac{L_E}{k} = \frac{48}{0.577} = 83.2$$

Last, we find the critical load:

$$P_{CR} = \frac{\pi^2 E A}{\left(\dfrac{L_E}{k}\right)^2} = \frac{\pi^2 (1.6 \times 10^6 \text{ lb})8 \text{ in.}^2}{\text{in.}^2 (83.2)^2}$$

$$P_{CR} = \textbf{18,300 lb}$$

This is four times the 4580-lb load the same column could carry with pinned-pinned end conditions.

Example Problem 20.4

A 50 mm × 150 mm timber is pinned on both ends along the X axis as shown in Fig. 20.6. If it is 4 m long and of southern pine, find its critical loads.

Solution

For the support shown the pin allows rotation in the 150 mm, or Y, direction (about the X axis). However, it does not allow rotation in the 50-mm, or X, direction (about the Y axis). Consequently, we must examine both modes of buckling. The critical load for the column will be the smaller of the two.

Buckling in the 150-mm Direction (Fig. 20.7)

The moment of inertia is about the X axis, so b is parallel to this axis. Thus $b = 50$ mm:

$$I_x = \frac{bh^3}{12} = \frac{50 \text{ mm}(150 \text{ mm})^3}{12} = 1.406 \text{ } E7 \text{ mm}^4$$

The radius of gyration is:

$$k_x = \sqrt{\frac{I_x}{A}} = \sqrt{\frac{1.406 \text{ } E7 \text{ mm}^4}{50 \text{ mm}(150 \text{ mm})}} = \sqrt{1.875 \text{ } E3 \text{ mm}^2} = 43.3 \text{ mm}$$

For this direction the end conditions are pinned-pinned, so $K = 1$ and the equivalent length is the actual length:

$$L_E = KL = 1(4 \text{ m}) = 4.00 \text{ m}$$

The slenderness ratio is:

$$\frac{L_E}{k_x} = \frac{4 \text{ m}}{0.0433 \text{ m}} = 92.4$$

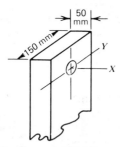

FIG. 20.6 Example Problem 20.4.

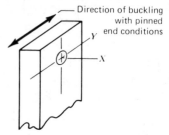

FIG. 20.7 Buckling in the Y direction.

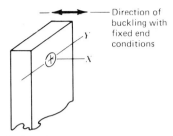

FIG. 20.8 Buckling in the X direction.

and the critical load is:

$$P_{CR} = \frac{\pi^2 EA}{\left(\dfrac{L_E}{k}\right)^2} = \frac{\pi^2(11.0\ E9\ \text{N})(0.150\ \text{m})(0.050\ \text{m})}{\text{m}^2(92.4)^2}$$

$$P_{CR} = 95.4\ \text{kN} \qquad \textbf{for the 150-mm direction}$$

Buckling on the 50-mm Direction (Fig. 20.8)

$$I_y = \frac{bh^3}{12} = \frac{150(50)^3}{12} = 1.562\ E6\ \text{mm}^4$$

$$k_y = \sqrt{\frac{I_y}{A}} = \sqrt{\frac{1.562\ E6\ \text{mm}^4}{50\ \text{mm}(150\ \text{mm})}} = 14.4\ \text{mm}$$

For this direction the end conditions are fixed-fixed, so $K = 0.5$ and the equivalent length is:

$$L_E = KL = 0.5(4\ \text{in.}) = 2.00\ \text{m}$$

The equivalent slenderness ratio is:

$$\frac{L_E}{k} = \frac{2\ \text{m}}{0.0144\ \text{m}} = 139$$

$$P_{CR} = \frac{\pi^2 EA}{\left(\dfrac{L_E}{k}\right)^2} = \frac{\pi^2(11.0\ E9\ \text{N})(0.150\ \text{m})(0.050\ \text{m})}{\text{m}^2(139)^2}$$

$$P_{CR} = 42.1\ \text{kN}$$

Thus the critical load for the column is 42.1 kN, and buckling will occur first in the 50-mm direction. Notice that in the critical load calculation the numbers are identical except for the slenderness ratios. We could have selected the failure mode by comparing slenderness ratios, saving one calculation.

20.5 SHORT COLUMNS AND LONG COLUMNS

In understanding column behavior it is useful to make a plot of Equation 20.11. The line *AB* in Fig. 20.9 is such a plot, and it indicates that for small slenderness ratios, the critical stress is very high. For very high slenderness ratios the stress is

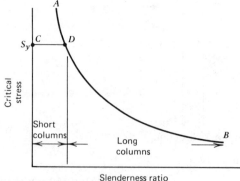

FIG. 20.9   Stress versus slenderness ratio.

very low. If we draw an additional line *CD*, we can illustrate some very important properties of columns. The line *CD* represents the yield strength of the material. If, on the one hand, the critical stress is greater than the yield strength (points on *AD*), the column will yield before buckling. On the other hand, if the critical stress is less than the yield strength, the column will buckle before yielding. Thus the line *CDB* represents failure of a column and the limiting compressive stress. From *C* to *D* the column will fail because of yielding and from *D* to *B* because of buckling. At *D* yielding and buckling are equally likely. We call a column governed by yield strength a *short column*. This will theoretically be from *C* to *D*. We call a column governed by Euler's equation a *long column*. This will theoretically be from *D* to *B* (and beyond).

We have hinted that the characterization of long and short columns is *theoretical*. This is true, especially as we approach point *D*. Column tests are difficult to conduct. Members are supposed to be perfectly straight and perfectly homogeneous. The load is perfectly axial and the end conditions approach the idealized state. Of course, these conditions are never absolutely realized, which leads to variation in the results. Near point *D* in Fig. 20.9, test results tend to fall under the theoretical curve. This undercutting is shown as the cross-hatched area in Fig. 20.10. The cross-hatching is bounded by points *E* and *F*. The region from

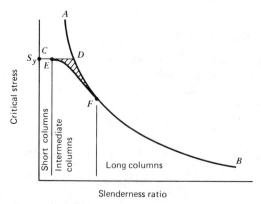

FIG. 20.10   Intermediate columns.

E to *F* represents *intermediate columns*. The region *C* to *E* represents *short col-umns*. These columns are governed by the yield strength. The region beyond *F* represents *long columns* which are governed by Euler's formula.

There are a number of design approaches for intermediate columns, most of them empirical. By empirical we mean we have an equation or procedure that fits the test results without necessarily having a theoretical basis. Some of these formulas take into account some eccentricity of the load as well. For the purpose of this text—developing an understanding of the buckling phenomenon—we return to the idealized analysis of Fig. 20.9, where columns are either long or short. We assume that they will fail on the basis of yield (or ultimate) strength or by buckling according to Euler's equation. We leave the various empirical methods to courses in structures or machine design. You should note that the *method presented here is not valid for columns with eccentric loading or columns in the intermediate domain.*

Example Problem 20.5

A mild steel column ($S_y = 35$ ksi, $E = 29,000$ ksi) is to carry 20 kips. Assuming the ends to be fixed, determine the factor of safety for this 12 ft S 8 × 18.4.

Solution

From Table A-10:

$$A = 5.41 \text{ in.}^2$$
$$r_x = 3.26 \text{ in.} = k_x$$
$$r_y = 0.831 \text{ in.} = k_y$$

Because the end conditions are the same in either direction, the critical stress will be limited by the smaller radius of gyration. From Table 20.1, the equivalent length factor *K* is 0.5. Then the equivalent length is:

$$L_E = KL = 0.5(12 \text{ ft})12 \text{ in./ft} = 72.0 \text{ in.}$$

and the equivalent slenderness ratio is:

$$\frac{L_E}{k} = \frac{72.0 \text{ in.}}{0.831 \text{ in.}} = 86.6$$

Then by Eq. 20.11 the critical stress is:

$$\sigma_{CR} = \frac{\pi^2 E}{(L/k)^2} = \frac{\pi^2(29,000 \text{ kips})}{\text{in.}^2(86.6)^2} = \mathbf{38.1 \text{ ksi}}$$

This is the stress the column can carry without buckling. The stress the column can carry without yielding is:

$$S_y = 35.0 \text{ ksi}$$

Since it is less than σ_{CR}, it will limit the load and this is a "short column." The allowable load is:

$$P_A = S_y A = 35.0(5.41 \text{ in.}^2) = 189 \text{ kips}$$

The factor of safety N is the allowable load divided by the actual load.

$$N = \frac{P_{allowable}}{P_{actual}} = \frac{187 \text{ kips}}{20 \text{ kips}} = \textbf{9.47}$$

20.6   IDEALIZED DESIGN OF COLUMNS

We have Euler's equation in two forms:

$$P_{CR} = \frac{\pi^2 EI}{L_E^2} \tag{20.9}$$

$$\frac{P_{CR}}{A} = \frac{\pi^2 E}{\left(\dfrac{L_E}{k}\right)^2} \tag{20.11}$$

Equation 20.11 is the more functional form of the equation as we seek to understand the buckling phenomenon. It is in terms of the slenderness ratio, which is a governing parameter for columns. Most of the empirical methods use the slenderness ratio as well. This equation also is useful for analysis, giving a critical stress that can be readily compared to the yield strength of the material to determine which one governs. The governing stress can then be compared with the applied stress to determine the adequacy of the column.

If our problem is not analysis but design, Eq. 20.11 is awkward. In design problems we seek a structural member that will carry the required load. Equation 20.11 has its geometric factors, A and k, separated. For design purposes, Eq. 20.9 is much more functional. We substitute the problem parameters, solve for I, and select an appropriate member from tables or geometric formulas. Finally, the column must be checked against its yield or ultimate strength.

Example Problem 20.6

Select a steel, equal-leg angle member for a column to carry a 10-kip load, with a safety factor of 3. The column is to be 14 ft long with each end rigidly fixed.

$$S_y = 35 \text{ ksi} \quad \text{and} \quad E = 29,000 \text{ ksi}$$

Solution

From Eq. 20.9:

$$P_{CR} = \frac{\pi^2 EI}{L_E^2}$$

Solving for I:

$$I = \frac{P_{CR} L_E^2}{\pi^2 E}$$

In the past we have applied the factor of safety to the strength of the material.

Since buckling does not depend on the strength of the material, that approach will not do here. If we apply the factor of safety to the load, we will take care of strength *and* buckling. Thus $P_{\text{allowable}} = NP_{\text{actual}}$

$$P_A = 3(10) = 30 \text{ kips}$$

For fixed-fixed ends K is 0.5 and the equivalent length is:

$$L_E = 0.5(14 \text{ ft})\left(\frac{12 \text{ in.}}{\text{ft}}\right) = 84.0 \text{ in.}$$

Then:

$$I = \frac{30 \text{ kips}(84 \text{ in.})^2(\text{in.}^2)}{\pi^2(29,000) \text{ kips}} = \textbf{0.740 in.}^4$$

Going to Table A-13 to select a number, note that r (our k) will be minimum about the Z–Z axis. This will require computing $I_z = Ak^2$, since only the radius of gyration is given in the table. We select the following candidates:

L 5 × 5 × $\frac{5}{16}$(10.3)	$3.03(0.994)^2 = 2.99 \text{ in.}^4$
L 4 × 4 × $\frac{1}{4}$(6.6)	$1.94(0.795)^2 = 1.23 \text{ in.}^4$
L $3\frac{1}{2}$ × $3\frac{1}{2}$ × $\frac{1}{4}$(5.8)	$1.69(0.694)^2 = 0.814 \text{ in.}^4$
L 3 × 3 × $\frac{1}{4}$(4.9)	$1.44(0.592)^2 = 0.505 \text{ in.}^4$ too small

The smallest member with sufficient I is the **L $3\frac{1}{2}$ × $3\frac{1}{2}$ × $\frac{1}{4}$ at 5.8 lb/ft.** Checking for direct stress, we write:

$$A = \frac{P}{S_y} = \frac{30 \text{ kips (in.}^2)}{35 \text{ kips}} = 0.857 \text{ in.}^2$$

The cross-sectional area of the specific angle iron is 1.69 in.^{2}, which is greater than required for yielding. So buckling governs. Use the **L $3\frac{1}{2}$ × $3\frac{1}{2}$ × $\frac{1}{4}$.**

20.7 DESIGN FORMULAS

The foregoing discussion has emphasized the concepts of buckling and how a member in compression may fail. It draws out the significance of such terms as slenderness ratio, effective length, end conditions, short columns, intermediate columns, and long columns. It emphasizes the relation between buckling and the applied load, the cross-sectional geometry, and the material properties. Having done all that, is it too much to ask that it also *actually* be a practical method for designing columns? In many cases, yes!

In our discussion we treated the problem in an idealized fashion, and we presumed to understand some things that are not so well understood. Beams usually are not "perfectly straight," loads are not "perfectly centered," and end conditions cannot be perfectly described as "pinned" or "fixed." Alas, the "real world" of columns, like so many "real worlds," is not perfect.

To account for these imperfections, numerous empirical equations have been developed for various applications. By empirical we mean equations that are based on experimental and/or field data. They describe our laboratory or field experience to some degree, but may not lend themselves to theoretical development.

One of the more common of these is the J. B. Johnson formula. It can be written as follows:

$$\frac{P_{CR}}{A} = a - b\left(\frac{L}{k}\right)^2 \tag{20.12}$$

where the constants a and b depend on the material properties and other factors. An equation that takes into account the eccentricity of the load is known as the *secant formula*:

$$\frac{P}{A} = \frac{S_y}{1 + \left(\dfrac{ec}{k^2}\right)\sec\left[\dfrac{L}{k}\sqrt{\dfrac{P}{4AE}}\right]} \tag{20.13}$$

In this formula e is the eccentricity of the load, that is, its distance from the centroid. The distance from the neutral axis to the extreme fiber is c, as it was in bending.

In addition to these fairly general forms, very specific forms have been specified by trade organizations concerned with steel, aluminum, wood, and other products. Some of these and others are also contained in building codes that are legally binding.

20.8 SUMMARY

Euler's equation is the basic governing equation for columns:

$$P_{CR} = \frac{\pi^2 EI}{L_E^2}$$

The load a column can carry without buckling, the critical load, depends on the column length, moment of inertia of its cross section, end conditions, and the modulus of elasticity. It does not depend on the strength of the material. In terms of critical stress, Euler's equation is:

$$\sigma_{CR} = \frac{P_{CR}}{A} = \frac{\pi^2 E}{\left(\dfrac{L_E}{k}\right)^2}$$

where L_E/k is the slenderness ratio. The equivalent length is:

$$L_E = KL$$

where K depends on the end conditions.

For *short* columns

$$\sigma_{CR} > \sigma_{yield}$$

and σ_{yield} governs.

For *long* columns:

$$\sigma_{CR} < \sigma_{yield}$$

and σ_{CR} governs.

Intermediate columns are transitional regions between short and long columns; here, empirical equations govern.

The equations above emphasize the phenomenon of buckling and its related parameters under ideal conditions. Empirical equations prescribed by trade organizations and codes supersede them.

PROBLEMS

For Problems 20.1 through 20.12, assume that the end effects apply in every direction.

20.1 Find the slenderness ratios for each assigned column in Table 20.2.

20.2 Find the slenderness ratios for each assigned column in Table 20.3.

20.3 Find the critical load for each assigned column in Table 20.2 if the column is pinned on each end.

20.4 Find the critical load for each assigned column in Table 20.2 if the column is fixed on each end.

20.5 Find the critical load for each assigned column in Table 20.2 if one end is fixed and the other free.

20.6 Find the critical load for each assigned column in Table 20.2 if one end is fixed and the other pinned.

TABLE 20.2 COLUMN PROPERTIES FOR PROBLEMS
20.1, 20.3–20.6: COLUMN LENGTH: 12 ft

	Cross Section	Material
(a)	2 × 4 actual size	Southern pine
(b)	4 × 12 (S4S)	Southern pine
(c)	S 8 × 23.0	Steel
(d)	3-in.-diameter standard weight pipe	Steel
(e)	3-in.-diameter solid shaft	Steel
(f)	L 4 × 4 × $\frac{3}{4}$	Steel
(g)	L 5 × $3\frac{1}{2}$ × $\frac{3}{4}$	Steel

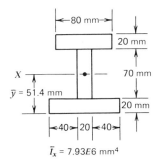

$\bar{I}_x$ = 7.93E6 mm⁴

FIG. 20.11 Problems 20.2, 20.7, 20.8, 20.9, 20.10.

20.7 Find the critical load for each assigned column in Table 20.3 if the column is pinned on each end.

20.8 Find the critical load for each assigned column in Table 20.3 if the column is fixed on each end.

20.9 Find the critical load for each assigned column in Table 20.3 if the column is fixed on one end and free on the other.

20.10 Find the critical load for each assigned column in Table 20.3 if the column is fixed on one end and pinned on the other.

20.11 The following members are to be used as columns. In each case calculate the load the column can carry based on its yield (or ultimate) strength and based on Euler's formula. Indicate which one will govern the design.

(a)   4 in. × 4 in. (S4S), 4-ft long, southern pine, fixed-fixed

(b)   6-in. pipe, 18-in. long, steel, fixed-fixed

(c)   L8 × 8 × 1, 6-ft long, steel, fixed-free

(d)   Do part (c) if the material is aluminum.

20.12 The following members are to be used as columns. In each case calculate the load the member can carry based on its yield (or ultimate) strength and based on Euler's formula. Indicate which one will govern the design.

(a)   100 mm × 100 mm, 1.40-m long, southern pine, fixed-fixed

(b)   150 mm (125-mm I.D.) pipe, 500-mm long, steel, fixed-fixed

(c)   Do part (b) if the material is aluminum.

TABLE 20.3   COLUMN PROPERTIES FOR PROBLEMS
20.2, 20.7–20.10: COLUMN LENGTH: 4 m

Cross Section	Material
(a) 50 mm × 100 mm	Southern pine
(b) 100 mm × 300 mm	Southern pine
(c) A pipe with 80 mm O.D. and 60 mm I.D.	Steel
(d) Cross section of Fig. 20.11	Steel

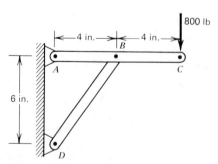

FIG. 20.12   Problem 20.13.

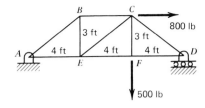

FIG. 20.13 Problem 20.16.

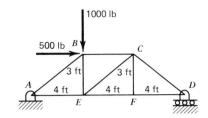

FIG. 20.14 Problem 20.17.

20.13 Member *BD* in Fig. 20.12 is to be a solid steel rod ($S_y = 35$ ksi). Find the diameter required. Check both buckling and yielding.

20.14 A flag pole sitter weighs 200 lb. He performs on top of a 30-ft pole. Using a factor of safety of 4, select an appropriate steel pipe for this flag pole.

20.15 A flag pole sitter weighs 900 N. He performs on top of a 10-m pole. Using a factor of safety of 4, select an appropriate steel pipe for this flag pole if I.D. = 0.80 O.D.

20.16 The truss in Fig. 20.13 is to be made of southern pine. Each member is to be square. Assume each joint to be pinned. Identify the members where buckling is of concern. Select the size of each indicated member.

(a) *AB*	(b) *AE*	(c) *BE*	(d) *BC*	(e) *EC*
(f) *EF*	(g) *CD*	(h) *CF*	(i) *FD*	

20.17 The truss in Fig. 20.14 is to be made of aluminum. Each member has a square cross section. Assume each joint to be pinned. Identify the members where buckling is of concern. Select the size of each indicated member.

(a) *AB*	(b) *AE*	(c) *BE*	(d) *BC*	(e) *EC*
(f) *EF*	(g) *CD*	(h) *CF*	(i) *FD*	

20.18 Identify all compression members in Fig. 20.15. Select a solid steel rod for each compression member.

20.19 Identify all compression members in Fig. 20.16. Select a solid steel rod for each compression member.

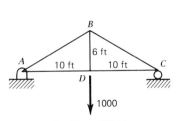

FIG. 20.15 Problem 20.18.

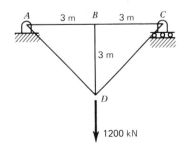

FIG. 20.16 Problem 20.19.

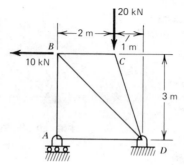

FIG. 20.17   Problem 20.20.

20.20 Identify all compression members in Fig. 20.17. Select a square bronze column for each member in compression.

21

Miscellaneous Applications

The material of Chapters 10 through 20 constitutes the basics of strength of materials. In this chapter we look at some additional applications, as well as some limitations. These are just a few of many applications but they illustrate how the principles may be applied in several important ways. Additional applications can be found in texts on machine design and structural analysis and design. These texts amplify further the limitations of the principles as they are applied.

21.1   CYLINDRICAL PRESSURE VESSELS

The results of the analysis of pressure vessels are important in themselves because of the wide use of pressure vessels. They are important to us beyond that, in that the analysis indicates how the principles may be applied to new problems.

First, we consider a cylindrical tank with plane ends (Fig. 21.1a). Note that these results are not limited to tanks with plane ends; however, this condition may make the analysis clearer for those not familiar with fluid mechanics. The internal pressure in the tank is p. A cutting plane is passed through the tank perpendicular to the longitudinal axis, resulting in Fig. 21.1b, which also shows the pressure acting on the flat end of the tank and the stress acting on the cross section of the tank. For a thin shell (thickness $t < 0.1$ times the radius R) any variation of this stress with the radial direction is ignored. This stress is in the longitudinal direction and is, therefore, called the *longitudinal stress*, σ_L.

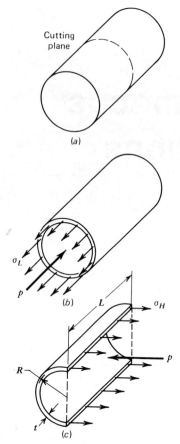

FIG. 21.1a–c Cylindrical pressure vessel.

We now sum the forces in the longitudinal direction. The force due to pressure will be the pressure times the area it acts over, or:

$$pA = p\pi R^2$$

where R is the radius of the tank.

The longitudinal stress acts on the area of the thin ring of thickness t. Thus it produces a force of:

$$\sigma_L A = \sigma_L(2\pi Rt)$$

Since these are the only forces acting longitudinally, they must be equal:

$$\sigma_L(2\pi Rt) = p\pi R^2$$

and

$$\sigma_L = p\left(\frac{R}{2t}\right) \tag{21.1}$$

We see that the longitudinal stress is equal to the internal pressure times the ratio of the radius to twice the thickness. Since we have required in our analysis that R be at least 10 times t, σ_L will be at least 5 times p.

We have assumed the end of the cylinder to be flat, to permit us to calculate the force due to pressure as simply pressure times area. Based on this, Eq. 21.1 would be valid only for tanks with flat ends. However, it turns out that the force in the longitudinal direction, because of pressure, is the same regardless of the shape of the end. Regardless of the shape, the force is the pressure times the *projected* area. The projected area is the area of a flat end, and Eq. 21.1 is valid for any cylindrical tank.

A second cutting plane is passed perpendicular to the longitudinal axis and a third through the longitudinal axis resulting in the C-shaped section of Fig. 21.1c. With this section we can examine the stresses acting in the circumferential direction. These are labeled σ_H and are called *hoop stresses*. Now we sum forces in the horizontal direction. The force due to internal pressure is the pressure times the projected area. Thus:

$$pA = p(2RL)$$

where L is the length of the section.

The force due to the hoop stress is:

$$\sigma_H A = \sigma_H(2tL)$$

Setting the two equal:

$$\sigma_H(2tL) = p(2RL)$$

Solving for the hoop stress gives:

$$\sigma_H = p\left(\frac{R}{t}\right) \tag{21.2}$$

This is twice the longitudinal stress and, therefore, will govern the design. As there are no shear stresses on these planes, the hoop and longitudinal stresses are the principal stresses, and the hoop stress, being the greater, will govern the design. Ductile failure of a cylindrical pressure vessel will often reveal this stress pattern by showing a longitudinal split in the vessel as the hoop stress pulls it apart.

The maximum normal stress in a cylindrical tank is the ratio of the radius to wall thickness times the pressure. This will be at least 10 times the pressure, typically greater. This stress will govern the design. These equations do not apply to "thick" pressure vessels in which the stress varies across the thickness of the vessel wall. Analysis of the stresses in thick vessels is a more advanced topic.

21.2 SPHERICAL PRESSURE VESSELS

In the section of a spherical pressure vessel shown in Fig. 21.2, a cutting plane has been passed through the center. The normal stress σ and the internal pressure p are indicated. The force due to the internal pressure is the pressure times the projected area.

$$pA = p(\pi R^2)$$

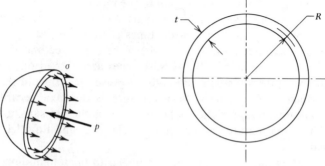

FIG. 21.2 Spherical pressure vessel.

The force due to the stress σ is the stress times the area of the thin ring it acts over:

$$\sigma A = \sigma(2\pi Rt)$$

Summing the forces horizontally sets the two equal:

$$\sigma(2\pi Rt) = p(\pi R^2)$$

Solving for σ gives:

$$\sigma = p\left(\frac{R}{2t}\right) \tag{21.3}$$

This is the same as the longitudinal stress given by Eq. 21.1, but only half the hoop stress given by Eq. 21.2. Hence the maximum stress produced in a spherical vessel is only half the maximum stress produced in a cylindrical one. A spherical vessel is inherently more efficient than a cylindrical one.

Plotting Mohr's circle for this pressure vessel produces a very interesting result. Although a vertical cutting plane was used for Fig. 21.2, its selection was arbitrary. Any other cutting plane through the center would produce a similar result. Thus we have equal normal stresses on perpendicular planes and no shear stress in Fig. 21.3a. To plot Mohr's circle, we plot $(\sigma_x, 0)$ and $(\sigma_y, 0)$. Since σ_x and σ_y are both defined by Eq. 21.3, these two points lie on top of each other, (Fig. 21.3b). In fact, the Mohr's circle for this state of stress is this point! Furthermore, the maximum stress, the minimum stress, and the stress on any plane are equal to this value. The shear stress on any plane is zero.

Example Problem 21.1

A cylindrical pressure vessel is to be 10 ft long and 4 ft in diameter. Find its thickness based on a yield strength of 36 ksi, if it is to carry 180 psi with a factor of safety of 4.

Solution

Equation 21.2 governs:

$$\sigma_H = p\left(\frac{R}{t}\right)$$

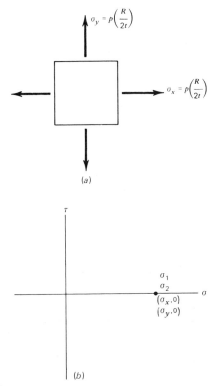

FIG. 21.3a–b   Mohr's circle for a spherical pressure vessel.

Solving for t gives:

$$t = \frac{p}{\sigma_H}(R)$$

The allowable stress is:

$$(\sigma_H)_A = \frac{36 \text{ ksi}}{4} = 9.00 \text{ ksi}$$

Then

$$t = \frac{180 \text{ psi}}{9000 \text{ psi}}(24 \text{ in.}) = \mathbf{0.480 \text{ in.}}$$

21.3   BOLTED AND RIVETED CONNECTIONS

We discuss bolts and rivets interchangeably in this chapter, since the design procedures for them are common. In Chapter 11 we examined simple riveted connections in shear. There, we looked only at the shear of the rivet. We now consider other factors in the design of a complete connection. In all our considerations, we

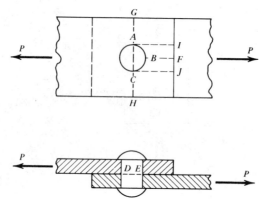

FIG. 21.4   Riveted connection.

assume a logical but somewhat idealistic single mode of failure. Actual failures are often more complex than those assumed. Nonetheless, the methods of analysis and design presented here do give workable results.

In this analysis we also ignore the transfer of load by friction forces. The friction load can play a significant role, and in fact with high strength bolts that are highly torqued, the entire load can be transferred by friction.

Figure 21.4 shows a single rivet in shear; this joint is called single riveted *lap joint*. In Chapter 11, when we investigated the failure of this connection in shear, we found that the load P must be supported by the cross-sectional area of the rivet, designated as DE in Fig. 21.4. That is only one of several possible modes of failure that must be evaluated for proper design of a riveted connection. Other modes are as follows.

There can be a bearing failure over the surface ABC (Fig. 21.4). This failure can occur in the rivet or in the plate. Only the weaker material needs to be evaluated, and that is normally the plate. Although the failure actually occurs on the curved surface ABC, the design is based on the projected rectangular plane area AC.

A tensile failure of the plate can also occur. In this case the area involved is GA and CH. There are also stress concentrations around the hole, which we will ignore for the present.

The last modes of failure we consider are tearing out of the end of the plate, area BF (Fig. 21.4), or shearing out the end of the plate, areas AI and CJ. Although we can make similar calculations for either of these failures, they are usually handled by following a rule of thumb that says to make the center of the rivet at least two diameters from the edge of the plate. Following this rule of thumb eliminates the need for calculating stresses associated with tear-out or end-plate shear.

Thus in a bolted or riveted connection we need to examine the fastener shear, the plate or fastener bearing stress, and the plate tensile stress. We have discussed these for a single rivet. If additional rivets are involved, a similar analysis may be used as long as the load is through the centroid of the rivet pattern. The problem is more complicated when the load is not through the centroid of the rivet pattern. That problem is left for more advanced texts. In analyzing the failure of a

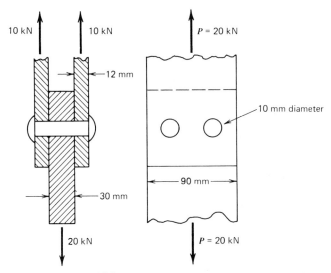

FIG. 21.5 Example Problem 21.2.

connection involving several rivets we assume the entire structure moves as a rigid body except at the regions of failure. This will be illustrated in Example Problem 21.2. When three plates are used, additional calculations may be needed, but they will be variations of the above. Typical properties of materials to be used in these problems are given below.

Plates:

Bearing strength	100 ksi (690 MPa)
Tensile strength	70 ksi (483 MPa)

Rivets:

Shear strength	50 ksi (345 MPa)

Example Problem 21.2

The joint shown in Fig. 21.5 carries 20 kN. Find all the design stresses for analyzing this joint.

Solution

Shear

Fig. 21.5 shows half a double-riveted butt joint. The rivets are in double shear, which means that the shear load is only half the total load, as shown in Fig. 21.6. Since there are two rivets, the load per rivet is half the 10-kN load per plate, or 5 kN. The average shear stress in the rivet is calculated:

$$\tau_{AV} = \frac{V}{A} = \frac{5\text{ kN}(4)}{\pi(10\text{ mm})^2} = \textbf{63.7 MPa}$$

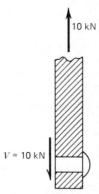

FIG. 21.6 Shear load.

FIG. 21.7 Projected area for bearing stresses.

Bearing Stresses

Two different bearing stresses must be analyzed: those on the center plate and those on the outside plates. Although it is the half cylindrical surface that is in bearing, calculations are based on the projected area, the shaded rectangular plane in Fig. 21.7. Again, since there are two rivets, the bearing load will be 5 kN per rivet on the outside plates and 10 kN per rivet on the center plate. For the outside plate and rivet:

$$\sigma_{OB} = \frac{P}{A} = \frac{5 \text{ kN}}{10 \text{ mm}(12 \text{ mm})} = \textbf{41.7 MPa}$$

For the center plate:

$$\sigma_{CB} = \frac{P}{A} = \frac{10 \text{ kN}}{10 \text{ mm}(30 \text{ mm})} = \textbf{33.3 MPa}$$

where σ_{OB}, being the greater, will govern if all the materials are the same or if the center plate is the strongest material (including the rivet).

Tensile Stresses

Again two situations must be evaluated, the center and the outside plates. The outside plates carry 10 kN. The minimum area in tension is the 12 × 90 cross section minus the two 10-mm holes.

$$\sigma_{OT} = \frac{P}{A} = \frac{10 \text{ kN}}{12 \text{ mm}[90 - 2(10)] \text{ mm}} = \textbf{11.9 MPa}$$

For the inside plate we have:

$$\sigma_{CT} = \frac{P}{A} = \frac{20 \text{ kN}}{30 \text{ mm}[90 - 2(10)] \text{ mm}} = \textbf{9.52 MPa}$$

where σ_{OT} will govern unless the center plate has a lower strength.

21.4 WELDMENTS

Welds are one of the most common methods of joining metals. They are widely used in pipelines, building structures, and all sorts of mass- and custom-produced items. Even works of art take advantage of this technology. In spite of the widespread use of the process in very sophisticated industries, the routine design of weldments remains simplistic and conservative. The conservatism seems well founded. The great industrialist and inventor, R. G. LeTourneau, once said he could teach monkeys to weld. As far as I know he was never successful in that endeavor, but I have seen weldments that suggest he may have been.

Weld designs are usually based on the *throat* area. The definition of the "throat" varies with the type of weld, but it is generally the minimum cross section in a weld. Figure 21.8 shows a *butt weld*. For a butt weld the throat area is the area of the plate being welded. Thus the area is h times the length of the weld. The rounded reinforcement shown in Fig. 21.8 adds strength in static loading but is not included in the design height h. This reinforcement is ground off for fatigue loading, since a stress concentration is developed at the corner where the reinforcement intersects the plate. This stress concentration is detrimental in fatigue loading but is of no consequence in static loading. The same throat area is used when the load is in shear. Thus we have for tensile or compressive loads:

$$\sigma = \frac{P}{hL} \tag{21.4}$$

where L is the length of the weld and:

$$\tau = \frac{P_s}{hL} \tag{21.5}$$

for shear loads where P_s is a shear load. The shear load P_s is perpendicular to the paper in Fig. 21.8.

Figure 21.9a shows a lap joint with a *fillet weld*. The size of the weld refers to the dimension w. The design of fillet welds is also based on the throat area, and it is assumed to fail in shear regardless of the direction of loading. The weld, shown in detail in Fig. 21.9b, looks like a 45° right triangle in cross section. Consequently, the throat depth will be:

$$h = w \cos 45° = 0.707w$$

The shear stress will be as given by Eq. 21.5, that is:

$$\tau = \frac{P}{hL}$$

FIG. 21.8 Butt weld.

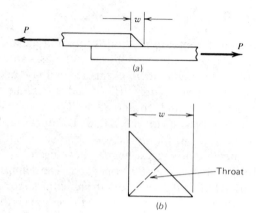

FIG. 21.9a–b Lap joint with fillet weld.

or

$$\tau = \frac{P}{0.707wL} \tag{21.6}$$

Typical allowable strengths for welds in structural steels are 20,000 psi (140 MPa) for tensile stress and 13,500 psi (93.1 MPa) for shear stress.

As in the case of bolted or riveted points, these loads *must be through the centroid of the total weld area.* When they are not, they have a tendency to twist the connection, and much greater stresses are generated. Many applications of weld design are governed by code. Of course, such codes should be observed when they apply.

Example Problem 21.3

Find the average shear stress in the 8-mm fillet weld shown in Fig. 21.10.

Solution

The total length of weld is:

$$L = 100 + 80 + 100 = 280 \text{ mm}$$

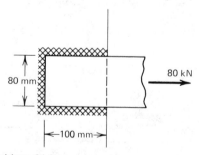

FIG. 21.10 Example Problem 21.3.

The throat depth is:

$$h = 0.707(8) = 5.66 \text{ mm}$$

and the total shear area is:

$$A = hL = 5.66(280) = 1580 \text{ mm}^2$$

The average shear stress is:

$$\tau = \frac{P}{hL} = \frac{80 \ E3 \ N}{1580 \text{ mm}^2} = \textbf{50.5 MPa}$$

Note that the load is through the centroid of the weld and has no tendency to twist it.

21.5 STRESS CONCENTRATION

All the stress equations developed thus far have assumed an absence of irregularities in the cross section in the vicinity of the section being analyzed. It was also assumed that the section was well removed from concentrated loads. If these conditions are not met, the stresses produced will be higher than those predicted by the stress equations, and the stress distribution will be different from what we have assumed or developed. Figure 21.11a shows a flat plate with a hole. From

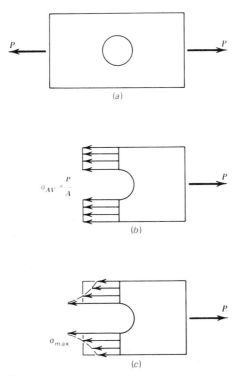

FIG. 21.11a–c The effect of stress concentration on axial stresses.

the method of Chapter 11 we calculate the stress from:

$$\sigma = \frac{P}{A} \tag{11.1}$$

and assume the stress distribution to be uniform as shown in Fig. 21.11b. The actual stress distribution is as shown in Fig. 21.11c. Clearly, it is not uniform, and the maximum stress can be two to three times as large as the average stress. This higher stress is the result of the sudden change in cross section. These rapid changes, called stress risers, are to be avoided in critical sections of machines and structures. Gradual changes in shape that minimize the effect of stress risers are desirable when changes in geometry are necessary.

The ratio of the maximum stress to the average stress is usually designated by the letter K, called the *stress concentration factor*. We write:

$$K = \frac{\sigma_{max}}{\sigma_{AV}}$$

or more commonly:

$$\sigma_{max} = K\sigma_{AV} \tag{21.7}$$

Or we may modify Eq. 11.1 to read:

$$\sigma_{max} = K\frac{P}{A} \tag{21.8}$$

In a similar manner the other stress equations we have developed may be written as follows:

$$\tau_{max} = K\frac{V}{A} \tag{21.9}$$

$$\tau_{max} = K\frac{Tc}{J} \tag{21.10}$$

$$\sigma_{max} = K\frac{Mc}{I} \tag{21.11}$$

We use Eqs. 21.8 through 21.11 just as we have the ones on which they are based. Generally the nominal stress calculation is based on the net area, but not always, so care must be taken. The stress concentration factor K can be determined from the theory of elasticity for very simple shapes. As the problem becomes more complex we must rely on experimental methods, primarily photoelasticity. This is a technique using polarized light and plastic models that respond to stresses by varying the transmission of light. Very colorful patterns result, indicating the direction and intensity of the principal stresses. More recently, stress concentration factors have been calculated using numerical methods on the digital computer.

Most machine design texts include an assortment of stress concentration factors similar to those shown in Fig. 21.12. In using these charts to determine stress concentration factors, care must be taken to apply the data correctly. Make sure that the loading is that described in your problem. Be sure that you are

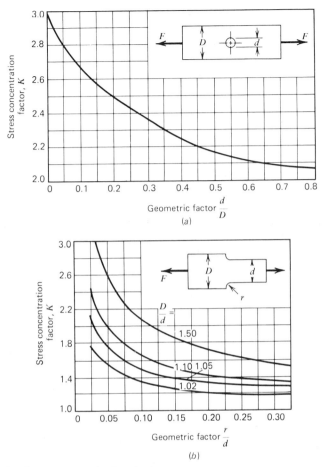

FIG. 21.12a–b Stress concentration factor for a flat bar. (From R. E. Peterson, Design Factors for Stress Concentration, *Machine Design*, Vol. 23, 1951. Used by permission.)

using the correct area. And finally, determine with certainty whether the chart is for a flat piece or a round one.

It should be noted from Fig. 21.12 that when the change in shape is very abrupt, characterized by relatively small holes and fillets, the stress concentrations are the highest. These abrupt changes should generally be avoided.

Now it's time for a bad news–good news story. The bad news is that stress risers increase the stress beyond the nominal value. The good news is that sometimes it does not matter, and in a few cases it is actually helpful. Specific rules about when and how to use them are best left to texts on machine design. However, a couple of generalities can be made:

1. When designing with ductile materials and static loads, stress risers may be ignored.

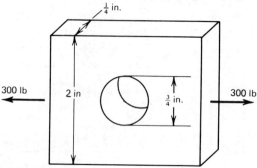

FIG. 21.13   Example Problem 21.4.

2. When designing with repeated loads, (fatigue) stress concentrations are used, although materials differ in their sensitivity to them.
3. When brittle materials with stress concentrations are used in critical sections under tensile loading . . . stay out from under it!

Example Problem 21.4

A $\frac{1}{4}$-in.-thick plate is 2 in. wide and has a $\frac{3}{4}$-in. hole cut in the center of it (Fig. 21.13). It carries a 300-lb load. Find the maximum stress in the plate.

> **Solution**
>
> The net area is:
>
> $$A = (2 - 0.75)(0.25) = \mathbf{0.312 \text{ in.}^2}$$
>
> The nominal stress is:
>
> $$\sigma = \frac{P}{A} = \frac{300 \text{ lb}}{0.312 \text{ in.}^2} = \mathbf{960 \text{ psi}}$$
>
> To read Fig. 21.12a we need d/D:
>
> $$\frac{d}{D} = \frac{0.75}{2} = 0.375$$
>
> From Fig. 21.12a we get:
>
> $$K = 2.27$$
>
> Hence:
>
> $$\sigma_{\max} = K\sigma_{AV} = 2.27(960) = \mathbf{2180 \text{ psi}}$$

21.6   FATIGUE

If you are still with us after having started umpteen chapters ago, you may be feeling something known as fatigue. Well, surprisingly, materials get tired too— in a sense. When a material gets tired we call it *fatigue* also. We can take a mild steel with an ultimate strength of say 60,000 psi (414 MPa) and a yield strength

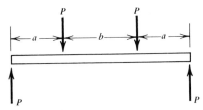

FIG. 21.14 Load configuration for Moore
fatigue test.

of say 40,000 psi (276 MPa). If we repeatedly load this material to perhaps 35,000 psi (241 MPa), below both the ultimate and yield strengths, it will fail after several hundred thousand cycles. This failure from cyclic loading is known as fatigue.

Fatigue failure is a failure that leaves its own characteristic signature and usually can be readily identified by materials experts. It is usually initiated at a point of stress concentration. The stress concentration may be due to an abrupt change in geometry, as discussed in Section 21.5, or due to a material flaw or even a surface scratch. A minute crack is initiated at one of the stress concentration locations. As the load is cycled, the crack grows, reducing the area available to carry the load. Suddenly the remaining portion fails, usually in a brittle fashion. Because this failure is sudden and without warning, it is frequently dangerous.

The foregoing type of failure has been studied extensively. It does not yield readily to analysis and shows considerable statistical scatter. Several methods have been developed to design against fatigue failure, but extensive testing is usually recommended as well. Fatigue analysis is needed in most machinery and equipment subject to dynamic loading such as internal combustion engines, electric motors, washing machines, airplanes, and helicopters—especially helicopters!

The most common laboratory test for fatigue is the *Moore rotating beam test*. The load configuration is as shown in Fig. 21.14. This loading results in a constant bending moment of magnitude *Pa* everywhere between the two central loads. All the loads are applied through bearings that allow the beam (often polished) to be continuously rotated. For each rotation of the beam, the stress on a given element on the beam cycles from plus the maximum stress to minus the maximum stress as indicated in Fig. 21.15. The maximum stress is set at a particular level. The beam is rotated until it fails; the number of cycles required for failure is recorded. This test is repeated on another specimen at a different stress level until

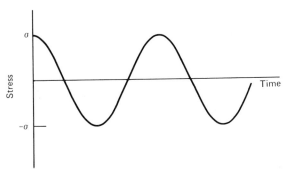

FIG. 21.15 Load cycle in fatigue test.

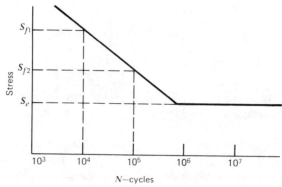

FIG. 21.16 S–N diagram.

enough data are collected to plot an *S–N diagram*. The *S–N* diagram is a plot of stress level (*S*) versus the number of cycles (*N*) required for failure. Figure 21.16 is typical of such plots. On the vertical axis the stress is plotted. On the horizontal axis the number of cycles to failure is plotted. A logarithmic scale is usually used for the number of cycles and frequently for the stress.

From the *S–N* diagram the *fatigue strength* may be determined. For instance, S_{f1} is the fatigue strength corresponding to 10,000 cycles in Fig. 21.16. Fatigue strength is always for a given number of cycles. A second fatigue strength S_{f2} is observed for 100,000 cycles, and so on. A last point S_e is known as the *endurance limit*. If the stress is below the endurance limit, failure will not occur regardless of the number of cycles. It is common to assume that a specimen that has not failed after 1 million cycles (or 10 million in some cases) will not fail. For steels the endurance limit is often estimated as half the ultimate strength.

21.7 SUMMARY

The equations for cylindrical pressure vessels are:

$$\sigma_L = p\left(\frac{R}{2t}\right)$$

$$\sigma_H = p\left(\frac{R}{t}\right)$$

Spherical pressure vessels:

$$\sigma = p\left(\frac{R}{2t}\right)$$

Bolted and rivet connections when the load is through the centroid of the pattern design for:

1. Shear in rivets.
2. Tensile failure in plates.
3. Bearing failure in plates or rivets.

Weldments:

$$\sigma = \frac{P}{hL}$$

$$\tau = \frac{P_s}{hL}$$

based on the throat or minimum area.

Stress concentration:

$$\sigma = K\frac{P}{A}$$

$$\sigma = K\frac{Mc}{I}$$

$$\tau = K\frac{V}{A}$$

$$\tau = K\frac{Tc}{J}$$

where K is the stress concentration factor. Stress concentration factors are obtained from data like Fig. 21.12.

Fatigue:

Fatigue strength is the strength of a part corresponding to a given number of cycles of the applied load.

The endurance limit is the strength of a part corresponding to an unlimited number of cycles.

An $S-N$ diagram is a plot of fatigue strength versus the corresponding number of cycles.

PROBLEMS

21.1 A cylindrical pressure tank is 6 ft in diameter and $\frac{3}{4}$ in. thick. If the pressure is 600 psi:

(a) Find the hoop stress.

(b) Find the longitudinal stress.

(c) Plot Mohr's circle for the stress element.

(d) Find the maximum shear stress in the cylinder.

21.2 A cylindrical pressure tank is 2 m diameter and 20 mm thick. If the pressure is 4.00 MPa:

(a) Find the hoop stress.

(b) Find the longitudinal stress.

(c) Plot Mohr's circle for the stress element.

(d) Find the maximum shear stress in the cylinder.

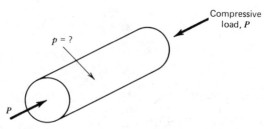

FIG. 21.17   Problems 21.10, 21.11.

21.3   A cylindrical pressure vessel is 3 ft in diameter and $\frac{1}{2}$ in. thick. Based on an allowable stress of 40,000 psi, what pressure can it hold?

21.4   A cylindrical pressure vessel is 1.2 m in diameter and 12 mm thick. Based on an allowable stress of 270 MPa, what pressure can it hold?

21.5   Find the maximum normal stress in a spherical pressure vessel that is 5 ft in diameter and 0.80 in. thick if the pressure is 800 psi.

21.6   Find the maximum normal stress in a spherical pressure vessel that is 1.5 m in diameter and 20 mm thick if the pressure is 5.0 MPa.

21.7   Design a spherical pressure vessel to hold 180 ft³ of gas at 500 psi based on a yield strength of 20 ksi.

21.8   Design a spherical pressure vessel to hold 2 m³ of gas at 3.5 MPa based on a yield strength of 140 MPa.

21.9   What is the norrmal stress in a balloon inflated to 8 psi when it is 6 in. in diameter and 0.065 in. thick?

21.10   A cylinder (Fig. 21.17) is 150 mm in diameter and 8 mm thick. It carries a compressive longitudinal load of 40 kN.

(a)   At what internal pressure will the longitudinal stress be zero?

(b)   What will be the corresponding hoop stress?

21.11   A cyclinder (Fig. 21.17) is 8 in. in diameter and 0.30 in. thick. It carries a compressive longitudinal load of 8000 lb.

(a)   At what pressure will the longitudinal stress be zero?

(b)   What will be the corresponding hoop stress?

21.12   The connnection shown in Fig. 21.18 is 2 in. wide. The rivet is $\frac{1}{2}$ in. in diameter and the plates are $\frac{1}{2}$ in. thick. Based on the properties given in Section 21.3, find the load this connection can carry.

21.13   The connection shown in Fig. 21.18 is 20 mm wide. The rivet is 12 mm in diameter and the plates are 12 mm thick. Based on the properties given in Section 21.3, find the load this connection can carry.

21.14   The joint shown in Fig. 21.19 consists of a single set of $\frac{1}{4}$-in. rivets. The external plates are $\frac{1}{4}$ in. thick and the internal ones are $\frac{3}{8}$ in. thick. The plates are $\frac{3}{4}$ in. wide. If the load on this joint is 1000 lb find:

(a)   The shear stress in the rivets

(b)   The tensile stress in the exterior plates

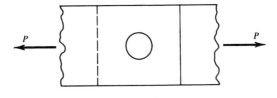

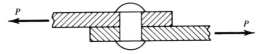

FIG. 21.18   Problems 21.12, 21.13.

(c)   The tensile stress in the interior plates

(d)   The bearing stress in the exterior plates

(e)   The bearing stress in the interior plates

21.15 Do Problem 21.14 if there are two sets of rivets and the plates are $1\frac{1}{4}$ in. wide.

21.16 Do Problem 21.14 if there are three sets of rivets and the plates are $1\frac{3}{4}$ in. wide.

21.17 The joint shown in Fig. 21.19 consists of a single set of 6-mm rivets. The external plates are 6 mm thick and the internal ones are 10 mm thick. The plates are 20 mm wide. If the load on this joint is 5000 N find:

(a)   The shear stress in the rivets

(b)   The tensile stress in the exterior plates

(c)   The tensile stress in the interior plates

(d)   The bearing stress in the exterior plates

(e)   The bearing stress in the interior plates

21.18 Do Problem 21.17 if there are two sets of rivets and the plates are 30 mm wide.

21.19 Do Problem 21.17 if there are three sets of rivets and the plates are 40 mm wide.

21.20 Find the load the joint described in Problem 21.14 can carry based on the properties given in Section 21.3.

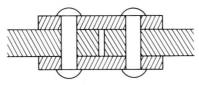

FIG. 21.19   Problems 21.14, 21.15, 21.16, 21.17, 21.18, 21.19, 21.20, 21.21.

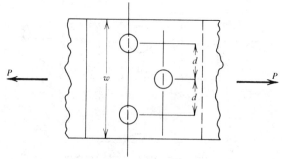

FIG. 21.20   Problems 21.22, 21.23, 21.24, 21.25.

21.21 Find the load the joint described in Problem 21.17 can carry based on the properties given in Section 21.3.

21.22 The simple lap joint in Fig. 21.20 has 1-in. rivets, and the load is 12,000 lb. The plates are $\frac{1}{2}$ in. thick. Make the relevant stress calculations for the design of this joint based on the following dimensions: $d = 2.5$ in. and $w = 8.0$ in.

21.23 The simple lap joint in Fig. 21.20 has 25-mm rivets and the load is 60 kN. The plates are 12 mm thick. Make the relevant stress calculations for the design of this joint based on the following dimensions: $d = 60$ mm and $w = 200$ mm.

21.24 Given the geometry of Problem 21.22, the material properties of Section 21.3, and a factor of safety of 4, what load can be carried by the joint of Fig. 21.20?

21.25 Given the geometry of Problem 21.23, the material properties of Section 21.3, and a factor of safety of 5, what load can be carried by the joint of Fig. 21.20?

21.26 For the lap joint shown in Fig. 21.21, what minimum weld size (w) is required if the weld is to be 2 in. long, the allowable stress is 13 ksi, and the load is 2000 lb?

21.27 For the lap joint shown in Fig. 21.21, what minimum weld size (w) is required if the weld is to be 80 mm long, the allowable stress is 90 MPa, and the load is 12 kN?

21.28 What size (w) fillet weld is needed for the weld design of Fig. 21.22 if an allowable stress of 90 MPa is used?

21.29 For the joint shown in Fig. 21.23 find the average shear stresss in the $\frac{1}{4}$-in. weld if A is 3 in. and the load is 800 lb.

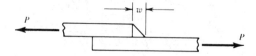

FIG. 21.21   Problems 21.26, 21.27.

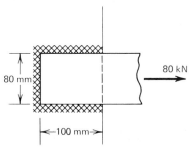

FIG. 21.22   Problem 21.28.

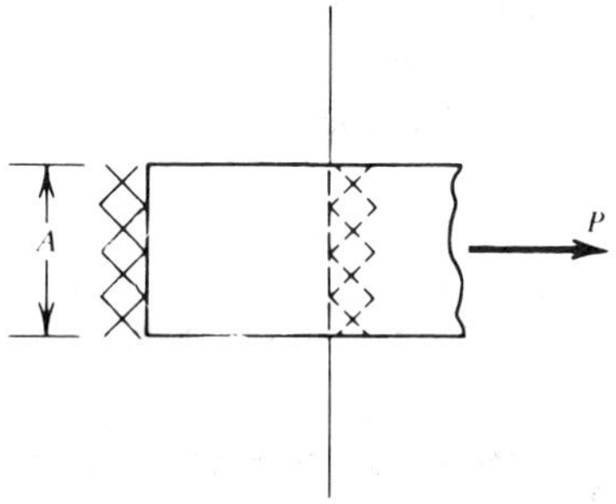

FIG. 21.23   Problems 21.29, 21.30, 21.31, 21.32, 21.33.

21.30 For the joint shown in Fig. 21.23, find the average shear stress in the 10-mm weld if A is 80 mm and the load is 4 kN.

21.31 If the load in Fig. 21.23 is 12,000 lb and the maximum value of A is 6 in., design an appropriate weld (length and width) for this connection based on an allowable stress of 14,000 psi.

21.32 If the load in Fig. 21.23 is 60 kN and the maximum value of A is 200 mm, design an appropriate weld (length and width) for this connection based on an allowable stress of 100 MPa.

21.33 If the strap in Fig. 21.23 is 2. in. wide, $\frac{3}{8}$ in. thick, and overlaps the $\frac{3}{8}$-in.-thick plate by 3 in., what is the maximum load P that can be carried based on an allowable stress of 14 ksi and a safety factor of 3?

21.34 A 5-in.-wide band is $\frac{1}{2}$ in. thick. It has a 1.5-in. hole cut in its center. It is to carry 2000 lb in tension. Find the maximum stress in the band, including the effect of stress concentration.

21.35 A 150-mm-wide band is 40 mm thick. It has a 80-mm hole cut in its center. It is to carry 15 kN in tension. Find the maximum stress in the band, including the effect of stress concentration.

21.36 A 5-in.-wide band is $\frac{1}{2}$ in. thick. It uniformly tapers to a 3-in. band using 1-in.-radius fillets. Find the maximum stress including stress concentration in the band if it is to carry 3000 lb in tension.

21.37 A 150-mm-wide band is 40 mm thick. It uniformly tapers to a 100-mm band using 25-mm radius fillets. Find the maximum stress including stress concentration in the band if it is to carry 25 kN in tension.

21.38 A 4-in.-wide steel strap has a 1-in. hole in it. How thick must this strap be to carry 1500 lb in tension based on an allowable stress of 20 ksi?

21.39 A 80-mm-wide steel strap has a 20-mm hole in it. How thick must this strap be to carry 6 kN in tension based on an allowable stress of 140 MPa?

22

Statically Indeterminate Members

Up to this point we have dealt with problems of a very convenient type—those whose external loads could be found by the methods of statics alone. Needing a name for all God's children, we call these creatures "statically determinate structures," meaning that from the principles of *statics* alone we can *determine* the loads on these structures. Fortunately, many real problems are statically determinate, and our effort is not in vain. An additional large class of problems may be treated as though they were statically determinate without introducing appreciable error in the analysis. (Considerable judgment–read "experience"—no, read, "You've done it wrong enough times to know better"—is required to know when loads may be safely neglected.) Alas, there are some problems that are not statically determinate, nor can they reasonably be approximated as such. These are said to involve *statically indeterminate* structures.

Statically indeterminate members occur any time the number of unknowns present exceeds the number of independent, nontrivial statics equations available. Thus such problems cannot be solved by the methods of statics alone. From algebra we know that we must have as many equations as there are unknowns for a problem to be solvable. Additional equations—beyond those available from statics—are obtained by considering the geometric constraints of the problem and the force–deflection relations that exist. Thus the force–deflection relations of Chapters 11, 13, and 16 are very important.

For any two-dimensional free body diagram there will be, at most, three statics equations. Therefore, any time our free body diagram shows more than three unknowns, we are potentially dealing with a statically indeterminate problem. As we shall see in the following sections, three or fewer unknowns sometimes result in statically indeterminate problems.

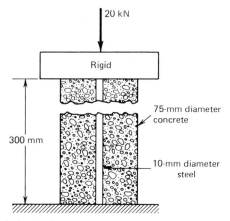

FIG. 22.1 Axially loaded member.

22.1 AXIALLY LOADED MEMBERS

The steel reinforced column shown in Fig. 22.1 is an axially loaded structure that presents a statically indeterminate problem. We wish to know what portion of the load is carried by the concrete and what is carried by the steel. A free body diagram is drawn in Fig. 22.2 after passing a cutting plane through an arbitrary section of the column. Summing forces vertically we get:

$$\sum F_y = 0 = -20kN + F_s + F_c \tag{22.1}$$

where F_s is the force in the steel and F_c is the resultant force in the concrete. The remaining two statics equations tell us only that zero equals zero. We call these equations trivial, since they offer no useful information. We are left with the single Eq. 22.1 that contains two unknowns, which, according to my abacus, is one too many.

What is needed is a second equation. The second equation is generated from geometric constraints and force–deflection relationships.

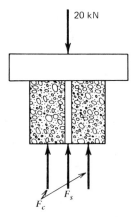

FIG. 22.2 Free body diagram.

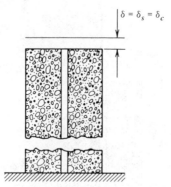

FIG. 22.3 Deflection diagram.

First, the geometric constraints. We note that the cap is rigid and will translate in the direction of the 20-kN load. Thus there is a compression of the column δ that will be common for the concrete and the steel, as shown in Fig. 22.3, and we may write:

$$\delta_s = \delta_c \qquad (22.2)$$

This equation represents the geometric constraints. It is generated by recognizing the deflection that takes place in the structure. This will be greatly aided if a detail sketch of the deflection is drawn. Now we have two equations (22.1 and 22.2), but four unknowns. (So far we have taken one step backward!)

But on to the deflection equations. Equation 11.5 relates axial load to axial deflection. Thus, we may write for the steel reinforcing rod:

$$\delta_s = \frac{F_s l}{A_s E_s} \qquad (22.3)$$

and for the concrete:

$$\delta_c = \frac{F_c l}{A_c E_c} \qquad (22.4)$$

Equations 22.3 and 22.4 may be substituted into Eq. 22.2, yielding:

$$\frac{F_s l}{A_s E_s} = \frac{F_c l}{A_c E_c} \qquad (22.5)$$

Now we have two equations (22.1 and 22.5), and two unknowns, F_s and F_c, and once more it's algebra.

Our problem here was to find F_s and F_c. Of course, once they have been found, we may compute the actual deflection of the column and the stress in the concrete and steel.

The principles above are basic to problems of this type. As their complexity increases, it will be necessary to apply the principle of superposition. The same approach is also useful for many problems involving stresses caused by temperature changes in a structure. This will be demonstrated in Example Problem 22.2.

Example Problem 22.1

For the problem in Fig. 22.1 find the force and stress in each member and the total deflection.

Solution

From the previous analysis we have:

$$F_c + F_s = 20 \qquad (22.1)$$

and

$$\frac{F_s l}{A_s E_s} = \frac{F_c l}{A_c E_c} \qquad (22.5)$$

Solving for F_s:

$$F_s = \frac{A_s E_s}{A_c E_c} F_c$$

$$A_s = \frac{\pi D_s^2}{4} = \frac{\pi (10 \text{ mm})^2}{4} = 78.5 \text{ mm}^2$$

$$A_c = \frac{\pi D_c^2}{4} - A_s = \frac{\pi (75 \text{ mm})^2}{4} - 78.5 = 4339 \text{ mm}^2$$

Then:

$$F_s = \frac{78.5(207\ E9)}{4340(14\ E9)} F_c = 0.267 F_c$$

Substituting into Eq. 22.1 gives:

$$F_c + 0.267\ F_c = 20$$

$$F_c = \frac{20}{1.267} = \textbf{15.8 kN}$$

$$F_s = \textbf{4.22 kN}$$

Then:

$$\sigma_s = \frac{F_s}{A_s} = \frac{4.22 \text{ kN}}{78.5 \text{ mm}^2} = \textbf{53.8 MPa}$$

$$\sigma_c = \frac{F_c}{A_c} = \frac{15.8 \text{ kN}}{4340 \text{ mm}^2} = \textbf{3.64 MPa}$$

and

$$\delta = \frac{F_s l}{A_s E_s} = \frac{4.22 \text{ kN } 300 \text{ mm(mm)}^2}{78.5 \text{ mm}^2\ 207\ E3\ \text{N}} = \textbf{77.9 } \boldsymbol{\mu}\textbf{m}$$

Example Problem 22.2

The concentric pipe assembly shown in Fig. 22.4 is firmly attached at both ends. Find the stress generated in each pipe if the assembly is heated 200°F.

$$A_S = 5.581 \text{ in.}^2 \qquad A_B = 1.075 \qquad L = 60 \text{ in.}$$

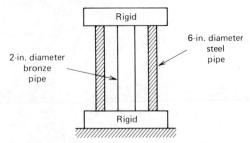

FIG. 22.4 Example Problem 22.2.

Solution

First we compute the change in each member that would occur due to change
in temperature if it were free (Fig. 22.5). From Eq. 11.9, we have:

$$\varepsilon_S = \alpha(\Delta T)$$

from which

$$\delta_S = \alpha L(\Delta T)$$

$$= 6.5 \frac{E\text{-}6}{°\mathrm{F}} (60 \text{ in.})(200°\mathrm{F})$$

$$\delta_S = \textbf{7.80 } \textbf{\textit{E}-2 in.}$$

Similarly,

$$\delta_B = 10 \frac{E\text{-}6}{°\mathrm{F}} (60 \text{ in.})(200°\mathrm{F}) = \textbf{1.20 } \textbf{\textit{E}-1 in.}$$

The bronze wants to expand more than the steel (Fig. 22.6), by the amount:

$$\delta = \delta_B - \delta_S = (1.20 \text{ } E\text{-}1) - (7.80 \text{ } E\text{-}2) = 4.20 \text{ } E\text{-}2 \text{ in.}$$

Hence it will stretch the steel an additional amount δ_{S-p}, generating a tensile
force P_S. The steel, on the other hand, will pull the bronze back by the amount
δ_{B-p}, generating a compressive force. Because of the rigid cap, the final length
of the two pipes must be equal. Thus, the stretching of the steel plus the com-

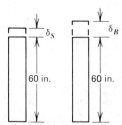

FIG. 22.5 Change in length due to
temperature change.

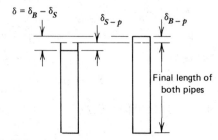

FIG. 22.6 Deflection diagram.

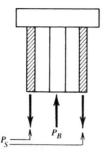

FIG. 22.7 Free body diagram.

pression of the bronze will close the gap created by the differences in deformation due to the temperature change and we may write

$$\delta = \delta_{S-p} + \delta_{B-p}$$

The deflection of each member due to its axial load is found by Eq. 11.5, giving:

$$\delta = \frac{P_S L}{A_S E_S} + \frac{P_B L}{A_B E_B}$$

The forces P_S and P_B are unknown in the equation above. We pass a cutting plane through the assembly and draw a free body diagram (Fig. 22.7). There being no external forces, we conclude:

$$P_B = P_S = P$$

Substituting into the equation above, we write:

$$\delta = \frac{PL}{A_S E_S} + \frac{PL}{A_B E_B} = PL\left(\frac{1}{A_S E_S} + \frac{1}{A_B E_B}\right)$$

$$P = \frac{\delta}{L\left(\dfrac{1}{A_S E_S} + \dfrac{1}{A_B E_B}\right)}$$

$$P = \frac{4.20\ E\text{-}2\ \text{in.}}{60\ \text{in.}\left[\dfrac{1\ \text{in.}^2}{5.581\ \text{in.}^2(30\ E6)\ \text{lb}} + \dfrac{1\ \text{in.}^2}{1.075\ \text{in.}^2(16\ E6)\ \text{lb}}\right]}$$

P = 10,900 lb

This is the load in each pipe. From it we calculate the following stresses:

$$\sigma_S = \frac{10,900}{5.581} = \textbf{1960 psi}$$

$$\sigma_B = \frac{10,900}{1.075} = \textbf{10,200 psi}$$

Note that the final deformation of the whole structure is greater than that for the steel alone, but less than that of the bronze alone.

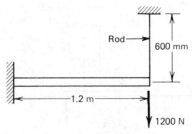

FIG. 22.8   Example Problem 22.3.

22.2 BEAMS

Beams show up in at least two ways in statically indeterminate problems. The first is just as another elastic element in a general indeterminate problem. It will be illustrated in Example Problem 22.3. The second deals specifically with the indeterminate beam, and it will be handled by the method of superposition in the next section.

Example Problem 22.3

For Fig. 22.8 find the load carried by the steel connecting rod with a cross section of 8 mm^2. The beam is steel, and $I = 4.17\ E6\ \text{mm}^4$.

Solution

We draw a free body diagram (Fig. 22.9), from which we get two equations and three unknowns: P_r, V, and M. The force equation is:

$$\sum F_y = 0 = V + P_r - 1200$$

An additional equation is obtained by observing that the deflection of the beam and the rod are the same (Fig. 22.10):

$$\delta_b = \delta_r$$

FIG. 22.9   Free body diagram.

FIG. 22.10   Deflection diagram.

From Chapter 11 the deflection of the rod due to the load on it, P_r, is:

$$\delta_r = \frac{PL}{AE} = \frac{P_r(600 \text{ mm}) \text{ mm}^2}{8 \text{ mm}^2(207 \text{ E3 N})} = (3.62 \text{ E-4})P_r$$

From Table A-18, Case 5, the deflection of the beam due to the *net* load on it, P_b, is:

$$\delta_b = \frac{P_b L^3}{3EI} = \frac{P_b(1200 \text{ mm})^3 \text{ mm}^2}{3(207 \text{ E3 N})(4.17 \text{ E6 mm}^4)} = 6.67 \text{ E-4}$$

Thus:

$$(3.62 \text{ E-4})P_r = (6.67 \text{ E-4})P_b$$

from which

$$P_r = 1.84P_b$$

Since P_b is the same as V, we can substitute into the first equation, giving:

$$P_b + 1.84P_b = 1200$$

$$P_b = \frac{1200}{2.84} = \textbf{422 N}$$

This is the net force on the right-hand end of the beam and the shear on the left-hand end. The force in the rod is:

$$P_r = 1.84P_b = \textbf{777 N}$$

22.3 BEAMS BY SUPERPOSITION

The problem of a statically indeterminate beam is illustrated in Fig. 22.11. This beam has three supports. A free body diagram (Fig. 22.12) shows three unknowns, R_A, R_B, and R_C. We can write two nontrivial equations. Thus there is one excess unknown, and the problem is said to be indeterminate to the first degree. Alternately, we may say there is one redundant support. To solve a problem of this type, we approach it in a manner similar to those considered earlier in this chapter, plus we use the method of superposition. We'll think of one of the reactions, R_B in this case, as simply another external load. We will then say, based on the method of superposition, that the solution for the unknowns in Fig. 22.12 is the sum of the solutions in Figs. 22.13 and 22.14. That is, if we add Fig. 22.14 to Fig. 22.13, we get Fig. 22.12. Therefore,

$$R_A = R_{A1} + R_{A2}$$
$$R_C = R_{C1} + R_{C2}$$

Now we still have an excessive unknown. It is handled by imposing the geometric constraints of the problem on the solution. We note that the deflection at the support at B (Fig. 22.12) is zero. Therefore, the deflection produced by the loading

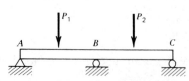

FIG. 22.11 Statically indeterminate beam.

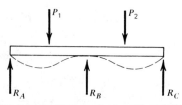

FIG. 22.12 Free body and deflection diagram.

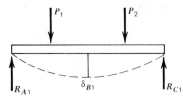

FIG. 22.13 Free body and deflection diagram with redundant support removed.

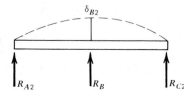

FIG. 22.14 Free body and deflection diagram with redundant support as an external load.

of Fig. 22.13 when added to that produced by Fig. 22.14 must produce a net deflection of zero for point B.

$$\delta_{B1} + \delta_{B2} = 0$$

Using equations from Table A-18 allows us to relate the deflection to the load and consequently the loads to each other. This generates the additional equation needed for solution. Example Problem 22.4 illustrates the method.

Example Problem 22.4

The beam of Fig. 22.11 is 16 ft long with the supports and loads equally spaced at 4-ft intervals. The beam is a steel S 8 × 23.0 which has an I of 64.9 in.[4] Find the reactions at supports A, B, and C if the loads P_1 and P_2 are each equal to 10 kips.

Solution

Referring to Figs. 22.13 and 22.14, as noted in the preceding discussion:

$$-\delta_{B1} = \delta_{B2}$$

From Table A-18, Case 3, we have

$$\delta_{B1} = \frac{Pa}{24EI}(3L^2 - 4a^2)$$

$$= \frac{10 \text{ kips}(4 \text{ ft})}{24EI}[3(16 \text{ ft})^2 - 4(4 \text{ ft})^2]$$

$$\delta_{B1} = \frac{1173}{EI} \text{ kips-ft}^3$$

and from Case 2, Table A-18:

$$\delta_{B2} = \frac{PL^3}{48EI} = \frac{R_B(16\ \text{ft})^3}{48EI} = \frac{85.3}{EI} R_B\ \text{ft}^3$$

Setting these equal, since they are of opposite sign:

$$\frac{85.3}{EI} R_B\ \text{ft}^3 = \frac{1173\ \text{kips-ft}^3}{EI}$$

$$R_B = \frac{1173}{85.3} = \textbf{13.75 kips}$$

Now that R_B has been found, we may use either the free body diagrams Figs. 22.13 and 22.14 or return to Fig. 22.12. In either case the problem has been reduced to one that is statically determinate. For Fig. 22.12, we have:

$$\sum M_A = 0 = -4(10) + 8(13.75) - 12(10) + 16R_c$$

$$R_c = \frac{40 - 110 + 120}{16} = \textbf{3.12 kips}$$

$$\sum F_y = 0 = R_A - 10 + 13.75 - 10 + 3.12$$
$$R_A = \textbf{3.12 kips}$$

The symmetric answer should have been anticipated.

22.4   SUMMARY

When the number of unknown forces exceeds the available statics equations, additional equations must be found. These are developed by observing the geometric constraints of the problem and using force–deflection relations. These principles coupled with the principle of superposition allow their solution.

Briefly we can summarize the general method of solution as follows:

1. Draw a free body diagram of the structure.
2. Write equilibrium equations and determine the degree of indeterminancy (number of excess unknowns).
3. Make a deflection sketch or sketches to develop a deflection equation for each excessive unknown. The principle of superposition may be necessary as well as additional free body diagrams.
4. Relate deflection to loads using force–deflection equations.
5. There should now be as many equations as there are unknowns. Carry out the algebra.

PROBLEMS

22.1   The 60-in.-long, 6-in.-diameter concrete column in Fig. 22.15 has two $\frac{1}{2}$-in. steel reinforcing rods.

   (a)   Find the loads carried by the concrete and the load carried by the steel if the applied load P is 2 kips.

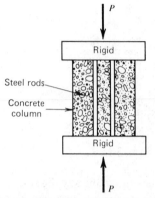

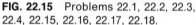

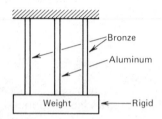

FIG. 22.15 Problems 22.1, 22.2, 22.3, 22.4, 22.15, 22.16, 22.17, 22.18.

FIG. 22.16 Problems 22.5, 22.6, 22.7, 22.8, 22.19, 22.20, 22.21, 22.22.

    (b)   Find the stress in the concrete and in the steel rods.

    (c)   Calculate the deflection in each to see if they are equal.

22.2   Do Problem 22.1 if there are four 1-in.-diameter rods.

22.3   The 1.5-m-long, 150-mm-diameter concrete column in Fig. 22.15 has two 12-mm steel reinforcing rods.

    (a)   Find the load carried by the concrete and the load carried by the steel if the applied load P is 20 kN.

    (b)   Find the stress in the concrete and in the steel rods.

    (c)   Calculate the deflection in each to see if they are equal.

22.4   Do Problem 22.3 if there are four 25-mm-diameter rods.

22.5   The bronze rods in Fig. 22.16 are $\frac{1}{2}$ in. in diameter; the aluminum one is $\frac{3}{4}$ in. All are 48 in. long. The weight is 3000 lb. Find:

    (a)   The load in each rod

    (b)   The stress in each rod

    (c)   The strain in each rod

    (d)   The total elongation of each rod

22.6   The bronze rods in Fig. 22.16 are $\frac{3}{4}$ in. in diameter; the aluminum one is 1 in. All are 36 in. long. The weight is 8000 lb. Find:

    (a)   The load in each rod

    (b)   The stress in each rod

    (c)   The strain in each rod

    (d)   The total elongation of each rod

22.7   The bronze rods in Fig. 22.16 are 10 mm in diameter; the aluminum one is 15 mm. All are 1.2 m long. The weight is 12 kN. Find:

    (a)   The load in each rod

    (b)   The stress in each rod

    (c)   The strain in each rod

    (d)   The total elongation of each rod

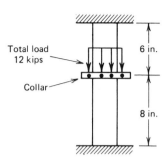

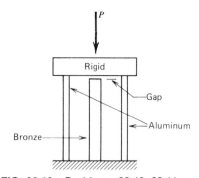

FIG. 22.17 Problem 22.9.

FIG. 22.18 Problems 22.10, 22.11, 22.12, 22.13, 22.23, 22.24.

22.8 The bronze rods in Fig. 22.16 are 18 mm in diameter; the aluminum one is 25 mm. All are 2.0 m long. The weight is 30 kN. Find:

(a) The load in each rod

(b) The stress in each rod

(c) The strain in each rod

(d) The total elongation of each rod

22.9 A 2-in.-diameter steel pipe carries a total load of 12,000 lb on the collar shown in Fig. 22.17. Find the reactions at the top and bottom of the support.

22.10 The two aluminum rods of Fig. 22.18 are exactly 18 in. long and have a cross section of 1.5 in.^{2} The bronze one has a cross section of 2.5 in.^{2} and is slightly short, leaving a gap of 0.008 in.

(a) What force P is required to close the gap?

(b) How will an additional 50,000 lb be carried in the members?

(c) What will be the final length of the aluminum rods?

22.11 The two aluminum rods of Fig. 22.18 are exactly 30 in. long and have a cross section of 2.0 in.^{2} The bronze one has a cross section of 3.0 in.^{2} and is slightly short, leaving a gap of 0.010 in.

(a) What force P is required to close the gap?

(b) How will an additional 30,000 lb be carried in the members?

(c) What will be the final length of the aluminum rods?

22.12 The two aluminum rods of Fig. 22.18 are exactly 500 mm long and have a cross section of 900 mm^2. The bronze one has a cross section of 1500 mm^2 and is slightly short, leaving a gap of 0.200 mm.

(a) What force P is required to close the gap?

(b) How will an additional 2.0 MN be carried in the members?

(c) What will be the final length of the aluminum rods?

22.13 The two aluminum rods of Fig. 22.18 are exactly 800 mm long and have a cross section of 1500 mm^2. The bronze one has a cross section of 3000 mm^2 and is slightly short, leaving a gap of 0.300 mm.

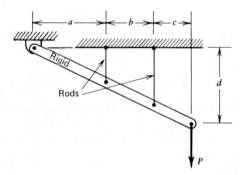

FIG. 22.19 Problem 22.14.

(a)   What force P is required to close the gap?

(b)   How will an additional 3.0 MN be carried in the members?

(c)   What will be the final length of the aluminum rods?

22.14 For Fig. 22.19 and the conditions given, find the load and elongation of each of the aluminum rods described below.

	a	b	c	d	P	Rod Area
(a)	5 ft	3 ft	2 ft	5 ft	1.5 kips	0.1 in.²
(b)	8 ft	4 ft	2 ft	14 ft	2.0 kips	0.2 in.²
(c)	2 m	4 m	2 m	4 m	10 kN	50 mm²
(d)	2 m	1 m	1 m	4 m	20 kN	80 mm²

22.15 The 60-in.-long, 6-in.-diameter concrete column in Fig. 22.15 has two $\frac{1}{2}$-in.-diameter steel reinforcing rods. There is no external load on the column but with the ends attached to both the concrete and steel, it is heated 400°F. Find the stress in the steel rods and the concrete.

22.16 The 2-m-long, 150-mm-diameter concrete column in Fig. 22.15 has two 12-mm-diameter steel reinforcing rods. There is no external load on the column, but with the ends attached to both the concrete and the steel, it is heated 300°C. Find the stress in the steel rods and the concrete.

22.17 If the column in Problem 22.15 also has a compressive load of 2 kips, find the stress in the steel and the concrete.

22.18 If the column in Problem 22.16 also has a compressive load of 20 kN, find the stress in the steel and the concrete.

22.19 Do Problem 22.5 if, in addition, the assembly is heated 300°F.

22.20 Do Problem 22.6, if, in addition, the assembly is heated 400°F.

22.21 Do Problem 22.7, if, in addition, the assembly is heated 250°C.

22.22 Do Problem 22.8, if, in addition, the assembly is heated 350°C.

22.23 The two aluminum rods of Fig. 22.18 are exactly 18 in. long and have a cross section of 1.5 in.² The bronze rod has a cross section of 2.5 in.² and is slightly short, leaving a gap of 0.008 in.

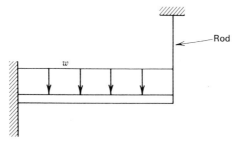

FIG. 22.20 Problems 22.25, 22.26, 22.27, 22.28.

(a) Find the change in temperature necessary to close the gap.

(b) Find the stress in each member if the temperature drops another 150°F.

(c) If 50,000 lb (compressive) is next loaded on the structure, what will be the stress in each member?

22.24 The two aluminum rods of Fig. 22.18 are exactly 500 mm long and have a cross section of 900 mm². The bronze rod has a cross section of 1500 mm² and is slightly short, leaving a gap of 0.200 mm.

(a) Find the change in temperature necessary to close the gap.

(b) Find the stress in each member if the temperature drops another 150°C.

(c) If 200 kN (compressive) is next loaded on the structure, what will be the stress in each member?

22.25 The steel rod in Fig. 22.20 is 10 ft long and 0.5 in.² in area. The steel beam has a moment of inertia of 1200 in.⁴ If the loading is 300 lb/ft along the 16-ft span of the beam, find the load in the rod and the deflection of the end of the beam.

22.26 The aluminum rod in Fig. 22.20 is 6 ft long and 0.10 in.² in area. The aluminum beam has a moment of inertia of 2400 in.⁴ If the load is 200 lb/ft along the 20-ft span of the beam, find the load in the rod and the deflection of the end of the beam.

22.27 The aluminum rod in Fig. 22.20 is 2 m long and 60 mm² in area. The aluminum beam has a moment of inertia of $6.0\,E6$ mm⁴. If the load is 3 kN/m along the 7-m span of the beam, find the load in the rod and the deflection of the end of the beam.

22.28 The steel rod in Fig. 22.20 is 4 m long and 300 mm² in area. The aluminum beam has a moment of inertia of $4.0\,E6$ mm⁴. If the load is 5 kN/m along the 5 m-span of the beam, find the load in the rod and the deflection of the end of the beam.

22.29 In Fig. 22.21 the steel beam AC has a 12-ft span and I is 14.0 in.⁴ Beam BD (perpendicular to AC) has a span of 16 ft, I of 20.0 in.⁴, and is steel. Find the deflection of point B and the reaction of A. The load P is 8000 lb.

22.30 In Fig. 22.21, the steel beam AC has an 8-ft span and I is 10.0 in.⁴ Beam BD (perpendicular to AC) has a span of 12 ft, I of 15 in.⁴, and is aluminum. Find the deflection of point B and the reaction of C. The load P is 10,000 lb.

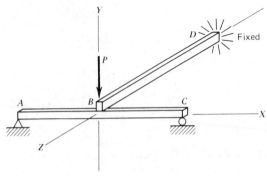

FIG. 22.21   Problems 22.29, 22.30, 22.31, 22.32.

22.31 In Fig. 22.21, the aluminum beam AC has a 3-m span and I is 5.0 $E6$ mm⁴. Beam BD (perpendicular to AC) has a span of 4 m, I of 5.0 $E6$ mm, and is aluminum. Find the deflection of point B and the reaction at D. The load P is 32 kN.

22.32 In Fig. 22.21, the aluminum beam AC has a 6-m span and I is 10 $E6$ mm⁴. Beam BD (perpendicular to AC) has a span of 6 m, I of 5.0 $E6$ mm⁴, and is aluminum. Find the deflection of point B and the reaction at A. The load P is 60 kN.

22.33 Find the reaction at each of the supports for the problems in Fig. 22.22.

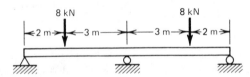

FIG. 22.22a   Problem 22.33a.

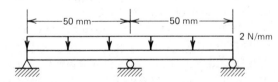

FIG. 22.22b   Problem 22.33b.

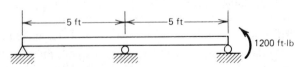

FIG. 22.22c   Problem 22.33c.

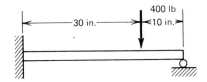

FIG. 22.22d   Problem 22.33d.

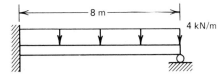

FIG. 22.22e   Problem 22.33e.

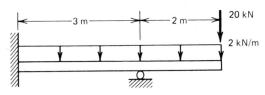

Fig. 22.22f   Problem 22.33f.

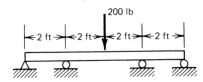

Fig. 22.22g   Problem 22.33g.

Appendix Tables

TABLE A-1 SPECIFIC WEIGHT OF COMMON MATERIALS

Material	lb/ft³	kN/m³
Solids		
Aluminum	169	26.6
Bronze	510	80.1
Concrete	149	23.3
Cast iron	449	70.6
Magnesium	112	17.6
Steel	487	76.5
Nylon	67.4	10.6
Copper	555	87.2
Lead	708	111
Silver	649	102
Brick	144	22.5
Glass	156	24.5
Rubber	74.9	11.8
Polyethylene	56.2	8.8
Liquids		
Water	62.4	9.80
Crude oil	50–60	7.8–9.4
Coors	61	9.6
Gasoline	45	7.1
Lubricating oil	55	8.6
Glycerine	78.6	12.3
Mercury	845	133
Salt water	71.8	11.3

TABLE A-2   METRIC AND ENGLISH UNITS

Dimension	SI (symbol)	Common English (symbol)
Length	meter (m)	foot (ft) or inch (in.)
Mass	kilogram (kg)	lb-s^2/ft or slug
Time	second (s)	second (s)
Force	newton (N) or kg·m/s^2	pound (lb) or kilopound (kip)
Stress or pressure	pascal (Pa) or N/m^2	lb/in.^{2} or (psi)
Energy or work	joule (J) or (N·m)	ft-lb
Angle	radian (rad)	degree (°)
Power	watt (W) or N·m/s or J/s	ft-lb/s, horsepower (hp), or watts (W), etc.
Area	m^2	in.^{2}, etc.
Volume	m^3	in.^{3}, etc.
Velocity	m/s	ft/s
Angular velocity	rad/s	revolution per minute (rpm)
Density	kg/m^3	lb-s^2/ft^4
Acceleration	m/s^2	ft/s^2
Moment of force	N·m	lb-ft

TABLE A-3   METRIC–ENGLISH CONVERSION FACTORS[a]

Length	Force	Angles
$\dfrac{0.3048 \text{ m}^b}{\text{ft}}$	$\dfrac{4.448 \text{ N}}{\text{lb}_{\text{force}}}$	$\dfrac{2\pi \text{ rad}^b}{360}$
$\dfrac{2.54 \text{ cm}^b}{\text{in.}}$	Stress	Power
Mass	$\dfrac{6895 \text{ Pa}}{\text{psi}}$	$\dfrac{745.7 \text{ W}}{\text{hp}}$
$\dfrac{0.4536 \text{ kg}}{\text{lb}_{\text{mass}}}$	Energy	$\dfrac{550 \text{ ft-lb/s}^b}{\text{hp}}$
	$\dfrac{1.356 \text{ J}}{\text{ft-lb}}$	

[a] Acceleration due to standard gravity: 9.807 m/s^2, 32.17 ft/s^2.
[b] Denotes conversion factors that are exact.

TABLE A-4   PREFERRED SI UNIT PREFIXES

Multiple	Computer Designation	Prefix	Symbol
10^{12}	E12	tera-	T
10^9	E9	giga-	G
10^6	E6	mega-	M
10^3	E3	kilo-	k
10^{-3}	E-3	milli-	m
10^{-6}	E-6	micro-	μ
10^{-9}	E-9	nano-	n
10^{-12}	E-12	pico-	p

TABLE A-5   TRIGONOMETRIC IDENTITIES

$$\cot \theta = \frac{1}{\tan \theta}$$

$$\sec \theta = \frac{1}{\cos \theta}$$

$$\csc \theta = \frac{1}{\sin \theta}$$

$$\tan \theta = \frac{\sin \theta}{\cos \theta}$$

$$\sin^2 \theta + \cos^2 \theta = 1$$
$$\sin(-\theta) = -\sin \theta$$
$$\cos(-\theta) = \cos \theta$$
$$\tan(-\theta) = -\tan \theta$$
$$\sin(\theta + \phi) = \sin \theta \cos \phi + \cos \theta \sin \phi$$
$$\sin(\theta - \phi) = \sin \theta \cos \phi - \cos \theta \sin \phi$$
$$\cos(\theta + \phi) = \cos \theta \cos \phi - \sin \theta \sin \phi$$
$$\cos(\theta - \phi) = \cos \theta \cos \phi + \sin \theta \sin \phi$$
$$\sin 2\theta = 2 \sin \theta \cos \theta$$
$$\cos 2\theta = \cos^2 \theta - \sin^2 \theta$$

Law of sines

$$\frac{a}{\sin A} = \frac{b}{\sin B} = \frac{c}{\sin C}$$

Law of cosines

$$a^2 = b^2 + c^2 - 2bc \cos A$$

TABLE A-6 DERIVATIVES OF FUNCTIONS

1. $\dfrac{d}{dx}(c) = 0$

7. $\dfrac{d}{dx}\left(\dfrac{u}{v}\right) = \dfrac{v\dfrac{du}{dx} - u\dfrac{dv}{dx}}{v^2}$

2. $\dfrac{d}{dx}(x) = 1$

8. $\dfrac{d}{dx}(\ln v) = \dfrac{1}{v}\dfrac{dv}{dx}$

3. $\dfrac{d}{dx}(u + v - w) = \dfrac{du}{dx} + \dfrac{dv}{dx} - \dfrac{dw}{dx}$

9. $\dfrac{d}{dx}(a^v) = a^v \ln a\,\dfrac{dv}{dx}$

4. $\dfrac{d}{dx}(cv) = \dfrac{c\,dv}{dx}$

10. $\dfrac{d}{dx}(\sin v) = \cos v\,\dfrac{dv}{dx}$

5. $\dfrac{d}{dx}(uv) = \dfrac{u\,dv}{dx} + \dfrac{v\,du}{dx}$

11. $\dfrac{d}{dx}(\cos v) = -\sin v\,\dfrac{dv}{dx}$

6. $\dfrac{d}{dx}(v^n) = nv^{n-1}\dfrac{dv}{dx}$

12. $\dfrac{d}{dx}(\tan v) = \sec^2 v\,\dfrac{dv}{dx}$

TABLE A-7 INTEGRATION OF STANDARD FORMS

1. $\int (du + dv) = \int dv + \int dv$ (u and v are variables)

2. $\int a\,dv = a\int dv$ (a is a constant)

3. $\int dx = x$

4. $\int x^n\,dx = \dfrac{x^{n+1}}{n+1}$ (n is a constant)

5. $\int \dfrac{dv}{v} = \ln v$

6. $\int e^x\,dx = e^x$

7. $\int \sin x\,dx = -\cos x$

8. $\int \cos x\,dx = \sin x$

TABLE A-8 TYPICAL PHYSICAL PROPERTIES OF COMMON MATERIALS

Material	Unit Weight, lb/in.³ (kN/m³)	Modulus of Elasticity, Mpsi (GPa)	Shear Modulus of Elasticity, Mpsi (GPa)	Poisson's Ratio	Coefficient of Thermal Expansion $\alpha \times E6$ /1°F (/1°C)[a]	Ultimate Strength, kpsi (MPa)	Yield Strength, kpsi (MPa)
Aluminum	0.098 (26.6)	10.3 (71.0)	3.8 (26)	0.33	13 (23)	60 (414)	40 (276)
Bronze	0.295 (80.1)	16 (110)	6.0 (41)	0.35	10 (18)	40 (275)	10 (70)
Concrete	0.086 (23.3)	2 (14)			6.0 (10.8)	2 compression (14)	
Cast iron	0.260 (70.6)	14.5 (100)	6.0 (41)	0.21	5.9 (10.6)	140 compression (965) 40 tension (476)	
Magnesium	0.065 (17.6)	6.5 (45)	2.4 (16)	0.35	14 (25)	44 (303)	31 (214)
Steel—carbon	0.282 (76.5)	30 (207)	11.5 (79.3)	0.29	6.5 (11.7)	50 (345)	36 (248)
Steel—nickel alloy	0.280 (76.0)	30 (207)	11.5 (79.3)	0.29	6.5 (11.7)	200 (1380)	150 (1030)
Stainless steel	0.280 (76.0)	27.6 (190)	10.6 (73.1)	0.30	6.2 (11.2)	110 (758)	40 (276)
Douglas fir	0.017 (4.6)	1.6 (11.0)	0.6 (4.1)	0.33		7.4 (51)	
Southern pine	0.021 (5.7)	1.6 (11.0)	0.6 (4.1)	0.33	3.0 (5.4)	8.4 (58)	
Nylon	0.039 (10.6)	1.8 (12.4)			80 (144)	7.4 (51)	6.0 (41)

[a] This means: $\alpha \times E6 = 13/°F$; therefore $\alpha = 13 \times E\text{-}6/°F$.

TABLE A-9 AREAS, CENTROIDS, AND CENTROIDAL
MOMENTS OF INERTIA

Rectangle

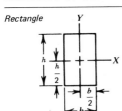

$$A = bh$$

$$\bar{I}_x = \frac{bh^3}{12}$$

Triangle

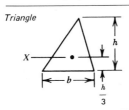

$$A = \frac{bh}{2}$$

$$\bar{I}_x = \frac{bh^3}{36}$$

Circle

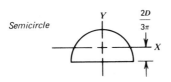

$$A = \frac{\pi D^2}{4}$$

$$\bar{I}_x = \frac{\pi D^4}{64}$$

$$\bar{J} = \frac{\pi D^4}{32}$$

Semicircle

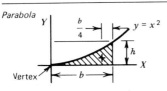

$$A = \frac{\pi D^2}{8}$$

$$\bar{I}_x = (6.86\ E\text{-}3)D^4$$

$$\bar{I}_y = \frac{\pi D^4}{128}$$

Parabola

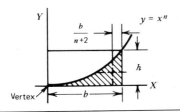

$$A = \frac{bh}{3}$$

$$A = \frac{bh}{n+1}$$

TABLE A-10   STANDARD BEAMS

I

S SHAPES
Properties for designing

Designation	Area A	Depth d	Flange		Web Thickness t_w	Elastic Properties					
			Width b_f	Thickness t_f		Axis X-X			Axis Y-Y		
						I	S	r	I	S	r
	In.²	In.	In.	In.	In.	In.⁴	In.³	In.	In.⁴	In.³	In.
S 24×120	35.3	24.00	8.048	1.102	0.798	3030	252	9.26	84.2	20.9	1.54
×105.9	31.1	24.00	7.875	1.102	0.625	2830	236	9.53	78.2	19.8	1.58
S 24×100	29.4	24.00	7.247	0.871	0.747	2390	199	9.01	47.8	13.2	1.27
× 90	26.5	24.00	7.124	0.871	0.624	2250	187	9.22	44.9	12.6	1.30
× 79.9	23.5	24.00	7.001	0.871	0.501	2110	175	9.47	42.3	12.1	1.34
S 20× 95	27.9	20.00	7.200	0.916	0.800	1610	161	7.60	49.7	13.8	1.33
× 85	25.0	20.00	7.053	0.916	0.653	1520	152	7.79	46.2	13.1	1.36
S 20× 75	22.1	20.00	6.391	0.789	0.641	1280	128	7.60	29.6	9.28	1.16
× 65.4	19.2	20.00	6.250	0.789	0.500	1180	118	7.84	27.4	8.77	1.19
S 18× 70	20.6	18.00	6.251	0.691	0.711	926	103	6.71	24.1	7.72	1.08
× 54.7	16.1	18.00	6.001	0.691	0.461	804	89.4	7.07	20.8	6.94	1.14
S 15× 50	14.7	15.00	5.640	0.622	0.550	486	64.8	5.75	15.7	5.57	1.03
× 42.9	12.6	15.00	5.501	0.622	0.411	447	59.6	5.95	14.4	5.23	1.07
S 12× 50	14.7	12.00	5.477	0.659	0.687	305	50.8	4.55	15.7	5.74	1.03
× 40.8	12.0	12.00	5.252	0.659	0.472	272	45.4	4.77	13.6	5.16	1.06
S 12× 35	10.3	12.00	5.078	0.544	0.428	229	38.2	4.72	9.87	3.89	0.980
× 31.8	9.35	12.00	5.000	0.544	0.350	218	36.4	4.83	9.36	3.74	1.00
S 10× 35	10.3	10.00	4.944	0.491	0.594	147	29.4	3.78	8.36	3.38	0.901
× 25.4	7.46	10.00	4.661	0.491	0.311	124	24.7	4.07	6.79	2.91	0.954
S 8× 23	6.77	8.00	4.171	0.425	0.441	64.9	16.2	3.10	4.31	2.07	0.798
× 18.4	5.41	8.00	4.001	0.425	0.271	57.6	14.4	3.26	3.73	1.86	0.831
S 7× 20	5.88	7.00	3.860	0.392	0.450	42.4	12.1	2.69	3.17	1.64	0.734
× 15.3	4.50	7.00	3.662	0.392	0.252	36.7	10.5	2.86	2.64	1.44	0.766
S 6× 17.25	5.07	6.00	3.565	0.359	0.465	26.3	8.77	2.28	2.31	1.30	0.675
× 12.5	3.67	6.00	3.332	0.359	0.232	22.1	7.37	2.45	1.82	1.09	0.705
S 5× 14.75	4.34	5.00	3.284	0.326	0.494	15.2	6.09	1.87	1.67	1.01	0.620
× 10	2.94	5.00	3.004	0.326	0.214	12.3	4.92	2.05	1.22	0.809	0.643
S 4× 9.5	2.79	4.00	2.796	0.293	0.326	6.79	3.39	1.56	0.903	0.646	0.569
× 7.7	2.26	4.00	2.663	0.293	0.193	6.08	3.04	1.64	0.764	0.574	0.581
S 3× 7.5	2.21	3.00	2.509	0.260	0.349	2.93	1.95	1.15	0.586	0.468	0.516
× 5.7	1.67	3.00	2.330	0.260	0.170	2.52	1.68	1.23	0.455	0.390	0.522

Courtesy American Institute of Steel Construction, Inc.

TABLE A-11 WIDE FLANGE BEAMS

W SHAPES
Properties for designing

Designation	Area A	Depth d	Flange		Web Thickness t_w	Elastic Properties					
			Width b_f	Thickness t_f		Axis X-X			Axis Y-Y		
						I	S	r	I	S	r
	In.²	In.	In.	In.	In.	In.⁴	In.³	In.	In.⁴	In.³	In.
W 36×300	88.3	36.72	16.655	1.680	0.945	20300	1110	15.2	1300	156	3.83
×280	82.4	36.50	16.595	1.570	0.885	18900	1030	15.1	1200	144	3.81
×260	76.5	36.24	16.551	1.440	0.841	17300	952	15.0	1090	132	3.77
×245	72.1	36.06	16.512	1.350	0.802	16100	894	15.0	1010	123	3.75
×230	67.7	35.88	16.471	1.260	0.761	15000	837	14.9	940	114	3.73
W 36×194	57.2	36.48	12.117	1.260	0.770	12100	665	14.6	375	61.9	2.56
×182	53.6	36.32	12.072	1.180	0.725	11300	622	14.5	347	57.5	2.55
×170	50.0	36.16	12.027	1.100	0.680	10500	580	14.5	320	53.2	2.53
×160	47.1	36.00	12.000	1.020	0.653	9760	542	14.4	295	49.1	2.50
×150	44.2	35.84	11.972	0.940	0.625	9030	504	14.3	270	45.0	2.47
×135	39.8	35.55	11.945	0.794	0.598	7820	440	14.0	226	37.9	2.39
W 33×240	70.6	33.50	15.865	1.400	0.830	13600	813	13.9	933	118	3.64
×220	64.8	33.25	15.810	1.275	0.775	12300	742	13.8	841	106	3.60
×200	58.9	33.00	15.750	1.150	0.715	11100	671	13.7	750	95.2	3.57
W 33×152	44.8	33.50	11.565	1.055	0.635	8160	487	13.5	273	47.2	2.47
×141	41.6	33.31	11.535	0.960	0.605	7460	448	13.4	246	42.7	2.43
×130	38.3	33.10	11.510	0.855	0.580	6710	406	13.2	218	37.9	2.38
×118	34.8	32.86	11.484	0.738	0.554	5900	359	13.0	187	32.5	2.32
W 30×210	61.9	30.38	15.105	1.315	0.775	9890	651	12.6	757	100	3.50
×190	56.0	30.12	15.040	1.185	0.710	8850	587	12.6	673	89.5	3.47
×172	50.7	29.88	14.985	1.065	0.655	7910	530	12.5	598	79.8	3.43
W 30×132	38.9	30.30	10.551	1.000	0.615	5760	380	12.2	196	37.2	2.25
×124	36.5	30.16	10.521	0.930	0.585	5360	355	12.1	181	34.4	2.23
×116	34.2	30.00	10.500	0.850	0.564	4930	329	12.0	164	31.3	2.19
×108	31.8	29.82	10.484	0.760	0.548	4470	300	11.9	146	27.9	2.15
× 99	29.1	29.64	10.458	0.670	0.522	4000	270	11.7	128	24.5	2.10

Courtesy American Institute of Steel Construction, Inc.

TABLE A-11 WIDE FLANGE BEAMS (*continued*)

W SHAPES
Properties for designing

Designation	Area A	Depth d	Flange Width b_f	Flange Thickness t_f	Web Thickness t_w	Axis X-X I	Axis X-X S	Axis X-X r	Axis Y-Y I	Axis Y-Y S	Axis Y-Y r
	In.²	In.	In.	In.	In.	In.⁴	In.³	In.	In.⁴	In.³	In.
W 27×177	52.2	27.31	14.090	1.190	0.725	6740	494	11.4	556	78.9	3.26
×160	47.1	27.08	14.023	1.075	0.658	6030	446	11.3	495	70.6	3.24
×145	42.7	26.88	13.965	0.975	0.600	5430	404	11.3	443	63.5	3.22
W 27×114	33.6	27.28	10.070	0.932	0.570	4090	300	11.0	159	31.6	2.18
×102	30.0	27.07	10.018	0.827	0.518	3610	267	11.0	139	27.7	2.15
× 94	27.7	26.91	9.990	0.747	0.490	3270	243	10.9	124	24.9	2.12
× 84	24.8	26.69	9.963	0.636	0.463	2830	212	10.7	105	21.1	2.06
W 24×160	47.1	24.72	14.091	1.135	0.656	5120	414	10.4	530	75.2	3.35
×145	42.7	24.49	14.043	1.020	0.608	4570	373	10.3	471	67.1	3.32
×130	38.3	24.25	14.000	0.900	0.565	4020	332	10.2	412	58.9	3.28
W 24×120	35.4	24.31	12.088	0.930	0.556	3650	300	10.2	274	45.4	2.78
×110	32.5	24.16	12.042	0.855	0.510	3330	276	10.1	249	41.4	2.77
×100	29.5	24.00	12.000	0.775	0.468	3000	250	10.1	223	37.2	2.75
W 24× 94	27.7	24.29	9.061	0.872	0.516	2690	221	9.86	108	23.9	1.98
× 84	24.7	24.09	9.015	0.772	0.470	2370	197	9.79	94.5	21.0	1.95
× 76	22.4	23.91	8.985	0.682	0.440	2100	176	9.69	82.6	18.4	1.92
× 68	20.0	23.71	8.961	0.582	0.416	1820	153	9.53	70.0	15.6	1.87
W 24× 61	18.0	23.72	7.023	0.591	0.419	1540	130	9.25	34.3	9.76	1.38
× 55	16.2	23.55	7.000	0.503	0.396	1340	114	9.10	28.9	8.25	1.34
W 21×142	41.8	21.46	13.132	1.095	0.659	3410	317	9.03	414	63.0	3.15
×127	37.4	21.24	13.061	0.985	0.588	3020	284	8.99	366	56.1	3.13
×112	33.0	21.00	13.000	0.865	0.527	2620	250	8.92	317	48.8	3.10
W 21× 96	28.3	21.14	9.038	0.935	0.575	2100	198	8.61	115	25.5	2.02
× 82	24.2	20.86	8.962	0.795	0.499	1760	169	8.53	95.6	21.3	1.99
W 21× 73	21.5	21.24	8.295	0.740	0.455	1600	151	8.64	70.6	17.0	1.81
× 68	20.0	21.13	8.270	0.685	0.430	1480	140	8.60	64.7	15.7	1.80
× 62	18.3	20.99	8.240	0.615	0.400	1330	127	8.54	57.5	13.9	1.77
× 55	16.2	20.80	8.215	0.522	0.375	1140	110	8.40	48.3	11.8	1.73
W 21× 49	14.4	20.82	6.520	0.532	0.368	971	93.3	8.21	24.7	7.57	1.31
× 44	13.0	20.66	6.500	0.451	0.348	843	81.6	8.07	20.7	6.38	1.27

Courtesy American Institute of Steel Construction, Inc.

TABLE A-11   WIDE FLANGE BEAMS (*continued*)

W SHAPES
Properties for designing

Designation	Area A	Depth d	Flange		Web Thickness t_w	Elastic Properties					
			Width b_f	Thickness t_f		Axis X-X			Axis Y-Y		
						I	S	r	I	S	r
	In.²	In.	In.	In.	In.	In.⁴	In.³	In.	In.⁴	In.³	In.
W 18×114	33.5	18.48	11.833	0.991	0.595	2040	220	7.79	274	46.3	2.86
×105	30.9	18.32	11.792	0.911	0.554	1850	202	7.75	249	42.3	2.84
× 96	28.2	18.16	11.750	0.831	0.512	1680	185	7.70	225	38.3	2.82
W 18× 85	25.0	18.32	8.838	0.911	0.526	1440	157	7.57	105	23.8	2.05
× 77	22.7	18.16	8.787	0.831	0.475	1290	142	7.54	94.1	21.4	2.04
× 70	20.6	18.00	8.750	0.751	0.438	1160	129	7.50	84.0	19.2	2.02
× 64	18.9	17.87	8.715	0.686	0.403	1050	118	7.46	75.8	17.4	2.00
W 18× 60	17.7	18.25	7.558	0.695	0.416	986	108	7.47	50.1	13.3	1.68
× 55	16.2	18.12	7.532	0.630	0.390	891	98.4	7.42	45.0	11.9	1.67
× 50	14.7	18.00	7.500	0.570	0.358	802	89.1	7.38	40.2	10.7	1.65
× 45	13.2	17.86	7.477	0.499	0.335	706	79.0	7.30	34.8	9.32	1.62
W 18× 40	11.8	17.90	6.018	0.524	0.316	612	68.4	7.21	19.1	6.34	1.27
× 35	10.3	17.71	6.000	0.429	0.298	513	57.9	7.05	15.5	5.16	1.23
W 16× 96	28.2	16.32	11.533	0.875	0.535	1360	166	6.93	224	38.8	2.82
× 88	25.9	16.16	11.502	0.795	0.504	1220	151	6.87	202	35.1	2.79
W 16× 78	23.0	16.32	8.586	0.875	0.529	1050	128	6.75	92.5	21.6	2.01
× 71	20.9	16.16	8.543	0.795	0.486	941	116	6.71	82.8	19.4	1.99
× 64	18.8	16.00	8.500	0.715	0.443	836	104	6.66	73.3	17.3	1.97
× 58	17.1	15.86	8.464	0.645	0.407	748	94.4	6.62	65.3	15.4	1.96
W 16× 50	14.7	16.25	7.073	0.628	0.380	657	80.8	6.68	37.1	10.5	1.59
× 45	13.3	16.12	7.039	0.563	0.346	584	72.5	6.64	32.8	9.32	1.57
× 40	11.8	16.00	7.000	0.503	0.307	517	64.6	6.62	28.8	8.23	1.56
× 36	10.6	15.85	6.992	0.428	0.299	447	56.5	6.50	24.4	6.99	1.52
W 16× 31	9.13	15.84	5.525	0.442	0.275	374	47.2	6.40	12.5	4.51	1.17
× 26	7.67	15.65	5.500	0.345	0.250	300	38.3	6.25	9.59	3.49	1.12

Courtesy American Institute of Steel Construction, Inc.

TABLE A-11 WIDE FLANGE BEAMS (*continued*)

W SHAPES
Properties for designing

Designation	Area A	Depth d	Flange Width b_f	Flange Thickness t_f	Web Thickness t_w	Axis X-X I	Axis X-X S	Axis X-X r	Axis Y-Y I	Axis Y-Y S	Axis Y-Y r
	In.²	In.	In.	In.	In.	In.⁴	In.³	In.	In.⁴	In.³	In.
W 14×730	215	22.44	17.889	4.910	3.069	14400	1280	8.18	4720	527	4.69
×665	196	21.67	17.646	4.522	2.826	12500	1150	7.99	4170	472	4.62
×605	178	20.94	17.418	4.157	2.598	10900	1040	7.81	3680	423	4.55
×550	162	20.26	17.206	3.818	2.386	9450	933	7.64	3260	378	4.49
×500	147	19.63	17.008	3.501	2.188	8250	840	7.49	2880	339	4.43
×455	134	19.05	16.828	3.213	2.008	7220	758	7.35	2560	304	4.37
W 14×426	125	18.69	16.695	3.033	1.875	6610	707	7.26	2360	283	4.34
×398	117	18.31	16.590	2.843	1.770	6010	657	7.17	2170	262	4.31
×370	109	17.94	16.475	2.658	1.655	5450	608	7.08	1990	241	4.27
×342	101	17.56	16.365	2.468	1.545	4910	559	6.99	1810	221	4.24
×314	92.3	17.19	16.235	2.283	1.415	4400	512	6.90	1630	201	4.20
×287	84.4	16.81	16.130	2.093	1.310	3910	465	6.81	1470	182	4.17
×264	77.6	16.50	16.025	1.938	1.205	3530	427	6.74	1330	166	4.14
×246	72.3	16.25	15.945	1.813	1.125	3230	397	6.68	1230	154	4.12
W 14×237	69.7	16.12	15.910	1.748	1.090	3080	382	6.65	1170	148	4.11
×228	67.1	16.00	15.865	1.688	1.045	2940	368	6.62	1120	142	4.10
×219	64.4	15.87	15.825	1.623	1.005	2800	353	6.59	1070	136	4.08
×211	62.1	15.75	15.800	1.563	0.980	2670	339	6.56	1030	130	4.07
×202	59.4	15.63	15.750	1.503	0.930	2540	325	6.54	980	124	4.06
×193	56.7	15.50	15.710	1.438	0.890	2400	310	6.51	930	118	4.05
×184	54.1	15.38	15.660	1.378	0.840	2270	296	6.49	883	113	4.04
×176	51.7	15.25	15.640	1.313	0.820	2150	282	6.45	838	107	4.02
×167	49.1	15.12	15.600	1.248	0.780	2020	267	6.42	790	101	4.01
×158	46.5	15.00	15.550	1.188	0.730	1900	253	6.40	745	95.8	4.00
×150	44.1	14.88	15.515	1.128	0.695	1790	240	6.37	703	90.6	3.99
×142	41.8	14.75	15.500	1.063	0.680	1670	227	6.32	660	85.2	3.97
W 14×320	94.1	16.81	16.710	2.093	1.890	4140	493	6.63	1640	196	4.17

Courtesy American Institute of Steel Construction, Inc.

TABLE A-11   WIDE FLANGE BEAMS (*continued*)

$Z = \dfrac{I}{c}$

section modulus.

			Flange		Web	Elastic Properties					
						Axis X-X			Axis Y-Y		
Designation	Area A	Depth d	Width b_f	Thickness t_f	Thickness t_w	I	S	r	I	S	r
	In.²	In.	In.	In.	In.	In.⁴	In.³	In.	In.⁴	In.³	In.
W 14×136	40.0	14.75	14.740	1.063	0.660	1590	216	6.31	568	77.0	3.77
×127	37.3	14.62	14.690	0.998	0.610	1480	202	6.29	528	71.8	3.76
×119	35.0	14.50	14.650	0.938	0.570	1370	189	6.26	492	67.1	3.75
×111	32.7	14.37	14.620	0.873	0.540	1270	176	6.23	455	62.2	3.73
×103	30.3	14.25	14.575	0.813	0.495	1170	164	6.21	420	57.6	3.72
× 95	27.9	14.12	14.545	0.748	0.465	1060	151	6.17	384	52.8	3.71
× 87	25.6	14.00	14.500	0.688	0.420	967	138	6.15	350	48.2	3.70
W 14× 84	24.7	14.18	12.023	0.778	0.451	928	131	6.13	225	37.5	3.02
× 78	22.9	14.06	12.000	0.718	0.428	851	121	6.09	207	34.5	3.00
W 14× 74	21.8	14.19	10.072	0.783	0.450	797	112	6.05	133	26.5	2.48
× 68	20.0	14.06	10.040	0.718	0.418	724	103	6.02	121	24.1	2.46
× 61	17.9	13.91	10.000	0.643	0.378	641	92.2	5.98	107	21.5	2.45
W 14× 53	15.6	13.94	8.062	0.658	0.370	542	77.8	5.90	57.5	14.3	1.92
× 48	14.1	13.81	8.031	0.593	0.339	485	70.2	5.86	51.3	12.8	1.91
× 43	12.6	13.68	8.000	0.528	0.308	429	62.7	5.82	45.1	11.3	1.89
W 14× 38	11.2	14.12	6.776	0.513	0.313	386	54.7	5.88	26.6	7.86	1.54
× 34	10.0	14.00	6.750	0.453	0.287	340	48.6	5.83	23.3	6.89	1.52
× 30	8.83	13.86	6.733	0.383	0.270	290	41.9	5.74	19.5	5.80	1.49
W 14× 26	7.67	13.89	5.025	0.418	0.255	244	35.1	5.64	8.86	3.53	1.08
× 22	6.49	13.72	5.000	0.335	0.230	198	28.9	5.53	7.00	2.80	1.04

W SHAPES — Properties for designing

Courtesy American Institute of Steel Construction, Inc.

TABLE A-11   WIDE FLANGE BEAMS (*continued*)

W SHAPES
Properties for designing

Designation	Area A	Depth d	Flange Width b_f	Flange Thickness t_f	Web Thickness t_w	Axis X-X I	Axis X-X S	Axis X-X r	Axis Y-Y I	Axis Y-Y S	Axis Y-Y r
	In.²	In.	In.	In.	In.	In.⁴	In.³	In.	In.⁴	In.³	In.
W 12×190	55.9	14.38	12.670	1.736	1.060	1890	263	5.82	590	93.1	3.25
×161	47.4	13.88	12.515	1.486	0.905	1540	222	5.70	486	77.7	3.20
×133	39.1	13.38	12.365	1.236	0.755	1220	183	5.59	390	63.1	3.16
×120	35.3	13.12	12.320	1.106	0.710	1070	163	5.51	345	56.0	3.13
×106	31.2	12.88	12.230	0.986	0.620	931	145	5.46	301	49.2	3.11
× 99	29.1	12.75	12.192	0.921	0.582	859	135	5.43	278	45.7	3.09
× 92	27.1	12.62	12.155	0.856	0.545	789	125	5.40	256	42.2	3.08
× 85	25.0	12.50	12.105	0.796	0.495	723	116	5.38	235	38.9	3.07
× 79	23.2	12.38	12.080	0.736	0.470	663	107	5.34	216	35.8	3.05
× 72	21.2	12.25	12.040	0.671	0.430	597	97.5	5.31	195	32.4	3.04
× 65	19.1	12.12	12.000	0.606	0.390	533	88.0	5.28	175	29.1	3.02
W 12× 58	17.1	12.19	10.014	0.641	0.359	476	78.1	5.28	107	21.4	2.51
× 53	15.6	12.06	10.000	0.576	0.345	426	70.7	5.23	96.1	19.2	2.48
W 12× 50	14.7	12.19	8.077	0.641	0.371	395	64.7	5.18	56.4	14.0	1.96
× 45	13.2	12.06	8.042	0.576	0.336	351	58.2	5.15	50.0	12.4	1.94
× 40	11.8	11.94	8.000	0.516	0.294	310	51.9	5.13	44.1	11.0	1.94
W 12× 36	10.6	12.24	6.565	0.540	0.305	281	46.0	5.15	25.5	7.77	1.55
× 31	9.13	12.09	6.525	0.465	0.265	239	39.5	5.12	21.6	6.61	1.54
× 27	7.95	11.96	6.497	0.400	0.237	204	34.2	5.07	18.3	5.63	1.52
W 12× 22	6.47	12.31	4.030	0.424	0.260	156	25.3	4.91	4.64	2.31	0.847
× 19	5.59	12.16	4.007	0.349	0.237	130	21.3	4.82	3.76	1.88	0.820
× 16.5	4.87	12.00	4.000	0.269	0.230	105	17.6	4.65	2.88	1.44	0.770
× 14	4.12	11.91	3.968	0.224	0.198	88.0	14.8	4.62	2.34	1.18	0.754

Courtesy American Institute of Steel Construction, Inc.

TABLE A-11 WIDE FLANGE BEAMS (*continued*)

W SHAPES
Properties for designing

Designation	Area A	Depth d	Flange Width b_f	Flange Thickness t_f	Web Thickness t_w	Axis X-X I	Axis X-X S	Axis X-X r	Axis Y-Y I	Axis Y-Y S	Axis Y-Y r
	In.²	In.	In.	In.	In.	In.⁴	In.³	In.	In.⁴	In.³	In.
W 10×112	32.9	11.38	10.415	1.248	0.755	719	126	4.67	235	45.2	2.67
×100	29.4	11.12	10.345	1.118	0.685	625	112	4.61	207	39.9	2.65
× 89	26.2	10.88	10.275	0.998	0.615	542	99.7	4.55	181	35.2	2.63
× 77	22.7	10.62	10.195	0.868	0.535	457	86.1	4.49	153	30.1	2.60
× 72	21.2	10.50	10.170	0.808	0.510	421	80.1	4.46	142	27.9	2.59
× 66	19.4	10.38	10.117	0.748	0.457	382	73.7	4.44	129	25.5	2.58
× 60	17.7	10.25	10.075	0.683	0.415	344	67.1	4.41	116	23.1	2.57
× 54	15.9	10.12	10.028	0.618	0.368	306	60.4	4.39	104	20.7	2.56
× 49	14.4	10.00	10.000	0.558	0.340	273	54.6	4.35	93.0	18.6	2.54
W 10× 45	13.2	10.12	8.022	0.618	0.350	249	49.1	4.33	53.2	13.3	2.00
× 39	11.5	9.94	7.990	0.528	0.318	210	42.2	4.27	44.9	11.2	1.98
× 33	9.71	9.75	7.964	0.433	0.292	171	35.0	4.20	36.5	9.16	1.94
W 10× 29	8.54	10.22	5.799	0.500	0.289	158	30.8	4.30	16.3	5.61	1.38
× 25	7.36	10.08	5.762	0.430	0.252	133	26.5	4.26	13.7	4.76	1.37
× 21	6.20	9.90	5.750	0.340	0.240	107	21.5	4.15	10.8	3.75	1.32
W 10× 19	5.61	10.25	4.020	0.394	0.250	96.3	18.8	4.14	4.28	2.13	0.874
× 17	4.99	10.12	4.010	0.329	0.240	81.9	16.2	4.05	3.55	1.77	0.844
× 15	4.41	10.00	4.000	0.269	0.230	68.9	13.8	3.95	2.88	1.44	0.809
× 11.5	3.39	9.87	3.950	0.204	0.180	52.0	10.5	3.92	2.10	1.06	0.787

Courtesy American Institute of Steel Construction, Inc.

TABLE A-11 WIDE FLANGE BEAMS (*continued*)

W SHAPES
Properties for designing

Designation	Area A	Depth d	Flange Width b_f	Flange Thick-ness t_f	Web Thick-ness t_w	Axis X-X I	Axis X-X S	Axis X-X r	Axis Y-Y I	Axis Y-Y S	Axis Y-Y r
	In.²	In.	In.	In.	In.	In.⁴	In.³	In.	In.⁴	In.³	In.
W 8×67	19.7	9.00	8.287	0.933	0.575	272	60.4	3.71	88.6	21.4	2.12
×58	17.1	8.75	8.222	0.808	0.510	227	52.0	3.65	74.9	18.2	2.10
×48	14.1	8.50	8.117	0.683	0.405	184	43.2	3.61	60.9	15.0	2.08
×40	11.8	8.25	8.077	0.558	0.365	146	35.5	3.53	49.0	12.1	2.04
×35	10.3	8.12	8.027	0.493	0.315	126	31.1	3.50	42.5	10.6	2.03
×31	9.12	8.00	8.000	0.433	0.288	110	27.4	3.47	37.0	9.24	2.01
W 8×28	8.23	8.06	6.540	0.463	0.285	97.8	24.3	3.45	21.6	6.61	1.62
×24	7.06	7.93	6.500	0.398	0.245	82.5	20.8	3.42	18.2	5.61	1.61
W 8×20	5.89	8.14	5.268	0.378	0.248	69.4	17.0	3.43	9.22	3.50	1.25
×17	5.01	8.00	5.250	0.308	0.230	56.6	14.1	3.36	7.44	2.83	1.22
W 8×15	4.43	8.12	4.015	0.314	0.245	48.1	11.8	3.29	3.40	1.69	0.876
×13	3.83	8.00	4.000	0.254	0.230	39.6	9.90	3.21	2.72	1.36	0.842
×10	2.96	7.90	3.940	0.204	0.170	30.8	7.80	3.23	2.08	1.06	0.839
W 6×25	7.35	6.37	6.080	0.456	0.320	53.3	16.7	2.69	17.1	5.62	1.53
×20	5.88	6.20	6.018	0.367	0.258	41.5	13.4	2.66	13.3	4.43	1.51
×15.5	4.56	6.00	5.995	0.269	0.235	30.1	10.0	2.57	9.67	3.23	1.46
W 6×16	4.72	6.25	4.030	0.404	0.260	31.7	10.2	2.59	4.42	2.19	0.967
×12	3.54	6.00	4.000	0.279	0.230	21.7	7.25	2.48	2.98	1.49	0.918
× 8.5	2.51	5.83	3.940	0.194	0.170	14.8	5.08	2.43	1.98	1.01	0.889
W 5×18.5	5.43	5.12	5.025	0.420	0.265	25.4	9.94	2.16	8.89	3.54	1.28
×16	4.70	5.00	5.000	0.360	0.240	21.3	8.53	2.13	7.51	3.00	1.26
W 4×13	3.82	4.16	4.060	0.345	0.280	11.3	5.45	1.72	3.76	1.85	0.991

Courtesy American Institute of Steel Construction, Inc.

TABLE A-12 CHANNELS

CHANNELS
AMERICAN STANDARD
Properties for designing

Designation	Area A	Depth d	Flange Width b_f	Flange Average thickness t_f	Web thickness t_w	Axis X-X I	Axis X-X S	Axis X-X r	Axis Y-Y I	Axis Y-Y S	Axis Y-Y r	$\bar{x}$
	In.²	In.	In.	In.	In.	In.⁴	In.³	In.	In.⁴	In.³	In.	In.
C 15×50	14.7	15.00	3.716	0.650	0.716	404	53.8	5.24	11.0	3.78	0.867	0.799
×40	11.8	15.00	3.520	0.650	0.520	349	46.5	5.44	9.23	3.36	0.886	0.778
×33.9	9.96	15.00	3.400	0.650	0.400	315	42.0	5.62	8.13	3.11	0.904	0.787
C 12×30	8.82	12.00	3.170	0.501	0.510	162	27.0	4.29	5.14	2.06	0.763	0.674
×25	7.35	12.00	3.047	0.501	0.387	144	24.1	4.43	4.47	1.88	0.780	0.674
×20.7	6.09	12.00	2.942	0.501	0.282	129	21.5	4.61	3.88	1.73	0.799	0.698
C 10×30	8.82	10.00	3.033	0.436	0.673	103	20.7	3.42	3.94	1.65	0.669	0.649
×25	7.35	10.00	2.886	0.436	0.526	91.2	18.2	3.52	3.36	1.48	0.676	0.617
×20	5.88	10.00	2.739	0.436	0.379	78.9	15.8	3.66	2.81	1.32	0.691	0.606
×15.3	4.49	10.00	2.600	0.436	0.240	67.4	13.5	3.87	2.28	1.16	0.713	0.634
C 9×20	5.88	9.00	2.648	0.413	0.448	60.9	13.5	3.22	2.42	1.17	0.642	0.583
×15	4.41	9.00	2.485	0.413	0.285	51.0	11.3	3.40	1.93	1.01	0.661	0.586
×13.4	3.94	9.00	2.433	0.413	0.233	47.9	10.6	3.48	1.76	0.962	0.668	0.601
C 8×18.75	5.51	8.00	2.527	0.390	0.487	44.0	11.0	2.82	1.98	1.01	0.599	0.565
×13.75	4.04	8.00	2.343	0.390	0.303	36.1	9.03	2.99	1.53	0.853	0.615	0.553
×11.5	3.38	8.00	2.260	0.390	0.220	32.6	8.14	3.11	1.32	0.781	0.625	0.571
C 7×14.75	4.33	7.00	2.299	0.366	0.419	27.2	7.78	2.51	1.38	0.779	0.564	0.532
×12.25	3.60	7.00	2.194	0.366	0.314	24.2	6.93	2.60	1.17	0.702	0.571	0.525
× 9.8	2.87	7.00	2.090	0.366	0.210	21.3	6.08	2.72	0.968	0.625	0.581	0.541
C 6×13	3.83	6.00	2.157	0.343	0.437	17.4	5.80	2.13	1.05	0.642	0.525	0.514
×10.5	3.09	6.00	2.034	0.343	0.314	15.2	5.06	2.22	0.865	0.564	0.529	0.500
× 8.2	2.40	6.00	1.920	0.343	0.200	13.1	4.38	2.34	0.692	0.492	0.537	0.512
C 5× 9	2.64	5.00	1.885	0.320	0.325	8.90	3.56	1.83	0.632	0.449	0.489	0.478
× 6.7	1.97	5.00	1.750	0.320	0.190	7.49	3.00	1.95	0.478	0.378	0.493	0.484
C 4× 7.25	2.13	4.00	1.721	0.296	0.321	4.59	2.29	1.47	0.432	0.343	0.450	0.459
× 5.4	1.59	4.00	1.584	0.296	0.184	3.85	1.93	1.56	0.319	0.283	0.449	0.458
C 3× 6	1.76	3.00	1.596	0.273	0.356	2.07	1.38	1.08	0.305	0.268	0.416	0.455
× 5	1.47	3.00	1.498	0.273	0.258	1.85	1.24	1.12	0.247	0.233	0.410	0.438
× 4.1	1.21	3.00	1.410	0.273	0.170	1.66	1.10	1.17	0.197	0.202	0.404	0.437

Courtesy American Institute of Steel Construction, Inc.

TABLE A-13   ANGLES: EQUAL LEGS

ANGLES
Equal legs
Properties for designing

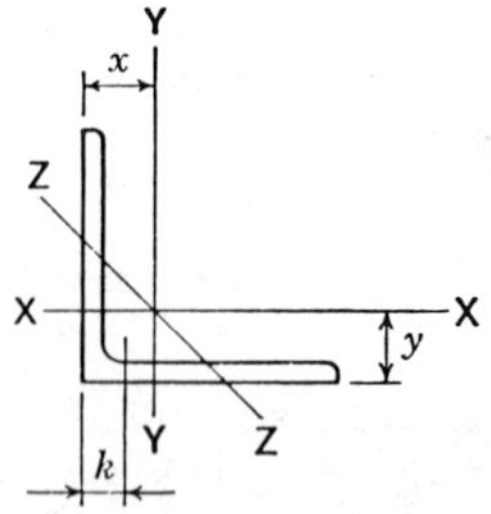

Size and Thickness	Weight per Foot	Area	AXIS X-X AND AXIS Y-Y				AXIS Z-Z
			I	S	r	x or y	r
In.	Lb.	In.²	In.⁴	In.³	In.	In.	In.
L 8 × 8 × 1⅛	56.9	16.7	98.0	17.5	2.42	2.41	1.56
1	51.0	15.0	89.0	15.8	2.44	2.37	1.56
⅞	45.0	13.2	79.6	14.0	2.45	2.32	1.57
¾	38.9	11.4	69.7	12.2	2.47	2.28	1.58
⅝	32.7	9.61	59.4	10.3	2.49	2.23	1.58
9/16	29.6	8.68	54.1	9.34	2.50	2.21	1.59
½	26.4	7.75	48.6	8.36	2.50	2.19	1.59
L 6 × 6 × 1	37.4	11.0	35.5	8.57	1.80	1.86	1.17
⅞	33.1	9.73	31.9	7.63	1.81	1.82	1.17
¾	28.7	8.44	28.2	6.66	1.83	1.78	1.17
⅝	24.2	7.11	24.2	5.66	1.84	1.73	1.18
9/16	21.9	6.43	22.1	5.14	1.85	1.71	1.18
½	19.6	5.75	19.9	4.61	1.86	1.68	1.18
7/16	17.2	5.06	17.7	4.08	1.87	1.66	1.19
⅜	14.9	4.36	15.4	3.53	1.88	1.64	1.19
5/16	12.4	3.65	13.0	2.97	1.89	1.62	1.20
L 5 × 5 × ⅞	27.2	7.98	17.8	5.17	1.49	1.57	.973
¾	23.6	6.94	15.7	4.53	1.51	1.52	.975
⅝	20.0	5.86	13.6	3.86	1.52	1.48	.978
½	16.2	4.75	11.3	3.16	1.54	1.43	.983
7/16	14.3	4.18	10.0	2.79	1.55	1.41	.986
⅜	12.3	3.61	8.74	2.42	1.56	1.39	.990
5/16	10.3	3.03	7.42	2.04	1.57	1.37	.994
L 4 × 4 × ¾	18.5	5.44	7.67	2.81	1.19	1.27	.778
⅝	15.7	4.61	6.66	2.40	1.20	1.23	.779
½	12.8	3.75	5.56	1.97	1.22	1.18	.782
7/16	11.3	3.31	4.97	1.75	1.23	1.16	.785
⅜	9.8	2.86	4.36	1.52	1.23	1.14	.788
5/16	8.2	2.40	3.71	1.29	1.24	1.12	.791
¼	6.6	1.94	3.04	1.05	1.25	1.09	.795

Courtesy American Institute of Steel Construction, Inc.

TABLE A-13   ANGLES: EQUAL LEGS (*continued*)

ANGLES
Equal legs
Properties for designing

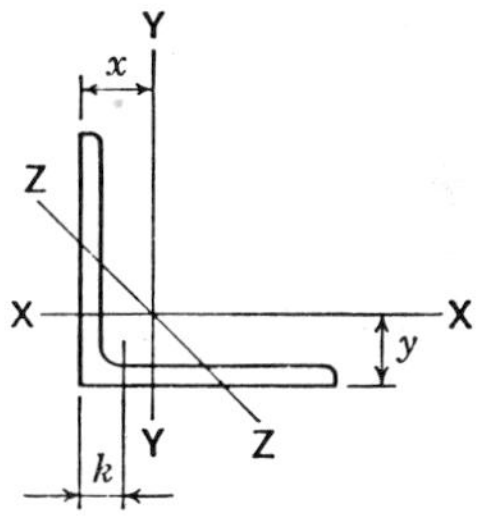

Size and Thickness		Weight per Foot	Area	AXIS X-X AND AXIS Y-Y				AXIS Z-Z
				I	S	r	x or y	r
In.		Lb.	In.^{2}	In.^{4}	In.^{3}	In.	In.	In.
L 3½ × 3½ × ½		11.1	3.25	3.64	1.49	1.06	1.06	.683
⁷⁄₁₆		9.8	2.87	3.26	1.32	1.07	1.04	.684
⅜		8.5	2.48	2.87	1.15	1.07	1.01	.687
⁵⁄₁₆		7.2	2.09	2.45	.976	1.08	.990	.690
¼		5.8	1.69	2.01	.794	1.09	.968	.694
L 3 × 3 × ½		9.4	2.75	2.22	1.07	.898	.932	.584
⁷⁄₁₆		8.3	2.43	1.99	.954	.905	.910	.585
⅜		7.2	2.11	1.76	.833	.913	.888	.587
⁵⁄₁₆		6.1	1.78	1.51	.707	.922	.869	.589
¼		4.9	1.44	1.24	.577	.930	.842	.592
³⁄₁₆		3.71	1.09	.962	.441	.939	.820	.596
L 2½ × 2½ × ½		7.7	2.25	1.23	.724	.739	.806	.487
⅜		5.9	1.73	.984	.566	.753	.762	.487
⁵⁄₁₆		5.0	1.46	.849	.482	.761	.740	.489
¼		4.1	1.19	.703	.394	.769	.717	.491
³⁄₁₆		3.07	0.92	.547	.303	.778	.694	.495
L 2 × 2 × ⅜		4.7	1.36	.479	.351	.594	.636	.389
⁵⁄₁₆		3.92	1.15	.416	.300	.601	.614	.390
¼		3.19	.938	.348	.247	.609	.592	.391
³⁄₁₆		2.44	.715	.272	.190	.617	.569	.394
⅛		1.65	.484	.190	.131	.626	.546	.398
L 1¾ × 1¾ × ¼		2.77	.813	.227	.186	.529	.529	.341
³⁄₁₆		2.12	.621	.179	.144	.537	.506	.343
⅛		1.44	.422	.126	.099	.546	.484	.347
L 1½ × 1½ × ¼		2.34	.688	.139	.134	.449	.466	.292
³⁄₁₆		1.80	.527	.110	.104	.457	.444	.293
⁵⁄₃₂		1.52	.444	.094	.088	.461	.433	.295
⅛		1.23	.359	.078	.072	.465	.421	.296
L 1¼ × 1¼ × ¼		1.92	.563	.077	.091	.369	.403	.243
³⁄₁₆		1.48	.434	.061	.071	.377	.381	.244
⅛		1.01	.297	.044	.049	.385	.359	.246
L 1 × 1 × ¼		1.49	.438	.037	.056	.290	.339	.196
³⁄₁₆		1.16	.340	.030	.044	.297	.318	.195
⅛		.80	.234	.022	.031	.304	.296	.196

Courtesy American Institute of Steel Construction, Inc.

TABLE A-14   ANGLES: UNEQUAL LEGS

ANGLES
Unequal legs
Properties for designing

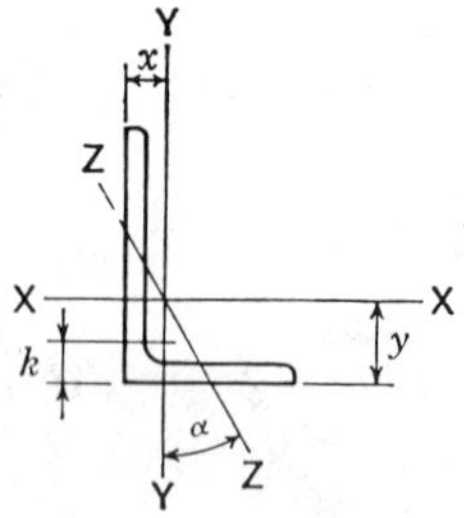

Size and Thickness	Weight per Foot	Area	AXIS X-X				AXIS Y-Y				AXIS Z-Z	
			I	S	r	y	I	S	r	x	r	Tan α
In.	Lb.	In.²	In.⁴	In.³	In.	In.	In.⁴	In.³	In.	In.	In.	
L 9 × 4 × 1	40.8	12.0	97.0	17.6	2.84	3.50	12.0	4.00	1.00	1.00	.834	.203
⅞	36.1	10.6	86.8	15.7	2.86	3.45	10.8	3.56	1.01	.953	.836	.208
¾	31.3	9.19	76.1	13.6	2.88	3.41	9.63	3.11	1.02	.906	.841	.212
⅝	26.3	7.73	64.9	11.5	2.90	3.36	8.32	2.65	1.04	.858	.847	.216
⁹⁄₁₆	23.8	7.00	59.1	10.4	2.91	3.33	7.63	2.41	1.04	.834	.850	.218
½	21.3	6.25	53.2	9.34	2.92	3.31	6.92	2.17	1.05	.810	.854	.220
L 8 × 6 × 1	44.2	13.0	80.8	15.1	2.49	2.65	38.8	8.92	1.73	1.65	1.28	.543
⅞	39.1	11.5	72.3	13.4	2.51	2.61	34.9	7.94	1.74	1.61	1.28	.547
¾	33.8	9.94	63.4	11.7	2.53	2.56	30.7	6.92	1.76	1.56	1.29	.551
⅝	28.5	8.36	54.1	9.87	2.54	2.52	26.3	5.88	1.77	1.52	1.29	.554
⁹⁄₁₆	25.7	7.56	49.3	8.95	2.55	2.50	24.0	5.34	1.78	1.50	1.30	.556
½	23.0	6.75	44.3	8.02	2.56	2.47	21.7	4.79	1.79	1.47	1.30	.558
⁷⁄₁₆	20.2	5.93	39.2	7.07	2.57	2.45	19.3	4.23	1.80	1.45	1.31	.560
L 8 × 4 × 1	37.4	11.0	69.6	14.1	2.52	3.05	11.6	3.94	1.03	1.05	.846	.247
⅞	33.1	9.73	62.5	12.5	2.53	3.00	10.5	3.51	1.04	.999	.848	.253
¾	28.7	8.44	54.9	10.9	2.55	2.95	9.36	3.07	1.05	.953	.852	.258
⅝	24.2	7.11	46.9	9.21	2.57	2.91	8.10	2.62	1.07	.906	.857	.262
⁹⁄₁₆	21.9	6.43	42.8	8.35	2.58	2.88	7.43	2.38	1.07	.882	.861	.265
½	19.6	5.75	38.5	7.49	2.59	2.86	6.74	2.15	1.08	.859	.865	.267
⁷⁄₁₆	17.2	5.06	34.1	6.60	2.60	2.83	6.02	1.90	1.09	.835	.869	.269
L 7 × 4 × ⅞	30.2	8.86	42.9	9.65	2.20	2.55	10.2	3.46	1.07	1.05	.856	.318
¾	26.2	7.69	37.8	8.42	2.22	2.51	9.05	3.03	1.09	1.01	.860	.324
⅝	22.1	6.48	32.4	7.14	2.24	2.46	7.84	2.58	1.10	.963	.865	.329
⁹⁄₁₆	20.0	5.87	29.6	6.48	2.24	2.44	7.19	2.35	1.11	.940	.868	.332
½	17.9	5.25	26.7	5.81	2.25	2.42	6.53	2.12	1.11	.917	.872	.335
⁷⁄₁₆	15.8	4.62	23.7	5.13	2.26	2.39	5.83	1.88	1.12	.893	.876	.337
⅜	13.6	3.98	20.6	4.44	2.27	2.37	5.10	1.63	1.13	.870	.880	.340

Courtesy American Institute of Steel Construction, Inc.

TABLE A-14   ANGLES: UNEQUAL LEGS (*continued*)

ANGLES
Unequal legs
Properties for designing

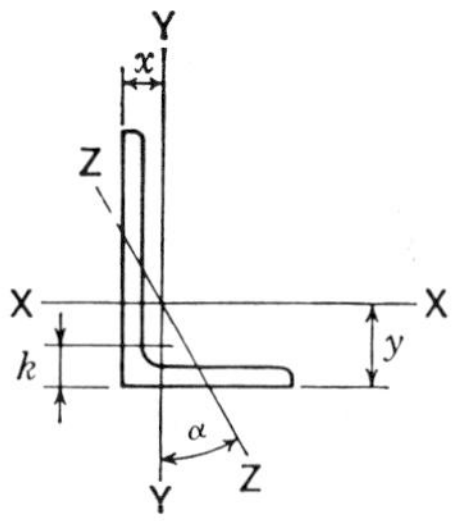

Size and Thickness	Weight per Foot	Area	AXIS X-X				AXIS Y-Y				AXIS Z-Z	
			I	S	r	y	I	S	r	x	r	Tan α
In.	Lb.	In.²	In.⁴	In.³	In.	In.	In.⁴	In.³	In.	In.	In.	
L 6 × 4 × ⅞	27.2	7.98	27.7	7.15	1.86	2.12	9.75	3.39	1.11	1.12	.857	.421
¾	23.6	6.94	24.5	6.25	1.88	2.08	8.68	2.97	1.12	1.08	.860	.428
⅝	20.0	5.86	21.1	5.31	1.90	2.03	7.52	2.54	1.13	1.03	.864	.435
9⁄16	18.1	5.31	19.3	4.83	1.90	2.01	6.91	2.31	1.14	1.01	.866	.438
½	16.2	4.75	17.4	4.33	1.91	1.99	6.27	2.08	1.15	.987	.870	.440
7⁄16	14.3	4.18	15.5	3.83	1.92	1.96	5.60	1.85	1.16	.964	.873	.443
⅜	12.3	3.61	13.5	3.32	1.93	1.94	4.90	1.60	1.17	.941	.877	.446
5⁄16	10.3	3.03	11.4	2.79	1.94	1.92	4.18	1.35	1.17	.918	.882	.448
¼	8.3	2.44	9.27	2.26	1.95	1.89	3.41	1.10	1.18	.894	.887	.451
L 6 × 3½ × ½	15.3	4.50	16.6	4.24	1.92	2.08	4.25	1.59	.972	.833	.759	.344
⅜	11.7	3.42	12.9	3.24	1.94	2.04	3.34	1.23	.988	.787	.767	.350
5⁄16	9.8	2.87	10.9	2.73	1.95	2.01	2.85	1.04	.996	.763	.772	.352
¼	7.9	2.31	8.86	2.21	1.96	1.99	2.34	0.847	1.01	.740	.777	.355
L 5 × 3½ × ¾	19.8	5.81	13.9	4.28	1.55	1.75	5.55	2.22	.977	.996	.748	.464
⅝	16.8	4.92	12.0	3.65	1.56	1.70	4.83	1.90	.991	.951	.751	.472
½	13.6	4.00	9.99	2.99	1.58	1.66	4.05	1.56	1.01	.906	.755	.479
7⁄16	12.0	3.53	8.90	2.64	1.59	1.63	3.63	1.39	1.01	.883	.758	.482
⅜	10.4	3.05	7.78	2.29	1.60	1.61	3.18	1.21	1.02	.861	.762	.486
5⁄16	8.7	2.56	6.60	1.94	1.61	1.59	2.72	1.02	1.03	.838	.766	.489
¼	7.0	2.06	5.39	1.57	1.62	1.56	2.23	.830	1.04	.814	.770	.492
L 5 × 3 × ½	12.8	3.75	9.45	2.91	1.59	1.75	2.58	1.15	.829	.750	.648	.357
7⁄16	11.3	3.31	8.43	2.58	1.60	1.73	2.32	1.02	.837	.727	.651	.361
⅜	9.8	2.86	7.37	2.24	1.61	1.70	2.04	.888	.845	.704	.654	.364
5⁄16	8.2	2.40	6.26	1.89	1.61	1.68	1.75	.753	.853	.681	.658	.368
¼	6.6	1.94	5.11	1.53	1.62	1.66	1.44	.614	.861	.657	.663	.371

Courtesy American Institute of Steel Construction, Inc.

TABLE A-14   ANGLES: UNEQUAL LEGS (*continued*)

ANGLES
Unequal legs
Properties for designing

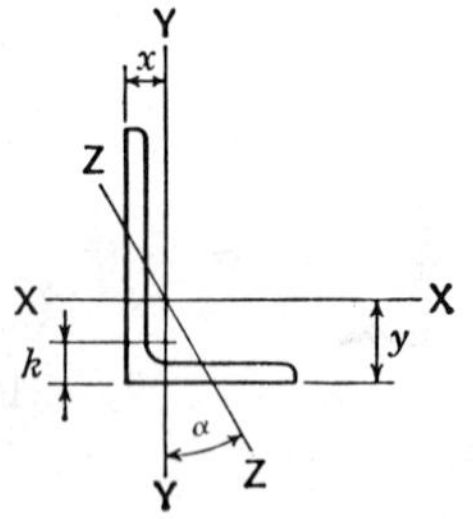

Size and Thickness	Weight per Foot	Area	AXIS X-X				AXIS Y-Y				AXIS Z-Z	
			I	S	r	y	I	S	r	x	r	Tan
In.	Lb.	In.²	In.⁴	In.³	In.	In.	In.⁴	In.³	In.	In.	In.	α
L 4 × 3½ × ⅝	14.7	4.30	6.37	2.35	1.22	1.29	4.52	1.84	1.03	1.04	.719	.745
½	11.9	3.50	5.32	1.94	1.23	1.25	3.79	1.52	1.04	1.00	.722	.750
⁷⁄₁₆	10.6	3.09	4.76	1.72	1.24	1.23	3.40	1.35	1.05	.978	.724	.753
⅜	9.1	2.67	4.18	1.49	1.25	1.21	2.95	1.17	1.06	.955	.727	.755
⁵⁄₁₆	7.7	2.25	3.56	1.26	1.26	1.18	2.55	.994	1.07	.932	.730	.757
¼	6.2	1.81	2.91	1.03	1.27	1.16	2.09	.808	1.07	.909	.734	.759
L 4 × 3 × ⅝	13.6	3.98	6.03	2.30	1.23	1.37	2.87	1.35	.849	.871	.637	.534
½	11.1	3.25	5.05	1.89	1.25	1.33	2.42	1.12	.864	.827	.639	.543
⁷⁄₁₆	9.8	2.87	4.52	1.68	1.25	1.30	2.18	.992	.871	.804	.641	.547
⅜	8.5	2.48	3.96	1.46	1.26	1.28	1.92	.866	.879	.782	.644	.551
⁵⁄₁₆	7.2	2.09	3.38	1.23	1.27	1.26	1.65	.734	.887	.759	.647	.554
¼	5.8	1.69	2.77	1.00	1.28	1.24	1.36	.599	.896	.736	.651	.558
L 3½ × 3 × ½	10.2	3.00	3.45	1.45	1.07	1.13	2.33	1.10	.881	.875	.621	.714
⁷⁄₁₆	9.1	2.65	3.10	1.29	1.08	1.10	2.09	.975	.889	.853	.622	.718
⅜	7.9	2.30	2.72	1.13	1.09	1.08	1.85	.851	.897	.830	.625	.721
⁵⁄₁₆	6.6	1.93	2.33	.954	1.10	1.06	1.58	.722	.905	.808	.627	.724
¼	5.4	1.56	1.91	.776	1.11	1.04	1.30	.589	.914	.785	.631	.727
L 3½ × 2½ × ½	9.4	2.75	3.24	1.41	1.09	1.20	1.36	.760	.704	.705	.534	.486
⁷⁄₁₆	8.3	2.43	2.91	1.26	1.09	1.18	1.23	.677	.711	.682	.535	.491
⅜	7.2	2.11	2.56	1.09	1.10	1.16	1.09	.592	.719	.660	.537	.496
⁵⁄₁₆	6.1	1.78	2.19	.927	1.11	1.14	.939	.504	.727	.637	.540	.501
¼	4.9	1.44	1.80	.755	1.12	1.11	.777	.412	.735	.614	.544	.506
L 3 × 2½ × ½	8.5	2.50	2.08	1.04	.913	1.00	1.30	.744	.722	.750	.520	.667
⁷⁄₁₆	7.6	2.21	1.88	.928	.920	.978	1.18	.664	.729	.728	.521	.672
⅜	6.6	1.92	1.66	.810	.928	.956	1.04	.581	.736	.706	.522	.676
⁵⁄₁₆	5.6	1.62	1.42	.688	.937	.933	.898	.494	.744	.683	.525	.680
¼	4.5	1.31	1.17	.561	.945	.911	.743	.404	.753	.661	.528	.684
³⁄₁₆	3.39	.996	.907	.430	.954	.888	.577	.310	.761	.638	.533	.688

Courtesy American Institute of Steel Construction, Inc.

TABLE A-14   ANGLES: UNEQUAL LEGS (*continued*)

ANGLES
Unequal legs
Properties for designing

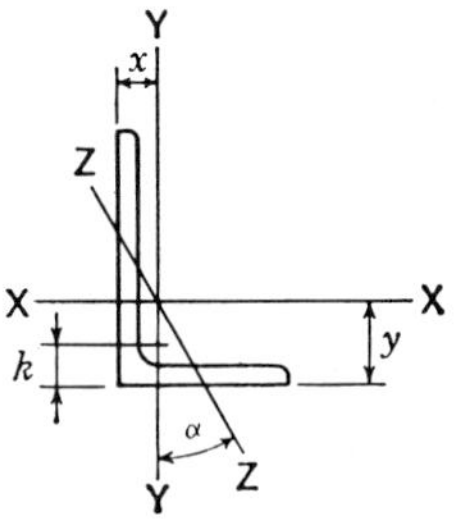

Size and Thickness	Weight per Foot	Area	AXIS X-X				AXIS Y-Y				AXIS Z-Z	
			I	*S*	*r*	*y*	*I*	*S*	*r*	*x*	*r*	Tan
In.	Lb.	In.²	In.⁴	In.³	In.	In.	In.⁴	In.³	In.	In.	In.	α
L 3 × 2 × ½	7.7	2.25	1.92	1.00	.924	1.08	.672	.474	.546	.583	.428	.414
⁷⁄₁₆	6.8	2.00	1.73	.894	.932	1.06	.609	.424	.553	.561	.429	.421
⅜	5.9	1.73	1.53	.781	.940	1.04	.543	.371	.559	.539	.430	.428
⁵⁄₁₆	5.0	1.46	1.32	.664	.948	1.02	.470	.317	.567	.516	.432	.435
¼	4.1	1.19	1.09	.542	.957	.993	.392	.260	.574	.493	.435	.440
³⁄₁₆	3.07	.902	.842	.415	.966	.970	.307	.200	.583	.470	.439	.446
L 2½ × 2 × ⅜	5.3	1.55	.912	.547	.768	.831	.514	.363	.577	.581	.420	.614
⁵⁄₁₆	4.5	1.31	.788	.466	.776	.809	.446	.310	.584	.559	.422	.620
¼	3.62	1.06	.654	.381	.784	.787	.372	.254	.592	.537	.424	.626
³⁄₁₆	2.75	.809	.509	.293	.793	.764	.291	.196	.600	.514	.427	.631
L 2½ × 1½ × ⁵⁄₁₆	3.92	1.15	.711	.444	.785	.898	.191	.174	.408	.398	.322	.349
¼	3.19	.938	.591	.364	.794	.875	.161	.143	.415	.375	.324	.357
³⁄₁₆	2.44	.715	.461	.279	.803	.852	.127	.111	.422	.352	.327	.364
L 2 × 1½ × ¼	2.77	.813	.316	.236	.623	.663	.151	.139	.432	.413	.320	.543
³⁄₁₆	2.12	.621	.248	.182	.632	.641	.120	.108	.440	.391	.322	.551
⅛	1.44	.422	.173	.125	.641	.618	.085	.075	.448	.368	.326	.558
L 2 × 1¼ × ¼	2.55	.750	.296	.229	.628	.708	.089	.097	.344	.333	.269	.378
³⁄₁₆	1.96	.574	.232	.177	.636	.686	.071	.075	.351	.311	.271	.387
⅛	1.33	.391	.163	.122	.645	.663	.050	.052	.359	.287	.274	.396
L 1¾ × 1¼ × ¼	2.34	.688	.202	.176	.543	.602	.085	.095	.352	.352	.267	.486
³⁄₁₆	1.80	.527	.160	.137	.551	.580	.068	.074	.359	.330	.269	.496
⅛	1.23	.359	.113	.094	.560	.557	.049	.051	.368	.307	.272	.506

Courtesy American Institute of Steel Construction, Inc.

TABLE A-15   PIPE

PIPE
Dimensions and properties

Dimension				Weight per Foot	Properties			
Nominal Diameter In.	Outside Diameter In.	Inside Diameter In.	Wall Thickness In.	Lbs. Plain Ends	A In.^{2}	I In.^{4}	S In.^{3}	r In.
Standard Weight								
½	.840	.622	.109	.85	.250	.017	.041	.261
¾	1.050	.824	.113	1.13	.333	.037	.071	.334
1	1.315	1.049	.133	1.68	.494	.087	.133	.421
1¼	1.660	1.380	.140	2.27	.669	.195	.235	.540
1½	1.900	1.610	.145	2.72	.799	.310	.326	.623
2	2.375	2.067	.154	3.65	1.07	.666	.561	.787
2½	2.875	2.469	.203	5.79	1.70	1.53	1.06	.947
3	3.500	3.068	.216	7.58	2.23	3.02	1.72	1.16
3½	4.000	3.548	.226	9.11	2.68	4.79	2.39	1.34
4	4.500	4.026	.237	10.79	3.17	7.23	3.21	1.51
5	5.563	5.047	.258	14.62	4.30	15.2	5.45	1.88
6	6.625	6.065	.280	18.97	5.58	28.1	8.50	2.25
8	8.625	7.981	.322	28.55	8.40	72.5	16.8	2.94
10	10.750	10.020	.365	40.48	11.9	161	29.9	3.67
12	12.750	12.000	.375	49.56	14.6	279	43.8	4.38
Extra Strong								
½	.840	.546	.147	1.09	.320	.020	.048	.250
¾	1.050	.742	.154	1.47	.433	.045	.085	.321
1	1.315	.957	.179	2.17	.639	.106	.161	.407
1¼	1.660	1.278	.191	3.00	.881	.242	.291	.524
1½	1.900	1.500	.200	3.63	1.07	.391	.412	.605
2	2.375	1.939	.218	5.02	1.48	.868	.731	.766
2½	2.875	2.323	.276	7.66	2.25	1.92	1.34	.924
3	3.500	2.900	.300	10.25	3.02	3.89	2.23	1.14
3½	4.000	3.364	.318	12.50	3.68	6.28	3.14	1.31
4	4.500	3.826	.337	14.98	4.41	9.61	4.27	1.48
5	5.563	4.813	.375	20.78	6.11	20.7	7.43	1.84
6	6.625	5.761	.432	28.57	8.40	40.5	12.2	2.19
8	8.625	7.625	.500	43.39	12.8	106	24.5	2.88
10	10.750	9.750	.500	54.74	16.1	212	39.4	3.63
12	12.750	11.750	.500	65.42	19.2	362	56.7	4.33
Double-Extra Strong								
2	2.375	1.503	.436	9.03	2.66	1.31	1.10	.703
2½	2.875	1.771	.552	13.69	4.03	2.87	2.00	.844
3	3.500	2.300	.600	18.58	5.47	5.99	3.42	1.05
4	4.500	3.152	.674	27.54	8.10	15.3	6.79	1.37
5	5.563	4.063	.750	38.55	11.3	33.6	12.1	1.72
6	6.625	4.897	.864	53.16	15.6	66.3	20.0	2.06
8	8.625	6.875	.875	72.42	21.3	162	37.6	2.76

The listed sections are available in conformance with ASTM Specification A53 Grade B or A501. Other sections are made to these specifications. Consult with pipe manufacturers or distributors for availability.

Courtesy American Institute of Steel Construction, Inc.

TABLE A-16 SCREW THREADS

THREADED FASTENERS

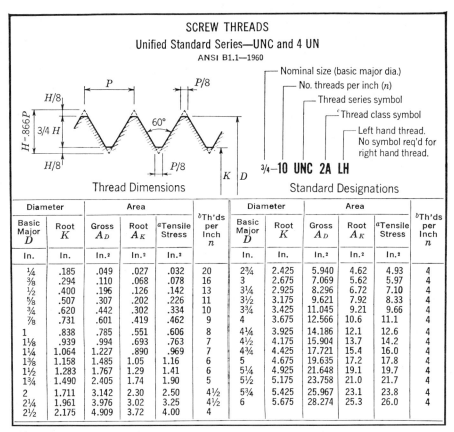

SCREW THREADS

Unified Standard Series—UNC and 4 UN

ANSI B1.1—1960

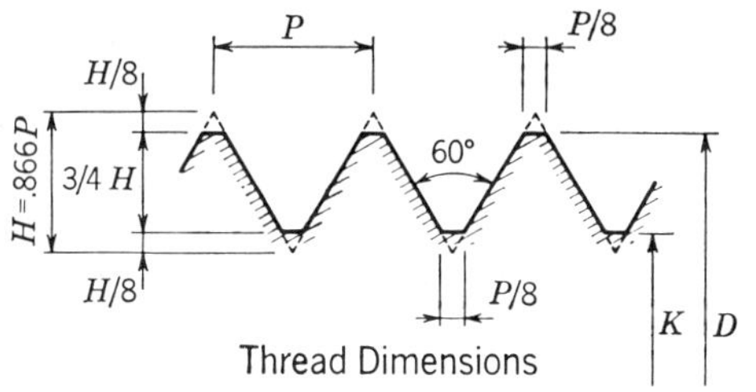
P
P/8
H/8
60°
H = .866P
3/4 H
H/8
P/8
K
D

Thread Dimensions

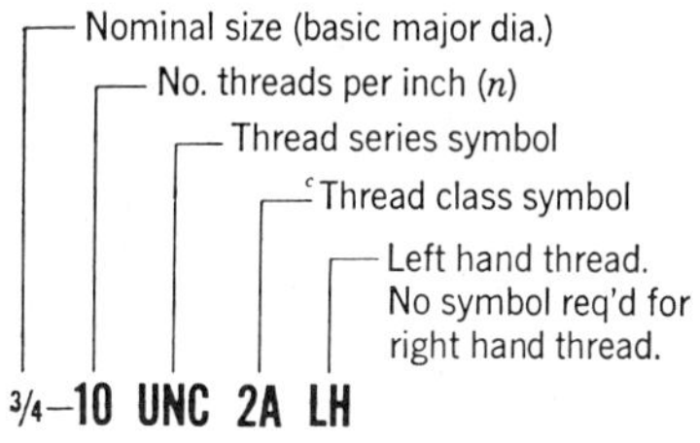
Nominal size (basic major dia.)
No. threads per inch (n)
Thread series symbol
[c]Thread class symbol
Left hand thread.
No symbol req'd for
right hand thread.
3/4–10 UNC 2A LH

Standard Designations

Diameter		Area			[b]Th'ds per Inch	Diameter		Area			[b]Th'ds per Inch
Basic Major D	Root K	Gross A_D	Root A_K	[a]Tensile Stress	n	Basic Major D	Root K	Gross A_D	Root A_K	[a]Tensile Stress	n
In.	In.	In.²	In.²	In.²		In.	In.	In.²	In.²	In.²	
1/4	.185	.049	.027	.032	20	2 3/4	2.425	5.940	4.62	4.93	4
3/8	.294	.110	.068	.078	16	3	2.675	7.069	5.62	5.97	4
1/2	.400	.196	.126	.142	13	3 1/4	2.925	8.296	6.72	7.10	4
5/8	.507	.307	.202	.226	11	3 1/2	3.175	9.621	7.92	8.33	4
3/4	.620	.442	.302	.334	10	3 3/4	3.425	11.045	9.21	9.66	4
7/8	.731	.601	.419	.462	9	4	3.675	12.566	10.6	11.1	4
1	.838	.785	.551	.606	8	4 1/4	3.925	14.186	12.1	12.6	4
1 1/8	.939	.994	.693	.763	7	4 1/2	4.175	15.904	13.7	14.2	4
1 1/4	1.064	1.227	.890	.969	7	4 3/4	4.425	17.721	15.4	16.0	4
1 3/8	1.158	1.485	1.05	1.16	6	5	4.675	19.635	17.2	17.8	4
1 1/2	1.283	1.767	1.29	1.41	6	5 1/4	4.925	21.648	19.1	19.7	4
1 3/4	1.490	2.405	1.74	1.90	5	5 1/2	5.175	23.758	21.0	21.7	4
2	1.711	3.142	2.30	2.50	4 1/2	5 3/4	5.425	25.967	23.1	23.8	4
2 1/4	1.961	3.976	3.02	3.25	4 1/2	6	5.675	28.274	25.3	26.0	4
2 1/2	2.175	4.909	3.72	4.00	4						

Courtesy American Institute of Steel Construction, Inc.

TABLE A-17   PROPERTIES OF STRUCTURAL LUMBER

Nominal size b(inches)d	Standard dressed size (S4S) b(inches)d	Area of Section A	Moment of inertia I	Section modulus S	Weight in pounds per linear foot of piece when weight of wood per cubic foot equals:					
					25 lb.	30 lb.	35 lb.	40 lb.	45 lb.	50 lb.
1 × 3	3/4 × 2-1/2	1.875	0.977	0.781	0.326	0.391	0.456	0.521	0.586	0.651
1 × 4	3/4 × 3-1/2	2.625	2.680	1.531	0.456	0.547	0.638	0.729	0.820	0.911
1 × 6	3/4 × 5-1/2	4.125	10.398	3.781	0.716	0.859	1.003	1.146	1.289	1.432
1 × 8	3/4 × 7-1/4	5.438	23.817	6.570	0.944	1.133	1.322	1.510	1.699	1.888
1 × 10	3/4 × 9-1/4	6.938	49.466	10.695	1.204	1.445	1.686	1.927	2.168	2.409
1 × 12	3/4 × 11-1/4	8.438	88.989	15.820	1.465	1.758	2.051	2.344	2.637	2.930
2 × 3	1-1/2 × 2-1/2	3.750	1.953	1.563	0.651	0.781	0.911	1.042	1.172	1.302
2 × 4	1-1/2 × 3-1/2	5.250	5.359	3.063	0.911	1.094	1.276	1.458	1.641	1.823
2 × 5	1-1/2 × 4-1/2	6.750	11.391	5.063	1.172	1.406	1.641	1.875	2.109	2.344
2 × 6	1-1/2 × 5-1/2	8.250	20.797	7.563	1.432	1.719	2.005	2.292	2.578	2.865
2 × 8	1-1/2 × 7-1/4	10.875	47.635	13.141	1.888	2.266	2.643	3.021	3.398	3.776
2 × 10	1-1/2 × 9-1/4	13.875	98.932	21.391	2.409	2.891	3.372	3.854	4.336	4.818
2 × 12	1-1/2 × 11-1/4	16.875	177.979	31.641	2.930	3.516	4.102	4.688	5.273	5.859
2 × 14	1-1/2 × 13-1/4	19.875	290.775	43.891	3.451	4.141	4.831	5.521	6.211	6.901
3 × 1	2-1/2 × 3/4	1.875	0.088	0.234	0.326	0.391	0.456	0.521	0.586	0.651
3 × 2	2-1/2 × 1-1/2	3.750	0.703	0.938	0.651	0.781	0.911	1.042	1.172	1.302
3 × 4	2-1/2 × 3-1/2	8.750	8.932	5.104	1.519	1.823	2.127	2.431	2.734	3.038
3 × 5	2-1/2 × 4-1/2	11.250	18.984	8.438	1.953	2.344	2.734	3.125	3.516	3.906
3 × 6	2-1/2 × 5-1/2	13.750	34.661	12.604	2.387	2.865	3.342	3.819	4.297	4.774
3 × 8	2-1/2 × 7-1/4	18.125	79.391	21.901	3.147	3.776	4.405	5.035	5.664	6.293
3 × 10	2-1/2 × 9-1/4	23.125	164.886	35.651	4.015	4.818	5.621	6.424	7.227	8.030
3 × 12	2-1/2 × 11-1/4	28.125	296.631	52.734	4.883	5.859	6.836	7.813	8.789	9.766
3 × 14	2-1/2 × 13-1/4	33.125	484.625	73.151	5.751	6.901	8.051	9.201	10.352	11.502
3 × 16	2-1/2 × 15-1/4	38.125	738.870	96.901	6.619	7.943	9.266	10.590	11.914	13.238
4 × 1	3-1/2 × 3/4	2.625	0.123	0.328	0.456	0.547	0.638	0.729	0.820	0.911
4 × 2	3-1/2 × 1-1/2	5.250	0.984	1.313	0.911	1.094	1.276	1.458	1.641	1.823
4 × 3	3-1/2 × 2-1/2	8.750	4.557	3.646	1.519	1.823	2.127	2.431	2.734	3.038
4 × 4	3-1/2 × 3-1/2	12.250	12.505	7.146	2.127	2.552	2.977	3.403	3.828	4.253
4 × 5	3-1/2 × 4-1/2	15.750	26.578	11.813	2.734	3.281	3.828	4.375	4.922	5.469
4 × 6	3-1/2 × 5-1/2	19.250	48.526	17.646	3.342	4.010	4.679	5.347	6.016	6.684
4 × 8	3-1/2 × 7-1/4	25.375	111.148	30.661	4.405	5.286	6.168	7.049	7.930	8.811
4 × 10	3-1/2 × 9-1/4	32.375	230.840	49.911	5.621	6.745	7.869	8.933	10.117	11.241
4 × 12	3-1/2 × 11-1/4	39.375	415.283	73.828	6.836	8.203	9.570	10.938	12.305	13.672
4 × 14	3-1/2 × 13-1/4	46.375	678.475	102.411	8.047	9.657	11.266	12.877	14.485	16.094
4 × 16	3-1/2 × 15-1/4	53.375	1034.418	135.66	9.267	11.121	12.975	14.828	16.682	18.536
5 × 2	4-1/2 × 1-1/2	6.750	1.266	1.688	1.172	1.406	1.641	1.875	2.109	2.344
5 × 3	4-1/2 × 2-1/2	11.250	5.859	4.688	1.953	2.344	2.734	3.125	3.516	3.906
5 × 4	4-1/2 × 3-1/2	15.750	16.078	9.188	2.734	3.281	3.828	4.375	4.922	5.469
5 × 5	4-1/2 × 4-1/2	20.250	34.172	15.188	3.516	4.219	4.922	5.675	6.328	7.031
6 × 1	5-1/2 × 3/4	4.125	0.193	0.516	0.716	0.859	1.003	1.146	1.289	1.432
6 × 2	5-1/2 × 1-1/2	8.250	1.547	2.063	1.432	1.719	2.005	2.292	2.578	2.865
6 × 3	5-1/2 × 2-1/2	13.750	7.161	5.729	2.387	2.865	3.342	3.819	4.297	4.774
6 × 4	5-1/2 × 3-1/2	19.250	19.651	11.229	3.342	4.010	4.679	5.347	6.016	6.684
6 × 6	5-1/2 × 5-1/2	30.250	76.255	27.729	5.252	6.302	7.352	8.403	9.453	10.503
6 × 8	5-1/2 × 7-1/2	41.250	193.359	51.563	7.161	8.594	10.026	11.458	12.891	14.323
6 × 10	5-1/2 × 9-1/2	52.250	392.963	82.729	9.071	10.885	12.700	14.514	16.328	18.142
6 × 12	5-1/2 × 11-1/2	63.250	697.068	121.229	10.981	13.177	15.373	17.569	19.766	21.962
6 × 14	5-1/2 × 13-1/2	74.250	1127.672	167.063	12.891	15.469	18.047	20.625	23.203	25.781
6 × 16	5-1/2 × 15-1/2	85.250	1706.776	220.229	14.800	17.760	20.720	23.681	26.641	29.601
6 × 18	5-1/2 × 17-1/2	96.250	2456.380	280.729	16.710	20.052	23.394	26.736	30.078	33.420
6 × 20	5 1/2 × 19-1/2	107.250	3398.484	348.563	18.620	22.344	26.068	29.792	33.516	37.240
6 × 22	5-1/2 × 21-1/2	118.250	4555.086	423.729	20.530	24.635	28.741	32.847	36.953	41.059
6 × 24	5-1/2 × 23-1/2	129.250	5948.191	506.229	22.439	26.927	31.415	35.903	40.391	44.878
8 × 1	7-1/4 × 3/4	5.438	0.255	0.680	0.944	1.133	1.322	1.510	1.699	1.888
8 × 2	7-1/4 × 1-1/2	10.875	2.039	2.719	1.888	2.266	2.643	3.021	3.398	3.776
8 × 3	7-1/4 × 2-1/2	18.125	9.440	7.552	3.147	3.776	4.405	5.035	5.664	6.293
8 × 4	7-1/4 × 3-1/2	25.375	25.904	14.803	4.405	5.286	6.168	7.049	7.930	8.811
8 × 6	7-1/2 × 5-1/2	41.250	103.984	37.813	7.161	8.594	10.026	11.458	12.891	14.323
8 × 8	7-1/2 × 7-1/2	56.250	263.672	70.313	9.766	11.719	13.672	15.625	17.578	19.531
8 × 10	7-1/2 × 9-1/2	71.250	535.859	112.813	12.370	14.844	17.318	19.792	22.266	24.740
8 × 12	7 1/2 × 11-1/2	86.250	950.547	165.313	14.974	17.969	20.964	23.958	26.953	29.948
8 × 14	7-1/2 × 13-1/2	101.250	1537.734	227.813	17.578	21.094	24.609	28.125	31.641	35.156
8 × 16	7-1/2 × 15-1/2	116.250	2327.422	300.313	20.182	24.219	28.255	32.292	36.328	40.365
8 × 18	7-1/2 × 17-1/2	131.250	3349.609	382.813	22.786	27.344	31.901	36.458	41.016	45.573
8 × 20	7-1/2 × 19-1/2	146.250	4634.297	475.313	25.391	30.469	35.547	40.625	45.703	50.781
8 × 22	7-1/2 × 21-1/2	161.250	6211.484	577.813	27.995	33.594	39.193	44.792	50.391	55.990
8 × 24	7-1/2 × 23-1/2	176.250	8111.172	690.313	30.599	36.719	42.839	48.958	55.078	61.198

Courtesy National Forest Products Association.

TABLE A-17 PROPERTIES OF STRUCTURAL LUMBER (*continued*)

Nominal size b(inches)d	Standard dressed size (S4S) b(inches)d	Area of Section A	Moment of inertia I	Section modulus S	Weight in pounds per linear foot of piece when weight of wood per cubic foot equals					
					25 lb.	30 lb.	35 lb.	40 lb.	45 lb.	50 lb.
10 x 1	9-1/4 x 3/4	6.938	0.325	0.867	1.204	1.445	1.686	1.927	2.168	2.409
10 x 2	9-1/4 x 1-1/2	13.875	2.602	3.469	2.409	2.891	3.372	3.854	4.336	4.818
10 x 3	9-1/4 x 2-1/2	23.125	12.044	9.635	4.015	4.818	5.621	6.424	7.227	8.030
10 x 4	9-1/4 x 3-1/2	32.375	33.049	18.885	5.621	6.745	7.869	8.993	10.117	11.241
10 x 6	9-1/2 x 5-1/2	52.250	131.714	47.896	9.071	10.885	12.700	14.514	16.328	18.142
10 x 8	9-1/2 x 7-1/2	71.250	333.984	89.063	12.370	14.844	17.318	19.792	22.266	24.740
10 x 10	9-1/2 x 9-1/2	90.250	678.755	142.896	15.668	18.802	21.936	25.069	28.203	31.337
10 x 12	9-1/2 x 11-1/2	109.250	1204.026	209.396	18.967	22.760	26.554	30.347	34.141	37.934
10 x 14	9-1/2 x 13-1/2	128.250	1947.797	288.563	22.266	26.719	31.172	35.625	40.078	44.531
10 x 16	9-1/2 x 15-1/2	147.250	2948.068	380.396	25.564	30.677	35.790	40.903	46.016	51.128
10 x 18	9-1/2 x 17-1/2	166.250	4242.836	484.896	28.863	34.635	40.408	46.181	51.953	57.726
10 x 20	9-1/2 x 19-1/2	185.250	5870.109	602.063	32.161	38.594	45.026	51.458	57.891	64.323
10 x 22	9-1/2 x 21-1/2	204.250	7867.879	731.896	35.460	42.552	49.644	56.736	63.828	70.920
10 x 24	9-1/2 x 23-1/2	223.250	10274.148	874.396	38.759	46.510	54.262	62.014	69.766	77.517
12 x 2	11-1/4 x 3/4	8.438	0.396	1.055	1.465	1.758	2.051	2.344	2.637	2.930
12 x 2	11-1/4 x 1-1/2	16.875	3.164	4.219	2.930	3.516	4.102	4.688	5.273	5.859
12 x 3	11-1/4 x 2-1/2	28.125	14.648	11.719	4.883	5.859	6.836	7.813	8.789	9.766
12 x 4	11-1/4 x 3-1/2	39.375	40.195	22.969	6.836	8.203	9.570	10.938	12.305	13.672
12 x 6	11-1/2 x 5-1/2	63.250	159.443	57.979	10.981	13.177	15.373	17.569	19.766	21.962
12 x 8	11-1/2 x 7-1/2	86.250	404.297	107.813	14.974	17.969	20.964	23.958	26.953	29.948
12 x 10	11-1/2 x 9-1/2	109.250	821.651	172.979	18.967	22.760	26.554	30.347	34.141	37.934
12 x 12	11-1/2 x 11-1/2	132.250	1457.505	253.479	22.960	27.552	32.144	36.736	41.328	45.920
12 x 14	11-1/2 x 13-1/2	155.250	2357.859	349.313	26.953	32.344	37.734	43.125	48.516	53.906
12 x 16	11-1/2 x 15-1/2	178.250	3568.713	460.479	30.946	37.135	43.325	49.514	55.703	61.892
12 x 18	11-1/2 x 17-1/2	201.250	5136.066	586.979	34.939	41.927	48.915	55.903	62.891	69.878
12 x 20	11-1/2 x 19-1/2	224.250	7105.922	728.813	38.932	46.719	54.505	62.292	70.078	77.865
12 x 22	11-1/2 x 21-1/2	247.250	9524.273	885.979	42.925	51.510	60.095	68.681	77.266	85.851
12 x 24	11-1/2 x 23-1/2	270.250	12437.129	1058.479	46.918	56.302	65.686	75.069	84.453	93.837
14 x 2	13-1/4 x 1-1/2	19.875	3.727	4.969	3.451	4.141	4.831	5.521	6.211	6.901
14 x 3	13-1/4 x 2-1/2	33.125	17.253	13.802	5.751	6.901	8.051	9.201	10.352	11.502
14 x 4	13-1/4 x 3-1/2	46.375	47.34	27.052	8.047	9.657	11.266	12.877	14.485	16.094
14 x 6	13-1/2 x 5-1/2	74.250	187.172	68.063	12.891	15.469	18.047	20.625	23.203	25.781
14 x 8	13-1/2 x 7-1/2	101.250	474.609	126.563	17.578	21.094	24.609	28.125	31.641	35.156
14 x 10	13-1/2 x 9-1/2	128.250	964.547	203.063	22.266	26.719	31.172	35.625	40.078	44.531
14 x 12	13-1/2 x 11-1/2	155.250	1710.984	297.563	26.953	32.344	37.734	43.125	48.516	53.906
14 x 16	13-1/2 x 15-1/2	209.250	4189.359	540.563	36.328	43.594	50.859	58.125	65.391	72.656
14 x 18	13-1/2 x 17-1/2	236.250	6029.297	689.063	41.016	49.219	57.422	65.625	73.828	82.031
14 x 20	13-1/2 x 19-1/2	263.250	8341.734	855.563	45.703	54.844	63.984	73.125	82.266	91.406
14 x 22	13-1/2 x 21-1/2	290.250	11180.672	1040.063	50.391	60.469	70.547	80.625	90.703	100.781
14 x 24	13-1/2 x 23-1/2	317.250	14600.109	1242.563	55.078	66.094	77.109	88.125	99.141	110.156
16 x 3	15-1/4 x 2-1/2	38.125	19.857	15.885	6.619	7.944	9.267	10.592	11.915	13.240
16 x 4	15-1/4 x 3-1/2	53.375	54.487	31.135	9.267	11.121	12.975	14.828	16.682	18.536
16 x 6	15-1/2 x 5-1/2	85.250	214.901	78.146	14.800	17.760	20.720	23.681	26.641	29.601
16 x 8	15-1/2 x 7-1/2	116.250	544.922	145.313	20.182	24.219	28.255	32.292	36.328	40.365
16 x 10	15-1/2 x 9-1/2	147.250	1107.443	233.146	25.564	30.677	35.790	40.903	46.016	51.128
16 x 12	15-1/2 x 11-1/2	178.250	1964.463	341.646	30.946	37.135	43.325	49.514	55.703	61.892
16 x 14	15-1/2 x 13-1/2	209.250	3177.984	470.813	36.328	43.594	50.859	58.125	65.391	72.656
16 x 16	15-1/2 x 15-1/2	240.250	4810.004	620.646	41.710	50.052	58.394	66.736	75.078	83.420
16 x 18	15-1/2 x 17-1/2	271.250	6922.523	791.146	47.092	56.510	65.929	75.347	84.766	94.184
16 x 20	15-1/2 x 19-1/2	302.250	9577.547	982.313	52.474	62.969	73.464	83.958	94.453	104.948
16 x 22	15-1/2 x 21-1/2	333.250	12837.066	1194.146	57.856	69.427	80.998	92.569	104.141	115.712
16 x 24	15-1/2 x 23-1/2	364.250	16763.086	1426.646	63.238	75.885	88.533	101.181	113.828	126.476
18 x 6	17-1/2 x 5-1/2	96.250	242.630	88.229	16.710	20.052	23.394	26.736	30.078	33.420
18 x 8	17-1/2 x 7-1/2	131.250	615.234	164.063	22.786	27.344	31.901	36.458	41.016	45.573
18 x 10	17-1/2 x 9-1/2	166.250	1250.338	263.229	28.863	34.635	40.408	46.181	51.953	57.726
18 x 12	17-1/2 x 11-1/2	201.250	2217.943	385.729	34.939	41.927	48.915	55.903	62.891	69.878
18 x 14	17-1/2 x 13-1/2	236.250	3588.047	531.563	41.016	49.219	57.422	65.625	73.828	82.031
18 x 16	17-1/2 x 15-1/2	271.250	5430.648	700.729	47.092	56.510	65.929	75.347	84.766	94.184
18 x 18	17-1/2 x 17-1/2	306.250	7815.754	893.229	53.168	63.802	74.436	85.069	95.703	106.337
18 x 20	17-1/2 x 15-1/2	341.250	10813.359	1109.063	59.245	71.094	82.943	94.792	106.641	118.490
18 x 22	17-1/2 x 21-1/2	376.250	14493.461	1348.229	65.321	78.385	91.450	104.514	117.578	130.642
18 x 24	17-1/2 x 23-1/2	411.250	18926.066	1610.729	71.398	85.677	99.957	114.236	128.516	142.795

Courtesy National Forest Products Association.

TABLE A-17 PROPERTIES OF STRUCTURAL LUMBER (*continued*)

Nominal size b(inches)d	Standard dressed size (S4S) b(inches)d	Area of Section A	Moment of inertia I	Section modulus S	Weight in pounds per linear foot of piece when weight of wood per cubic foot equals:					
					25 lb.	30 lb.	35 lb.	40 lb.	45 lb.	50 lb.
20 × 6	19-1/2 × 5-1/2	107.250	270.359	98.313	18.620	22.344	26.068	29.792	33.516	37.240
20 × 8	19-1/2 × 7-1/2	146.250	685.547	182.813	25.391	30.469	35.547	40.625	45.703	50.781
20 × 10	19-1/2 × 9-1/2	185.250	1393.234	293.313	32.161	38.594	45.026	51.458	57.891	64.323
20 × 12	19-1/2 × 11-1/2	224.250	2471.422	429.813	38.932	46.719	54.505	62.292	70.078	77.865
20 × 14	19-1/2 × 13-1/2	263.250	3998.109	592.313	45.703	54.844	63.984	73.125	82.266	91.406
20 × 16	19-1/2 × 15-1/2	302.250	6051.297	780.813	52.474	62.969	73.464	83.958	94.453	104.948
20 × 18	19-1/2 × 17-1/2	341.250	8708.984	995.313	59.245	71.094	82.943	94.792	106.641	118.490
20 × 20	19-1/2 × 19-1/2	380.250	12049.172	1235.813	66.016	79.219	92.422	105.625	118.828	132.031
20 × 22	19-1/2 × 21-1/2	419.250	16149.859	1502.313	72.786	87.344	101.901	116.458	131.016	145.573
20 × 24	19-1/2 × 23-1/2	458.250	21089.047	1794.813	79.557	95.469	111.380	127.292	243.203	159.115
22 × 6	21-1/2 ×/ 5-1/2	118.250	298.088	108.396	20.530	24.635	28.741	32.847	36.953	41.059
22 × 8	21-1/2 × 7-1/2	161.250	755.859	201.563	27.995	33.594	39.193	44.792	50.391	55.990
22 × 10	21-1/2 × 9-1/2	204.250	1536.130	323.396	35.460	42.552	49.644	56.736	63.828	70.920
22 × 12	21-1/2 × 11-1/2	247.250	2724.901	473.896	42.925	51.510	60.095	68.681	77.266	85.851
22 × 14	21-1/2 × 13-1/2	290.250	4408.172	653.063	50.391	60.469	70.547	80.625	90.703	100.781
22 × 16	21-1/2 × 15-1/2	333.250	6671.941	860.896	57.856	69.427	80.998	92.569	104.141	115.712
22 × 18	21-1/2 × 17-1/2	376.250	9602.211	1097.396	65.321	78.385	91.450	104.514	117.578	130.642
22 × 20	21-1/2 × 19-1/2	419.250	13284.984	1362.563	72.786	87.344	101.901	116.458	131.016	145.573
22 × 22	21-1/2 × 21-1/2	462.250	17806.254	1656.396	80.252	96.302	112.352	128.403	144.453	160.503
22 × 24	21-1/2 × 23-1/2	505.250	23252.023	1978.896	87.717	105.260	122.804	140.347	157.891	175.434
24 × 6	23-1/2 × 5-1/2	129.250	325.818	118.479	22.439	26.927	31.415	35.903	40.391	44.878
24 × 8	23-1/2 × 7-1/2	176.250	826.172	220.313	30.599	36.719	42.839	48.958	55.078	61.198
24 × 10	23-1/2 × 9-1/2	223.250	1679.026	353.479	38.759	46.510	54.262	62.014	69.766	77.517
24 × 12	23-1/2 × 11-1/2	270.250	2978.380	517.979	46.918	56.302	65.686	75.069	84.453	93.837
24 × 14	23-1/2 × 13-1/2	317.250	4818.234	713.813	55.078	66.094	77.109	88.125	99.141	110.156
24 × 16	23-1/2 × 15-1/2	364.250	7292.586	940.979	63.238	75.885	88.533	101.181	113.828	126.476
24 × 18	23-1/2 × 17-1/2	411.250	10495.441	1199.479	71.398	85.677	99.957	114.236	128.516	142.795
24 × 20	23-1/2 × 19-1/2	458.250	14520.797	1489.313	79.557	95.469	111.380	127.292	143.203	159.115
24 × 22	23-1/2 × 21-1/2	505.250	19462.648	1810.479	87.717	105.260	122.804	140.347	157.891	175.434
24 × 24	24-1/2 × 23-1/2	552.250	25415.004	2162.979	95.877	115.052	134.227	153.403	172.578	191.753

Courtesy National Forest Products Association.

TABLE A-18 BEAM DEFLECTION FORMULAS

Loading	Deflection

1.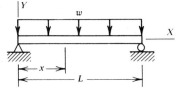

$$y = -\frac{wx}{24EI}(L^3 - 2Lx^2 + x^3)$$

$$y_{max} = -\frac{5}{384}\frac{wL^4}{EI} \qquad \text{at } x = L/2$$

2.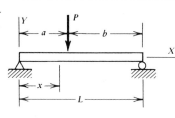

$$y = -\frac{Pbx}{6EIL}(L^2 - b^2 - x^2) \qquad \text{for } x < a$$

When $a = b = L/2$:

$$y = -\frac{Px}{48EI}(3L^2 - 4x^2) \qquad \text{for } x < L/2$$

$$y_{max} = -\frac{PL^3}{48EI} \qquad \text{at } x = L/2$$

3.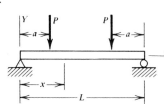

$$y = -\frac{Px}{6EI}(3La - 3a^2 - x^2) \qquad \text{for } x < a$$

$$y = -\frac{Pa}{6EI}(3Lx - 3x^2 - a^2) \qquad \text{for } a < x < L - a$$

$$y = -\frac{Pa^2}{6EI}(3L - 4a) \qquad \text{at } x = a$$

$$y_{max} = -\frac{Pa}{24EI}(3L^2 - 4a^2) \qquad \text{at } x = L/2$$

4.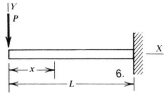

$$y = -\frac{Mx}{6EIL}(L^2 - x^2)$$

$$y_{max} = -\frac{ML^2}{9\sqrt{3}EI} \qquad \text{at } x = \frac{L}{\sqrt{3}}$$

5.

$$y = -\frac{P}{6EI}(2L^3 - 3L^2x + x^3)$$

$$y_{max} = -\frac{PL^3}{3EI} \qquad \text{at } x = 0$$

6.

$$y = -\frac{w}{24EI}(x^4 - 4L^3x + 3L^4)$$

$$y_{max} = -\frac{wL^4}{8EI} \qquad \text{at } x = 0$$

TABLE A-18 BEAM DEFLECTION FORMULAS (*continued*)

Loading	Deflection
7. 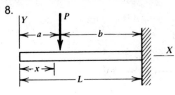	W is total load $y = -\dfrac{W}{60EIL^2}(x^5 - 5L^4 x + 4L^5)$ $y_{max} = -\dfrac{WL^3}{15EI}$ at $x = 0$

7.

W is total load

$$y = -\frac{W}{60EIL^2}(x^5 - 5L^4 x + 4L^5)$$

$$y_{max} = -\frac{WL^3}{15EI} \quad \text{at } x = 0$$

8.

$$y = -\frac{Pb^2}{6EI}(3L - 3x - b) \quad \text{for} \quad x < a$$

$$y = -\frac{P(L-x)^2}{6EI}(3b - L + x) \quad \text{for} \quad x > a$$

$$y_{max} = -\frac{Pb^2}{6EI}(3L - b) \quad \text{at } x = 0$$

Answers to Problems

Answers are generally omitted for every third problem.

CHAPTER 1

1.1 (a) 866700, 867000, 870000, 900000
(b) 942.1, 942, 940, 900
(c) 0.0001234, 0.000123, 0.00012, 0.0001
(d) 2.000, 2.00, 2.0, 2
(e) 0.02000, 0.200, 0.020, 0.02
(f) 3.142, 3.14, 3.1, 3
1.2 (a) 15.8 to 24.8: 15 to 25   (b) 19.55 to 20.45: 19.5 to 20.5
(c) 19.955 to 20.045: 19.95 to 20.05
1.4 (a) 207 kPa   (b) 6.09 m^3 (c) 24.1 km/hr   (d) 3280 N/m   (e) 45.2 W
1.5 (a) 508 in. lb   (b) 8.68 $lb/in.^2$ (c) 4.09 $E9$ ft lb   (d) 134000 $lb/in.^2$
(e) 68.1 rad/s
1.7 (a) 22.4 in., 26.6°, 63.4°
(b) 26.0 m, 30.0°, 60.0°
(c) 22.4 ft, 48.2°, 41.8°
(d) 25.1 km, 30.9 km, 54.4°
(e) 8.08 mi, 21.6 mi, 68.0°
(f) 47.0, 10.0, 48.1 and an infinite number of other solutions which are proportional
(g) 46.5 yd, 29.3 yd, 32.2°
(h) 11.5 mm, 2.31 mm, 60.0°
(i) 33.3 lb, 44.8 lb, 48.0°
1.8 (a) 22.3°, 49.5°, 108.2°
(b) 17.3 m, 90.0°, 60.0°
(c) 28.0 ft, 14.5°, 135.5°
(d) 12.4 km, 96.2°, 53.8°
(e) 157 mi, 79.8 mi, 30.0°
(f) 138 yd, 122 yd, 70.0°
(g) 15.3, 10.0, 13.5 and an infinite number of other solutions which are proportional
(h) 983 mm, 121.0°, 9.0°
(i) 137 lb, 200 lb, 70.0°

CHAPTER 2

Note: graphical solutions generally will *not* agree to three significant figures.

2.1 (a) 40.6 N @ $-56.4°$ (b) 166 kN @ 2.70 rad   (c) 104 N @ 116.9°
(d) 14.4 kN @ -1.90 rad

2.2 (a) 40.6 N @ −56.4°   (b) 166 kN @ 2.70 rad   (c) 104 N @ 116.9°
(d) 14.4 kN @ −1.90 rad

2.4 (a) 140 lb @ 60.4°   (b) 140 lb @ 44.6°   (c) 1130 lb @ 90.0°
(d) 56.7 kips @ 176.5°   (e) 608 N @ −54.7°   (f) 26.9 kN @ 0.405 rad
(g) 24.4 kN @ 1.95 rad

2.5 63.6 N @ 112.6°

2.7 (a) 277 lb @ 52.5°   (b) 49.6 kips @ −175.8°   (c) 36.8 kN @ 64.7°
(d) 1580 N @ 131.9°

2.8 (a) 86.6 lb, 50.0 lb   (b) 50.0 lb, 86.6 lb   (c) 25.9 lb, 96.6 lb
(d) 47.8 lb, 14.8 lb   (e) 41.3 kN, 28.2 kN   (f) 27.0 kN, 42.1 kN

2.10 (a) 14.7 tons, 10.3 tons   (b) 14.7 tons, −10.3 tons
(c) −10.3 tons, −14.7 tons   (d) −10.3 tons, 14.7 tons
(e) −14.7 tons, −10.3 tons   (f) −14.7 tons, 10.3 tons

2.11 (a) 17.7 kN, 17.7 kN   (b) 17.7 kN, −17.7 kN   (c) −17.7 kN, 17.7 kN
(d) −17.7 kN, −17.7 kN   (e) −17.7 kN, −17.7 kN   (f) −17.7 kN, 17.7 kN

2.13 (a) 140 lb @ 60.4°   (b) 140 lb @ 44.6°   (c) 1130 lb @ 90.0°
(d) 56.7 kips @ 176.5°   (e) 608 N @ −54.7°   (f) 26.9 kN @ 0.405 rad
(g) 24.4 kN @ 1.95 rad

2.14 (a) 40.6 N @ −56.4°   (b) 166 kN @ 2.70 rad   (c) 104 N @ 116.9°
(d) 14.4 kN @ −1.90 rad

2.16 721 kN @ −175.8°

2.17 (a) 277 lb @ 52.5°   (b) 49.6 kips @ −175.8°   (c) 36.8 kN @ 64.7°
(d) 1580 N @ 131.9°

2.19 (a) $22.5i − 338j$ (N)   (b) $−150.7i + 70.7j$ (kN)   (c) $−46.9i + 92.6j$ (N)
(d) $−4.66i − 13.58j$ (kN)

2.20 $−155.4i + 57.1j$ (kN)

2.22 (a) $69.2i + 121.6j$ (lb)   (b) $99.5i + 98.3j$ (lb)   (c) $1130j$ (lb)
(d) $−56.6i + 3.4j$ (kips)   (e) $351i + 496j$ (N)   (f) $24.8i + 10.6j$ (kN)
(g) $−9.0i + 22.7j$ (kN)

2.23 (a) $7.00i + 11.0j$ (N)   (b) $13.0i + 17.0j$ (N)   (c) $−23.0i − 31.0j$ (N)

CHAPTER 3

3.1

3.2

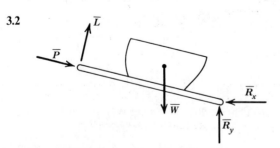

3.4

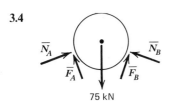

75 kN

3.5

$\overline{A}_y$ $\overline{B}$ $\overline{F}_c$

$\overline{A}_x$

$\overline{N}_c$

40 lb

3.7   3350 lb @ $-116.6°$
3.8   1500 N @ $-53.1°$
3.10 10.7 N @ $-37.1°$
3.11 (a) 46.6 lb @ $0.0°$, 110 lb @ $115.0°$ (b) 145 kN @ $15.0°$, 145 kN @ $165.0°$
3.13 26.6°, 44.7 N
3.14 12.0 lb, 32.9 lb
3.25 143 lb @ $-153.5°$
3.26 648 N @ $43.0°$
3.28 1.90 kN @ $180.0°$ (the wall must *pull*), 16.8 kN @ $60.0°$
3.29 4.00 kN, 7.72 kN @ $75.0°$, 4.00 kN, 7.39 kN @ $67.5°$ The tension is unchanged but the pin reaction will vary with θ.
3.31 32.0 N, 32.0 N
3.32 (a) 500 lb   (b) $DF = KH = 100$ lb, $BC = EJ = 500$ lb   (c) 940 lb @ $70.0°$
3.34 120 lb, $BC = DE = FG = 40.0$ lb, $HI = 80.0$ lb
3.35 900 kN, $BC = DE = FG = 900$ kN, $HI = 1800$ kN
3.49 (a) 447 N, 200 N   (b) 862 N, 320 N   (c) 2160 N, 1800 N
3.50 (a) 33.5 tons, 30.0 tons   (b) 16.8 tons, 7.50 tons   (c) 531 lb, 469 lb
3.52 424 lb, 473 lb
3.53 0.0 kN, 70.7 kN
3.55 $-1500\mathbf{i} - 3000\mathbf{j}$ (lb)
3.56 $900\mathbf{i} - 1200\mathbf{j}$ (N)
3.58 $8.51\mathbf{i} - 6.43\mathbf{j}$ (N)
3.61 $-128\mathbf{i} - 64.0\mathbf{j}$ (lb)
3.62 $474\mathbf{i} + 442\mathbf{j}$ (N)

CHAPTER 4

4.1   (a) 301 N·m ccw   (b) 600 kN·m cw   (c) 82.3 in.-lb ccw   (d) 600 ft-kips ccw
4.2   (a) 240 N·m ccw   (b) 900 kN·m ccw   (c) 0   (d) 1440 ft-kips ccw
4.4   167 N, decrease the drum diameter
4.5   (a) -26.0 ft-lb   (b) -46.0 ft-lb   (c) -136 ft-lb   (d) -156 ft-lb
          (e) -246 ft-lb   (f) -266 ft-lb   (g) 4.00 ft-lb   (h) 64.0 ft-lb
4.7   (a) 301 N·m ccw   (b) 600 kN·m cw   (c) 82.3 in.-lb ccw
          (d) 600 ft-kips ccw
4.8   (a) 240 N·m ccw   (b) 900 kN·m ccw   (c) 0   (d) 1440 ft-kips ccw
4.10 (a) -11.6 kN·m   (b) -65.0 kN·m   (c) -21.2 kN·m   (d) 18.0 kN·m
4.11 (e) -47.4 kN·m
          (a) 2350 in.-lb   (b) 2580 in.-lb   (c) 2930 in.-lb   (d) -967 in.-lb
          (e) -3320 in.-lb

4.13 564 N·m, 500 N
4.14 750 in.-lb, 150 lb
4.16 −40 N·m
4.17 −80.0 N·m
4.19 1440 in.-lb
4.20 1920 in.-lb
4.23 60.0 N, perpendicular
4.25 (a–g) 0, −26.8 in.-kips
4.26 (a–g) −53.6 in.-kips
4.28 (a–c) 27.7 in.-oz
4.29 40.0 lb
4.32 (a) −300 kN, −600 kN·m   (b) −300 kN, 900 kN·m
4.34 −60.0 lb, −737 in.-lb
4.35 30.0 lb at −150.0°, 173 in.-lb
4.37 35.0 kN at 45.0°, 2.12 m above and 2.12 m to the left of A.

4.38 (a) 50.0 kips at $\overset{3}{\underset{4}{\diagdown}}$, 1000 ft-kips

4.40 R = 31.6 lb at 71.6° and:
(a) −26.0 ft-lb   (b) −46.0 ft-lb   (c) −136 ft-lb   (d) −156 ft-lb
4.41 31.6 lb at 71.6°, 0.780 ft to the left and 0.260 ft above A.
4.43 12.8 N at 38.7°, 2.49 m to the right and 3.11 m below A.
4.44 R = 12.2 kN at 118.9° and:
(a) −11.6 kN·m   (b) −65.0 kN·m   (c) −21.2 kN·m   (d) 18.0 kN·m
4.46 R = 316 lb at −3.5° and:
(a) 2350 in.-lb   (b) 2580 in.-lb   (c) 2930 in.-lb   (d) −967 in.-lb
4.47 316 lb at −3.5°, 0.457 in. to the left and 7.41 in. below A.
4.49 (a) −150 lb, 2400 ft-lb   (b) −150 lb, 3150 ft-lb
4.50 −150 lb, 16.0 ft left of A.
4.52 110 N, 24.5 mm left of A.
4.53 −40.0 lb, −560 in.-lb, −40.0 lb, −680 in.-lb

CHAPTER 5

5.1 (a) 32.0 lb, 48.0 lb   (b) 45.0 lb, 75.0 lb   (c) 6.70 N, 13.3 N
(d) 13.3 kN, 26.7 kN
5.2 (a) −53.0 lb, 133 lb   (b) −72.0 lb, 192 lb   (c) −100 N, 300 N
(d) −20.0 kN, 60.0 kN
5.4 12.4 kN, 4.60 kN
5.5 5.80 kips, 10.2 kips
5.7 4.00 kips, 28.0 ft-kips
5.8 −20.0 N, 1.60 N·m
5.10 −60.0 N, −240 N·m
5.11 300 lb, 1600 ft-lb
5.13 4.40 kips, 15.6 kips
5.14 −1.00 kN, 1.00 kN
5.16 A_x = −7.86 lb, A_y = 17.9 lb, C_x = 32.2 lb, C_y = −32.2 lb
5.17 A_y = 60.0 N, B_x = −122 N, B_y = −26.2 N
5.19 A_x = −60.0 kN, A_y = −20.0 kN, C_x = 60.0 kN, C_y = −80.0 kN
5.20 A_x = 123 lb, A_y = 183 lb, B = 154 lb
5.22 A_x = −2.50 kips, A_y = 1.46 kips, B = 2.87 kips
5.23 A_x = 56.6 N, A_y = 171 N, B = 85.9 N

5.25 $A_x = -9.00$ kN, $A_y = 6.00$ kN, $M_A = 86.0$ kN·m

5.26 $A_x = -120$ lb, $A_y = -50.0$ lb, $M_A = 540$ in.-lb

5.28 $A_x = 5.20$ lb, $A_y = 33.2$ lb, $M_A = -236$ in.-lb

5.29 $A_x = 0$, $A_y = 450$ lb, $M_A = 2700$ ft-lb

5.31 (a) $F = -3500$ lb, $N = 2000$ lb, 56.4 ft/s^2
(b) $F = -18.0$ kN, $N = 10.0$ kN, 17.7 m/s^2

5.32 $R_B = 11.3$ oz at $-45.9°$
$A_x = -8.00$ oz, $A_y = 8.00$ oz, $M_A = 6.00$ in.-oz

5.34 (a) $A_x = 560$ lb, $A_y = 560$ lb, $M_A = 16{,}800$ in.-lb
(b) $B = 290$ lb at 255.0°, $C = 560$ lb at 90.0°, $D = 970$ lb at 240.0°

5.35 (a) $A_x = 0$, $A_y = 7.00$ N, $M_A = 560$ N·mm
(b) $B = 9.18$ N at $-22.5°$, $C = 9.18$ N at 202.5°, $D = 17.0$ N at 90.0°

5.37 $A_x = -143$ lb, $A_y = 393$ lb, $D = 179$ lb

5.38 $A_x = -800$ lb, $A_y = -200$ lb, $D = 1000$ lb

5.40 $A = 1000$ lb, $B_x = 800$ lb, $B_y = 0$

5.41 $A = 10.0$ kips, $C_x = 14.1$ kips, $C_y = 11.9$ kips

5.43 $A = 496$ lb, $B_x = -291$ lb, $B_y = 50.8$ lb

5.44 $A = 2.40$ kips, $B_x = 10.0$ kips, $B_y = 13.3$ kips

5.46 $D = 26.0$ kN, $E_x = -22.5$ kN, $E_y = 7.00$ kN

5.47 $B = 16.0$ kips, $E_x = 0$, $E_y = 8.00$ kips

5.49 $A = -550$ lb, $B_x = 400$ lb, $B_y = 250$ lb

5.50 $A_x = 300$ N, $A_y = -30.0$ N, $B = 430$ N

5.52 $A_x = -93.8$ lb, $A_y = 425$ lb, $D = 156$ lb

5.53 $A_x = -287$ N, $A_y = 260$ N, $C = 387$ N

5.55 $A_x = -19.5$ lb, $A_y = 44.0$ lb, $P = 52.7$ lb

5.56 $A_x = -14.2$ lb, $A_y = 35.9$ lb, $P = 47.0$ lb

CHAPTER 6

6.1 (a) 1280 N, $-13{,}400$ N·m, 10.5 m   (b) 1280 N, $-13{,}600$ N·m, 10.6 m

6.2 (a) 440 N, 840 N   (b) 430 N, 850 N

6.4 (a) 1400 lb, 1000 lb   (b) 1400 lb, 1000 lb

6.5 (a) 540 N, -17.1 N·m, 31.5 mm   (b) 540 N, -16.4 N·m, 30.4 mm

Note: Answers to Problems 6.7 through 6.10 are not unique.

6.7 (a) 752 N at 5.62 m   (b) 740 N at 5.50 m

6.8 (a) 400 N, 352 N   (b) 401 N, 339 N

6.10 (a) 3.23 kips, 4.57 kips   (b) 3.22 kips, 4.88 kips

6.11 427 N, 853 N

6.13 360 N, 180 N

6.14 9.17 kips, 20.8 kips

6.16 26.4 kN, 8.56 kN

6.17 941 N, 859 N

6.19 100 N, 51.5 kN·m

6.20 -1500 lb, 33000 in.-lb

6.22 180 lb

6.23 21.2 kN, 265 kN·m

6.25 468 N, 1.06 kN·m

6.26 208 lb, 1630 ft-lb

6.28 (a) 2.48 $E6$ lb   (b) 1.01 $E6$ lb

6.29 3.77 kN, 1.88 kN

6.31 333 lb, 665 lb

6.32 (a) 832 lb, 1160 lb   (b) 41.6 lb, 208 lb
6.34 (a) 16300 ft-lb   (b) 14900 ft-lb
6.35 0.735 m
6.37 (a) 1.34 kN
6.38 252 mm

CHAPTER 7

7.1 $AB = 70.0$ N T $AC = 85.4$ N C $AD = 329$ N T $BC = 85.4$ N C
$CD = 171$ N T
7.2 $AB = 353$ lb C $AD = 271$ lb T $BC = 104$ lb C $BD = 249$ lb C
$CD = 67.1$ lb T
7.4 $AB = 972$ lb C $= BC$ $AD = 831$ lb C $= CD$ $BD = 1000$ lb T
7.5 $AB = 600$ kN C $= BC$ $AD = 849$ kN T $= CD$ $BD = 0$
7.7 $AB = 16.7$ kN C $AD = 0$ $BC = 6.67$ kN C $BD = 23.6$ kN T
$CD = 21.1$ kN C
7.8 $AB = 55.5$ lb T $AE = 756$ lb T $BC = 44.4$ lb T $BE = 33.3$ lb C
$CD = 889$ lb C $CE = 55.5$ lb T $CF = 500$ lb T $EF = 711$ lb T $= DF$
7.10 $AB = 15.0$ kN C $AI = 18.0$ kN T $BC = 15.0$ kN C $BI = 0$
$CD = 22.5$ kN C $CH = 5.00$ kN T $CI = 9.01$ kN C $DE = 30.0$ kN C
$DG = 10.0$ kN T $DH = 12.5$ kN C $EF = 15.0$ kN T $EG = 16.8$ kN C
$FG = 45.1$ kN T $GH = 36.1$ kN T $HI = 27.0$ kN T
7.11 $BC = 0 = BG = CG = CD = DE = DF = CF$ $FG = 11.3$ kips C $= EF$
7.13 $AB = 9.69$ kips T $AD = 1.40$ kips T $BC = 4.00$ kips T $BD = 10.5$ kips C
$CD = 10.8$ kips C
7.14 See 7.1
7.16 $AB = 2890$ lb C $AE = 1440$ lb T $BC = 1730$ lb C $BE = 577$ lb T
$CD = 4040$ lb C $CE = 577$ lb C $DE = 2020$ lb T
7.17 See 7.4
7.19 $AB = 140$ lb T $AD = 200$ lb T $BC = 198$ lb T $BD = 272$ lb C
$CD = 48.7$ lb C
7.20 See 7.7
7.22 $AB = 903$ lb C $AE = 1220$ lb T $BC = 1220$ lb C $BE = 458$ lb C
$CD = 764$ lb C $CE = 764$ lb T $CF = 0$ $DF = 611$ lb T $= EF$
7.23 See 7.10
7.25 Fig. 7.31–34, 7.38: none; Fig. 7.35 *BD*, Fig. 7.36 *AD*, Fig. 7.39 *CF*,
Fig. 7.40 *BI*, Fig. 7.41 *DF, CF, CG*.
7.26 Fig. 7.31–7.33, 7.35, 7.40–7.41: none; Fig. 7.34 *D*, Fig. 7.36 *A*, Fig. 7.37 *A*, Fig. 7.38 *F*,
Fig. 7.39 *F*
7.28 See 7.16
7.29 See 7.8
7.31 See 7.10
7.32 See 7.10

CHAPTER 8

(Loads at joints are magnitudes only)

8.1 $A_x = -120$ lb, $A_y = -40.0$ lb $C_x = 60.0$ lb, $C_y = 100$ lb
$B_x = 120$ lb, $B_y = 100$ lb
8.2 $B_x = 0$, $B_y = 120$ N $C_x = 80.0$ N, $C_y = -200$ N $A_x = 0$, $A_y = 200$ N

8.4 $A_x = 12.0$ MN, $A_y = -0.27$ MN $E_x = -5.00$ MN, $E_y = 10.9$ MN
$C_x = 5.00$ MN, $C_y = 10.9$ MN

8.5 $A_x = 0$ $E_y = 100$ lb $= A_y$ $B_x = 40.0$ lb $= D_x = C_x$ $B_y = 100$ lb $= D_y$
$C_y = 0$

8.7 $E_x = -2250$ lb, $E_y = 1500$ lb $D_x = 2250$ lb
$B_x = 2250$ lb, $B_y = 4500$ lb $= C_y = F_y$ $C_x = 4500$ lb $= F_x$

8.8 $C_y = 600$ lb $= E_y$ $A_x = D_x = B_x = 1200$ lb $B_y = 0 = A_y = D_y$

8.10 $A_x = 750$ lb, $A_y = 2400$ lb $C_x = -750$ lb, $C_y = -1200$ lb $B_x = D_x = 2000$ lb
$B_y = 800$ lb, $D_y = 2000$ lb

8.11 $A_x = -83.3$ kN, $A_y = 54.5$ kN $E_x = 83.3$ kN, $E_y = 45.5$ kN
$C_x = 83.3$ kN, $C_y = 45.5$ kN

8.13 $A_x = -10.0$ MN, $A_y = -4.00$ MN $E_x = 10.0$ MN, $E_y = 24.0$ MN
$C_x = 10.0$ MN, $C_y = 4.00$ MN

8.14 $B_x = 0$, $B_y = 120$ N $C_x = 80.0$ N, $C_y = 280$ N

8.16 $A_x = -4.40$ MN, $A_y = 24.0$ MN $E_x = -5.00$ MN, $E_y = -7.04$ MN

8.17 $A_x = -100$ lb, $A_y = -25.0$ lb $E_y = 225$ lb $B_x = D_x = 140$ lb
$B_y = D_y = 100$ lb

8.19 $A_x = -3.33$ kN, $A_y = 40.9$ kN $E_x = 53.3$ kN, $E_y = 29.1$ kN
$C_x = 50.0$ kN $= C_y$

8.20 $A_x = 0$, $A_y = 140$ lb $D_x = 80.0$ lb, $D_y = -100$ lb

8.22 Forces are in lb

	P	A_x	A_y	B_x	B_y	C_x	C_y
(a)	645	645	-310	645	310	645	310
(b)	733	733	-277	733	277	733	277
(c)	989	989	-256	989	256	989	256
(d)	1860	1860	-242	1860	242	1860	242

8.23 Forces are in kN, moments in N·m.

	M	A_x	A_y	B_x	B_y	C_x	C_y
(a)	1260	20.0	-5.27	20.0	5.27	20.0	5.27
(b)	1750	20.0	-9.19	20.0	9.19	20.0	9.19
(c)	1350	20.0	-9.51	20.0	9.51	20.0	9.51
(d)	662	20.0	-5.96	20.0	5.96	20.0	5.96

8.25 50.0 N, $R_x = 0$, $R_y = 350$ N

8.26 Forces are in lb.

	P	A_x	A_y	B_x	B_y	D_x	D_y
(a)	38.6	38.6	2.30	38.6	17.7	38.6	17.7
(b)	14.4	14.4	5.00	14.4	15.0	14.4	15.0
(c)	5.63	5.63	11.9	5.63	8.08	5.63	-8.08

8.28 $D = 233$ N, $E = 1170$ N, $A_x = 933$ N, $A_y = 933$ N, $B_x = E_x = 933$ N,
$B_y = E_y = 2330$ N

8.29 $D = 667$ N, $F = 1330$ N, $B_x = E_x = 1070$ N, $B_y = E_y = 2670$ N, $A_x = 1070$ N,
$A_y = 667$ N

8.31 $A_A = 6.59$ MN, $A_S = 10.0$ MN $B_A = 0$, $B_S = -20$ MN
$C_A = -6.59$ MN, $C_S = 10.0$ MN

8.32 $A_A = 93.5$ lb, $A_S = 35.5$ lb $B_A = -79.3$ lb, $B_S = -72.9$ lb
$C_A = -14.2$ lb, $C_S = 37.4$ lb

8.34 $D_A = 94.9$ kN, $D_S = 0$ $E_A = -94.9$ kN, $E_S = 0$

8.35 $A_A = -1.91$ MN, $A_S = -10.6$ MN $B_A = 10.6$ MN, $B_S = 17.0$ MN
$C_A = -8.69$ MN, $C_S = -6.36$ MN

8.37 $A_A = 11.5$ lb, $A_S = -9.97$ lb $B_A = 5.79$ lb, $B_S = 20.0$ lb
$C_A = -17.3$ lb, $C_S = -10.0$

8.38 (a) $A_x = B_x = C_x = D_x = 2800$ lb, $A_y = B_y = C_y = 2800$ lb, $D_y = 4800$ lb
(b) $A_x = B_x = C_x = D_x = 2380$ lb, $A_y = B_y = C_y = 1900$ lb, $D_y = 3170$ lb
(c) $A_x = B_x = C_x = D_x = 17.8$ kN, $A_y = B_y = C_y = 13.3$ kN, $D_y = 23.3$ kN
(d) $A_x = B_x = C_x = D_x = 13.6$ kN, $A_y = B_y = C_y = 13.6$ kN, $D_y = 25.0$ kN

CHAPTER 9

9.1 (a) 237 lb, 36.3 lb
(b) 300 N, 160 N, assumption false
(c) 2.60 kips, 1.50 kips, assumption false
(d) 1170 N, 366 N

9.2 (a) 155 lb   (b) 220 N

9.4 (a) 54.9 lb   (b) 100 lb

9.5 (a) 0   (b) 27.6 N

9.7 (a) 85.8 lb   (b) 84.4 lb   (c) 120 lb

9.8 (a) 36.3 kN, 16.9 kN   (b) 67.8 N, 42.4 N   (c) 19.0 tons, 6.18 tons
(d) 12.3 oz., 2.17 oz.

9.10 (a) 155 lb   (b) 220 N

9.11 (a) 1.89 kips   (b) 836 N

9.13 (a) 0   (b) 27.6 N

9.14 (a) 67.9 lb   (b) 0.109 N   (c) 48.2 MN

9.16 (a) 1260 lb   (b) 321 N   (c) 1960 kN

9.17 (a) 1380 lb   (b) 377 N   (c) 3260 kN

9.19 13.5 kN

9.20 0.105

9.22 (a) 2.83 kN·m   (b) self-locking, 0.223 kN·m

9.23 (a) 16.2 kN·m   (b) self-locking, 6.41 kN·m

9.25 (a) 9670 in.-lb   (b) self-locking, 6360 in.-lb

9.26 583 lb, 737 lb

9.28 (a) 1.68 in.   (b) 1.56 in.

9.29 (a) 38.9 mm   (b) 28.9 mm

9.31 6.68 ft

9.32 (a) 400 N, 1340 N, $A_x = 840$ N, $A_y = 400$ N

9.34 (a) no motion   (b) no motion

9.35 19.2 in.

9.37 6.00 N, no

9.38 1680 lb

9.40 2.77 kN

9.41 5.76 kN

9.43 10.1 in.

9.44 (a) 41.0 N   (b) 2.44 MN

9.46 0.205

9.47 2.11, 4.22

9.49 (a) 2.11 kN·m   (b) 30.2 kN·m

9.50 (a) 4390 in.-lb   (b) 16900 in.-lb

9.52 79.9 kN

9.53 $A = 295$ lb, $B = 84.0$ lb
9.55 $A = 26.2$ lb, $B = 90.0$ lb
9.56 $A = 309$ lb, $B = 90.0$ lb
9.58 (a) 3.53 N   (b) 0.258 N
9.59 (a) 5.05 lb   (b) 15.0 lb

CHAPTER 10

10.1 (a) $18x$ (b) $16x + 2$ (c) $4\cos 2x$ (d) $3/x$ (e) $\dfrac{x}{2}\cos\dfrac{x}{2} + \sin\dfrac{x}{2}$

10.2 (a) 4   (b) 24, 48, 72   (c) 2, 0, -2 (d) 1   (e) 3, 0.750, 0.333
10.4 (a) 648   (b) 26.2   (c) 0.117   (d) 22.9   (e) 0.943
10.5 (a) 352   (b) 1410   (c) 592
10.7 129 ft/s

CHAPTER 11

11.1 10.0 psi, 3.33 psi
11.2 27.1 lb, 3.38 psi, 0.562 psi
11.4 127 psi
11.5 127 MPa
11.7 7.98 mm
11.8 (a) 20.4 ksi   (b) 10.2 ksi
11.10 92.9 psi
11.11 600 kPa
11.13 48.3 kN
11.14 AB: 59.1 psi AE: 804 psi BC: 47.3 psi BE: 35.5 psi CD: 946 psi
CE: 59.1 psi CF: 532 psi DF: 757 psi EF: 757 psi
11.16 AB: 1.97 E-6, 1.18 E-4 in. AE: 2.68 E-5, 1.29 E-3 in.
BE: 1.18 E-6, 4.26 E-5 in. BC: 1.58 E-6, 7.57 E-5 in.
EC: 1.97 E-6, 1.18 E-4 in. EF: 2.52 E-5, 1.21 E-3 in.
CD: 3.15 E-5, 1.89 E-3 in. CF: 1.77 E-5, 6.38 E-4 in.
FD: 2.52 E-5, 1.21 E-3 in.
11.17 AB: -1.08 E-6, -9.23 μ in. AC: 1.31 E-6, 6.87 μ in.
AD: 3.55 E-6, 21.30 μ in. BC: 1.31 E-6, 6.87 μ in. DC: 2.63 E-6, 13.74 μ in.
11.19 407 MPa, 5.74 E-3, 2.30 mm
11.20 50.9 ksi, 2.50 E-4, 204 E 3 ksi
11.22 619 MPa, 0.100, 6.19 GPa
11.23 27.2 ksi, 2.78 E-4, 9.79 E 7 psi
11.25 28.8 E 6 psi
11.26 280 MPa, 421 MPa, 20.1%
11.28 61400 lb/in.
11.29 9.75 E 6 N/m
11.31 603 MPa, 6100 μ, 98.8 GPa, 0.320
11.32 3.00 E-3, 160 ksi, 53.3 E 3 ksi, -4.54 E-4 in.
11.34 0.426 mm, 0.544 mm^2
11.35 2.34 E-2 in., 6.03 E 4 lb
11.37 0.00200 in., 3200 lb
11.38 34.4 kips

11.40 $-231°F$, $+115°F$, $+231°F$
11.41 10700 lb
11.43 (a) 350 N   (b) 400 N   (c) 333 N
11.44 (a) 30.0 ksi   (b) 72.0 ksi   (c) 45.0 ksi
11.46 0.300 in.
11.47 9.29 E-5, 5.80 E-6 in.
11.49 31.2 GPa
11.50 (a) 0.341, 0.300   (b) 0.208, 0.354
11.52 5.79 mm
11.53 0.199 in.
11.56 AB: 0.602 in.^{2} AE: 0.815 in.^{2} BC: 0.815 in.^{2} BE: 0.306 in.^{2}
  CD: 0.509 in.^{2} CE: 0.509 in.^{2} CF: 0 FD: 0.407 in.^{2} FE: 0.407 in.^{2}
11.58 243 psi, 8.10 E-6, 1.13 E-3 in.
11.59 200 MPa, 2.82 E-3, 8.45 mm
11.61 0.259 in.
11.62 -1.91 E-3, 5.45 E-3
11.64 16.7 kN, 51.3 MPa, 722 E-6, 2.17 mm
11.65 140 lb T, 317 psi, 10.6 E-6, 6.34 E-4 in.
11.67 4.24 mm
11.68 1130 MPa, -46.4 mm, 0.127 mm

CHAPTER 12

12.1 (a) 6.00 in., 432 in.^{3}, 3.00 in., 216 in.^{3}
  (b) 2.00 m, 18.0 m^3, 2.00 m, 18.0 m^3
  (c) 0, 0, 1.70 ft, 42.7 ft^3
  (d) 90.0 mm, 7.07 $E5$ mm^3, -70.0 mm, -5.50 $E5$ mm^3
12.2 (a) 144 in.^{3} (b) 360 in.^{3} (c) 0   (d) 63.0 m^3
  (e) -36.0 m^3 (f) 0   (g) -101 ft^3 (h) -57.9 ft^3
  (i) 101 ft^3 (j) 7.85 $E4$ mm^3 (k) 0   (l) 0
12.4 3.00 in.
12.5 9.64 m
12.7 46.7 mm
12.8 26.7 mm
12.10 6.54 ft
12.11 3.75 in.
12.13 (7.29 in., 4.72 in.)
12.14 (4.23 in., 3.13 in.)
12.16 (8.49 in., 5.00 in.)
12.17 (5.00 in., 6.90 in.)
12.19 9.00 ft^2, 36.0 ft^3, 4.00 ft
12.20 9.00 ft^2, 9.00 ft^3, 1.00 ft
12.22 10.5 in.^{2}, 13.5 in.^{3}, 1.29 in.
12.23 864 in.^{4}, 216 in.^{4}
12.25 101 ft^4, 28.1 ft^4
12.26 4.91 $E6$ mm^4, 4.91 $E6$ mm^4
12.28 13.5 ft^4
12.29 417 mm^4
12.31 177 m^4
12.32 24.8 in.^{4}
12.34 107 in.^{4}
12.35 (a) 3460 in.^{4} (b) 54.0 m^4 (c) 101 ft^4 (d) 6.85 $E7$ mm^4

12.37 (a) 288 in.^{4} (b) 594 m^4 (c) 201 ft^4 (d) 6.03 $E7$ mm^4
12.38 (a) 1152 in.^{4} (b) 40.5 m^4 (c) 40300 ft^4 (d) 2.45 $E7$ mm^4
12.40 4050 m^4, 7070 m^4
12.41 4.44 $E6$ mm^4, 1.56 $E6$ mm^4
12.43 346 in.^{4}, 398 in.^{4}
12.44 792 in.^{4}, 784 in.^{4}
12.46 1410 in.^{4}, 579 in.^{4}
12.47 260 in.^{4}, 581 in.^{4}
12.49 205 in.^{4}, 264 in.^{4}
12.50 6.14 $E5$ mm^4, 17.7 mm
12.52 17.2 in.^{4}
12.53 32.0 in.^{4}, 72.0 in.^{4}, 104 in.^{4}
12.55 236 in.^{4}, 4.00 in.
12.56 81.5 in.^{4}, 2.35 in.
12.58 (a) 1600 in.^{4}, 5.21 in.   (b) 619 in.^{4}, 3.24 in.
12.59 (a) 868 in.^{4}, 4.72 in.   (b) 198 in.^{4}, 2.25 in.

CHAPTER 13

13.1 158 ft-lb
13.2 215 N·m
13.4 118 W
13.5 2.19 lb
13.7 2360 in.-lb
13.8 245 N·m
13.10 118 MPa
13.11 74.8 hp
13.13 2.52 in.
13.14 66.3 mm
13.16 10.2 ksi
13.17 1.59 MPa, 1.59 MPa
13.19 1610 in.-lb
13.20 145 N·m
13.22 126 MPa
13.23 51.1 hp
13.25 3.60 in.
13.26 91.7 mm
13.28 18.2 MPa
13.29 3630 in.-lb, 6820 psi
13.31 12600 in.-lb, 0.0800 rad
13.32 2.33 kN·m, 6.47 E-2 rad
13.34 1.87 kN·m, 0.0642 rad
13.35 79.3 hp, 12.7 ksi, 6.64 E-2 rad
13.37 1300 ft-lb, 2950 psi, 0.0372 rad
13.38 1780 N·m, 2.78 E-2 rad, 21.4 MPa
13.40 60.2 kW, 158 MPa, 0.120 rad
13.41 1300 ft-lb, 5.70 ksi, 7.18 E-2 rad
13.43 14100 in.-lb
13.44 20400 in.-lb
13.46 16.9 MPa, 9.88 MPa, 4.50 E-3 rad
13.47 $\tau_0 = 0$ $\tau_{.5} = 1260$ psi $\tau_{1.0} = 2520$ psi $\tau_{1.5} = 3770$ psi

13.49   10.3 ksi
13.50   75.0 MPa
13.52   6.95 E-4 rad ccw
13.53   513 lb, 1310 psi
13.55   1.30 rad, 5600 ksi
13.56 $N_{2-3} = 600$ rpm, $N_{out} = 300$ rpm
$T_{in} = 29.2$ ft-lb, $T_{2-3} = 87.5$ ft-lb, $T_{out} = 175$ ft-lb
$D_{in} = 0.606$ in., $D_{2-3} = 0.874$ in., $D_{out} = 1.101$ in.

CHAPTER 14

14.1 $V_2 = 8.00$ kN, $M_2 = 16.0$ kN·m $V_8 = 0$, $M_8 = 24.0$ kN·m
14.2 $V_2 = 4.00$ kip, $M_2 = -20.0$ kip-ft $V_8 = 0$, $M_8 = 0$
14.4 $V_2 = 0.400$ kip, $M_2 = 4.80$ kip-ft $V_{8L} = -5.60$ kips, $M_{8L} = -19.8$ kip-ft
14.5 $V_2 = 134$ lb, $M_2 = 578$ ft-lb $V_8 = -133$ lb, $M_8 = 136$ ft-lb
14.7 $V_2 = 800$ lb, $M_2 = -1070$ ft-lb $V_6 = 0$, $M_6 = 0$
14.8 $V_2 = -60.0$ N, $M_2 = -120$ N·m $V_6 = -20.0$ N, $M_6 = -320$ N·m
14.10

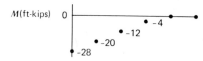

14.11

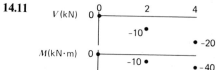

14.13

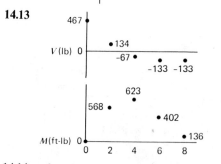

14.14

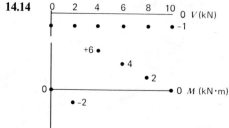

14.16

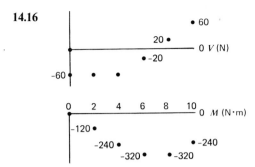

14.17 0 to 3: $V = 8$ $M = 8x$, 3 to 9: $V = 0$ $M = 24$, 9 to 12: $V = -8$
$M = 96 - 8x$

14.19 0 to 4: $V = -5x$ $M = -2.5x^2$

14.20 0 to 5: $V = 4.4 - 2x$ $M = 4.4x - x^2$, 5 to 8: $V = -5.6$ $M = -5.6x + 25$,
8 to 10: $V = 10$ $M = 10x - 99.8$

14.22 0 to 3: $V = -1$ $M = -x$, 3 to 10: $V = -1$ $M = 10 - x$

14.23 0 to 6: $V = 1800 - 600x + 50x^2$ $M = -3600 + 1800x - 300x^2 + 16.7x^3$,
6 to 8: $V = 0 = M$

14.25

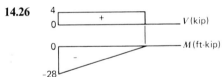

14.26

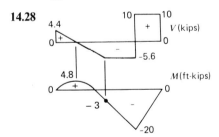

14.28

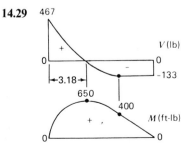

14.29

14.31

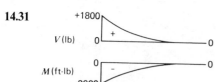

14.32

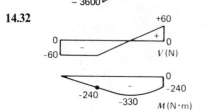

14.34

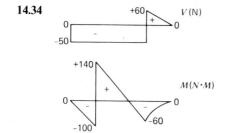

14.35

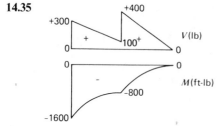

14.37

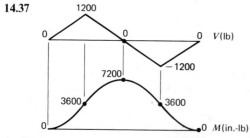

14.38

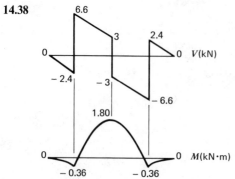

CHAPTER 15

15.1 28.0 ft-kips, 7.50 ksi T
15.2 56.0 ft-kips, 5.81 ksi C
15.4 4.36 ksi
15.5 13.2 ksi
15.7 $1.79T$, $1.49T$, $0.609T$, 0, $0.568C$, 1.16 ksi C
15.8 $830C$, $577C$, $325C$, 0, $181T$, $433T$, 686 psi T
15.10 2.22 MPa
15.11 (a) 576 MPa   (b) 288 MPa   (c) 177 MPa   (d) 477 MPa
        (e) 541 MPa   (f) 270 MPa   (g) 166 MPa   (h) 448 MPa
        (i) 72.0 MPa   (j) 36.0 MPa   (k) 22.1 MPa   (l) 59.6 MPa
        (m) 793 kPa   (n) 396 kPa   (o) 243 kPa   (p) 657 kPa
15.13 (a) 101 mm   (b) 120 mm   (c) 66.9 mm   (d) 11.2 mm
15.14 (a) 63.6 mm wide   (b) 75.4 mm wide   (c) 42.4 mm wide
        (d) 7.07 mm wide
15.16 8.30 ksi C
15.17 8.54 ksi
15.19 39.5 ksi
15.20 442 psi
15.22 $W\ 14 \times 30$
15.23 $W\ 12 \times 14$
15.25 $W\ 21 \times 49$
15.26 $W\ 4 \times 13$
15.28 18.5 MPa
15.29 $\sigma_{\text{flat}} = 2\sigma_{\text{edge}}$
15.31 (a) $C\ 7 \times 9.8$ (b) $L\ 7 \times 4 \times 7/16$ (c) $L\ 6 \times 6 \times 9/16$
        (d) 5 in. standard weight
15.32 3×12

CHAPTER 16

16.1 $\dfrac{1}{\text{ft}} = \dfrac{1}{\text{ft}}$

16.2 8330 in.-lb, 8330 psi
16.4 146 in.-lb, 28.1 ksi
16.5 20.3 N·m, 207 MPa
16.7 1.25 m
16.8 (a) $M = 200 - 300x + x^3$, $w = 6x$ (b) $M = 384x - 0.750x^4$, $w = -9x^2$
        (c) $M = -12x^2 + 108x - 360$ $w = -24$
16.10 $w = 0$, $V(0) = -200N$, $M(0) = 0$, $\theta(1.5) = 0$, $y(1.5) = 0$
16.11 $w = -w$, $V(0) = 0$, $M(0) = 0$, $\theta(L) = 0$, $y(L) = 0$

16.13 $M = C_1 x + C_2$, $EIy = \dfrac{C_1 x^3}{6} + \dfrac{C_2 x^2}{2} + C_3 x + C_4$

16.14 $M = -\dfrac{wx^2}{2} + C_1 x + C_2$, $EIy = \dfrac{-wx^4}{24} + \dfrac{C_1 x^3}{6} + \dfrac{C_2 x^2}{2} + C_3 x + C_4$

16.16 $V = -200$, $M = -200x$, $EI\theta = -100x^2 + 225$, $EIy = -33.3x^3 + 225x - 225$,
        $y = -0.952$ mm

16.17 $V = -wx$ $M = \dfrac{-wx^2}{2}$ $EI\theta = \dfrac{-w}{6}(x^3 - L^3)$

$EIy = \dfrac{-w}{24}(x^4 - 4L^3x + 3L^4)$

16.19 $\dfrac{-225 \text{ N·m}^3}{EI}$

16.20 $-\dfrac{wL^4}{8EI}$

16.22

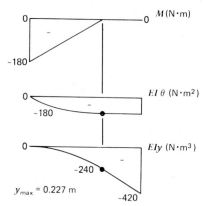

16.23

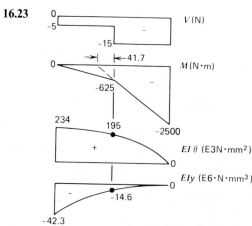

$y_{max} = 17.8$ mm

16.25 $M = -10x^2 + 200x - 1000, \quad EIy = -\dfrac{5x^4}{6} + \dfrac{100x^3}{3} - 500x^2$

16.26 $M = -200x, \quad EIy = -\dfrac{100x^3}{3} + 225x - 225$

16.28 $M = 90x - 180, \quad EIy = 15x^3 - 90x^2$

16.29 $M = -20x^2 + 160x - 320$, $EIy = -\dfrac{5x^4}{3} + \dfrac{80x^3}{3} - 160x^2$

16.31 $\dfrac{-25000}{EI}$ lb-ft^3

16.32 $\dfrac{-225}{EI}$ N·m^3

16.34 -0.227 m

16.35 -17.8 mm

16.37 $y(0) = -225/EI$ $y(0.3) = -158/EI$ $y(0.6) = -97.2/EI$
$y(0.9) = -46.8/EI$ $y(1.2) = -12.6/EI$ $y(1.5) = 0$

16.38 $y(0) = 0$ $y(.5) = 11.2$ mm $y(1.0) = 40.6$ mm $y(1.5) = 82.1$ mm
$y(2.0) = 130$ mm $y(2.5) = 178$ mm $y(3.0) = 228$ mm

16.40   0.548 m

16.41   6.66 mm

16.43   (a) 9.67 E-3 in.   (b) 6.66 mm

16.44   (a) -2.04 E-4 rad, -5.99 E-3 in.

16.46 $EIy = 2.5x^4 - 250x^2 - 5000x$

16.47 $EIy = -16.7x^4 - 1330x^3 + 751000$

16.49   0.0451 in.

16.50   max $y = -\dfrac{1200}{EI}$ N·m^3 at $x = 0$

16.52   (a) $\theta = \dfrac{-w}{24EI}(L^3 - 6Lx^2 + 4x^3)$ (b) $\theta = \dfrac{-M}{6EIL}(L^2 - 2x^2)$

(c) $\theta = \dfrac{-P}{6EI}(-3L^2 + 3x^2)$ (d) $\theta = \dfrac{-W}{60EIL^2}(5x^4 - 5L^4)$

16.53   (a) $\theta = \dfrac{-Pb}{6EIL}(L^2 - b^2 + 3x^2)$ (b) $\theta = \dfrac{-P}{6EI}(3La - 3a^2 - 3x^2)$ (c) $\theta = \dfrac{Pb^2}{2EI}$

(d) $\theta = \dfrac{-P}{2EI}\left[L^2 - Lb - 2(L - b)x + 3x^2\right]$

16.55   (a) L6 × 4 × 3/8, 36.1 ksi   (b) 2 × 14, 2.73 ksi   (c) 2.23 in. × 6.69 in., 7.25 ksi

CHAPTER 17

17.1   0, 51.3, 87.9, 110, 117, 110, 87.9, 51.3, 0 psi

17.2   0, 12.0, 18.0, 18.0, 12.0, 0 MPa

17.4   150, 140, 112, 65.6, 0 MPa

17.5   234, 230, 220, 202, 176, 143, 102, 54.9, 0 psi

17.7   284 psi, 7500 psi

17.8   341 psi, 12900 psi

17.10   691 psi on right 5 ft, 8300 psi at 10 K load

17.11   3.10 ksi, 8.52 ksi

17.13   2.48 ksi, 3.47 ksi

17.14   5.03 ksi, 5.03 ksi

17.16 (a)   2.40 MPa   (b) 2.40 MPa   (c) 4.67 MPa   (d) 4.24 MPa
     (e)   4.50 MPa   (f) 4.50 MPa   (g) 8.76 MPa   (h) 7.95 MPa
     (i)   300 kPa   (j) 300 kPa   (k) 584 kPa   (l)   530 kPa
     (m–p) 0

17.17 (a) 2.40 MPa, 576 MPa   (b) 2.40 MPa, 288 MPa   (c) 4.67 MPa, 177 MPa
     (d) 4.24 MPa, 477 MPa   (e) 6.00 MPa, 962 MPa   (f) 6.00 MPa, 480 MPa
     (g) 11.7 MPa, 295 MPa   (h) 10.6 MPa, 796 MPa   (i) 300 kPa, 168 MPa
     (j) 300 kPa, 83.9 MPa   (k) 584 kPa, 51.5 MPa   (l) 530 kPa, 139 MPa
     (m) 180 kPa, 793 kPa   (n) 180 kPa, 396 kPa   (o) 351 kPa, 243 kPa
     (p) 318 kPa, 657 kPa

17.19 267 N/mm, 30.0 mm
17.20 528 lb/in.
17.22 1.15 kip/in.
17.23 2.36 kip/in.
17.25 1.34 kip/in., 0.261 in.
17.26 (b) 699 in.^{4} (c) 6.49 ksi   (d) 0.355 ksi   (e) 0.912 in.   (f) 2.29 kip/in.
     (g) 0.349 in.

CHAPTER 18

18.1 (a) 3.75 MPa C, 1.25 MPa T (b) 0, 4.17 MPa T
18.2 3.12 MPa T, 6.25 MPa C
18.4 15.6 ksi T, 14.4 ksi C
18.5 $x = \pm 13.3$ mm, $y = \pm 20.0$ mm
18.7 1890 psi T, 2040 psi C
18.8 990 psi T
18.10 100 MPa T
18.11 125 MPa C
18.13 5330 psi C
18.14 6670 psi T
18.16 21.9 ksi T
18.17 34.0 ksi T
18.19 293 MPa C
18.20 87.5 psi C
18.22 2.59 MPa C
18.23 3.32 MPa T
18.25 19.8 kN
18.26 53.0 ksi T, 44.8 ksi C
18.28 3.73 MPa, 168 MPa, 172 MPa
18.29 71.6 lb
18.31 (a) 11,300 psi   (b) 10,900 psi   (c) 10,400 psi   (d) 10,900 psi
18.32 (a) 90.5 psi   (b) 724 psi   (c) 1540 psi   (d) 724 psi
18.34 (a) 0.46 in.
18.35 (a) 260 MPa   (b) 239 MPa   (c) 218 MPa   (d) 239 MPa
18.37 133 mm
18.38 97 mm
18.40 22.8 MPa
18.41 0.34 in.
18.43 287 ksi, 16
18.44 263 MPa, 15
18.46 196 N

CHAPTER 19

19.1 (a) 280 psi, 75.0 psi   (b) 225 psi, 130 psi   (c) 150 psi, 150 psi
19.2 (a) −1.46 GPa, −1.46 GPa   (b) −1.46 GPa, 1.46 GPa   (c) 0, 4.00 GPa
19.4 (a) 476 kPa, −91.6 kPa   (b) 282 kPa, −440 kPa
         (c) −90.2 kPa, 583 kPa
19.5 (a) 11.5 ksi, −8.28 ksi   (b) 9.36 ksi, −2.32 ksi   (c) 14.5 ksi, −11.8 ksi
19.7 (a) 280 psi, −75.0 psi   (b) 225 psi, −130 psi   (c) 20.1 psi, 75.0 psi
         (d) 75.0 psi, 130 psi   (e) 20.1 psi, −75.0 psi
19.8 (a) −1.46 GPa, −1.46 GPa   (b) −1.46 GPa, 1.46 GPa
         (c) 9.46 GPa, 1.46 GPa   (d) 9.46 GPa, −1.46 GPa
         (e) 5.46 GPa, 5.46 GPa
19.10 (a) 476 kPa, −91.6 kPa   (b) 282 kPa, −440 kPa   (c) −676 kPa, 129 kPa
         (d) −482 kPa, 440 kPa   (e) −290 kPa, −551 kPa
19.11 (a) 11.5 ksi, −8.28 ksi   (b) 9.36 ksi, 2.32 ksi   (c) 38.5 ksi, 8.28 ksi
         (d) 40.6 ksi, −2.32 ksi   (e) 19.2 ksi, 14.7 ksi
19.13 (a) 0, 90°   (b) 22.5°, 112.5°   (c) 13.3°, 103.3°   (d) 15.5°, 105.5°
         (e) 35.8°, 125.8°   (f) 39.3°, 129.3°
19.14 (a) 0, 300 psi   (b) 9.66, −1.66 ksi   (c) 10.9, −6.94 ksi
         (d) −683, 483 kPa   (e) 40.8, 9.19 ksi   (f) −50.5, 0.495 ksi

19.16

	(a)	(b)	(c)	(d)	(e)	(f)
θ	psi	GPa	ksi	kPa	ksi	MPa
0	0	8.00	10.0	−600	30.0	−30.0
15	20.1	9.64	10.9	−683	36.8	−41.8
30	75.0	9.64	9.46	−610	40.5	−49.2
45	150	8.00	6.00	−400	40.0	−50.0
60	225	5.64	1.46	−110	35.5	−44.2
75	280	2.54	−2.93	183	28.2	−33.2
90	300	0	−6.00	400	20.0	−20.0
105	280	−1.46	−6.92	483	13.2	−8.17
120	225	−1.46	−5.46	410	9.51	−0.85
135	150	0	−2.00	200	10.0	0
150	75.0	2.54	2.54	−90.2	14.5	−5.85
165	20.1	5.64	6.92	−383	21.8	−16.8
180	0	8.00	10.0	−600	30.0	−30.0
max	300	9.66	10.9	483	40.8	0.50
min	0	−1.66	−6.94	−683	9.19	−50.5

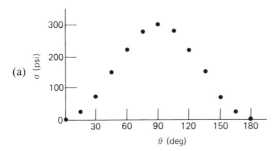

19.17 (a) 45°, 135° (b) −22.5°, 67.5° (c) −31.7°, 58.3° (d) −29.5°, 60.5°
(e) −9.22° 80.8° (f) −5.65°, 84.3°

19.19 (a) 150, 150 psi (b) 5.66, 4.00 GPa (c) 8.94, 2.00 ksi
(d) 583, −100 kPa (e) 15.8, 25.0 ksi (f) 25.5, −25.0 MPa

19.20

σ

θ	(a) psi	(b) GPa	(c) ksi	(d) kPa	(e) ksi	(f) MPa
0	0	4.00	4.00	−300	15.0	−25.0
15	75	1.46	−0.54	−10	10.5	−19.2
30	130	−1.46	−4.93	283	3.2	−8.2
45	150	−4.00	−8.00	500	−5.0	5.0
60	130	−5.46	−8.93	583	−11.8	16.8
75	75	−5.46	−7.46	510	−15.5	24.2
90	0	−4.00	−4.00	300	−15.0	25.0
105	−75	−1.46	0.54	10	−10.5	19.2
120	−130	1.46	4.93	−283	−3.2	8.2
135	−150	4.00	8.00	−500	5.0	−5.0
150	−130	5.46	8.93	−583	11.8	−16.8
165	−75	5.46	7.46	−510	15.5	−24.2
180	0	4.00	4.00	−300	15.0	−25.0
max	150	−5.66	8.94	583	−15.8	25.5

(a)

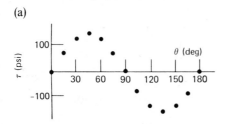

19.22 (a)

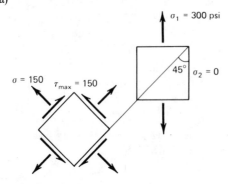

(b)

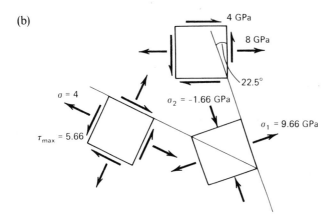

(c)

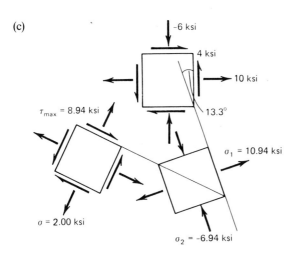

(d)

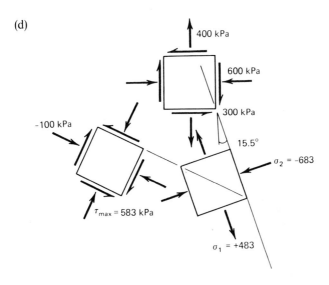

(e)

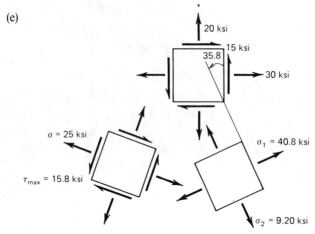

(f)

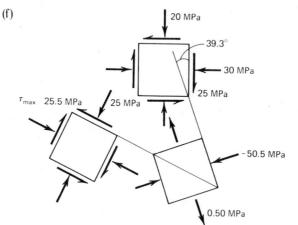

19.23 (a) 225, 130 psi   (b) 5.46, 5.47 GPa   (c) 9.46, 4.92 ksi   (d) −99.8, 583 psi
         (e) 40.0, 4.99 ksi   (f) 0, 5.04 MPa
19.25 50.0, 100, 0 MPa
19.26 62.5, 0, −125 MPa
19.28 3.34, 6.67, 0 ksi
19.29 (a) 10.9, 10.9, −10.9 ksi   (b) 11.3, 11.3, −11.3 ksi   (c) 21.1, 3.0, −39.2 ksi
         (d) 90.5, 90.5, −90.5 psi   (e) 18.1, 0.0, −36.2 ksi   (f) 90.5, 90.5, −90.5 psi
         (g) 54.3, 0, −109 ksi

CHAPTER 20

20.1 (a) 249, 125   (b) 143, 44.3   (c) 180, 46.5   (d) 124   (e) 192
        (f) 185, 121   (g) 193, 152, 92.9
20.2 (a) 277, 139   (b) 139, 46.2   (c) 160   (d) 100, 177
20.4 (a) 8.16 kips   (b) 122 kips   (c) 251 kips   (d) 172 kips   (e) 227 kips
        (f) 188 kips   (g) 185 kips

20.5   (a) 0.51 kips   (b) 7.60 kips   (c) 15.7 kips   (d) 10.7 kips   (e) 14.2 kips
(f) 11.8 kips   (g) 11.5 kips

20.7   (a) 7.07 kN   (b) 169 kN   (c) 176 kN   (d) 328 kN

20.8   (a) 28.3 kN   (b) 676 kN   (c) 704 kN   (d) 1310 kN

20.10   (a) 14.1 kN   (b) 338 kN   (c) 352 kN   (d) 655 kN

20.11   Lower value will govern
(a) 103, 343 kips   (b) 201, 103000 kips   (c) 540, 521 kips
(d) 600, 179 kips

20.13   0.288 in.

20.14   2.5 in. standard

20.16   *BE, CD*
(a) 0.081 in.   (b) 0.300 in.   (c) 0.063 in.   (d) 0.072 in.   (e) 0.081 in.
(f) 0.291 in.   (g) 0.325 in.   (h) 0.243 in.   (i) 0.291 in.

20.17   *AB, BE, BC, CD*
(a) 0.787 in.   (b) 0.175 in.   (c) 0.514 in.   (d) 0.759 in.   (e) 0.138 in.
(f) 0.124 in.   (g) 0.406 in.   (h) 0   (i) 0.124 in.

20.19   *AB*: 85.7 mm   *BC*: 85.7 mm

20.20   *AB*: 35.9 mm   *CD*: 39.1 mm   *BC*: 23.3 mm

CHAPTER 21

21.1   (a) 28.8 ksi   (b) 14.4 ksi   (d) 7.20 ksi

21.2   (a) 200 MPa   (b) 100 MPa   (d) 50.0 MPa

21.4   5.40 MPa

21.5   15.0 ksi

21.7 $D = 7.01$ ft, $t = 0.525$ in.

21.8 $D = 1.56$ m, $t = 9.77$ mm

21.10   (a) 2.26 MPa   (b) 21.2 MPa

21.11   (a) 159 psi   (b) 2120 psi

21.13   39.0 kN

21.14   (a) 10.2 ksi   (b) 4.00 ksi   (c) 5.33 ksi   (d) 8.00 ksi   (e) 10.7 ksi

21.16   (a) 3.40 ksi   (b) 2.00 ksi   (c) 2.67 ksi   (d) 2.67 ksi   (e) 3.56 ksi

21.17   (a) 88.4 MPa   (b) 29.8 MPa   (c) 35.7 MPa   (d) 69.4 MPa
(e) 83.3 MPa

21.19   (a) 29.4 MPa   (b) 18.9 MPa   (c) 22.7 MPa   (d) 23.1 MPa
(e) 27.8 MPa

21.20   4.91 kips

21.22   Shear: 5.09 ksi   Bearing: 8.00 ksi   Tensile: 4.00 ksi

21.24   Shear: 40.7 MPa   Bearing: 66.7 MPa   Tensile: 33.3 MPa

21.25   102 kN

21.26   0.109 in.

21.28   4.49 mm

21.29   754 psi

21.31   6 in. by 0.101 in.

21.32   5 mm by 84.9 mm

21.34   2710 psi

21.35   11.5 MPa

21.37   10.2 MPa

21.38   0.0608 in.

CHAPTER 22

22.1   (a) 1660, 345 lb   (b) 58.5, 878 psi   (c) 1.76 E-3 in.
22.2   (a) 696, 1300 lb   (b) 27.7, 415 psi   (c) 8.30 E-4 in.
22.4   (a) 7.02, 13.0 kN   (b) 0.447, 6.61 MPa   (c) 47.9 μm
22.5   (a) 870, 1260 lb   (b) 4430, 2850 psi   (c) 277, 277μ (d) 13.3 E-3 in.
22.7   (a) 3.48, 5.04 kN   (b) 44.3, 28.6 MPa   (c) 402, 402μ (d) 0.483 mm
22.8   (a) 9.24, 11.5 kN   (b) 36.3, 23.4 MPa   (c) 330, 330μ (d) 0.661 mm
22.10 (a) 13.7 kips   (b) Aluminum: 10.9 kips each, Bronze: 28.2 kips
           (c) 17.979 in.
22.11 (a) 22.8 kips   (b) Aluminum: 6.93 kips each, Bronze: 16.1 kips
           (c) 29.973 in.
22.13 (a) 79.9 kN   (b) Aluminum: 588 kN each, Bronze: 1820 kN
           (c) 795.28 mm
22.14 (a) 1150 lb and 0.0336 in., 1150 lb and 0.0538 in.
           (b) 1400 lb and 0.0652 in., 1400 lb and 0.0979 in.
           (c) 10.0 kN and 2.82 mm, 10.0 kN and 8.45 mm
           (d) 16.0 kN and 5.63 mm, 16.0 kN and 8.45 mm
22.16 47.0 MPa C, 0.602 MPa T
22.17 5850 psi C, 10.5 psi T
22.19 Bronze: 2060 lb T, 10500 psi T, 3.66 E-3, 0.175 in.
           Aluminum: 1120 lb C, 2530 psi C, 3.66 E-3, 0.175 in.
22.20 Bronze: 5630 lb T, 12700 psi T, 4.80 E-3, 0.173 in.
           Aluminum: 3260 lb C, 4150 psi C, 4.80 E-3, 0.173 in.
22.22 Bronze: 28.0 kN T, 110 MPa T, 7.30 E-3, 14.6 mm
           Aluminum: 26.1 kN C, 53.2 MPa C, 7.30 E-3, 14.6 mm
22.23 (a) $-148°$F   (b) Aluminum: 2610 psi T, Bronze: 3140 psi C
           (c) Aluminum: 4650 psi C, Bronze: 14400 psi C
22.25 1600 lb, 0.0128 in.
22.26 1450 lb, 0.101 in.
22.28 9.37 kN, 0.604 mm
22.29 1.14 in., 3850 lb
22.31 49.4 mm, 822 N
22.32 369 mm, 29.1 kN

Index